2002

MILLER

GAAS GUIDE

A Comprehensive Restatement of
Standards for Auditing, Attestation,
Compilation, and Review

LARRY P. BAILEY, PH.D., CPA

ASPEN LAW & BUSINESS
A Division of Aspen Publishers, Inc.
New York   Gaithersburg
(Formerly published by Harcourt Professional Publishing)

This publication is designed to provide accurate and authoritative information in regard to the subject matter covered. It is sold with the understanding that the publisher is not engaged in rendering legal, accounting, or other professional services. If legal advice or other professional assistance is required, the services of a competent professional person should be sought.
—From a *Declaration of Principles* jointly adopted by a Committee of the American Bar Association and a Committee of Publishers and Associations

Copyright © 2002 by Aspen Law & Business
A Division of Aspen Publishers, Inc.
A Wolters Kluwer Company
www.aspenpublishers.com

All rights reserved. No part of this publication may be reproduced or transmitted in any form or by any means, electronic or mechanical, including photocopy, recording, or any information storage and retrieval system, without permission in writing from the publisher. Requests for permission to make copies of any part of the work should be mailed to:

> Permissions
> Aspen Law & Business
> 1185 Avenue of the Americas
> New York, NY 10036
> (212) 597-0200

Portions of this work were published in previous editions.

Miller GAAS Guide is a trademark of Aspen Law & Business

Printed in the United States of America

ISBN: 0-7355-2686-9
ISSN: 1088-9159

00 01 02 03   WBC   4 3 2 1

About Aspen Law & Business

Aspen Law & Business is a leading publisher of authoritative treatises, practice manuals, services, and journals for attorneys, corporate and bank directors, accountants, auditors, environmental compliance professionals, financial and tax advisors, and other business professionals. Our mission is to provide practical solution-based how-to information keyed to the latest original pronouncements, as well as the latest legislative, judicial, and regulatory developments.

We offer publications in the areas of accounting and auditing; antitrust; banking and finance; bankruptcy; business and commercial law; construction law; corporate law; criminal law; environmental compliance; government and administrative law; health law; insurance law; intellectual property; international law; legal practice and litigation; matrimonial and family law; pensions, benefits, and labor; real estate law; securities; and taxation.

Other Aspen Law & Business products treating accounting and auditing issues include:

- **Accounting Irregularities and Financial Fraud**
- **Audit Committees: A Guide for Directors, Management, and Consultants**
- **Construction Accounting Deskbook**
- **CPA's Guide to Developing Effective Business Plans**
- **CPA's Guide to Effective Engagement Letters**
- **CPA's Guide to E-Business**
- **Federal Government Contractor's Manual**
- **How to Manage Your Accounting Practice**
- **Medical Practice Management Handbook**
- **Miller Audit Procedures**
- **Miller Compilations and Reviews**
- **Miller European Accounting Guide**
- **Miller GAAP Financial Statement Disclosures Manual**
- **Miller GAAP Guide**
- **Miller GAAP Practice Manual**
- **Miller GAAS Practice Manual**
- **Miller Governmental GAAP Guide**
- **Miller International Accounting Standards Guide**
- **Miller Local Government Audits**
- **Miller Not-for-Profit Organization Audits**
- **Miller Not-for-Profit Reporting**
- **Miller Single Audits**
- **Professional's Guide to Value Pricing**

ASPEN LAW & BUSINESS
A Division of Aspen Publishers, Inc.
A Wolters Kluwer Company
www.aspenpublishers.com

SUBSCRIPTION NOTICE

This Aspen Law & Business product is updated on a periodic basis with supplements to reflect important changes in the subject matter. If you purchased this product directly from Aspen Law & Business, we have already recorded your subscription for the update service.

If, however, you purchased this product from a bookstore and wish to receive future updates and revised or related volumes billed separately with a 30-day examination review, please contact our Customer Service Department at 1-800-234-1660, or send your name, company name (if applicable), address, and the title of the product to:

ASPEN LAW & BUSINESS
A Division of Aspen Publishers, Inc.
7201 McKinney Circle
Frederick, MD 21704

Our Peer Review Policy

Thank you for ordering the 2002 *Miller GAAS Guide*. Each year we bring you the best engagement guides available, with accompanying electronic workpapers and practice aids. To confirm the technical accuracy and quality control of our materials, Aspen Law & Business (formerly Harcourt Professional Publishing) voluntarily submitted to a peer review of our publishing system and our publications (see the Peer Review Statement on the following page).

In addition to peer review, our publications undergo strict technical and content reviews by qualified practitioners. This ensures that our books, workpapers, and practice aids meet "real world" standards and applicability.

Our publications are reviewed every step of the way—from conception to production—to ensure that we bring you the finest guides on the market.

Updated annually, peer reviewed, technically accurate, convenient, and practical—the 2002 *Miller GAAS Guide* shows our commitment to creating books and workpapers you can trust.

Peer Review Statement

Caldwell, Becker, Dervin, Petrick & Co., L.L.P.
CERTIFIED PUBLIC ACCOUNTANTS

May 26, 2000

Board of Directors
Aspen Publishers, Inc.

We have reviewed the system of quality control for the development and maintenance of <u>MILLER GAAS GUIDE: 2001 EDITION</u> (materials) of Aspen Publishers, Inc. (the Company) (formerly materials of Harcourt, Inc.) in effect for the year ended April 30, 2000, and the resultant materials in effect at April 30, 2000, in order to determine whether the materials are reliable aids to assist users in conforming with those professional standards the materials purport to encompass. The design of the system, and compliance with it, are the responsibilities of the company. Our responsibility is to express an opinion on the design of the system, and the company's compliance with that system based on our review. Our review did not cover the development and maintenance of the continuing education programs included in the materials.

Our review was conducted in accordance with the standards for reviews of quality control materials established by the peer review committee of the SEC practice section of the AICPA Division for CPA Firms. In performing our review, we have given consideration to the following general characteristics of a system of quality control. A company's system for the development and maintenance of quality control materials encompasses its organizational structure and the policies and procedures established to provide the users of its materials with reasonable assurance that the quality control materials are reliable aids to assist them in conforming with professional standards in conducting their accounting, auditing, and attest practices. The extent of a company's quality control policies and procedures for the development and maintenance of the materials and the manner in which they are implemented will depend upon a variety of factors, such as the size and organizational structure of the company and the nature of quality control materials provided to users. Variance in individual performance and professional interpretation affects the degree of compliance with prescribed quality control policies and procedures. Therefore, adherence to all policies and procedures in every case may not be possible.

Our review and tests were limited to the system of quality control for the development and maintenance of the aforementioned materials of Aspen Publishers, Inc. (formerly materials of Harcourt, Inc.) and to the materials themselves and did not extend to the application of these materials by users of the materials nor to the policies and procedures of individual users.

In our opinion, the system of quality control for the development and maintenance of the quality control materials of Aspen Publishers, Inc. (formerly materials of Harcourt, Inc.) was suitably designed and was being complied with during the year ended April 30, 2000, to provide users of the materials with reasonable assurance that the materials are reliable aids to assist them in conforming with those professional standards the materials purport to encompass. Also, in our opinion, the quality control materials referred to above are reliable aids at April 30, 2000.

CALDWELL, BECKER, DERVIN, PETRICK & CO., LLP.
CALDWELL, BECKER, DERVIN, PETRICK & CO., L. L. P.

20750 Ventura Boulevard, Suite 140 • Woodland Hills, CA 91364
(818) 704-1040 • (323) 873-1040 • FAX (818) 704-5536

Contents

Our Peer Review Policy v
Peer Review Statement vi
Preface xi
About the Author xiv

AU 100: Introduction

Section 110: Responsibilities and Functions
of the Independent Auditor 3

Section 150: Generally Accepted Auditing Standards 4

Section 161: The Relationship of Generally Accepted Auditing
Standards to Quality Control Standards 7

AU 200: The General Standards

Section 201: Nature of the General Standards 13

Section 210: Training and Proficiency of the
Independent Auditor 14

Section 220: Independence 16

Section 230: Due Care in the Performance of Work 20

AU 300: The Standards of Field Work

Section 310: Appointment of the Independent Auditor 27

Section 311: Planning and Supervision 32

Section 312: Audit Risk and Materiality in Conducting an
Audit 48

Section 313: Substantive Tests Prior to the Balance Sheet Date 67

Section 315: Communications between Predecessor and
Successor Auditors 72

Section 316: Consideration of Fraud in a Financial
Statement Audit 80

Section 317: Illegal Acts by Clients 91

Section 319: Consideration of Internal Control in a Financial
Statement Audit 97

Section 322: The Auditor's Consideration of the Internal Audit
Function in an Audit of Financial Statements 118

Section 324: Service Organizations 124

Section 325: Communication of Internal Control
   Related Matters Noted in an Audit 140
Section 326: Evidential Matter 151
Section 329: Analytical Procedures 156
Section 330: The Confirmation Process 171
Section 331: Inventories 185
Section 332: Auditing Derivative Instruments, Hedging Activities,
   and Investments in Securities 192
Section 333: Management Representations...200
Section 334: Related Parties 209
Section 336: Using the Work of a Specialist...216
Section 337: Inquiry of a Client's Lawyer Concerning Litigation,
   Claims, and Assessments..223
Section 339: Working Papers 232
Section 341: The Auditor's Consideration of an Entity's Ability
   to Continue as a Going Concern 238
Section 342: Auditing Accounting Estimates 248
Section 350: Audit Sampling..256
Section 380: Communication with Audit Committees 297
Section 390: Consideration of Omitted Procedures after the
   Report Date 303

AU 400: The First, Second, and Third Standards of Reporting

Section 410: Adherence to Generally Accepted Accounting
   Principles 309
Section 411: The Meaning of "Present Fairly in Conformity
   with Generally Accepted Accounting Principles"..............................311
Section 420: Consistency of Application of Generally
   Accepted Accounting Principles 318
Section 431: Adequacy of Disclosures in Financial Statements 325
Section 435: Segment Information 336

AU 500: The Fourth Standard of Reporting

Section 504: Association with Financial Statements 339
Section 508: Reports on Audited Financial Statements 346
Section 530: Dating of the Independent Auditor's Report 381
Section 532: Restricting the Use of an Auditor's Report 384

Contents ix

Section 534: Reporting on Financial Statements Prepared
   for Use in Other Countries 392
Section 543: Part of Audit Performed by Other Independent
   Auditors 398
Section 544: Lack of Conformity with Generally Accepted
   Accounting Principles 406
Section 550: Other Information in Documents Containing
   Audited Financial Statements 408
Section 551: Reporting on Information Accompanying the Basic Financial
   Statements in Auditor-Submitted Documents 411
Section 552: Reporting on Condensed Financial Statements
   and Selected Financial Data 415
Section 558: Required Supplementary Information 419
Section 560: Subsequent Events 426
Section 561: Subsequent Discovery of Facts Existing at the
   Date of the Auditor's Report 432

AU 600: Other Types of Reports

Section 622 (Withdrawn): Engagements to Apply Agreed-Upon
   Procedures to Specified Elements, Accounts, or Items of a
   Financial Statement 441
Section 623: Special Reports..442
Section 625: Reports on the Application of Accounting
   Principles..465
Section 634: Letters for Underwriters and Certain Other
   Requesting Parties 471

AU 700: Special Topics

Section 711: Filings under Federal Securities Statutes 499
Section 722: Interim Financial Information 505

AU 800: Compliance Auditing

Section 801: Compliance Auditing Considerations in Audits
   of Governmental Entities and Recipients of Governmental
   Financial Assistance 531

AU 900: Special Reports of the Committee on Auditing Procedure

Section 901: Public Warehouses—Controls and Auditing
   Procedures for Goods Held 537

AT Section: Statements on Standards for Attestation Engagements

AT Section 101: Attest Engagements 541

AT Section 201: Agreed-Upon Procedures Engagements.........................563

AT Section 301: Financial Forecasts and Projections 571

AT Section 401: Reporting on Pro Forma Financial Information..............595

AT Section 501: Reporting on an Entity's Internal Control Over Financial Reporting 605

AT Section 601: Compliance Attestation 620

AT Section 701: Management's Discussion and Analysis 635

AR Section: Statements on Standards for Accounting and Review Services

AR Section 100: Compilation and Review of Financial Statements 667

AR Section 200: Reporting on Comparative Financial Statements 762

AR Section 300: Compilation Reports on Financial Statements in Certain Prescribed Forms 776

AR Section 400: Communications between Predecessor and Successor Accountants 779

AR Section 600: Reporting on Personal Financial Statements Included in Written Personal Financial Plans 782

Accounting Resources on the Web   785

Cross-Reference   787

Index   805

About the CD-ROM   841

CD-ROM Contents   843

For the latest information, refer to the *Miller GAAS Update Service* and the Miller GAAS Library, at http://www.MillerSeries.com.

Preface

Your *Miller GAAS Guide* describes the engagement standards, practices, and procedures in use today—including Statements on Auditing Standards (SASs) and their Interpretations, Statements on Standards for Attestation Engagements (SSAEs) and their Interpretations, and Statements on Standards on Accounting and Review Services (SSARS) and their Interpretations.

The 2002 edition of the *Miller GAAS Guide* has been updated to incorporate the most recent pronouncements, including the following:

- SAS-92—Auditing Derivative Instruments, Hedging Activities, and Investments in Securities

- SAS-93—Omnibus Statement on Auditing Standards—2000

- SAS-94—The Effect of Information Technology on the Auditor's Consideration of Internal Control in a Financial Statement Audit

- SSAE-10—Attestation Standards: Revision and Recodification

- SSARS-8—Amendments to Statement on Standards for Accounting and Review Services No. 1, Compilation and Review of Financial Statements

- Auditing Interpretation (December 2000)—The Meaning of the Term Misstatement

- Auditing Interpretation (December 2000)—Evaluating Differences in Estimates

- Auditing Interpretation (December 2000)—Quantitative Measures of Materiality in Evaluating Audit Findings

- Auditing Interpretation (December 2000)—Considering the Qualitative Characteristics of Misstatements

The book's sensible organization follows the arrangement of the AICPA's *Profession Standards* (Volumes I and II), so that you can easily go from the AICPA's original language to our analyses of the standards. All the exhibit material in the book appears on the accompanying CD-ROM. All the sample letters, reports, and checklists found in the text can be printed and customized to meet all your auditing needs.

Within each section, an organizational structure is used that is both simple and insightful. Each section begins with "Authoritative Pronouncements," listing the auditing-related documents that are pertinent to the section. An "Overview" is then provided, followed by a "Promulgated Procedures Checklist" that identifies the essential professional responsibilities that must be satisfied in each part of your engagement. Next, under "Analysis and Application of Reporting Standards," you'll find a concise discussion of how each specific promulgated procedure should be applied. Finally, many of the sections have "Practitioner's Aids" that will help you apply the promulgated standards to your specific engagements.

Also within each section you are alerted to key guidance that will help you meet your professional responsibilities and better plan and execute your engagements. This guidance is classified as (1) a Risk Assessment Point, (2) an Engagement Strategy, (3) a Planning Aid Reminder, or (4) an Observation. With this highlighting you can feel comfortable that key, but subtle, guidance is being brought to your attention in a timely manner.

This 2002 edition continues to provide what has always been the most important feature of the *Miller GAAS Guide*—readability. The utmost care has been exercised to avoid the difficult language and organization of many of the original AICPA pronouncements. Essential material is placed at your fingertips for quick integration into your practice. There is no more need to wonder exactly what a standard means or how it is to be used in a "real" engagement.

CPE Available

Aspen Law & Business is offering a self-study CPE course that can be used in conjunction with *Miller GAAS Guide*. Our goal is to provide you with the clearest, most concise, and up-to-date accounting and auditing information to help further your professional development, as well as a convenient method to help you satisfy your continuing professional educational requirements.

The CPE course has the following characteristics:

> **Prerequisites:** Basic knowledge of auditing
> **Recommended CPE Credit:** 10 hours
> **Level of Knowledge:** Intermediate—Builds on a basic level of understanding in order to relate fundamental principles or skills to practical situations and extend them to a broader range of applications. This level is for participants with some exposure to the subject.
> **Field of Study:** Auditing

If you are interested in taking the CPE course and examination, please contact:

Aspen CPE
c/o ACCPE
2419 Hollywood Boulevard
Hollywood, FL 33020
800-394-6275
http://www.ACCPE.com

Automate your Miller Engagement Guides with ePaceENGAGEMENT

By integrating your Miller Engagement guides with ePaceENGAGEMENT, you can achieve a fully paperless audit workflow. ePaceENGAGEMENT, the newest member of the CCH ProSystem *fx* Office suite, enables firms to increase convenience and efficiency by automating workpaper preparation, management, and workflow within a state-of-the-art paperless engagement system. ProSystem *fx* and Aspen Publishers are pleased to offer this high quality combination of software and content to the accounting community. To sample ePaceENGAGEMENT, contact ePace! Software at (949) 553-8001 or click on http://www.ePaceSoftware.com/.

Acknowledgments

Thanks are due Vincent Love, CPA, of New York, New York, and Thomas F. Cardegna, CPA, of Towson, Maryland, for their thoughtful, thorough reviews of the 2002 edition.

Larry P. Bailey
Mt. Laurel, New Jersey

About the Author

Larry P. Bailey is a Professor of Accounting at Rider University in Lawrenceville, New Jersey, where he teaches auditing and financial accounting. Dr. Bailey earned a B.S. degree in business from Concord College and a Masters and Ph.D. from the University of Pennsylvania. He is a Certified Public Accountant (Virginia) and has worked in public accounting (Arthur Young & Company), in government (intern for the State of New Jersey), and as an educational consultant.

Professor Bailey is a member of the American Institute of Certified Public Accountants and the American Accounting Association. His research interests include auditing and governmental financial reporting, and he has published numerous articles in such journals as *Management Accountant*, *The CPA Journal*, and *Government Accountants Journal*. He is also the author of four books (including the *Miller Governmental GAAP Guide* and *Miller Compilations and Reviews*), the *Miller Governmental GAAP Update Service*, and various pamphlets.

AU 100

Introduction

Section 110: Responsibilities and Functions
of the Independent Auditor 3

Section 150: Generally Accepted Auditing Standards 4

Section 161: The Relationship of Generally Accepted Auditing
Standards to Quality Control Standards 7

SECTION 110

RESPONSIBILITIES AND FUNCTIONS OF THE INDEPENDENT AUDITOR

Authoritative Pronouncements

SAS-1—Codification of Auditing Standards and Procedures (Section 110, Responsibilities and Functions of the Independent Auditor)

Overview

The purpose of an audit engagement is to express an opinion in an auditor's report on a client's financial statements. The opinion may be unqualified, qualified, or adverse; in some circumstances, however, the auditor may disclaim an opinion on the financial statements. Although the auditor expresses an opinion on the client's financial statements, the responsibility for the financial statements rests with management. Nonetheless, the auditor can makes suggestions to the client about the form and content of the financial statements or may draft the financial statements based on information the client provides.

In order to perform the role of an auditor of financial statements, the auditor must be possess an appropriate educational background and have adequate experience. An auditor is not expected to have the background necessary to accept the responsibilities of another profession. For example, an auditor is not expected to fulfill the role of an attorney or asset appraiser.

In order to express an opinion on a client's financial statements, an auditor is expected to exercise professional judgment in a number of areas, ranging from selecting auditing procedures to determining the appropriateness of an accounting principle or method. The financial judgment made by an auditor is that of an qualified professional, but that judgment is not infallible.

Finally, an auditor has a responsibility to his or her profession to observe professional standards, including the AICPA's Code of Professional Conduct.

SECTION 150

GENERALLY ACCEPTED AUDITING STANDARDS

Authoritative Pronouncements

SAS-1—Codification of Auditing Standards and Procedures (Section 150, Generally Accepted Auditing Standards)

SAS-43—Omnibus Statement on Auditing Standards (Generally Accepted Auditing Standards)

Overview

Auditing standards deal with the quality of an audit performed by an independent auditor. The members of the American Institute of Certified Public Accountants (AICPA) have approved and adopted ten generally accepted auditing standards (GAAS), divided into three groups: (1) general standards, (2) standards of fieldwork, and (3) standards of reporting. Under Rule 202 of the Code of Professional Conduct, every member of the AICPA must comply with GAAS. To the extent that the standards are relevant in the circumstances, they are applicable to all services governed by Statements on Auditing Standards (SASs), unless the Auditing Standards Board specifies otherwise.

General standards

The most important factor in any profession is the people who make up the profession. The personal characteristics of an auditor are described below in a discussion of the three general standards. Desirable traits are difficult to describe in any individual, much less a profession. Therefore, these general standards are quite broad and are open to a considerable degree of reasonable interpretation.

- *General Standard No. 1*—The audit is to be performed by a person or persons having adequate technical training and proficiency as an auditor.
- *General Standard No. 2*—In all matters relating to the assignment, an independence in mental attitude is to be maintained by the auditor or auditors.
- *General Standard No. 3*—Due professional care is to be exercised in the planning and performance of the audit and the preparation of the report.

Standards of fieldwork

- *Standard of Fieldwork No. 1*—The work is to be adequately planned and assistants, if any, are to be properly supervised.

- *Standard of Fieldwork No. 2*—A sufficient understanding of internal control is to be obtained to plan the audit and to determine the nature, timing, and extent of tests to be performed.

- *Standard of Fieldwork No. 3*—Sufficient competent evidential matter is to be obtained through inspection, observation, inquiries, and confirmations to afford a reasonable basis for an opinion regarding the financial statements under audit.

Standards of reporting

- *Reporting Standard No. 1*—The report shall state whether the financial statements are presented in accordance with generally accepted accounting principles (GAAP).

- *Reporting Standard No. 2*—The report shall identify those circumstances in which such principles have not been consistently observed in the current period in relation to the preceding period.

- *Reporting Standard No. 3*—Informative disclosures in the financial statements are to be regarded as reasonably adequate unless otherwise stated in the report.

- *Reporting Standard No. 4*—The report shall contain either an expression of opinion regarding the financial statements taken as a whole, or an assertion to the effect that an opinion cannot be expressed. When an overall opinion cannot be expressed, the reasons therefore should be stated. In all cases where an auditor's name is associated with financial statements, the report should contain a clear-cut indication of the character of the auditor's work, if any, and the degree of responsibility the auditor is taking.

Again, generally accepted auditing standards are broad in nature and require the exercise of professional judgment in order to effectively apply them to a particular audit engagement. Two concepts that are fundamental to the application of the standards (especially the standards of fieldwork and reporting) to an engagement are materiality and audit risk. Both concepts give direction to the audit strategy.

> **ENGAGEMENT STRATEGY:** Materiality and audit risk provide guidance to the auditor because those account balances or elements of an account balance that are relatively more im-

portant to the financial statements should generally get more attention. Additionally, those items that are more susceptible to misstatement would likewise have an effect on the planning of an engagement. For example, cash transactions are generally more susceptible to irregularities than capital transactions, and transactions with a related party are more likely to be misstated (not presented at fair value) than transactions with an external party.

OBSERVATION: The AICPA has issued an Exposure Draft (ED) entitled "Generally Accepted Auditing Standards." If it is adopted, the ED would supersede the current material in Section 150 by (1) clarifying the authority of auditing publications, (2) identifying publications that must be observed by auditors, and (3) listing AICPA auditing publications and how they may be obtained.

SECTION 161

THE RELATIONSHIP OF GENERALLY ACCEPTED AUDITING STANDARDS TO QUALITY CONTROL STANDARDS

Authoritative Pronouncements

SAS-25—The Relationship of Generally Accepted Auditing Standards to Quality Control Standards

SQCS-2—System of Quality Control for a CPA Firm's Accounting and Auditing Practice

SQCS-3—Monitoring a CPA Firm's Accounting and Auditing Practice

Overview

An accounting firm must adopt a system of controls to provide reasonable assurance that generally accepted auditing standards (GAAS) are followed by the professional staff of the firm (SAS-25). The AICPA Auditing Standards Board has the authority to issue pronouncements on quality control standards for CPA firms that are members of the American Institute of Certified Public Accountants (AICPA).

The actual design of the system of quality controls will vary from firm to firm, depending on such factors as the size of the professional staff, the number of offices, and the geographical location of the offices.

Quality control standards are based on Statement on Quality Control Standards (SQCS) No. 2 (System of Quality Control for a CPA Firm's Accounting and Auditing Practice) and SQCS-3 (Monitoring a CPA Firm's Accounting and Auditing Practice). The concepts and guidance discussed in SQCS-2 and SQCS-3 are summarized below.

The standards established by SQCSs apply to a firm's *accounting and auditing practice,* which is defined as follows by SQCS-2:

> Accounting and auditing practice refers to all audit, attest, accounting and review, and other services for which standards have been established by the AICPA Auditing Standards Board or the AICPA Accounting and Review Services Committee under Rules 201 or 202 of the AICPA Code of Professional Conduct.

The 1999/2000 *Audit Risk Alert* notes the following common audit engagement deficiencies that have been identified in peer reviews:

- No assessment of the risk of fraud, as required by SAS-82 (AU 316)
- No documentation of the auditor's consideration of a client's internal control, as required by SAS-55 (AU 319)
- No written audit programs, as required by SAS-22 (AU 311)
- No legal representation letter when an attorney was consulted, as required by SAS-12 (AU 337)
- No management representation letter, as required by SAS-84 (AU 315)
- Issuance of an inappropriate audit report when the auditor was not independent
- Audit report did not use language consistent with the critical elements of the standards of reporting
- Audit report was not appropriately modified to reflect (a) scope limitations of the audit engagement or (b) departures from the basis of accounting used to prepared the financial statements
- Audit report was not modified for departures from generally accepted accounting principles (GAAP)
- No report was issued on compliance or internal control for audits subject to *Government Auditing Standards* (GAS)

The above deficiencies are characterized by the *Audit Risk Alert* as "those that are considered to be material to understanding the report or financial statements, or that represent critical auditing procedures."

Promulgated Quality Control Component Checklist

A public accounting firm should consider the following components in the design of an effective quality control system:

____ Independence, integrity, and objectivity

____ Personnel management

____ Acceptance and continuance of clients and engagements

____ Engagement performance

____ Monitoring

§161 • The Relationship of GAAS to Quality Control Standards

Although these components are discussed separately in the following analysis, an effective system of quality control recognizes that all of the components are interrelated.

Analysis and application of quality control components

Independence, integrity, and objectivity

Controls should be established to reasonably assure that personnel are independent. For example, a firm may periodically distribute a client list to staff members and have them acknowledge that they have no financial interest in the client businesses or that none of their relatives holds a key position with a client.

Personnel management

Quality controls related to personnel management should encompass "hiring, assigning personnel to engagements, professional development, and advancement activities." SQCS-2 specifically states that controls should be designed to reasonably assure that the following are achieved:

- Employees possess the appropriate characteristics to enable them to perform competently.

- Work is assigned to personnel who have the technical training and proficiency required to complete the assignment.

- Professional personnel participate in general and industry-specific continuing professional education (CPE) and other professional development activities that enable personnel to fulfill their responsibilities and to satisfy applicable CPE requirements of the AICPA and regulatory agencies.

- Personnel selected for advancement have the qualifications necessary to fulfill their new responsibilities.

Acceptance and continuance of clients and engagements

Controls should be in place to determine whether the firm should continue to be associated with clients and prospective clients. These controls should be designed to assess the integrity of management. For example, a firm may require a thorough investigation of the integrity of the principals associated with existing and prospective clients. Although the firm must be concerned with the integrity of management, the evaluation performed by the firm does not vouch for the integrity of its management.

In addition to requiring an assessment of management, SQCS-2 requires that controls be established to provide reasonable assurance that the following objectives related to an engagement are achieved:

- Undertake only those engagements that the firm can reasonably expect to be completed with professional competence
- Appropriately consider the risk associated with providing professional services in a particular circumstance

Engagement performance

Quality controls should be designed to reasonably assure that an engagement is performed in a manner that satisfies "professional standards, regulatory requirements, and the firm's standards of quality." These controls should encompass all phases of the engagement—from its initial acceptance to the preparation of the accountant's report. An integral part of engagement performance includes consultation, ranging from references to authoritative literature to discussions with personnel who have expertise relevant to the engagement.

Monitoring

Controls should be established to determine whether the foregoing quality controls are being observed by the firm.

AU 200
The General Standards

Section 201: Nature of the General Standards 13

Section 210: Training and Proficiency of the
    Independent Auditor 14

Section 220: Independence 16

Section 230: Due Care in the Performance of Work 20

SECTION 201

NATURE OF THE GENERAL STANDARDS

Authoritative Pronouncements

SAS-1—Codification of Auditing Standards and Procedures (Section 201, Nature of the General Standards)

Overview

The general standards of generally accepted auditing standards (GAAS) are personal and relate to the qualifications of the auditor and to the professional care exercised in a particular engagement. However, the general standards, standards of fieldwork, and reporting standards are all interrelated and must be applied accordingly.

SECTION 210

TRAINING AND PROFICIENCY OF THE INDEPENDENT AUDITOR

Authoritative Pronouncements

SAS-1—Codification of Auditing Standards and Procedures (Section 210, Training and Proficiency of the Independent Auditor)

Overview

General Standard No. 1 states that "the audit is to be performed by a person or persons having adequate technical training and proficiency as an auditor." This first standard addresses two characteristics that an auditor must possess: adequate technical training and proficiency as an auditor.

A technical body of accounting and auditing knowledge must be mastered as a prerequisite for the successful practice of auditing. This body of knowledge encompasses an understanding of generally accepted accounting principles (GAAP) and generally accepted auditing standards (GAAS). Much of this knowledge can be acquired by the completion of an accounting degree at a college or university.

However, adequate technical training goes beyond the completion of certain accounting courses. Accounting educators and practitioners do not agree on what specific courses a prospective auditor should complete. In one respect, the practitioner's problem of technical training has been solved by the state boards of accountancy, in that these boards establish the minimum number of credits a candidate must complete before taking the certified public accounting (CPA) examination.

For a number of reasons, the practitioner should not take a passive role in accepting the state boards' prescribed course requirements. Not all newly hired auditors will take the CPA examination; some may never meet the state-mandated requirements. In addition, the needs of a particular firm might require that an employee have specialized accounting or auditing training. But most important, adequate technical training is a dynamic concept and the need for it should not apply only to newly hired employees. Having passed the CPA examination ten years ago does not necessarily mean that a CPA is adequately trained today. Thus, a CPA firm must view technical training in the context of its clientele and (1) establish minimum courses that an employee should complete and (2) design a training program that reflects changes in the accounting profession.

§210 • Training and Proficiency of the Independent Auditor

Adequate technical training for an auditor does not go beyond the bounds of accounting and auditing knowledge. A firm may encounter a situation in which the practitioner needs technical training in other disciplines in order to successfully complete an audit engagement. For example, the fairness of the financial statements may be dependent on geological conclusions or actuarial computations. SAS-73 (AU 336) (Using the Work of a Specialist) recognizes the technical limitations of an auditor and establishes guidelines for the use of members of other disciplines. In much the same way, SAS-12 (AU 337) (Inquiry of a Client's Lawyer Concerning Litigation, Claims, and Assessments) provides guidelines for the use of a lawyer in applying Financial Accounting Standards Board Statement (FAS) No. 5 (CT C59) (Accounting for Contingencies).

The second part of the first general standard refers to an auditor's need for proficiency. Success in auditing goes beyond the need for education and training. An auditor should be able to apply his or her knowledge in an actual engagement. Thus, proficiency is gained through on-the-job experience. It should be noted that the basis for proficiency is adequate training and education. Therefore, the practitioner must apply the first general standard on an integrated basis, recognizing the interrelationship of training and proficiency.

> **PLANNING AID REMINDER:** If the first general standard were applied literally to an engagement, only experienced auditors could be used, because of the proficiency requirement. However, General Standard No. 1 must be evaluated in conjunction with the first standard of fieldwork, which notes that assistants must be properly supervised. Thus, professional standards can be achieved if a firm matches the background of its staff with the complexities of a particular engagement and designs a plan of supervision that reflects both the background and the complexities.

SECTION 220

INDEPENDENCE

Authoritative Pronouncements

SAS-1, Codification of Auditing Standards and Procedures (Section 220, Independence)

Overview

General Standard No. 2 states that "in all matters relating to the assignment, an independence in mental attitude is to be maintained by the auditor or auditors." Although every profession should demand that its members be trained and proficient, the second general standard is unique to the auditing profession. The need for independence is a result of the auditor's responsibility to users of the financial statements. Since the users of financial statements have no way of verifying the fairness of the statement, they must rely on the work of an independent auditor. If it is suspected that the auditor is not independent, then the integrity and fairness of the financial statements are questionable.

The Code of Professional Conduct provides guidelines for accounting practitioners in the conduct of their professional affairs. A member of the American Institute of Certified Public Accountants (AICPA) must observe the Rules of Conduct. The applicability of the Code of Professional Conduct is based on the guidance provided by the AICPA, paraphrased as follows:

- The Rules of Conduct that follow apply to all professional services performed except (a) where the wording of the rule indicates otherwise and (b) that a member who is practicing outside the United States will not be subject to discipline for departing from any of the rules stated herein as long as the member's conduct is in accord with the rule of the organized accounting profession in the country in which he or she is practicing. Where a member's name is associated with financial statements under circumstances that entitle the reader to assume that United States practices were followed, however, the member must comply with the requirements of Rules 202 and 203.

- All persons associated with a member in the practice of public accounting and who are either under the member's supervision or are the member's partners or shareholders may hold the member responsible for compliance with the rules.

- A member shall not permit others to carry out on his or her behalf, either with or without compensation, acts which, if carried out by the member, would place the member in violation of the rules.

A member of the AICPA must also be aware of Interpretations of the AICPA Rules of Conduct. After exposure to state societies and state boards of accountancy, Interpretations of the AICPA Rules of Conduct are published, modified, or deleted by the Executive Committee of the Professional Ethics Division. Interpretations are not intended to limit the scope or application of the Rules of Conduct. A member of the AICPA who departs from the guidelines provided in the Interpretations has the burden of justifying such departure in any AICPA disciplinary hearings.

> **OBSERVATION:** Most state societies and boards of accountancy have similar rules or adopt the AICPA model.

Rule 101—Independence

A member in public practice shall be independent in the performance of professional services as required by standards promulgated by bodies designated by AICPA Council.

"Independence" is a highly subjective term, because it concerns an individual's ability to act with integrity and objectivity. Integrity relates to an auditor's honesty, while objectivity is the ability to be neutral during the conduct of the engagement and the preparation of the auditor's report. Two facets of independence are independence in fact and independence in appearance. The second general standard of generally accepted auditing standards (GAAS) requires that an auditor be independent in mental attitude in all matters relating to an engagement. In essence, the second standard embraces the concept of independence in fact. However, independence in fact is impossible to measure, since it is a mental attitude; the Code of Professional Conduct takes a more pragmatic approach to the concept of independence.

Rule 101 is applicable to professional services provided by a CPA that require independence. Engagements that require that a CPA be independent include the following:

- Professional services subject to Statements on Auditing Standards (SASs)

    — Audits of financial statements prepared in accordance with generally accepted accounting principles (GAAP)

    — Audits of financial statements prepared in accordance with a comprehensive basis of accounting other than GAAP [SAS-62 (AU 623) (Special Reports)]

- Reports expressing an opinion on one or more specified elements, accounts, or items of a financial statement [SAS-62 (AU 623)]
- Reports on compliance with aspects of contractual agreements or regulatory requirements related to audited financial statements [SAS-62 (AU 623)]
- Reports on information accompanying the basic financial statements in auditor-submitted documents [SAS-29 (AU 551) (Reporting on Information Accompanying the Basic Financial Statements in Auditor-Submitted Documents)]
- Reports on reviews of interim financial information [SAS-71 (AU 722) (Interim Financial Information)]
- Reports on condensed financial statements and selected financial data [SAS-42 (AU 552) (Reporting on Condensed Financial Statements and Selected Financial Data)]
- Special-purpose reports on internal accounting control at service organizations [SAS-70 (AU 324) (Service Organizations)]
- Reports on financial statements prepared for use in other countries [SAS-51 (AU 534) (Reporting on Financial Statements Prepared for Use in Other Countries)]

- Professional services subject to Statements on Standards for Attestation Engagements (SSAE)
  - Agreed-upon procedures (AUP) engagements
  - Financial forecasts and projections engagements
  - Reporting on pro forma financial information engagements
  - Reporting on an entity's internal control over financial reporting engagements
  - Compliance with requirements of specified laws, regulations, rules, contracts, and grants engagements
  - Reporting on the effectiveness of an entity's internal control over compliance with specified requirements
  - Reporting on management's discussion and analysis engagements

- Professional services subject to Statements on Standards for Accounting and Review Services (SSARS)
  - Reviews of financial statements prepared by nonpublic entities
  - Compilations of financial statements prepared by nonpublic entities

> **PLANNING AID REMINDER:** A CPA may conduct a compilation engagement when he or she is not independent, but the compilation report must be modified to disclose the lack of independence.

- Professional services subject to Statements on Standards for Accountants' Services on Prospective Financial Information

  — Examinations, compilations, or applications of agreed-upon procedures to financial forecasts and projects

  > **PLANNING AID REMINDER:** Statements on Standards for Accountants' Services on Prospective Financial Information have been codified as Statements on Standards for Attestation Engagements.

- Professional services subject to Statements on Standards for Attestation Engagements (SSAE)

  — Examinations, reviews, or applications of agreed-upon procedures to engagements where the accountant expresses a written conclusion about the reliability of a written assertion that is the responsibility of another party

  > **ENGAGEMENT STRATEGY:** The 1999/2000 *Audit Risk Alert* reminds auditors that state societies, state boards of accountancy, and state regulatory agencies may have additional requirements for assessing whether independence has been compromised. Also, if the client is a public entity, regulations established by the Securities and Exchange Commission and Independence Standards Board must be considered.

SECTION 230

DUE CARE IN THE PERFORMANCE OF WORK

Authoritative Pronouncements

SAS-1—Codification of Auditing Standards and Procedures (Section 230, Due Professional Care in the Performance of Work)

Overview

General Standard No. 3 states that "due professional care is to be exercised in the planning and performance of the audit and the preparation of the report." The final general standard requires that the auditor exercise due professional care in planning and performing an audit engagement, including preparing the auditor's report. This general standard recognizes that even if an auditor is competent and independent, these qualities alone will not necessarily result in a successful audit. Besides possessing these qualities, an auditor must be conscientious in conducting the engagement.

In some respects, the standard of due professional care encompasses the other nine generally accepted auditing standards (GAAS). The auditor must observe the standards of fieldwork and reporting in order to comply with the concept of due professional care. The fieldwork and reporting standards can be achieved only if the auditor is adequately trained and experienced and has an independent mental attitude.

On the other hand, the standard of due professional care is more than just the observance of the other nine standards. This standard is the synthesizer for the entire audit process. The auditor is expected to pull together all the facts gathered during the engagement and to use his or her experience and professional judgment to reach a conclusion about the fairness of the financial statements or some other specific facet of the engagement. Two fundamental aspects of this audit process are (1) professional skepticism and (2) reasonable assurance.

Professional skepticism

Every task performed by a professional person is approached with a mental attitude. In an audit engagement, that mental attitude is described as professional skepticism. Professional skepticism does not suggest that the auditor assumes the client's management is dishonest or that everything management says is incorrect. According to SAS-1, the appropriate mental state the auditor assumes is "an attitude that includes a questioning mind and a critical assessment of audit evidence." For example, as a gesture of courtesy, a client's

§230 • Due Care in the Performance of Work   21

employee might offer to mail confirmations that the auditor has just prepared. While the auditor is almost certain that the offer is genuine, professional skepticism would require that the auditor exercise due care in performing the audit and deliver the confirmations directly to the U.S. Postal Service.

Reasonable assurance

The performance of an audit is a complex process, and no matter how professionally it may be performed the auditor cannot offer a guarantee (absolute assurance) that the financial statements are not materially misstated. Fundamentally, the audit process is based on professional judgment in planning the engagement and determining the nature, timing, and extent of audit procedures.

For example, an audit generally involves the selective testing of data, rather than a 100% examination. There is no guarantee that material errors or fraud rest in the items not tested. Even for those items tested, the auditor must use judgment in assessing the implications for the audit, and as in all professional services, the assessment might not always be correct. Besides, the accounting process is based on numerous estimates and judgments, which may or may not be confirmed by future events. In the audit environment, the best an auditor can do is to collect competent and sufficient evidence that is persuasive rather than convincing. For this reason, the auditor's opinion on the financial statements is a reasonable assurance and not an absolute assurance.

While the use of professional judgment in determining the scope of the engagement and the assessment of accounting estimates are fundamental to every audit engagement, fraud is another factor that restricts the level of assurance that the auditor can offer. There is always a chance, even when an engagement has been properly planned and executed, that the auditor may fail to detect a material misstatement of the financial statements caused by fraud. For example, it may be difficult to detect fraud that is based on collusion between management personnel and third parties. Auditing standards do not require the authentication of documentation by auditors, and auditors are not experts in such authentication.

SAS-1 concludes that "the subsequent discovery that a material misstatement, whether from error or from fraud, exists in the financial statements does not, in and of itself, evidence (a) failure to obtain reasonable assurance; (b) inadequate planning, performance, or judgment; (c) the absence of due professional care; or (d) a failure to comply with generally accepted auditing standards."

Practitioner's Aids

Professional skepticism is a key element of observing the General Standard No. 3 of GAAS. The practitioner's aid presented in Exhibit AU 230-1 is based on the guidance provided in the AICPA's Practice Alert 98-2 (Professional Skepticism and Related Topics). Practice Alerts are based on existing auditing standards and are issued by the AICPA to help practitioners improve the efficiency and effectiveness of their audits.

EXHIBIT AU 230-1—PROFESSIONAL SKEPTICISM

Key Questions on Skepticism	Suggested Guidance Provided by Practice Alert 98-2
• What is professional skepticism?	Professional skepticism is an attitude that includes a questioning mind and working practices that en compass a critical assess ment of audit evidence.
• Should professional skepticism be exercised throughout the audit?	Because audit evidence is gathered and evaluated throughout an engagement, professional skepticism must be exercised during the entire engagement.
• Does professional skepticism mean that statements made by management should never be accepted?	The auditor should strike a balance between disbelief and unquestioning acceptance.
• What level of evidence should the auditor obtain in exercising professional skepticism?	Evidence should be persuasive.
• Do representations by management provide persuasive evidence?	Representations by management, without further corroboration, rarely provide persuasive evidence.
• What are some audit areas that may demand particular scrutiny?	Management responses to questions resulting from analytical reviews
	Representations regarding recoverability of assets or deferred charges

§230 • Due Care in the Performance of Work

- Which conditions related to nonstandard journal entries may suggest heightened skepticism with respect to a particular account balance?

  Accruals (or lack thereof), particularly for unusual events or transactions

  Substance of large and unusual (particularly period-end) transactions

  Vague contract terms or conditions

  Existence of nonstandard journal entries (see discussion below)

  Lack of copies of original documents (see discussion below)

  Journal entries processed outside the normal course of business

  Transactions that are complex or unusual in nature

  Estimates and period-end adjustments.

  Journal entries indicative of potential problems with the accounting systems

  Item has been prone to client error in the past

  Item has not been reconciled on a timely basis or contains old reconciling items

  Represents a particular risk specific to the client's industry

  Represents account balances affecting the company's book value and liquidity (e.g., account balances that are used in determining loan covenant ratios).

- Does the use of photocopies or draft copies (rather than originals) have effect on audit skepticism?

    Yes; it may be more difficult to identify alterations on photocopied material, and draft copies might not include all relevant information. With the use of scanners, original documents can be altered in a way that makes detection especially difficult.

- When originals are not available, what alternative procedures are available to the auditor?

    The auditor should consider whether the originals should be obtained and inspected.

- Should the auditor accept facsimile (fax) confirmation responses?

    The auditor should consider whether one (a) to confirm the information over the telephone and/or (b) to request that the original confirmation be returned directly to the auditor.

AU 300

The Standards of Field Work

Section 310: Appointment of the Independent Auditor....................27

Section 311: Planning and Supervision 32

Section 312: Audit Risk and Materiality in Conducting an Audit 48

Section 313: Substantive Tests Prior to the Balance Sheet Date 67

Section 315: Communications between Predecessor and Successor Auditors 72

Section 316: Consideration of Fraud in a Financial Statement Audit 80

Section 317: Illegal Acts by Clients...91

Section 319: Consideration of Internal Control in a Financial Statement Audit 97

Section 322: The Auditor's Consideration of the Internal Audit Function in an Audit of Financial Statements 118

Section 324: Service Organizations 124

Section 325: Communication of Internal Control Related Matters Noted in an Audit 140

Section 326: Evidential Matter 151

Section 329: Analytical Procedures...156

Section 330: The Confirmation Process 171

Section 331: Inventories 185

Section 332: Auditing Derivative Instruments, Hedging Activities, and Investments in Securities 192

Section 333: Management Representations 200

Section 334: Related Parties 209

Section 336: Using the Work of a Specialist 216

Section 337: Inquiry of a Client's Lawyer Concerning Litigation,
    Claims, and Assessments 223

Section 339: Working Papers..232

Section 341: The Auditor's Consideration of an Entity's Ability
    to Continue as a Going Concern 238

Section 342: Auditing Accounting Estimates..............................248

Section 350: Audit Sampling 256

Section 380: Communication with Audit Committees....................297

Section 390: Consideration of Omitted Procedures after the
    Report Date 303

SECTION 310

APPOINTMENT OF THE INDEPENDENT AUDITOR

Authoritative Pronouncements

SAS-83—Establishing an Understanding with the Client

SAS-89—Audit Adjustments

Overview

The auditor should communicate (1) the objectives and limitations of an audit engagement, (2) the responsibilities of the auditor, and (3) the responsibilities of the client. This is all part of establishing an understanding with the client.

Promulgated Procedures Checklist

The auditor should perform the following procedures in determining whether an appropriate understanding has been established with the client:

_____ Identify the basic understandings related to an engagement.

_____ Consider other matters that should be part of the understanding.

_____ Document the understanding in the workpapers.

Analysis and Application of Procedures

Identify the basic understandings related to an engagement

SAS-83 notes that, generally, the understanding should encompass the following items:

- That the purpose of an audit is to express an opinion on the financial statements
- That management is responsible for its financial statements
- That management is responsible for establishing and maintaining effective internal control over financial reporting

- That management is responsible for identifying the laws and regulations applicable to its activities and ensuring that the entity complies with these laws and regulations
- That management is responsible for making all financial records and related information available to the auditor
- That at the conclusion of the engagement management will provide the auditor with a letter that confirms certain representations made during the audit.
- That management is responsible for adjusting the financial statements to remove any material misstatements
- That management is responsible for stating in the representation letter that any misstatements identified by the auditor and not corrected are immaterial, "both individually and in the aggregate," with respect to the financial statements taken as a whole
- That the auditor is responsible for conducting the audit in accordance with generally accepted auditing standards (GAAS). GAAS standards require that the auditor obtain a reasonable, rather than an absolute, assurance about whether the financial statements are free of material misstatement and whether misstatements are caused by error or by fraud. Accordingly, a material misstatement might remain undetected. Also, an audit is not designed to detect error or fraud that is immaterial to the financial statements. If for any reason the auditor is unable to complete the audit or is unable to form or has not formed an opinion, he or she may decline to express an opinion or to issue a report as a result of the engagement.
- That an audit includes obtaining an understanding of internal control sufficient to plan the audit and to determine the nature, timing, and extent of audit procedures to be performed. An audit is not designed to provide assurance on internal control or to identify reportable conditions. However, the auditor is responsible for ensuring that the audit committee or others with equivalent authority or responsibility are aware of any reportable conditions that come to the auditor's attention.

Consider other matters that should be part of the understanding

SAS-83 also notes that an auditor may include other matters, such as the following, as part of the understanding with the client:

- Arrangements regarding the conduct of the engagement (timing, client assistance regarding the preparation of schedules, and the availability of documents)

§310 • Appointment of the Independent Auditor 29

- Arrangements concerning involvement of specialists or internal auditors, if applicable
- Arrangements involving a predecessor auditor
- Arrangements regarding fees and billing
- Any limitation or other arrangements regarding the liability of the auditor or the client, such as indemnification to the auditor for liability arising from known misrepresentations to the auditor by management (SAS-83 notes that regulators, including the Securities and Exchange Commission, may restrict or prohibit such liability limitation arrangements.)
- Conditions under which access to the auditor's workpapers may be granted to others
- Additional services to be provided relating to regulatory requirements
- Arrangements regarding other services to be provided in connection with the engagement

Document the understanding in the workpapers

Auditing standards require that the understanding with the client be documented in the workpapers (preferably in the form of a client engagement letter). If the auditor believes that an understanding with the client has not been established, the engagement should not be accepted (or performed).

> **PLANNING AID REMINDER:** The guidance established by SAS-83 is written in the context of an audit engagement; however, the understanding should be modified to reflect the type of service provided by the auditor. For example, modifications would be required by an engagement subject to SAS-71 (AU 722) (Interim Financial Information), SAS-74 (AU 801) (Compliance Auditing Considerations in Audits of Governmental Entities and Recipients of Governmental Financial Assistance), and SAS-75 (AU 622) (Engagements to Apply Agreed-Upon Procedures to Specified Elements, Accounts, or Items of a Financial Statement).

Exhibit AU 310-1 presents an example of an engagement letter that establishes an appropriate understanding with the client.

Practitioner's Aids

EXHIBIT AU 310-1—ENGAGEMENT LETTER

Mr. Robert J. Bray, President
Averroes Company
1800 Carolina Avenue
Cherry Hill, NJ 08003

Dear Mr. Bray:

In accordance with the agreement reached in our conference on October 14, 20X5, we are to perform an audit of the balance sheet of Averroes Company as of December 31, 20X5, and of the related statements of income, retained earnings, and cash flows for the fiscal year then ended. The audit report will be mailed to you and to the Board of Directors. During our conference we discussed a number of factors, and we have reached the following understanding with you and your management:

- The purpose of our audit is to express an opinion on the financial statements of Averroes Company based on the performance of generally accepted auditing standards. Those standards require that we obtain reasonable rather than absolute assurance about whether the financial statements are free of material misstatement, whether caused by error or by fraud. Accordingly, a material misstatement may remain undetected. Also, our audit is not designed to detect error or fraud that is immaterial to the financial statements. If, for any reason, we are unable to complete the audit or we are unable to form an opinion on the financial statement, we may decline to express an opinion or decline to issue a report as a result of the engagement.
- You and your management are responsible for (a) the financial statements, (b) establishing and maintaining effective internal control over financial reporting, (c) identifying and ensuring that the company complies with the laws and regulations applicable to its activities and (d) making all financial records and related information available to the auditor.
- At the conclusion of the engagement, we will request that your management provide us with a letter that confirms certain representations made during the audit.

- Our audit will include obtaining an understanding of internal control sufficient to plan the audit and to determine the nature, timing, and extent of audit procedures to be performed. An audit is not designed to provide assurance on internal control or to identify reportable conditions. However, we are responsible for ensuring that the audit committee is aware of any reportable conditions that come to our attention.

In addition to the performance of an audit of your financial statements, we will prepare the federal and state income tax returns for the fiscal year ending December 31, 20X5.

Based on our discussion with your personnel and the predecessor auditor and after a preliminary review of your accounting records, we estimate that the cost of the audit engagement, including the preparation of the related tax returns, will be between $75,000 and $80,000. It should be recognized that the estimated fee could be affected by unusual circumstances we cannot foresee at this time. However, if we should encounter such problems, we will contact you to discuss the implications of the new developments.

Whenever possible, we will attempt to use your company's personnel. This effort should substantially reduce our time requirements and help us perform an efficient audit.

We appreciate the opportunity to serve your company. Do not hesitate to contact us if you have questions about the engagement or desire other professional services.

If the terms designated in this letter are satisfactory, please sign in the space provided below and return the copy of the letter to us.

Sincerely,
Penny J. Nichols, CPA

Accepted by:
Title:
Date:

SECTION 311

PLANNING AND SUPERVISION

Authoritative Pronouncements

SAS-22—Planning and Supervision

SAS-47—Audit Risk and Materiality in Conducting an Audit

SAS-48—The Effects of Computer Processing on the Examination of Financial Statements

SAS-77—Amendments to Statements on Auditing Standards No. 22, "Planning and Supervision," No. 59, "The Auditor's Consideration of an Entity's Ability to Continue as a Going Concern," and No. 62, "Special Reports"

Auditing Interpretation (February 1980)—Communications Between the Auditor and Firm Personnel Responsible for Non-Audit Services

Auditing Interpretation (February 1986)—Responsibility of Assistants for the Resolution of Accounting and Auditing Issues

Overview

The first standard of fieldwork requires that an engagement be adequately planned and that assistants be properly supervised. This standard recognizes that the successful completion of an audit engagement is a difficult task and, like most difficult tasks, requires proper planning. Adequate planning of an audit encompasses features such as understanding the basic characteristics of the client, determining personnel requirements, and determining how to use a firm's resources in an effective manner.

Part of the first standard of fieldwork also requires that staff assistants be properly supervised. In most audit engagements, several auditors with varying degrees of experience will be used. When two or more auditors are involved in an engagement, there must be a system of review and supervision. The degree of supervision will depend on a variety of factors, such as the background of the assistant and the nature of the work being performed by the assistant.

Promulgated Procedures Checklist

The auditor should perform the following procedures in determining whether the audit engagement has been (1) adequately planned and (2) properly supervised (if assistants are used):

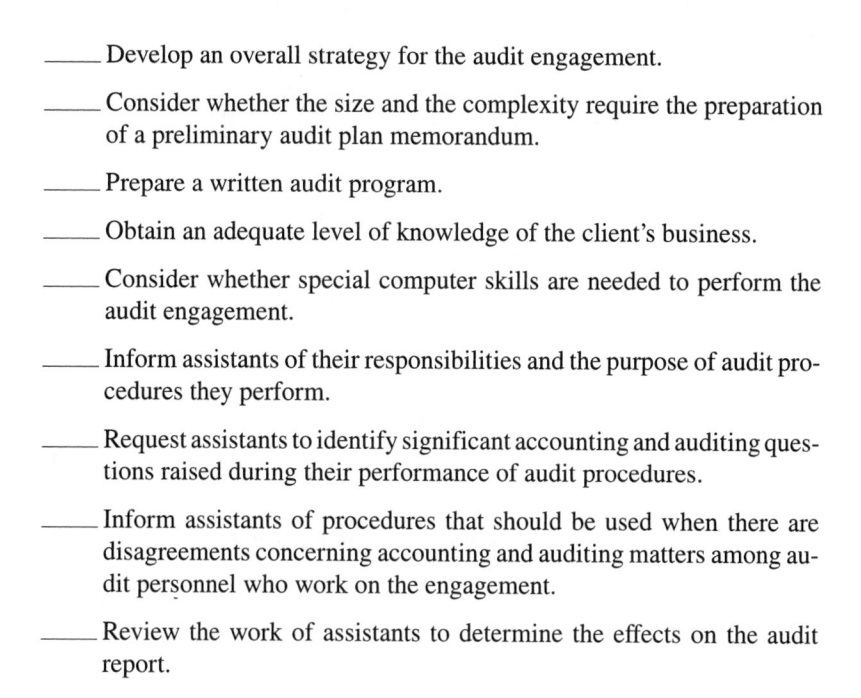

§311 • Planning and Supervision

___ Develop an overall strategy for the audit engagement.

___ Consider whether the size and the complexity require the preparation of a preliminary audit plan memorandum.

___ Prepare a written audit program.

___ Obtain an adequate level of knowledge of the client's business.

___ Consider whether special computer skills are needed to perform the audit engagement.

___ Inform assistants of their responsibilities and the purpose of audit procedures they perform.

___ Request assistants to identify significant accounting and auditing questions raised during their performance of audit procedures.

___ Inform assistants of procedures that should be used when there are disagreements concerning accounting and auditing matters among audit personnel who work on the engagement.

___ Review the work of assistants to determine the effects on the audit report.

Analysis and Application of Procedures

Develop an overall strategy for the audit engagement

The specific audit strategy for an engagement is based on the characteristics of the client. Specific factors that the auditor should consider include the following:

- Characteristics of the client's business and the related industry
- Accounting controls used by the client
- Data processing methods used by the client, especially the role of computers
- The planned assessed level of control (see AU Section 319)
- Preliminary materiality levels
- Conditions that may require the modification of audit procedures, such as the risk of fraud or related-party transactions

If firm personnel have performed nonaudit services for the client, the auditor should consider whether these services have affected the financial statements (tax planning and the affect on the tax accrual) and the performance of audit procedures (design of a cost accounting system and the effect on the valuation of inventories and related costs).

Specific procedures that the auditor may use as part of the planning of the audit engagement include the following:

- Review correspondence files, current audit files, permanent audit files, and prior years' audit reports
- Inquire about current industrial, economic, and regulatory developments that may be relevant to the audit engagement
- Read the current year's interim financial statements that are available
- Discuss in general the preliminary audit strategy with key client personnel, members of the board of directors, and members of the audit committee
- Evaluate the potential impact of new accounting standards on the client's financial statements
- Consider the use of client personnel in the execution of the audit engagement
- Consider the need for special expertise in the conduct of the audit engagement
- Determine a preliminary timing for the performance of the engagement
- Identify staff requirements, and coordinate the requirements with other firm personnel

Consider whether the size and the complexity of the engagement require the preparation of a preliminary audit plan memorandum

For small engagements it may not be necessary to prepare an audit plan memorandum; however, to facilitate the planning and supervision of a large and complex engagement, the auditor should considered whether such an memorandum is essential.

Prepare a written audit program

Every audit engagement should include a set of written audit programs, which should incorporate the following guidance:

- The procedures should be reasonably detailed.
- The form of the audit programs should be based on the initial planning considerations.

§311 • Planning and Supervision

Obtain an adequate level of knowledge of the client's business

The auditor should develop a background of the client's business that will enable him or her to have an adequate understanding of the events, transactions, and practices that may have a significant impact on the client's financial statements.

An adequate understanding of the client's business includes factors such as the following:

- The client's industry, competitive forces within the industry, and the degree of regulation
- The structure of the organization, including compensation packages and pay incentives
- The operating characteristics, including distribution systems and strategies
- Major sources of financing, including major stockholders and creditors
- Operating personnel, including key management players
- Any related parties or related organizations
- The role of technology in product development and distribution
- Past financial statements, creditor reports, and other relevant reports

This understanding will enable the auditor to recognize situations that may affect such matters as management's representations, the need for and reasonableness of estimates, and the appropriateness of specific accounting principles.

> **ENGAGEMENT STRATEGY:** An auditor who is unfamiliar with the basic characteristics of the client's industry may develop an adequate insight by reading the relevant AICPA Accounting and Audit Guides (one has been developed for the client's industry). Also, a tremendous amount of information is available through the Internet using search engines such as Yahoo! and the Open Directory Project.

Consider whether special computer skills are needed to perform the audit engagement

The auditor should be alert early in the planning stage of an engagement to determine whether the client information system is computerized in a manner that is beyond the auditor's expertise. Factors that the auditor should consider during the planning stage with respect to the client's computerized system include the following:

- The degree to which the computer is used to process accounting information
- The degree of complexity of the client's computerized system
- The use of outside services to process accounting data
- The form of data and documentation that is available to the auditor
- The possible use of computer-assisted audit techniques by the auditor

The auditor may resolve this issue by using firm personnel or outside consultants.

> **RISK ASSESSMENT POINT:** When outside computer personnel are used, the auditor must have sufficient computer background to be able to describe the objective of the work that the outside party will perform and to evaluate the results of the procedures performed in order to determine whether they satisfy the requirements of the engagement.

Inform assistants of their responsibilities and the purpose of audit procedures they perform

Assistants used in an engagement should know their role in relationship to specific audit objectives and the reason they are performing audit procedures outlined in an audit program. The degree of instruction will vary depending on the experience of assistants and the complexity of the procedures to be performed.

> **SUPERVISION AID REMINDER:** Often there is an inverse relationship between the time spent with an assistant in the planning stage and the time needed to review the assistant's workpapers. A little extra time spent up front with an assistant may avoid the need to redo work later.

Request assistants to identify significant accounting and auditing questions raised during their performance of audit procedures

An engagement can be performed more efficiently if the audit supervisor stays in reasonably close contact with assistants and lets them know that accounting and auditing issues should be discussed earlier, rather than later, in an engagement.

Inform assistants of procedures that should be used when there are disagreements concerning accounting and auditing matters among audit personnel who work on the engagement

An effective audit team is one that recognizes that concerns and disagreements can be aired and resolved in a professional and responsible manner. Often, assistants' willingness to raise these issues is based not so much on procedures established by the firm as on the personality of the supervising auditor.

> **RISK ASSESSMENT POINT:** In order to avoid embarrassing situations that may arise when an engagement is evaluated by an outside party, it is important to have established (written) procedures concerning the resolution of disagreements over auditing and accounting issues that may arise. The firm's policy must make it clear that each assistant has the right and responsibility to document any position taken if he or she chooses not to be associated with the final resolution of a matter.

Review the work of assistants to determine the effects on the audit report

The supervising auditor should allow adequate time to review the results of the assistants' workpapers to make sure that those results are consistent with the audit conclusion that is being expressed in the report.

Practitioner's Aids

Use a planning checklist

The auditor may use an engagement planning checklist to control the planning phase of the audit engagement. An example of such a checklist is presented in Exhibit AU 311-1.

EXHIBIT AU 311-1—AUDIT ENGAGEMENT PLANNING CHECKLIST

Use the following checklist as a guide for planning audit procedures in a continuing engagement. The checklist is only a guide, and professional judgment should be exercised to determine how the checklist should be modified by revising questions listed or adding questions to the checklist where appropriate.

Check the appropriate response. If the question is not relevant to this particular audit engagement, place "N/A" (not applicable) in the space provided for the workpaper reference. If additional explanation is needed with respect to a question, provide a proper cross-reference to another workpaper.

Client Name: _____

Date of Financial Statements: _____

	Yes	No	Workpaper Reference
1. Is the scope of the audit engagement limited to a single financial statement?	___	___	_____
• If yes, have we identified the notes and other disclosures that are appropriate for a single financial statement presentation?	___	___	_____
• If yes, are the other financial statements going to be available for our perusal in order to identify events, transactions, and balances that may have implications for the audited financial statements?	___	___	_____
2. Are comparative financial statements presented?	___	___	_____
• If yes, are we responsible for reporting on the previous year's financial statements?	___	___	_____
3. If a predecessor CPA is reporting on the previous year's financial statements, have we:			
• Asked the client for permission to discuss relevant matters with the predecessor CPA?	___	___	_____
• Considered what matters to discuss with the predecessor CPA?	___	___	_____
• Arranged to communicate matters discovered in the current engagement to the predecessor CPA?	___	___	_____
• Arranged to provide the predecessor with a preliminary draft of the current and previous year's financial statements and our audit report?	___	___	_____

§311 • Planning and Supervision

			Workpaper
	Yes	No	*Reference*

- Considered the format and content of the representation letter to be issued to the predecessor CPA? ___ ___ _____

4. Have we considered the effect on audit procedures if the client has decided not to present a statement of cash flows? ___ ___ _____

5. If the client has decided to present supplementary information, which is not part of the basic financial statements, are we engaged to review the supplementary information? ___ ___ _____

6. If a portion of the financial statements is audited by another CPA, have we determined whether we can serve as the principal CPA? ___ ___ _____

7. If we can serve as the principal CPA, have we considered whether to refer in ouraudit report to the work done by the other CPA? ___ ___ _____

8. Have we identified the bases (operating income, total assets, etc.) and percentages of those amounts that should be used by subordinates to identify material misstatement? ___ ___ _____

9. In designing the specific inquiries to be made, have we considered: ___ ___ _____

    - The nature and materiality of items? ___ ___ _____
    - The likelihood of misstatement? ___ ___ _____
    - Knowledge obtained during current and previous engagements? ___ ___ _____
    - The stated qualifications of the entity's accounting personnel? ___ ___ _____
    - The extent to which a particular item is affected by management's judgment? ___ ___ _____
    - The inadequacies in the entity's underlying financial data? ___ ___ _____

Prepared By: _____

Date: _____

_____

Prospective client The degree of planning of an audit engagement is greatly affected by whether an engagement is new or recurring. Exhibit AU 311-2 is a prospective client evaluation form that can be helpful in determining whether a client should be accepted. Once a client is accepted, the form can be used as an integral part of the planning of the accepted engagement.

EXHIBIT AU 311-2—PROSPECTIVE CLIENT EVALUATION FORM

Use this form to document the evaluation of a prospective client who has requested audited financial statements. The memo format is only a guide. The auditor should exercise professional judgment to determine how the form should by modified by adding, deleting, or revising captions to the memo format.

The evaluation process does not imply that our firm is vouching for the integrity or reliability of the prospective client.

Name of Prospective Client: _____

Date of Financial Statements: _____

1. Describe how contact was established with the prospective client.

   _____
   _____
   _____

2. Provide a background of the principals that represent the client.

   _____
   _____
   _____

3. Describe the nature of the products and/or services provided by the prospective client.

   _____
   _____
   _____

§311 • Planning and Supervision 41

4. Describe the services and dates of services provided by the predecessor CPA.

   _____
   _____
   _____

5. Explain the reason(s) why the prospective client has decided to seek the services of another CPA.

   _____
   _____
   _____

6. Summarize the explanation for the change of accountants as understood by the predecessor CPA. (If the predecessor CPA firm has not been contacted, provide the reason that contact was not made.)

   _____
   _____
   _____

7. Summarize the history of the prospective client and other CPA firms (other than the predecessor CPA firm) that have provided service for the past 10 years.

   _____
   _____
   _____

8. Explain why the client desires audited financial statements, and identify external parties who may rely on the statements.

   _____
   _____
   _____

9. Describe any litigation that the client and its principals have been involved in during the past 5 years.

   _____
   _____
   _____

10. Summarize information obtained from credit bureaus, etc., concerning the credit rating of the client and its principals.

    _____
    _____
    _____

11. Other information:

   _____

   _____

   _____

Prepared By: _____

Date: _____

Client Accepted (Yes or No): _____

Acceptance Date: _____

Signature of CPA: _____

   _____

Continuing engagement questionnaire

If the client is a continuing engagement, the auditor may use a questionnaire such as the one illustrated in Exhibit AU 311-3.

EXHIBIT AU 311-3—AUDIT QUESTIONNAIRE CHECKLIST —CONTINUING ENGAGEMENT

Use the following checklist as a guide for planning audit procedures in a continuing engagement. The checklist is only a guide, and professional judgment should be exercised to determine how the checklist should be modified by revising questions listed or adding questions to the checklist where appropriate.

Initial and date each question as it is considered. If the question is not relevant to this particular audit engagement, place "N/A" (not applicable) in the space provided for an initial. If the answer to the question is "no" or if additional explanation is needed with respect to a question, provide a proper cross-reference to another workpaper.

Client Name: _____

Date of Financial Statements: _____

§311 • Planning and Supervision

	Yes	No	*Workpaper Reference*

1. Have we acquired an adequate understanding of specialized accounting principles and practices of the client's industry by:

   - Reviewing relevant AICPA Accounting /Audit Guides? ___ ___ _____

   - Reviewing financial statements of other entities in the same industry? ___ ___ _____

   - Consulting with other individuals familiar with accounting practices in the specialized industry? ___ ___ _____

   - Reading periodicals, textbooks, and other publications? ___ ___ _____

   - Performing other procedures? (Describe.) ___ ___ _____

2. Have we developed an understanding of the client's organization, including:

   - The form of business organization? ___ ___ _____

   - The history of the client? ___ ___ _____

   - The principals involved in the organizational chart or similar analysis? ___ ___ _____

   - Other relevant matters? (Describe.)

3. Have we developed an understanding of the client's operating characteristics, including:

   - An understanding of the client's products and services? ___ ___ _____

   - Identification of operating locations? ___ ___ _____

   - An understanding of production methods? ___ ___ _____

   - Other operating characteristics? (Describe.) ___ ___ _____

	Yes	No	Workpaper Reference

4. Have we developed an understanding of the nature of the client's assets, liabilities, revenues, and expenses by:
   - Reviewing the client's chart of accounts? ___ ___ _____
   - Reviewing the previous year's financial statements?
   - Considering the relationships between specific accounts and the nature of the client's business? ___ ___ _____
   - Performing other procedures? (Describe.) ___ ___ _____
5. Have we made inquiries concerning accounting principles, practices, and methods? ___ ___ _____
6. Have we made inquiries concerning the accounting procedures used by the client, including:
   - Recording transactions? ___ ___ _____
   - Classifying transactions? ___ ___ _____
   - Summarizing transactions? ___ ___ _____
   - Accumulating information for making disclosures in the financial statements? ___ ___ _____
   - Other accounting procedures? (Describe.) ___ ___ _____
7. Have we made inquiries concerning the effect on the financial statements due to actions taken at meetings of:
   - Stockholders? ___ ___ _____
   - The board of directors? ___ ___ _____
   - Other committees? (Describe.) ___ ___ _____
8. If there were changes in the application of accounting principles:
   - Did the change in accounting principle include the adoption of another acceptable accounting principle? ___ ___ _____

§311 • Planning and Supervision 45

	Yes	No	*Workpaper Reference*

- Was the change properly justified?
- Were the effects of the change presented in the financial statements, including adequate disclosure, in a manner consistent with APB-20? ___ ___ _____
- Were there other matters that we took into consideration? ___ ___ _____

9. Have we made inquiries concerning changes in the client's business activities that may require the adoption of different accounting principles, and have we considered the implication of this change for the financial statements? ___ ___ _____

10. Have we made inquiries concerning the occurrence of events subsequent to the date of the financial statements that may require:

    - Adjustments to the financial statements? ___ ___ _____
    - Disclosures in the financial statements? ___ ___ _____

11. Have we considered whether other professional services are needed in order to complete the audit engagement, including:

    - Preparing a working trial balance? ___ ___ _____
    - Preparing adjusting journal entries? ___ ___ _____
    - Consulting matters fundamental to the preparation of acceptable financial statements? ___ ___ _____
    - Preparing tax returns? ___ ___ _____
    - Providing bookkeeping or data processing services that do not include the generation of financial statements? ___ ___ _____
    - Other services considered necessary before a audit can be performed? (Describe.) ___ ___ _____

	Yes	No	*Workpaper Reference*

12. Have we obtained reports from other CPA(s) who reported on the financial statements of components of the client-reporting entity if we have decided to rely on their reports? ___ ___ _____

Reviewed By: _____

Date: _____

Supervision checklist

The auditor may use a supervision checklist, such as the one illustration in Exhibit AU 311-4, in an engagement.

EXHIBIT AU 311-4—AUDIT ENGAGEMENT SUPERVISION CHECKLIST

Use the following checklist as a guide for supervising an audit engagement. The checklist is only a guide, and professional judgment should be exercised to determine how the checklist should be modified by revising questions listed or adding questions to the checklist where appropriate.

Check the appropriate response. If the question is not relevant to this particular audit engagement, place "N/A" (not applicable) in the space provided for the workpaper reference. If additional explanation is needed with respect to a question, provide a proper cross-reference to another workpaper.

Client Name: _____

Date of Financial Statements: _____

In-Charge Accountant: _____

Assistants: _____

§311 • Planning and Supervision

	Yes	No	Workpaper Reference

1. Have assistants been adequately prepared for the engagement, including: ___ ___ _____

   - Reviewing the previous year's workpapers? ___ ___ _____

   - Reviewing the previous year's financial statements? ___ ___ _____

   - Informing them of developments that affect the current engagement? ___ ___ _____

   - Discussing engagement budget? ___ ___ _____

   - Other matters? (Describe.) ___ ___ _____

2. Have assistants been instructed to communicate significant problems to the in-charge accountant on a timely basis? ___ ___ _____

3. Have we made arrangements to review work-papers on a timely basis? ___ ___ _____

4. Have assistants been instructed to discuss their disagreements concerning professional matters with the in-charge accountant? ___ ___ _____

5. Have assistants been informed about procedures available to document their disagreements concerning professional matters? ___ ___ _____

6. Have other matters relative to supervising the engagement been identified? (Describe.) ___ ___ _____

Reviewed By: _____

Date: _____

SECTION 312

AUDIT RISK AND MATERIALITY IN CONDUCTING AN AUDIT

Authoritative Pronouncements

SAS-47—Audit Risk and Materiality in Conducting an Audit

Auditing Interpretation (December 2000)—The Meaning of the Term Misstatement

Auditing Interpretation (December 2000)—Evaluating Differences in Estimates

Auditing Interpretation (December 2000)—Quantitative Measures of Materiality in Evaluating Audit Findings

Auditing Interpretation (December 2000)—Considering the Qualitative Characteristics of Misstatements

Overview

In determining the nature, timing, and extent of audit procedures, the auditor should consider, among other factors, materiality and audit risk. "Materiality" is defined in the FASB's Statement of Financial Accounting Concepts No. 2 (Qualitative Characteristics of Accounting Information) as "the magnitude of an omission or misstatement of account information that, in the light of surrounding circumstances, makes it probable that the judgment of a reasonable person relying on the information would have been changed or influenced by the omission or misstatement." "Audit risk" is "the risk that the auditor may unknowingly fail to appropriately modify his or her opinion on financial statements that are materially misstated." The concept of audit risk is based on the reality that the audit process can result in only a reasonable assurance (not an absolute assurance) that the auditor will detect materially misstated financial statements (whether from error or from fraud). SAS-47 [(Audit Risk and Materiality in Conducting an Audit) as amended by SAS-82 (AU 316)] explains how the auditor should integrate the concepts of materiality and audit risk into the planning and execution of an audit engagement.

ENGAGEMENT STRATEGY: The Auditing Interpretation (December 2000) titled "The Meaning of the Term Misstatement" points out that a misstatement in the financial statements in-

§312 • Audit Risk and Materiality in Conducting an Audit   49

clude (1) a difference between the amount, classification, or presentation of a reported financial statements element, account, or item and the amount, classification, or presentation that would have been reported under GAAP; (2) the omission of a financial statement element, account, or item; (3) a financial statement disclosure that is not presented in accordance with GAAP; or (4) the omission of information required to be disclosed in accordance with GAAP.

OBSERVATION: Audit risk and materiality in an audit engagement relate to the assertions that are explicitly stated or implied in the financial statements. There are five broad categories of assertions identified in SAS-31 (AU 326) (Evidential Matter).

An auditor's opinion refers to materiality of the financial statements in the context of the financial statements taken as a whole. SAS-47 concludes that "financial statements are materially misstated when they contain misstatements whose effect, individually or in the aggregate, is important enough to cause them not to be presented fairly in all material respects, in conformity with generally accepted accounting principles." An auditor has no responsibility to plan and perform an engagement in order to obtain a reasonable assurance that immaterial misstatements (from error or from fraud) will be discovered.

Errors refer to unintentional misstatements or omissions of amounts or disclosures from financial statements, whereas fraud is based on the perpetrator's deceit; however, the auditor's responsibility with respect to material misstatement in the financial statements is the same for errors as for fraud. On the other hand, the auditor's reaction to the discovery of an error during an engagement is different from the auditor's identification of fraud during an engagement. That difference, as described in SAS-47, is illustrated as follows: Generally, an isolated, immaterial error in processing accounting data or applying accounting principles is not significant to the audit. In contrast, when fraud is detected, the auditor should consider the implications for the integrity of management or employees and the possible effect on other aspects of the audit.

OBSERVATION: The auditor is concerned with audit risk and materiality levels during both the planning phase and the evaluation phase of an engagement. Although conceptually possible, generally, the assessment of materiality levels will not be the same at the planning stage as at the evaluation stage. This is because, toward the end of the engagement, the auditor will have more complete information to better assess materiality for a particular engagement. In fact, if the level of materiality is significantly less at the evaluation stage than at the planning stage, the auditor will generally need to "reevaluate the sufficiency of the audit procedures he or she has performed."

Promulgated Procedures Checklist

The auditor should design the audit approach so that materiality and audit risk is integrated into the audit engagement at the following points:

_____ Determine audit risk and materiality during the planning phase of the engagement.

_____ Assess the audit risk based on the results of substantive tests.

Analysis and Application of Procedures

Determine audit risk and materiality during the planning phase of the engagement

During the planning phase of the engagement, the auditor must consider audit risk and materiality (1) at the financial statements level and (2) at the individual account-balance or class-of-transactions level.

Financial statement level

Audit risk and materiality are considered during the planning phase of the engagement in order for the auditor to determine the nature, timing, and extent of audit procedures. SAS-47 provides little guidance in determining audit risk except to conclude that it should be "limited to a low level that is, in [the auditor's] professional judgment, appropriate for expressing an opinion on the financial statements." Since audit risk deals with the chance that the financial statements are misstated and yet the misstatements are undetected by the auditor, it is appropriate for the professional standards to require that all engagements be planned and executed with a low level of audit risk.

The level of audit risk may be expressed in quantitative terms or nonquantitative terms. For example, the auditor may conclude that audit risk should be established at 5% and use this threshold as a basis for the planning and the performance of audit procedures—a quantitative measure. On the other hand, an auditor can plan and perform audit procedures based on a nonquantitative measure and not attempt to be specific concerning audit risk.

> **RISK ASSESSMENT POINT:** In practice, auditors often express audit risk in both quantitative terms and nonquantitative terms.

For example, when statistical sampling is used for one or more parts of the engagement, audit risk must be quantified. Many areas of the engagements will not be susceptible to statistical sampling, however, and the auditor will use the nonquantitative guideline of low audit risk in order to guide the planning and execution of audit procedures. Also, due to the complexity of an audit engagement and the numerous variables that must be considered in determining audit risk, it is likely that an auditor would not be comfortable with a conclusion about audit risk expressed entirely in quantitative terms. For example, to conclude at the end of an audit engagement that the audit opinion is based on, say, 5% audit risk is to misunderstand the nature of the audit process and the environment in which it is applied.

SAS-47 lists the following factors that should be considered in determining audit risk and materiality at the financial statement level:

- The size and complexity of the engagement
- The auditor's experience with the client
- The auditor's knowledge of the client's business

During the planning phase of the engagement, the auditor must assess the risk that the financial statements may be materially misstated because of error or fraud. An auditor's understanding of a client's internal control may have an impact on the assessment of material misstatement. At the planning stage, that understanding may be based on the auditor's previous experience with the client. Additionally, SAS-47 [as amended by SAS-82 (AU 316)] states that "the auditor should specifically assess the risk of material misstatement of the financial statements due to fraud" in determining audit risk. If the auditor concludes that there is significant risk of material misstatement, the nature, timing, and extent of audit procedures should take this assessment into consideration. Additionally, the assignment of staff and the level of supervision should reflect an increase in the assessed risk of material misstatement.

The assessment of risk of material misstatement should also be related to an audit of a client with operations in multiple components or locations. SAS-47 requires that, in determining whether the activities at a location or at a component should be considered in the planning of the engagement, the auditor should consider factors such as the following:

- The nature and amount of assets and transactions executed at the location or component
- The degree of centralization of records or information processing

- The effectiveness of the control environment, particularly with respect to management's direct control over the exercise of authority delegated to others and its ability to effectively supervise activities at the location or component
- The frequency, timing, and scope of monitoring activities by the entity or others at the location or component
- Judgments about materiality of the location or component

The auditor must use professional judgment to establish materiality levels for an engagement based on the characteristics unique to that engagement. There are no specific standards for determining materiality levels; however, in general terms the auditor must consider both quantitative and qualitative factors.

From a quantitative perspective, an auditor generally focuses on various amounts that appear in the financial statements as a basis for determining materiality levels. These amounts may include such financial statement elements as revenue, gross profit, net income, total assets, current assets, and total liabilities. Using the FASB's broad definition of "materiality," the auditor must determine, in his or her opinion, what amount of misstatement in the various numbers contained in the financial statements may result in a material misstatement. For example, assume that the auditor has established the following analysis as a preliminary step in establishing materiality levels in an engagement:

Financial Statement Element	Financial Statements Amount (unaudited)	Percentage Misstatement Considered Material	Amount Misstatement Considered Material
Gross profit	$4,000,000	6%	$240,000
Income before taxes and irregular items	3,000,000	7%	210,000
Total assets	4,000,000	10%	400,000
Current assets	3,000,000	8%	240,000

RISK ASSESSMENT POINT: The Auditing Interpretation (December 2000) titled "Quantitative Measures of Materiality in Evaluating Audit Findings" points out that in some instances income or loss from continuing operations includes significant, unusual, or infrequently occurring items. Under these circumstances the Interpretation notes that it may be appropriate to exclude the unusual or infrequent items in developing a base for measuring materiality.

PLANNING AID REMINDER: In the above example, materiality levels are based on unaudited financial statement amounts. In some situations, the auditor may have to make preliminary estimates of current financial statement amounts based on annualized interim financial statements or financial statements from previous periods. SAS-47 recognizes that materiality judgments may have to be based on preliminary or unadjusted amounts, and it concludes that such an approach is acceptable as long as "recognition is given to the effects of major changes in the entity's circumstances (for example, a significant merger) and relevant changes in the economy as a whole or the industry in which the entity operates."

While the auditor may be concerned with the misstatement of several financial statement elements, generally the smallest materiality level is used in the planning phase of the engagement. This approach is justified because of the interrelationship of the financial statements and the need for audit efficiency. In the current example, the overall materiality level for the financial statements (balance sheet, statement of income, and statement of cash flows) would be $210,000.

ENGAGEMENT STRATEGY: When the auditor uses a single materiality threshold for all of the financial statements, the planned audit risk is lower for those items that have a materiality threshold level higher than the single materiality level selected for planning purposes. In the current example, the planned audit risk is lower for the balance sheet (total assets) because the materiality level is $210,000 rather than $400,000.

Besides establishing a quantitative materiality level during the planning phase of the engagement, the auditor should also be sensitive to possible misstatements that could be qualitatively material. Qualitative factors include such items as the discovery of a fraudulent transition in the previous engagement, or the existence of a loan covenant that, if violated, provides a creditor with the right to demand immediate payment of an obligation. SAS-47 concludes that it is not ordinarily possible, however, to plan audit procedures based on the possibility of material misstatements that are of a qualitative nature.

ENGAGEMENT STRATEGY: The Auditing Interpretation (December 2000) titled "Considering the Qualitative Characteristics of Misstatements" notes that "the significance of an item to a particular entity (for example, inventories to a manufacturing company), the pervasiveness of the misstatement (such as whether it affects the amounts and presentation of numerous financial statement items), and the effect of the misstatement on the financial statements taken as a whole are all factors to be considered in making a judgment regarding materiality." The Interpretation also provides a list of qualitative factors that an auditor may consider in assessing the materiality of an item. (See "Practitioner's Aids" at the end of this section.)

PLANNING AID REMINDER: There is an inverse relationship between audit risk and materiality, which can be expressed in the following generalizations: (a) the risk that an item could be misstated by an extremely large amount is generally low and (b) the risk that an item could be misstated by an extremely small amount is generally high. Thus, as the planned level of materiality is reduced, the scope of the audit approach must be increased.

Individual account-balance or class-of-transactions level

SAS-47 provides the following basic guidance for determining the nature, timing, and extent of audit procedures at the individual account-balance or class-of-transactions level:

> ... the auditor should design procedures to obtain reasonable assurance for detecting misstatements that he or she believes, based on the preliminary judgment about materiality, could be material when aggregated with misstatements in other balances or classes to the financial statements taken as a whole.

The auditor must use professional judgment to determine how preliminary judgments concerning materiality should affect the audit of a specific account balance or class of transactions. To illustrate one approach, assume that, based on the previous example (where materiality was set at $210,000), the auditor is considering the effect of materiality on the selection of audit procedures for the following balance sheet accounts:

Account Title	Balance	Materiality Level for Each Account (5.25%)
Cash	$ 500,000	$ 26,250
Accounts receivable	1,400,000	73,500
Inventories	1,100,000	57,750
Property, plant, and equipment (net)	1,000,000	52,500
	$4,000,000	$210,000

In the current example, the overall preliminary materiality level is 5.25% ($210,000/$4,000,000). The auditor could decide that a misstatement of 5.25% for each account or financial statement element individually is to be

§312 • Audit Risk and Materiality in Conducting an Audit

considered material or the auditor could allocate the total materiality amount among the items based on professional judgment. For example, the auditor may decide to allocate the $210,000 in the following manner:

Account Title	Balance	Materiality Level for Each Account (5.25%)
Cash	$ 500,000	$ 10,000
Accounts receivable	1,400,000	50,000
Inventories	1,100,000	50,000
Property, plant, and equipment (net)	1,000,000	100,000
Total	$4,000,000	$210,000

PLANNING AID REMINDER: Factors that may be relevant in determining how to allocate the overall materiality amount to specific accounts include the extent of errors in a particular account discovered during previous audit engagements, or the sensitivity of an account balance to external factors (such as the relationship of the business cycle to the estimate of doubtful accounts).

Selecting a materiality level at the individual account-balance level or class-of-transactions level affects the scope of the audit approach for each individual item. For example, SAS-47 notes that as the level of materiality is reduced for a particular account (holding other planning considerations equal), the auditor must do one or more of the following:

- Select a more effective auditing procedure (nature of procedures)
- Perform auditing procedures close to year-end (timing of procedures)
- Increase the extent of a particular auditing procedure (extent of procedures)

The determination of the audit scope during the planning stage is important because it provides a basis for the auditor to "restrict audit risk at the individual balance or class level in such a way that will enable him or her, at the completion of the examination, to express an opinion on the financial statements taken as a whole at an appropriately low level of audit risk." To evaluate audit risk at this level, the auditor must consider the following three types of risk:

1. Inherent risk
2. Control risk
3. Detection risk

Inherent risk and control risk relate to misstatements caused by both error and fraud.

Inherent risk

The nature of the account balance or class of transactions and the fundamental characteristics of the entity being audited determine the level of inherent risk. SAS-47 defines "inherent risk" as "the likelihood of a misstatement existing in an account balance or class of transactions that would be material when aggregated with misstatement(s) in other accounts or classifications, assuming that there were no related controls."

There are many factors that can affect inherent risk but, in general, these factors relate to broad characteristics of the entity as well as factors unique to the individual account balance or class of transactions. Factors to be considered include the need for estimates, sensitivity to external economic forces, and characteristics of the industry in which the company operates.

As a general rule, there is less inherent risk associated with an account that is based on actual transactions than with an account based on estimates. For example, there is less risk associated with rent expense than with warranty expense based on this single factor (estimate-based), and there is more inherent risk associated with the inventory of a company that is part of an industry experiencing rapid technological changes. SAS-47 notes that "if an auditor concludes that the effort required to assess inherent risk for an assertion would exceed the potential reduction in the extent of auditing procedures derived from such an assessment, the auditor should assess inherent risk as being at the maximum when designing auditing procedures."

Control risk

The client's design of internal control will have an impact on the level of audit risk. "Control risk" is defined by SAS-47 as "the possibility of a misstatement occurring in an account balance or class of transactions that (1) could be material when aggregated with misstatement(s) in other balances or classes and (2) will not be prevented or detected on a timely basis by the entity's internal control." Control risk, like inherent risk, cannot be changed by the auditor.

The client's internal control that produces the current financial statements must be treated as a given factor. Of course, the auditor can make recommendations for improving internal control, which may affect the audit engagement of the next period. In general, the stronger (in both design and operation) the internal control, the greater the likelihood that the system will prevent or detect material misstatements (either through error or through fraud).

§312 • Audit Risk and Materiality in Conducting an Audit

The level of control risk will be based on the auditor's consideration of the client internal control. SAS-47 notes that "if the auditor believes controls are unlikely to pertain to an assertion or are unlikely to be effective, or believes that evaluating their effectiveness would be inefficient, he or she would assess control risk for that assertion at the maximum."

> **PLANNING AID REMINDER:** Often, inherent risk and control risk are evaluated as a single risk factor because it is sometimes difficult to classify risk conditions. For example, the risk of inventory loss through theft may be a combination of poor internal controls as well as the physical nature of the inventory.

Detection risk

Even though the auditor performs a variety of audit procedures, it is possible that a material misstatement will not be detected. SAS-47 defines "detection risk" as "the risk that an auditor will conclude that a misstatement in an account balance or class of transactions that could be material (when aggregated with a misstatement in other accounts or classes) does not exist when, in fact, such a misstatement does exist." In part, detection risk arises because all items that make up an account balance are not examined (sampling misstatement) and audit procedures are not properly applied (nonsampling misstatement).

During planning phase of the engagement, the auditor must consider inherent risk, control risk, and detection risk and must select an audit strategy that will result in a low level of audit risk once the engagement is complete. There is an inverse relationship between the auditor's assessment of inherent and control risks and the level of detection risk. If inherent risk and control risks are high, the auditor should establish a low level of detection risk.

The level of detection risk has an impact on the design of the auditor's substantive tests. In general, if a low level of detection risk is appropriate, based on the assessment of inherent risk and control risk, the auditor would (1) expand the sample of substantive tests (extent of procedures), (2) be less likely to perform substantive tests at interim dates (timing of procedures), and/or (3) perform audit procedures that result in more competent evidential matter (nature of procedures).

SAS-47 concludes that "it is not appropriate, however, for an auditor to rely completely on assessments of inherent risk and control risk to the exclusion of performing substantive tests of account balances and classes of transactions where misstatements could exist that might be material when aggregated with misstatements in other balances or classes."

At the individual account-balance or class-of-transactions level, the auditor can express the interrelationship of the various risk factors as follows:

$$\text{Audit Risk} = \text{Inherent Risk} \times \text{Control Risk} \times \text{Detection Risk}$$

As stated earlier, control risk and inherent risk exist based on the client's characteristics. It is the auditor's responsibility to assess inherent risk and control risk at the appropriate levels based on those characteristics. Furthermore, as required by professional standards, audit risk must be set at an appropriately low level. Thus, the auditor's ability to change risk factors is limited to detection risk. For these reasons and for analytical purposes, the formula presented above can be manipulated with the following results:

$$\text{Detection Risk} = \frac{\text{Audit Risk}}{\text{Inherent Risk} \times \text{Control Risk}}$$

For example, if the auditor establishes audit risk at 5%, and inherent risk and control risk are both assessed at 40%, the detection risk would be established at about 31%, as shown below:

$$31\% = \frac{.05}{.4 \times .4}$$

PLANNING AID REMINDER: The formula to compute detection risk is more conceptual than mathematical. That is, the formula shows the interrelationship of the various risk factors, but in practice it is useful as a broad guide as well as a technique for quantifying detection risk.

If inherent risk and control risk are assessed at higher levels—say, 60%—the auditor would decrease the detection risk to about 14%, as shown below:

$$14\% = \frac{.05}{.6 \times .6}$$

The auditor uses detection risk to plan the nature, timing, and extent of substantive audit procedures. For example, as the detection risk is reduced, the size of the required audit sample increases.

The identification of audit risk and materiality at the individual account-balance and class-of-transactions level is preliminary and necessary in order for the auditor to plan the scope of the engagement; however, the professional judgments made are tentative. The audit process is cumulative in that as the engagement progresses the auditor should consider additional information obtained. For this reason, the auditor may need to reassess risk factors and adjust the scope of the engagement accordingly. For example,

§312 • Audit Risk and Materiality in Conducting an Audit

the auditor may discover excessive misstatements that were not anticipated in the preliminary planning stage of the engagement and that require a reduction in the level of materiality initially considered appropriate.

Assess the audit risk based on the results of substantive tests

Once substantive tests have been performed, the auditor must assess the audit risk in the context of the materiality level that has been used in determining the nature, timing, and extent of audit procedures. Initially the auditor should identify the known misstatement (actual misstatements discovered) based on the performance of audit procedures. Next, the known misstatement should be used as a basis to estimate the likely misstatement. In a simple example, an auditor may identify a known misstatement of $20,000 based on testing and may project a likely misstatement of $80,000 if the sample tested represents 25% of the total account balance. Additionally, the auditor would combine the quantitative results of his or her misstatement analysis with relevant qualitative factors to determine the risk that material misstatements exist.

> **RISK ASSESSMENT POINT:** The Auditing Interpretation (December 2000) titled "Evaluating Differences in Estimates" provides guidance for determining the amount of the likely misstatement to be aggregated. If the auditor has concluded, based on audit procedures employed, that a particular balance likely falls within a range, then the likely misstatement is the difference between the balance according to the financial statement and the upper or lower boundary of the range. For example, if the range is likely to be between $200,000 and $300,000 and the actual balance is $315,000, the misstatement to be aggregated is $15,000 ($315,000 − $300,000). However, if the auditor's assessment of the balance is based on a point estimate (say, $290,000) rather than a range, the misstatement to be aggregated is the difference between the point estimate and the financial statement balance [in this case $25,000 ($315,000 − $290,000)].

An auditor may apply analytical procedures to an account balance or a class of transactions; however, due to the nature of analytical procedures, it is ordinarily unlikely that the auditor would identify specific known misstatements and draw a conclusion concerning whether a material misstatement exists. Thus, the auditor's application of analytical procedures can provide only an indication that an account balance or class of transactions may be misstated. SAS-47 notes that when such an indication exists, "the auditor ordinarily would have to employ other procedures to enable him or her to estimate the likely misstatement in the balance or class."

As noted earlier, there is more audit risk for an account balance or a class of transactions that is based on estimates. A projected amount for an account balance or a class of transactions based on audit sampling will seldom be equal to the actual estimated amount in the financial statements. Generally, this difference should not be treated as a misstatement as long as the auditor believes the difference is reasonable. If the auditor believes the difference is not reasonable, the difference between the amount on the financial statements and the closest reasonable estimate should be treated as a misstatement. Next, the difference should be aggregated with other likely misstatements in determining whether a material misstatement exists in the financial statements taken as a whole.

Although each account balance or class of transactions is audited individually, the auditor should take a broader perspective to determine whether the client has a bias to misstate all or most of its estimated amounts. SAS-47 concludes that "if each accounting estimate included in the financial statements was individually reasonable, but the effect of the difference between each estimate and the estimate best supported by the audit evidence was to increase income, the auditor should reconsider the estimates taken as a whole."

After estimating the total misstated projected amount (likely misstatement) for all accounts or classes of transactions, the auditor should compare that amount to materiality. If the likely misstatement is greater than the amount designated as material, the auditor should request the client to investigate the financial statement balance. If additional procedures are not performed or if the client refuses to modify the financial statements in order to eliminate the material misstatement, the auditor would express either a qualified opinion or an adverse opinion on the financial statements. If the likely misstatement is less than the materiality amount, the auditor must use professional judgment to assess audit risk; for example, as the likely misstatement approaches the materiality amount, the level of audit risk rises. As noted earlier, SAS-47 concludes that the audit risk should be established at a relatively low level. Thus, the comparison and the analysis of the relationship of the likely misstatement and the level of materiality are critical. For example, if the auditor has estimated the aggregate likely misstatement to be $200,000 and the level of materiality is $210,000, it is likely that audit risk is too great to conclude that the financial statements are fairly stated. On the other hand, if the estimated aggregate likely misstatement had been $50,000 rather than $200,000, it is more likely that the auditor would conclude that a low level of audit risk had been achieved.

> **RISK ASSESSMENT POINT:** The current year's financial statements may be affected by misstatements from the prior year's engagement financial statements because such misstatements were not considered material and therefore no adjustment was

made in the prior year. If the auditor believes that "there is an unacceptably high risk" that the current year's financial statements are materially misstated when the prior year's misstatements are taken into consideration, the auditor should include the likely misstatement amount due to the prior year's misstatement with the current year's likely misstatement amount to determine whether the current year's financial statements appear to be materially misstated.

RISK ASSESSMENT POINT: During the engagement, the auditor may identify a minimum level of misstatement that may not be used to determine known misstatements and the likely misstatement. The amount must be set low enough, however, so that "any such misstatements, either individually or when aggregated with other such misstatements, would not be material to the financial statements, after the possibility of further undetected misstatements is considered."

Practitioner's Aids

Checklist of qualitative factors in determining materiality

The following (based on the Auditing Interpretation (December 2000) entitled "Considering the Qualitative Characteristics of Misstatements") are qualitative factors that may be relevant in determining the materiality of an item:

- ❏ Items that have an effect on trends (particularly profitability trends)
- ❏ Items that change losses to income
- ❏ Items that have an impact on segment information
- ❏ Items that are relevant in determining whether loan covenants and similar items have been violated
- ❏ Items that have an effect on materiality thresholds that are established by statute or regulation
- ❏ Items that increase management's compensation
- ❏ Items that affect the sensitivity of possible fraud, illegal acts, or other similar situations
- ❏ Particular nature of the item misstated (such as recurring items versus nonrecurring items)
- ❏ Items that are misclassified (such as misclassification of an item that should be considered operating but is classified as nonoperating)

- ❏ The significance of the item in relationship to known user needs
- ❏ The character of the item (for example, the degree to which an item is based on an estimate)
- ❏ The possible motivation of management
- ❏ The existence of offsetting effects of individually significant items
- ❏ The possibility that a currently immaterial item could have a material impact on subsequent financial statements
- ❏ The cost of making a correction
- ❏ The risk that other undetected misstatements would affect the auditor's opinion

SEC Staff Accounting Bulletin—materiality

The Financial Accounting Standards Board (FASB) and the American Institute of Certified Public Accountants (AICPA) have provided little guidance for determining what constitutes a material item in financial statements. The Securities and Exchange Commission (SEC) has addressed this issue in a Staff Accounting Bulletin (SAB) titled "Materiality." Although the SEC addresses only publicly traded companies, this Bulletin, discussed below, provides valuable guidance in the performance of audits in general. This Practitioner's Aid summarizes the guidance in the SAB.

Assessing Materiality

Statements of Financial Accounting Concepts No. 2 (Qualitative Characteristics of Accounting Information) characterizes "materiality" as follows:

> The omission or misstatement of an item in a financial report is material if, in the light of surrounding circumstances, the magnitude of the item is such that it is probable that the judgment of a reasonable person relying upon the report would have been changed or influenced by the inclusion or correction of the item.

While everyone agrees with this description of materiality, applying the concept in practice requires a considerable amount of professional judgment. In many engagements, an auditor establishes a material threshold or a rule of thumb, such as 5% or 10%, and a misstatement(s) that is less than the specific threshold is not considered material. SEC SAB-99 points out that the creation of a specific materiality percentage or dollar value for determining whether a particular item is material "has no basis in the accounting literature or the law."

§312 • Audit Risk and Materiality in Conducting an Audit

An auditor deals with two broad types of materiality during an engagement. First, in order to help plan an engagement, the auditor must identify a materiality factor. That is, the auditor must make some determination of what may be material in determining the nature, timing, and extent of audit procedures. Generally, as the materiality threshold falls from, say, 10% to 5%, the extent of audit procedures that are necessary to achieve the auditor's objective is increased. The SEC has no problem with an auditor using preliminary definitions of "materiality" in determining the audit approach in a particular engagement.

The second type of materiality the auditor must address in an engagement is to determine whether specific misstatements are in the aggregate large enough for the auditor to conclude that the financial statements may be materially misstated. The SEC points out that in this phase of the audit engagement, using hard and fast materiality thresholds is not appropriate. That is, concluding whether an item is material is not a procedural process (asking whether an item exceeds a specific threshold) but rather an analytical process (asking whether it could affect one's assessment of a particular company). To support the argument that acceptance of the analytical process is the appropriate approach, the SEC referred to the following legal conclusion: "Magnitude by itself, without regard to the nature of the item and the circumstances in which the judgment has to be made, will not generally be a sufficient basis for a materiality judgment." That is, the SEC reminds auditors that both quantitative and qualitative factors must be considered in determining whether an item is material to the financial statements taken as a whole.

SEC SAB-99 points out that the qualitative factors used to evaluate a matter that is below the quantitative threshold should include the following:

- Whether the misstatement arises from an item capable of precise measurement or from an estimate and, if from an estimate, the degree of imprecision inherent in the estimate
- Whether the misstatement masks a change in earnings or other trends
- Whether the misstatement hides a failure to meet analysts' consensus expectations for the enterprise
- Whether the misstatement changes a loss into income or vice versa
- Whether the misstatement concerns a segment or other portion of the registrant's business that has been identified as playing a significant role in the registrant's operations or profitability
- Whether the misstatement affects the registrant's compliance with regulatory requirements
- Whether the misstatement affects the registration's compliance with loan covenants or other contractual requirements

- Whether the misstatement has the effect of increasing management's compensation—for example, by satisfying requirements for the award of bonuses or other forms of incentive compensation
- Whether the misstatement involves concealment of an unlawful transaction

The SEC also notes that an auditor must be particularly careful when audit results suggest that management has intentionally made errors in the preparation of its financial statements that appear to have the objective of "managing earnings." In this regard, the Staff Accounting Bulletin makes the following observation:

> The staff believes that investors generally would regard as significant a management practice to over- or under-state earnings up to an amount just short of a percentage threshold in order to "manage" earnings. Investors presumably also would regard as significant an accounting practice that, in essence, rendered all earnings figures subject to a management-directed margin of misstatement.

Based on the SEC's reasoning and plain common sense, an auditor should not establish a materiality threshold and then blindly apply it in an engagement. That is not exercising judgment; it is reducing the audit process to a mechanical process that can be more efficiently performed by a computer.

Aggregating and Netting Misstatements

In determining whether financial statements are materially misstated, the misstatement should be evaluated both individually and in the aggregate. This determination should be made on the basis of both quantitative thresholds and qualitative factors (such as those discussed in the previous section), and the analysis should be directed to "individual line item amounts, subtotals, or totals in the financial statements."

When an individual item by itself is material, it is incorrect to offset its significance with another item that has the opposite impact on the financial statements. For example, if sales are materially overstated and cost of goods sold is materially overstated by more or less the same amount, it would not be proper to suggest that the income statement is not materially misstated because net income is not materially affected by the offsetting misstatements.

The Staff Bulletin warns auditors that they must be careful when aggregating the effects of two or more misstatements that net to a smaller effect on a particular total or subtotal. This is especially true when two misstatements are offset and one is based on an estimate while the other is based on a precise measurement.

> **ENGAGEMENT STRATEGY:** The auditor must take into consideration in the current engagement misstatements that were made in previous years but were considered immaterial. Those previous years' misstatements could have a material impact on the current year's financial statements, since the quantitative and qualitative factors that are relevant to identifying material items in the current engagement may have changed.

Immaterial Misstatements That Are Intentional

SAB-99 raises the question of whether a client can make deliberate adjustments to its financial statements that are inconsistent with generally accepted accounting principles (GAAP) even though the effect is immaterial. The SEC takes the position that such action by a client is inappropriate and may in fact be in violation of securities laws that require that the books and records be accurate in "reasonable detail." The "reasonable detail" is more stringent than the materiality threshold. In determining what is reasonable detail, the auditor should consider the materiality factors (quantitative and qualitative factors discussed earlier) as well as additional factors such as the following:

- *The significance of the misstatement*—Though the staff does not believe that registrants need to make finely calibrated determinations of significance with respect to immaterial items, plainly it is "reasonable" to treat misstatements whose effects are clearly inconsequential differently than more significant ones.

- *How the misstatement arose*—It is unlikely that it is ever "reasonable" for registrants to record misstatements or not to correct known misstatements—even immaterial ones—as part of an ongoing effort directed by or known to senior management for the purposes of "managing" earnings. On the other hand, insignificant misstatements that arise from the operation of systems or recurring processes in the normal course of business generally will not cause a registrant's books to be inaccurate "in reasonable detail."

- *The cost of correcting the misstatement*—The books and records provisions of the Exchange Act do not require registrants to make major expenditures to correct small misstatements. Conversely, where there is little cost or delay involved in correcting a misstatement, failing to do so is unlikely to be "reasonable."

- *The clarity of authoritative accounting guidance with respect to the misstatement*—Where reasonable minds may differ about the appropriate accounting treatment of a financial statement item, a failure to correct it may not render the registrant's financial statements inaccurate "in reasonable detail." Where, however, there is little ground for reasonable disagreement, the case for leaving a misstatement uncorrected is correspondingly weaker.

The Auditor's Response to Intentional Misstatements

Both securities laws and auditing standards [SAS-54 (AU 317) and SAS-82 (AU 316)] require that an auditor report fraudulent acts to the appropriate level of management. SAB-99 notes that "the clear implication of SAS-82 is that immaterial misstatements may be fraudulent financial reporting."

> **ENGAGEMENT STRATEGY:** In addition to reporting fraudulent acts to the appropriate level of management, the auditor must also consider how the discovery of such facts affects the nature, timing, and extent of audit procedures. In some instances it may be appropriate, after seeking competent legal advice, for the auditor to resign from an engagement.

GAAP Precedent over Industry Practice

When there is a conflict between GAAP and industry accounting practice, clearly GAAP must be observed. Thus, if a client prepares a portion of its financial statements to conform to industry accounting practices that are inconsistent with GAAP, these departures must be evaluated to determine whether the financial statements are materially misstated.

General Comments

The SEC recognizes that determining when financial statements are materially misstated can be a complex process. This is especially true when the application of GAAP to a particular transaction or balance is not clear. Under these conditions, a client may account for an item "based on analogies to similar situations or other factors." When these conditions arise, an auditor is encouraged to discuss ambiguous accounting and reporting issues with the SEC staff on a timely basis.

> **ENGAGEMENT STRATEGY:** When the client is not a public company, the auditor should have in place procedures that encourage staff accountants to discuss difficult reporting issues with appropriate personnel within the firm.

SECTION 313

SUBSTANTIVE TESTS PRIOR TO THE BALANCE SHEET DATE

Authoritative Pronouncements

SAS-45—Omnibus Statement on Auditing Standards—1983

Overview

Audit planning, the consideration of internal control, and the application of substantive tests are frequently conducted by the auditor prior to the balance sheet date. In this manner, the auditor may become aware of significant matters that affect the year-end financial statements, including (1) related party transactions, (2) changing economic conditions, (3) recent accounting pronouncements, and (4) other items that may require adjustment at the balance sheet date. Substantive tests involve testing the details of a particular asset or liability account, along with other types of substantive tests, including the following:

- Tests of details of the additions to and reductions from accounts such as property, investments, debt, and equity
- Tests of details of transactions affecting income and expense accounts
- Tests of accounts that are not to be audited by testing the details of items composing the balance, such as warranty reserves, clearing accounts, and certain deferred charges
- Analytical procedures applied to income and expense accounts

Substantive tests can be applied to the above types of transactions for any selected dates prior to the balance sheet date and completed as part of the year-end audit procedures. However, the auditor must consider certain factors before principal substantive tests can be applied to the details of particular asset or liability accounts as of a date (interim date) that is prior to the balance sheet date.

Promulgated Procedures Checklist

The auditor should perform the following procedures when substantive tests for assets and liability accounts are performed prior to the client's balance sheet date:

_____ Consider the difficulty of controlling incremental audit risk before applying principal substantive tests to asset and liability accounts at an interim date.

_____ Design substantive tests to include the period between the interim test date and the balance sheet date (the remaining period).

Analysis and Application of Procedures

Consider the difficulty of controlling incremental audit risk

The performance of principal substantive tests prior to the balance sheet date increases audit risk, because misstatements that could exist at the balance sheet date might not be detected by the auditor as of the interim audit date. This potential audit risk increases as the period increases between the date of the interim date substantive tests and the balance sheet date. However, the auditor can control the increased audit risk by properly designing the substantive tests that are applied during the period between the interim date substantive tests and the balance sheet date.

Before applying principal substantive tests to the details of asset or liability accounts at an interim date, the auditor should consider the following factors:

- The cost of the additional substantive tests during the period between the interim date of the principal substantive tests and the balance sheet date
- The difficulty of controlling the increased audit risk

The auditor should first determine whether performing principal substantive tests on the details of balance sheet accounts at an interim date is cost-effective. If the auditor can assess control risk as low during the period between the interim date of the principal substantive tests and the balance sheet date, the additional substantive tests that are necessary during this period may be restricted to the extent that they are cost-effective. In this event, the auditor may have a reasonable basis for extending the audit conclusions from the interim date of the principal substantive tests to the balance sheet date. On the other hand, if the auditor cannot assess control risk as low during the period between the interim date of the principal substantive tests and the balance sheet date, the additional substantive tests that are necessary during this period may not be restricted as long as they are cost-effective.

ENGAGEMENT STRATEGY: To achieve a reasonable basis of extending the audit conclusions from the interim date of the principal substantive tests to the balance sheet date, the auditor

§313 • Substantive Tests Prior to the Balance Sheet Date

does not have to assess control risk as low. In this event, the auditor must exercise care in determining the effectiveness of the substantive tests performed during the period from the interim date of the principal substantive tests to the balance sheet date. If the auditor concludes that the effectiveness of the tests is impaired, the tests should be performed at the balance sheet date.

Because of rapidly changing business conditions or other circumstances occurring during the period between the interim date of the principal substantive tests and the balance sheet date, the auditor must consider the possibility of management misstating the financial statements. If these conditions exist, the auditor may conclude that the principal substantive tests should not be performed at the interim audit date.

The auditor should consider the nature of the balance sheet account to determine whether the interim-audit-date balance is likely to be similar to the balance-sheet-date balance. The auditor must consider the predictability of the amount and the significance and composition of the particular balance sheet account that is selected for interim principal substantive tests. Finally, the client's accounting procedures must be sufficiently adequate to permit the auditor to analyze the year-end account balances and the transactions occurring in the account between the interim date of the principal substantive tests and the balance sheet date.

Design substantive tests to include the remaining period

When the auditor decides to perform principal substantive tests to the details of a balance sheet account at an interim date, additional substantive tests should be applied to the transactions that occurred in the account between the interim date and the balance sheet date. The additional substantive tests must be selected to ensure that the overall audit objective for the particular balance sheet account is achieved. Generally, the tests should include the following procedures:

- Comparison of details of the interim and year-end balances in the account
- Performance of analytical procedures and/or substantive tests of details to provide a basis for extending to the balance sheet date the audit conclusion reached at the interim date of the principal substantive tests

If significant monetary misstatements are discovered at the interim date of the principal substantive tests, the auditor may be required to modify the nature, timing, or extent of the additional substantive tests that are performed during the period between the interim date and the balance sheet date. Under these circumstances, the auditor must exercise professional judgment.

RISK ASSESSMENT POINT: The performance of principal substantive tests to the details of a balance sheet account at an interim date must be coordinated with other audit procedures related to the same balance sheet account. Coordinating auditing procedures should be based on the auditor's planned assessed level of control risk related to the particular balance sheet account.

Practitioner's Aids

Professional judgment must be used to determine which balance sheet accounts can be subjected to substantive tests prior to the balance sheet date. To illustrate how this approach may be applied, assume that an auditor has decided to confirm accounts receivable at an interim date. The confirmation procedures normally applied at year-end would be applied to the trial balance of accounts receivable as of the interim date. Returned confirmation would be evaluated, and the auditor would develop various confirmation statistics. For transactions occurring after the interim date, the auditor would rely upon the client's internal control to process data in an acceptable manner. Summary data in the sales journal and cash receipts journal would be reviewed for unusual items. In addition, the client could be requested to prepare an aged trial balance at the end of the year, and the auditor could do the analysis. During the review, the auditor would look for significant amounts from customers that were not listed on the interim trial balance. Other items that are unusual or that otherwise come to the attention of the auditor could be subject to confirmation as of the year-end date.

Exhibit AU 313-1 illustrates a workpaper format that an auditor could use to document the approach of perform substantive tests on data processed by the client after the interim date.

EXHIBIT AU 313-1—SAMPLE WORKPAPER FORMAT

Averroes Company
Analysis of Accounts Receivable from
Interim to Year-End Date   12/31/X5

Accounts Receivable Balance @ 9/30/X5		450,000
		See workpaper @ AR110
Sales—October (a)	80,000	
November (a)	85,000	
December (a)	82,000	
		247,000
Cash receipts—October (b)	78,000	
November (b)	81,000	
December (b)	79,000	
		236,000
Write-offs—October (c)	450	
November (c)	230	
December (c)	1,850	
		−2,530
Accounts Receivable Balance @ 12/31/X5		458,470
		See workpaper @ AR100

(a) Traced to Sales Journal—Footed November and December journals
(b) Traced to Cash Receipts Journal—Footed October
(c) Traced to approvals and reviewed with credit manager

Prepared By : ___JB_____
Date: ___1/29/X6_____   AR101

SECTION 315

COMMUNICATIONS BETWEEN PREDECESSOR AND SUCCESSOR AUDITORS

Authoritative Pronouncements

SAS-84 — Communications Between Predecessor and Successor Auditors

SAS-93 — Omnibus Statement on Auditing Standards — 2000

Overview

A variety of auditing problems can arise when a client changes from one auditor to another auditor. SAS-84 defines a "predecessor auditor" as an auditor with either of the following characteristics.

- An auditor who has reported on the most recent audited financial statements or was engaged to perform but did not complete the engagement of any subsequent financial statements.

- An auditor who has resigned, has declined to stand for reappointment, or has been notified that his or her services have been or may be terminated.

> **RISK ASSESSMENT POINT:** SAS-93 clarifies the original language used in SAS-84 in order to emphasize that the definition of "predecessor auditor" includes "any auditor who is engaged to perform, but does not complete, an audit."

When an auditor is replaced before an engagement is completed, the replaced auditor is considered a predecessor auditor. In this circumstance there are two predecessor auditors: the auditor who performed the audit and the auditor who was replaced during the engagement. A successor auditor is the auditor who is considering accepting an audit engagement but has not communicated with the predecessor auditor or who has not accepted the audit engagement.

> **PLANNING AID REMINDER:** The standards established by SAS-84 do not apply to an engagement if the most recently audited financial statements are dated more than two years prior to the earliest period being audited by the successor auditor.

Promulgated Procedures Checklist

The auditor should perform the following procedures when a predecessor/successor auditor relationship arises or when issues related to a new client arise:

§315 • Communications Between Predecessor/Successor Auditors

_____ The successor auditor should communicate with the successor auditor.

_____ The predecessor auditor should cooperate with reasonable requests made by a successor auditor.

In addition, the change of auditors may create the need to perform the following audit procedures:

_____ Obtain audit evidence to support beginning account balances.

_____ Perform audit procedures related to a reaudit engagement.

_____ Perform audit procedures related to the discovery of misstatements in previously issued financial statements.

Analysis and Application of Procedures

The successor auditor should communicate with the predecessor auditor

A successor auditor is required to communicate with a predecessor auditor before accepting an engagement; however, an auditor may make a proposal on an engagement before the communication has been made. The responsibility to initiate the communication, which can be either oral or written, rests with the successor auditor.

Communications before an engagement is accepted

SAS-84 requires that an auditor attempt to communicate with the predecessor auditor before accepting an engagement. This communication is necessary to determine whether there are prior client-auditor problems that might cause the successor auditor to refuse the engagement.

> **RISK ASSESSMENT POINT:** Rule 301 of the Code of Professional Conduct prohibits an auditor from disclosing confidential information except when the client agrees to the disclosure. To reconcile the requirements of SAS-84 with Rule 301, the successor auditor should ask the prospective client to grant permission to discuss the impending engagement with the predecessor auditor. The client should not place any restrictions on the exchange of information between the successor and predecessor auditors. If the successor auditor cannot obtain required information from the predecessor auditor because of client restrictions, the successor auditor should consider the reasons for the restrictions and take the circumstances into consideration when deciding whether to accept the client.

SAS-84 notes that inquiries directed by the successor auditor to the predecessor auditor should be "specific and reasonable" and should include matters such as the following:

- Information related to the integrity of management
- Disagreements between the predecessor auditor and the client concerning accounting principles, audit procedures, or other "similarly significant matters"
- Predecessor auditor's communications with the client audit committee (or others with equivalent authority and responsibility, such as the members of the board of directors or the trustees or an owner-manager) concerning fraud, illegal acts by the client, and matters related to the client's internal control
- The predecessor auditor's reason for the change in auditors

Other communications

Communications between the predecessor auditor and the successor auditor, other than the type listed above, may be helpful in planning the audit engagement, but they do not have to be made before the successor auditor accepts the client. For example, the successor auditor should request access to the predecessor auditor's workpapers, and in turn the predecessor auditor should make him- or herself available to the successor auditor.

Although the predecessor auditor must use professional judgment in determining which workpapers should be made available to and copied by the successor auditor, SAS-84 points out that generally the predecessor auditor should grant the successor access to workpapers, such as those documenting (1) planning the engagement; (2) internal control; (3) audit results; and (4) matters related to continuing accounting and auditing significance, such as analyses of balances and contingencies.

The predecessor auditor should cooperate with reasonable requests made by a successor auditor

During the change of auditors, more than one auditor may make a proposal on the same engagement. Under this circumstance, the predecessor auditor is not expected to respond to inquiries made by the auditor until (1) the client has selected a successor auditor and (2) the successor auditor has accepted the engagement subject to the consideration of the responses received from the predecessor auditor. Once these conditions are satisfied, the predecessor auditor should respond promptly to inquiries made by the successor auditor. However, the predecessor auditor may decide not to respond

§315 • Communications Between Predecessor/Successor Auditors

to the inquiries or to respond in a limited way under unusual circumstances such as pending litigation or disciplinary proceedings.

> **OBSERVATION:** If the predecessor auditor is owed fees for prior work, the auditor does not need to comply with a request until those fees are paid.
>
> **PLANNING AID REMINDER:** When the most recent financial statements have been compiled or reviewed, a successor-predecessor auditor relationship does not exist; however, the auditor is not prohibited from following the guidance established by SAS-84.

Before allowing access to workpapers, the predecessor auditor should reach an understanding with the successor auditor as to the use of the workpapers. This understanding may be documented in a letter prepared by the predecessor auditor and acknowledged by the successor. An example of such a letter is illustrated in Exhibit AU 315-1. In order to further document the process related to the review of the predecessor auditor's workpapers, the predecessor auditor may request a consent and acknowledgment letter from the client. An example of such a letter is reproduced as Exhibit AU 315-2.

Obtain audit evidence to support beginning account balances

Beginning balances and the consistency standard

In order to express an opinion on the financial statements for an initial engagement, the successor auditor must obtain sufficient competent evidential matter (1) relating to the opening balances of balance sheet accounts and (2) satisfying the consistency standard. Auditing standards conclude that evidential matter to support these audit objectives may be obtained from the following:

- Reading of the previous year's financial statements and the related predecessor auditor's report
- Inquiries made of the predecessor auditor
- Review of the predecessor auditor's workpapers
- Audit procedures applied to the current year's transactions that substantiate opening balances (for example, the review of subsequent cash collections that apply to the opening balance of accounts receivable)
- Audit procedures applied by the successor auditor to opening balances and transactions from the previous year

With respect to the client's opening balances and the investigation of the application of the consistency standard, the successor auditor's approach may be influenced by the review of the predecessor auditor's workpapers. However, ultimately the nature, timing, and extent of audit procedures used during the initial engagement will be based solely on the successor auditor's professional judgment.

> **RISK ASSESSMENT POINT:** Although he or she is not required to do so by the standards established by SAS-84, an auditor may decide to make inquiries concerning the reputation of the predecessor auditor based on guidance established by SAS-1, AU Section 543 (Part of Audit Performed by Other Independent Auditors). However, even though the successor auditor may be influenced by the work performed by the predecessor auditor, the successor auditor's report on the current year's financial statements should not refer to the work performed by the predecessor auditor.

Perform audit procedures related to a reaudit engagement

In some instances the successor auditor is requested to reaudit the financial statements that were previously audited by the predecessor auditor. A reaudit engagement creates a successor auditor–predecessor auditor relationship, and the communications described above must be followed—except that the successor auditor must explain to the predecessor auditor that the purpose of the request for information is the performance of a reaudit. The workpapers that the successor auditor requests to review should include the predecessor auditor's workpapers for the year under reaudit and for the previous year. However, information the successor auditor obtains through inquiries made of the predecessor auditor or through review of the predecessor auditor's workpapers is not sufficient to enable the successor auditor to express an opinion on the previous year's financial statements.

The successor auditor must plan the reaudit in a manner that, based on the successor auditor's professional judgment, will satisfy generally accepted auditing standards (GAAS). If GAAS cannot be satisfied, the successor auditor should express a qualified opinion or disclaim an opinion on the previous year's financial statements based on the circumstances of the reaudit engagement. Evidence obtained by the successor auditor during the audit of the current year's financial statements, if appropriate, "may be considered in planning and performing the reaudit of the preceding period or periods and may provide evidential matter that is useful in performing the reaudit."

Of course, the successor auditor will be unable to observe inventory or perform other related procedures as described in SAS-1, AU Section 331, paragraphs 9–11. In determining the nature, timing, and extent of audit procedures related to inventory balances (beginning and ending) in the financial

§315 • Communications Between Predecessor/Successor Auditors 77

statements subject to reaudit, the successor auditor may take into consideration knowledge obtained from the review of the predecessor auditor's workpapers and inquiries of the predecessor. However, SAS-84 requires that the successor auditor "observe or perform some physical counts of inventory at a date subsequent to the period of the reaudit, in connection with a current audit or otherwise, and apply appropriate tests of intervening transactions." The appropriate tests may include tests of transactions, review of records showing prior physical counts, and the use of analytical procedures.

SAS-84 draws the following conclusions with respect to the reaudit engagement:

- The successor cannot assume responsibility for the predecessor auditor's work or assume divided responsibility with the predecessor auditor in a manner described in SAS-1, AU Section 543 (Part of Audit Performed by Other Independent Auditors).

- The work of the predecessor auditor should not be considered the work by a specialist as described in SAS-73 (AU 336) (Using the Work of a Specialist).

- The work of the predecessor auditor should not be considered work by an internal auditor as described in SAS-65 (AU 322) (The Auditor's Consideration of the Internal Audit Function in an Audit of Financial Statements).

Perform audit procedures related to the discovery of misstatements in previously issued financial statements

During the audit or reaudit of the new client's financial statements, the successor auditor may discover information that suggests that the financial statements reported on by the predecessor auditor were misstated. Under this circumstance, the successor auditor should inform the client of the situation and request the client to inform the predecessor auditor of the matter. In addition, the successor auditor should communicate information to the predecessor auditor that will enable the predecessor auditor to evaluate the situation based on the guidance established by SAS-1, AU Section 561 (Subsequent Discovery of Facts Existing at the Date of the Auditor's Report). Also, report guidance established by AU Section 561 should be observed.

When the successor auditor discovers a possible misstatement, ideally the three parties meet and resolve the issue. However, if the client refuses to inform the predecessor auditor of the matter or if the successor is not satisfied with resolution of the matter, SAS-84 concludes that the successor auditor should consider, perhaps after consultation with legal counsel, whether it is appropriate to resign from the engagement.

Practitioner's Aids

Exhibit AU 315-1 is an example of a letter of understanding between the predecessor and successor auditors. This letter is reproduced, with minor modifications, from Appendix B of SAS-84.

EXHIBIT AU 315-1—LETTER OF UNDERSTANDING BETWEEN PREDECESSOR AND SUCCESSOR AUDITOR

We have previously audited, in accordance with generally accepted auditing standards, the December 31, 20X7, financial statements of Averroes Company. We rendered a report on those financial statements and have not performed any audit procedures subsequent to the audit report date. In connection with your audit of Averroes Company's 20X8 financial statements, you have requested access to our workpapers prepared in connection with that audit. Averroes Company has authorized our firm to allow you to review the workpapers.

Our audit, and the workpapers prepared in connection therewith, of Averroes Company's financial statements was not planned or conducted in contemplation of your review. Therefore, items of possible interest to you may not have been specifically addressed. Our use of professional judgment and the assessment of audit risk and materiality for the purpose of our audit mean that matters may have existed that would have been assessed differently by you. We make no representation as to the sufficiency or appropriateness of the information in our workpapers for your purposes.

We understand that the purpose of your review is to obtain information about Averroes Company and that our 20X7 audit results will assist you in planning your 20X8 audit of Averroes Company. For that purpose only, we will provide you access to our workpapers that relate to that objective.

Upon request, we will provide copies of those workpapers that provide factual information about Averroes Company. You agree to subject any such copies or information otherwise derived from our workpapers to your normal policy for retention of workpapers and protection of confidential client information. Furthermore, in the event of a third-party request for access to your workpapers prepared in connection with your audits of Averroes Company, you agree to obtain our permission before voluntarily allowing any such access to our workpapers or information otherwise derived from our workpapers, and to obtain on our behalf any releases that you obtain from such third party. You agree to notify us promptly of any such third-party request and provide us with a copy of any subpoena, summons, or other court order for access to your workpapers that include copies of our workpapers or information otherwise derived therefrom.

Please confirm your agreement with the foregoing by signing and dating a copy of this letter and returning it to us.

Very truly yours,
[Predecessor Auditor]
By:

Accepted:
[Successor Auditor]
By:
Date:

SAS-84 notes that in order to further document the process related to the review of the predecessor auditor's workpapers, the predecessor auditor may request a consent and acknowledgment letter from the client. An example of such a letter (reproduced from Appendix A of SAS-84) appears in Exhibit AU 315-2.

EXHIBIT AU 315-2—CLIENT CONSENT AND ACKNOWLEDGMENT LETTER

You have given your consent to allow [name of successor CPA firm], as successor independent auditors for Averroes Company, access to our workpapers for our audit of the December 31, 20X7, financial statement of Averroes Company. You also have given your consent to us to respond fully to [name of successor CPA firm] inquiries. You understand and agree that the review of our workpapers is undertaken solely for the purpose of obtaining an understanding of Averroes and certain information about our audit of the December 31, 20X8, financial statement of Averroes Company.

Please confirm your agreement with the foregoing by signing and dating a copy of this letter and returning it to us.

Attached is the form of the letter we will furnish [name of successor CPA firm] regarding the use of the workpapers.

Very truly yours,
[Predecessor Auditor]
By:

Accepted:
[Averroes Company]
By:
Date:

SECTION 316

CONSIDERATION OF FRAUD IN A FINANCIAL STATEMENT AUDIT

Authoritative Pronouncements

SAS-82—Consideration of Fraud in a Financial Statement Audit

Overview

In the audit of financial statements, the auditor is concerned with two types of intentional misstatements on the financial statements, namely, misstatements arising (1) from fraudulent financial reporting and (2) from misappropriation of assets.

Fraudulent financial reporting

The intentional misstatements of information (through either commission or omission) in financial statements is referred to as fraudulent financial reporting. SAS-82 lists the following as examples of fraudulent financial reporting:

- Manipulation, falsification, or alteration of accounting records or supporting documents from which financial statements are prepared (e.g., the inclusion of false amounts in the accounts receivable subsidiary ledger).

- Misrepresentation in, or intentional omission from, the financial statements of events, transactions, or other significant information [e.g., not capitalizing leases that are *in-substance purchases* as defined by FAS-13 (CT L10)].

- Intentional misapplications of accounting principles relating to amounts, classification, manner of presentation, or disclosure [e.g., disclosing a loss contingency based on the standards established by FAS-5 (Accounting for Contingencies) when, in fact, the contingency should be accrued].

Misappropriation of assets

The theft of assets that results in the misstatement of financial statements is referred to as misappropriation of assets (defalcation). Misappropriation can result from a variety of deliberate actions, such as the unauthorized removal of inventory and the payment for assets that have never been received by the client.

§316 • Consideration of Fraud in a Financial Statement Audit

> **RISK ASSESSMENT POINT:** Fraud may be committed by a single individual, or it may involve collusion among employees, perhaps in conjunction with external parties. The factors that may lead to fraud are numerous and often can be discussed in only the most general of terms. For this reason, SAS-82 notes that an auditor is able to obtain only reasonable assurance that material misstatements in the financial statements, including misstatements resulting from fraud, have been detected.

Fundamentally, an engagement should be planned, and audit procedures executed, based on the guidance established by SAS-22 (AU 311) (Planning and Supervision). Audit risk should be assessed using the guidance provided in SAS-47 (AU 312) (Audit Risk and Materiality in Conducting an Audit). "Audit risk" is the "risk that the auditor may unknowingly fail to appropriately modify his opinion on financial statements that are materially misstated," and it includes the risk related to misstatement due to fraud. Specifically, SAS-82 requires that the assessment of risk should take into consideration risk factors related to (1) misstatements arising from fraudulent financial reporting and (2) misstatements arising from misappropriation of assets.

> **PLANNING AID REMINDER:** The 1999/2000 *Audit Risk Alert* points out that common characteristics of recent litigation related to fraudulent financial statements include (1) accepting management's representations without obtaining corroborative evidence, (2) allowing management to influence the scope of audit procedures, and (c) ignoring conditions that suggest that there is an unreasonable degree of risk related to the engagement.

Promulgated Procedures Checklist

The auditor should perform the following procedures in considering the possibility that fraud related to financial statements exists in an audit engagement:

_____ Assess the risk factors related to misstatements arising from fraudulent financial reporting.

_____ Assess the risk factors related to misstatements arising from misappropriation of assets.

_____ Consider the audit impact from the assessment of risk factors.

_____ Evaluate overall audit risk when the engagement is complete.

_____ Document audit results.

_____ Communicate acts of fraud discovered.

Analysis and Application of Procedures

Assess the risk factors related to misstatements arising from fraudulent financial reporting

The auditor should consider the following risk factors:

- Risk factors related to fraudulent financial reporting
- Factors related to management's characteristics and influence over the control environment
- Factors related to industry conditions
- Factors related to operating characteristics and financial stability

Risk factors related to fraudulent financial reporting

In assessing risk related to fraudulent financial reporting, the auditor may consider three broad categories of factors, namely, (1) management's characteristics and influence over the control environment, (2) industry conditions, and (3) the client's operating characteristics and financial stability.

> **ENGAGEMENT STRATEGY:** There is no specific list of factors that will ensure that the auditor will always or almost always identify fraud when it exists. The auditor must be sensitive to the possible existence of fraud and use professional judgment in identifying relevant factors that may suggest the possibility of fraud occurring under a particular set of circumstances. Not surprisingly, much of the discussion in SAS-82 is based on examples rather than generalizations or specific guidelines, with the intention of having the auditor develop a particular mindset regarding fraud.

Factors related to management's characteristics and influence over the control environment

Fundamental factors that may indicate the existence of an environment conducive to fraud relate to characteristics of management personnel and management's attitude toward the control environment. SAS-82 lists the following as circumstances that may be relevant in this category:

- There are motivational reasons for management to engage in fraudulent financial reporting (e.g., a significant portion of key members of the management team's compensation is based on profitability).
- Management indirectly communicates to its employees its lack of concern or interest in adequate internal controls and procedures related to the

§316 • Consideration of Fraud in a Financial Statement Audit 83

preparation of financial reports (e.g., significant internal control deficiencies are ignored).

- Nonfinancial management personnel have an unusual interest in the selection of accounting principles or the establishment of accounting estimates.
- There is a high turnover rate among senior management, legal counsel, and/or members of the board.
- There are poor relations between management and the previous auditor.
- There is a pattern of securities law violations identified with the client or its principals.

Factors related to industry conditions

Industry conditions can provide insights into situations that may suggest a higher possibility of the occurrence of fraud when compared to other industries. SAS-82 lists the following as examples that may be relevant in this category:

- A change in accounting, statutory, or regulatory requirements may have a significant impact on the financial position or profitability of the client.
- The industry may be highly competitive.
- The industry as a whole may be in a decline, characterized by numerous bankruptcies.
- The industry is subject to rapid changes in technology or product offerings.

Factors related to operating characteristics and financial stability

The auditor should also be aware of conditions that exert unusual pressure on the client's operating results and financial stability. SAS-82 lists the following as examples that may be relevant in this category:

- Cash flows from operations are greater than reported earnings.
- Competitive pressures require significant capital investments.
- Estimated amounts reported on the financial statements are highly tentative, and the entity's stability could be compromised if the amounts prove incorrect.
- Significant related party transactions exist that are either audited by another CPA or unaudited.
- Unusual or complex transactions, especially those executed toward the end of the accounting period, raise the concern of substance over form.

- Operations exist in tax-haven jurisdictions for no apparent reason.
- Organizational structure is unduly complex for no apparent reason.
- Control over the client is difficult to identify.
- Operations are characterized by unusual growth or profitability.
- Stability of the client is unusually sensitive to changes in interest rates.
- Stability of the client is unusually sensitive to debt service requirements or debt covenants.
- Sales or profitability incentive programs are unrealistic.
- Stability of the client is in question because of imminent bankruptcy or foreclosure or hostile takeover.
- Stability is dependent on pending transactions.
- The client's debts have been guaranteed by management, and currently the client's financial position is poor or deteriorating.

Assess the risk factors related to misstatements arising from misappropriation of assets

In assessing risk related to misstatements arising from misappropriations of assets, the auditor may consider two broad categories of factors, namely, (a) susceptibility of assets to misappropriation and (b) controls.

Factors related to susceptibility of assets to misappropriation

Fraudulent actions may result in the misappropriation of assets. SAS-82 lists the following circumstances that suggest conditions may exist for the possible misappropriation of assets:

- A large amount of cash is held on the premises or is processed.
- Inventory items have characteristics (such as small size or high value) that may encourage misappropriation.
- Assets exist that are easily converted into cash (bearer bonds, precious stones, etc.).
- Fixed assets have characteristics (such as a ready market or lack of ownership identification) that may encourage misappropriation.

Factors related to controls

The likelihood that fraudulent acts will occur depends to some degree on the controls the client institutes. SAS-82 lists the following as examples that may be relevant in this category:

- There is a lack of appropriate managerial oversight.

§316 • Consideration of Fraud in a Financial Statement Audit

- There is little or no background investigation of personnel who have access to assets susceptible to misappropriation.
- There are inadequate records to provide a basis for accounting for assets susceptible to misappropriation.
- There is inappropriate segregation of duties or inappropriate independent checks.
- There is an inadequate authorization system and inadequate transaction approval.
- There are inadequate physical safeguards over assets susceptible to misappropriation.
- There is inadequate timely documentation to support transactions.
- There is no enforcement of vacations for employees who perform sensitive control functions.

> **PLANNING AID REMINDER:** SAS-82 notes that the auditor does not have to plan an engagement to discover information that indicates financial stress of employees or adverse relationships between the entity and its employees. If such information (such as pending employee layoffs) becomes known to the auditor, however, the auditor should consider such factors in assessing the possible misstatement of financial statements through the misappropriation of assets.
>
> Although the auditor may identify a variety of factors related to fraud, there is of course no specific guidance for identifying which factors or combination of factors is of most concern to the auditor. That is, the auditor must exercise professional judgment to assess risk factors, using the client's basic characteristics as context. For example, the size, complexity, and type of industry in which the client exists would provide background for assessing risk factors.
>
> In many respects, it is difficult to segregate the assessment of a client's internal controls and the assessment of fraud-related risk factors. SAS-82 concludes that for this reason, the auditor's understanding of the entity's internal control will often affect the auditor's consideration of the significance of fraud risk factors. Although there is an interrelationship between the two assessments, it is preferable for the auditor to address the assessment of fraud-related risk factors in a separate memorandum.
>
> **ENGAGEMENT STRATEGY:** SAS-82 notes that a client may establish a program that is designed to "prevent, deter, and detect fraud," and the auditor may decide to consider the program's effectiveness. As part of that evaluation, the auditor should determine whether specific fraud risk factors have been identified as part of the program's implementation.

The assessment of fraud-related risk factors is an ongoing process, and it should consider the results of performing other segments of the audit. For example, as part of the performance of substantive procedures, the auditor might discover unexplained items on bank reconciliations. Under this circumstance, the auditor should reconsider the initial assessment of fraud risk factors and modify subsequent audit procedures accordingly.

Consider the audit impact from the assessment of risk factors

Using professional judgment, the auditor must determine whether the assessment of risk factors related to the possible occurrence of fraud should have an effect on planned audit procedures. In some instances, even when some risk factors exist, the auditor may conclude that there is no need to modify the nature, timing, or extent of planned audit procedures. On the other hand, the results of the assessments may require the auditor to modify audit procedures in order to "limit audit risk to a low level that is, in the auditor's professional judgment, appropriate for expressing an opinion on the financial statements." When the auditor concludes that the assessment of risk factors requires a change in the planned audit procedures, the modification may require an overall modification, an approach that is directed to a particular account balance, class of transaction, or assertion, or to a combination of account balance and assertion or transaction and assertion.

Overall modification

SAS-82 concludes that an overall modification of the audit approach due to the impact of the assessment of risk factors may affect (1) professional skepticism, (2) assignment of personnel, (3) accounting principles and policies, and (4) controls.

Professional skepticism In an audit engagement, "skepticism" is defined as "an attitude that includes a questioning mind and a critical assessment of audit evidence." It should be the auditor's mental attitude throughout the engagement. Professional skepticism requires the auditor not to assume that management is either honest or dishonest but rather to base his or her opinion on the financial statements on the evidence gathered during the engagement. If the auditor believes, however, that the overall audit approach should be modified because of the result of the assessment of risk factors related to the possibility of fraud, the level of professional skepticism should be increased. Generally, an increase in professional skepticism will result in a modification of the nature, timing, and extent of planned audit procedures. For example, oral representations made by management may be subject to corroboration from other parties, both within and without the organization.

§316 • Consideration of Fraud in a Financial Statement Audit

Assignment of personnel Besides increasing the professional skepticism in an engagement, the fraud risk factors may suggest that the auditor more carefully consider the assignment of personnel. For example, it may no longer be appropriate for an inexperienced staff auditor to perform certain audit procedures if the circumstances suggest that fraud risk factors are somewhat greater than anticipated. Likewise, such circumstances would indicate that the supervision level should be increased in order to reasonably ensure that the financial statements are not misstated because of fraud.

Accounting principles and policies Another aspect of modifying the overall audit approach relates to the client's selection of accounting principles and policies. The auditor may decide to more carefully evaluate the selection of accounting principles and policies, especially those related to revenue recognition, asset valuation, and capitalization versus expensing policies, in order to determine whether selections made are "being applied in an inappropriate manner to create a material misstatement of the financial statements."

Controls SAS-82 points out that when fraud risk factors have control implications, the auditor's ability to assess control risk below the maximum may be reduced. This circumstance does not suggest, however, that the auditor should not obtain an adequate understanding of the relevant internal controls. As noted in SAS-82, "such an understanding may be of particular importance in further understanding and considering any controls (or lack thereof) the entity has in place to address the identified fraud risk factors." In any case, the auditor should consider the possibility of management's ability to override the controls in question.

Modification directed to a particular account balance, class of transaction, or assertion

In some instances, the fraud risk factors are not related to the client's fundamental characteristics; instead, they are directed to narrow issues whereby the direction of specific audit modifications is likewise more narrowly focused. In general, the auditor must modify the approach so that audit risk will be assessed at an appropriate level when considered in the context of the identified risk factors. Again, it is impossible to generalize about which audit procedures should be performed, since each situation will dictate the appropriate response by the auditor. SAS-82 presents a number of examples, including the following:

- For significant and unusual transactions, particularly those occurring at or near year-end, investigate (1) the possibility of related parties and (2) the sources of financial resources supporting the transactions.

- If the work of a specialist becomes particularly significant with respect to its potential impact on the financial statements, the auditor should perform additional procedures with respect to some or all of the specialist's assumptions, methods, or findings to determine that the findings are not unreasonable; or the auditor should engage another specialist for the purpose.

Evaluate overall audit risk when the engagement is complete

When the audit engagement is complete, the auditor must make an assessment to determine whether the level of audit risk initially planned for has been achieved. This assessment is primarily a qualitative judgment. If the auditor concludes that an appropriate level of audit risk has not been achieved as a result of applying various audit procedures, he or she must consider the need to enhance the level of audit evidence acquired.

SAS-82 concludes that when the auditor has identified misstatements in the financial statements, he or she should consider whether the misstatements result from fraudulent acts. If misstatements have arisen from fraud but their results are immaterial, the auditor should nonetheless consider the implications of such acts, especially the original level at which the fraud occurred. For example, the auditor would be far more concerned with fraud that involves a high-level member of management than with fraudulent acts perpetrated by the petty cash custodian. In the former case, the auditor should reconsider the assessment of the risk of material misstatement due to fraud as it relates to (1) the nature, timing, and extent of tests of balances or transactions; (2) the assessment of control risk (if risk was assessed at a level less than the maximum; and (3) the appropriate assignment of personnel to the engagement.

When the auditor concludes that the financial statement misstatement is (or may be) based on a fraudulent act, and concludes that either (1) the fraudulent act may have a material effect on the financial statements or (2) the level of materiality has not been determined, SAS-82 requires that some of the following audit procedures be implemented:

- Consider the implication of the fraudulent act to other components of the engagement.
- Discuss the fraudulent act and its effect on the audit approach with appropriate management personnel (at least one level above the incident of the fraud) and with senior management.
- Attempt to perform appropriate audit procedures in order to determine whether the effect of the fraud has, or could have, a material impact on the financial statements and the audit report.
- If appropriate, suggest that the client discuss the matter with legal counsel.

§316 • Consideration of Fraud in a Financial Statement Audit

In some circumstances, the significance of the fraudulent act(s) may be so great that the auditor may decide to withdraw from the engagement. The reasons for withdrawing from the engagement should be communicated to the audit committee (or others with equivalent authority and responsibility).

> **PLANNING AID REMINDER:** Although each situation is different, professional judgment must be used to determine whether withdrawal from an engagement is appropriate. SAS-82 notes that the degree of cooperation of and response from senior management or the board of directors are two factors that may play a role in that determination.

Document audit results

Fraud risk factors may be identified as part of the planning of the engagement, or they may be identified subsequent to the planning stage. When fraud risk factors have been identified, the documentation should include the following:

- Identification of the specific fraud risk factors
- Modification of the audit approach that was taken to address the specific fraud risk factors identified

Communicate acts of fraud discovered

The discovery of acts of fraud, whether significant or inconsequential, should be communicated to an appropriate level of management. An understanding should be reached with the audit committee regarding what communications would be appropriate if a lower-level employee is involved in a fraudulent act. Acts involving senior management that result in a material misstatement of the financial statements should be reported to the audit committee (or others with equivalent authority and responsibility).

> **ENGAGEMENT STRATEGY:** Fraud risk factors that have continuing control implications and that have been discovered during the engagement should be evaluated to determine whether they represent reportable conditions as described in SAS-60 (AU 325) (Communication of Internal Control Related Matters Noted in an Audit). SAS-82 also notes that the auditor may want to communicate other fraud risk factors when the entity can reasonably take actions to address the risk.

Generally, the auditor is not responsible for communicating the existence or possible existence of fraud to external parties. In fact, such communication could violate the confidential relationship that exists between the client and the auditor; however, a disclosure obligation may exist under the following circumstances:

- Based on law or regulations that govern the client
- Based on standards established by SAS-84 (AU 314) (Communications Between Predecessor and Successor Auditors)
- In response to a subpoena
- Based on requirements established by a funding agency or other specified agency when the client receives governmental financial assistance

> **RISK ASSESSMENT POINT:** In most instances, it would be prudent for the auditor to discuss with legal counsel the appropriateness of communicating information about fraudulent acts to management, to the audit committee, and to external parties.

SECTION 317

ILLEGAL ACTS BY CLIENTS

Authoritative Pronouncements

SAS-54—Illegal Acts by Clients

Auditing Interpretation (October 1978)—Consideration of the Internal Control Structure in a Financial Statement Audit and the Foreign Corrupt Practices Act

Auditing Interpretation (October 1978)—Material Weakness in Internal Control and the Foreign Corrupt Practices Act

Overview

Although the purpose of an audit is not to detect illegal acts, an auditor should be aware that such acts could occur. SAS-54 (Illegal Acts by Clients) defines "illegal acts" as "violations of laws or governmental regulations," including acts committed by management and the entity's employees acting on behalf of the entity. An illegal act, for purposes of SAS-54, does not include acts arising from the personal conduct of an employee of the entity unrelated to business activities.

An entity must observe many laws and regulations. In general, the auditor lacks the expertise to identify and evaluate all illegal acts. For purposes of determining the auditor's responsibilities for detecting illegal acts, illegal acts are classified as either those with direct effects on the financial statements or those with indirect effects on the financial statements.

Illegal acts with direct effects on financial statements

Some laws and regulations directly apply to financial statements and are, therefore, taken into consideration when the auditor plans his or her audit procedures. For example, the auditor may determine whether a provision for income taxes has been properly reflected in the financial statements to comply with Internal Revenue Code (IRC) and related regulations. The auditor's responsibility for detecting illegal acts relating to laws and regulations having a direct and material effect on the financial statements is the same as the responsibility relating to the detection of errors and fraud [see previous discussion of SAS-82 (AU 316)]. The auditor must design the audit to provide reasonable assurance of detecting such acts.

> **RISK ASSESSMENT POINT:** The Auditing Interpretation (October 1978) titled "Consideration of the Internal Control Struc-

ture in a Financial Statement Audit and the Foreign Corrupt Practices Act" notes that the auditor is not required to expand the scope of the audit engagement because of the Foreign Corrupt Practices Act of 1977, beyond the normal scope required by the second standard of fieldwork.

Illegal acts with indirect effects on financial statements

Most laws and regulations have only an indirect effect on financial statements; that is, when an illegal act related to this type of law or regulation has occurred, the effects are often indirect in that they require disclosure in the financial statements based on their classification as a contingent liability. Illegal acts of this type are generally related to the operations of the organization rather than to the financial and accounting aspects of the entity. Furthermore, under many circumstances, the auditor has no basis for determining whether this type of law or regulation has been violated.

SAS-54 addresses illegal acts relating to laws and regulations that have an indirect effect on financial statements. Although the auditor is not responsible for the detection of illegal acts, during various phases of the engagement specific information may be discovered that raises questions about whether illegal acts have occurred. SAS-54 lists the following as examples of specific information that may raise questions about the existence of illegal acts:

- Unauthorized transactions, improperly recorded transactions, or transactions not recorded in a complete or timely manner in order to maintain accountability for assets

- Investigation by a governmental agency, an enforcement proceeding, or payment of unusual fines or penalties

- Violations of laws or regulations cited in reports of examinations by regulatory agencies made available to the auditor

- Large payments for unspecified services to consultants, affiliates, or employees

- Sales commissions or agents' fees that appear excessive in relation to those normally paid by the client or to the services actually received

- Unusually large payments in cash, purchases of bank cashiers' checks in large amounts payable to bearer, transfers to numbered bank accounts, or similar transactions

- Unexplained payments made to government officials or employees

- Failure to file tax returns or pay government duties or similar fees common to the entity's industry or the nature of its business

§317 • Illegal Acts by Clients

PLANNING AID REMINDER: SAS-54 establishes professional standards relating to the auditor's responsibility for detecting illegal acts in the course of the audit of the entity's financial statements. An auditor might accept other engagements that impose a different responsibility for detecting illegal acts. Such engagements include professional services subject to governmental auditing standards or special engagements designed to determine compliance with specific laws or regulations.

PLANNING AID REMINDER: The Auditing Interpretation (October 1978) titled "Material Weakness in Internal Control and the Foreign Corrupt Practices Act" notes that when a material weakness comes to the auditor's attention in an engagement covered by the Act, the auditor should discuss with management and the auditor's legal counsel whether the material weakness is a violation of the Act.

Promulgated Procedures Checklist

The auditor should perform the following procedures with respect to illegal acts in an audit engagement:

_____ Perform audit procedures that are appropriate when there is no suspicion of illegal acts.

_____ Perform audit procedures that are appropriate when there is suspicion of illegal acts.

_____ Evaluate the results of performing procedures related to illegal acts.

_____ Communicate illegal acts to the client's audit committee.

_____ Determine the effects of an illegal act on the audit report.

Analysis and Application of Procedures

Perform audit procedures that are appropriate when there is no suspicion of illegal acts

Typically, the engagement does not include audit procedures specifically directed to identifying illegal acts when no specific information has come to the attention of the auditor that would suggest that any illegal acts occurred. Nonetheless, the auditor should make the following inquiries of management:

- Entity's compliance with laws and regulations
- Entity's policies that may prevent illegal acts
- Entity's directives and periodic representations obtained by the entity concerning compliance with laws and regulations

> **PLANNING AID REMINDER:** Also, the auditor should request a written representation from the entity stating that no violations or possible violations of laws or regulations have occurred that may require accrual or disclosure in the financial statements.

Perform audit procedures that are appropriate when there is suspicion of illegal acts

If an auditor is aware of information concerning an illegal act, the auditor should (1) understand the nature of the act, (2) understand the circumstances surrounding the act, and (3) obtain sufficient information to evaluate the effects of the act on the financial statements. If possible, the auditor should deal with management at least one level above those involved in the act.

When management cannot provide sufficient information to demonstrate that an illegal act did not take place, the auditor should:

- Consult with the entity's legal counsel or other specialists (the entity should make the arrangements for meeting with its legal counsel).
- If necessary to obtain a further understanding of the act, perform additional procedures such as the following:
  — Inspect supporting documentation and compare it with the accounting record
  — Confirm information with other parties and intermediaries
  — Determine if the transaction has been properly authorized
  — Consider whether similar transactions have occurred, and attempt to identify them

Evaluate the results of performing procedures related to illegal acts

When an illegal act has occurred or probably occurred, the auditor should evaluate the effects of the act.

> **RISK ASSESSMENT POINT:** The possible loss arising from the illegal act should be evaluated to determine whether the amount is material. All costs related to the loss, such as penal-

ties and fines, should be considered. The need for accrual and/or disclosure in the financial statements should be evaluated in the context of guidelines established by FAS-5 (Accounting for Contingencies).

The illegal act should also be evaluated to determine whether other aspects of the engagement are affected. This is particularly applicable to the evaluation of the reliability of management representations. Such facts as the perpetrators involved, the methods of concealment, and the nature of internal control procedures overridden should be considered in the evaluation.

Communicate illegal acts to the client's audit committee

An auditor should ensure that an illegal act has been communicated to the client's audit committee (or to "individuals with a level of authority and responsibility equivalent to an audit committee in organizations that do not have one, such as the board of directors, the board of trustees, an owner in an owner-managed enterprise, or others who may have engaged the auditor"). The communication should include the following:

- Description of the illegal act
- Circumstances surrounding the illegal act
- Auditor's evaluation of the effects of the illegal act on the financial statements

> **ENGAGEMENT STRATEGY:** If members of senior management are involved in the illegal act, the auditor should communicate directly with the audit committee (or equivalent individuals). The communication can be written or oral, and in either case it should be adequately documented in the workpapers.

Notifying parties other than management and the audit committee (or equivalent individuals) about the occurrence of an illegal act is not required; however, SAS-54 notes that under the following circumstances the auditor may be called on to inform another party of an illegal act:

- SEC disclosure requirements based on a change of auditors
- Inquiries received from a successor auditor
- Subpoena issued by a court
- Governmental audit requirements applicable to entities that have received financial aid

RISK ASSESSMENT POINT: Because of the confidential relationship between the entity and the auditor, the auditor may find it advisable to contact legal counsel before illegal acts are disclosed to outside parties.

Determine the effects of an illegal act on the audit report

If the effects of an illegal act are not properly accrued for or are not properly disclosed in the financial statements, either an adverse opinion or a qualified opinion should be expressed. If the entity does not allow the auditor to collect sufficient competent evidential matter to determine whether an illegal act has taken place or whether an illegal act has a material effect on the financial statements, usually a disclaimer of opinion should be expressed. If the entity refuses to accept the modified auditor's report, the auditor should withdraw from the engagement and notify the board of directors and the audit committee (or equivalent individuals) of the reason for the withdrawal.

In some circumstances it may not be possible to determine whether an illegal act has occurred, because evidential matter does not exist to resolve the issue or because there is disagreement about the interpretation of the law or regulation. In this case, the auditor is faced with an uncertainty and must determine whether the auditor's report should be modified (see the discussion in Section 508, titled "Auditor's Reports").

SECTION 319

CONSIDERATION OF INTERNAL CONTROL IN A FINANCIAL STATEMENT AUDIT

Authoritative Pronouncements

SAS-55—Consideration of Internal Control in a Financial Statement Audit

SAS-94—The Effect of Information Technology on the Auditor's Consideration of Internal Control in a Financial Statement Audit

Overview

SAS-55 describes "internal control" as follows:

> Internal control is a process—effected by an entity's board of directors, management, and other personnel—designed to provide reasonable assurance regarding the achievement of objectives in the following categories: (a) reliability of financial reporting, (b) effectiveness and efficiency of operations, and (c) compliance with applicable laws and regulations.

SAS-94 points out that internal controls of interest to the auditor include manual procedures as well as information technology (IT).

Once management establishes objectives, it must also establish a process that encourages employees to follow and meet those established objectives. Thus, a critical part of the success of the internal control process is the following five components:

1. *Control environment*—Control environment sets the tone of an organization, which influences the control consciousness of its employees. The control environment is the foundation for all other components of internal control, because it provides discipline and structure.

2. *Risk assessment*—Risk assessment is the process that an entity must conduct to identify and assess any relevant risks to its objectives. Once this is done, management must determine how the risks should be managed.

3. *Control activities*—Control activities are the polices and procedures that help ensure that management directives are carried out.

4. *Information and communication*—These two key elements help management carry out its responsibilities. Management must establish a timely and effective process for relaying information.
5. *Monitoring*—Monitoring is a process that an entity uses to assess the quality of its internal control performance over time.

SAS-55 provides a broad definition of "internal control," ranging from financial reporting matters to the efficient execution of operational activities. However, the purpose of an audit of financial statements is narrow: Determine whether the financial statements are prepared in accordance with generally accepted accounting principles (GAAP) [or any other comprehensive basis of accounting (OCBOA)]. For this reason, the auditor is concerned with the internal control process and its components as they relate to the reliability of financial reporting. The following discussion of the five components of internal control is limited to the internal control objective related to financial reporting.

Control environment

The success or failure of implementing internal controls will depend on the environment in which the internal control process takes place. It is unlikely that specific internal control activities, no matter how well designed, can be effective if those activities must be executed in a flawed control environment. SAS-55 identifies the following as elements that affect an entity's control environment:

- Integrity and ethical values
- Commitment to competence
- Participation of board of directors or audit committee
- Management's philosophy and operating style
- Organizational structure
- Assignment of authority and responsibilities
- Human resource policies and practices

Risk assessment

The design of internal controls related to financial reporting should include management's assessment of risk factors that may prevent financial statements from being prepared in accordance with GAAP. When designing internal controls, management should consider "external and internal events and circumstances that may occur and adversely affect an entity's ability to record, process, summarize, and report financial data consistent with the assertions of management in the financial statements." Risk assessment is an ongoing process, and SAS-55 notes that the initial assessment of risk can change for the following reasons:

- Changes can occur in the operating environment.
- New personnel can become involved.
- Information system(s) can change.
- The entity can experience rapid growth.
- New technologies can be introduced into the production process or the information processing system.
- The client can introduce new business models, products, or services.
- Corporate restructuring can occur.
- Foreign operations can be expanded.
- New accounting pronouncements can be adopted.

Control activities

SAS-94 notes that a client's information system consist of "infrastructure (physical and hardware components), software, people, procedures (manual and automated), and data."

In addition to creating an effective control environment and a risk assessment process, the client should include specific control activities (policies and procedures) in its internal controls. SAS-55 classifies control activities as (1) performance reviews, (2) information processing, (3) physical controls, and (4) segregation of duties.

Information and communication

Internal control features related to the information and communication component focus on the entity's information systems (both automated and manual) and the "methods and records established to record, process, summarize, and report entity transactions (as well as events and conditions) and to maintain accountability for the related assets, liabilities, and equity." SAS-55 notes that an entity's accounting information system should include methods and records that do the following:

- Identify and record all valid transactions
- Provide a timely description of transactions so they can be properly classified
- Properly measure recorded transactions
- Record transactions in the appropriate accounting period

As part of the communication process, individuals who have internal control responsibilities within the accounting system should understand how their activities relate to the activities performed by other individuals within the organization. That is, the accounting system should not be viewed as a separate activity but rather as an integral part of the process by which the organization achieves its objectives. For example, individuals who have responsibilities related to the accounting system should know what constitutes an exception to the normal informational process and who should be informed when an exception occurs. Effective communication may be achieved through the preparation of accounting manuals and policy statements and through oral statements made by management.

Monitoring

Once internal controls are implemented, management will need to assess the controls (both from a design perspective and an operational perspective) on a timely basis and make modifications when appropriate. SAS-55 notes that ongoing monitoring should be part of the routine activities of effective internal control. In some entities the routine monitoring will be supplemented by the internal auditor function, which does not have to be performed by a formal internal audit department. In such instances, strengths and weaknesses of internal controls are identified and communicated to appropriate managerial personnel. In addition, external parties can have an important role in monitoring internal controls. For example, as part of its role a regulatory agency may evaluate internal controls or the client's customers may complain about billing errors or incorrect shipment of materials. All of these factors make up the monitoring component of internal control.

Other factors to be considered

Although the five components of internal control apply to all entities, the concepts are broad and must be applied in a manner that reflects the characteristics of a particular entity. SAS-55 concludes that in addition to the size of the entity, the auditor should consider the following factors when evaluating internal controls of a particular client:

- The organization and ownership characteristics of the client
- The nature of the client's business
- The diversity and complexity of the client's activities
- The legal and regulatory environment in which the client operates
- The nature and complexity of the client's systems that make up internal control (including the use of service organizations)

Limitations of internal controls

The basic characteristics of internal controls provide a reasonable assurance that the entity's objectives will be achieved; however, the controls cannot provide absolute assurance that those objectives will be attained. No matter how well internal controls are designed, they do have inherent limitations. For example, one of the design principles of internal controls is that the duties and responsibilities of departments and individuals need to be properly segregated. If collusion exists, the effectiveness of this principle may be completely invalidated. Additionally, internal controls can be circumvented by management. Other factors, such as employee carelessness, misunderstanding of instructions, and errors in judgment, have a similar impact on the effectiveness of internal controls. Finally, a basic concept in the design of internal controls is the realization that controls must be cost-effective. That is, the benefits derived from an internal control procedure should exceed the cost of adopting the procedure. When designing internal controls, an entity cannot measure the cost-benefit relationship precisely, but a reasonable analysis combined with appropriate judgment and estimates is useful.

The Effect of Information Technology

In considering an entity's internal control, an auditor recognizes that IT as well as manual controls can affect the fundamental manner by which transactions are initiated, recorded, processed, and reported. While the auditor is well versed in controls related to a manual system, such as written authorization for a transaction and appropriate segregation of duties and responsibilities, special attention often must be paid to advantages and disadvantages of a client's use of IT controls. SAS-94 points out that the use of IT controls can benefit internal control because of the following:

- Predefined business rules and complicated calculations can be consistently applied to a large number of similar transactions.

- Information can be processed accurately and be available to internal users in a timely fashion.
- A variety of analytical tools can be applied to processed information.
- An entity's activities and its policies and procedures can be better monitored.
- The risk that controls can be circumvented can be reduced.
- Security controls for applications, databases, and operating systems can be implemented to enhance the effective segregation of duties.

On the other hand, SAS-94 reminds auditors that the use of IT controls introduces a variety of specific risks related to the internal control environment, including the following:

- A reliance on automated procedures that are incorrectly processing data or processing incorrect data
- An introduction of data into the system that is unauthorized
- An unauthorized change of data in a master file
- An unauthorized change to a system or program
- The failure to make necessary changes to a system or program
- The inappropriate intervention due to a manual control
- A potential loss of data

Each client will design IT controls and procedures based on its needs and expertise as well as the availability of resources. The auditor recognizes that "the nature and characteristics of an entity's use of IT in its information system affect the entity's internal control."

Promulgated Procedures Checklist

The auditor should take into consideration a client's internal controls by performing the following procedures:

_____ Understand (relevant/related to financial statement assertions) internal control and determine whether related controls are in operation.

_____ Document the understanding of the internal controls.

_____ Determine the planned assessed level of control risk.

§319 • Internal Control in a Financial Audit   103

_____ Perform tests of controls to provide support for the planned assessed level of control risk.

_____ Evaluate whether the planned assessed level of control risk is supported by the results of tests of controls.

_____ Document the assessed level of control risk and the basis if it is assessed at less than the maximum level.

_____ Design substantive tests based on assessed level of control risk.

Analysis and Application of Procedures

Understand (relevant/related to financial statement assertions) internal control and determine whether related controls are in operation

In all audit engagements, the auditor must adequately understand those internal controls that are relevant to the audit of the financial statements. As noted earlier, relevant controls are concerned with the recording, processing, summarizing, and reporting of financial data consistent with the assertions embodied in the financial statements. Thus, the auditor needs to understand internal controls that increase the likelihood that the financial statements will be prepared in accordance with GAAP.

Financial statement assertion

SAS-31 (AU 326) (Evidential Matter) defines and describes "financial statement assertions." An example of how financial statement assertions and internal controls are related is presented in Exhibit AU 319-1.

Relevant controls

Generally, relevant internal controls are concerned only with financial data; however, controls related to nonfinancial data also may be of interest to the auditor. For example, quality control data may be useful for testing the assertion in the financial statement that the allowance for returned goods is properly valued. On the other hand, controls that relate to effectiveness, economy, and efficiency usually are not useful in testing assertions embodied in the financial statements.

Developing an understanding

SAS-55 concludes that the auditor must obtain an understanding of the design of internal controls for all five control components in every audit engagement. The auditor's understanding must be sufficient to plan the audit engagement to achieve the following:

- Identify misstatements that could occur in the financial statements
- Identify factors that affect the degree of risk for misstatements in financial statements
- Identify factors that determine whether tests of controls should be performed
- Identify factors relevant to the design of substantive tests

Although the auditor is required to obtain an understanding of all five components of the client's internal controls, the specific nature, timing, and extent of the audit procedures used to obtain such an understanding will not be the same for all engagements. Specifically, SAS-55 notes that the following factors will have an impact on the extent of the auditor's understanding of a client's internal controls during the planning stage of the audit engagement:

- The size and complexity of the client
- Previous client engagements, if any
- The nature of specific controls implemented by the client, including the entity's use of IT
- The nature and extent of changes in systems and operations
- The degree to which specific controls are documented by the client

PLANNING AID REMINDER: During the planning stage of the audit engagement, the auditor's responsibility to gain an understanding of internal controls is limited to determining whether internal controls are in place; it does not include determining whether those control are being used effectively. (Determining whether controls are being used effectively is part of tests of controls, which are discussed later.)

While the auditor is developing an understanding of internal controls, he or she may encounter circumstances indicating that the financial statements cannot be audited. These circumstances include the following:

- The lack of management integrity raises doubts about the overall reliability of internal controls.

§319 • Internal Control in a Financial Audit

- The accounting records are inadequate and do not provide sufficient competent evidential matter on which an opinion may be based.

Obtaining an understanding of the control environment

SAS-55 concludes that the auditor should develop an understanding of the client's control environment "to understand management's and the board of directors' attitude, awareness, and actions concerning the control environment considering both the substance of controls and their collective effect." The auditor should develop a broad view of the control environment, taking into consideration how various elements of the environment relate to other components of the client's internal control. For example, SAS-55 points out that while a client might have effective hiring practices that relate to financial and accounting personnel, those practices might be invalidated by "a strong bias by top management to overstate earnings."

Obtaining an understanding of risk assessment

The auditor should acquire an understanding of how the client identifies risks related to the possible occurrence of errors for particular transactions, events, and balances. For example, if the client receives a significant amount of returned goods, the auditor should understand how management identifies such goods and similar financial reporting risks and how risks of this nature are managed so that the financial statements are not materially misstated.

Obtaining an understanding of control activities

The auditor should obtain an understanding of control activities so that he or she can be reasonably assured that management's objectives related to financial reporting are achieved. As noted earlier, control activities relate to (1) performance reviews, (2) information processing, (3) physical controls, and (4) segregation of duties. SAS-55 notes that "ordinarily, auditing planning does not require an understanding of the control activities related to each account balance, transaction class, and disclosure component in the financial statements or to every assertion relevant to them."

> **ENGAGEMENT STRATEGY:** Although the auditor is required to obtain an understanding of all five components of internal control, that does not suggest that this gathering of information is accomplished as five distinct tasks. The auditor, for example, may develop an understanding of some control activities as part of obtaining information about the information and communication component of internal control.

Obtaining an understanding about information and communication

The auditor should gain an understanding of the information and communication component of internal control so that the auditor can achieve the following:

- Understand the classes of transactions in the entity's operations that are significant to its financial statements
- Understand how those transactions are initiated
- Understand the accounting records, supporting documents, machine-readable and machine-transmitted information, and specific accounts in the financial statements involved in the processing and reporting of transactions
- Understand the accounting process, from the initiation of a transaction to its inclusion in the financial statements, including how the computer is used to process data
- Understand the financial reporting process for preparing financial statements, including significant accounting estimates and disclosures

Finally, the auditor should acquire an understanding of how the client communicates "financial reporting roles and responsibilities and significant matters relating to financial reporting" to appropriate personnel.

Obtaining an understanding about monitoring

The auditor should develop an understanding of how the client monitors its internal controls to see whether those controls are effective. SAS-55 notes that obtaining an understanding about monitoring activities should be based on guidance established by SAS-65 (AU 322) (The Auditor's Consideration of the Internal Audit Function in an Audit of Financial Statements).

Procedures used to obtain an understanding of components

The auditor may use the following procedures to obtain an understanding of an entity's internal controls:

- Review workpapers from previous assignments.
- Make inquiries of appropriate management, supervisory, and staff personnel.
- Inspect relevant documents and records.
- Observe the entity's activities and operations.

§319 • Internal Control in a Financial Audit

The extent to which such procedures are used depends on the characteristics of the engagement. Characteristics that should be considered include the following:

- Size and complexity of the entity, including its use of IT
- Level of previous experience with the entity
- Nature of relevant controls identified
- Manner of documentation of relevant controls used by the entity
- Assessments of inherent risks
- Judgments about materiality levels with respect to specific accounts and transactions

The effect of IT on understanding internal control

In many engagements that are not complex and for which an owner-manager approves and reviews transactions and accounting records the auditor may need a limited understanding of internal control in order to adequately plan the engagement. On the other hand when the client uses a complex automated system, a considerable amount of effort may be needed to develop an adequate understanding of internal control.

In some instances an engagement requires specialized IT skills to understand IT controls, or to design and perform tests of IT controls or substantive tests. The necessary IT skills may be possessed by a member of the firm or it may be necessary to consult an outside professional. SAS-94 points out that in determining whether specialized IT skills are necessary in an engagement, factors such as the following should be considered:

- The complexity of the entity's system and the IT controls utilized in the system
- The modification of existing systems or the integration of new systems during the year
- The extent data are shared among systems
- The extent to which a client is involved in electronic commerce
- The use of emerging technologies
- The degree to which audit evidence is available only in an electronic format

While the auditor may assign various IT duties to a staff person or an outside professional, "the auditor should have sufficient IT-related knowledge to communicate the auditor's objectives to the professional, to evaluate whether the specified procedures will meet the auditor's objectives, and to evaluate the results of the procedures as they relate to the nature, timing, and extent of other planned procedures."

> **PLANNING AID REMINDER:** When the auditor decides to use an outside professional with specialized IT skills, the guidance established by SAS-73 (AU 336) (Using the Work of a Specialist) should be followed.

Document the understanding of the internal controls

Once the auditor has gained an adequate understanding of the entity's internal control, that understanding should be documented in the workpapers. Methods of documentation include the preparation of flowcharts, internal control questionnaires, and narrative descriptions. The auditor must use professional judgment to determine which methods are best for documenting the understanding.

Determine the planned assessed level of control risk

Once the auditor has obtained an understanding of the internal control, he or she must determine the planned assessed level of control risk. Such an approach is based on the interrelationship of audit risk and other risk factors, defined below.

Audit risk refers to the probability that an auditor will not detect a material error that exists in the financial statements and includes inherent risk, control risk, and detection risk. SAS-55 defines these risks as follows:

- *Inherent risk*—The susceptibility of an assertion to a material misstatement, assuming there are no related internal control policies or procedures
- *Control risk*—The risk that a material misstatement that could occur in an assertion will not be prevented or detected on a timely basis by an entity's internal controls
- *Detection risk*—The risk that the auditor will not detect a material misstatement that exists in an assertion

> **OBSERVATION:** These risk factors are discussed in Section 312.

Once the auditor has obtained an understanding of the client's internal control, it is possible to assess the level of control risk for a particular engagement. At this point, the assessment is primarily analytical. The auditor has documented the system and, based on the documentation, has identified potential strengths and weaknesses in the internal control.

§319 • Internal Control in a Financial Audit 109

SAS-94 points out that the following factors should be taken into consideration when determining whether control risk for specific assertions should be assessed at the maximum level or at a lower level:

- Nature of the assertion
- Volume of transactions/data related to the assertion
- Nature and complexity of system (including the use of IT) related to the assertion
- Nature of evidential matter (including that available only in electronic form) related to the assertion

> **ENGAGEMENT STRATEGY:** In some instances it is not possible to reasonably substantiate an assertion only through evidence obtained through the use of substantive tests when the information that supports the assertion is electronically initiated, recorded, processed, or reported. Under these circumstances the auditor should identify and test the effectiveness of IT controls.

> **RISK ASSESSMENT POINT:** The assessment of the level of control risk provides the auditor with a general strategy for planning the remaining internal control evaluation. If the auditor believes the internal control is well designed, the level of control risk will be assessed at a relatively low level for a given assertion. On the other hand, if the internal control appears to be poorly designed, a higher level of control risk will be assigned to the internal control.

> **ENGAGEMENT STRATEGY:** In circumstances where the auditor believes the internal control is not reliable, the auditor should ignore a substantial portion of the structure and depend almost exclusively on evidential matter collected as part of the performance of substantive tests. When the control risk is assessed at a relatively low level, the auditor will perform tests of controls.

Perform tests of controls to provide support for the planned assessed level of control risk

Generally, an audit is more efficient when the auditor can rely to some degree on the client's internal control. However, that reliance can occur only under the following circumstances:

- When specific internal controls related to specific assertions can be identified
- When tests of controls are performed

When the auditor performs a test of automated controls, the test should include not only the computerized control but also any related control that tests the effectiveness of the overall system. For example, an automated control might include a procedure whereby a transaction is identified as an exception based on a number of predetermined criteria. The auditor should not only test that the automated control is working effectively but also that the exception report is being used in the manner that was anticipated by the client when the control was initially designed. However, the nature of testing each of those elements of internal control is often different. That is, the automated control might require limited testing because once the control is implemented it functions the same way each time unless the program is changed. The auditor may test this automated control at the time it is implemented or at a later date and also test that program changes have not been made since the inception of the control. The nature of testing the automated control may require the use of special IT skills as discussed earlier. Finally, the nonautomated control is often tested in a different manner that may require drawing an adequate sample from the population and applying conventional testing methods, such as recomputation, inquiry, and observation.

> **OBSERVATION:** SAS-55 refers to this strategy as "assessing control risk at a level less than the maximum." The auditor must identify specific internal controls relevant to the prevention or detection of material misstatements in specific assertions embodied in the financial statements. Internal controls may be evaluated based on their breadth of influence and degree of relevance. The auditor should consider both of these factors when determining whether he or she is justified in identifying policies and controls that may serve as a basis for the reduction of the assessed level of control risk.

SAS-94 points out that in some instances where a client's "initiation, recording, or processing of financial data exists only in electronic form" it may be unlikely that an acceptable level of detection risk can be achieved with the performance of only substantive tests.

Breadth of influence

Some internal controls have a pervasive effect on accounts and classes of transactions. Generally, controls related to the control environment and the accounting system have a pervasive effect. For example, methods of assign-

§319 • Internal Control in a Financial Audit

ing authority and responsibility have implications for all assertions embodied in the financial statements. Control procedures, on the other hand, tend to be directed to specific assertions related to account balances and classes of transactions.

Degree of relevance

Some controls are directly related to specific assertions, while other controls are related only indirectly to specific assertions. The more direct the relationship between controls and an assertion, the more likely it is that controls can provide a basis for reducing the level of assessed control risk.

> **RISK ASSESSMENT POINT:** The performance of tests of controls is the second step in the process of determining whether the planned assessed level of control risk is appropriate. Tests of controls are used to determine the effectiveness of (1) the design of controls and (2) the operations of controls.

Evaluation of effectiveness of design

To evaluate the effectiveness of design, the auditor determines whether controls are adequate to prevent or detect material misstatements of financial statement assertions. The process of evaluating the design of controls is more analytical than corroborative in nature; that is, the auditor is concerned with the design of controls rather than with their operational effectiveness. Audit procedures used to evaluate the effectiveness of design generally include the following:

- Inquiries of appropriate personnel (possibly through the preparation of an internal control questionnaire)
- Inspection of documents and reports to determine how information is collected
- Observation of the application of specific controls to determine which controls are in place
- Evaluation of documentation

Evaluation of operational effectiveness

The evaluation of the operational effectiveness of internal controls requires the collection of corroborative evidence to determine (1) who performed the procedures, (2) whether procedures were performed correctly, and (3) to what extent the procedures were performed throughout the accounting period. Audit procedures used to evaluate the operational effectiveness of controls generally include the following:

- Inquiries of appropriate personnel to determine who performed a procedure
- Inspection of documents and reports to determine how a procedure was executed and who executed the procedure
- Observation of the application of specific controls to determine who performed a procedure
- Reperformance of the procedure to substantiate that the procedure was performed correctly

> **PLANNING AID REMINDER:** In practice, both elements of the tests of controls (effective design and operational effectiveness) will be performed concurrently. The auditor is not concerned with the classification of specific audit procedures but rather with the evaluation and substantiation of internal controls.
>
> **OBSERVATION:** The tests of details of transactions are classified as substantive tests; however, the auditor may use tests of details of transactions as tests of controls when they are useful in determining the effectiveness of internal controls.

Evaluate whether the planned assessed level of control risk is supported by the results of tests of controls

If an auditor decides to perform tests of controls, the results of the tests should be used to determine whether the planned assessed level of control risk can be justified. The auditor must obtain sufficient competent evidential matter to support the assessment of control risk at the planned assessed level. Professional judgment must be used to determine what constitutes sufficient competent evidential matter; the following factors should be used in making this judgment:

- Nature (type) of evidential matter
- Source of evidential matter
- Timeliness of evidential matter
- Interrelationships of evidential matter
- Extent of evidential matter

§319 • Internal Control in a Financial Audit

Interrelationship of evidential matter

There is seldom, if ever, a perfect one-to-one relationship between the results of performing a single test of controls procedure and a single assertion embodied in the financial statements. To properly evaluate evidence gathered as part of tests of controls, the auditor must recognize that interrelationships exist among evidential matter. Generalizations about these interrelationships can be summarized as follows:

- Assessment of risk concerning an assertion will usually be based on evidence gathered from various audit (tests of controls) procedures.
- Evidence gathered through tests of controls must be evaluated in the context of the control environment and the accounting system.
- Various types of evidence that support a similar conclusion increase the assurance about the effectiveness of controls.
- Various types of evidence that support dissimilar conclusions decrease the assurance about the effectiveness of controls.
- Evidence is accumulated throughout an engagement, and it may be necessary for the auditor to reassess the level of control risk.

Document the assessed level of control risk and the basis if it is assessed at less than the maximum level

The assessment of control risk for a particular assertion (or group of assertions related to an account balance or class of transactions) must be documented. The assessment must be related to the results of the performance of tests of controls. While specific documentation methods and levels cannot be established, SAS-55 notes that the following factors will influence the auditor's documentation:

- Assessed level of control risk
- Nature of the entity's internal control
- Nature of the entity's documentation of its internal control

> **RISK ASSESSMENT POINT:** A variety of control risks can be assessed in a single engagement. As demonstrated in the discussion in this chapter, the auditor can assess a maximum level and a level less than the maximum. In practice, it is likely that different control risks will be assessed for different account balances and classes of transactions and for different assertions related to the same account balance or class of transactions.

Design substantive tests based on assessed level of control risk

Based on the auditor's (1) assessment of inherent risk and (2) assessment of control risk resulting from the understanding of the entity's internal control and perhaps tests of control, the auditor determines an acceptable level of detection risk. "Detection risk" is the risk that the auditor will not detect a material misstatement in an assertion. The lower the assessment of inherent risk and control risk, the higher the acceptable detection risk. In other words, the auditor is willing to accept a relatively higher detection risk when other risk factors (inherent and control) are relatively low.

"Substantive tests" are defined in SAS-55 as "tests of details and analytical procedures performed to detect material misstatements in the account balance, transaction class, and disclosure components of financial statements." The establishment of a level of acceptable detection risk is used as a basis for determining the nature, timing, and extent of substantive tests. For example, as the level of detection risk is decreased:

- Audit procedures that create more competent evidential matter are employed (nature of procedures).
- Audit procedures are more likely to be applied to year-end balances than to interim balances (timing of procedures).
- The size of the sample selected for testing becomes larger (extent of procedures).

> **ENGAGEMENT STRATEGY:** The above generalizations are reasonable. If the auditor desires a lower level of detection risk, the quality and/or quantity of audit evidence collected through substantive tests must increase.

As suggested earlier, there is interplay among the risk factors. By establishing an overall audit risk and assessing inherent risk and control risk, the auditor selects an appropriate level of detection risk that, when combined with inherent and control risks, will result in the attainment of the overall audit risk sought by the auditor.

> **RISK ASSESSMENT POINT:** Under no circumstances could assessed low levels of inherent risk and control risk suggest that there is no need to perform substantive tests to achieve the overall audit risk.

> **PLANNING AID REMINDER:** Tests of details of transactions are principally substantive tests and therefore are concerned with the identification of material misstatements in the financial

§319 • Internal Control in a Financial Audit

statements. Tests of details of transactions may be applied secondarily as tests of controls to evaluate the design and operational effectiveness of internal controls. In order for tests of details of transactions to simultaneously function as substantive tests and tests of controls, the auditor must consider carefully whether tests of details of transactions have been adequately designed to satisfy both purposes.

Practitioner's Aids

EXHIBIT AU 319-1—RELATIONSHIP OF FINANCIAL STATEMENT ASSERTIONS AND RELEVANT INTERNAL CONTROLS

SAS-31 (AU 326) (Evidential Matter) defines the following financial statement assertions:

- *Existence or occurrence*—The auditor should determine whether assets or liabilities of the entity exist at a given date and whether recorded transactions have occurred during a given period.

- *Completeness*—The auditor should determine whether all transactions and accounts that should be presented in the financial statements are included.

- *Rights and obligations*—The auditor should determine whether assets are the rights of the entity and liabilities the obligations of the entity at a given date.

- *Valuation or allocation*—The auditor should determine whether assets, liabilities, revenue, and expense components have been included in the financial statements at appropriate amounts.

- *Presentation and disclosure*—The auditor should determine whether particular components of the financial statements are properly classified, described, and disclosed.

The interrelationship of assertions embodied in the financial statements and relevant internal controls for inventory is illustrated below.

Assertions in the Financial Statements Related to Inventories	*Relevant Internal Controls*
Inventory is held for resale (existence).	Portions of the inventory are counted every four months. Counts are compared to the perpetual inventory amounts.

Assertions in the Financial Statements Related to Inventories	Relevant Internal Controls
Purchases of inventory for the period are recorded (completeness).	Prenumbered receiving reports are prepared and used for the receipt of all inventory. Receiving reports are accounted for every two months.
Inventory on hand is owned (rights).	A perpetual inventory system is maintained for goods received from consignors. Every three months, recorded amounts are compared to actual counts.
Inventory is valued at first in, first out (FIFO) (valuation).	Perpetual inventory system is maintained for both quantities and cost.
Inventory is a current asset (presentation and disclosure).	Inventory turnover rates on a test basis for certain inventory items are computed to identify slow-moving and obsolete inventory.

§319 • Internal Control in a Financial Audit

EXHIBIT AU 319-2—THE APPLICATION OF INTERNAL CONTROL CONCEPTS TO SMALL AND MIDSIZED ENTITIES

Internal control is a critical element in helping the client to prepare financial statements that reflect generally accepted accounting principles (GAAP). However, SAS-55 recognizes that internal control for a large publicly held company is different from internal control for a small company or even a midsized company. The five components of internal control should be present in every client's internal control, but how control objectives are achieved can vary from client to client. For example, the following features of a small or midsized entity's internal control may be as effective as the features adopted by a public company.

- *Control environment*—Controls related to the control environment might not be as extensively documented in a formal manner but, rather, may be communicated orally to affected personnel. However, although a formal code of conduct might not be formally documented, the essence of such a code might be part of the culture of the entity.

- *Risk assessment*—Risk assessment related to the preparation of financial statements might be less formal in a small company; however, key managerial personnel (including owner-managers), because of their involvement in the day-to-day operations of the entity, may be fully aware of the relationship between various operational activities and financial reporting objectives.

- *Control activities*—Control activities might be concentrated, to some extent, in a relatively small number of personnel; however, managerial personnel may have an extensive awareness of normal levels of activity and would likely become aware of transactions that appear to be questionable.

- *Information and communication*—Documentation of the information system and communication of related control features might not be extensive or formal in a small company; however, extensive involvement by a relatively small number of managerial personnel might not require formal accounting manuals or involved accounting records.

- *Monitoring*—There may be limited ongoing monitoring of daily activities; however, management's day-to-day involvement in operational activities may provide an adequate separate evaluation of the effectiveness of the design and operations of internal controls.

SECTION 322

THE AUDITOR'S CONSIDERATION OF THE INTERNAL AUDIT FUNCTION IN AN AUDIT OF FINANCIAL STATEMENTS

Authoritative Pronouncements

SAS-65—The Auditor's Consideration of the Internal Audit Function in an Audit of Financial Statements

Overview

As suggested earlier, an internal audit function, if it exists, is part of the client's internal control. SAS-65 (The Auditor's Consideration of the Internal Audit Function in an Audit of Financial Statements) describes how the auditor should evaluate the internal audit function in order to plan the audit engagement (designing the nature, timing, and extent of subsequent audit procedures).

An internal audit function may consist of a variety of activities, some or all of which might not be related to the recording, processing, and reporting of financial information. The auditor should obtain an understanding of the internal audit function as part of obtaining an understanding of the client's internal control. While special circumstances of each engagement will dictate the specific audit approach, the auditor should initially develop an understanding of the purpose and scope of the internal audit function and its location in the organizational hierarchy. In addition, the auditor might read reports prepared by internal auditors, determine how staff members are allocated within the internal audit function (operational versus financial audit activities), and refer to assessments of internal audit activities that were part of previous audits of the client's financial statements.

Promulgated Procedures Checklist

If the auditor concludes that relevant activities are being performed by internal auditors, and it appears that it would be efficient to rely on those activities in assessing internal control risk, the auditor should perform the following:

____ Assess the objectivity and competence of the internal audit function

____ Determine the effect of the internal audit function on understanding the internal control

§322 • The Internal Audit Function

_____ Determine the effect of the internal audit function on the assessed risk

_____ Determine the effect of the internal audit function on the design of substantive procedures

_____ Determine the degree of reliance on the internal audit function

_____ Evaluate the internal audit work

> **PLANNING AID REMINDER:** SAS-65 requires that, in all engagements, the auditor develop some understanding of the internal audit function and determine whether that function is relevant to the assessment of control risk. Thus, if there is an internal audit function, it must be evaluated. The evaluation is not optional.

Analysis and Application of Procedures

Assess the objectivity and competence of the internal audit function

The auditor should evaluate the objectivity of internal auditors by determining the organizational status of the internal audit function and by examining the policies that may enhance the likelihood that the internal auditors are objective.

> **RISK ASSESSMENT POINT:** The standard of objectivity is different from the standard of independence. Although it could be argued that it is simply a matter of semantics, the differentiation is based on the reasonable assumption that an internal auditor cannot achieve independence, because he or she is an employee of the client.

SAS-65 states that factors relevant to determining organizational status of the internal audit function include the following:

- Direct reporting to an officer, which implies broad audit coverage and adequate consideration of audit findings
- Direct access and reporting to the board of directors, the audit committee, or the owner/manager
- For internal audit employment decisions, oversight responsibility that rests with the board of directors, the audit committee, or the owner/manager

In addition, policies that minimize the placement of internal auditors in situations where they have an existing relationship (for example, auditing a department where a spouse works) or may have a future relationship (possible assignment to a department once the internal audit stint is completed) can contribute to the objectivity of the internal audit function and should be considered by the auditor.

In assessing the competence of the internal auditors, the auditor should review background information on the internal auditors, such as their educational achievements (degrees, certifications, continuing education) and professional experience. In addition, the auditor should consider operational practices such as the assignment of internal auditors, supervision and review of personnel within the department, quality of workpapers, and specific performance evaluations.

SAS-65 concludes that in some instances it may be necessary to test the effectiveness of the client's controls on objectivity and competency. For example, rather than simply accepting an assertion that the audit committee is involved in the hiring of internal auditors, the auditor may decide to interview members of the committee and ask them specifically about their roles in hiring a particular internal auditor.

> **ENGAGEMENT STRATEGY:** The degree to which the effectiveness of controls will be tested should be based on the anticipated degree to which the internal audit function will be a factor in the planning of subsequent audit procedures: The greater the reliance on the internal audit function, the greater the degree to which the controls should be tested.

If the auditor concludes that the internal audit function possesses an acceptable level of objectivity and competence, the auditor should determine the effect of the function on (1) the understanding of the internal control, (2) the assessment of risk, and (3) the design of substantive procedures.

Determine the effect of the internal audit function on understanding the internal control

The understanding of the client's internal control generally consists of an analytical phase and a tests-of-controls phase. Work performed by internal auditors may affect one or both of these phases of the engagement. For example, internal auditors may have documented the cash disbursements system by preparing a flowchart and supportive narrative descriptions. In addition, the internal auditors may have inspected canceled voucher packages to determine whether certain specific control procedures depicted on the flowchart were followed. The auditor could rely on this documentation to gain an initial understanding of the cash disbursement system (analytical phase) and could review the number and types of control deviations discovered by the internal auditors (tests-of-controls phase).

Determine the effect of the internal audit function on the assessed risk

The auditor assesses risk at the financial statement level and at the account balance or class-of-transaction level. Risk at the financial statement level is broad in nature in that it applies to assessing the risk of material misstatement in one of the financial statements. Generally, factors related to the control environment have a broad effect on risk assessment. Thus, an evaluation of the internal audit function as an element of the client's internal control can have an effect on the auditor assessment's of risk at the financial statement level.

Risk at the account balance or class-of-transaction level is directed to specific control activities and the related assertions that appear in the financial statements. Having internal auditors perform tests of controls may influence the level of risk assessed at the account balance level or class-of-transaction level. For example, if internal auditors have tested the cash disbursement system, the auditor reviewing the tests may decide that control risk as it relates to assertions concerning certain operating expenses (such as advertising expense and utilities expense) can be assessed at a level less than maximum.

Determine the effect of the internal audit function on the design of substantive procedures

SAS-65 states that if the internal auditors are requested to directly assist in the audit, the auditor should follow the guidelines listed below:

- Assess the competence and objective of the internal auditors

- Supervise, review, evaluate, and test the work performed by the internal auditors

- Describe to the internal auditors their responsibilities

- Describe the objective of the work that is being performed

- Describe circumstances that could affect the nature, timing, and extent of audit procedures

- Direct internal auditors to inform the auditor of all significant accounting and auditing issues that arise during the performance of their work

Determine the degree of reliance on the internal audit function

Although the role of the internal audit function can be considered in understanding internal control, assessing risk, and designing substantive procedures, the independent auditor is solely responsible for the opinion expressed on the financial statements. For this reason, the auditor should carefully consider the extent to which the internal audit function should influence the audit approach. The fundamental guidance for determining the role the internal audit function should play in the audit is simple: Evidential matter obtained indirectly from an internal auditor is less reliable than the same evidential matter developed directly by the independent auditor.

> **RISK ASSESSMENT POINT:** SAS-65 concludes that the auditor should consider three factors—(1) the materiality of balances or classes of transactions, (2) the degree of inherent risk and control risk, and (3) the degree of subjectivity needed to evaluate evidence to support assertions in the financial statements—in determining the degree of reliance on the internal audit function. As each one of these factors increases, the degree of reliance on work performed by internal auditors should decrease (and vice versa).

SAS-65 reiterates that when assertions related to material amounts are characterized by a high risk of material misstatement or a high degree of subjectivity (or both), the auditor must be in a position to accept sole responsibility for satisfying the standards of fieldwork with respect to these assertions and the related internal control. Furthermore, the work of the internal auditors cannot solely be used as a basis for eliminating the auditor's performance of substantive tests on those assertions. SAS-65 suggests that the following assertions have either a high degree of risk or a high degree of subjectivity in the evaluation of audit evidence:

- Significant accounting estimates that are the basis for valuing assets or liabilities
- Existence and disclosure of related party transactions
- Existence and disclosure of contingencies and other uncertainties
- Existence and disclosure of subsequent events

While the work of internal auditors may be used in a variety of circumstances, SAS-65 concludes that the following judgments should be made by the auditor and not by internal auditors:

- Assessments of inherent risk and control risk
- Sufficiency of audit tests performed
- Evaluation of significant accounting estimates

Other similar judgments also should be made exclusively by the auditor.

§322 • The Internal Audit Function

Evaluate internal audit work

When the auditor concludes that the work of internal auditors may be used to determine an understanding of internal control, to assess risk, or as substantive procedures, the auditor should evaluate the quality of that work. Factors that might be considered in assessing the work of internal auditors are the following:

- Whether the scope of the work is consistent with audit objectives
- Adequacy of internal audit programs
- Adequacy of workpaper documentation, including evidence of supervision and review
- Appropriateness of conclusions drawn
- Whether the internal audit reports are consistent with the nature of the work performed

The auditor's evaluation of the effectiveness of the procedures conducted by internal auditors should include the testing of the internal auditors' work related to significant financial statement assertions. The auditor can satisfy the need for such evaluation either by (1) examining controls, transactions, or balances examined by the internal auditors or by (2) examining similar controls, transactions, or balances not actually examined by the internal auditors. The auditor should then compare his or her own results to those of the internal auditors. The degree to which the auditor performs such tests is a matter of professional judgment.

SECTION 324

SERVICE ORGANIZATIONS

Authoritative Pronouncements

SAS-70—Service Organizations

SAS-88—Service Organizations and Reporting on Consistency

Auditing Interpretation (April 1995)—Describing Tests of Operating Effectiveness and the Results of Such Tests

Auditing Interpretation (April 1995)—Service Organizations That Use the Services of Other Service Organizations (Subservice Organizations)

Overview

The standards established by SAS-70 (as amended by SAS-88) apply to the audit of a client that uses the services of another entity (service organization), whereby those services are considered to be part of the client's information system because they affect one or more of the following:

- The initiation of an entity's transactions
- The client's accounting records, supporting information, and specific accounts in the financial statements
- The procedures used to process accounting transactions (from the initiation of a transaction to the impact of the transaction on the financial statements)
- The process used to prepare the client's financial statements (including significant accounting estimates and disclosures)

For example, a mortgage company may use the services of another entity to receive and process monthly mortgage payments from its customers, or a company may engage a computer processing service to record and process routine transactions related to payroll, trade receivables, and trade payables.

The activities performed by the other company may be considered part of the client's internal control and therefore may require that the auditor develop a sufficient understanding of the controls in place at the other company's facilities. However, it may be costly to have the client's auditor visit the other organization to obtain such an understanding. Also, it could be disruptive to the other organization to have several of its customers' auditors review and test its internal control.

To provide a reasonable solution to this problem, the American Institute of Certified Public Accountants (AICPA) issued SAS-70 (Service Organizations). SAS-70 identifies and defines the following four parties relative to reporting on processing of transactions by service organizations:

1. *User organization*—The entity that has engaged a service organization and whose financial statements are being audited

2. *User auditor*—The auditor who reports on the financial statements of the user organization

3. *Service organization*—The entity (or segment of an entity) that provides services to the user organization

4. *Service auditor*—The auditor who reports on the processing of transactions by a service organization

> **PLANNING AID REMINDER:** The standards established by SAS-70 are also applicable to service organizations that develop, provide, and maintain the software used by user organizations. On the other hand, the standards are not applicable to the audit of a client's transactions that arise from financial interests in partnerships, corporations, and joint ventures, when the entity's proprietary interest is accounted for and reported. In addition, SAS-70 would not apply when the service organization executes transactions based on specific authorization granted by the user organization. For example, the user auditor would not consider the control procedures of a broker that simply executes security transactions for the user organization.

ROLE OF THE USER AUDITOR

When a user organization employs a service organization, the user organization's ability to institute effective internal controls over the activities performed by the service organization can vary.

In many instances, internal controls of the service organization are an extension of the user organization's accounting system. Generally, transactions authorized by the user organization are transferred to the service organization for additional processing, and internal controls are maintained by both the user and the service organization. In other instances, the service organization may execute transactions and maintain related accountability, and the user organization might not have effective internal controls over such transactions.

Promulgated Procedures Checklist—User Auditor

The user auditor should perform the following procedures in determining the degree to which the work of the service auditor should be utilized:

____ Determine the degree of understanding that should be obtained about the service organization's internal controls.

____ Consider the internal controls at the service organization in assessing the audit control risk.

____ Determine the effects of substantive tests performed by the service auditor.

____ Make inquiries concerning the service auditor's professional reputation.

____ Determine whether the work of the service auditor can be used.

Analysis and Application of Procedures—User Auditor

Determine the degree of understanding that should be obtained about the service organization's internal controls

When a service organization's activities are considered to be part of the client's information system (as described earlier), the requirements established in SAS-55 (AU 319) (Consideration of Internal Control in a Financial Statement Audit) apply to the tasks performed by the service organization. That is, the auditor must obtain an understanding of the related controls instituted by both the client and the service organization in order to achieve the following:

- Identify the nature of potential misstatements that might occur
- Consider relevant factors that affect the risk of a material misstatement in the financial statements
- Design substantive tests

Relevant controls instituted by a service organization can be identified from a number of sources, including the following:

- User manuals
- System overviews

§324 • Service Organizations

- Technical manuals
- The contract between the two parties
- Reports by other parties including the service auditor, internal auditors, and regulatory authorities

SAS-88 notes that when the activities performed by the service organization are routine and highly standardized, a review of the user auditor's previous reports might be useful in planning the current engagement.

On the basis of these factors, and others that the user auditor may consider relevant, the user auditor should decide whether the service organization should be contacted. If the user auditor concludes that there is sufficient information about the service organization's internal control to plan the audit, there is no need to contact the service organization.

> **PLANNING AID REMINDER:** However, if it is concluded that the information is insufficient for adequate planning of the audit, the user auditor should consider contacting the service organization (through the client). The user auditor could (1) request additional information from the service organization, (2) request that a service auditor be engaged by the service organization (see later discussion titled "Role of the Service Auditor"), or (3) visit the service organization and obtain the desired information.

Consider the internal controls at the service organization in assessing the audit control risk

When assessing control risk, the user auditor should consider controls that are employed by the service organization, as well as those established by the user organization. SAS-55 (AU 319) concludes that control risk can be assessed at a level below the maximum level only when (1) specific controls relate to specific financial statements assertions and (2) those procedures are subject to tests of controls. The user auditor can obtain evidence arising from tests of controls in the following ways:

- By performing tests of controls at the user organization's location
- By performing tests of controls at the service organization
- By obtaining a service auditor's report on controls placed in operation, as well as tests of operating effectiveness
- By obtaining a service auditor's report on the application of agreed-upon procedures that describes appropriate tests of controls

> **RISK ASSESSMENT POINT:** Although the user auditor can obtain information about tests of controls in a variety of ways, the information should be carefully evaluated to determine whether it is relevant to and sufficient for the assessment of control risk at a level that is less than the maximum level.

Determine the effects of substantive tests performed by the service auditor

The service auditor may perform audit procedures that substantiate transactions and balances that appear in the user organization's financial statements. Such procedures should be agreed to by the user organization, user auditor, service organization, and service auditor. Similarly, governmental auditing regulations or other arrangements might require the service auditor to perform specific substantive tests. The user auditor might take into consideration the results of performing such procedures.

Make inquiries concerning the service auditor's professional reputation

As suggested earlier, the user auditor might obtain a service auditor's report on (1) controls placed in operations (used to obtain an understanding of internal control in order to plan the engagement) or (2) controls placed in operation and tests of operating effectiveness (used to obtain an understanding of internal control in order to plan the engagement and assess control risk). Before either of these reports is relied on, the user auditor should make inquiries concerning the service auditor's professional reputation. Guidance for making such inquiries can be found in SAS-1, AU Section 543 (Part of Audit Performed by Other Independent Auditors).

> **ENGAGEMENT STRATEGY:** Although the user auditor may rely on the work of the service auditor, there should be no reference to such work in the user auditor's report on the financial statements of the user organization. This is not a "division of responsibility" reporting circumstance as described in SAS-1, AU Section 543.

Determine whether the work of the service auditor can be used

If it is concluded that the service auditor's professional reputation is acceptable, there should be a determination of whether the work performed by the service auditor is sufficient to achieve the user auditor's objectives. To make this determination, the user auditor should consider performing one or more of the following procedures:

- Communicating with the service auditor and discussing the application and results of audit procedures performed
- Reviewing the audit programs used by the service auditor
- Reviewing the audit workpapers of the service auditor

> **PLANNING AID REMINDER:** If it is concluded that the work of the service auditor does not fully meet the needs of the user auditor, (1) the user auditor might request (with the permission of the user organization and the service organization) that the service auditor perform agreed-upon procedures or (2) the user auditor might perform appropriate procedures at the service organization's location.

ROLE OF THE SERVICE AUDITOR

When a service auditor reports on the processing of transactions by a service organization, the general standards—and the relevant standards of fieldwork and reporting—should be observed. Although the service auditor must be independent with respect to the service organization, it is not necessary to be independent from every user organization.

If the service auditor becomes aware of illegal acts, fraud, or uncorrected errors (that are other than inconsequential) that affect a user organization, the service auditor should determine whether the user organization has been informed of the matter. If such matters have not been communicated to the user organization, the service auditor should inform the service organization's audit committee (or equivalent party) of the matter. If, after being informed of the matter, the audit committee does not take appropriate action, the service auditor should consider withdrawing from the engagement.

The service organization should determine what type of engagement the service auditor should perform; however, in an ideal situation, the user organization would discuss the matter with the service organization and its auditors to ensure that all parties will be satisfied with the service auditor's report.

The service auditor should observe the following guidance:

- Prepare an appropriate service audit report.
- Obtain written representations from the service organization.

Analysis and Application of Procedures—Service Auditor

Prepare an appropriate service audit report

SAS-70 defines a *report on controls placed in operation* (PPPO report) as follows:

> A service auditor's report on a service organization's description of its internal controls that may be relevant to a user organization's internal control, on whether such controls were suitably designed to achieve specified control objectives, and on whether they had been placed in operation as of a specific date.

A *report on controls placed in operation and tests of operating effectiveness* (PPPO/TOE report) is defined as follows:

> A service auditor's report on a service organization's description of its controls that may be relevant to a user organization's internal control, on whether such controls were suitably designed to achieve specified control objectives, on whether they had been placed in operation as of a specific date, and on whether the controls that were tested were operating with sufficient effectiveness to provide reasonable, but not absolute, assurance that the related control objectives were achieved during the period specified.

The user auditor may use the PPPO report to obtain an understanding of the user organization's internal control as it relates to the activities performed by the service organization. The report may be used to plan tests of controls and substantive tests in the audit of the user organization's financial statements, but it cannot be the basis for reducing the user auditor's assessment of control risk below the maximum level. A PPPO/TOE report, however, can be used by the user auditor to reduce the assessment of control risk below the maximum level, as well as to obtain an understanding and plan tests.

The service auditor issuing a PPPO report or a PPPO/TOE report should obtain an description of the relevant controls of the service organization's internal control that satisfies the needs of the user auditor. To determine whether the service organization has placed the controls in operation, the service auditor should consider the following audit procedures:

- Refer to results from previous experience with the service auditor (may include results from the audit of the service organization's financial statements)

§324 • Service Organizations

- Make inquiries of appropriate service organization personnel
- Inspect relevant documents and records of the service organization
- Observe activities conducted by the service organization

> **ENGAGEMENT STRATEGY:** When issuing a PPPO/TOE report, the service auditor should complete the above procedures and also perform tests of controls based on guidance established in SAS-55 (AU 319) and SAS-39 (AU 350) (Audit Sampling) to determine the effectiveness of the relevant controls identified.

The service auditor should make inquiries about changes in controls that may have occurred before fieldwork was begun. If there have been significant changes in controls (limited to changes within the last 12 months), those controls should be included in the description of the service organization's controls. If such changes are not included in the description of the service organization's controls, the service auditor should include them in his or her report.

For PPPO reports and PPPO/TOE reports, the description of relevant controls placed in operation at the service organization may be prepared by the service organization or by the service auditor. In either case, the representations made in the description are those of the management of the service organization. In order for the service auditor to express an opinion on the description, the following conditions must exist:

- There must be an appropriate identification and description of control objectives and the relevant controls.
- The service auditor must evaluate the relationships between the control objective and the relevant controls.
- The service auditor must obtain sufficient evidence to provide a basis for expressing an opinion on the description.

During the engagement, the service auditor should consider whether there are significant deficiencies in the service organization's controls that suggest that control objectives could not be satisfied. In addition, the service auditor should consider any additional information, whether or not it is related to specific control objectives, that (1) questions the ability of the service organization to record, process, summarize, or report financial data to user organization without error and (2) indicates that the user organizations generally would not have controls in place to discover errors.

PLANNING AID REMINDER: The service auditor should evaluate the control objectives (unless they are established by an outside party) to determine whether they are reasonable and consistent with the service organization's contractual obligations.

In addition to including a description of relevant controls, a service auditor's PPPO/TOE report on the processing of transactions by the service organization should be accompanied by a separate description of tests of specified service organization controls designed to obtain evidence about the operating effectiveness of the relevant controls. That description should include the following:

- Controls that were tested
- Control objectives that the controls were intended to achieve
- Tests applied to the controls
- Results of the tests applied
- Description of the nature, timing, and extent of tests (presented in sufficient detail to enable user auditors to determine the effect on the assessment of control risk for the user organizations)
- Relevant information about exceptions discovered by the service auditor, including causative factors and corrective actions taken

The service organization determines which control objectives will be subjected to tests of controls. The service auditor determines which controls are relevant to achieving specific control objectives and then establishes the nature, timing, and extent of audit procedures to test their effectiveness. The test period for relevant controls should generally cover a period of not less than six months, and sample items should be selected over the entire period.

SAS-70 establishes the following procedures for preparing PPPO and PPPO/TOE reports:

- Refer to the applications, services, products, or other aspects of the service organization covered by the report.
- Describe the scope and nature of the procedures performed.
- Identify the party that specified the control objectives.
- Indicate the purpose of the engagement.
- State an opinion on whether the description presents fairly, in all material respects, the relevant aspects of the service organization's controls that had been placed in operation as of a specific date.

- State the inherent limitations of the potential effectiveness of controls and the risk of projecting to future periods any evaluation of the description.
- Identify the parties for which the report is intended.

A PPPO report should also state an opinion on whether the controls were suitably designed to provide reasonable assurance that the specified control objectives would be achieved if those controls were satisfactorily complied with, and it should disclaim an opinion on the operating effectiveness of the controls.

A PPPO/TOE report, on the other hand, should also state an opinion on whether the controls tested were operating with sufficient effectiveness to provide a reasonable assurance that the related control objectives were achieved during the period. Therefore, in this type of report, the service auditor must also:

- Refer to the description of tests of specified service organization controls.
- Disclose the period covered by tests of specified controls.
- State an opinion on whether controls tested were operating with sufficient effectiveness to provide a reasonable assurance that the related control objectives were achieved during the period.
- State that the effectiveness of specific service organization controls depends on their interaction with individual user organizations' controls, and other factors.
- If all control objectives listed in the description of controls were not covered by tests of operating effectiveness, state that the opinion is not applicable to those control objectives not listed in the description of tests performed.
- State that the service auditor has not performed procedures to determine the effectiveness of controls for user organizations.

According to SAS-70, PPPO reports and PPPO/TOE reports should be addressed to the service organization. An example of a PPPO report (Exhibit AU 324-1) and an example of a PPPO/TOE report (Exhibit AU 324-2) are presented at the end of this section.

If the service auditor concludes that the description that accompanies the PPPO or PPPO/TOE report is inaccurate or incomplete, the report should state this, and it should contain additional details to provide the user auditor with an appropriate understanding of the controls.

An effective design of internal controls at the service organization may be based on the assumption that complementary controls are in place at the user organization. Under this circumstance, the user organization's complementary controls should be part of the description of the service organization's relevant internal controls. Also, when the user organization's controls are considered necessary to achieve the stated control objectives, the report should be modified by adding an additional statement to the phrase "complied with satisfactorily" in the scope paragraph (first paragraph) and the opinion paragraph (third paragraph in the PPPO report, second paragraph in the PPPO/TOE report). The additional phrase is

> . . . and user organizations applied the internal controls contemplated in the design of the Service Organization's controls.

When the service auditor concludes that the description of controls is inaccurate or incomplete, the report should be changed by adding an explanatory paragraph (placed immediately before the opinion paragraph) that describes the deficiency and by qualifying the opinion paragraph. SAS-70 presents the following as an example of a qualified PPPO or PPPO/TOE report on a service organization's controls.

> [Explanatory paragraph:]
>
> The accompanying description states that X Service Organization uses operator identification numbers and passwords to prevent unauthorized access to the system. Based on inquiries of staff personnel and inspections of activities, we determined that such procedures are employed in Applications A and B but are not required to access the system in Applications C and D.
>
> [Opinion paragraph:]
>
> In our opinion, except for the matter referred to in the preceding paragraph, the accompanying description of the aforementioned application presents fairly, in all material respects, the relevant aspects of X Service Organization's controls that had been placed in operation as of [*identify date*]. Also, in our opinion, the controls, as described, are suitably designed to provide reasonable assurance that the specified control objectives would be achieved if the described controls were complied with satisfactorily.

When the service auditor concludes that there are significant deficiencies in the design or operation of relevant controls, the report should be changed by adding an explanatory paragraph (placed immediately before the opinion paragraph) that describes the deficiency and by qualifying the opinion paragraph. SAS-70 presents the following as an example of a qualified PPPO or PPPO/TOE report on a service organization's controls:

[Explanatory paragraph:]

As discussed in the accompanying description, from time to time the Service Organization makes changes in application programs to correct deficiencies or to enhance capabilities. The procedures followed in determining whether to make changes, designing the changes, and implementing them do not include review and approval by authorized individuals who are independent from those involved in making the changes. There are also no specified requirements to test such changes or to provide test results to an authorized reviewer prior to implementing the changes.

[Opinion paragraph:]

In our opinion, the accompanying description of the aforementioned application presents fairly, in all material respects, the relevant aspects of X Service Organization's controls that had been placed in operation as of [*identify date*]. Also, in our opinion, except for the deficiency referred to in the preceding paragraph, the controls, as described, are suitably designed to provide reasonable assurance that the specified control objectives would be achieved if the described controls were complied with satisfactorily.

Obtain written representations from the service organization

The service auditor should obtain a written representation from the service organization that includes the following matters:

- Acknowledgment that management is responsible for establishing and maintaining appropriate controls related to the processing of transactions for user organizations
- Acknowledgment of the appropriateness of the control objectives specified
- Statement that the description of controls presents fairly, in all material respects, the aspects of the service organization's controls that may be relevant to a user organization's internal control
- Statement that controls, as described, had been placed in operation as of a specified date
- Statement that management has disclosed any significant changes in controls that have occurred since the service organization's last examination

- Statement that management has disclosed any illegal acts, fraud, or uncorrected errors that may affect one or more user organizations
- Statement that management has disclosed all design deficiencies in controls of which it is aware, including those for which the costs may exceed the benefits
- Statement that management has disclosed all instances, of which it is aware, when controls have not operated with sufficient effectiveness to achieve the specified control objectives (required only for PPPO/TOE reports)

> **RISK ASSESSMENT POINT:** The Auditing Interpretation (April 1995) of SAS-70 titled "Describing Tests of Operating Effectiveness and the Results of Such Tests" concludes that the report on the controls placed in operation and tests of operating effectiveness should provide a sufficient description of the tests performed and their results to enable the user auditor to adequately assess control risk for financial statement assertions related to the tasks performed by the service organization.

> **PLANNING AID REMINDER:** Another Interpretation of SAS-70, titled "Service Organizations That Use the Services of Other Service Organizations (Subservice Organizations)," concludes that the user auditor must consider evaluating controls of a subservice organization that performs work for the service organization.

Practitioner's Aids

Exhibit AU 324-1 is an example of a controls-placed-in-operation report and Exhibit AU 324-2 is an example of a controls-placed-in-operation and tests of operating effectiveness report.

EXHIBIT AU 324-1—REPORT ON CONTROLS PLACED IN OPERATION AT A SERVICE ORGANIZATION

We have examined the accompanying description of controls related to the [*identify service applications*] of X Service Organization. Our examination included procedures to obtain reasonable assurance about whether (1) the accompanying description presents fairly, in all material respects, the aspects of X Service Organization's controls that may be relevant to a user organization's internal control; (2) the controls included in the description were suitably designed to achieve the control objectives specified in the description, if those controls were complied with satisfactorily; and (3) such controls had been placed in operation as of [*identify specific date*]. The control objectives were specified by [*identify party who specified control objectives*]. Our examination was performed in accordance with standards established by the American Institute of Certified Public Accountants and included those procedures we considered necessary in the circumstances to obtain a reasonable basis for rendering our opinion.

We did not perform procedures to determine the operating effectiveness of controls for any period. Accordingly, we express no opinion on the operating effectiveness of any aspects of X Service Organization's controls, individually or in the aggregate.

In our opinion, the accompanying description of the aforementioned application presents fairly, in all material respects, the relevant aspects of X Service Organization's controls that had been placed in operation as of [*identify date*]. Also, in our opinion, the controls, as described, are suitably designed to provide reasonable assurance that the specified control objectives would be achieved if the described controls were complied with satisfactorily.

The description of controls at X Service Organization is as of [*identify date*], and any projection of such information to the future is subject to the risk that, because of change, the description may no longer portray the controls in existence. The potential effectiveness of specific controls at the Service Organization is subject to inherent limitations and, accordingly, errors or fraud may occur and not be detected. Furthermore, the projection of any conclusions, based on our findings, to future periods is subject to the risk that changes may alter the validity of such conclusions.

This report is intended solely for use by the management of X Service Organization, its customers, and the independent auditors of its customers.

EXHIBIT AU 324-2—REPORT ON CONTROLS PLACED IN OPERATION AT A SERVICE ORGANIZATION AND TESTS OF OPERATING EFFECTIVENESS

We have examined the accompanying description of controls related to the [*identify service applications*] of X Service Organization. Our examination included procedures to obtain reasonable assurance about whether (1) the accompanying description presents fairly, in all material respects, the aspects of X Service Organization's controls that may be relevant to a user organization's internal control as it relates to an audit of financial statements, (2) the controls included in the description were suitably designed to achieve the control objectives specified in the description, if those controls were complied with satisfactorily, and (3) such controls had been placed in operation as of [*identify specific date*]. The control objectives were specified by [*identify party who specified control objectives*]. Our examination was performed in accordance with standards established by the American Institute of Certified Public Accountants and included those procedures we considered necessary in the circumstances to obtain a reasonable basis for rendering our opinion.

In our opinion, the accompanying description of the aforementioned application presents fairly, in all material respects, the relevant aspects of X Service Organization's controls that had been placed in operation as of [*identify date*]. Also, in our opinion, the controls, as described, are suitably designed to provide reasonable assurance that the specified control objectives would be achieved if the described controls were complied with satisfactorily.

In addition to the procedures we considered necessary to render our opinion as expressed in the previous paragraph, we applied tests to specific controls, listed in Schedule A, to obtain evidence about their effectiveness in meeting the control objectives, described in Schedule A, during the period from [*identify period covered*]. The specific controls and the nature, timing, extent, and results of the tests are listed in Schedule A. This information has been provided to user organizations of X Service Organization and to their auditors to be taken into consideration, along with information about the internal control at user organizations, when making assessments of control risk for user organizations. In our opinion the controls that were tested, as described in Schedule A, were operating with sufficient effectiveness to provide reasonable, but not absolute, assurance that the control objectives specified in Schedule A were achieved during the period [*identify period covered*].

The relative effectiveness and significance of specific controls at X Service Organization and their effect on assessments of control risk at user organizations are dependent on their interaction with the controls, and other factors present at individual user organizations. We have performed no procedures to evaluate the effectiveness of controls at individual user organizations.

The description of controls at X Service Organization is as of [*identify date*], and information about tests of the operating effectiveness of specified controls covers the period from [*identify period cov-

ered]. Any projection of such information to the future is subject to the risk that, because of change, the description may no longer portray the system in existence. The potential effectiveness of specified controls at the Service Organization is subject to inherent limitations and, accordingly, errors or fraud may occur and not be detected. Furthermore, the projection of any conclusions, based on our findings, to future periods is subject to the risk that changes may alter the validity of such conclusions.

This report is intended solely for use by the management of X Service Organization, its customers, and the independent auditors of its customers.

> **OBSERVATION:** If all of the control objectives identified in the description of controls were not subject to tests of controls, the following should be added as the last sentence to the third paragraph in the preceding example:
>
> However, the scope of our engagement did not include tests to determine whether control objectives not listed in Schedule A were achieved; accordingly, we express no opinion on the achievement of control objectives not included in Schedule A.

SECTION 325
COMMUNICATION OF INTERNAL CONTROL RELATED MATTERS NOTED IN AN AUDIT

Authoritative Pronouncements

SAS-60—Communication of Internal Control Structure Related Matters Noted in an Audit

Auditing Interpretation (February 1989)—Reporting on the Existence of Material Weaknesses

Overview

During an audit engagement, the auditor may discover matters related to the entity's internal control that should be reported to the entity's audit committee or to individuals with responsibilities equivalent to an audit committee. SAS-60 (Communication of Internal Control Related Matters Noted in an Audit) refers to these matters as "reportable conditions" and defines such conditions as follows:

> Reportable conditions are matters coming to the auditor's attention that, in his (or her) judgment, should be communicated to the audit committee because they represent significant deficiencies in the design or operation of the internal control, which could adversely affect the organization's ability to record, process, summarize, and report financial data consistent with the assertions of management in the financial statements.

> **RISK ASSESSMENT POINT:** SAS-60 supersedes SAS-20 (Required Communication of Material Weaknesses in Internal Accounting Control) and introduces a new, lower threshold of communication for reportable conditions. The main purpose of SAS-60 is to require the communication of conditions that are less significant than those identified in SAS-20. In fact, SAS-60 notes that some conditions might not be considered reportable but might nonetheless be communicated to management or other appropriate parties. The standards established by SAS-60 apply to all engagements, regardless of whether the client has an audit committee. Reportable conditions related to the client's internal control must be communicated to someone (e.g., owner/manager).

Promulgated Procedures Checklist

The auditor should perform the following procedures with respect to the communication of internal control matters:

_____ Identify those matters related to internal control that are considered reportable conditions.

_____ Consider the communication of other internal control matters to the audit committee.

_____ Prepare an appropriate report to communicate the internal control matter to the audit committee, or document an oral communication in the workpapers.

_____ Consider whether a reportable condition is a material weakness.

Analysis and Application of Procedures

Identify those matters related to internal control that are considered reportable conditions

An audit is not structured to identify all reportable conditions. Once discovered, however, a reportable condition should be communicated to the audit committee (or to "individuals with a level of authority and responsibility equivalent to an audit committee in organizations that do not have one, such as the board of directors, the board of trustees, an owner in an owner-managed enterprise, or others who may have engaged the auditor"). What constitutes a reportable condition is a matter of professional judgment. Factors to consider in making such a judgment include size and complexity of the entity, organizational structure, and characteristics of ownership. In some instances, management may be aware of reportable conditions but decide to accept the risk associated with the deficiency rather than incur the cost of additional control procedures. If the audit committee (or equivalent individuals) is aware of the deficiency and has acknowledged an understanding of the risk related to the condition, there is no need for the auditor to report the condition. Nonetheless, at subsequent dates, the auditor may decide periodically to remind the audit committee (or equivalent individuals) of the reportable condition.

> **PLANNING AID REMINDER:** Reportable conditions might be discovered during various phases of the engagement, including during the evaluation of the internal control and the tests of financial statement balances. Deficiencies can be related to

any of the five components of internal control. In addition, deficiencies can arise because of poor design or poor execution within internal control. For example, a reportable condition could be related to lack of proper segregation of duties and responsibilities (design within internal control) or lack of timely preparation of bank reconciliations (execution within internal control).

Exhibit AU 325-1 provides guidance regarding what items may be considered reportable conditions as envisioned by SAS-60.

Consider the communication of other internal control matters to the audit committee

A client may request that an auditor communicate control structure related matters that are not necessarily "reportable conditions" as defined in SAS-60. Such agreed-upon arrangements include reporting deficiencies that might not be as significant as reportable conditions or reporting results from applying additional procedures when the client is already aware of a deficiency. The auditor should expand the audit approach in an appropriate manner to satisfy the agreed-upon requirements.

> **ENGAGEMENT STRATEGY:** SAS-60 does not prohibit the auditor from informing the client of conditions that might increase the efficiency or effectiveness of the client's operations, even when there is no understanding that the auditor will do so.

Prepare an appropriate report to communicate the internal control matter to the audit committee, or document an oral communication in the workpapers

Reportable conditions or conditions related to agreed-upon criteria should be communicated in writing; however, if the conditions are communicated orally, the communication should be adequately documented in the workpapers.

The written report should include a scope paragraph, which is a paragraph(s) that describes the reportable condition, and a paragraph stating that the report is only for the use of the audit committee, management, and others within the organization. An example of this type of report is presented in Exhibit AU 325-2.

If governmental regulations require submission of the report, the report should contain a reference to the regulatory agency.

§325 • **Internal Control Related Matters** 143

The standard report format may be expanded to include, for example, a description of the inherent limitations of internal control or other matters that describe the basis for the report.

> **RISK ASSESSMENT POINT:** When the auditor discovers no reportable conditions during the engagement, a report to the audit committee (or equivalent individuals) stating that fact should not be prepared, because of the possible misunderstanding of the report and the assurance provided by the report.

> **PLANNING AID REMINDER:** *Government Auditing Standards* require a written report on the internal control in all audits. When no reportable conditions have been discovered during the engagement, an auditor complies with *Government Auditing Standards* by issuing a report that essentially states that no material weaknesses were discovered. The form of the report is discussed in SAS-74 (AU 801) (Compliance Auditing Considerations in Audits of Governmental Entities and Recipients of Governmental Financial Assistance).

> **RISK ASSESSMENT POINT:** When the report describes both reportable conditions and other conditions identified as part of the agreed-upon criteria, the auditor may find it appropriate to identify which comments are applicable to which category.

Consider whether a reportable condition is a material weakness

A reportable condition might have such a potentially detrimental effect on an entity's internal control that it can be considered a material weakness. SAS-60 defines a "material weakness" as follows:

> A reportable condition in which the design or operation of the specific internal control elements do not reduce to a relatively low level the risk that errors or fraud in amounts that would be material in relation to the financial statements being audited may occur and not be detected within a timely period by employees in the normal course of performing their assigned functions.

The auditor may choose or the entity may request to have the material weakness separately identified and reported to the audit committee (or equivalent individuals).

At the discretion of the auditor or at the request of the entity, the auditor may report on a reportable condition while also reporting that the reportable condition is not considered to be a material weakness. Under this reporting circumstance, the following two paragraphs (placed before the last standard paragraph) would be added to the standard, three-paragraph report illustrated earlier:

> A material weakness is a reportable condition in which the design or operation of one or more of internal control components does not reduce to a relatively low level the risk that errors or fraud in amounts that would be material in relation to the financial statements being audited may occur and not be detected within a timely period by employees in the normal course of performing their assigned functions.
>
> Our consideration of internal control would not necessarily disclose all matters in the internal control that might be reportable conditions and, accordingly, would not necessarily disclose all reportable conditions that are also considered to be material weaknesses as defined above. However, none of the reportable conditions described above is believed to be a material weakness.

Exhibit AU 324-3 presents examples of possible material weaknesses that can exist in the audit of a small business enterprise.

The auditor should issue a report on reportable conditions or other matters on a timely basis. In some instances, this may require issuance of the report before the completion of the engagement. The timing of the issuance of the report will depend on such factors as the nature and significance of the reportable condition and the need for immediate remedial action.

The Auditing Interpretation (February 1989) of SAS-60 titled "Reporting on the Existence of Material Weaknesses" concludes that an auditor is not prohibited from issuing a report on material weaknesses that is separate from the report on reportable conditions. A separate report on material weaknesses should be consistent with the following guidelines:

- State that the purpose of the audit was to report on the financial statements and not to provide assurances concerning internal control.
- Provide a definition of a material weakness.
- State that the report is to be used solely by the audit committee, management, and others within the organization. (If the report is required by a governmental agency, reference may be made to the governmental agency.)
- Do not state that no reportable conditions were discovered.

An example of a separate report on material weaknesses is illustrated in Exhibit AU 324-3.

§325 • Internal Control Related Matters

In some instances, the auditor is asked to issue a separate report on material weaknesses and also to comment on matters relating to internal control or other matters. For example, the auditor might be asked to comment on specific internal control procedures. Under this circumstance, the auditor should modify the separate report on material weaknesses as follows:

- Clearly identify the internal control feature or other matter that is the subject of the report.
- Distinguish the additional matter being reported on from internal control.
- Describe in reasonable detail the scope of the investigation of the additional matter.
- Express a conclusion in language that is comparable to the language used in the separate report on material weaknesses illustrated above.

> **RISK ASSESSMENT POINT:** In wording the separate report, the auditor should be careful not to report on the internal control.
>
> **ENGAGEMENT STRATEGY:** The Auditing Interpretation (October 1978) of SAS-54 titled "Material Weaknesses in the Internal Control Structure and the Foreign Corrupt Practices Act" states that in audits of entities subject to the Foreign Corrupt Practices Act of 1977, the auditor should consult with the client's management and legal counsel if he or she finds a material weakness in internal control. If the client takes no corrective action, the auditor should consider withdrawing from the engagement.

Practitioner's Aids

Exhibit AU 325-1 reproduces items listed in SAS-60 as possible reportable conditions. Exhibit AU 325-2 is an example of a separate report on material weaknesses.

EXHIBIT AU 325-1—EXAMPLES OF POSSIBLE REPORTABLE CONDITIONS

- *Deficiencies in internal control design*

    — Inadequate overall internal control design

    — Absence of appropriate segregation of duties consistent with appropriate control objectives

— Absence of appropriate reviews and approvals of transactions, accounting entries, or systems output

— Inadequate procedures for appropriately assessing and applying accounting principles

— Inadequate provisions for safeguarding assets

— Absence of other control techniques considered appropriate for the type and level of transaction activity

— Evidence that a system fails to provide complete and accurate output that is consistent with objectives and current needs because of design flaws

- *Failures in the operation of internal control*

    — Evidence of failure of identified controls in preventing or detecting misstatements of accounting information

    — Evidence that a system fails to provide complete and accurate output consistent with the entity's control objectives, because of the misapplication of control procedures

    — Evidence of failure to safeguard assets from loss, damage, or misappropriation

    — Evidence of intentional override of internal control by those in authority to the detriment of the overall objectives of the system

    — Evidence of failure to perform tasks that are part of internal control, such as reconciliations not prepared or not prepared in a timely manner

    — Evidence of willful wrongdoing by employees or management

    — Evidence of manipulation, falsification, or alteration of accounting records or supporting documents

    — Evidence of intentional misapplication of accounting principles

    — Evidence of misrepresentation by client personnel to the auditor

    — Evidence that employees or managers lack the qualifications and training to fulfill their assigned functions

- *Other*

    — Absence of a sufficient level of control consciousness within the organization

- Failure to follow up on and to correct previously identified internal control deficiencies
- Evidence of significant or extensive undisclosed related party transactions
- Evidence of undue bias or lack of objectivity by those responsible for accounting decisions

EXHIBIT AU 325-2—EXAMPLE OF A REPORT ON A REPORTABLE CONDITION

In planning and performing our audit of the financial statements of the X Company for the year ended December 31, 20X5, we considered its internal control in order to determine our auditing procedures for the purpose of expressing our opinion on the financial statements and not to provide assurance on the internal control. However, we noted certain matters involving the internal control and its operation that we consider to be reportable conditions under standards established by the American Institute of Certified Public Accountants. Reportable conditions involve matters coming to our attention relating to significant deficiencies in the design or operation of internal control that, in our judgment, could adversely affect the organization's ability to record, process, summarize, and report financial data consistent with the assertions of management in the financial statements.

[*Describe reportable condition in separate paragraph(s).*]

This report is intended solely for the information and use of the audit committee [*board of directors, board of trustees, or owners in owner-managed enterprises*], management, and others within the organization [*or specified regulatory agency*] and is not intended to be and should not be used by anyone other than these specified parties.

EXHIBIT AU 325-3—EXAMPLES OF POSSIBLE MATERIAL WEAKNESSES—SMALL BUSINESS ENTERPRISE

NOTE: A "material weakness" is defined as "a reportable condition in which the design or operation of the specific internal control elements do not reduce to a relatively low level the risk that errors or fraud in amounts that would be material in relation to the financial statements being audited may occur and not be detected within a timely period by employees in the normal course of performing their assigned functions."

Determining whether a specific condition is a material weakness is based on exercising professional judgment in the context of the existing characteristics of a particular client. The following list includes examples of conditions that the auditor may identify as a material weakness for a small business enterprise. The list is illustrative only and is not intended to be comprehensive. Also, because the assumption is that the client is a small business enterprise, there is an emphasis on cash and related cash transactions, inventory, and property, plant, and equipment.

- *Cash and credit sales*

    —Credit sales are approved by the bookkeeper, who is responsible for the write-off of bad debts.

    —A bookkeeper maintains cash receipts records, opens the mail, and prepares the bank deposit.

    —Cash payments for expenditures using cash receipts for the day.

    —Cash receipts are deposited at the end of the week, net of expenditures paid during the week.

    —Several sales clerks have access to the single cash drawer used during the day to record cash sales.

    —Cash registers used during the day are not read and reconciled after the end of each shift.

    —A bookkeeper is responsible for the purchase of goods and services.

    —There is no formal documentation that shows that goods purchased were received.

    —Documentation to support cash disbursements is maintained on a haphazard basis.

    —The office manager authorizes the payment of invoices, prepares checks, and reconciles the bank statements.

- *Cash and purchases of goods and services*

    —Purchase orders are not used to authorize the acquisition of goods and services.

    —Invoices and other supporting documentation are not marked as "canceled or paid."

— The hiring and firing of employees is not centralized.

— Paychecks are given to an immediate supervisor for distribution.

— The number of hours or days worked is not controlled through the use of time clocks or otherwise approved by supervisory personnel.

— An unusually large amount of petty cash is maintained, and support for expenditures is lacking.

— Numerous checking accounts are used, and renumbered checks are not accounted for.

— Numerous employees are authorized to sign checks.

— Checks are often written to "cash."

— Bank reconciliations are seldom prepared.

- *Inventory controls*

— The periodic inventory count is not under the control of the owner or manager.

— The inventory is not subject to reasonable limited access (for both employees and customers) based on the characteristics of the business.

— Inventory shipments to customers are not based on appropriate shipping authorization.

— Inventory receipts are not properly counted and inspected.

— The year-end inventory summarization is not analyzed and evaluated by the owner or manager for unusual variations in gross profit percentages, obsolete inventory lines, unreasonable inventory counts, missing items, inappropriate cost data, etc.

- *Property, plant, and equipment*

— A plant ledger is not maintained.

— The owner or manager does not periodically verify the existence and condition of property items.

— The sale of used property items is not approved by the owner or manager.

EXHIBIT AU 325-4—EXAMPLE OF A SEPARATE REPORT ON MATERIAL WEAKNESSES

In planning and performing our audit of the financial statements of X Company for the year ended December 31, 20X5, we considered its internal control in order to determine our auditing procedures for the purpose of expressing our opinion on the financial statements and not to provide assurance on the internal control. Our consideration of internal control would not necessarily disclose all matters in internal control that might be material weaknesses under standards established by the American Institute of Certified Public Accountants.

A material weakness is a condition in which the design or operation of the specific internal control does not reduce to a relatively low level the risk that errors or fraud in amounts that would be material in relation to the financial statements being audited may occur and not be detected within a timely period by employees in the normal course of performing their assigned functions. However, we noted no matters involving internal control and its operation that we consider to be material weaknesses as defined above.

This report is intended solely for the information and use of the audit committee [*board of directors, board of trustees, or owners in owner-managed enterprises*], management, and others within the organization [*or specified regulatory agency*] and is not intended to be and should not be used by anyone other than these specified parties.

NOTE: The auditor may add the following sentence to the above report:

> These conditions were considered in determining the nature, timing, and extent of the procedures to be performed in our audit of the 20X5 financial statements, and this report does not affect our report on these financial statements dated February 15, 20X6.

If material weaknesses are discovered, the last sentence in the first paragraph of the above illustration should be changed to read:

> However, we noted the following matters involving internal control and its operation that we consider to be material weakness as defined above.

A description of the material weaknesses should follow.

SECTION 326

EVIDENTIAL MATTER

Authoritative Pronouncements

SAS-31—Evidential Matter

SAS-48—The Effects of Computer Processing on the Examination of Financial Statements

SAS-80—Amendment to Statement on Auditing Standards No. 31, Evidential Matter

Auditing Interpretation (October 1980)—Evidential Matter for an Audit of Interim Financial Statements

Auditing Interpretation (March 1981)—The Effect of an Inability to Obtain Evidential Matter Relating to Income Tax Accruals

Auditing Interpretation (April 1986)—The Auditor's Consideration of the Completeness Assertion

Auditing Interpretation (August 1998)—Applying Auditing Procedures to Segment Disclosures in Financial Statements

Overview

Evidential matter is competent when it is both valid and relevant; however, generalizing about what constitutes reliable evidence is difficult, because the particular circumstances of each audit must be considered. Nonetheless, the following generalizations can be made about evidential matter:

- Evidence is more reliable if it is obtained from an independent source.
- The more effective the internal control, the more reliable the evidence.
- Evidence that the auditor obtains directly through physical examination, observation, computation, and inspection is more persuasive than information he or she obtains indirectly.

> **RISK ASSESSMENT POINT:** The Auditing Interpretation (October 1980) titled "Evidential Matter for an Audit of Interim Financial Statements" notes that the third standard of fieldwork (sufficient competent evidential matter) must be satisfied when an auditor expresses an opinion on financial statements, including interim financial statements.

Promulgated Procedures Checklist

The auditor should satisfy the following audit objectives as part of collecting and evaluating evidential matter to support his or her opinion on the client's financial statements:

- Collect sufficient evidential matter during the audit engagement.
- Design substantive tests that will test significant assertions contained in the client's financial statements.
- Evaluate the effect that the client's information technology has on the audit process.

Analysis and Application of Procedures

Collect sufficient evidential matter during the audit engagement

The term "sufficient" refers to the amount of evidence collected. Audit judgment is used to determine when sufficiency is achieved, just as judgment is used to determine the competency of evidential matter. The concept of sufficiency recognizes that the auditor can never reduce audit risk to zero, and a fundamental concept in auditing is that the accumulation of evidence should be persuasive rather than convincing. This concept is consistent with the idea that the auditor is not free to collect unlimited amounts of evidence, since he or she must work within economic limits. Cost cannot, however, be the sole basis for the quantity or quality of audit procedures.

Evidential matter can be classified as (1) underlying accounting data and (2) corroborating evidence. Underlying accounting data consist of general and specialized journals, ledgers, manuals, and supporting worksheets, spreadsheets, and other analyses. Generally, the auditor tests underlying accounting data by retracing transactions through the accounting system, recomputing allocations, and performing other mathematical calculations.

Although underlying accounting data are an important part of evidential matter, such data are not adequate to determine whether financial statements are fairly presented in accordance with generally accepted accounting principles. Therefore, the auditor needs to collect corroborating evidence before he or she can express an opinion on the financial statements. Corroborating evidence consists of documentary evidence, such as vendor's invoices, confirmations, and observations, stored either in hard copy form or electronically.

ENGAGEMENT STRATEGY: FAS-14 (Financial Reporting for Segments of a Business Enterprise) provided guidance for the reporting of segment information for certain companies, and

§326 • **Evidential Matter**

SAS-21 (Segment Information) provided guidance for the audit of segment information. In June 1997, FAS-131 (CT S-20) (Disclosures about Segments of an Enterprise and Related Information) superseded FAS-14, and because the audit guidance provided by SAS-21 was inappropriate for the standards established by FAS-131, SAS-21 was rescinded. Audit guidance for segment information is now covered by an Auditing Interpretation (August 1998) titled "Applying Auditing Procedures to Segment Disclosures in Financial Statements." The Interpretation concludes that the objective of applying audit procedures to segment disclosures is similar to the objective related to other disclosures in the audited financial statements. That is, "the auditor is not required to apply procedures as extensive as would be necessary to express an opinion on the segment information taken by itself." More specific procedures are detailed in the Interpretation. The standards established by FAS-131 do not apply to nonpublic companies and not-for-profit organizations.

Design substantive tests that will tests significant assertions contained in the client's financial statements

The collection and evaluation of sufficient competent evidential matter can be described, and should be applied, as a logical process. SAS-31 attempts to provide the logical framework for the audit process. Conceptually, the auditor should design a substantive tests audit program by relating assertions made in the financial statements to specific audit procedures that are designed to test the validity of the assertions. Five assertions generally are identified with a balance sheet account and the related account(s) on the income statement:

1. *Existence or occurrence*—The financial statements assert that an asset or a liability exists at the balance sheet date and that a nominal account represents transactions that occurred during an accounting period.

2. *Completeness*—The financial statements assert that all items that make up an asset, a liability, or a nominal account are represented.

3. *Rights and obligations*—The financial statements assert that assets properly represent rights owned by the client and that liabilities represent obligations of the client.

4. *Valuation and allocation*—The financial statements assert that all accounts are valued in accordance with generally accepted accounting principles.

5. *Presentation and disclosure*—The financial statements assert that accounts and related information are properly classified, described, and disclosed.

Using the five broad assertions in SAS-31 as a starting point, the auditor can identify related audit objectives. Generally, a single assertion will lead to more than one audit objective. For example, a balance sheet may represent that inventories are valued at a particular amount. In turn, this single financial statement assertion may lead to the following audit objectives: (1) inventories are stated at first in, first out (FIFO) cost and (2) defective inventories are stated at net realizable value. Having identified an audit objective, the auditor selects audit procedures to achieve the particular audit objective. Of course, an audit objective may require that more than one audit procedure be employed. Likewise, a single audit procedure may, in part, contribute information to the evaluation of other audit objectives.

ENGAGEMENT STRATEGY: An auditor's reliance on the internal control and the written representations of management does not provide sufficient audit evidence to support the assertion that all account balances and transactions have been properly included in the financial statements (completeness assertion).

RISK ASSESSMENT POINT: The Auditing Interpretation (April 1986) titled "The Auditor's Consideration of the Completeness Assertion" states that an auditor's reliance on the internal control and the written representations of management does not provide sufficient audit evidence to support the assertion that all account balances and transactions have been properly included in the financial statements (completeness assertion, paragraph 3 of SAS-31). An auditor must evaluate the audit risk of omission and whether any accounts and/or transactions have been improperly omitted from the financial statements. Substantive tests that are designed to obtain evidence about the completeness assertion are used to reduce the audit risk of omission. These substantive tests should include analytical procedures and tests of details of related account balances. The type and quantity of substantive tests may vary depending on the auditor's assessment of control risk.

Evaluate the effect that the client's information technology has on the audit process

SAS-80 amends SAS-31 by providing basic guidance on how information technology relates to the audit process. The client's use of digital technology to process financial data does not change the auditor's fundamental responsibility, which is to collect sufficient competent evidence upon which to base an opinion on the financial statements. The client's use of technology, however, can have an effect on the design of the audit strategy and specific audit procedures that may be employed in an engagement.

PLANNING AID REMINDER: In fact, SAS-80 notes that in some instances it may be "difficult or impossible for the auditor to access certain information for inspection, inquiry, or confirmation without using information technology." For example, some clients store documents, such as purchase orders and vendor invoices, only in electronic form; others convert a hard copy document to electronic images and not retain the original source document. In other instances, even electronic forms are retained only for a specific period of time. The auditor must plan the timing of tests of controls and substantive tests accordingly.

In general, it may also be impossible to reduce detection risk to an acceptable level without performing tests of controls. This generalization applies to all types of systems, including those that rely heavily on electronic data processing procedures. For example, SAS-80 notes that for a client "where significant information is transmitted, processed, maintained, or accessed electronically," it may be impractical or impossible to reduce detection risk for some financial statement assertions to an acceptable level by performing only substantive tests. In this circumstance, it would be necessary to perform tests of controls and to consider the results of these tests in the assessment of control risk.

ENGAGEMENT STRATEGY: Does SAS-80 require that the auditor perform tests of control when the client relies heavily on computerized systems to process and report accounting information? The answer is no—except when it is impractical or impossible to reduce detection risk to an acceptable level.

RISK ASSESSMENT POINT: Even though the assessed level of control risk may be lowered because of the performance of tests of controls related to a client's computerized accounting system, the auditor must nonetheless perform some substantive tests for related significant account balances and transaction classes.

ENGAGEMENT STRATEGY: The Auditing Interpretation (March 1981) titled "The Effect of an Inability to Obtain Evidential Matter Relating to Income Tax Accruals" notes that the auditor is required to prepare tax workpapers. If necessary, the evidential matter can take the form of a tax accrual memorandum. The auditor must exercise professional judgment and expertise in obtaining and examining tax accrual information and cannot rely solely on the opinion of the client's outside or in-house tax counsel.

SECTION 329

ANALYTICAL PROCEDURES

Authoritative Pronouncements

SAS-56—Analytical Procedures

Overview

Analytical procedures are used to determine whether information is consistent with the auditor's expectations. For example, if an auditor is aware that a client has invested heavily in new machinery, depreciation expense would be expected to be significantly greater in the current period than in the prior period. To successfully employ analytical procedures, an auditor must have a thorough knowledge of the client and the industry in which it operates. Because analytical procedures are applied in a broad manner in the collection of evidence and because such an approach has limitations in achieving audit objectives, analytical procedures should only be employed by (or supervised closely by) experienced staff.

Expectations concerning financial information and assumptions that affect financial information may be developed from sources such as the following:

- Prior-period financial information (if appropriate, modified for new conditions and events)
- Budgeted, forecasted, and projected financial information
- Interrelationships of financial information
- Industrial characteristics
- Nonfinancial information that may affect financial information

Promulgated Procedures Checklist

The auditor should perform the following procedures as part of implementing analytical procedures as part of the audit engagement:

_____ Perform analytical procedures as part of the planning of the engagement.

_____ Perform analytical procedures as part of the overall review of financial information.

§329 • Analytical Procedures

_____ Consider performing analytical procedures as part of substantive tests.

> **PLANNING AID REMINDER:** Analytical procedures must be used in planning the nature, timing, and extent of audit procedures and in conducting an overall review of the financial information. The auditor must use professional judgment to determine whether analytical procedures should be used as a substantive test to collect evidential matter related to account balances or classes of transactions.

> **ENGAGEMENT STRATEGY:** Although SAS-56 does not require that analytical procedures be used as part of substantive testing, it does imply that it may be difficult to achieve certain audit objectives efficiently without applying them as a substantive test.

Analysis and Application of Procedures

Perform analytical procedures as part of the planning of the engagement

An auditor must perform analytical procedures to provide a basis for determining the nature, timing, and extent of subsequent audit procedures. Analytical procedures are employed to reduce to an acceptable level the possibility that a material misstatement or omission in the financial statements may occur (detection risk). When establishing an acceptable level of detection risk, the auditor must consider the susceptibility of an account to be misstated (inherent risk), the control structure related to the account (control risk), and materiality.

> **ENGAGEMENT STRATEGY:** Analytical procedures applied early in the engagement can help the auditor understand factors that must be used to establish a satisfactory level of detection risk.

The planning phase of an engagement should include review of financial information that is generally aggregated to identify unexpected relationships or trends. This may be accomplished through comparisons of general ledger balances with similar balances from prior periods and with budgeted or forecasted balances. Various ratios or trends may be computed to facilitate the analysis; however, the evaluation should be sensitive to changing conditions that may explain unexpected variations or may raise expectations that variations should in fact be present in the financial information. For example, the balance in the current legal expense account may be consistent with both last year's amount and the budgeted amount, but such expense stability may be unwarranted because the client has experienced unanticipated legal problems. In planning subsequent audit procedures, the auditor should select procedures to determine whether the client's legal counsel is billing its services on a timely basis.

Formulating Expectation

An auditor should be careful to use analytical procedures in this stage of the engagement as a positive and directional tool. That is, in some engagements, auditors may see analytical procedures as a nuisance and not as an integral part of the engagement. Under this circumstance, it may be easy to gather corroborative evidence and then, based on the audit results, let the evidence drive the documentation of the "expectations" that should have been driven by the original performance of analytical procedures. For example, an auditor may conclude, as a result of performing procedures related to the substantiation of bad debts expense, that bad debts expense as a percentage of credit sales has fallen significantly compared with the previous year's engagement because more rigorous credit review policies have been implemented during the year. This is a backward approach to the use of analytical procedures and is a violation of professional standards.

To encourage staff personnel to use analytical procedures correctly, it may be useful to document the preliminary expectations that result from the use of analytical procedures. That documentation should include the expected impact of the results of the analytical procedures on the design of the timing, extent, and nature of audit procedures to be used as part of substantive tests. A Practitioner's Aid at the end of this section illustrates how preliminary expectations may be documented in an engagement.

> **PLANNING AID REMINDER:** In addition to financial information, nonfinancial data may be taken into consideration as part of the performance of analytical procedures. For example, quality control reports prepared near year-end may identify production problems, which may suggest that significant amounts of inventory sold during the latter part of the year may be returned or may significantly increase future warranty claims.

Perform analytical procedures as part of the overall review of financial information

An auditor must perform analytical procedures as part of the final review of the audited financial information in order to determine whether the anticipated opinion on the financial statements appears to be warranted.

§329 • Analytical Procedures

Consider performing analytical procedures as part of substantive tests

Analytical procedures may be used as part of substantive tests (tests of financial statement balances) to achieve desired audit objectives or to achieve those objectives in an efficient manner. In general, the auditor uses analytical procedures as part of substantive testing by evaluating aggregated information to form conclusions about specific assertions contained in the financial statements. For example, an aged trial balance may be prepared and analyzed to test the assertion that accounts receivable are presented at net realizable value. In many instances the auditor will use both analytical procedures and tests of details to examine financial statement balances and classes of transactions.

In determining whether and to what extent analytical procedures should be used, an auditor should consider the following factors:

- Nature of the assertion being tested
- Plausibility and predictability of the relationship
- Reliability and availability of the data used to develop the expectation
- Precision of the expectation

These four factors should be considered in assessing the relative efficiency and effectiveness of analytical procedures as compared to tests of details.

The nature of the assertion being tested should be evaluated to determine whether analytical procedures may satisfy the related audit objective in a more efficient and effective way than tests of details. In general, it may be more appropriate to test assertions related to the completeness assertion (all transactions and accounts are reflected in the financial statements) by using analytical procedures. For example, the validity of an allowance for returned merchandise may be more effectively tested by using analytical procedures (review of sales volume, history of returned goods, maintenance of production standards, etc.) than by using tests of details (vouching actual sales returned).

The applicability of analytical procedures depends on the plausibility and predictability of the relationship between data. There is seldom a one-to-one relationship between data; however, the stronger the relationship, the more likely it is that analytical procedures can satisfy some audit objectives. The following generalizations may be useful in identifying plausible relationships:

- Relationships in a relatively stable environment tend to be more predictable than those in an unstable environment. (For example, bad debts expense and credit sales tend to be closely related to a stable economic environment.)

- Relationships among data on the income statement tend to be more predictable than relationships among data on the balance sheet. (For example, sales and sales commission expense tend to be more closely related than trade accounts payable and inventories.)
- Relationships that are subject to management discretion are more difficult to evaluate. (For example, loss contingency accruals associated with the number of pending lawsuits tend not to be predictable.)

For the auditor to be able to draw an inference about an account balance or a class of transactions based on applying analytical procedures, the data from which the inference is made must be reliable and available. In evaluating the reliability of data, the following generalizations are useful:

- Audited data (current or prior years) are more reliable than unaudited data.
- Internal data tend to be more reliable when developed from records maintained by personnel who are not responsible for the audited amount.
- Internal data tend to be more reliable when developed under an adequate control structure.
- Data from an external source tend to be more reliable.
- Reliability of expectations increases as sources of data increase.

Because analytical procedures generally lead to fairly broad conclusions about assertions in the financial statements, an auditor should consider the precision of the established expectation. In some instances, an auditor may be satisfied with a fairly imprecise expectation. For example, expectations concerning the relationship between warranty expense and sales subject to warranty may be imprecise (say, from 1% to 8% of sales) if significant changes in warranty expenses are unlikely to have a material effect on the financial statements. On the other hand, a more precise expectation may be demanded for sales returns when the client is in an industry that experiences significant returns and a change of a percentage point or two could have a material effect on the financial statements. Some of the factors that affect the precision of an expectation include:

- The number of relevant variables that affect a relationship (the more variables, the more precise the expectation)

§329 • Analytical Procedures

- The number of relevant variables that are evaluated by the auditor (the more variables evaluated, the more precise the expectation)
- The level of detail in the data used to construct the expectation (the more detailed the data, the more precise the expectation)

> **RISK ASSESSMENT POINT:** When planning analytical procedures, the auditor should set the materiality thresholds for acceptable deviations from expected amounts. The amount of an acceptable deviation from the expected amount should be less than what is considered material when those deviations are combined with other errors in other account balances and classes of transactions.

When a significant deviation from an expected amount is encountered, the auditor should attempt to identify and corroborate reasons to explain the deviation. The corroborative process may include the following:

- Use of information obtained in other parts of the examination
- Explanation provided by the client
- Use of extended audit procedures

> **ENGAGEMENT STRATEGY:** The corroborative process is employed to reasonably ensure that the significant deviation is caused by factors other than errors. The more precise and reliable an expectation, the lower the probability that a significant deviation is the result of factors other than errors. Under this latter circumstance, an auditor must be more skeptical about explanations that seek to justify a significant deviation.

Practitioner's Aids

Exhibits AU 329-1 and AU 329-2 are examples of workpapers that could be used to document the performance and results of analytical procedures.

EXHIBIT AU 329-1—DOCUMENTATION OF THE EFFECT OF ANALYTICAL PROCEDURES ON THE PLANNING OF SUBSTANTIVE AUDIT PROCEDURES

Use this workpaper to document the effect of analytical procedures on planned substantive audit procedures. The evaluation of the preliminary condition's effect on planned substantive audit procedures is preliminary, and the nature, extent, and timing of audit procedures may be revised based on additional information obtained during the engagement.

Client Name: _____

Date of Financial Statements: _____

Preliminary Condition	Implication of Preliminary Condition on Planning Substantive Audit Procedures	Substantive Workpapers Reference
• **Account Balance/Transaction:** Description of preliminary condition:	Nature of Procedure: Timing of Procedure: Extent of Procedure:	
• **Account Balance/Transaction:** Description of preliminary condition:	Nature of Procedure: Timing of Procedure: Extent of Procedure:	
• **Account Balance/Transaction:** Description of preliminary condition:	Nature of Procedure: Timing of Procedure: Extent of Procedure:	
• **Account Balance/Transaction:** Description of preliminary condition:	Nature of Procedure: Timing of Procedure: Extent of Procedure:	
• **Account Balance/Transaction:** Description of preliminary condition:	Nature of Procedure: Timing of Procedure: Extent of Procedure:	

§329 • Analytical Procedures

- **Account Balance/Transaction:** Nature of Procedure:
Description of preliminary condition:

    Timing of Procedure:
    Extent of Procedure:

- **Account Balance/Transaction:** Nature of Procedure:
Description of preliminary condition:

    Timing of Procedure:
    Extent of Procedure:

- **Account Balance/Transaction:** Nature of Procedure:
Description of preliminary condition:

    Timing of Procedure:
    Extent of Procedure:

- **Account Balance/Transaction:** Nature of Procedure:
Description of preliminary condition:

    Timing of Procedure:
    Extent of Procedure:

- **Account Balance/Transaction:** Nature of Procedure:
Description of preliminary condition:

    Timing of Procedure:
    Extent of Procedure:

- **Account Balance/Transaction:** Nature of Procedure:
Description of preliminary condition:

    Timing of Procedure:
    Extent of Procedure:

Analysis Performed by: _____

Date: _____

Reviewed by: _____

Date: _____

EXHIBIT AU 329-2—ANALYTICAL PROCEDURES FOR A REVIEW ENGAGEMENT

Use this form to document the performance of analytical procedures for a review engagement. The form is only a guide, and professional judgment should be exercised to determine how the form should be modified by omitting or adding analytical procedures.

Client Name: _____

Date of Financial Statements: _____

COMPARISON OF CURRENT FINANCIAL STATEMENTS WITH COMPARABLE PRIOR-PERIOD FINANCIAL STATEMENTS

The following ratios were computed:

____Using financial data that reflects adjustments proposed to date.

____Using financial data that does not reflect adjustments.

	Formula
LIQUIDITY RATIOS	
1. Current ratio	Current Assets / Current Liabilities
2. Acid-test ratio	Quick Assets / Current Liabilities
3. Days' sales in accounts receivable	Average Accounts Receivable × 365 Days / Net Credit Sales
4. Current liabilities to total assets	Current Liabilities / Total Assets
ACTIVITY RATIOS	
1. Inventory turnover	Cost of Goods Sold / Average Inventory
2. Receivable turnover	Net Credit Sales / Average Accounts Receivable

§329 • Analytical Procedures

	Formula
OTHER RATIOS	
3. Asset turnover	$\dfrac{\text{Net Sales}}{\text{Average Total Assets}}$
4. Gross profit percentage	$\dfrac{\text{Gross Profit}}{\text{Net Sales}}$
PROFITABILITY RATIOS	
1. Bad debt to sales	$\dfrac{\text{Bad Debt Expense}}{\text{Net Sales}}$
2. Rate of return	$\dfrac{\text{Net Income}}{\text{Total Assets}}$
	$\dfrac{\text{Net Income}}{\text{Total Equity}}$
3. Net margin	$\dfrac{\text{Net Income}}{\text{Net Sales}}$
COVERAGE RATIOS	
1. Debt to total assets	$\dfrac{\text{Total Debt}}{\text{Total Assets}}$
2. Interest expense to sales	$\dfrac{\text{Interest Expense}}{\text{Net Sales}}$
3. Number of times interest earned	$\dfrac{\text{Income before Interest and Taxes}}{\text{Interest Expenses}}$
1. Effective tax rate	$\dfrac{\text{Income Taxes}}{\text{Income before Taxes}}$
2. Bad debt rate	$\dfrac{\text{Allowance for Bad Debts}}{\text{Accounts Receivable}}$
3. Depreciation rate	$\dfrac{\text{Depreciation Expense}}{\text{Depreciable Property}}$
4. Accounts payable to purchases	$\dfrac{\text{Accounts Payable}}{\text{Purchases}}$

	Formula
5. Dividend rate	$\dfrac{\text{Dividends}}{\text{Common Stock (Par)}}$
6. Interest rate	$\dfrac{\text{Interest Expense}}{\text{Average Interest-Bearing Debt}}$
7. Payroll rate	$\dfrac{\text{Payroll Expense}}{\text{Net Sales}}$
8. Dividend return	$\dfrac{\text{Dividend Income}}{\text{Average Equity Investments}}$
9. Interest income return	$\dfrac{\text{Interest Income}}{\text{Average Debt Investments}}$

OTHER

COMPARISON OF CURRENT FINANCIAL STATEMENTS WITH ANTICIPATED RESULTS

20XX

Acct #	*Account Name*	*Actual*	*Budgeted*	*Difference*
	Cash in bank—name			
	Cash in bank—name			
	Petty cash			
	Cash in bank—payroll			
	Investment marketable equity securities (current)			
	Allowance for decline in market value—marketable equity securities (current)			
	Accounts receivable			
	Allowance for doubtful accounts			
	Other receivables (current)			
	Accrued interest receivable			
	Notes receivable (current)			
	Discount on notes receivable			
	Dividends receivable			
	Inventory (year-end balance)			

§329 • **Analytical Procedures** 167

		_20XX_		
Acct #	_Account Name_	_Actual_	_Budgeted_	_Difference_
	Prepaid insurance			
	Prepaid rent			
	Prepaid advertising			
	Land			
	Buildings			
	Accumulated depreciation—buildings			
	Delivery equipment			
	Accumulated depreciation—delivery equipment			
	Fixtures			
	Accumulated depreciation—fixtures			
	Office equipment			
	Accumulated depreciation—Office equipment			
	Property—capital leases			
	Investment—marketable equity securities (noncurrent)			
	Allowance for decline in market value—marketable equity securities (noncurrent)			
	Deferred bond issuance costs			
	Other receivables (noncurrent)			
	Investment—convertible bonds			
	Land held for investment			
	Accounts payable			
	Accrued liabilities			
	Payroll taxes and other withholdings			
	Interest payable			
	Notes payable			
	Discounts/premiums—notes payable			
	Obligations—capital leases (current)			
	Dividends payable			

		20XX		
Acct #	Account Name	Actual	Budgeted	Difference

- Income taxes payable
- Notes payable (noncurrent)
- Bonds payable
- Discounts/premiums—bonds payable
- Obligation—capital leases (noncurrent)
- Common stock
- Paid-in capital in excess of par
- Unappropriated retained earnings
- Appropriated retained earnings
- Unrealized loss—marketable equity securities (noncurrent)
- Sales
- Sales returns and allowances
- Sales discounts
- Cost of goods sold
- Purchases
- Freight-in
- Bad debt expense
- Utilities expense
- Travel expense
- Advertising expense
- Delivery expense
- Miscellaneous expense
- Insurance expense
- Rent expense
- Professional fees expense
- Salaries and wages expense
- Payroll taxes expense
- Depreciation expense—buildings
- Depreciation expense—delivery equipment
- Depreciation expense—fixtures

Depreciation expense—
   office equipment
Depreciation expense—
   capital leases
Repairs and maintenance
   expense
Miscellaneous income
Extraordinary items
Dividend income
Interest income
Interest expense
Loss/gain on sale of assets
Unrealized loss—mar-
   ketable equity securities
Recovery of market reduc-
   tion of marketable equity
   securities (current)
   recorded in prior years
Loss on exchange of assets
Loss due to permanent de-
   cline in value of security
   investments
Loss/gain on sale of invest-
   ments
Income tax expense
Totals

Prepared By: _____

Reviewed By: _____

STUDY OF FINANCIAL STATEMENT ELEMENTS AND UNEXPECTED RELATIONSHIPS

Unexpected Relationships	Summary of Analysis
_____	_____
_____	_____
_____	_____
_____	_____
_____	_____
_____	_____
_____	_____
_____	_____
_____	_____
_____	_____
_____	_____

OTHER ANALYTICAL PROCEDURES

Summary of findings: _____

_____

_____

_____

_____

_____

_____

_____

_____

_____

_____

Prepared By: _____

Date: _____

Reviewed By: _____

Date: _____

SECTION 330

THE CONFIRMATION PROCESS

Authoritative Pronouncements

SAS-67—The Confirmation Process

Overview

The auditor can obtain evidential matter by confirming with, or acquiring information from, third parties. The confirmation process can be used as part of the audit of a number of account balances, transactions, and other information. For example, accounts receivable and payable may be confirmed with customers and vendors, respectively; a complex transaction may be confirmed with the counterparty; and the relationship between two (related) parties may be explained by the other party.

In general, audit evidence obtained through the confirmation process is considered very reliable. SAS-31 (AU 326) (Evidential Matter) reinforces this position by stating that "when evidential matter can be obtained from independent sources outside an entity, it provides greater assurance of reliability for the purposes of an independent audit than that secured solely within the entity."

Promulgated Procedures Checklist

The auditor should perform the following procedures for the confirmation process to provide reliable evidence:

_____ Design the confirmation request to satisfy audit objectives.

_____ Perform confirmation procedures to satisfy audit objectives.

_____ Evaluate confirmation information received from the third party.

Analysis and Application of Procedures

Design the confirmation request to satisfy audit objectives

When designing a confirmation request, the auditor should identify related audit objectives and then format the confirmation request so that those objectives will be achieved. Audit objectives are established to test the numerous assertions (both explicit and implicit) that are included in a client's financial statements. These assertions can be grouped into the following five categories:

- Existence and occurrence
- Completeness
- Rights and obligations
- Valuation or allocation
- Presentation and disclosure

Although confirmation requests may be designed to enable the auditor to obtain evidence to support all five assertions, evidence acquired through confirmation generally is either not relevant to all five assertions or more persuasive in testing one assertion than the others. For example, when an account receivable is confirmed, the evidential matter created through confirmation is very persuasive with respect to the existence assertion, but is almost irrelevant to the valuation assertion. Thus, when evaluating the evidence from confirmation requests, the auditor should recognize the limitations of the confirmation process.

If an important assertion will not be tested as part of the confirmation process, the auditor must select other audit procedures that will satisfactorily test the remaining assertions.

In designing the confirmation request, factors such as the following should be considered.

- Confirmation request form
- Prior auditor experience
- Information being confirmed
- Characteristics of respondents

Confirmation request form

An auditor may use either a positive confirmation form or a negative confirmation form.

A positive confirmation form may be designed in two ways. The information to be confirmed may be indicated in the confirmation request, or the request may be blank, requiring the respondent to fill in the missing information.

> **RISK ASSESSMENT POINT:** There is a trade-off between selecting the complete format and selecting the incomplete format. When a respondent completes and returns an incomplete

form, more competent evidence is created than when the respondent is simply asked to sign a complete confirmation form. However, when the incomplete form is used, the response rate generally will be lower (sufficiency of evidence matter), and it may be necessary to perform alternative audit procedures to supplement the confirmation process. When a positive confirmation is used and the request is not returned, no evidence is created.

A negative confirmation form requires the respondent to return the confirmation only if there is disagreement. When negative confirmations are not returned, the evidence generated is different from that generated when positive confirmations are used. That is, the lack of returned negative confirmations provides only implicit evidence that the information is correct.

RISK ASSESSMENT POINT: Unreturned negative confirmations do not provide explicit evidence that the intended third parties received the confirmation requests and verified that the information contained on them is correct.

Because of the limitation described above, the negative confirmation form should be used only when all of the following conditions are met:

- The combined assessed level of inherent risk and control risk is low.

- The audit population contains a large number of relatively small individual balances.

- There is no reason to believe that respondents will not give adequate attention to confirmation requests.

ENGAGEMENT STRATEGY: Even under the conditions described above, there is a concern that the use of negative confirmations will not generate sufficient competent evidential matter, and the auditor should consider performing other substantive procedures to supplement the use of negative confirmations. For example, if the auditor uses negative confirmations to test the existence of accounts receivable, it may also be advisable to use additional tests (such as reviewing subsequent cash collections and vouching) to determine with reasonable assurance that accounts receivable do exist.

When a response is received from a negative confirmation, the auditor should investigate the reason for the disagreement. If there are a number of disagreements or if the disagreements appear to be significant, the auditor should reconsider the original assessment of the level of inherent and control risk. This reassessment may lead to the conclusion that the combined assessed level of inherent risk and control risk is not low, in which case the auditor should appropriately modify the originally planned audit approach.

Prior auditor experience

In designing confirmation requests, the auditor should consider prior experience with the client and with similar clients. Prior experience may suggest, for example, that a confirmation form was improperly designed or that previous response rates were so low that audit procedures other than confirmations should be considered.

Information being confirmed

The auditor should consider the capabilities of the respondent in determining what should be included in the confirmation request. Respondents can confirm only what they are capable of confirming, and there will be a tendency to confirm only what is relatively easy to confirm. For example, in designing an accounts receivable confirmation, the auditor should consider whether respondents are more capable of verifying an individual account balance or transactions that make up a single receivable balance. The auditor's understanding of the nature of transactions as they relate to respondents is fundamental to determining what information should be included in a confirmation request.

Information to be confirmed with respondents should not be limited to dollar or other amounts. For example, in complex transactions it may be appropriate to confirm terms of contracts or other documentation that support such transactions. In addition, it may be appropriate to confirm information that is based on oral modifications and therefore not part of the formal documentation. The following guidance from SAS-67 may be useful with respect to oral modifications:

> When the auditor believes there is a moderate or high degree of risk that there may be significant oral modifications, he or she should inquire about the existence and details of any such modifications to written agreements.

If the client's response to the auditor's inquiry is that there are no oral modifications to an agreement, the auditor should consider confirming with the *other* party to the agreement that no oral modifications exist.

Characteristics of respondents

Confirmation requests should be addressed to respondents who, when they respond to the requests, will generate meaningful and competent evidential matter. Factors to be considered include the following:

§330 • The Confirmation Process

- Competence of respondent
- Knowledge of respondent
- Objectivity of respondent

If information concerning the above factors (as well as other relevant factors) comes to the auditor's attention and that information suggests that meaningful and competent evidential matter will not result from the confirmation process, the auditor should consider using other audit procedures to test financial statement assertions.

> **RISK ASSESSMENT POINT:** The auditor should be aware that under some circumstances the level of professional skepticism should be increased, resulting in a closer scrutiny of the respondent. For example, increased skepticism is appropriate when there has been an unusual transaction or a significant balance or transaction. For these as well as other circumstances, SAS-67 does not state specifically what the auditor's actions should be. Presumably, the auditor could decide to investigate the characteristics of the respondents more closely or to employ other audit procedures to reduce the risk of material misstatements in the financial statements.

Perform confirmation procedures to satisfy audit objectives

The confirmation process should be executed so that the client does not have an opportunity to intercept requests when they are mailed or when they are returned from respondents. However, the work of internal auditors may be used in the confirmation process if the guidance established by SAS-65 (AU 322) (The Auditor's Consideration of the Internal Audit Function in an Audit of Financial Statements) is observed.

The confirmation process ideally involves the auditor mailing a confirmation request directly to a respondent and receiving the returned confirmation directly from the respondent. When positive confirmations are used, and there is no response, the auditor should consider sending second and possibly third requests.

SAS-67 does recognize that other means of confirmation may be used, but it notes that the auditor must consider using additional audit procedures to reasonably ensure that a response is authentic and relevant. Specifically, SAS-67 discusses the use of fax and oral responses.

When the auditor receives a fax from a respondent as part of the confirmation process, the same degree of uncertainty concerning the source of the information arises. To reduce that risk, the auditor may employ procedures such as the following:

- Verify the source and content of the fax through a telephone call to the respondent.
- Request the respondent to mail the original confirmation directly to the auditor.

> **ENGAGEMENT STRATEGY:** When information is confirmed orally, the content of and circumstances surrounding the confirmation should be documented in the workpapers. If the information confirmed orally is significant, the information should be confirmed in writing.

> **RISK ASSESSMENT POINT:** Information may be received from a respondent via a fax machine. As with other evidential matter, the auditor must take reasonable precautions to ensure that the fax is authentic. For example, a fax received directly by the client is similar to a returned confirmation that has been opened by the client. To avoid this problem, the auditor may receive the fax on an auditor-controlled telephone line, or reconfirm the information contained on the fax through a telephone conversation with the respondent. In general, the auditor must be careful not to reduce his or her level of professional skepticism just because technology has changed the way evidence is created.

Evaluate confirmation information received from the third party

The auditor often is unable to obtain a 100% response rate when positive confirmations are used. When information has not been confirmed, alternative audit procedures frequently must be used. The specific nature of alternative procedures depends on the account balance or transaction and the adequacy of the client's internal control. For example, when a customer will not confirm an account receivable, the existence of the account could be substantiated through the review of a subsequent cash collection(s) or the inspection of documentation for the transaction(s) that created the year-end balance.

It may be acceptable to omit the use of alternative procedures if both of the following two circumstances exist:

1. Unconfirmed balances do not appear to be unique.
2. Unconfirmed balances are immaterial when projected as 100% misstatements.

Unconfirmed balances do not appear to be unique

The auditor should review those accounts that respondents will not confirm to determine whether they are unusual. While it is difficult to define "unusual," transactions that are complex and not routine, or balances that do not follow a dollar-value pattern, would increase the level of audit risk and generally would preclude the auditor from omitting alternative procedures. For example, most auditors would be skeptical if most of the unconfirmed accounts receivable were from customers that also had other relationships with the client.

Unconfirmed balances are immaterial

The auditor may treat all accounts that respondents do not confirm as misstatements if collectively those misstatements could not have a material effect on the financial statements. In determining the misstatements, the auditor must project the assumed misstatements from the unconfirmed balances to the total population.

Based on the evidence obtained through the confirmation process and the use of alternative audit procedures, the auditor should determine whether related assertions have been sufficiently tested. The auditor should consider the following factors when making this determination:

- The reliability of evidence obtained through the confirmation process and alternative procedures
- The nature and implications of exceptions discovered
- Evidence that may have been obtained through the use of procedures other than confirmation and alternative audit procedures

> **PLANNING AID REMINDER:** If the auditor anticipates that evidential matter obtained through the confirmation process, alternative audit procedures, and other audit procedures may not be sufficient to substantiate relevant assertions in the financial statements, additional evidence must be obtained. The additional evidence may be acquired by employing whatever procedures the auditor may deem appropriate, including additional confirmations, tests of details, and analytical procedures.

> **PLANNING AID REMINDER:** Auditors must be cautious when confirming the fair value of assets with parties that were originally involved in the acquisition of the assets being investigated. Because the respondent party might not provide objec-

tive evidence, the auditor should consider whether it is necessary to communicate with a party that is not involved in the transaction in order to collect competent evidential matter concerning the fair value of an asset.

Procedures for the confirmation of accounts receivable

In addition to providing standards for employing the confirmation process, SAS-67 specifically addresses the confirmation of accounts receivable. The term "accounts receivable" is defined as follows:

- The entity's claims against customers that have arisen from the sale of goods or services in the normal course of business
- A financial institution's loans

> **OBSERVATION:** Although SAS-67 defines the term "accounts receivable," that definition also encompasses notes receivable and other receivables that use descriptive terms, assuming the account balance arose from the sale of goods or services in the normal course of business.

The confirmation of accounts receivable is a generally accepted auditing procedure and should be employed in all audit engagements, except under one or more the following circumstances:

- The accounts receivable balance is immaterial.
- It is expected that the use of confirmations would be ineffective (for example, prior experience may suggest that the response rate is too low or responses are expected to be unreliable).
- Confirmation is not necessary to reduce audit risk to an acceptably low level.

The last circumstance arises when the combined assessed level of inherent and control risk is low, and the expected evidence created from analytical procedures and other substantive tests of details results in the achievement of an acceptable level of audit risk

> **PLANNING AID REMINDER:** Although the confirmation of accounts receivable is not necessary when audit risk can otherwise be reduced to an "acceptably low level," SAS-67 appears to warn auditors that such a situation is unusual by stating that "in many situations, both confirmation of accounts receivable and other substantive tests of details are necessary

to reduce audit risk to an acceptably low level for the applicable financial statement assertions."

When the auditor concludes that it is not necessary to confirm accounts receivable, that position must be documented in the workpapers. Thus, the workpapers must include a full explanation based on one or more of the three circumstances listed above.

Practitioner's Aids

In the confirmation of accounts receivable the auditor may use a positive confirmation or a negative confirmation or a combination of both. An example of a positive confirmation is presented in Exhibit AU 330-1. An example of a negative confirmation is presented in Exhibit AU 330-2. Positive and negative confirmations may take a variety of forms. For example, the negative confirmation may be a stamp or a sticker placed directly on the monthly statements sent to the client's customers; for a positive confirmation it may be a letter in a format similar to the one used in Exhibit AU 330-1.

The standards related to the confirmation process apply to all confirmations, not just those that involve the confirmation of receivables. Exhibits AU 330-3 and AU 330-4 illustrate other types of confirmations, namely, the confirmation of a lease obligation and a mortgage obligation.

Exhibit AU 330-5 illustrates an audit program for the confirmation of accounts receivable.

Exhibit AU 330-6 provides an example of an workpaper that summarizes the results of the accounts receivable confirmation process.

EXHIBIT AU 330-1—POSITIVE CONFIRMATION

[*Client's Letterhead*]

[*Customer's Name and Address*]

Dear _____:

In accordance with the request of our auditors, please confirm the correctness of your account as listed below.

Account # _____
Date of Account Balance _____
(Confirmation Date)
Account Balance $_____

If the amount is correct, sign in the space proved and return this letter to our auditor in the enclosed self-addressed envelope.

If the amount is incorrect, sign in the space provided, explain the difference on the back of this letter, and return this letter to our auditor in the enclosed self-addressed envelope

This is not a request for payment.

Thank you for your prompt attention to this matter.

Very truly yours.

[Client's Signature]

The above balance at the confirmation date is correct, except as noted on the back of this letter.

[Customer's Signature]

[Title]

EXHIBIT AU 330-2 — NEGATIVE CONFIRMATION

CONFIRMATION REQUEST

Please examine this statement carefully. If it is not correct, please notify our auditors of any differences. For your convenience a stamped, self-addressed envelope is enclosed.

If you do not reply to this request, it will be assumed that the balance is correct.

This is not a request for payment.

EXHIBIT AU 330-3 — OBLIGATION UNDER LONG-TERM LEASES

[Client's Letterhead]

[Lessor's Name and Address]

Dear _____:

In accordance with the request of our auditors, please confirm the correctness of terms of our lease (and related matters) with your company.

    Initial date of lease: _____

    Monthly payments: $_____

    Number of months covered by the lease: _____

    Renewal date (if applicable): _____

        Monthly renewal payments $_____

        Period covered by renewal options: From:_____To:_____

Purchase option (if applicable)
   Purchase option price: $_____
   Dates covered by purchase option: From:_____ To:_____
Date of last lease payment received: _____
Other information:

_____

_____

_____

_____

If the above information is correct, sign in the space provided and return this letter to our auditor in the enclosed self-addressed envelope.

If the above information is incorrect, sign in the space provided, explain the difference on the back of this letter, and return this letter to our auditor in the enclosed self-addressed envelope.

Thank you for your prompt attention to this matter.

Very truly yours,

_____
[Client's Signature]

The above information is correct, except as noted on the back of this letter.

_____
[Lessor's Signature]   *[Title]*

EXHIBIT AU 330-4—MORTGAGE OBLIGATION

[Client's Letterhead]

[Mortgagor's Name and Address]

Dear _____:
In accordance with the request of our auditors, please confirm the correctness of terms of our mortgage (and related matters) with your company.

Initial date of mortgage: _____
Monthly payments: $_____
Number of months covered by the mortgage: _____
Interest rate: _____%
Unpaid balance as of (Date): $_____

Date of last lease payment received: _____
Purpose of mortgage:

_____

_____

Description of mortgaged property:

_____

_____

Escrow amount held by you: $_____
Amount of property taxes paid during (Date): $_____
Amount of insurance paid during (Date): $_____
Other information:

_____

_____

If the above information is correct, sign in the space proved and return this letter to our auditor in the enclosed self-addressed envelope.

If the above information is incorrect, sign in the space provided, explain the difference on the back of this letter, and return this letter to our auditor in the enclosed self-addressed envelope.

Thank you for your prompt attention to this matter.

Very truly yours,

_____

[*Client's Signature*]

The above information is correct, except as noted on the back of this letter.

_____

[*Mortgagor's Signature*]   [*Title*]

EXHIBIT AU 330-5 — AUDIT PROGRAM — CONFIRMATION OF ACCOUNTS RECEIVABLE

Use the following procedures as a guide for confirming accounts receivable. The audit program is only a guide, and professional judgment should be exercised to determine how the procedures should be modified by revising procedures listed or adding procedures to the audit program.

Initial and date each procedure as it is completed. If the procedure is not relevant to this particular audit engagement, place "N/A" (not applicable) in the space provided for an initial.

§330 • The Confirmation Process

Client Name: _____

Date of Financial Statements: _____

Date of Fieldwork: _____

	Yes	No	*Workpaper Reference*

1. Obtain or prepare an aged trial balance of accounts receivable. ___ ___ _____

2. Foot and crossfoot the aged trial balance and trace the total to the general ledger. ___ ___ _____

3. Trace a sample of accounts listed on the aged trial balance to the account in the accounts receivable subsidiary ledger. ___ ___ _____

4. Trace a sample of accounts in the accounts receivable subsidiary ledger to the aged trial balance. ___ ___ _____

5. From the aged trial balance select a sample of account balances for confirmation. ___ ___ _____

6. If confirmations are prepared by the client, substantiate the information on the confirmation with information contained in the subsidiary ledger. ___ ___ _____

7. Mail confirmations directly with the U.S. postal system and include in the mailings a self-addressed return envelope. ___ ___ _____

8. Trace returned confirmation to information contained in the list of confirmations mailed. ___ ___ _____

9. Investigate exceptions noted in returned confirmation. ___ ___ _____

10. Send second requests for confirmations not returned. ___ ___ _____

11. Apply alternative procedures (such as review of subsequent cash collection and inspection of documentation that substantiate the original balance) to confirmations not returned. ___ ___ _____

			Workpaper
	Yes	No	Reference

12. Prepare summary statistics based on confirmations mailed and results of confirmation process. ___ ___ _____

Reviewed By: _____

Date: _____

EXHIBIT AU 330-6—SUMMARY OF ACCOUNTS RECEIVABLE CONFIRMATION STATISTICS

Averroes Company
Accounts Receivable Confirmation Statistics
12/31/X5

			Relative to Total Accounts Receivable		Relative to Total Confirmations Sent	
	Dollar Value	Number of Accounts	Dollar Value	Number of Accounts	Dollar Value	Number of Accounts
Total Accounts Receivable	$351,574.31	426				
Total Confirmations Mailed	223,876.12	235	63.70%	55.20%		
Accounts Confirmed (including exceptions cleared)	184,392.13	177	52.50%	41.60%	82.40%	75.30%
Unconfirmed Accounts Verified through Alternative Procedures	36,726.75	43	10.40%	10.10%	16.40%	18.30%
Exceptions not cleared [a]	2,757.24	15	0.80%	3.50%	1.20%	4.40%
Totals	$223,876.12	235	63.70%	55.20%	100.00%	100.00%

(a)—See analysis of exceptions not cleared at AR201.

Prepared By: __JB__
Date: __2/18/X6__   AR200

SECTION 331

INVENTORIES

Authoritative Pronouncements

SAS-1, Codification of Auditing Standards and Procedures (Section 331, Inventories)

Overview

The observation of inventories is a mandatory generally accepted auditing procedure. The observation requirement may be satisfied in a number of ways.

Promulgated Procedures Checklist

The auditor should observe the following broad guidelines in order to substantiate the existence of inventories owned by the client:

_____ Observe inventories when inventory quantities are determined solely by a physical count.

_____ Observe inventories when well-kept perpetual inventory records are maintained.

_____ Observe inventories when statistical sampling is used to estimate the inventory count.

_____ Substantiate the inventory count made in a previous year.

_____ Substantiate the inventory held in a public warehouse or by another outside custodian.

> **ENGAGEMENT STRATEGY:** AU Section 311 addresses only issues related to the substantiation of the inventory count.

Analysis and Application of Procedures

Observe inventories when inventory quantities are determined solely by a physical count

When a client determines the inventory quantity solely by a physical count as of the balance sheet date (or within a reasonable time period before or after the date of the balance sheet), the auditor should observe the physical inventory count. The objective of the observation is to determine the physical existence of the inventory and its condition.

Observe inventories when well-kept perpetual inventory records are maintained

When the client effectively maintains perpetual inventory records and substantiates the balances in these records by appropriate physical counts throughout the year, the auditor's observation tests can generally be performed either during the year or after year-end.

Observe inventories when statistical sampling is used to estimate the inventory count

A client may determine its inventory by using a statistical sampling method. When statistical sampling is used, the auditor must determine the validity and application of the statistical plan and observe such counts as he or she deems necessary.

> **RISK ASSESSMENT POINT:** If an auditor has not substantiated the existence of inventory based on one of the approaches described above, testing solely the client's inventory records will not be sufficient to satisfy professional standards. SAS-1 concludes that under this circumstance the auditor should observe the client's count or should actually make inventory counts of the inventory and test intervening transactions between the count date and the balance sheet date. These procedures should be performed in concert with documentation created and procedures performed by the client.

Substantiate inventory count made in a previous year

In some instances an auditor will be requested to audit the financial statements of a previous year as part of the current- year engagement. The auditor may substantiate inventory quantities for the previous year by using procedures such as tests of prior transactions, reviews of the client's inventory count, and gross profit tests. This can be successful only if the auditor is satisfied with the client's current inventory count.

Substantiate inventory held in a public warehouse or by another outside custodian

Generally, the direct confirmation of the inventory held by outside custodians provides sufficient evidence to validate the existence and ownership of

§331 • Inventories

the inventory. However, if the inventory held by an external party is significant in relation to current assets and total assets, confirmation must be supplemented with the performance of the following procedures:

- Discuss with the client (owner of the goods) the client's control procedures in investigating the warehouseman, including tests of related evidential matter.
- Observe the warehouseman's or client's count of goods whenever practical and reasonable.
- If warehouse receipts have been pledged as collateral, confirm details with the lenders to the extent the auditor deems necessary.
- Obtain an independent auditor's report on the warehouseman's control procedures relevant to custody of goods and, if applicable, pledge receipts; or apply alternative procedures at the warehouse to gain reasonable assurance that information received from warehouseman is reliable.

> **PLANNING AID REMINDER:** Some companies are in the business of counting, recording, and pricing inventories. The auditor's responsibility for the count and other tasks performed by an inventory-taking company is similar to the responsibility for tasks normally performed directly by the client. Therefore, the auditor should (1) review the client's inventory-counting program, (2) make or observe a test of physical counts, (3) make appropriate mathematical checks, and (4) test the valuation of the inventory.

Practitioner's Aids

EXHIBIT AU 331-1—AUDIT PROGRAM: INVENTORY OBSERVATION PROCEDURES

Use the following procedures as a guide for the observation of inventories. The audit program is only a guide, and professional judgment should be exercised to determine how the procedures should be modified by revising procedures listed or adding procedures to the audit program.

Initial and date each procedure as it is completed. If the procedure is not relevant to this particular review engagement, place "N/A" (not applicable) in the space provided for an initial.

Client Name: _____

Date of Financial Statements: _____

Date of Fieldwork: _____

			Workpaper
	Yes	*No*	*Reference*

Planning Phase

1. Review with appropriate personnel the inventory count procedures to be used by the client. ___ ___ _____

2. Attend meetings in which the client instructs personnel concerning the inventory count. ___ ___ _____

3. Identify inventory count issues that need special attention (such as the use of a specialist, inventory held by consignees, inventory held for other parties). ___ ___ _____

4. Determine the number of staff personnel and level of experience needed to cover the client's inventory count. ___ ___ _____

Inventory Count Phase

5. Meet with client personnel to identify any new issues that need to be addressed before the count begins. ___ ___ _____

6. Determine whether inventory that should not be counted (such as consigned goods, inventory to be shipped during the day) has been appropriately segregated or otherwise identified. ___ ___ _____

7. Obtain inventory control count information (such as range of ticket numbers or count sheet numbers to be used during the count). ___ ___ _____

8. Obtain inventory cutoff information from the shipping department (such as bill of lading numbers) and the receiving department (such as receiving report numbers). ___ ___ _____

9. Test inventory counts on a sample basis, and determine whether items are being counted and described correctly and identified as obsolete or damaged if appropriate. ___ ___ _____

§331 • Inventories

	Yes	No	*Workpaper Reference*

10. Record some test counts that can be used later to test the client's summarization of inventory counts. ___ ___ _____

11. Determine whether all inventory items are counted and clearly marked as "counted." ___ ___ _____

12. Determine whether inventory that is moved from one location to another is appropriately identified to avoid double counting or omission from the count. ___ ___ _____

13. Once the inventory count is completed, obtain inventory control information (such as last ticket or counting sheet number used).

Inventory Count Summary Phase

14. Trace inventory test counts made during the inventory count to client inventory summarization sheets. ___ ___ _____

15. Determine whether inventory numbers used in the client's summarization sheets are consistent with inventory control information obtained at the conclusion of the physical inventory count. ___ ___ _____

16. Select inventory amount in the inventory summarization, and trace to either (1) inventory test count information or (2) consistency of ticket control information. ___ ___ _____

17. Determine whether inventory items identified as damaged or obsolete during the inventory count were appropriately identified in the client's inventory summarization. ___ ___ _____

18. Determine whether inventory cutoff information obtained during the inventory count is consistent with sales information and purchases information shortly before and after the year-end date. ___ ___ _____

Reviewed By: _____

Date: _____

EXHIBIT AU 331-2 — CONFIRMATION REQUEST FOR INVENTORY HELD BY ANOTHER PARTY

[*Client's Letterhead*]

[*Custodian's Name and Address*]

Dear _____:

In accordance with the request of our auditors, please confirm the correctness of the inventory items owned by us but held by your company as of December 31, 20X5. For your convenience we have included with this correspondence a list of these items based on our records.

Also, please answer the following questions:

1. How did you determine the number of inventory items held by you as of December 31, 20X5?

2. Are any of the items held by you for us damaged?

3. Are there any negotiable or nonnegotiable warehouse receipts issued, and if so, to your knowledge have any of the receipts been assigned or pledged?

4. Are there any liens against the inventory?

§331 • Inventories

5. Do we owe you any amount of money as of December 31, 20X5?

_____

_____

_____

If the amounts and descriptions included in the attachment are correct, please sign the space proved and return this letter to our auditor in the enclosed self-addressed envelope.

If the amounts are incorrect or there is other relevant information that you want to communicate to our auditors, sign in the space provided, explain the difference in a separate letter, and return this letter and any other relevant information to our auditor in the enclosed self-addressed envelope.

Thank you for your prompt attention to this matter.

Very truly yours,

_____

[*Client's Signature*]

The above balance at the confirmation date is correct, except as noted on the back of this letter.

_____

[*Custodian's Signature*]   [*Title*]

SECTION 332

AUDITING DERIVATIVE INSTRUMENTS, HEDGING ACTIVITIES, AND INVESTMENTS IN SECURITIES

Authoritative Pronouncements

SAS-92—Auditing Derivative Instruments, Hedging Activities, and Investments in Securities

Overview

SAS-92 supersedes the auditing standards originally established by SAS-81 (Auditing Investments). The standards established by SAS-92, which are much broader than those addressed by SAS-81, include both guidance for the audit of derivative instruments and hedging activities and securities.

For derivative instruments and hedging activities SAS-92 provides guidance for the accounting and reporting standards established in FAS-133 (CT F80) (Accounting for Derivative Instruments and Hedging Activities). FAS-133 defines a derivative instrument as a financial instrument or other contract with all three of the following characteristics:

1. It has (1) one or more underlyings and (2) one or more notional amounts or payment provisions or both. Those terms determine the amount of the settlement or settlements, and, in some cases, whether or not a settlement is required.

2. It requires no initial net investment or an initial net investment that is smaller than would be required for other types of contracts that would be expected to have a similar response to changes in market factors.

3. Its terms require or permit net settlement, it can readily be settled net by a means outside the contract, or it provides for delivery of an asset that puts the recipient in a position not substantially different from net settlement.

For purposes of financial reporting, all derivative instruments must be classified as follows:

- No hedge designation
- Fair value hedge
- Cash flow hedge
- Foreign currency hedge

§ 332 • Auditing Investments   193

SAS-92 provides guidance for "hedging activities in which the entity designates a derivative or a nonderivative financial instrument as a hedge of exposure for which FASB Statement No. 133 permits hedge accounting."

Securities

The standards established by SAS-92 apply to all securities (both debt securities and equity securities) held by an entity. The financial accounting and reporting standards that a client should follow depend on the client's characteristics. For example, commercial enterprises must observe the standards established by FAS-115 (CT I89) (Accounting for Certain Investments in Debt and Equity Securities); not-for-profit entities must follow the guidance established by FAS-124 (CT N05) (Accounting for Certain Investments Held by Not-for-Profit Organizations), and governmental entities must refer to the standards identified in GASB-31 (I 50) (Accounting and Financial Reporting for Certain Investments and for External Investment Pools).

> **ENGAGEMENT STRATEGY:** SAS-92 applies to both marketable and nonmarketable debt and equity securities. The standards also apply to securities accounted for using the equity method as described in APB Opinion 18 (The Equity Method of Accounting for Investments in Common Stock).

Promulgated Procedures Checklist

The auditor should perform the following procedures to obtain sufficient competent evidential matter to substantiate the presentation of derivative instruments and securities:

- Develop an understanding of the derivative/security
- Consider audit risk and materiality
- Design appropriate substantive procedures
- Consider management's intent in hedge transactions
- Consider management's intent in security transactions

Analysis and Application of Procedures

Develop an understanding of the derivative/security

Some derivatives and securities have complicated characteristics, and in order to properly audit these items an auditor must have an adequate understanding of them. SAS-92 presents the following audit procedures that may be needed in this area:

- Understand the nature of a derivative/security and related generally accepted accounted principles (GAAP)
- Understand the information system used to process and account for the derivative or security (including the use of an outside service organization)
- Obtain skills necessary to understand how computer applications are used to transmit, process, maintain, and access derivative or security transactions and balances
- Understand various models that may be used to determine the fair value of a derivative or security
- Assess inherent risk and control risk related to the assertions related to derivatives that are used in hedge transactions

Consider audit risk and materiality

AU Section 312 (Audit Risk and Materiality in Conducting an Audit) provides general guidance for planning and executing audit procedures in an engagement. Two important elements in the planning of audit procedures are the assessments of inherent risk and control risk.

> **PLANNING AID REMINDER:** If an auditor decides to use the work of a client's internal auditor in this part of the engagement, the guidance established by AU Section 322 (The Auditor's Consideration of the Internal Audit Function in an Audit of Financial Statements) should be followed.

Assessment of Inherent Risk

SAS-55 (AU 319) (Consideration of the Internal Control in a Financial Statement Audit) defines inherent risk as "the susceptibility of an assertion to a material misstatement, assuming there are no related internal control policies or procedures." SAS-92 lists the following as examples of factors that can affect an auditor's assessment of inherent risk for a derivative or security:

- Management's objective for acquiring a derivative or security
- The complex nature of the derivative or security

§332 • Auditing Investments

- Whether cash was used in the origination of the derivative or security
- Past experience with the derivative or security
- Whether the derivative is freestanding or an embedded feature of an agreement
- Whether external factors, such as credit, market, basis, or legal risk, affect the related assertions in the financial statements
- The newness of the derivative and whether accounting standards address the related measurement and reporting issues
- The degree to which the client understands how a derivative is valued
- Whether GAAP requires the development of assumptions about future conditions

Assessment of Control Risk

SAS-55 (AU 319) defines control risk as "the risk that a material misstatement that could occur in an assertion will not be prevented or detected on a timely basis by an entity's internal controls." SAS-92 points out that control features that may be adopted by a client who uses derivative transactions extensively include the following:

- Separate monitoring by personnel who are fully independent of derivative activities
- Required approval by senior management of derivative transactions that exceed previously approved transaction limits
- Senior management's determination of the appropriateness of actions that deviated from previously approved derivative strategies
- Controls that determine whether the communication of derivative positions in the risk measurement system have been accurate
- Controls that determine whether there has been appropriate reconciliations "to ensure data integrity across the full range of derivatives"
- Controls to ensure that derivative strategies have been properly evaluated by derivative traders, risk managers, and senior management
- Identification of an appropriate group to review controls and financial results of derivative activities and strategies
- Established reviews when limits that relate to strategies, risk tolerance, and market conditions are changed

The auditor's assessment of control related to derivatives and securities transactions is performed based on the guidance established by professional standards including SAS-55 (AU 319) and SAS-70 (AU 324).

Design Appropriate Substantive Procedures

The nature, timing, and extent of substantive procedures for financial statement assertions related to derivatives and securities are based on the auditor's assessment of inherent risk and control risk. While this approach is conceptually the same for all assertions included in financial statements, SAS-92 identifies several illustrative procedures, which are enumerated in a "Practitioner's Aid" at the end of this section and that may be appropriate substantive procedures for derivative and securities.

Management Representations

The auditor should obtain written representations from management "confirming aspects of management's intent and ability that affect assertions about derivative and securities, such as its intent and ability to hold a debt security until its maturity or to enter into a forecasted transaction for which hedge accounting is applied."

Implications of Using a Service Organization

In those instances where a service organization performs duties that are an important part of a client's information system, the auditor must incorporate this circumstance into the design of the nature, timing, and extent of audit procedures. Professional judgment must be used to determine how the role of the service organization might affect the design of the audit plan; however, SAS-92 provides the examples in Exhibit AU 332-1 of services that would affect substantive procedures.

EXHIBIT AU 332-1—SERVICES THAT AFFECT SUBSTANTIVE PROCEDURES

Activity Performed By The Service Organization	Effect on Substantive Tests
Documentation that supports derivative/security transactions is maintained at the service organization	Relevant documentation should be inspected by either (a) the principal auditor, (b) an auditor employed by the principal auditor, or (c) an auditor employed by the service auditor

Activity Performed By The Service Organization	Effect on Substantive Tests
Significant information about the client's securities may be accessed by external parties, including data processors and investor advisers	Principal auditor may have to identify and test the operating effectiveness of related controls at the client and/or service organization in order to reduce audit risk to an acceptable level
Security transactions may be initiated by the service organization and may be held and serviced by the organization	Principal auditor may have to evaluate the controls at the service organization (such as segregation of duties) in order to determine the level of detection risk for substantive tests

Practitioner's Aid

Exhibit AU 332-2 illustrates substantive procedures that may be appropriate for the audit of derivatives and securities.

EXHIBIT AU 332-2—ILLUSTRATIVE SUBSTANTIVE PROCEDURES FOR DERIVATIVES AND SECURITIES

Existence or occurrence financial statement assertion—The financial statements assert that an asset or a liability exists at the balance sheet date and that a nominal account represents transactions that occurred during an accounting period:

- ❏ Confirm balances or transactions with the issuer
- ❏ Confirm securities with holder or confirm derivatives with counterparty
- ❏ Confirm settled transaction with broker-dealer or counterparty
- ❏ Physically inspect security or derivative contract
- ❏ Read executed partnership or similar agreement
- ❏ Inspect underlying agreements and related documentation for (1) amount reported, (2) evidence that would preclude the sales treatment of a transfer, or (3) unrecorded repurchase agreement
- ❏ Inspect underlying documentation for settlements made after year-end
- ❏ Perform analytical procedures

Completeness financial statement assertion—The financial statements assert that all items that make up an asset, a liability, or a nominal account are represented:

- Request a counterparty or holder to provide a complete description of the transaction
- Query previously active counterparties or holders that current accounting records indicate presently have no involvement in derivative/security transactions about whether they are a party to a current transaction
- Inspect current documentation to determine whether agreements include embedded derivatives
- Review documentation for activities that occurred subsequent to the year-end date
- Perform analytical procedures
- Identify transactions that have been settled to determine whether treating them as sales was appropriate
- Read other information such as minutes of meetings of the board of directors or relevant committees

Rights and obligations financial statement assertion—The financial statements assert that assets properly represent rights owned by the client and that liabilities represent obligations of the client:

- Confirm significant terms of an agreement with the counterparty or holder
- Inspect documentation that supports derivative or security transactions
- Consider evidence obtained in other areas of the engagement

Valuation and allocation financial statement assertion—The financial statements assert that all accounts are valued in accordance with GAAP:

- For items reported at historical cost, inspect appropriate documentation
- For items reported based on the valuation of an investee's financial results, review the financial statements and consider obtaining additional evidence related to other matters such as (1) significant differences in fiscal year-ends, (2) changes in ownership, (3) material transactions between the investor and investee companies, and (4) the issuance of unaudited financial statements

- For items reported at fair value, determine whether the method of valuation is specified by GAAP, fully understand how the method is employed (such as pricing models), determine whether it is necessary to obtain information from more than one source, and where appropriate follow the guidance established by SAS-70 (AU 324) and SAS-73 (AU 336)
- For items that are required to be evaluated for possible impairment losses that are other than temporary, obtain relevant information concerning the loss of value of a particular item
- For derivatives that are hedges, obtain evidence that demonstrates that management has complied with the hedge accounting requirements of GAAP
- For securities, obtain evidence that demonstrates that management has complied with the investment accounting requirements of GAAP

Presentation and disclosure financial statement assertion—The financial statements assert that accounts and related information are properly classified, described, and disclosed:

- Determine that the accounting method used is acceptable and appropriate under the circumstances
- Determine that the financial statements are "informative of matters that may affect their use, understanding, and interpretation"
- Determine that the financial statements are classified and summarized in a reasonable manner
- Determine that the financial statements reflect the underlying transactions and events within a range of acceptable limits

SECTION 333

MANAGEMENT REPRESENTATIONS

Authoritative Pronouncements

SAS-85—Management Representations

SAS-89—Audit Adjustments

Auditing Interpretation (March 1979)—Management Representations on Violations and Possible Violations of Laws and Regulations

Overview

During the course of an engagement, the client's personnel make a variety of representations in response to questions raised by the auditor. Generally accepted auditing standards require that in order to reduce the likelihood of misunderstandings between the client and the auditor, written representations be obtained from the client to confirm explicit and implicit representations made by management during the engagement.

Written representations received from management are evidential matter, and they often support other evidential matter the auditor obtains. For example, the auditor may inspect client documentation to determine whether there are liens against certain capital assets; however, the auditor should obtain a written representation from management stating that no liens exist. In other instances, written representations by management may be the primary source of evidential matter to support an assertion stated or implied in the financial statements. For example, certain current liabilities may be classified as noncurrent based on the guidance established by FAS-6 (CT BO5) (Classification of Short-Term Obligations Expected to Be Refinanced). Part of that guidance requires that management must intend to refinance the obligation on a long-term basis. Under this circumstance, the auditor's primary support for management's intent may be management's written representation rather than other sources of evidential matter.

Written representations should be addressed to the auditor and should apply to all periods covered in the auditor's report. Even though current management may not have been present during all of the periods covered by the report, written representations must cover all periods. The representations should be made by management as of a date no earlier than the date of the auditor's report and should be signed by the chief executive officer and chief financial officer or others "with overall responsibility for financial and operating matters whom the auditor believes are responsible for and knowl-

§333 • Management Representations

edgeable about, directly or through others in the origination, the matters covered by the written representations."

Promulgated Procedures Checklist

The auditor should perform the following procedures with respect to management representations in an audit engagement:

_____ Obtain certain minimum written management representations from management.

_____ Consider whether written management representations beyond the minimum required should be obtained.

_____ Evaluate inconsistencies between representations made by management and evidence otherwise obtained.

_____ Consider whether written representations should be obtained from parties other than management.

_____ Consider whether an "updating representation letter" should be obtained.

_____ If applicable, consider the circumstances under which management has refused to prove written representations.

Analysis and Application of Procedures

Obtain certain minimum written representations from management

SAS-85 requires that in all audit engagements, the auditor must obtain from a client written representations that relate to the following matters and must include management's acknowledgment of the following:

- Financial statements
  — Responsibility for the fair presentation in the financial statements of financial position, results of operations, and cash flows in conformity with generally accepted accounting principles
  — The belief that the financial statements are fairly presented in conformity with generally accepted accounting principles

— The belief that any misstatements identified by the auditor and not corrected are immaterial, "both individually and in the aggregate" with respect to the financial statements taken as a whole. (The representation letter or an attachment should summarize the uncorrected errors.)

- Completeness of information

   — The availability of all financial records and related data

   — The completeness and availability of all minutes of meetings of stockholders, directors, and committees of directors

   — The completeness of communications from regulatory agencies concerning noncompliance with or deficiencies in financial reporting practices

   — The absence of unrecorded transactions

- Recognition, measurement, and disclosure

   — The existence of information concerning fraud involving (a) management, (2) employees who have significant roles in internal control, or (3) others where the fraud could have a material effect on the financial statements

   — The existence of plans or intentions that may affect the carrying value or classification of assets or liabilities

   — The existence of information concerning related-party transactions and amounts receivable from or payable to related parties

   — The existence of guarantees, whether written or oral, under which the entity is contingently liable

   — Significant estimates and material concentrations known to management exist that are required to be disclosed in accordance with the AICPA's Statement of Position 94-6 (Disclosure of Certain Significant Risks and Uncertainties)

   — The existence of violations or possible violations of laws or regulations whose effects should be considered for disclosure in the financial statements or as a basis for recording a loss contingency

   — The existence of unasserted claims or assessments that the entity's lawyer has advised are probable of assertion and must be disclosed in accordance with Financial Accounting Standards Board Statement No. (FAS) 5 (CT C59) (Accounting for Contingencies)

   — The existence of other liabilities and gain or loss contingencies that are required by FAS-5 to be accrued or disclosed

§333 • Management Representations

— The existence of satisfactory title to assets, liens, or encumbrances on assets, and assets pledged as collateral

— Compliance with aspects of contractual agreements that may affect the financial statements

- Subsequent events

    — The existence of information concerning subsequent events

> **PLANNING AID REMINDER:** The minimum representations also apply to financial statements that use a comprehensive basis of accounting other than accrual accounting as described in SAS-62 (AU 623) (Special Reports).

SAS-85 notes that representations made by management may be limited to items that are material to the client's financial statements, if "management and the auditor have reached an understanding on materiality for this purpose." That understanding, expressed either in quantitative or qualitative terms, may be part of the management representation letter. However, some items that are the basis for management representations do not relate to dollar values and therefore are not affected by materiality considerations. For example, the management representation that all financial records and related data have been made available to the auditor is not subject to a materiality threshold.

As noted above, management must represent to the auditor that any uncorrected misstatements discovered during the audit are immaterial and that there should be a summary of these items in or attached to the representation letter. SAS-89 notes that if management does not agree with the auditor about a particular misstatement, the following may be added to the representation letter:

> We do not agree that items [*identify the items*] constitute misstatements because [*give reasons for the disagreement*].

In addition, SAS-47 (AU 312) (Audit Risk and Materiality in Conducting an Audit) points out that an auditor may establish a minimum amount that a misstatement must reach before it is accumulated by the auditor. The representation letter need not list these misstatements.

> **RISK ASSESSMENT POINT:** SAS-85 specifically notes that materiality does not apply to representations related to fraud involving management and employees who have significant roles in internal control.

Consider whether written management representations beyond the minimum required should be obtained

In addition to the specific representations listed above, the auditor must use professional judgment to determine whether additional representations are appropriate based on the characteristics of the engagement, including the industry in which the client operates. For example, SAS-85 points out that certain AICPA Audit Guides identify a variety of written representations that the auditor should consider. These additional representations could relate to such matters as the client's use of the cost method when the client owns less than 20% of an investee company's voting stock, the recognition of losses arising from purchase commitments, and the provision for losses related to environmental issues.

Evaluate inconsistencies between representations made by management and evidence otherwise obtained

When a management representation contradicts evidence the auditor has obtained, "the auditor should investigate the circumstances and consider the reliability of the representation made." Depending on the results of the investigation, the auditor should consider whether the inconsistency of the management representation has implications for other areas of the audit engagement.

> **RISK ASSESSMENT POINT:** By quoting the guidance provided in SAS-82 (AU 316) (Consideration of Fraud in a Financial Statement Audit), SAS-85 provides some practical insight into the auditor's reliance on statements made by management. It states, "The auditor neither assumes that management is dishonest nor assumes unquestioned honesty. In exercising professional skepticism, the auditor should not be satisfied with less than persuasive evidence because of a belief that management is honest."

Consider whether written representations should be obtained from parties other than management

SAS-85 notes that under some circumstances, such as the following, the auditor may obtain written representations from other individuals:

- Written representations concerning completeness may be obtained from the individual responsible for keeping the minutes of meetings of stockholders, board of directors, and committees of the board of directors.

- Written representations concerning matters such as related party transactions may be obtained from a parent company when the auditor's engagement is limited to expressing an opinion on a subsidiary's financial statements.

Consider whether an "updating representation letter" should be obtained

Under some circumstances, such as the following, an auditor should obtain an "updating representation letter" from management:

- A predecessor auditor has been requested to reissue previously issued reports covering financial statements that will be presented on a comparative basis with financial statements audited by a successor auditor.
- The auditor is performing subsequent audit procedures related to a filing under the Securities Act of 1933.

The updating written representations should state (1) whether subsequent information has come to the attention of management that would affect written representations previously expressed and (2) whether any subsequent events have occurred that would require adjustment or disclosure in the latest financial statement reported on by the auditor.

> **PLANNING AID REMINDER:** SAS-1, AU Section 530 (Dating of the Independent Auditor's Report), provides guidance for situations in which the auditor's report should be "dual-dated." SAS-85 points out that the auditor should consider whether it is appropriate to obtain a written representation about the subsequent event that created the dual-dating situation.

If applicable, consider the circumstances under which management has refused to provide written representations

If management is unwilling to provide appropriate written representations, the auditor should consider whether that refusal has an affect on the auditor's reliance on other representations made by management during the engagement. Based on professional judgment, the auditor must determine whether it is necessary to withdraw from the engagement or disclaim an opinion on the financial statements because of the scope limitation. SAS-85 does note that "based on the nature of the representations not obtained or the circumstances of the refusal, the auditor may conclude that a qualified opinion is appropriate." However, the expression of an unqualified opinion on the financial statements is precluded.

The Auditing Interpretation (June 1983) of SAS-12 (AU 337) titled "Client Has Not Consulted Lawyer" states that when a client has not consulted outside legal counsel concerning litigation, claims, and assessments, the auditor usually will rely on internal documentation and representations made by management. In this event, the client's representation may read as follows:

> We are not aware of any impending or threatened litigation, claims, or assessments, or unasserted claims or assessments, that are required to be accrued or disclosed in the financial statements in accordance with FAS-5. We have not consulted a lawyer concerning litigation, claims, or assessments.
>
> **ENGAGEMENT STRATEGY:** The Auditing Interpretation (March 1979) titled "Management Representations on Violations and Possible Violations of Laws and Regulations" states that the auditor's request for written representations from management on significant violations or possible violations of laws and regulations need not include matters beyond those described in FAS-5.

Practitioner's Aids

Exhibit AU 333-1 illustrates a management representation letter similar to the one included in the appendix of SAS-85.

EXHIBIT AU 333-1—MANAGEMENT REPRESENTATION LETTER

We are providing this letter in connection with your audit(s) of the [*identify financial statements*] of [*name of entity*] as of [*dates*] and the [*periods*] for the purpose of expressing an opinion as to whether the (consolidated) financial statements present fairly, in all material respects, the financial position, results of operations, and cash flows of [*name of entity*] in conformity with generally accepted accounting principles. We confirm that we are responsible for the fair presentation of the (consolidated) financial statements of financial position, results of operations, and cash flows in conformity with generally accepted accounting principles.

Certain representations in this letter are described as being limited to matters that are material. Items are considered material, regardless of size, if they involve an omission or misstatement of accounting information that, in the light of surrounding circumstances, makes it probable that the judgment of a reasonable person relying on the information would be changed or influenced by the omission or misstatement.

We confirm, to the best of our knowledge and belief [*as of (date of auditor's report)*], the following representations made to you during your audit(s).

1. The financial statements referred to above are fairly presented in conformity with generally accepted accounting principles.
2. We have made available to you all
   a. Financial records and related data.
   b. Minutes of the meetings of stockholders, directors, and committees of directors, or summaries of actions of recent meetings for which minutes have not yet been prepared.
3. No communications from regulatory agencies have been received concerning noncompliance with or deficiencies in financial reporting practices.
4. All material transactions have been properly recorded in the accounting records underlying the financial statements.
5. No fraud exists involving
   a. Management or employees who have significant roles in internal control.
   b. Others that could have a material effect on the financial statements.
6. The company has no plans or intentions that may materially affect the carrying value or classification of assets and liabilities.
7. We believe that the uncorrected misstatements in the financial statements that are summarized in the accompanying schedule are immaterial, both individually and in the aggregate, to the financial statements taken as a whole.
8. The following have been properly recorded or disclosed in the financial statements:
   a. Related-party transactions, including sales, purchases, loans, transfers, leasing arrangements, and guarantees, and amounts receivable from or payable to related parties.
   b. Guarantees, whether written or oral, under which the company is contingently liable.
   c. Significant estimates and material concentrations known to management that are required to be disclosed in accordance with the AICPA's Statement of Position 94-6 (Disclosure of

Certain Significant Risks and Uncertainties). (Significant estimates are estimates at the balance sheet date that could change materially within the next year; concentrations refer to volumes of business, revenues, available sources of supply, or markets or geographic areas for which events could occur that would significantly disrupt normal finances within the next year.)

9. There are no
   a. Violations or possible violations of laws or regulations whose effects should be considered for disclosure in the financial statements or as a basis for recording a loss contingency.
   b. Unasserted claims or assessments that our lawyer has advised us are probable of assertion and must be disclosed in accordance with FAS-5 (Accounting for Contingencies).
   c. Other liabilities or gain or loss contingencies that are required to be accrued or disclosed by FAS-5.
10. The company has satisfactory title to all owned assets, and there are no liens or encumbrances on such assets nor has any asset been pledged as collateral.
11. The company has complied with all aspects of contractual agreements that would have a material effect on the financial statements in the event of noncompliance.

To the best of our knowledge and belief, no events have occurred subsequent to the balance sheet date and through the date of this letter that would require adjustment to our disclosure in the aforementioned financial statements.

SECTION 334

RELATED PARTIES

Authoritative Pronouncements

SAS-45—Omnibus Statement on Auditing Standards 1983

Auditing Interpretation (April 1979)—Examination of Identified Related Party Transactions with a Component

Auditing Interpretation (April 1979)—Exchange of Information Between the Principal and Other Auditor on Related Parties

Auditing Interpretation (May 1986)—The Nature and Extent of Auditing Procedures for Examining Related Party Transactions

Auditing Interpretation (May 2000)—Management's and Auditor's Responsibilities With Regard to Related Party Disclosures Prefaced by Terminology Such As "Management Believes That"

Overview

An auditor must be alert for the possible occurrence of related party transactions and should evaluate them with a higher degree of skepticism than transactions that are executed by parties that are not related. SAS-45 establishes guidelines for evaluating related party transactions that are discovered during an audit engagement.

An accounting transaction generally reflects the resources exchanged and obligations incurred when parties to a transaction are unrelated. The auditor may verify the values assigned to the accounts by examining the supporting documentation. For example, if a client purchases machinery for $10,000 cash, inspection of the vendor invoice will usually satisfy the auditor that the fair value of the asset acquired at the transaction date was in fact $10,000. However, if the parties to the transaction are related, it cannot always be assumed that the recorded amounts properly reflect the true economic substance of the transaction. Moreover, the inspection of supporting documentation may not provide the auditor with competent evidential matter. Professional guidelines for related party transactions were established in SAS-45 and FAS-57 (CT R36) (Related Party Disclosures).

> **PLANNING AID REMINDER:** The Auditing Interpretation (April 1979) of SAS-45 titled "Exchange of Information Between the Principal and Other Auditor on Related Parties" states that the

principal auditor and other auditors of related entities should exchange information on the names of known related parties in the early stages of their examinations.

Promulgated Procedures Checklist

The auditor should perform the following procedures with respect to related party transactions:

____ Determine whether conditions exist for related party transactions.

____ Select audit procedures that are likely to identify related party transactions.

____ Determine whether the client has made appropriate disclosures for related party transactions that have been identified.

Analysis and Application of Procedures

Determine whether conditions exist for related party transactions

A related party transaction occurs when one party to a transaction has the ability to impose contract terms that would not have occurred if the parties had been unrelated. FAS-57 concludes that related parties consist of all affiliates of an enterprise, including (1) its management and their immediate families; (2) its principal owners and their immediate families; (3) investments accounted for by the equity method; (4) beneficial employee trusts that are managed by the management of the enterprise; and (5) any party that may, or does, deal with the enterprise and has ownership, control, or significant influence over the management or operating policies of another party to the extent that an arm's-length transaction may not be achieved.

> **PLANNING AID REMINDER:** The Auditing Interpretation (April 1979) of SAS-45 titled "Examination of Identified Related Party Transactions with a Component" states that principal auditors ordinarily should allow access to the relevant portions of their workpapers to other auditors who are auditing a component or subsidiary of the entity. This enables other auditors to understand the related party transactions.

In addition to relationships that may lead to the auditor's identification of a related party transaction, certain transactions suggest that the parties may be related. SAS-45 lists the following as examples:

§334 • Related Parties

- Contracts that carry no interest rate or that carry an unrealistic interest rate
- Real estate transactions that are made at a price significantly different from appraised values
- Nonmonetary transactions that involve the exchange of similar assets
- Loan agreements that contain no repayment schedule

Finally, certain conditions may increase the possibility that a related party transaction may occur. These conditions include the following:

- Inadequate working capital or lines of credit
- Management's desire for strong earnings to support the market price of the company's stock
- Earnings forecast that was too optimistic
- A declining industry
- Excess capacity
- Significant legal problems
- Exposure to technological changes

> **RISK ASSESSMENT POINT:** Although these conditions do not usually result in related party transactions, they indicate that the auditor must be more alert to the increased possibility.

Select audit procedures that are likely to identify related party transactions

FAS-57, which is reviewed at the end of this Section, covers related party transactions and how they should be identified and disclosed in the financial statements. SAS-45 concludes that until special accounting rules are promulgated, the auditor should evaluate related party transactions in the context of existing generally accepted accounting principles and should consider whether material transactions are adequately disclosed in the financial statements.

The Interpretation (May 1986) of SAS-45 titled "The Nature and Extent of Auditing Procedures for Examining Related Party Transactions" states that the auditor should apply sufficient audit procedures to provide reasonable assurance that related party transactions are adequately disclosed in the financial statements and that material misstatements associated with identified related party transactions do not exist.

> **RISK ASSESSMENT POINT:** Since the audit risk associated with management's assertions concerning related party transactions is generally higher than the audit risk associated with other transactions, the audit procedures that are applied to related party transactions should be more extensive or effective. For example, to obtain additional evidence or a better understanding of a related party transaction, the auditor may apply selected audit procedures to, or may actually audit, the financial statements of the related party.

Initially the auditor should select audit procedures that are likely to identify transactions with related parties. These procedures are as follows:

- Supply the names of known related parties of the client and its divisions, segments, etc., to all audit personnel.
- Read the minutes of the board of directors meetings and executive or operating committee meetings.
- Review proxy and other material filed with the SEC and comparable data filed with other regulatory agencies for information on material related party transactions.
- Read conflict-of-interest statements prepared by the client's key personnel.
- Review major transactions for indications of previously undisclosed relationships.
- Consider if any transactions are not being recorded.
- Review significant or nonroutine transactions, especially those occurring near the end of the accounting period.
- Review confirmations of compensating-balance agreements for suggestions that balances are or were maintained for or by related parties.
- Review invoices from law firms to see whether a related party is involved.
- Review loan confirmations to determine if guarantees exist.

> **PLANNING AID REMINDER:** The auditor should consider obtaining written representations from senior management of an entity and its board of directors regarding whether they or other related parties were involved in transactions with the entity.

When a related party transaction is identified, the auditor should consider performing the following procedures:

- Understand the purpose of the transaction.
- Read documentation that supports the transaction.
- Test the reasonableness of numbers compiled for possible disclosure in the financial statements.
- If appropriate, arrange for the audit of intercompany account balances. Use the same audit date cutoff for all balances.
- If appropriate, arrange for the examination of transactions by the auditors for each of the parties.
- Determine the transferability and value of collateral, if any.

> **ENGAGEMENT STRATEGY:** If the auditor is not satisfied with the results of the above procedures, he or she may select additional procedures to obtain a complete understanding of the nature of the transaction. These procedures may include confirming data with the other party, discussing transactions with banks or other parties, inspecting documents held by others, or verifying the existence of the other party by referring to trade journals or other sources.

The Interpretation (May 2000) titled "Management's and Auditor's Responsibilities With Regard to Related Party Disclosures Prefaced by Terminology Such As 'Management Believes That'" points out that management may use phraseology such as "management believes that" or "it is the Company's belief that" in describing a related party transaction. The use of this or similar terminology does not change management's responsibility to substantiate its representations concerning a related party transaction that it believes was executed on terms equivalent to those similar to an arm's-length transaction.

> **RISK ASSESSMENT POINT:** If management does not adequately substantiate its representation with respect to the related party transaction, the auditor should express a qualified or adverse opinion on the financial statements if the matter is considered material.

Determine whether the client has made appropriate disclosures for related party transactions that have been identified

The Financial Accounting Standards Board (FASB) requires disclosure of related party transactions that (1) are not eliminated in consolidated or combined financial statements and (2) are necessary to understand the entity's financial statements.

If separate financial statements of an entity that has been consolidated are presented in a financial report that includes the consolidated financial statements, duplicate disclosure of the related party transactions is not necessary. Thus, disclosure of the related party transactions in the consolidated statements is all that is required. However, disclosure of related party transactions is required in separate financial statements of (1) a parent company, (2) a subsidiary, (3) a corporate joint venture, or (4) an investee that is less than 50% owned. The minimum financial statement disclosures required by FAS-57 for related party transactions that (1) are not eliminated in consolidation or combination and (2) are necessary to the understanding of the financial statements are as follows:

1. The nature of the related party relationship. The name of the related party should also be disclosed if it is essential to the understanding of the relationship.
2. A description of the related party transactions, including amounts and other pertinent information for each period in which an income statement is presented.
3. Related party transactions of no amount, or of nominal amounts, must also be disclosed. In other words, all information that is necessary for an understanding of the effects of the related party transactions on the financial statements must be disclosed, assuming this information is material.
4. The effects of any change in terms between the related parties from terms used in prior periods. In addition, the dollar amount of transactions for each period in which an income statement is presented must be disclosed.
5. If not apparent in the financial statements, (1) the terms of related party transactions; (2) the manner of settlement to related party transactions; and (3) the amount due to, or due from, related parties must all be disclosed.
6. The nature of any control relationship, even if there were no transactions between the related parties, must be disclosed in all circumstances.

The amount of detail disclosed for related party transactions must be sufficient for the user of the financial statements to be able to understand the related party transaction. Thus, the disclosure of the total amount of a specific type of related party transaction, or the effects of the relationship between the related parties, may be all that is necessary. The auditor must determine whether the related party transaction affects the financial statements to such a degree that they are materially misstated and must modify the report accordingly.

> **RISK ASSESSMENT POINT:** One cannot assume that a related party transaction is consummated in the same manner as an arm's-length transaction. Disclosures or other representations of related party transactions in financial statements should not, under any circumstances, indicate that the transaction was made on the same basis as an arm's-length transaction.

SECTION 336

USING THE WORK OF A SPECIALIST

Authoritative Pronouncements

SAS-73—Using the Work of a Specialist

Auditing Interpretation (October 1998)—The Use of Legal Interpretations as Evidential Matter to Support Management's Assertion That a Transfer of Financial Assets Has Met the Isolation Criterion in Paragraph 9(a) of Financial Accounting Standards Board Statement 125

Overview

In some instances the dollar amounts reflected in the financial statements are based on evidential matter that an auditor is not capable of evaluating. For example, pension costs depend on an actuarial analysis that is usually beyond the expertise of an auditor. SAS-73, which supersedes SAS-11 (Using the Work of a Specialist), was issued to provide guidance in an engagement requiring the services of a specialist. Although there is no complete list of circumstances that require the use of a specialist, SAS-73 provides the following examples:

- Valuation of inventories, property, plant, and equipment, financial instruments, and works of art for which the question of a writedown due to the application of the lower of cost or market rule or the cost recoverability rule is relevant
- Valuation of an environmental contingency
- Physical measurements (tons, barrels, etc.) of raw materials
- Dollar valuations based on specialized measurement techniques such as actuarial computations
- Interpretation of technical material such as legal documents and regulatory standards and guidance

> **PLANNING AID REMINDER:** SAS-73 did not change the requirement established by SOP 92-4 (Auditing Insurance Entities' Loss Reserves) that a "loss reserve specialist," not an employee or officer of the client, must be used to audit the loss reserve for property and liability insurance companies.

> **ENGAGEMENT STRATEGY:** SAS-73 concludes that the auditor has the expertise necessary to consider the financial statement implications (accrual, disclosure, and presentation) of income tax matters. This presupposes an understanding of income tax laws and regulations that apply to a particular client and the standards established by FAS-109 (CT 127) (Accounting for Income Taxes) and other related pronouncements.

SAS-73 does not provide guidelines for the use of a lawyer who is requested to make representations concerning litigation, claims, or assessments [see SAS-12 (Inquiry of A Client's Lawyer Concerning Litigation, Claims, and Assessments) (AU 337)]; however, the standard does apply to using the expertise of a lawyer in other circumstances.

The standards established by SAS-73 apply to the audit of financial statements prepared in accordance with generally accepted accounting principles (GAAP) as well as to engagements discussed in SAS-62 (AU 623) (Special Reports); however, they do not apply to specialists employed by the auditor when those specialists are part of the audit team. When a auditor employs a specialist as a member of the audit team in an engagement, the standards established by SAS-22 (AU 311) (Planning and Supervision) must be observed.

An auditing firm must apply the standards established by SAS-73 in the following circumstances:

- When management employs a specialist and the auditor is considering using the work of the specialist as part of substantive testing

- When management employs a specialist to perform advisory services, and the auditor employs the specialist to perform services related to substantive testing (Under this circumstance, the auditor should consider the effect on independence.)

- When the auditor employs a specialist as part of substantive testing

> **ENGAGEMENT STRATEGY:** SAS-73 was issued in part to clarify when professional standards apply to the work of a specialist. Based on the above list, it is obvious that such standards apply only as part of substantive testing. Thus, the standards apply when it is necessary to use the work of a specialist to determine whether specialized inventory must be written down below its original cost of purchase or production. On the other hand, the standards would not apply when a real estate appraisal is part of the internal control procedures a mortgage company uses to determine whether to make a loan.

Promulgated Procedures Checklist

Once an auditor determines that a specialist is appropriate in an engagement, the following procedures should be performed:

_____ Determine the qualifications of the specialists.

_____ Evaluate the effects of using a specialist on audit evidence.

_____ Determine the extent to which the work of the specialist should be used.

_____ Consider the effect of using the work of a specialist on the audit report.

_____ If applicable, consider using the work of a specialist to determine whether there has been a transfer of financial assets as defined by FAS-125 (CT F25).

Analysis and Application of Procedures

Determine the qualifications of the specialists

Initially, the auditor must determine the nature of the work to be performed by a specialist as it relates to substantive testing. That is, the auditor should identify the *assertions* [as defined by SAS-31 (AU 326) (Evidential Matter)] in the financial statements (either explicitly or implicitly) that can be substantiated only through evidence obtained or developed by a specialist. For example, presentation and disclosure assertions related to the projected benefit obligation that appear in a note to the financial statements [as required by FAS-87 (Employers' Accounting for Pensions)] require the expertise of an actuary. Specifically, SAS-73 requires that the auditor obtain an understanding of the following with respect to nature of the services to be provided by a specialist:

- The objectives and scope of the specialist's services
- The relationship between the specialist and the client
- The methods and assumptions to be used in the work
- A comparison of the methods and assumptions proposed for the current engagement with those used in the previous engagement

§336 • Using the Work of a Specialist

- The appropriateness of the work of the specialist in relationship to the assertions to be substantiated
- The form and content of the results of work of the specialist and how they relate to the auditor's need to evaluate that work

> **RISK ASSESSMENT POINT:** SAS-73 notes that the auditor may need to inform the specialist that his or her work will be used to substantiate certain assertions in the financial statements. Although SAS-73 does not provide any guidance on when this contact may be appropriate, it generally would be necessary to ensure that the specialist understands the need to provide a "usable link" between the specialist's work and the assertions to be substantiated. Essentially, the prudent auditor must make sure that the technical nature of the specialist's work makes sense in the context of the audit engagement.

Before the auditor places reliance on the work of a specialist, the qualifications and experience of the specialist should be established, for example, by identifying the professional designations (certification, license, etc.) and the professional reputation earned by the specialist. In addition, professional work experience provides insight into whether the qualifications of the specialist are acceptable.

Evaluate the effects of using a specialist on audit evidence

Perhaps the most sensitive aspect of using the work of a specialist is the relationship between the specialist and the client, and the effect of that relationship on an auditor's collection of competent and sufficient evidential matter. If the specialist is biased in favor of the client, the information created by the specialist and used as evidence by the auditor will be tainted.

Ideally, the specialist would not have a relationship with the client that could provide an opportunity for the client to "directly or indirectly control or significantly influence the specialist." The concept of a *relationship* is broad and encompasses such circumstances as that of an employer/employee or a member of the same family. If there is no relationship between the client and the specialist (that is, the auditor hires the specialist and there are no other direct or indirect relationships between the client and the specialist), there is a greater chance that the work the specialist performs will be reliable.

> **ENGAGEMENT STRATEGY:** SAS-73 notes that the term *relationship* includes (but is not limited to) those relationships included in Note 1 of SAS-45. The SAS-45 note is based on the definition of "related parties" contained in SAS-57.

If a relationship does exist between the client and the specialist, the auditor is required to obtain an understanding of the relationship, as the existence of a relationship does not in itself preclude the auditor from relying on the specialist's work. In this circumstance, SAS-73 requires that the auditor "assess the risk that the specialist's objectivity might be impaired." If the auditor concludes that the specialist's objectivity might be impaired, the auditor must perform additional procedures. These procedures should focus on "some or all of the specialist's assumptions, methods, or findings." When the results of performing the additional procedures do not dispel the auditor's concern with the specialist's objectivity, the auditor should engage another specialist.

Determine the extent to which the work of the specialist should be used

The auditor's role in the evaluation of the evidence created by a specialist is to determine whether the specialist's findings are reasonable. SAS-73 concludes that the auditor should use the following approach to assess the reasonableness of the findings:

- Obtain an understanding of the specialist's methods and assumptions.
- Test the data provided to the specialist by the client. (The nature, timing, and extent of the testing should be based on the auditor's assessment of the client's control risk.)
- Evaluate whether the relevant assertions in the financial statements are substantiated by the specialist's findings.

> **PLANNING AID REMINDER:** If, on the basis of the above and other procedures deemed appropriate by the auditor, the auditor concludes that the findings are reasonable, the evidence can be relied on as the basis for forming an opinion on the financial statements. On the other hand, if the auditor's evaluation does not suggest that the findings are reasonable, SAS-73 requires that the auditor perform additional procedures. If the matter still is unresolved after the performance of additional procedures, the auditor should obtain the opinion of another specialist.

Consider the effect of using the work of a specialist on the audit report

When the auditor concludes that the specialist's findings support the particular assertions in the financial statements, the third standard of fieldwork has been satisfied. An unqualified opinion, without reference to the work of the specialist, can be expressed.

§336 • Using the Work of a Specialist

On the other hand, when the findings of the specialist do not support the relevant assertions in the financial statements, the auditor should perform additional procedures to try to resolve the problem. If the auditor cannot resolve the issue by performing additional procedures or obtaining the services of another specialist, the auditor must determine whether the circumstance is (1) a deviation from GAAP or (2) a scope limitation.

A deviation from GAAP arises when the auditor concludes that the relevant assertions in the financial statements are not supported by findings of the specialist and by other procedures (perhaps including the work of another specialist) that the auditor may perform. Under this circumstance, the auditor should express either a qualified opinion or an adverse opinion on the financial statements.

A scope limitation arises when the auditor concludes that the performance of additional audit procedures would not provide a reasonable basis for either substantiating or refuting the relevant assertions in the financial statements. Under this circumstance, the auditor should either express a qualified opinion or disclaim an opinion on the financial statements.

SAS-73 concludes that, generally, the auditor's report, whether unqualified or modified, should not make reference to the findings of a specialist, because the reference may be interpreted as (1) a qualification or (2) an attempt to divide the responsibility for the report between the auditor and the specialist. However, SAS-73 allows the auditor to add explanatory language to an unqualified report or a modified report if "the auditor believes such reference will facilitate an understanding of the reason for the explanatory paragraph or the departure from the unqualified opinion." Thus, the auditor may decide to express an unqualified opinion and add an explanatory paragraph (after the opinion paragraph but with no reference in the opinion paragraph to the explanatory paragraph) that refers to the findings of a specialist. In addition, the auditor may decide to express an opinion that is other than unqualified, and the paragraph that describes the basis for the report modification could then refer to the findings of a specialist. In each circumstance, the explanatory paragraph may refer to and identify the specialist.

If applicable, consider using the work of a specialist to determine whether there has been a transfer of financial assets as defined by FAS-125

FAS-125 (Accounting for Transfers and Servicing of Financial Assets and Extinguishments of Liabilities) requires that the transfer of financial assets must satisfy the following condition in order for the transaction to be accounted for as a sale:

> The transferred assets have been isolated from the transferor—put presumptively beyond the reach of the transferor and its creditors, even in bankruptcy or other receivership.

An Audit Interpretation (February 1998) concludes that determining whether the above condition (the isolation criterion) has been satisfied is "largely a matter of law." The Interpretation addresses the circumstances under which it may be appropriate to use the work of a specialist to make that determination. The Interpretation notes that the need for the work of a specialist generally depends on the complexity of the transaction. For example, a specialist may not be necessary when "there is a routine transfer of financial assets that does not result in any continuing involvement by the transfer." On the other hand, when the transfer involves "complicated legal structures, continuing involvement by the transferor, or other legal issues" it may be appropriate to use the work of a specialist to determine whether the isolation criterion exists.

When the auditor concludes that the services of a specialist should be used, the following factors may be considered in evaluating the work of the specialist according to the Interpretation:

- The legal experience of the specialist in the area (including exposure to the U.S. Bankruptcy Code and other relevant statutes)
- The assumptions the specialist uses to form a reasoned legal opinion on the matter
- The performance of appropriate tests on relevant information that has been provided to the specialist by management

> **RISK ASSESSMENT POINT:** The Interpretation notes that the specialist's work is usually expressed "in the form of a reasoned legal opinion that is restricted to particular facts and circumstances relevant to the specific transaction." If the auditor concludes that the legal opinion provided by the specialist is inadequate or inappropriate, the auditor must determine how the audit report should be modified.

SECTION 337

INQUIRY OF A CLIENT'S LAWYER CONCERNING LITIGATION, CLAIMS, AND ASSESSMENTS

Authoritative Pronouncements

SAS-12—Inquiry of a Client's Lawyer Concerning Litigation, Claims and Assessments

Auditing Interpretation (March 1977)—Specifying Relevant Date in an Audit Inquiry Letter

Auditing Interpretation (March 1977)—Relationship Between Date of Lawyer's Response and Auditor's Report

Auditing Interpretation (March 1977)—Form of Audit Inquiry Letter When Client Represents That No Unasserted Claims and Assessments Exist

Auditing Interpretation (March 1977)—Documents Subject to Lawyer–Client Privilege

Auditing Interpretation (June 1983)—Alternative Wording of the Illustrative Audit Inquiry Letter to a Client Lawyer

Auditing Interpretation (June 1983)—Client Has Not Consulted a Lawyer

Auditing Interpretation (February 1997)—Assessment of a Lawyer's Evaluation of the Outcome of Litigation

Auditing Interpretation (June 1983)—Use of the Client's Inside Counsel in the Evaluation of Litigation, Claims, and Assessments

Auditing Interpretation (February 1990)—Use of Explanatory Language About the Attorney-Client Privilege or the Attorney Work-Product Privilege

Auditing Interpretation (January 1997)—Use of Explanatory Language Concerning Unasserted Possible Claims or Assessments in Lawyer's Response to Audit Inquiry Letters

Overview

SAS-12 provides guidance for the collection of evidential matter to determine whether litigation, claims, and assessments have been properly reflected in the financial statements in accordance with generally accepted accounting principles (GAAP). Financial reporting standards with respect to litigation, claims, and assessments were established by FAS-5 (Accounting for Contingencies). FAS-5 requires that a loss contingency be accrued if (1) information available before the issuance of the financial statements indicates that it is probable that an asset had been impaired or a liability incurred at the date of the financial statements and (2) the amount of loss can be reasonably estimated. If these two conditions are not both met but there is a reasonable possibility that a loss or an additional loss may be incurred, the loss contingency must be disclosed in the financial statements, usually in a note.

Promulgated Procedures Checklist

The auditor should perform the following procedures with respect to the identification of litigation, claims and assessments:

_____ Identify litigation, claims, and assessments that may have to be accrued or disclosed in the financial statements.

_____ Obtain a letter of audit inquiry from the client's lawyer.

_____ Consider whether it is appropriate to accept oral representations made by the client's lawyer.

_____ Determine the effect on the audit report when the client's lawyer does not respond to the letter of audit inquiry.

Analysis and Application of Procedures

Identify litigation, claims, and assessments that may have to be accrued or disclosed in the financial statements

Although the point is not explicitly stated, SAS-12 recognizes that the auditor lacks the expertise to evaluate litigation, claims, and assessments in the context of the financial reporting requirements established by FAS-5. For this reason, the auditor must rely a great deal on the client's lawyer. It is the auditor's responsibility to collect evidential matter (1) to identify circumstances that may result in a loss contingency, (2) to identify the period in which the event occurred that may lead to the loss contingency, (3) to support the probability of the loss, and (4) to support the estimated amount of the loss or the estimated range of the loss. To achieve these audit objectives, the auditor should employ the following procedures:

§337 • Inquiry of a Client's Lawyer

- Obtain a list and evaluation of litigation, claims, and assessments from the client.
- Obtain a representation from the client, preferably in writing, that FAS-5 requirements have been observed with respect to litigation, claims, and assessments.
- Examine documents relative to legal liability matters, including correspondence and invoices from lawyers.
- Obtain from the client a statement in writing that the client has disclosed unasserted claims that the lawyer believes will probably be asserted.
- After obtaining permission from the client, notify the client's lawyer that the client has made the assurances described immediately above. Notification may be in the form of a separate letter or as part of the letter of audit inquiry.
- Send letters of inquiry to lawyers who have been consulted concerning legal matters.
- Read contracts, loan agreements, leases, and correspondence from taxing authorities.
- Obtain information from banks concerning loan agreements.
- Review other documents for possible guarantees the client has made.

> **PLANNING AID REMINDER:** The Auditing Interpretation (June 1983) titled "Client Has Not Consulted Lawyer" states that SAS-12 is expressly limited to inquiries of lawyers with whom management has consulted. If the client has not consulted a lawyer during the period, the auditor should rely on (1) the review of internal information available and (2) written representations from management stating it had not consulted a lawyer about litigation, claims, and assessments.
>
> **RISK ASSESSMENT POINT:** The Auditing Interpretation (March 1977) of SAS-12, titled "Documents Subject to Lawyer-Client Privilege," states that it is not necessary for the auditor to examine documents held by the client that are subject to the lawyer-client privilege.

Obtain a letter of audit inquiry from the client's lawyer

Representations that the client makes with respect to litigation, claims, and assessments must be substantiated by letters of audit inquiry to the client's lawyers. Letters of audit inquiry should be sent to those lawyers who have the primary responsibility for and knowledge about particular litigation, claims, and assessments. In some circumstances the client's in-house counsel will be the recipient of the letter and may provide the auditor with the necessary corroboration concerning litigation, claims, and assessments. A letter of audit inquiry typically would include, but is not limited to, the following matters:

1. Identification of the client and the date

2. A list that describes and evaluates pending and threatened litigation, claims, and assessments, prepared by management or legal counsel

3. A list prepared by management that describes and evaluates unasserted claims

4. A request that the lawyer reply directly to the independent auditor if his or her views differ from management's regarding item 2, above

5. A statement that the client understands that whenever its lawyer has formed a professional conclusion concerning a possible claim or assessment, the lawyer has so advised the client and has consulted with the client concerning the question of disclosure provided for by GAAP

6. A request that the lawyer confirm item 5, above

7. A request that the lawyer identify the nature of and reasons for any limitation in his or her response

Exhibit AU 337-1, which is taken from Appendix A of SAS-12, illustrates an audit inquiry letter to legal counsel.

Exhibit AU 337-2, which is based on the Auditing Interpretation (June 1983) titled "Alternative Wording of the Illustrative Audit Inquiry Letter to a Client's Lawyer," illustrates an audit inquiry letter whereby management has requested that the lawyer prepare the list of pending or threatened litigation, claims, and assessments.

The Auditing Interpretation (January 1997) titled "Use of Explanatory Language Concerning Unasserted Possible Claims or Assessments in Lawyer's Response to Audit Inquiry Letters" notes that some lawyers include the following or similar language in their response to the auditor's letter of inquiry:

> Please be advised that, pursuant to clauses (b) and (c) of Paragraph 5 of the ABA Statement of Policy (American Bar Association's Statement of Policy Regarding Lawyers' Responses to Auditors' Requests for Information) and the related Commen-

§337 • Inquiry of a Client's Lawyer

tary referred to in the last paragraph of this letter, it would be inappropriate for this firm to respond to a general inquiry relating to the existence of unasserted possible claims or assessments involving the Company. We can only furnish information concerning those unasserted possible claims or assessments upon which the Company has specifically requested in writing that we comment. We also cannot comment upon the adequacy of the Company's listing, if any, of unasserted possible claims or assessments or its assertions concerning the advice, if any, about the need to disclose same.

The Interpretation notes that inclusion of this type of language does not limit the scope of the audit engagement.

> **ENGAGEMENT STRATEGY:** The Auditing Interpretation (June 1983) titled "Use of the Client's Inside Counsel in the Evaluation of Litigation, Claims, and Assessments" notes that audit inquiry letters "should be sent to those lawyers, which may be either inside counsel or outside lawyers, who have the primary responsibility for, and knowledge about, particular litigation, claims and assessments."

Consider whether it is appropriate to accept oral representations made by the client's lawyer

Under special circumstances, the lawyer may make representations orally. For example, the details and accounting implications of complex litigation may best be evaluated in a conference attended by the client, the lawyer, and the auditor.

> **RISK ASSESSMENT POINT:** Another Interpretation (March 1977) of SAS-12, titled "Specifying Relevant Date in an Audit Inquiry Letter," states that the audit inquiry letter to a client's attorney should specify (1) the earliest acceptable effective date of the attorney's response and (2) the latest date for return to the auditor. A two-week period between the dates is recommended. If the attorney does not specify an effective date of the response, the effective date is assumed to be the date of the response. Another Interpretation (March 1977), "Relationship Between Date of Lawyer's Response and Auditor's Report," recommends that the effective date requested in a letter to the client's attorney be as close as possible to the date of the auditor's report.

> **PLANNING AID REMINDER:** The Interpretation (February 1990) of SAS-12 titled "Use of Explanatory Language About

the Attorney-Client Privilege or the Attorney Work-Product Privilege" notes that some clients state in their letter of audit inquiry that the letter is not intended to infringe on the attorney-client privilege or the attorney work-product privilege. Likewise, legal counsel's response to the letter may state that counsel has been advised by the client that the request for information is not intended to waive the privileged relationship with the client. Such comments in the client letter of audit inquiry or counsel's response to the letter do not result in a limitation of the scope of an audit.

Determine the effect on the audit report when the client's lawyer does not respond to the letter of audit inquiry

Under some circumstances a lawyer may not respond to the auditor's letter of audit inquiry. If the lawyer decides not to respond, there is a scope limitation, and the auditor should issue a qualified opinion or a disclaimer of opinion. When the lawyer cannot reasonably respond to the letter because of significant uncertainties surrounding the possible outcome of a certain legal matter, there is an uncertainty, and the auditor's report should be so modified.

> **ENGAGEMENT STRATEGY:** The Interpretation (June 1983) of SAS-12 titled "Assessment of a Lawyer's Evaluation of the Outcome of Litigation" states that when the auditor is uncertain about the meaning of the lawyer's evaluation of litigation, claims, or assessments, he or she should request clarification either in a follow-up letter or in a conference with the client and lawyer. The clarification should be adequately documented in the auditor's workpapers.
>
> **RISK ASSESSMENT POINT:** The lawyer's response to the auditor's letter of audit inquiry should be addressed to the auditor, should apply to circumstances that existed from the date of the balance sheet through the auditor's report date, and should have an effective date within two or three weeks of the report date.

Practitioner's Aids

EXHIBIT AU 337-1—ILLUSTRATIVE AUDIT INQUIRY LETTER TO LEGAL COUNSEL

In connection with an audit of our financial statements at [*balance sheet date*] and for the [*period*] then ended, management of the Company has prepared, and furnished to our auditors [*name and address of auditors*], a description and evaluation of certain contingencies, including those set forth below involving matters with respect to which you have been engaged and to which you have devoted substantive attention on behalf of the Company in the form of legal consultation or representation. These contingencies are regarded by management of the Company as material for this purpose [*management may indicate a materiality limit if an understanding has been reached with the auditor*]. Your response should include matters that existed at [*balance sheet date*] and during the period from that date to the date of your response.

Pending or Threatened Litigation [excluding unasserted claims]

[Ordinarily the information would include the following: (1) the nature of the litigation, (2) the progress of the case to date, (3) how management is responding or intends to respond to the litigation (for example, to contest the case vigorously or to seek an out-of-court settlement), and (4) an evaluation of the likelihood of an unfavorable outcome and an estate, if one can be made, of the amount or range of potential loss.]

Please furnish to our auditors such explanation, if any, that you consider necessary to supplement the foregoing information, including an explanation of those matters as to which your views may differ from those stated and an identification of the omission of any pending or threatened litigation, claims, and assessments or a statement that the list of such matters is complete.

Unasserted Claims and Assessments [considered by management to be probable of assertion and that, if asserted, would have at least a reasonable possibility of an unfavorable outcome]

[Ordinarily, management's information would include the following: (1) the nature of the matter, (2) how management intends to respond if the claim is asserted, and (3) an evaluation of the likelihood of an unfavorable outcome and an estimate, if one can be made, of the amount or range of potential loss.]

Please furnish to our auditors such explanation, if any, that you consider necessary to supplement the foregoing information, including an explanation of those matters as to which your views may differ from those stated.

We understand that whenever, in the course of performing legal services for us with respect to a matter recognized to involve an unasserted possible claim or assessment that may call for financial statement disclosure, if you have formed a professional conclusion that we should disclose or consider disclosure concerning such possible claim or assessment, as a matter of professional responsibility to us, you will so advise us and will consult with us concerning the question of such disclosure and the applicable requirements of Statement of Financial Accounting Standards No. 5. Please specifically confirm to our auditors that our understanding is correct.

Please specifically identify the nature of and reasons for any limitation on your response.

[The auditor may request the client to inquire about additional matters—for example, unpaid or unbilled charges—or specified information on certain contractually assumed obligations of the company, such as guarantees or indebtedness of others.]

> **PLANNING AID REMINDER:** The Interpretation (March 1977) titled "Form of Audit Inquiry Letter When Client Represents That No Unasserted Claims and Assessments Exist" notes that when the client believes there are no unasserted claims or assessments to be identified that are probable of assertion and that, if asserted, would have a reasonable possibility of an unfavorable outcome, that section of the letter may be replaced with the following:
>
>> *Unasserted claims and assessments*—We have represented to our auditors that there are no unasserted possible claims that you have advised us are probable of assertion and must be disclosed, in accordance with Statement of Financial Accounting Standards No. 5. The second paragraph in the letter illustrated above would not be changed.

EXHIBIT AU 337-2—ILLUSTRATIVE AUDIT INQUIRY LETTER TO LEGAL COUNSEL WHEREBY MANAGEMENT HAS REQUESTED THAT THE LAWYER PREPARE THE LIST OF PENDING OR THREATENED LITIGATION, CLAIMS, AND ASSESSMENTS

In connection with an audit of our financial statements as of [*balance sheet date*] and for the [*period*] then ended, please furnish our auditors, [*name and address of auditors*], with the information requested below concerning certain contingencies involving matters with respect to which you have devoted substantive attention on behalf of the Company in the form of legal consultation or representation. [When a materiality limit has been established based on an understanding between management and the auditor, the following sentence should be added: This request is limited to contingencies amount to (amount) individually or items involving lesser amounts that exceed (amount) in the aggregate.]

Pending or Threatened Litigation, Claims, and Assessments

Regarding pending or threatened litigation, claims, and assessments, please include in your response (1) the nature of each matter; (2) the progress of each matter to date; (3) how the Company is responding or intends to respond (for example, to contest the case vigorously or seek an out-of-court settlement); and (4) an evaluation of the likelihood of an unfavorable outcome and an estimate, if one can be made, of the amount or range or potential loss.

Unasserted Claims and Assessments

We have represented to our auditors that there are no unasserted possible claims or assessments that you have advised us are probable of assertion and must be disclosed in accordance with FASB Statement No. 5. We understand that whenever, in the course of performing legal services for us with respect to a matter recognized to involve an unasserted possible claim or assessment that may call for financial statement disclosure, you have formed a professional conclusion that we should disclose or consider disclosure concerning such possible claim or assessment, as a matter of professional responsibility to us, you will so advise us and will consult with us concerning the question of such disclosure and the applicable requirements of FASB Statement No. 5. Please specifically confirm to our auditors that our understanding is correct.

Other Matters

Your response should include matters that existed as of [*balance-sheet date*] and during the period from that date to the effective date of your response.

Please specifically identify the nature of and reasons for any limitations on your response.

Our auditors expect to have the audit completed about [*expected completion date*]. They would appreciate receiving your reply by that date with a specified effective date no earlier than [*ordinarily two weeks before expected completion date*].

SECTION 339

WORKING PAPERS

Authoritative Pronouncements

SAS-41—Working Papers

Auditing Interpretation (June 1996)—Providing Access to, or Photocopies of, Working Papers to a Regulator

> **OBSERVATION:** The AICPA has issued an Exposure Draft that would replace SAS-41. The ED requires that audit documentation should "(a) enable a reviewer with relevant knowledge and experience to understand from the information contained therein the nature, timing, extent, and results of auditing procedure performed, and the evidence obtained, and (b) indicate the engagement team member(s) who performed and reviewed the work." In addition, the ED proposes specific documentation requirements for several other existing SASs.

Overview

The work performed and the conclusions reached by the auditor should be adequately documented in the audit workpapers. The actual quantity and nature of the workpapers for any particular engagement will differ depending on the specific circumstances of the engagement. The following circumstances may have an effect on the content of workpapers:

- Nature of engagement
- Nature of auditor's report
- Nature of financial data subject to auditor's report, including the financial statements, schedules, and other financial information
- Nature and condition of client's records
- Assessed level of control risk
- Degree of supervision and review required

> **PLANNING AID REMINDER:** Workpapers are the property of the auditor, and appropriate procedures should be established to protect the confidentiality of the information. Workpapers should be retained for a period that meets legal requirements and meets the needs of the auditor.

Promulgated Procedures Checklist

The auditor should observe the following procedures with respect to workpapers for an audit engagement:

§339 • Working Papers

_____ Develop workpapers that demonstrate that the standards of fieldwork have been observed.

_____ If applicable, provide regulators with access to the workpapers.

Analysis and Application of Procedures

Develop workpapers that demonstrate that the standards of fieldwork have been observed

In general, workpapers must demonstrate that the three standards of fieldwork have been achieved and that the accounting records agree or reconcile with the financial statements being reported on. Workpapers may include memos, audit programs, flowcharts, completed internal control questionnaires, confirmations, and other documents that demonstrate the accumulation of evidence by the auditor. Finally, workpapers are an essential product of an audit. They aid in the control of an engagement and serve as a basis for performing a review of the work completed.

With respect to the second standard of fieldwork, proper documentation would include completed internal control questionnaires, flowcharts, narrative descriptions, and audit programs. An important concept of the second standard of fieldwork is the effect of the study and assessment of control risk on the nature, timing, and extent of substantive testing. It is therefore advisable that an auditor prepare so-called bridging workpapers. This type of workpaper typically includes headings (1) for the identification of weaknesses, (2) for the possible effect on the financial statements, and (3) for the impact on subsequent audit procedures. The bridging workpapers should also identify strengths in the system that may permit the auditor to curtail some audit procedures.

Although SAS-41 does not attempt to prescribe the detailed content of an auditor's workpapers, it should be remembered that some SASs require that certain items be included in the auditor's workpapers. These requirements and related standards are listed below:

- Letter of inquiry sent to the client's lawyer [SAS-12 (AU 337) (Inquiry of a Client's Lawyer Concerning Litigation, Claims, and Assessments) superseded by SAS-85 (Management Representation)]

- Client representation letters [SAS-19 (Client Representations) superseded by SAS-85 (Management Representations)]

- Notation in the workpapers, or a copy of the written communication sent to the client, that describes reportable conditions in the internal control [SAS-60 (AU 325) (Communication of Internal Control Related Matters Noted in an Audit)]

- Written audit programs [SAS-22 (AU 311) (Planning and Supervision)]
- Understanding of internal control [(SAS-55 (AU 319) (Consideration of the Internal Control in a Financial Statement Audit)]
- Oral communication of illegal acts [SAS-54 (AU 317) (Illegal Acts by Clients)]
- Oral communication to an audit committee [SAS-61 (AU 380) (Communication with Audit Committees)]
- Explanation of why accounts receivable were not confirmed [SAS-67 (AU 330) (The Confirmation Process)]

If applicable, provide regulators with access to the workpapers

Although workpapers are the property of the auditor, governmental regulators may have the right to them based on law, regulation, or the audit contract. An Auditing Interpretation (July 1994) of SAS-41 titled "Providing Access to or Photocopies of Working Papers to a Regulator" states that when regulators have requested access to workpapers, the auditor should observe the following guidance:

- Consider notifying the client that regulators have requested access to the workpapers, and state that the auditor intends to comply with the request.
- Make arrangements (time, date, place, etc.) with the regulators concerning access to the workpapers.
- Establish procedures that allow the auditor to maintain control over the workpapers.

In addition to the above procedures, the auditor should consider sending a letter to the regulatory agency (probably requesting a signed acknowledgment of receipt of the letter) that explains the role of the auditor and the nature of the workpapers. (Exhibit AU 339-1 is an example of such a letter.) The auditor should not agree to transfer the ownership of the workpapers to the regulatory agency.

When a regulatory agency requests the auditor's workpapers but there is no legal basis for the request (no applicable law, regulation, or audit contract requirement), the auditor should evaluate the purpose for the request. That evaluation may include consultation with legal counsel. If the auditor agrees with the request, the auditor should obtain permission for access to the workpapers from the client (preferably in writing). In some instances the client may request an inspection of the workpapers before granting the regulatory agency access to them. If the auditor agrees to the client's request, the auditor should maintain control over the workpapers.

Some regulatory agencies may hire a third party to inspect workpapers. Under this circumstance, the auditor should follow the same procedures that would apply if the regulatory agency itself were inspecting the workpapers. In addition, the auditor should obtain from the regulatory agency a statement (preferably in writing) that the third party is "acting on behalf of the regulator and agreement from the third party that he or she is subject to the same restriction on disclosure and use of workpapers and the information contained therein as the regulator."

> **RISK ASSESSMENT POINT:** The guidance established by the Interpretation does not apply to requests from (1) the Internal Revenue Service, (2) peer review programs (and similar programs) established by the AICPA or state societies of CPAs, (3) proceedings arising from alleged violations of ethical standards, or (4) subpoenas.

Practitioner's Aids

Exhibit AU 339-1 is an example of a letter that may be sent to a regulatory agency when that agency requests access to the auditor's workpapers.

EXHIBIT AU 339-1—LETTER FOR REGULATORY AGENCY THAT REQUESTS ACCESS TO AUDIT WORKPAPERS

Your representatives have requested access to our workpapers in connection with our audit of the December 31, 20X5, financial statements of X Company. It is our understanding that the purpose of your request is to facilitate your regulatory examination.

Our audit of X Company's December 31, 20X5, financial statements was conducted in accordance with generally accepted auditing standards, the objective of which is to form an opinion on whether the financial statements, which are the responsibility and representations of management, present fairly, in all material respects, the financial position, results of operations and cash flows in conformity with generally accepted accounting principles. Under generally accepted auditing standards, we have the responsibility, within the inherent limitations of the auditing process, to design our audit to provide reasonable assurance the errors and fraud that have a material effect on the financial statements will be detected, and to exercise due care in the conduct of our audit. The concept of selective testing of the data being audited, which involves judgment both as to the number of transactions to be audited and as to the areas to be tested, has been generally accepted as a valid and sufficient basis for an auditor to express an opinion on financial statements. Thus, our audit, based on the concept of selective testing, is subject to the inherent risk that material errors or fraud, if they exist, would not be detected. In addition, an audit does not address the possibility that material errors or fraud may occur in the future. Also, our use of professional judgment and the assessment of materiality for the purpose of our audit means that matters may have existed that would have been assessed differently by you.

The workpapers were prepared for the purpose of providing the principal support for our report on X Company's December 31, 20X5, financial statements and to aid in the conduct and supervision of our audit. The workpapers document the procedures performed, the information obtained, and the pertinent conclusions reached in the engagement. The audit procedures that we performed were limited to those we considered necessary under generally accepted auditing standards to enable us to formulate and express an opinion on the financial statements taken as a whole. Accordingly, we make no representation as to the sufficiency or appropriateness, for your purposes, of either the information contained in our workpapers or our audit procedures. In addition, any notations, comments, and individual conclusions appearing on any of the workpapers do not stand alone, and should not be read as an opinion on any individual amounts, accounts, balances, or transactions.

Our audit of X Company's December 31, 20X5, financial statements was performed for the purpose stated above and has not been planned or conducted in contemplation of your regulatory examination or for the purpose of assessing X Company's compliance with laws and regulations. Therefore, items of possible interest to you may not have been specifically addressed. Accordingly, our audit and the workpapers prepared in connection therewith should not supplant other inquiries and procedures that should be undertaken by the [*name of regulatory agency*] for the purpose of monitoring and regulating the financial affairs of X Company. In addition, we have not audited any financial statements of X Company since December 31, 20X5, nor have we performed any audit procedures since February 22, 20X6, the date of our auditor's report, and significant events or circumstances may have occurred since that date.

The workpapers constitute and reflect work performed or information obtained by [*name of CPA firm*] in its capacity as independent auditor for X Company. The documents contain trade secrets and confidential commercial and financial information of our firm and X Company that is privileged and confidential, and we expressly reserve all rights with respect to disclosures to third parties. Accordingly, we request confidential treatment under the Freedom of Information Act or similar laws and regulations when requests are made for the workpapers or information contained therein or any documents created by the [*name of regulatory agency*] containing information derived therefrom. We further request that written notice be given to our firm before distribution of the information in the workpapers (or photocopies thereof) to others, including other governmental agencies, except when such distribution is required by law or regulation.

The above illustrative letter should be appropriately modified to reflect the circumstances of the engagement. Some of the modifications that may be needed include the following:

- When the audit has been conducted in accordance with GAAS and other established auditing procedures (such as generally accepted governmental auditing standards), the letter should be appropriately modified.

- When the audit was conducted in accordance with the Single Audit Act of 1984, and other federal audit requirements, the letter should be modified to explain the object of the audit.

- When the letter is sent to the regulatory agency at the request of management (rather than by law, regulation, or audit contract), the letter should state that "the management of X Company has authorized us to provide you access to our workpapers in order to facilitate your regulatory examination."

- When the financial statements are based on regulatory accounting principles, the letter should be appropriately modified.

- When the regulatory agency has asked for photocopies of the workpapers, the letter should state that "any photocopies of our workpapers we agree to provide you will be identified as 'Confidential Treatment Request by [*name of auditor, address, telephone number*].'"

- When the audit engagement has not been completed, the letter should be modified to describe that fact and to put the regulatory agency on guard that the workpapers may change based on the performance of additional audit procedures (generally, the auditor should not agree to supply the regulatory agency with incomplete workpapers).

SECTION 341

THE AUDITOR'S CONSIDERATION OF AN ENTITY'S ABILITY TO CONTINUE AS A GOING CONCERN

Authoritative Pronouncements

SAS-59—The Auditor's Consideration of an Entity's Ability to Continue as a Going Concern

Auditing Interpretation (August 1995)—Eliminating a Going Concern Explanatory Paragraph from a Reissued Report

Overview

Financial statements are usually prepared on the assumption that the entity will continue as a going concern. When a company decides or is forced to liquidate, the going-concern concept is not appropriate, and assets should be presented at their estimated net realizable values and legally enforceable liabilities should be classified according to priorities established by law.

SAS-59 (The Auditor's Consideration of an Entity's Ability to Continue as a Going Concern) concludes that as part of an examination, the auditor should evaluate conditions or events discovered during the engagement that raise questions about the appropriateness of the going-concern concept. The auditor may identify such conditions or events at various points during the engagement, including during the performance of analytical procedures, when reading of responses received from the entity's legal counsel, and when evaluating the entity's compliance with restrictions imposed by loan agreements.

> **PLANNING AID REMINDER:** Information that raises questions about going concern generally relates to the entity's ability to meet its maturing obligations without selling operating assets, restructuring debt, or revising operations based on outside pressures or similar strategies. SAS-59 concludes that the projection of the going-concern concept is limited to a "reasonable period of time," which is defined as not exceeding one year beyond the date of the audited financial statements.

Promulgated Procedures Checklist

The auditor should perform the following procedures when considering an entity's ability to continue as a going concern:

§341 • Entity's Ability to Continue as a Going Concern

_____ Evaluate relevant information obtained during the course of the engagement.

_____ Identify and evaluate management's plans related to going concern.

_____ Consider the effect of the evidence on disclosures and the audit report.

Analysis and Application of Procedures

Evaluate relevant information obtained during the course of the engagement

Although not specifically required to employ procedures to identify conditions or events that might raise a substantial-doubt question, the auditor should be sensitive to evidential matter collected and implications relative to going concern.

SAS-59 provides the examples in Exhibit AU 341-1 as conditions and events that may raise a substantial-doubt question.

EXHIBIT AU 341-1— CONDITIONS AND EVENTS THAT MAY RAISE A SUBSTANTIAL-DOUBT QUESTION

Condition or Event	Specific Example
Negative trends	• Recurring operating losses • Working capital deficiencies • Negative cash flows from operations • Adverse key financial ratios
Other indications of possible agreements	• Default on loan or similar financial difficulties • Arrearages in dividends
Other indications of possible financial difficulties	• Denial of usual trade credit from vendors • Restructuring of debt • Noncompliance with statutory capital requirements • Need to seek new sources of financing • Need to sell substantial assets

Condition or Event	Specific Example
Internal matters	• Labor difficulties, such as work stoppages • Substantial dependence on the success of a particular project • Uneconomic long-term commitments • Need to significantly revise operations
External matters or similar matters that might affect the entity's ability to continue operations	• Legal proceedings, legislation • Loss of key franchise, license, or patent • Loss of principal customer or vendor • Occurrence of uninsured catastrophe

When the evidential matter raises a substantial-doubt question, the auditor may obtain additional evidence that may remove the question of substantial doubt.

Identify and evaluate management's plans related to going concern

If the auditor concludes that there is substantial doubt about the continued existence of the entity as a going concern for a reasonable period of time, he or she should identify and evaluate management's plans to mitigate the effects of the adverse conditions or events. SAS-59 identifies the examples in Exhibit AU 341-2 as plans and factors that are relevant to the evaluation of those plans.

EXHIBIT AU 341-2—PLANS AND FACTORS RELEVANT TO THE EVALUATION OF MANAGEMENT'S PLANS

Planned Action	Factors Relevant to Evaluation of Planned Action
Sale of assets	• Restrictions on the sale of assets • Likely marketability of assets • Effects from sale of assets

Planned Action	Factors Relevant to Evaluation of Planned Action
Borrow or restructure debt	• Likelihood of raising funds based on existing or committed debt arrangements • Existing or committed arrangements for restructuring debt or obtaining guarantees for loans • Restrictions on ability to borrow or use assets as collateral
Reduce or delay expenditures	• Feasibility of reducing or postponing expenditures • Effects of reducing or postponing expenditures
Increase ownership equity	• Feasibility of increasing equity based on existing or committed arrangements • Flexibility of dividend policy • Ability to raise funds from affiliates or other investors

The auditor should consider obtaining evidential matter to support planned actions that are significant to the substantial-doubt question.

Some management strategies may in part be evaluated through the auditor's investigation of management's prospective financial statements. The specific audit procedures that the auditor may employ include the following:

- Read the prospective financial statements.

- Identify fundamental assumptions used to prepare the prospective financial statements.

- Evaluate the prospective financial statements on the basis of the auditor's familiarity with the client's operations.

- Compare the prospective financial statements for prior periods with actual results.

- Compare the prospective financial statements for the current period with actual results to date.

During the evaluation of fundamental assumptions used to prepare the prospective financial statements, the auditor should direct special emphasis to the following assumptions:

- Assumptions that have a material effect on the prospective financial statements
- Assumptions that have a high degree of uncertainty
- Assumptions that are inconsistent with past patterns

> **RISK ASSESSMENT POINT:** If the auditor discovers material factors that are not reflected in the preparation of the prospective financial statements, such discoveries should be discussed with management with the understanding that the statements may have to be revised.

Consider the effect of the evidence on disclosures and the audit report

Once the auditor has evaluated management's strategies designed to mitigate the adverse effects of conditions or events that raise a question about continued existence, the auditor must determine whether substantial doubt exists about the going-concern concept.

If substantial doubt does not exist, there is no need to modify the auditor's report. However, the auditor should consider whether the conditions or events that originally created the question about going concern should be disclosed in the financial statements. The disclosure might include the possible effect of the conditions or events and mitigating factors (including management's plans).

If the auditor concludes that substantial doubt exists, the effects of conditions or events should be considered as they relate to (1) adequate disclosures in the financial statements and (2) modification to the auditor's report.

Adequate disclosures

If the auditor concludes that substantial doubt exists about the client's ability to continue in existence, care must be taken to ensure that presentations and related disclosures in the financial statements properly reflect the (1) recoverability and classification of assets and (2) amount and classification of liabilities. In addition, the auditor should consider whether disclosures related to the possible discontinuation of operations are adequate in the financial statements. SAS-59 notes that the disclosure might include the following:

§341 • Entity's Ability to Continue as a Going Concern

- Conditions or events that gave rise to the substantial doubt concerning continued existence
- Possible effects of the conditions or events
- Management's assessments concerning the significance of the conditions or events
- Other factors that may aggravate or mitigate the conditions or events
- Management's strategies that will attempt to deal with the adverse conditions or events
- Possible discontinuance of operations

> **ENGAGEMENT STRATEGY:** The financial statement effects described above are relevant when there is substantial doubt about continued existence. If the auditor concludes that the going-concern concept is not applicable, the financial statements must be prepared on a liquidation basis. Guidance for reporting on liquidation-based financial statements can be found in the Auditing Interpretation (December 1984) titled "Reporting on Financial Statements Prepared on a Liquidation Basis of Accounting."

Report modifications

If an auditor concludes that substantial doubt exists about the continued existence of the client, the audit report should be modified by adding an explanatory paragraph. When the auditor believes that the financial statements can still be relied on, the report modification is limited to a reference to the going-concern matter in the report, but the opinion expressed is unqualified.

The substantial-doubt question is discussed in an explanatory paragraph following the opinion paragraph. SAS-64 (AU 341, AU 508, AU 543) (Omnibus Statement on Auditing Standards—1990) requires that the explanatory paragraph include the phrase "substantial doubt about its [the entity's] ability to continue as a going concern," or similar wording. If similar wording is used, the terms "substantial doubt" and "going concern" must be used in the phrase.

When an auditor concludes that there is substantial doubt about an entity's ability to continue as a going concern, the audit report should not use language that suggests that the conclusion is conditional on future events. Specifically, SAS-77 (AU 311, AU 341, AU 623) notes that the use of conditional terminology—such as "if the company is unable to obtain refinancing, there may be substantial doubt about the company's ability to continue as a going concern"—is precluded.

The introductory, scope, and opinion paragraphs make no reference to the explanatory paragraph. An example of an explanatory paragraph based on a substantial-doubt question is presented below:

> The accompanying financial statements have been prepared assuming that the Company will continue as a going concern. As discussed in Note X to the financial statements, the Company is involved in litigation concerning alleged patent infringement. Because operations of the Company could be substantially impeded if the charges are upheld, the pending litigation raises substantial doubt about its ability to continue as a going concern. Management's plans in regard to the litigation are also described in Note X. The financial statements do not include any adjustments that might result from the outcome of this uncertainty.

> **ENGAGEMENT STRATEGY:** An auditor can no longer express a "subject to" qualified opinion because of an uncertainty.

When the auditor concludes that the uncertainty related to the substantial-doubt question is so significant that an opinion cannot be expressed on the financial statements, a disclaimer of opinion may be expressed.

The modification of the auditor's report because of a substantial-doubt question in the current year does not imply that the auditor's report on a prior year's financial statements (presented on a comparative basis) should also be modified.

During the current year, a question of substantial doubt contained in an auditor's report on a prior year's financial statements may no longer be applicable. Under this circumstance, the explanatory paragraph should not be repeated in the auditor's report on the comparative financial statements.

> **ENGAGEMENT STRATEGY:** To *not* include the explanatory paragraph is not a change in the opinion expressed by the auditor; therefore, not including the paragraph does not require that the auditor observe the report guidelines established in SAS-58 concerning changes of opinions.

Although the auditor is responsible for including an explanatory paragraph in the auditor's report when a substantial-doubt question arises, the auditor is not responsible for predicting the outcome of future events. Thus, the liquidation of an entity (even within one year of the date of the financial statements) does not imply that the audit was substandard when an explanatory paragraph has not been included in the auditor's report. Similarly, the

§341 • Entity's Ability to Continue as a Going Concern

lack of including an explanatory paragraph in the auditor's report should not be taken as an assurance that the entity will continue as a going concern within a reasonable period of time.

SAS-77 (AU 311, AU 341, AU 623) prohibits the use of conditional language when a substantial-doubt explanatory paragraph is presented. Two examples of unacceptable language that are provided by SAS-77 (AU 311, AU 341, AU 623) are as follows:

> If the company continues to suffer recurring losses from operations and continues to have a net capital deficiency, there may be substantial doubt about its ability to continue as a going concern.
>
> The company has been unable to renegotiate its expiring credit agreements. Unless the company is able to obtain financial support, there is substantial doubt about its ability to continue as a going concern.

The going-concern paragraph should be included in subsequent auditor's reports as long as substantial doubt about the entity's existence continues. If the substantial-doubt condition ceases in a future period, there is no need to include the substantial-doubt explanatory paragraph for reports that cover previous periods in which the substantial-doubt condition was originally applicable.

> **RISK ASSESSMENT POINT:** SAS-59 does not discuss the conditions related to substantial doubt about an entity's ability to continue as a going concern that may lead to a disclaimer of opinion; however, it does note that nothing in the Statement is intended to preclude an auditor from declining to express an opinion in cases involving uncertainties.

After the auditor has issued a report that refers to a going-concern issue, the client may request the auditor to reissue the report and remove the going-concern reference because the client believes the circumstances that led to the uncertainty have been changed. Since the request by the client constitutes a new engagement, the auditor is not obligated to accept it. If the auditor accepts the engagement, the circumstances related to the going-concern issue should be examined to determine whether it is appropriate to revise the report.

The Auditing Interpretation (August 1995) titled "Eliminating a Going-Concern Explanatory Paragraph from a Reissued Report" notes that the auditor is not obligated to reissue a report; however, if the auditor decides to do so, he or she should perform the following procedures:

- Audit the event or transaction that prompted the request to delete the going-concern paragraph.
- Perform procedures related to subsequent events as described in AU 560.11–AU 560.12.
- Consider the factors related to the going-concern concept as described in AU 341.06–AU 341.11.

> **ENGAGEMENT STRATEGY:** In addition to the listed procedures, the auditor should conduct other procedures he or she deems appropriate. Based on the results of applying those procedures, the auditor should reassess the going-concern status of the client.

Practitioner's Aids

EXHIBIT AU 341-3—EVALUATING AN ENTITY'S ABILITY TO CONTINUE AS A GOING CONCERN

Use the following procedures, which are adapted from guidance found in SAS-59 (The Auditor's Consideration of an Entity's Ability to Continue as a Going Concern), as a guide for evaluating an entity's ability to continue as a going concern. The program is only a guide, and professional judgment should be exercised to determine how the guidance established should be adapted to a particular engagement.

Initial and date each procedure as it is completed. If the procedure is not relevant to this engagement, place "N/A" (not applicable) in the space provided for an initial.

Client Name: _____

Date of Financial Statements: _____

	Initials	Date	Workpaper Reference
1. Evaluate relevant information obtained during the course of the engagement.	_____	_____	_____
2. Identify and evaluate management's plans related to going concern.	_____	_____	_____
3. Consider the effect of the evidence on disclosures and the engagement report.	_____	_____	_____

	Initials	Date	Workpaper Reference

4. Consider whether the following disclosures in the financial statements are appropriate: _____ _____ _____

  - Factors that are the basis for raising the question of going concern _____ _____ _____

  - Possible effects on the financial statements of the factors that raised the question of going concern _____ _____ _____

  - Management's assessment of the significance of the factors and any mitigating circumstances _____ _____ _____

  - Possible discontinuance of operations _____ _____ _____

  - Management's plans to deal with the current circumstances (including relevant prospective information) _____ _____ _____

  - Information related to asset recoverability and classification and the amount and classification of liabilities _____ _____ _____

Other engagement procedures: _____

_____

_____

_____

Reviewed by: _____

Date: _____

OBSERVATION: If through performing other audit procedures the auditor identifies conditions and events that may raise questions about the entity's ability to continue as a going concern and management has not developed plans to address the issue, the Interpretation notes that the auditor ordinarily would conclude that doubts about the going-concern issue are valid and would consider modifying the auditor's report in a manner required by SAS-59.

SECTION 342

AUDITING ACCOUNTING ESTIMATES

Authoritative Pronouncements

SAS-57—Auditing Accounting Estimates

Auditing Interpretation (February 1993)—Performance and Reporting Guidance Related to Fair Value Disclosures

Overview

SAS-57 (Auditing Accounting Estimates) defines "accounting estimate" as "an approximation of a financial statement element, item, or account." Accounting estimates are made to measure past transactions or events (loss contingency arising from pending lawsuits) or to measure assets (net realizable value of accounts receivable) or liabilities (accrual related to warranty contracts).

It is management's responsibility to establish reasonable accounting estimates—by reviewing past experiences and evaluating these experiences in the context of current and expected future conditions. Thus, accounting estimates are based on both objective factors (past transactions and events) and subjective factors (projecting the likely outcome of future transactions and events). Although management is responsible for accounting estimates, the auditor must collect sufficient evidential matter to determine that accounting estimates are reasonable. Because of the uncertainty related to accounting estimates and the higher possibility of misstatement, an auditor must have a greater degree of skepticism when planning and performing procedures related to the audit of accounting estimates.

Management's internal control

As for all classes of transactions and events that affect the financial statements, management should adopt, either formally or informally, a process for developing accounting estimates. The process should include identifying circumstances that require accounting estimates, and collecting and evaluating information that leads to the development of reasonable accounting estimates.

Many factors, such as the availability of reliable data and the required complexity of the evaluation process, have an effect on the risk of material misstatement in the financial statements because of unreasonable accounting estimates. In addition, when assessing the risk factor for misstatement

§342 • Auditing Accounting Estimates

the auditor should consider the entity's internal control relating to the development of accounting estimates. The entity's internal control should include the following elements:

- Use of controls that allow the entity to identify circumstances requiring the development of accounting estimates
- Development of sufficient and reliable data
- Use of competent personnel
- Review and approval of accounting estimates by appropriate personnel (including the review of relevant factors and assumptions and the determination of whether there is a need for a specialist)
- Comparison of previous accounting estimates with actual results
- Determination that accounting estimates are consistent with management's plans

Promulgated Procedures Checklist

The auditor should perform the following procedures with respect to accounting estimates in an audit of a client's financial statements:

____ Determine whether all circumstances that give rise to accounting estimates have been identified by the entity.

____ Determine whether accounting estimates are reasonable.

____ Determine whether accounting estimates are presented in accordance with generally accepted accounting principles (GAAP).

____ Obtain sufficient evidential matter to support fair value disclosures.

Analysis and Application of Procedures

Determine whether all circumstances that give rise to accounting estimates have been identified by the entity

To determine whether the entity has identified all circumstances that require accounting estimates, the auditor should consider the entity's operating characteristics and the industry in general—including any new pronouncements that affect the industry. On the basis of a review of these factors, the auditor should consider performing the following procedures:

- Read the financial statements, and identify those assertions implied in the financial statements that may require an accounting estimate.
- Refer to evidence gathered in other parts of the engagement, including the following:
  — Changes made or contemplated by the entity or the industry that would affect the operations of the business
  — Changes made in the manner in which information is accumulated
  — Identified litigation and other contingencies
  — Relevant information contained in minutes of the board of directors, stockholders, and other significant committees
  — Relevant information contained in regulatory reports, supervisory correspondence, and similar information from relevant regulatory agencies
- Discuss with management situations that may require an accounting estimate.

Determine whether accounting estimates are reasonable

To determine which specific accounting estimates are reasonable, an auditor should concentrate on fundamental factors and assumptions that are material to an estimate and for which changes in the factor or assumption would have a significant effect on the accounting estimate. In addition, attention should be directed to factors and assumptions that are different from past patterns or that are highly subjective.

The audit approach should encompass an understanding of the entity's process for developing accounting estimates. Having gained such an understanding, the auditor should adopt one or a combination of the following approaches:

- Review and test the accounting estimation process.
- Develop an independent estimate.
- Review subsequent events or transactions.

Procedures that the auditor should consider when deciding to review and test the accounting estimation process include the following:

- Identify management controls and supporting data.
- Identify sources of data and factors used by management.

- Consider whether data and factors are relevant, reliable, and sufficient to support the estimate.
- Determine whether other factors or assumptions are appropriate.
- Determine if assumptions are internally consistent with other assumptions and supporting data.
- Determine that historical data used are comparable and consistent with data of the period under audit and that such data are reliable.
- Determine whether changes during the current period require that other factors be considered in developing assumptions.
- Review documentation supporting assumptions used to make accounting estimates.
- Inquire about other plans management may have adopted that could have an effect on assumptions related to accounting estimates.
- Determine whether a specialist is needed to evaluate assumptions.
- Recompute calculations made to convert assumptions and key factors into the accounting estimate.

The auditor may test the reasonableness of accounting estimates by making an independent calculation. In making the calculation, the auditor should use other factors or alternative assumptions that he or she considers relevant.

Finally, the auditor may decide to test the reasonableness of an accounting estimate by reviewing subsequent events or transactions that occur after the date of the balance sheet but before the completion of fieldwork. Such information may make it unnecessary to evaluate factors and assumptions related to the accounting estimate. In other circumstances, the uncertainty related to the evaluation of factors and assumptions may be significantly reduced.

> **RISK ASSESSMENT POINT:** As stated earlier, the purpose of the audit of accounting estimates is to determine whether estimates are reasonable. Thus, an auditor might conclude that an estimate is reasonable even though it is not the best estimate. The difference between the reasonable estimate and the best estimate should not necessarily be treated as a misstatement; however, if most estimates appear to reflect a particular bias, such as the tendency to understate expenses, the auditor should consider whether all misstatements combined could result in a material misstatement.

Determine whether accounting estimates are presented in accordance with GAAP

Once the auditor has determined that an accounting estimate has been identified and properly valued, the auditor must determine whether the accounting estimate is properly presented and disclosed in the financial statements; and he or she must consider the nature of the accounting estimate, relevant accounting and reporting standards, and the general rule of disclosure when making this determination.

> **ENGAGEMENT STRATEGY:** The Auditing Interpretation (February 1993) of SAS-57 titled "Performance and Reporting Guidance Related to Fair Value Disclosures" concludes that, when auditing estimates related to FAS-107 (Disclosures about Fair Value of Financial Instruments), the auditor should collect sufficient competent evidential matter to reasonably assure (1) that valuation methods are acceptable, are applied consistently, and are adequately documented; and (2) that estimation methods and significant assumptions are disclosed.

Obtain sufficient evidential matter to support fair value disclosures

FAS-107 (CT F25) (Disclosures about Fair Value of Financial Instruments) requires that "an entity shall disclose, either in the body of the financial statements or in the accompanying notes, the fair value of financial instruments for which it is practicable to estimate that value." Some companies may disclose only the information required by FAS-107, while others may voluntarily disclose the fair value of assets and liabilities not required by FAS-107. The Auditing Interpretation (February 1993) of SAS-57 titled "Performance and Reporting Guidance Related to Fair Value Disclosures" provides guidance for auditing and reporting on fair value disclosures:

> The auditor must collect sufficient evidential matter to satisfy the following:
>
> - Valuation principles are acceptable.
> - Valuation principles are consistently applied and their application is adequately documented.
> - Estimation methods used and significant assumptions made are properly disclosed.

Reporting on required information

When a client reports only the disclosures required by FAS-107 and the auditor has satisfied the three conditions listed above, a standard auditor's report is issued with no reference to the fair value disclosures. If the required disclosures are not made, the auditor must decide, depending on his or her assessment of the materiality of the disclosures omitted from the financial statements, whether to modify the standard report (qualified opinion or adverse opinion).

> **ENGAGEMENT STRATEGY:** The Interpretation notes that it may be appropriate to expand the standard report by adding an emphasis-of-a-matter paragraph when fair value is based on management's best estimate rather than on quoted market prices.

Reporting on required and voluntary information

When voluntary information on fair values is presented, that information may be audited only when the following conditions are met:

1. Criteria used to measure and disclose the information are reasonable.
2. Application of the disclosure and measurement criteria by competent persons would result in similar information.

The Interpretation concludes that voluntary disclosures may result in the presentation of essentially a complete balance sheet or an incomplete balance sheet based on fair values.

Complete balance sheet

The Interpretation concludes that if the fair value disclosures (both required and voluntary) encompass all material items in the balance sheet, the auditor should expand the report by adding the following paragraph:

> We have also audited in accordance with generally accepted auditing standards the supplemental fair value balance sheet of X Company as of December 31, 20X5. As described in Note X, the supplemental fair value balance sheet has been prepared by management to present relevant financial information that is not provided by the historical-cost balance sheets and is not intended to be a presentation in conformity with generally accepted accounting principles. In addition, the supplemental fair value balance sheet does not purport to present the net realizable, liquidation, or market value of X Company as a whole. Furthermore, amounts ultimately realized by X Company from the disposal of assets may vary significantly from the fair val-

ues presented. In our opinion, the supplemental fair value balance sheet referred to above presents fairly, in all material respects, the information set forth therein as described in Note X.

Incomplete balance sheet

If the fair value disclosures do not include all of the material items in the balance sheet and the disclosures are made either on the face of the financial statements or in notes, the Interpretation concludes that there is no need to make reference to the disclosures in the auditor's report. However, if the disclosures are presented in a supplemental schedule or exhibit, the auditor should add the following paragraph to the report:

> Our audit was conducted for the purpose of forming an opinion on the basic financial statements taken as a whole. The fair value disclosures contained in Schedule X are presented for purposes of additional analysis and are not a required part of the basic financial statements. Such information has been subjected to the auditing procedures applied in the audit of the basic financial statements and, in our opinion, is fairly stated in all material respects in relation to the basic financial statements taken as a whole.

Reporting when disclosures are not audited

The auditor may not be requested to audit voluntary fair value disclosures or may be unable to audit the information because the conditions listed earlier may not be satisfied. When voluntary fair value disclosures are not audited but are presented in an auditor-submitted document, and they appear on the face of the financial statements, in the notes, or in a supplemental schedule to the basic financial statements, the disclosures should be labeled "unaudited" and the paragraph below should be added to the auditor's report:

> Our audit was conducted for the purpose of forming an opinion on the basic financial statements taken as a whole. The fair value disclosures contained in Schedule X are presented for purposes of additional analysis and are not a required part of the basic financial statements. Such information has not been subjected to the auditing procedures applied in the audit of the basic financial statements, and, accordingly, we express no opinion on them.

PLANNING AID REMINDER: When the unaudited voluntary disclosures are presented in a client-prepared document and the information is included on the face of the financial statements, in the notes, or in a supplemental schedule, the disclosures should be labeled "unaudited." There is no need to disclaim an opinion on the information. If the unaudited voluntary disclosures are not presented on the face of the financial statements, in the notes, or in a supplemental schedule, the auditor should read the information in a manner consistent with the guidance established by SAS-8 (Other Information in Documents Containing Audited Financial Statements).

SECTION 350

AUDIT SAMPLING

Authoritative Pronouncements

SAS-39—Audit Sampling

Auditing Interpretation (January 1985)—Audit Sampling: Auditing Interpretations of Section 350

Overview

The third standard of fieldwork requires that sufficient competent evidential matter the auditor gather as a basis for formulating an opinion on the financial statements. "Evidence" may be defined as any information that has an effect on determining whether the financial statements are presented in accordance with generally accepted accounting principles.

Examining the documentation for every transaction of a business is costly and time-consuming. Since most audit objectives do not require that amount of evidence, an auditor will frequently use sampling techniques and procedures. SAS-39 (Audit Sampling) notes that there may be reasons other than sampling why an auditor would examine fewer than all of the items in a given population, such as (1) to gain an understanding of the nature of an entity's operations or (2) to clarify his or her understanding of the design of the entity's internal control. Under these circumstances, guidelines established in SAS-39 are not applicable.

Nonsampling plans

Although sampling is an important audit strategy in many engagements, a sampling approach is not appropriate for many situations. The Auditing Interpretation (January 1985) titled "Audit Sampling: Auditing Interpolations of Section 350" states that when less than 100% of the items in a given population are not examined, the following circumstances would not be considered sampling:

- The auditor does not intend to extend the sample results to the remainder of the items in the population.

- Although he or she might not be examining all of the items in the population, the auditor might be examining 100% of the items that make up a subgroup of the entire population.

- The auditor is performing tests of controls on an undocumented procedure (e.g., observing the client counting his or her inventory).

- The auditor is not performing a substantive test of details (e.g., applying analytical procedures).

For example, an auditor examining a client's trial balance of accounts receivable may discover that the balance is composed of only four accounts, and each amount due is individually significant. In this circumstance it would be appropriate, for example, to confirm each of the four receivables and evaluate each for likelihood of collection.

Nonstatistical sampling plans

The strategy of sampling is to examine less than 100% of the items in a given population and to draw from this examination a conclusion about certain characteristics of the total population. The conclusion can be expressed in quantitative terms (statistical sampling) or nonquantitative terms (nonstatistical sampling). For example, a sample of customer credit orders may be examined to determine whether appropriate credit approval has been made on each order. If the auditor has used nonstatistical sampling, he or she may say in the conclusion, "Based on the number of errors and the nature of those errors, I believe that the credit approval process is working effectively." On the other hand, if the auditor has used statistical sampling, he or she may conclude, "Based on the number of errors and the nature of those errors, I am 95% certain that the maximum error rate for nonapproval of credit is 1.2%."

SAS-39 was issued to provide guidance for the auditor's design and implementation of audit sampling plans. SAS-39 endorses both a nonstatistical approach and a statistical approach to sampling by concluding that either approach can provide sufficient evidential matter, as required by the third standard of fieldwork. Both nonstatistical sampling and statistical sampling are based on judgment, and the same factors are used in both approaches in order to determine the appropriate sample size and to evaluate the sample results.

The difference between the two approaches is that in statistical sampling the sample approach and the sample results are quantified, whereas in nonstatistical sampling qualitative terms are used to express the sampling results. Because of the similarities of the professional judgments in the two approaches, the following discussion applies to both nonstatistical and statistical sampling. It should be emphasized that while the concepts used in SAS-39 appear to be directed to statistical sampling, those concepts (and terminology) apply equally to nonstatistical sampling.

When an auditor designs a nonstatistical sampling plan or a statistical sampling plan, the purpose of the plan is to draw a conclusion about either an attribute or a dollar value. Attribute sampling measures the frequency of a specific occurrence in a particular population. This sampling technique is used to discover how often exceptions occur in the population under examination. Thus, attribute sampling is concerned with the qualitative characteristics of a sample. Generally, attribute sampling is associated with tests of controls, the results of which are the basis for assessing control risk at a level less than the maximum level.

Variable sampling is used to estimate the dollar value of a population and to determine the reasonableness of specific balances on the financial statements. Thus, variable sampling is concerned with the quantitative characteristics of a population. Generally, variable sampling is associated with substantive tests, which are performed to gather evidential matter concerning the validity and the propriety of specific transactions and balances.

Audit risk

Even when every transaction and balance is examined 100%, there is always a degree of audit risk present in an engagement. This degree of audit risk is referred to in SAS-39 as a combination of nonsampling risk and sampling risk. Examples of nonsampling risk are (1) the selection of inappropriate auditing procedures and (2) the failure to identify an error on a document that the auditor is examining. Nonsampling risk cannot be measured, but it can be reduced to an acceptable level if the auditor implements an effective quality control system.

Sampling risk occurs because fewer than 100% of the sample units in a population are reviewed. For this reason, the auditor can reduce sampling risk by increasing the size of the sample. Sampling risks are classified as follows:

- *Risk of assessing control risk too low (tests of controls)*—The risk that the assessed level of control risk based on the sample is less than the true operating effectiveness of the control structure policy or procedure. In other words, the internal control is not as effective as the auditor believes it to be.

- *Risk of assessing control risk too high (tests of controls)*—The risk that the assessed level of control risk based on the sample is greater than the true operating effectiveness of the control policy or procedure. In other words, the internal control is more effective than the auditor believes it to be.

- *Risk of incorrect acceptance (substantive tests)*—The risk that the selected sample supports the auditor's conclusion that the recorded account balance is not materially misstated, when in fact the recorded account balance is materially misstated. In other words, on the basis of the selected sample, the auditor concludes that the recorded account balance is not materially misstated, when in fact, based on the total population, the recorded account balance is materially misstated.

- *Risk of incorrect rejection (substantive tests)*—The risk that the selected sample supports the auditor's conclusion that the recorded account balance is materially misstated, when in fact the recorded account balance is not materially misstated. In other words, on the basis of the selected sample, the auditor concludes that the recorded account balance is materially misstated, when in fact, based on the total population, the recorded account balance is not materially misstated.

Both the risk of incorrectly assessing control risk too high and the risk of incorrect rejection of a recorded account balance are associated with the efficiency of the audit. For example, by assessing control risk at a high level (when in fact the control risk is lower), the auditor may increase the extent of substantive testing unnecessarily. Thus, the audit was not performed efficiently, because the auditor could have selected, for example, a smaller sample for substantive testing.

Both the risk of incorrectly assessing control risk too low on internal control and the risk of incorrect acceptance of a recorded account balance are associated with the effectiveness of the audit. For example, when an auditor concludes that a recorded account balance is correct when in fact the balance is not correct, the effectiveness of the audit is impaired.

Thus, the risk of assessing control risk too high and the risk of incorrect rejection may affect the efficiency of an audit, whereas the risk of assessing control risk too low and the risk of incorrect acceptance may affect the effectiveness of an audit. An auditor is more concerned with the risk of assessing control risk too low and the risk of incorrect acceptance than with the risk of assessing control risk too high and the risk of incorrect rejection, because the effectiveness of the audit is more important than the efficiency of the audit. For this reason, the risk of assessing control risk too low and the risk of incorrect acceptance of an incorrectly recorded account balance are emphasized in SAS-39.

The implications of testing less than 100% of a population

Sampling is concerned with selecting less than 100% of the items that make up a population to project the results of testing the sample to the total population. For example, an auditor may select a sample of accounts to be confirmed and, based on the results of the confirmed items, make a statement about a characteristic of the total accounts receivable balance. This approach is sampling and is subject to the guidance established by SAS-39.

However, the fact that an auditor tests less than 100% of a population does not mean that the approach is always sampling and, therefore, subject to the guidance established by SAS-39. For example, an auditor may decide to confirm all receivables that have a balance of $1,000 or more. The 1999/2000 Audit Risk Alert points out that in this case an auditor cannot project the results of the confirmed items to the total balance of accounts receivable, because the auditor has not drawn a sample from all of the receivables. The auditor cannot project the results of sampling to the population as a whole unless all of the items in the total population have had some chance for selection.

SAMPLING TESTS OF CONTROLS (NONSTATISTICAL AND STATISTICAL SAMPLING APPROACHES)

As stated earlier, attribute sampling measures the frequency of a specific occurrence in a particular population. This sampling technique is used to discover how often exceptions occur in the population under examination. Thus, attribute sampling is concerned with the qualitative characteristics of a sample—with tests of controls, which the auditor must perform in order to assess control risk at less than the maximum level.

Promulgated Procedures Checklist

The auditor may use the following steps to apply attribute sampling to tests of controls:

_____ 1. Determine the objectives of the test.
_____ 2. Define the deviation conditions.
_____ 3. Define the population.
        a. Define the period covered by the test.
        b. Define the sampling unit.
        c. Consider the completeness of the population.
_____ 4. Determine the method of selecting the sample.
        a. Random-number sampling
        b. Systematic sampling
        c. Other sampling

____ 5. Determine the sample size.
   a. Consider the allowable risk of assessing control risk too low.
   b. Consider the maximum rate of deviations from prescribed internal controls that would support the auditor's planned assessed level of control risk (tolerable rate).
   c. Consider the expected population deviation rate.
   d. Consider the effect of the population size.
   e. Consider statistical or nonstatistical sampling methods.
____ 6. Perform the sampling plan.
____ 7. Evaluate the sample results.
   a. Calculate the deviation rate.
   b. Consider the sampling risk.
   c. Consider the qualitative aspects of the deviations.
   d. Reach an overall conclusion.
____ 8. Document the sampling procedures.

Analysis and Application of Procedures

Step 1—Determine the objectives of the test

Generally, the use of sampling techniques in tests of controls applies only to those internal controls that generate documentary evidence. Thus, sampling techniques generally cannot be used in tests of controls for segregation of duties or the competency of personnel.

Tests of controls are concerned with determining whether a client's internal control is operating in accordance with prescribed policies. Each internal control procedure has an objective and prescribed rules to obtain that objective. For example, in the credit department of a business, a control may state that orders must be appropriately approved for acceptance of credit risk before being processed. The objective of this control is to ensure that credit is approved before an order is accepted. This control must also include the prescribed rules for attaining the objective. One of the rules for attaining this particular objective for the credit department may state that no additional credit may be extended to any customer who has an outstanding balance more than sixty days old. The head of the credit department will be responsible for ensuring that this control and its prescribed rules are consistently followed.

Every control objective must have one or more stated control techniques, which are designed to achieve the control objective.

Controls may be classified as preventive or detective. Preventive controls are established to prevent errors from occurring. Detective controls are established to detect errors that have occurred.

When performing tests of controls, the auditor must determine whether a specific internal control is operating as designed and whether the control objective is being achieved. In this respect the auditor may be concerned with (1) who performed the control, (2) where the control was performed, and (3) whether the control was performed in accordance with prescribed policy.

The audit objective must be defined in terms of specific compliance characteristics that can be tested.

Step 2—Define the deviation conditions

A *deviation* is a departure from the prescribed internal control. The auditor must identify any significant deviation conditions that exist in a control. A significant deviation condition exists when a necessary step to achieve a particular internal control objective is not performed as prescribed. The auditor may consider that some internal controls, such as multiple approvals, are unimportant and need not be tested.

Step 3—Define the population

The population selected for examination must be complete and must provide the auditor with the opportunity to satisfy the established audit objective. A sample should be selected in a manner that is representative of the population from which it is selected. If the population is not complete in all respects, the selected sample will not be representative of the complete population. For example, the audit objective may be to determine whether all goods that are shipped are properly billed. For this audit objective, the auditor should define the population as bills of lading or other shipping records prepared during the audit period—rather than sales invoices, which may or may not represent goods that have been shipped.

Step 3a—Define the period covered by the test

A conclusion can be drawn about a population only if all items in the population have a chance of being selected for examination. The population from which the sample is selected should include all transactions for the accounting period under examination. However, professional standards recognize that it may be appropriate to perform tests of controls at interim dates and review subsequent transactions when the auditor performs year-end audit procedures.

§350 • Audit Sampling

Step 3b—Define the sampling unit

A population consists of a number of sampling units, such as canceled checks or sales invoices. For example, if the audit objective is to determine whether vouchers have been properly approved, the sampling items may be the line items in the voucher register rather than the checks used to pay the vouchers. Once the auditor adequately defines the population, the sample unit should not be difficult to define.

Step 3c—Consider the completeness of the population

The physical representation of the population must be consistent with the definition of the population. For example, the auditor may be concerned with all cash disbursements made during the period and define the population as all canceled checks during the period. The auditor must determine that the defined population is complete; otherwise, a representative sample cannot be drawn from the population.

Step 4—Determine the method of selecting the sample

Sampling units must be selected from the defined population so that each sampling unit has a chance of being selected. SAS-39 requires that a representative sample be selected for both nonstatistical sampling and statistical sampling. When statistical sampling is used, the sample must be selected on a random basis.

> **ENGAGEMENT STRATEGY:** SAS-39 does not define "representative sample," but there is an implied difference between a representative sample and a random sample. In order for a selection method to be random, each item in the population must have an equal chance of selection. Often auditors use a random selection method even for a nonstatistical sampling plan, so that they can be sure that a representative sample has been selected.

Step 4a—Random-number sampling

A sample may be selected from the population on a random basis using random numbers generated by a computer or numbers chosen from a random-number table.

Step 4b—Systematic sampling

The auditor may select a random sample using the systematic-selection method, whereby every *n*th item is selected. Systematic selection is also referred to as sequential sampling. The following steps should be observed when systematic selection is used:

1. Determine the population (N).
2. Determine the sample size (n).
3. Compute the interval size by dividing N by n.
4. Select a random start (a random-number table can be used to determine the starting point).
5. Determine the sample items selected by successively adding the interval to the random starting point.

To illustrate the systematic-selection method, assume that the auditor has defined the population as 3,000 sales invoices listed in the sales journal (N) and would like to select 100 sales invoices for testing (n). Thus, the interval is every thirtieth sales invoice (3,000/100). If it is assumed that the auditor selects the number 12 as a random starting point, the first sales invoice selected would be the twelfth invoice, the second would be the forty-second invoice (12 + 30), and so on, until the sample of 100 items is selected.

A client may summarize or group a population in a specific order, and thus such a population would not be random. A sample selected from a nonrandom population using the systematic-selection method may not be appropriate for drawing statistical conclusions about a population, unless the auditor takes steps to solve the problem. The auditor should examine the population to determine whether it has been grouped or summarized in a particular order. Inquiries of client personnel may also be made to ascertain how individual transactions are accumulated or individual balances listed. If the population is in a specific order, it should be stratified and proportional samples drawn from each stratum. In this event, the auditor may want to test one or more of the strata more extensively.

Even if the population is not in a specific order, it usually is advisable for the auditor to have two or more random starts.

Step 4c—Other sampling

Block sampling refers to selecting contiguous sampling units, such as all checks numbered from 420 to 440. Generally, block sampling cannot be used when the auditor uses a statistical sampling approach. When the auditor uses only a few blocks to select the sample, block sampling also would be inappropriate for a nonstatistical sampling approach.

Haphazard sampling consists of selecting sampling units without any conscious bias. For example, the selection would be biased if the auditor had a tendency to select vendor folders that had the most vendor invoices in them. If properly applied, haphazard sampling can be used for nonstatistical sampling but not for a statistical sampling approach.

Step 5—Determine the sample size

A considerable amount of professional judgment is necessary to determine the proper sample size. The method for reaching a decision for determining the sample size is the same for nonstatistical sampling as it is for statistical sampling. In statistical sampling, the auditor will quantify the factors that are used to determine the sample size; in nonstatistical sampling, the factors will be described in subjective terms. For example, in statistical sampling, the auditor may conclude that a 10% factor should be assigned to the risk of assessing control risk too low. In nonstatistical sampling, the auditor may conclude that the client's internal controls appear to be well-designed. Both conclusions are highly subjective and are based on the same fundamental analysis, although the conclusion associated with statistical sampling is more precise.

The audit decision process as described in SAS-39 is summarized in Exhibit AU 350-7.

Step 5a—Consider the allowable risk of assessing control risk too low

The level of sampling risk is influenced by the size of the sample. There is always a risk that the auditor will not draw a representative sample. The larger the sample, the more audit hours it takes to test the sample. Achieving an acceptable level of sampling risk is the result of a trade-off between trying to avoid overauditing on the one hand and underauditing on the other.

Establishing an allowable risk of assessing control risk too low is a function of the degree of assurance indicated by the evidential matter selected as part of the sample process. If the auditor desires a high degree of assurance, it is necessary to establish a relatively small risk of assessing control risk too low. Establishing a small risk of assessing control risk too low will require that (assuming all other factors remain constant) the auditor increase the size of the sample. The larger the sample size, the higher the degree of assurance the auditor can offer about the effectiveness of internal control. For example, if using a nonstatistical sample, the auditor must select a larger sample in order to establish a low risk of underestimating control risk rather than establishing a moderate risk of assessing control risk too low. When using statistical sampling, the auditor must select a larger sample size in order to make a statement about the maximum error rate at a 99% confidence level (or a 1% allowable risk of assessing control risk too low) rather than at a 90% confidence level.

Step 5b — Consider the tolerable rate

The "tolerable rate" is the maximum percentage of deviations (errors) in a population that an auditor will tolerate without changing the planned assessed level of control risk. SAS-39 concludes that the establishment of a tolerable rate in an engagement is based on (1) the planned assessed level of control risk and (2) the degree of assurance indicated by the evidential matter in the sample.

The planned assessed level of control risk results from obtaining an understanding of the client's internal control. Thus, having gained an understanding of the client's internal control, the auditor establishes the planned level of control risk, which in turn is a factor in determining the sample size for tests of control. For example, if an internal control is considered highly relevant to a critical financial statement assertion, the auditor initially would plan to rely relatively heavily on the control procedure and there would be a tendency to establish a small tolerable rate.

Step 5c — Consider the expected population deviation rate

The purpose of attribute sampling for nonstatistical as well as statistical sampling is to provide some insight into the deviation rate of a particular characteristic in a population. For example, the auditor may be interested in the rate of pricing errors the client made in preparing customer invoices. However, before sampling can begin, the auditor must make a preliminary estimate of the deviation rate. The expected population deviation rate is the anticipated deviation rate in the entire population. Ideally, the estimate should be based on the results of audits of prior years, taking into consideration any subsequent modifications of the client's internal control. The auditor may review workpapers for the last few years to obtain an idea of the expected population deviation rate. In a new engagement, the auditor can estimate the expected population deviation rate by selecting and auditing a preliminary sample of about 25 items. The results of the test should be properly documented, because the preliminary sample becomes part of the final sample.

As the expected population deviation rate approaches the tolerable rate that the auditor established, the required sample size increases because the auditor must make an allowance for sampling risk. That is, if the auditor establishes a tolerable rate of 5% but the preliminary estimate of the deviation rate is 4%, in most situations the risk is too great that the actual deviation rate is more than 5%. In nonstatistical and statistical sampling it is misleading to think of estimating a single error rate. It is more useful to think of estimating an error range. In the current example, if the auditor is using nonstatistical sampling, it is better to think of the preliminary estimate of the deviation rate of being somewhere around 4%. If statistical sampling is used, the auditor may state that the estimated deviation rate is 4% plus or minus 2% (a range between 2% and 6%). Clearly, when the expected population deviation rate for a particular internal control is equal to or greater than the tolerable rate, the auditor should establish the control risk at its maximum level and generally not complete the test of controls, at least for the particular control(s) under investigation.

Step 5d—Consider the effect of the population size

In most circumstances, the size of the population has little and sometimes no effect on the determination of the required sample size in attribute sampling.

Step 5e—Consider a statistical or nonstatistical sampling method

The auditor may use either a nonstatistical sampling method or a statistical sampling method.

Sample size and nonstatistical sampling When using nonstatistical sampling, the auditor takes into consideration the risk of assessing control risk too low, the tolerable rate, and the expected population deviation rate, and determines the sample size by professional judgment. The auditor should observe the following generalizations in determining the sample size when nonstatistical sampling is employed:

- As the risk of assessing control risk too low increases, the required sample size decreases.
- As the risk of assessing control risk too low decreases, the required sample size increases.
- As the tolerable rate increases, the required sample size decreases.
- As the tolerable rate decreases, the required sample size increases.
- As the expected population deviation rate increases, the required sample size increases.
- As the expected population deviation rate decreases, the required sample size decreases.

Sample size and statistical sampling For statistical sampling, the auditor can use tables to determine the appropriate sample size. Exhibit AU 350-1 is based on a 5% risk of assessing control risk too low. To use Exhibit AU 350-1 the auditor should observe the following procedures:

**EXHIBIT AU 350-1—
STATISTICAL SAMPLE SIZES FOR TESTS OF CONTROLS
WITH A 5% RISK OF ASSESSING CONTROL RISK TOO LOW
(WITH NUMBER OF EXPECTED ERRORS IN PARENTHESES)**

Tolerable Rate

Expected Population Deviation Rate	2%	3%	4%	5%	6%	7%	8%	9%	10%	15%	20%
0.00%	149(0)	99(0)	74(0)	59(0)	49(0)	42(0)	36(0)	32(0)	29(0)	19(0)	14(0)
.25	236(1)	157(1)	117(1)	93(1)	78(1)	66(1)	58(1)	51(1)	46(1)	30(1)	22(1)
.50	*	157(1)	117(1)	93(1)	78(1)	66(1)	58(1)	51(1)	46(1)	30(1)	22(1)
.75	*	208(1)	117(1)	93(1)	78(1)	66(1)	58(1)	51(1)	46(1)	30(1)	22(1)
1.00	*	*	156(2)	124(2)	78(1)	66(1)	58(1)	51(1)	46(1)	30(1)	22(1)
1.25	*	*	156(2)	124(2)	78(1)	66(1)	58(1)	51(1)	46(1)	30(1)	22(1)
1.50	*	*	192(3)	124(2)	103(2)	66(1)	58(1)	51(1)	46(1)	30(1)	22(1)
1.75	*	*	227(4)	153(3)	103(2)	88(2)	77(2)	51(1)	46(1)	30(1)	22(1)
2.00	*	*	*	181(4)	127(3)	88(2)	77(2)	68(2)	46(1)	30(1)	22(1)
2.25	*	*	*	208(5)	127(3)	88(2)	77(2)	68(2)	61(2)	30(1)	22(1)
2.50	*	*	*	*	150(4)	109(3)	77(2)	68(2)	61(2)	30(1)	22(1)
2.75	*	*	*	*	175(5)	109(3)	95(3)	68(2)	61(2)	30(1)	22(1)
3.00	*	*	*	*	195(6)	129(4)	95(3)	84(3)	61(2)	30(1)	22(1)
3.25	*	*	*	*	*	148(5)	112(4)	84(3)	61(2)	30(1)	22(1)
3.50	*	*	*	*	*	167(6)	112(4)	84(3)	76(3)	40(2)	22(1)
3.75	*	*	*	*	*	185(7)	129(5)	100(4)	76(3)	40(2)	22(1)
4.00	*	*	*	*	*	*	146(6)	100(4)	89(4)	40(2)	22(1)
5.00	*	*	*	*	*	*	*	158(8)	116(6)	40(2)	30(2)
6.00	*	*	*	*	*	*	*	*	179(11)	50(3)	30(2)
7.00	*	*	*	*	*	*	*	*	*	68(5)	37(3)

*Sample size is too large to be cost-effective for most audit applications.

NOTE: This table assumes a large population.

Copyright © 1983 by the American Institute of Certified Public Accountants, Inc. (The title of the table has been changed to conform to the terminology used in SAS-55.)

§350 • Audit Sampling

- Find the table with the risk of assessing control risk too low that the auditor has established. (Exhibit AU 350-1 is based on a 5% risk of assessing control risk too low.)

- Refer to the column in Exhibit AU 350-1 that corresponds to the auditor's tolerable rate.

- Refer to the row in Exhibit AU 350-1 that corresponds to the auditor's estimate of the expected population deviation rate.

- The sample size is located where the tolerable rate column and the expected population deviation row intersect. (The number in parentheses is the number of expected errors.)

To illustrate the above steps, assume that the risk of assessing control risk too low has been established at 5% (Exhibit AU 350-1 is based on 5%), the tolerable rate is 9%, and the expected population deviation rate is 4%. The sample size is located where the tolerable rate column (9%) and the expected population deviation row (4%) intersect. Thus, the required sample size is 100.

Step 6—Perform the sampling plan

After the sample has been selected, the auditor should apply audit procedures to each sampling unit to determine whether there has been a deviation from the established internal control procedure. Usually, a deviation occurs if the auditor is unable to perform an audit procedure or apply alternative audit procedures to a sampling unit. As a general rule, sampling units that are selected but not examined, such as voided transactions or unused documents, should be replaced with new sampling units. Voided transactions or unused documents are not considered deviations if the established procedure of accounting for these items has been properly followed.

Step 7—Evaluate the sample results

After the audit procedures have been applied to each sampling unit, and the deviations, if any, from the prescribed internal controls have been summarized, the auditor must evaluate the results of the sampling.

Step 7a—Calculate the deviation rate

The deviation rate is computed by dividing the number of deviations by the number of units in the sample. The sample deviation rate is the auditor's best estimate of the population deviation rate.

EXHIBIT AU 350-2—
STATISTICAL SAMPLE RESULTS EVALUATION
TABLE FOR TESTS OF CONTROLS
UPPER LIMITS AT 5% RISK OF ASSESSING CONTROL RISK TOO LOW

Actual Number of Deviations Found

Sample Size	0	1	2	3	4	5	6	7	8	9	10
25	11.3	17.6	*	*	*	*	*	*	*	*	*
30	9.5	14.9	19.6	*	*	*	*	*	*	*	*
35	8.3	12.9	17.0	*	*	*	*	*	*	*	*
40	7.3	11.4	15.0	18.3	*	*	*	*	*	*	*
45	6.5	10.2	13.4	16.4	19.2	*	*	*	*	*	*
50	5.9	9.2	12.1	14.8	17.4	19.9	*	*	*	*	*
55	5.4	8.4	11.1	13.5	15.9	18.2	*	*	*	*	*
60	4.9	7.7	10.2	12.5	14.7	16.8	18.8	*	*	*	*
65	4.6	7.1	9.4	11.5	13.6	15.5	17.4	19.3	*	*	*
70	4.2	6.6	8.8	10.8	12.6	14.5	16.3	18.0	19.7	*	*
75	4.0	6.2	8.2	10.1	11.8	13.6	15.2	16.9	18.5	20.0	*
80	3.7	5.8	7.7	9.5	11.1	12.7	14.3	15.9	17.4	18.9	*
90	3.3	5.2	6.9	8.4	9.9	11.4	12.8	14.2	15.5	16.8	18.2
100	3.0	4.7	6.2	7.6	9.0	10.3	11.5	12.8	14.0	15.2	16.4
125	2.4	3.8	5.0	6.1	7.2	8.3	9.3	10.3	11.3	12.3	13.2
150	2.0	3.2	4.2	5.1	6.0	6.9	7.8	8.6	9.5	10.3	11.1
200	1.5	2.4	3.2	3.9	4.6	5.2	5.9	6.5	7.2	7.8	8.4

*Over 20%

NOTE: This table presents upper limits as percentages. This table assumes a large population.

Copyright © 1983 by the American Institute of Certified Public Accountants, Inc. (The title of the table has been changed to conform to the terminology used in SAS-55.)

§350 • Audit Sampling

Step 7b—Consider the sampling risk

The auditor must consider the degree of sampling risk involved in the sample results. Sampling risk arises because the auditor does not examine all of the sampling units in a population. An auditor can reach an entirely different conclusion on the basis of sample results than if the entire population is examined. When the auditor's estimate of the population deviation is less than the tolerable rate for the population, there is still a possibility that the true deviation rate in the population (maximum population deviation) is greater than the tolerable rate. The auditor can determine the degree of sampling risk in the sample results by computing the maximum population deviation rate.

Sampling risk and nonstatistical sampling When the auditor employs nonstatistical sampling, the sampling risk cannot be quantified; the auditor should nonetheless take that risk into consideration in determining whether the potential error rate in the population is unacceptable. The auditor should observe the following generalizations when evaluating the results of nonstatistical sampling:

- The auditor may rely on the planned assessed level of control risk when the auditor's best estimate of the population deviation rate (based on the sample results) is equal to or less than the expected population deviation rate.

- The auditor cannot rely on the planned assessed level of control risk when the auditor's best estimate of the population deviation rate is greater than the expected population deviation rate.

When the deviation rate is greater than the tolerable rate, the planned assessed level of control risk is not justified. Thus, the auditor may, for example, decide not to rely on the client's internal control (assess control risk at the maximum) in the performance of substantive tests.

Sampling risk and statistical sampling When using statistical sampling, the auditor can use tables to measure the allowance for sampling risk. Exhibit AU 350-2 is based on upper limits at a 5% risk of assessing control risk too low. By using Exhibit AU 350-2, the auditor can determine the maximum population deviation rate. To use Exhibit AU 350-2 the auditor should observe the following procedures:

- Find the table with the risk of assessing control risk too low established by the auditor. (Exhibit AU 350-2 is based on a 5% risk factor, and tables are available for other percentages.)

- Refer to the column in Exhibit AU 350-2 that corresponds to the number of actual deviations found in the sample.
- Refer to the row in Exhibit AU 350-2 that corresponds to the sample size.
- The maximum population deviation rate is located where the column for the actual number of deviations found in the sample and the sample-size row intersect.

To illustrate the above procedures, assume that the risk the auditor has established for assessing control risk too low is 5% (Exhibit AU 350-2 is based on 5%), the sample size established by the auditor is 100, the tolerable rate established by the auditor is 9%, and the expected population deviation rate established by the auditor is 4%. If the auditor examines the 100 sample units and discovers two errors, the maximum population deviation rate is 6.2%, as shown on Exhibit AU 350-2 where the actual number of deviations found (2) intersects with a sample size of 100. The maximum population deviation rate is also referred to as the upper limits or the upper precision limits.

In the above illustration, the auditor can be 95% certain that the maximum population deviation rate is 6.2%. The 95% certainty percentage is the complement of the 5% risk factor (100% minus 5%). Since the maximum deviation rate of 6.2% is less than the tolerable rate of 9% established by the auditor, the planned assessed level of control risk is not changed. However, when the maximum population deviation rate is greater than the tolerable rate established by the auditor, the planned assessed level of control risk is not justified.

Step 7c—*Consider the qualitative aspects of the deviations*

The auditor should consider the qualitative aspects of each deviation. The nature and cause of each deviation should be analyzed and deviations should be classified into unintentional deviations (errors) or intentional deviations (acts of fraud). The auditor should make a determination about whether the deviation resulted from a misunderstanding of instructions or from carelessness. The discovery of an act of fraud would require more attention from the auditor than the discovery of an error.

Step 7d—*Reach an overall conclusion*

The auditor must determine whether the overall audit approach supports the planned assessed level of control risk. To make this overall evaluation, the auditor should consider the following factors:

§350 • Audit Sampling

- Sample results of tests of controls
- Results of inquiries about controls that do not leave an audit trail
- Results of observations concerning control procedures that are based on the segregation of responsibilities

Professional judgment is required in reaching a conclusion on how the results of the tests of controls will affect the nature, timing, and extent of the subsequent substantive tests.

Step 8—Document the sampling procedures

To satisfy the requirements of SAS-41 (AU 339) (Working Papers), the auditor should consider the following matters for documentation in the auditor's workpapers:

- Description of internal controls tested
- Objective of the tests of controls
- Definition of population and sampling unit
- Definition of deviation conditions
- Method of determining sample size
- Method of sample selection
- Description of audit procedures employed and list of deviations discovered by the auditor [deviations should be classified as unintentional and (suspected) intentional acts]
- Evaluation of sample results and overall conclusions

SAMPLING IN SUBSTANTIVE TESTS OF DETAILS (NONSTATISTICAL AND STATISTICAL SAMPLING APPROACHES)

Variable sampling—used in the performance of substantive tests of transactions and balances—is used to estimate the dollar value of a population and to determine the reasonableness of financial statement balances. The purpose of substantive tests is to obtain evidence of the validity and propriety of accounting balances and classes of transactions.

Promulgated Procedures Checklist

The auditor may use the following steps to apply variable sampling to substantive tests:

_____ 1. Determine the audit objective of the test.
_____ 2. Define the population.
   a. Define the sampling unit.
   b. Consider the completeness of the population.
   c. Identify individually significant items.
_____ 3. Choose an audit sampling technique.
_____ 4. Determine the sample size.
   a. Consider variations within the population.
   b. Consider the acceptable level of risk.
   c. Consider the tolerable misstatement.
   d. Consider the expected amount of error.
   e. Consider the population size.
_____ 5. Determine the method of selecting the sample.
_____ 6. Perform the sampling plan.
_____ 7. Evaluate the sample results.
   a. Project the misstatement to the population and consider sampling risk.
   b. Consider the qualitative aspects of misstatements and reach an overall conclusion.
_____ 8. Document the sampling procedures.

Analysis and Application of Procedures

Step 1—Determine the audit objective of the test

The audit objective of performing substantive tests is to determine whether the dollar value assigned by management to an account balance or group of transactions is reasonable.

Step 2—Define the population

The population the auditor defines must include all items that are related to the audit objective of the test. If items relevant to the audit objective are omitted from the population, the audit objective of the test will not be achieved. For example, the audit objective may be to determine whether the repairs and maintenance expense account is reasonably stated. The definition of the population could be all line items that make up the detail of the account, but such a definition would probably be deficient because other accounts—especially property, plant, and equipment—could contain expenditures that were capitalized when they should have been expensed. A better definition of the population would be all repairs and maintenance work orders authorized during the period.

Step 2a—Define the sampling unit

The population is made up of individual sampling units that may be individual transactions, documents, customer or vendor balances, or an individual entry. The auditor must consider the efficiency of the audit when selecting the sampling unit. For example, it may be more efficient to define the sampling unit as the individual sales invoice—rather than as the individual accounts receivable, which may be made up of several invoices.

Step 2b—Consider the completeness of the population

The physical representation of the population must be consistent with the definition of the population. For example, the auditor may be concerned with all cash disbursements made during the period and define the population as all canceled checks during the period. The auditor must determine that the defined population is complete; otherwise, a representative sample cannot be drawn from the population.

Step 2c—Identify individually significant items

The population should be reviewed for items that should be individually examined because of the audit exposure related to these items. Items that should be examined individually include large dollar items, related party transactions, and accounts with a history of errors. When items are examined individually, they are not part of the sampling results; however, these items must be considered in determining the possible misstatement in the population. There is, therefore, no sampling risk associated with these items.

Step 3—Choose an audit sampling technique

Initially, the auditor must determine whether a nonstatistical or a statistical sampling approach should be employed. As stated earlier, SAS-39 indicates no preference of one over the other. Whether a nonstatistical or a statistical sampling approach is used, many different types of sampling techniques are used in practice. Irrespective of the sampling approach or specific sampling technique the auditor uses, he or she must observe the following steps as established by SAS-39 in the performance of substantive tests based on sampling.

Step 4—Determine the sample size

The auditor must use professional judgment to determine the sample size. The decision process for determining the sample size is the same for nonstatistical sampling as it is for statistical sampling. In statistical sampling the auditor will quantify the relevant factors, whereas in nonstatistical sampling the factors will be described in a less structured manner.

The audit decision process for determining the sample size as described in SAS-39 is summarized in Exhibit AU 350-8.

Step 4a—Consider variations within the population

A basic concept in sampling is the need to obtain a representative sample from the population. If the population is composed of various items, the auditor must examine a sufficiently large sample to be reasonably assured that a representative sample has been selected.

For accounting populations, the variation within a population may be expressed in dollar amounts. It is not unusual for an accounting population to be composed of a few large balances, several medium balances, and numerous smaller balances. The required sample size increases as the variability in the population increases.

When nonstatistical sampling is employed, the auditor may review the population or the prior years' workpapers to acquire an understanding of the variation within the population. When a classical variable statistical sampling technique is employed, the auditor measures the variation in the population by computing the estimate of the standard deviation of the sample mean.

It may be efficient to stratify a population with a high degree of variation. "Stratification" simply means that the population is divided into groups (strata) of sampling units that have the same or approximately the same dollar values, and samples are selected from each group. Stratification is necessary to reduce the effect of the variation in the population on the size of the sample. (In both nonstatistical sampling and statistical sampling, as the variation increases, the auditor needs to select a larger sample size.)

> **ENGAGEMENT STRATEGY:** When probability proportional to size (PPS) sampling is used, there is no need to consider the variation within the population, because this technique automatically considers that factor since it is a combination of both attribute sampling and variable estimation.

Step 4b—Consider the acceptable level of risk

When considering whether to accept or reject the results of a sample, the auditor is faced with the risks of (1) incorrect rejection of a balance and (2) in-

§350 • Audit Sampling

correct acceptance of a balance. The risk of incorrect rejection of a balance is the risk that the results of a sample will lead the auditor to conclude that the recorded account balance is materially misstated when, in fact, the recorded account balance is not materially misstated. The risk of incorrect acceptance of a balance is the risk that the results of a sample will lead the auditor to conclude that the recorded account balance is not materially misstated when, in fact, the recorded account balance is materially misstated.

In determining an acceptable level of risk of incorrect acceptance for substantive tests of details, the auditor should consider (1) inherent risk, (2) control risk, and (3) the risk that other relevant substantive tests (including analytical procedures) would not detect a material misstatement. These risk factors and interrelationships must be considered in nonstatistical sampling plans as well as in statistical sampling plans. These relationships are illustrated in an appendix to SAS-39 in the following manner:

$$TD = AR/(IR \times CR \times AP)$$

where:

- AR = the allowable audit risk that monetary misstatements equal to tolerable misstatement might remain undetected for the account balance or class of transactions and related assertions after the auditor has completed all audit procedures deemed necessary.

- IR = the susceptibility of an assertion to a material misstatement assuming there are no related internal controls.

- CR = the risk that a material misstatement that could occur in an assertion will not be prevented or detected on a timely basis by the entity's internal controls. (The auditor may assess control risk at the maximum, or may assess control risk below the maximum on the basis of the sufficiency of evidential matter obtained to support the effectiveness of internal controls.)

- AP = the risk that analytical procedures and other relevant substantive tests would fail to detect misstatements that could occur in an assertion equal to tolerable misstatement, given that such misstatements occur and are not detected by the internal control.

- TD = the allowable risk of incorrect acceptance for the substantive test of details, given that misstatements equal to tolerable misstatement occur in an assertion and are not detected by internal control or analytical procedures and other relevant substantive tests.

The above equation emphasizes relationships among the various factors that the auditor must consider when determining the allowable risk of incorrect acceptance. For example, as control risk rises, the allowable risk of incorrect acceptance must decrease to achieve a stated level of audit risk. That relationship is based on the simple logic that as the perceived effectiveness of internal control decreases, the auditor is less willing to establish a high allowable risk of incorrect acceptance of an account balance. Stated in terms of its effect on sample size, it is necessary to increase the size of the sample as control risk increases to reduce the level of risk of incorrect acceptance. Thus, from the perspective of sample size and all other factors remaining constant, there is an inverse relationship between control risk and the allowable risk of incorrect acceptance.

While the relationships established in the above equation are intuitive, it is unlikely that an auditor would assign an absolute value to audit risk, but rather would evaluate the risk in an abstract manner. Even when statistical sampling is employed, most auditors would use the relationships established by the equation as a guide and would avoid a strict and comprehensive quantitative approach by simply plugging in risk factors. Even if an auditor insists on a strictly quantitative approach, that does not imply that judgment has been removed from the process. In the latter circumstance, the process may appear to be unbiased, but as discussed in this section, the risk factors are based on a number of decisions that depend heavily on professional judgments. Those judgments are the same for nonstatistical sampling and statistical sampling.

Step 4c—Consider the tolerable misstatement

The tolerable misstatement is an estimate of the maximum monetary misstatement that may exist in an account balance or group of transactions when combined with misstatement in other accounts, without causing the financial statements to be materially misstated. The tolerable misstatement is based on the auditor's definition of "materiality," or the maximum amount by which the financial statements could be misstated and still be in accordance with generally accepted accounting principles. There is an inverse relationship between the tolerable misstatement and the required sample size. Thus, the sample size must be increased when the tolerable misstatement is decreased.

Step 4d—Consider the expected amount of misstatement

An estimate of the expected amount of misstatement in a particular account balance or group of transactions is based on the following factors:

- Understanding of the entity's business
- Prior years' tests of the population

§350 • Audit Sampling

- Results of a pre-audit sample
- Results of tests of controls

The required sample size increases as the auditor's estimate of the expected amount of misstatement in the population increases.

> **PLANNING AID REMINDER:** In practice it is often difficult to determine the expected amount of misstatement, but this can be overcome by combining the effects of the tolerable misstatement and the expected amount of misstatement. This can be accomplished by establishing a materiality threshold and then dividing that amount by "about 2" in order to establish the tolerable misstatement. For example, if materiality is established at $100,000, then the tolerable misstatement would be about $50,000 ($100,000/2). Then only the (adjusted) tolerable misstatement would be used to determine the required sample size.

Step 4e — Consider the population size

The population size generally has an effect on the sample size, depending on which sampling technique the auditor employs.

Step 5 — Determine the method of selecting the sample

The auditor must select sampling units from the defined population in such a way that each sampling unit has a chance of being selected. The auditor's objective is to select a representative sample of all items from the population. If statistical sampling is used, the sample selection must be random.

Step 6 — Perform the sampling plan

Once the sample has been selected, the auditor should apply appropriate audit procedures. If the auditor is unable to perform an audit procedure on a sampling unit selected for examination, alternative audit procedures should be considered. If the sampling unit does not have an effect on the conclusion the auditor reaches concerning the acceptability of the population, alternative audit procedures do not have to be applied, and the sampling unit may be treated as an misstatement for evaluation purposes. In addition, the auditor should determine whether the inability to apply an audit procedure has an effect on the assessed level of control risk or the assessment of risk on representations made by the client.

Step 7—Evaluate the sample results

After testing the sample units, the auditor should evaluate the sample results to determine whether the account balance or group of transactions is correct and in accordance with generally accepted accounting principles.

Step 7a—Project the misstatement to the population and consider sampling risk

The misstatements discovered in the sampling units should be projected to the total population. In its simplest form, a $2,000 misstatement in a sample that represents 20% of the population would be projected as a total misstatement of $10,000 ($2,000/20%). The method of projecting the misstatement to the total population will depend on the type of sampling technique the auditor uses.

If the projected misstatement is greater than the tolerable misstatement, the account balance cannot be accepted as correct. If the projected misstatement is significantly less than the tolerable misstatement, the auditor may conclude that the account balance is not materially misstated. For example, if the projected misstatement is $10,000 and the tolerable misstatement is $50,000, in most instances the risk of accepting an incorrect balance would be acceptable. As the projected misstatement approaches the tolerable misstatement, the risk of accepting an incorrect balance increases, and the auditor must use professional judgment in deciding whether to accept a balance as correct. For example, if the projected misstatement is $40,000 and the tolerable misstatement is $50,000, in most instances the risk of accepting an incorrect balance would not be acceptable.

Step 7b—Consider the qualitative aspects of misstatements and reach an overall conclusion

Each misstatement the auditor discovers by testing the sample should be evaluated to determine why the misstatement was made and whether the misstatement has an effect on other phases of the engagement. For example, the discovery of a fraudulent act would have broader implication to the auditor than the discovery of a routine error.

The results of the substantive tests may suggest that the assessed level of control risk was too low. Such a condition would require the auditor to consider whether substantive tests should be expanded.

Step 8—Document the sampling procedures

To satisfy the requirements of SAS-41 (AU 339), the auditor should consider the following matters for documentation in the auditor's workpapers:

- Description of audit procedures and objectives tested
- Definition of population and sampling unit
- Definition of a misstatement
- Basis for establishment of risk of incorrect acceptance, incorrect rejection, tolerable misstatement, and expected misstatement
- Audit sampling technique used
- Method of sampling selection
- Description of sampling procedures performed and list of misstatements discovered [deviations should be classified as unintentional and (suspected) intentional acts]
- Evaluation of sample and summary of overall conclusions

NONSTATISTICAL SAMPLING FOR SUBSTANTIVE TESTS OF DETAIL

This section is based on the discussion in the previous section, but it focuses exclusively on nonstatistical sampling for substantive tests of detail. The guidance provided in this section is based on the AICPA's Auditing Practice Release (APR) titled "Audit Sampling" (Chapter 5).

Promulgated Procedures Checklist

The auditor may use the following steps to apply nonstatistical sampling concepts to substantive tests of details.

____ Identify individually significant items

____ Determine the sample size

____ Select the sample

____ Evaluate the sample results

Analysis and Application of Procedures

Identify individually significant items

Initially the auditor should review the items that make up the population to determine whether certain items should be tested 100% rather than sampled.

The items selected for 100% testing might be based on the dollar value of the item or unusual characteristics of the item. For example, an auditor may review the trial balance of accounts receivable and decide that all receivables that exceed $1,000 should be selected for confirmation. Generally items are selected for 100% testing if individually their misstatement could exceed the tolerable error amount.

Determine the sample size

The size of the sample in nonstatistical sampling is based on professional judgment. The auditor cannot simply decide to use a rule of thumb in all engagements and expect to satisfy professional standards or to perform an effective engagement. For example, if the auditor has a rule of thumb that he or she always confirms 10% of the dollar value of accounts receivable, that approach is a violation of generally accepted auditing standards.

The APR points out that when an auditor uses nonstatistical sampling to perform substantive test of details, the following factors (which were discussed in the previous section) must be taken into consideration:

- Population variation
- Risk of incorrect acceptance
- Tolerable misstatement and expected misstatement
- Population size

Although these four factors sound like concepts that are found in a statistics course, they are actually based on common sense.

> **PLANNING AID REMINDER:** Although the auditor must take the four factors listed above into consideration in determining the size of the sample, the auditor does not have to quantify these factors. Also, some auditors believe that there is some simple solution to determining sample size that does not have to take into consideration the four factors listed above. There is no simple rule-of-thumb solution. An auditor must take these factors into consideration and use professional judgment to determine the size of a sample, even when nonstatistical sampling is used.

Population variation

In general, the more homogenous the population, the smaller the sample size can be. That is, for example, if the trial balance of accounts receivable is made up of balances that range from $150 to $220, there is little variation in the population. For this reason, an auditor can test relatively few items in order to get a representative sample of the accounts receivable. On the other hand, if the range of balances in accounts receivable is from $5 to $25,000, this population exhibits more variability and it would be necessary to test a larger number of accounts receivable.

> **ENGAGEMENT STRATEGY:** In practice it is unlikely that an accounting population will have as small degree of variation as suggested in the above paragraph; however, it is possible to divide the population into groupings (population stratification) and thus significantly reduce the degree of variation in each grouping. Also, it should be remembered that a group of the population may be tested 100% (as discussed earlier) and evaluated separately. Stratification and testing some of the items 100% will almost always reduce the overall size of the sample.

The auditor can get a feel for the variation within a population by reviewing the items that make up the population. For example, a simple review of the trial balance of accounts receivable should give the auditor a reasonable impression of the variability of the population. A more precise measurement of variability may be determined quickly if the trial balance is digitized and can be subjected to analysis by various file analyzers. For example, if the trial balance of accounts receivable is maintained in a spreadsheet file, such as an Excel spreadsheet, it may be possible to create statistics such as the variance or standard deviation of the population.

Risk of incorrect acceptance

As discussed earlier in this section, an interplay exists among audit risk, inherent risk, and control risk. These relationships can be summarized as follows:

- When the combined inherent and control risks are assessed at a lower level, a greater risk of incorrect acceptance for planned substantive tests can be established. Under this circumstance, the required sample size is decreased.

- When the combined inherent and control risks are assessed at a higher level, a lower risk of incorrect acceptance for planned substantive tests can be established. Under this circumstance, the required sample size is increased.

- When the auditor relies more heavily on other substantive tests (including analytical procedures) to achieve the same audit objective, a greater risk of incorrect acceptance for planned substantive tests can be established. Under this circumstance, the required sample size is decreased.

- When the auditor relies less heavily on other substantive tests (including analytical procedures) to achieve the same audit objective, a lesser risk of incorrect acceptance for planned substantive tests can be established. Under this circumstance, the required sample size is increased.

Tolerable misstatement and expected misstatement

The establishment of a sample size in nonstatistical sampling must take into consideration the tolerable misstatement (the size of the error that the auditor considers to be tolerable) and the expected misstatement. In general, as the size of the tolerable misstatement increases, the required sample size decreases. For example, if the auditor believes that a tolerable error in the accounts receivable balance is $30,000 rather than $10,000, the number of items that must be in the sample is decreased.

In determining the size of a sample, the auditor should also take into consideration the expected misstatement in the population. As the expected misstatement in the population increases, the required sample size must be increased. That is, if an auditor does not have much faith in the balances under investigation, common sense would required an auditor to test more items from the population.

Population size

The size of the population has little effect on the size of the sample. Thus, if one trial balance of accounts receivable has 2,000 line items and another trial balance has 4,000 line items, assuming all other factors are equal, both populations would require essentially the same sample size.

> **ENGAGEMENT STRATEGY:** It is easy for auditors to overemphasize the size of the population in determining the required sample size for a particular balance. For example, if the auditor has a rule of thumb that he or she samples 10% of the items of the population, the result is a misapplication of auditing standards. In the previous example, the auditor would select 200 items from the first population and 400 items from the second, but that doubling of the sample size in the second population is not supported by sampling concepts. It is far more important for the auditor to thoughtfully look at the other three factors discussed above, rather than population size, in determining the required sample size for a population.

Consider the interplay of the four factors The auditor uses professional judgment to evaluate the four factors described above and, based on this evaluation, determines the required sample size. There is no single approach that an auditor should use to make this determination; however, for illustrative purpose the APR describes the following as an approach that an auditor may consider.

- Consider the level of inherent risk
- Consider the effectiveness of controls related to the financial statement assertions
- Establish the risk of incorrect acceptance
- Establish a tolerable misstatement level
- Evaluate the effect of other related substantive tests of details
- Determine the population reported amount
- Compute the preliminary sample size
- Adjust the preliminary sample size

> **ENGAGEMENT STRATEGY:** The APR is careful not to endorse any particular method for determining sample size but describes the usefulness of the approach described above as follows: The model is provided only to illustrate the relative effect of different planning considerations on sample size; it is not intended as a substitute for professional judgment. The auditor can find this approach useful to get a feel for how various assessments of the four factors described earlier can have on the required sample size.

Consider the level of inherent risk Initially the auditor assesses the level of inherent risk related to the particular assertions in the financial statements that will be tested once the sample is selected. SAS-47 (AU 312) (Audit Risk and Materiality in Conducting an Audit) defines inherent risk as "the likelihood of a misstatement existing in an account balance or class of transactions that would be material when aggregated with misstatement(s) in other accounts or classifications, assuming that there were no related controls." SAS-31 (AU 326) (Evidential Matters) attempts to provide the logical framework for the audit process by identifying the following broad assertions that must be tested in the audit of account balances and transactions:

- *Existence or occurrence*—The financial statements assert that an asset or a liability exists at the balance sheet date and that a nominal account represents transactions that occurred during an accounting period.
- *Completeness*—The financial statements assert that all items that comprise an asset, a liability, or a nominal account are represented.

- *Rights and obligations*—The financial statements assert that assets properly represent rights owned by the client and that liabilities represent obligations of the client.
- *Valuation and allocation*—The financial statements assert that all accounts are valued in accordance with generally accepted accounting principles.
- *Presentation and disclosure*—The financial statements assert that accounts and related information are properly classified, described, and disclosed.

> **OBSERVATION:** For a discussion of inherent risk see AU Section 312, and for a discussion of financial statements assertions see AU Section 325.

Consider the effectiveness of controls related to the financial statement assertions Once the specific financial statement assertions are identified, the auditor should consider the effectiveness of the controls related to the prevention and detection of material misstatements related to the assertions. SAS-47 (AU 312) defines control risk as "the possibility of a misstatement occurring in an account balance or class of transactions that (1) could be material when aggregated with misstatement(s) in other balances or classes and (2) will not be prevented or detected on a timely basis by the entity's internal control."

Establish the risk of incorrect acceptance The judgments made in the first two steps should be combined and the auditor should determine the risk of incorrect acceptance (which was described earlier in this section). That is, inherent risk and control risk related to specific assertions included in the financial statements provide insight into how much risk the auditor is willing to accept for those particular assertions. Although there are innumerable levels that could be identified in practice, the APR suggests that the following risk assessment levels may be used:

- Maximum
- Slightly below maximum
- Moderate
- Low

If the auditor believes that particular assertions have a high inherent risk and that the controls related to the assertions are weak, the maximum level of incorrect acceptance should be established. On the other hand, if there is relatively low inherent risk related to assertions and the related controls are effective, a low level of incorrect acceptance should be established.

Establish a tolerable misstatement level The tolerable misstatement is an estimate of the maximum monetary misstatement that may exist in an account balance or group of transactions when combined with misstatement in other accounts, without causing the financial statements to be materially misstated.

> **OBSERVATION:** For a discussion of tolerable misstatement, see AU Section 350.

Evaluate the effect of other related substantive tests of details When a single audit procedure is performed, the results of that test often test the validity of more than one assertion that appears in the financial statements. For this reason, the auditor should assess the risk that other audit procedures may have an impact on the assertions that are the focus of the current sample determination. The APR provides the following guidance in assessing this risk:

- *Maximum risk*—No other substantive procedures are performed to test the same assertions

- *Moderate risk*—Other substantive procedures that are performed to test the same assertions are expected to be moderately effective in detecting material misstatements in those assertions

- *Low risk*—Other substantive procedures that are performed to test the same assertions are expected to be highly effective in detecting material misstatements in those assertions

Determine the population reported amount The dollar value of the population is simply the amount reported in the financial statements less items that make up this value that are to be tested 100%.

Compute the preliminary sample size The preliminary size of the sample is computed based on the following formula:

$$\frac{\text{Population reported amount}}{\text{Tolerable misstatement}} \times \text{Assurance factor} = \text{Sample size}$$

The population reported amount and tolerable misstatement were discussed earlier. The assurance factor is based on the table in Exhibit AU 350-3, which is adapted from the APR (page 54).

EXHIBIT AU 350-3—ASSURANCE FACTOR

Assessment of Inherent and Control Risk	Risk That Other Substantive Procedures Will Fail to Detect a Material Misstatement			
	Maximum	Slightly Below Maximum	Moderate	Low
Maximum	3.0	2.7	2.3	2.0
Slightly below maximum	2.7	2.4	2.0	1.6
Moderate	2.3	2.1	1.6	1.2
Low	2.0	1.6	1.2	1.0

Adjust the preliminary sample size The preliminary sample size must be adjusted upward because nonstatistical rather than statistical sampling is used. The ARP notes "auditors typically adjust the sample size from 10% to 50% if the sample is not selected in a statically efficient manner." For example, if a population that has a great deal of variation has not been stratified, the auditor should increase the preliminary sample size.

To illustrate this approach, assume an auditor is trying to decide the sample size for the confirmation of accounts receivable under the following conditions:

- *Consider the level of inherent risk*—This particular audit procedure is concerned with the existence of accounts receivable, and the level of inherent risk is considered to be moderate based on the nature of accounts receivable and other factors related to the client.

- *Consider the effectiveness of controls related to the financial statement assertions*—Based on the evaluation of the client's internal control structure related to the processing of accounts receivable and cash receipts, the auditor has concluded that internal controls are weak and control risk is assessed at the maximum level.

- *Establish the risk of incorrect acceptance*—Based on the assessment of the level of inherent risk (moderate) and control risk (maximum), the auditor decides to assess the risk of incorrect acceptance at a level *slightly below maximum*.

- *Establish a tolerable misstatement level*—Based on the assessment of materiality, the auditor decides to establish a tolerable misstatement level of $9,000.

- *Evaluate the effect of other related substantive tests of details*—The auditor has identified another audit procedure that will help to determine the existence of accounts receivable (for example, the review of subsequent cash receipts) and has assessed the risk that other substantive procedures will fail to detect a material misstatement as *moderate*.

- *Determine the population reported amount*—The general ledger balance of accounts receivable is reported at $250,000 but accounts receivable that exceed $4,000 will be tested 100%. The accounts that will be tested 100% are reported at $20,000. Thus, the population subject to sampling has a reported amount of $230,000.

- *Compute the preliminary sample size*—Based on the assessments of inherent and control risk (slightly below maximum) and the risk that other substantive procedures will fail to detect a material misstatement (moderate), the assurance factor (as reported in the table reproduced above) is 2.0 and the sample size is computed as follows:

$$= \frac{\text{Population reported amount}}{\text{Tolerable misstatement}} \times \text{Assurance factor}$$

$$= \frac{\$230{,}000}{\$9{,}000} \times 2.0$$

$$= 52 \text{ Sample items}$$

- *Adjust the preliminary sample size*—The auditor, based on the review of the trial balance of accounts receivable, decided not to stratify the sample (except for the items that are tested 100%), even though there was a moderate amount of variation in the account balances. For this reason, the auditor decided to increase the size of the sample by 30%. Thus, the required sample size is 68 (52 x 1.3).

Select the sample

Once the sample size has been determined, the sample itself should be selected so that each item in the population has a chance of selection (representative sample). One way to select the sample is to divide the population into categories based on dollar values, selecting more items from the category with the greatest dollar value. The allocation in Exhibit AU 350-4 illustrates this approach based on the example presented earlier in this section.

EXHIBIT AU 350-4—SELECTING THE SAMPLE

Categories	Reported Amounts	Allocation Fraction	Total Required Sample Size	Sample Size for Category
$1 to $500	100,000	100/230	68	29
$501 to $2,000	80,000	80/230	68	24
$2001 to $4,000	50,000	50/230	68	15
Totals	$230,000			68

Thus, 29 receivables will be selected from those receivables that have a balance of $500 or less, and so on. Within each category, the specific items selected for confirmation could be selected on a random basis or an interval basis.

OBSERVATION: The population has been stratified for sample selection purposes but not for sample evaluation purposes.

Evaluate the sample results

In order to evaluate the sample results when a nonstatistical sampling approach is used, the auditor must do the following:

- Project the misstatement in the population
- Consider the sampling risk
- Consider qualitative characteristics

Project the misstatement in the population

Once the specific items are selected for testing, the appropriate audit procedures are performed. Based on the performance of the audit procedures, the auditor would determine the amount of the misstatements found in the sample items. This misstatement must then be projected to the total population. To continue with the current illustration, assume the auditor discovered misstatements equal to $200, for a sample with a total dollar value that was 5% of the dollar value of the total population. The projected total misstatement for the sampled population would be $4,000 ($200/5%).

When the auditor has tested a segment of the population 100%, the misstatement found for these items must be added to the projected total misstatement for the sampled item in order to determine the projected total misstatement for the total population. For example, in the current illustration all receivables with a balance greater than $4,000 were tested. If the misstatement discovered in this group of receivables was $1,000, the projected total misstatement for the population would be $5,000 ($4,000 + $1,000).

Consider sampling risk

Once the auditor has determined the projected total misstatement for the population, he or she must be careful not to draw a conclusion about the population based on this single estimate. That is, the auditor cannot say that the best estimate of the misstatement is a specific amount ($11,000 in the current example), but rather he or she must recognize that sampling risk must be considered. Sampling risk arises because not all the items in the population were tested; therefore, the best estimate of the misstatement is not a single amount but a range around that single amount.

Determining, based on the sampling results, whether a population's dollar value is probably not misstated involves a considerable amount of professional judgment. The focus of the judgment is the relationship between the tolerable misstatement and the projected misstatement. The broad generalizations in Exhibit AU 350-5 are helpful in making that judgment.

EXHIBIT AU 350-5—MISSTATEMENTS AND PROFESSIONAL JUDGMENT

Relationship of Projected Misstatement and Tolerable Misstatement for the Sample	Examples	Analysis and Judgment
The projected misstatement is significantly less than the tolerable misstatement.	Assume the projected misstatement is $1,000 and the tolerable misstatement is $9,000.	The projected misstatement is so much less than the tolerable misstatement, it is probably unlikely that the actual misstatement (if the entire population were sampled) would be greater than the tolerable misstatement. *Conclusion*: The auditor is reasonably sure that the population balance is not misstated.

Relationship of Projected Misstatement and Tolerable Misstatement for the Sample	Examples	Analysis and Judgment
The projected misstatement is equal to or greater than the tolerable misstatement	Assume the projected misstatement is $10,000 and the tolerable misstatement is $9,000.	The projected misstatement implies that the balance is materially misstated. *Conclusion*: The auditor may request that the client review the population for possible adjustment. Once adjustments are made, the auditor should reevaluate the balance to determine whether it is acceptable.
The projected misstatement is neither close to nor far from the tolerable misstatement.	Assume the projected misstatement is $7,500 and the tolerable misstatement is $9,000.	When the projected misstatement is neither close to nor far from the tolerable misstatement, the decision process becomes more difficult because the conclusion that can be drawn is not as obvious as it is in the two situations described above. *Conclusion*: Under this circumstance, the auditor may want to (a) increase the sample size (concluding that the original sample may not have been representative) or (b) perform alternative audit procedures in order to obtain additional evidence concerning the possible misstatement of the population.

Consider qualitative characteristics

When a misstatement is discovered, an auditor should not mechanically respond to the misstatement as simply part of the projection of the total misstated amount in the population. Each misstatement should be analyzed to determine whether it arose from an error (an unintentional action) or from possible fraud (an intentional action). If fraud is suspected, the auditor should follow the guidance established in AU Section 316 (Consideration of Fraud in a Financial Statement Audit).

Practitioner's Aids

EXHIBIT AU 350-6—REQUIRED SAMPLE SIZE FOR NONSTATISTICAL SUBSTANTIVE TESTS OF DETAILS

Use the following procedures as a guide for determining the required sample size for the performance of substantive tests of details based on a nonstatistical sampling approach. The checklist is only a guide, and professional judgment should be exercised to determine how the procedures should be modified by revising or adding procedures to the checklist. Initial and date each procedure as it is completed. Each procedure should be cross referenced to a workpaper that is the basis for the judgment or factor that is used to determine the required sample size.

Client Name: _____

Account Balance or Transactions Tested: _____

Date of Financial Statements: _____

	Initials	Date	*Workpaper Reference*

1. Establish the level of inherent risk.
    ____ Maximum
    ____ Slightly below maximum
    ____ Moderate
    ____ Low

2. Consider the effectiveness of controls related to the financial statement assertions (control risk).
    ____ Maximum
    ____ Slightly below maximum
    ____ Moderate
    ____ Low

	Initials	Date	Workpaper Reference

3. Establish the risk of incorrect acceptance.
   ___ Maximum
   ___ Slightly below maximum
   ___ Moderate
   ___ Low

4. Establish a tolerable misstatement level.

   $_____

5. Evaluate the effect of other related substantive tests of details.
   ___ Maximum
   ___ Slightly below maximum
   ___ Moderate
   ___ Low

6. Determine the population reported amount.

   $_____

7. Compute the preliminary sample size based on the following formula:

   $$\frac{\text{Population reported amount}}{\text{Tolerable misstatement}} \times \text{Assurance factor}$$

   Preliminary sample size: _____

	Initials	Date	Workpaper Reference

8. Adjust the preliminary sample size.

   Required sample size: _____

Reviewed by: _____

Date: _____

§350 • Audit Sampling

EXHIBIT AU 350-7—
Audit Judgment Factors Used in Nonstatistical and in Statistical Sampling to Determine Sample Size for Tests of Controls

Basis for Audit Judgment in Determining Factors Affecting Sample Size → **Factors Affecting Sample Size**

- Prior Years' Working Papers or Pre-Audit Sample Rate → Consider the Expected Population Deviation Rate
- Planned Assessed Level of Control Risk → Consider the Tolerable Rate
- Degree of Assurance Desired → Consider the Tolerable Rate; Allowable Risk of Assessing Control Risk Too Low
- Allowable Risk of Assessing Control Risk Too Low

→ Using Professional Judgment, Determine the Required Sample Size

Consider the Effects of Population Size ----→ Using Professional Judgment, Determine the Required Sample Size

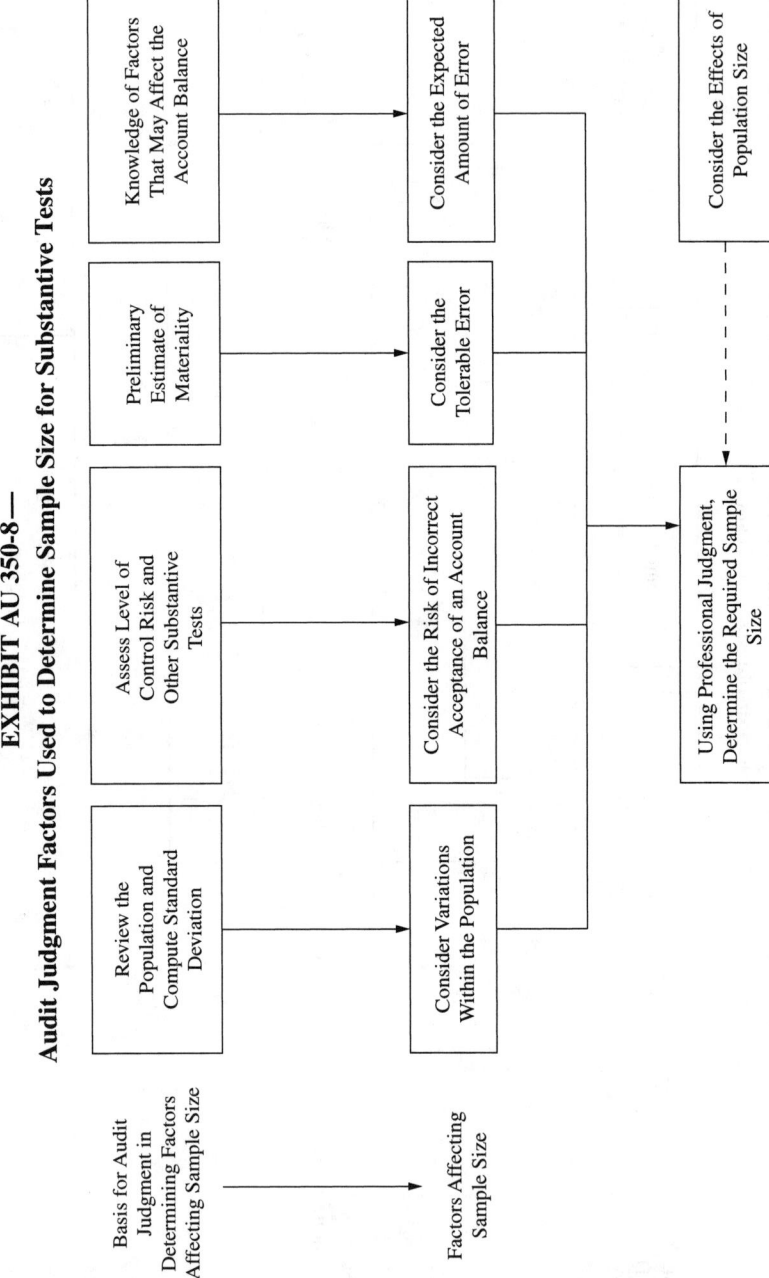

EXHIBIT AU 350-8—
Audit Judgment Factors Used to Determine Sample Size for Substantive Tests

Basis for Audit Judgment in Determining Factors Affecting Sample Size	→	Factors Affecting Sample Size

Review the Population and Compute Standard Deviation	Assess Level of Control Risk and Other Substantive Tests	Preliminary Estimate of Materiality	Knowledge of Factors That May Affect the Account Balance
↓	↓	↓	↓
Consider Variations Within the Population	Consider the Risk of Incorrect Acceptance of an Account Balance	Consider the Tolerable Error	Consider the Expected Amount of Error

→ Using Professional Judgment, Determine the Required Sample Size

Consider the Effects of Population Size ---→ Using Professional Judgment, Determine the Required Sample Size

SECTION 380

COMMUNICATION WITH AUDIT COMMITTEES

Authoritative Pronouncements

SAS-61—Communication with Audit Committees

SAS-89—Audit Adjustments

SAS-90—Audit Committee Communications

Auditing Interpretation (August 1993)—Applicability of Section 380

Overview

An element that a client should consider when designing its internal control system is the establishment of an audit committee. An audit committee should be composed mostly of board members who are not employees of the company. The role of the committee usually consists of nominating the independent auditor and reviewing the scope and the results of the audit. Selection of an audit committee may enhance the independence of the auditor, because the auditor can request the audit committee to encourage management to cooperate more fully, if necessary.

SAS-61 (Communication with Audit Committees) concludes that certain matters related to the audit should be communicated to those who have responsibility for oversight of the financial reporting process. The recipient of the communication will be the audit committee (or "individuals with a level of authority and responsibility equivalent to an audit committee in organizations that do not have one, such as the board of directors, the board of trustees, an owner in an owner-managed enterprise, or others who may have engaged the auditor"). Although the audit committee is to receive the communication, the auditor may also provide the information to the entity's management or others within the entity that may benefit from the communication.

> **ENGAGEMENT STRATEGY:** The guidance in SAS-60, SAS-54, and SAS-71 (Interim Financial Information), and SAS-82 identifies additional circumstances under which the auditor should communicate with the audit committee.

The communication requirements established by SAS-61 apply to the following situations:

- Engagements in which the client has established an audit committee or formally designated a group equivalent to an audit committee to have oversight responsibility with respect to the financial reporting process.

- Engagements is which the client is a registrant that files periodic reports with the SEC under the Investment Company Act of 1940 or the Securities Exchange Act of 1934 [except a broker or dealer registered only because of section 15(a) of the 1934 Act].

> **RISK ASSESSMENT POINT:** The Auditing Interpretation (August 1993) of SAS-61 titled "Applicability of Section 380" concludes that if the auditee's governing or oversight body has not established an audit committee or formally designated a group equivalent to an audit committee, the standards established by SAS-61 do not apply. For entities that do not have an audit committee or other formally designated group but have a board of directors, the auditor may communicate the information required by SAS-61 to the board, but is not required to do so.

Promulgated Procedures Checklist

The auditor should perform the following procedures in determining the nature of communications with the client's audit committee:

_____ Determine the form of the communication with the audit committee.

_____ Determine the specific matters that should be communicated to the audit committee.

_____ Discuss the quality of accounting principles (for SEC clients only).

Analysis and Application of Procedures

Determine the form of the communication with the audit committee

The communication with the audit committee may be written or oral. If written, the communication should note that the report is intended solely for the "audit committee or the board of directors, and, if appropriate, management, and is not intended to be and should not be used by anyone other than these specified parties." If the communication is oral, the matters communicated and other relevant factors related to the oral communication should be documented in the workpapers.

> **RISK ASSESSMENT POINT:** SAS-90 points out that when the audit committee prepares minutes of its meetings it may be appropriate to review these minutes to see if they are consistent with the auditor's communications with the committee.

§380 • Communication with Audit Committees

The communication with the audit committee should occur on a timely basis, either before or after the issuance of the auditor's report, depending on the circumstances.

Determine the specific matters that should be communicated to the audit committee

The purpose of the communication is to provide the audit committee with additional information regarding the scope and results of the audit that may assist the audit committee in overseeing the financial reporting and disclosure process for which management is responsible.

Exhibit AU 380-1 summarizes the topics that SAS-61 concludes should be communicated to the audit committee.

> **ENGAGEMENT STRATEGY:** In some cases, it may be more appropriate for management rather than the auditor to communicate some of the information; however, when management makes the communication, the auditor must be satisfied that the communication was actually made.

Discuss the quality of accounting principles (for SEC clients only)

SAS-90 requires that the auditor discuss with the audit committee the quality of the entity's accounting principles used to prepare its financial reports. Matters that should be included in the discussion include the following:

- The consistency of its accounting policies and their application

- The clarity and completeness of the financial statements based on the accounting principles selected by management

- The use of accounting principles that have a significant impact on the representational faithfulness, verifiability, and neutrality of information contained in the financial statements (these concepts are discussed in FAS concept Statement No. 2 (Qualitative Characteristics of Accounting Information)

The analysis of the quality of specific accounting principles could include estimates used by management, the treatment of unusual transactions, and the policies used to determine the timing of transactions.

> **PLANNING AID REMINDER:** The guidance established by SAS-90 puts a new and significant burden on the auditor. While there are, for some transactions, different methods that may be used to account for the same transaction, there is little professional guidance for determining the quality of any particular accounting method. This new requirement is a reaction by the

profession to the pressure by the SEC and other interested parties to increase the auditor's role in determining whether financial statements portray the actual economic conditions of the audited company. For this reason, it is important for an auditor to fully understand the fundamental characteristics of an industry (including unique products, technological changes, and global competition) and current economic developments in order to be in a position to apply his or her judgment about the quality of an entity's accounting principles

Practitioner's Aids

Exhibit AU 380-1 presents examples of topics that the auditor should communicate to the client audit committee.

EXHIBIT AU 380-1—TOPIC AND NATURE OF COMMUNICATIONS WITH THE CLIENT'S AUDIT COMMITTEE

Topic of Communication	Nature of Communication
Auditor's responsibility under generally accepted auditing standards	• Level of assurance by the auditor with respect to engagements conducted in accordance with accepted auditing standards • The concept of reasonable assurance, including supporting concepts such as materiality and audit tests • Auditor's responsibility for detecting weaknesses in the internal control, errors, fraud, and similar matters
Significant accounting policies	• Selection and application of significant accounting policies • Methods used to account for unusual transactions • Effects of significant accounting policies used to account for transactions and events when there is a lack of consensus about how the items should be accounted for and disclosed

§380 • Communication with Audit Committees

Topic of Communication	Nature of Communication
Management judgments and estimates	• Process used to make accounting estimates • Auditor's basis for determining reasonableness of accounting estimates
Audit adjustments	• Implications of significant audit adjustments proposed and recorded • Implications of audit adjustments proposed but not recorded • Uncorrected misstatements aggregated by the auditor that management believes are immaterial
Quality of accounting principles (for SEC clients only)	• Consistency of accounting policies • Clarity and completeness of financial statements • Use of accounting principles that have a significant impact on the qualitative characteristics of financial statements.
Other information in documents containing audited financial statements	• Auditor's responsibility with respect to other information in documents that include the audited financial statements
Disagreements with management	• Significant disagreements with management concerning applicability of accounting principles, scope of engagement, or wording of audit report (does not include differences based on incomplete information that were later resolved)
Consultation with other accountants	• Auditor's view of management's consultation with other accountants concerning applicability of accounting principles, scope of engagement, or wording of audit report [see SAS-50 (AU 625)]

Topic of Communication	Nature of Communication
Major issues discussed with management prior to retention	• Major issues discussed with management (such as applicability of accounting principles and audit standards) as part of the auditor retention process
Difficulties encountered in performing the audit	• Significant matters (such as availability of personnel and provision of information that impeded the audit process)

SECTION 390

CONSIDERATION OF OMITTED PROCEDURES AFTER THE REPORT DATE

Authoritative Pronouncements

SAS-46—Consideration of Omitted Procedures after the Report Date

Overview

SAS-46 provides guidance when the auditor concludes, subsequent to the date of the auditor's report, that one or more procedures were omitted from an engagement. This situation is different from the circumstance where the auditor, subsequent to the date of the report, discovers facts existing at the date of the auditor's report.

> **OBSERVATION:** Disclosure that procedures were omitted often comes as a result of a quality review or peer review of the auditor's engagement.

Promulgated Procedures Checklist

The auditor should perform the following procedures when it is suspected that audit procedures were omitted:

_____ Assess the significance of omitted procedures and consider whether to apply audit procedures.

_____ Determine the proper course of action if significant procedures or alternative procedures cannot be performed.

Analysis and Application of Procedures

Assess the significance of omitted procedures and consider whether to apply audit procedures

Initially, the auditor should assess the importance of the omitted audit procedure within the context of the engagement. This assessment may include a review of the workpapers and discussions with other personnel within the firm. The auditor must determine whether the third standard of fieldwork (evidential matter) was observed. If it is concluded that a significant audit procedure was omitted, and it is likely that the financial statements are being relied on or will be relied on by others, the auditor must take corrective action. If possible, the auditor should apply the omitted audit procedure or an alternative audit procedure.

Determine the proper course of action if significant procedures or alternative procedures cannot be performed

If the auditor is unable to apply the omitted or the alternative audit procedure, he or she should consult an attorney and discuss the appropriateness of the following actions:

- Notification of regulatory authorities (SEC, etc.)
- Notification of persons relying, or likely to rely, on the financial statements

> **ENGAGEMENT STRATEGY:** Applying the omitted audit procedure or an alternative audit procedure may lead the auditor to conclude that facts did exist at the date of the report that could have had an effect on the audit approach or the auditor's report.

Practitioner's Aids

EXHIBIT AU 390-1—OMISSION OF ENGAGEMENT PROCEDURES DISCOVERED AFTER THE REPORT DATE

Use the following procedures, which are adapted from guidance found in SAS-46 (Consideration of Omitted Procedures after the Report Date), as a guide for evaluating the omission of engagement procedures discovered after the report date. The program is only a guide, and professional judgment should be exercised to determine how the guidance established in the auditing standards should be adapted to a particular engagement.

Initial and date each procedure as it is completed. If the procedure is not relevant to this engagement, place "N/A" (not applicable) in the space provided for an initial.

Client Name: _____

Date of Financial Statements: _____

§390 • Omitted Procedures after the Report Date

	Initials	Date	Workpaper Reference

1. Establish the level of inherent risk. _____ _____ _____

1. Assess the significance of omitted procedures and consider whether to apply audit procedures. _____ _____ _____

2. Determine the proper course of action if significant procedures or alternative procedures cannot be performed. _____ _____ _____

Other engagement procedures: _____

Reviewed by: _____

Date: _____

AU 400

The First, Second, and Third Standards of Reporting

Section 410: Adherence to Generally Accepted Accounting
   Principles 309

Section 411: The Meaning of "Present Fairly in Conformity
   with Generally Accepted Accounting Principles" 311

Section 420: Consistency of Application of Generally
   Accepted Accounting Principles 318

Section 431: Adequacy of Disclosures in Financial Statements 325

Section 435: Segment Information 336

SECTION 410

ADHERENCE TO GENERALLY ACCEPTED ACCOUNTING PRINCIPLES

Authoritative Pronouncements

SAS-1—Codification of Auditing Standards and Procedures (Section 410, Adherence to Generally Accepted Accounting Principles)

Auditing Interpretation (February 1997)—The Impact of the Auditor's Report of a FASB Statement Prior to the Statement's Effective Date

Overview

The first standard of reporting requires that "the report shall state whether the financial statements are presented in accordance with generally accepted accounting principles." At the conclusion of an engagement, the auditor offers an opinion as to whether the financial statements are prepared in accordance with generally accepted accounting principles. Note that the auditor offers an opinion on the financial statements rather than a statement of fact. An opinion is based on various judgments that must be made during the audit engagement and by its very nature is not a statement of fact that can be verified in a manner that results in a guarantee that the financial statements conform to generally accepted accounting principles. If the auditor is unable to perform the audit procedures that are considered appropriate for a particular engagement, a qualified opinion or disclaimer of opinion must be expressed on the financial statements.

> **RISK ASSESSMENT POINT:** If a client's financial statements are based on a comprehensive basis of accounting other than generally accepted accounting principles, the auditor satisfies the first standard of reporting by stating in the audit report that "the statements have been prepared in conformity with another comprehensive basis of accounting other than generally accepted accounting principles" and by expressing an opinion on a basis of accounting identified in AU Section 623 (Special Reports).

> **PLANNING AID REMINDER:** The Auditing Interpretation (October 1979) on adherence to GAAP, titled "The Impact on an Auditor's Report of an FASB Statement Prior to the Statement's Effective Date," states that the auditor must evaluate the ade-

quacy of the client's disclosure of the use of an accounting principle that currently is acceptable but (1) will not be acceptable in the future because of the effective date of a new FASB Statement and (2) the new FASB Statement requires the restatement of prior years' financial statements when it is adopted.

SECTION 411

THE MEANING OF "PRESENT FAIRLY IN CONFORMITY WITH GENERALLY ACCEPTED ACCOUNTING PRINCIPLES"

Authoritative Pronouncements

SAS-69—The Meaning of "Present Fairly in Conformity with Generally Accepted Accounting Principles"

SAS-91—Federal GAAP Hierarchy

Auditing Interpretation (March 1995)—The Auditor's Consideration of Management's Adoption of Accounting Principles for New Transactions or Events

Overview

SAS-1 describes "generally accepted accounting principles" as a "technical accounting term that encompasses the conventions, rules, and procedures necessary to define accepted accounting practice at a particular time." Thus, generally accepted accounting principles include broad guidelines of general application (for example, the concept of depreciation) as well as detailed practices and procedures (straight-line deprecation). SAS-1 requires that in determining whether a client's financial statements are presented fairly in conformity with generally accepted accounting principles, the auditor must make the following judgments:

- The accounting principles selected an applied have generally acceptance.
- The accounting principles are appropriate in the circumstances.
- The financial statements, including the related notes, are informative of matters that may affect their use, understanding, and interpretation (see AU Section 431—Adequacy of Disclosure in Financial Statements).
- The information presented in the financial statements is classified and summarized in a reasonable manner; that is, it is neither too detailed nor too condensed (see AU Section 43).
- The financial statements reflect the underlying transactions and events in a manner that presents the financial position, results of operations, and cash flows stated within a range of acceptable limits, that is, within limits that are reasonable and practicable to attain in financial statements.

To determine how a particular transaction or event should be accounted for and reported in the financial statements, the auditor must refer to the generally accepted accounting principles (GAAP) hierarchy in SAS-69, which establishes a private-sector accounting hierarchy, a public-sector accounting hierarchy, and a federal GAAP hierarchy. The private-sector accounting hierarchy should be used in the preparation of financial statements of commercial enterprises and not-for-profit organizations. The public-sector accounting hierarchy should be used in the preparation of statements for state and local governmental entities. The federal GAAP hierarchy should be used to prepare the financial statements for federal governmental entities.

> **ENGAGEMENT STRATEGY:** SAS-69 notes that state and local governmental entities include public benefit corporations and authorities, public employee retirement systems, governmental utilities, governmental hospitals and other governmental health care providers, and public colleges and universities.

The private-sector, public-sector, and federal accounting hierarchies are presented in Exhibits AU 411-1, AU 411-2, and AU 411-3, respectively. In these hierarchies, the specific sources of generally accepted accounting principles are ranked by their level of authoritative support. Thus, for example, an accounting principle established by a Financial Accounting Standards Board (FASB) Statement would be more authoritative than an accounting principle identified in an American Institute of Certified Public Accountants (AICPA) Accounting or Audit Guide.

> **PLANNING AID REMINDER:** For public companies, Level A would include rules and interpretive releases of the Securities and Exchange Commission (SEC). SAS-69 notes that the SEC staff issues Staff Accounting Bulletins, which deal with SEC disclosure requirements, but SAS-69 does not specifically identify where Staff Accounting Bulletins should be classified in the accounting hierarchy. Presumably, it is in Level A. Also, SAS-69 notes that the SEC will challenge any accounting method that differs from a consensus established by the FASB's Emerging Issues Task Force (EITF).

> **ENGAGEMENT STRATEGY:** SAS-69 does not refer to the fifth level in the two accounting hierarchies as Level E, but rather labels the category as "other accounting literature." This clearly establishes Levels A through D as "must know" GAAP, departures from which violate Rule 203 or 202 of the AICPA Code of Professional Conduct.

The absence of official pronouncements or unofficial writings forces an enterprise to review other actual accounting and reporting practices.

Practitioners can identify specific practices by reviewing surveys and reports published by professional organizations. For example, the AICPA annually publishes *Accounting Trends and Techniques*, which summarizes the accounting practices followed by 600 large business enterprises. Periodically the AICPA publishes its *Financial Report Survey*, which discusses the actual reporting practices of many companies for a specific accounting topic. Many accounting firms maintain departments that answer questions raised by professional staff members or clients about accounting methods or practices. As specific problems are solved, they are documented by the firm. This serves as a basis for the selection of accounting methods in similar situations. Some accounting firms have an informal arrangement whereby they share experiences and technical opinions with other accounting firms.

New transactions or events

The Auditing Interpretation (March 1995) titled "The Auditor's Consideration of Management's Adoption of Accounting Principles for New Transactions or Events" makes the following points for when a client adopts accounting principles for new transactions or events that are not specifically addressed by Levels A through D of the accounting hierarchies:

- The auditor should understand the basis by which the client determined how to account for the item.
- In determining the appropriateness of the basis used by the client, the auditor may consider analogous transactions or events for which accounting principles have been established.
- In determining the appropriateness of the basis the client used, the auditor may consider other accounting literature (as discussed in the other accounting literature category of the accounting hierarchies) depending on (1) its relevance to the new transaction or event, (2) the specificity of the guidance, and (3) the "general recognition of the issuer or author as an authority."

The Interpretation also notes that in engagements that are covered by the standards established by AU Section 380 (Communication with Audit Committees), the auditor should determine that the audit committee (or its equivalent) has been informed of the newly adopted accounting principle. The audit committee should also be informed of accounting methods used "to account for significant unusual transactions and the effect of significant accounting policies in controversial or emerging areas for which there is a lack of authoritative guidance or consensus."

Practitioner's Aids

EXHIBIT AU 411-1—PRIVATE-SECTOR ACCOUNTING HIERARCHY

Authoritative GAAP

Level A
- FASB Statements
- FASB Interpretations
- Accounting Principles Board (APB) Opinions
- AICPA Accounting Research Bulletins

Level B
- FASB Technical Bulletins
- AICPA Industry Audit and Accounting Guides
- AICPA Statements of Position

Level C
- FASB Emerging Issues Task Force consensus positions
- AICPA Practice Bulletins

Level D
- AICPA Accounting Interpretations
- Implementation Guides (Qs and As) published by the FASB staff
- Practices widely recognized and prevalent generally or in industry

Other Nonauthoritative Accounting Literature
- FASB Statements of Financial Accounting Concepts
- APB Statements
- AICPA Issues Papers
- International Accounting Standards of the International Accounting Standards Committee
- Government Accounting Standards Board (GASB) Statements
- GASB Interpretations
- GASB Technical Bulletins
- Pronouncements of other professional associations or regulatory agencies
- AICPA Technical Practice Aids

§411 • The Meaning of Present Fairly in Conformity with GAAP   315

- Accounting textbooks
- Handbooks
- Articles

EXHIBIT AU 411-2—PUBLIC-SECTOR ACCOUNTING HIERARCHY

Authoritative GAAP

Level A

- GASB Statements
- GASB Interpretations
- FASB pronouncements made applicable by a GASB Statement or GASB Interpretation
- AICPA pronouncements made applicable by a GASB Statement or GASB Interpretation

Level B

- GASB Technical Bulletins
- AICPA Industry Audit and Accounting Guides made applicable by the AICPA
- AICPA Statements of Position made applicable by the AICPA

Level C

- AICPA Practice Bulletins made applicable by the AICPA
- GASB Emerging Issues Task Force consensus positions (if created)

Level D

- GASB Implementation Guides (Qs and As)
- Practices widely recognized and prevalent in state and local governments

Other Nonauthoritative Accounting Literature

- GASB Concepts Statements
- Sources identified in Levels A through D in the private-sector accounting hierarchy that have not been made applicable by the action of the GASB
- APB Statements

- FASB Statements of Financial Accounting Concepts
- AICPA Issues Papers
- International Accounting Standards of the International Accounting Standards Committee
- Pronouncements of other professional associations or regulatory agencies
- AICPA Technical Practice Aids
- Accounting textbooks
- Handbooks
- Articles

EXHIBIT AU 411-3—FEDERAL GAAP HIERARCHY

Authoritative GAAP

Level A

- FASAB (Federal Accounting Standards Advisory Board) Statements
- FASAB Interpretations
- AICPA and FASB pronouncements made applicable by a FASAB Statement or Interpretation

Level B

- FASAB Technical Bulletins
- AICPA Industry Audit and Accounting Guides made applicable by the AICPA and cleared by the FASAB
- AICPA Statements of Position made applicable by the AICPA and cleared by the FASAB

Level C

- AICPA AcSEC Practice Bulletins if made applicable and cleared by the FASAB
- Technical releases of the Accounting and Auditing Policy Committee of the FASAB

Level D

- FASAB Implementation Guides
- Practices widely recognized and prevalent in the federal government

Other Nonauthoritative Accounting Literature
- FASAB Concepts Statements
- Sources identified in Levels A through D in the private-sector accounting hierarchy that have not been made applicable by the action of the FASAB
- GASB Concepts Statements
- GASB Statements, Interpretations, Technical Bulletins, and Concepts Statements
- AICPA Issues Papers
- International Accounting Standards of the Internal Accounting Standards Committee
- Pronouncements of other professional associations or regulatory agencies
- AICPA Technical Practice Aids
- Accounting textbooks
- Handbooks
- Articles

SECTION 420

CONSISTENCY OF APPLICATION OF GENERALLY ACCEPTED ACCOUNTING PRINCIPLES

Authoritative Pronouncements

SAS-1—Codification of Auditing Standards and Procedures (Section 420, Consistency of Application of Generally Accepted Accounting Principles)

Auditing Interpretation (February 1974)—The Effect of APB Opinion 28 on Consistency

Auditing Interpretation (December 1980)—Change in Presentation of Accumulated Benefit Information in the Financial Statements of a Defined Benefit Pension Plan

Auditing Interpretation (April 1989)—Impact of the Auditor's Report of FIFO to LIFO Change in Comparative Financial Statements

Auditing Interpretation (June 1993)—The Effect of Accounting Changes by an Investee on Consistency

Overview

The second standard of reporting states that the report shall "identify those circumstances in which such principles have not been consistently observed in the current period in relation to the preceding period."

Accounting Principles Board (APB) Opinion No. 20 (Accounting Changes) classifies "accounting changes" as (1) changes in an accounting principle, (2) changes in a reporting entity, and (3) changes in an accounting estimate. For each accounting change, APB Opinion No. 20 establishes appropriate accounting and reporting standards. In general, changes in accounting principles result in either a cumulative-effect adjustment that is reported on the statement of income (no restatement of prior-period financial statements) or an adjustment to the beginning balance of retained earnings (restatement of prior-period financial statements).

Under the following conditions, the auditor does not refer to the consistent application of accounting principles in the standard three-paragraph report:

- There have been no changes in the application of accounting principles in the preparation of the current year's financial statements.

- There have been changes in the application of accounting principles in the preparation of the current year's financial statements, but the effects of the changes are considered immaterial.

§420 • Consistency of Application of GAAP

When there has been a change in the application of an accounting principle and the effects of the change are considered material, an explanatory paragraph should be added to the standard auditor's report. The explanatory paragraph should immediately follow the opinion paragraph and should include the following:

- Reference to the note to the financial statements that discusses the change in accounting principle
- Discussion of the nature of the change in accounting principle

The following is an example of an explanatory paragraph resulting from a change in an accounting principle:

> As discussed in Note X to the financial statements, the Company changed its method of valuing inventories in 20X5.

Even though there has been a violation of the consistency standard, the auditor's report is not qualified, and there is no reference to the explanatory paragraph in the opinion paragraph.

> **PLANNING AID REMINDER:** The Auditing Interpretation (June 1993) titled "The Effect of Accounting Changes by an Investee on Consistency" concludes that the auditor's report on an investor company that uses the equity method to account for its interest in an investee company must include an explanatory paragraph when the investee company changes an accounting principle.

> **PLANNING AID REMINDER:** The Auditing Interpretation (December 1980) titled "Change in Presentation of Accumulated Benefit Information in the Financial Statements of a Defined Benefit Pension Plan" concludes that changes in the formatting of information related to the presentation of accumulated benefits are reclassifications and not changes in an accounting principles and therefore do not require the addition of an explanatory paragraph.

Promulgated Reporting Checklist

The auditor should consider the effect on the consistency standard under the following circumstances:

_____ Report covers only a single (current) year

_____ Reporting subsequent to the year of change

___ Change in the format of the statement of cash flows

___ Changing to an acceptable accounting principle

___ Correction of an error

___ Change in an accounting estimate

___ Change in an accounting principle inseparable from an estimate

___ Change in the reporting entity

___ Substantially different transactions or events

___ Change that may have a material effect in the future

Analysis and Application of Reporting Standards

Report covers only a single (current) year

When the auditor's report covers only a single (current) year, the auditor must determine whether generally accepted accounting principles have been consistently applied in the current year and in the previous year. When the auditor's report covers two or more years, the auditor must determine whether generally accepted accounting principles have been applied on a consistent basis (1) between or among the financial statements reported on and (2) between the earliest set of financial statements reported on and the immediately previous year's set of financial statements (not reported on) if the previous year's statements are presented.

Reporting subsequent to the year of change

Reporting a change in an accounting principle in a period after the change has occurred is dependent on whether (1) the change was accounted for through the retroactive restatement of prior years' financial statements and (2) the change was from FIFO (first in, first out) to LIFO (last in, first out).

Retroactive restatement

When a change in an accounting principle is accounted for by the retroactive restatement of prior years' financial statements, there is comparability among the financial statements since all financial statements are prepared (after restatement) using the same accounting principles. For this reason, an explanatory paragraph (as illustrated earlier) describing a change in accounting principle needs to be added to the standard auditor's report only in the year of the change.

No retroactive restatement

When a change in an accounting principle is accounted for in a manner that does not result in the retroactive restatement of prior years' financial statements, there is a lack of complete comparability among financial statements due to the cumulative-effect adjustment reflected in the financial statements for the year of the change. For this reason, an explanatory paragraph describing the change in accounting principle must be added to the standard auditor's report for as long as the financial statements for the year of the change are presented with subsequent statements.

FIFO to LIFO change

APB Opinion No. 20 provides specific guidance when an entity changes from the FIFO inventory method to the LIFO inventory method. A change from FIFO to LIFO requires neither a cumulative-effect adjustment nor a retroactive restatement of prior years' financial statements. An Auditing Interpretation on consistency (April 1989) titled "Impact on the Auditor's Report of FIFO to LIFO Change in Comparative Financial Statements" concludes that a FIFO to LIFO accounting change would require an explanatory paragraph in the auditor's report for (1) the year of the change and (2) all subsequent years until the year of change is the earliest year reported on by the auditor.

> **PLANNING AID REMINDER:** Another Interpretation on consistency (February 1974), titled "The Effect of APB Opinion No. 28 on Consistency," states that the auditor should not add an explanatory paragraph in those circumstances in which accounting principles and practices used in preparing the annual financial information have been modified in accordance with APB Opinion No. 28 (Interim Financial Reporting).

Change in the format of the statement of cash flows

FAS-95 (CT C25) (Statement of Cash Flows) allows some flexibility in the preparation of the statement of cash flows. For example, either the direct method or the indirect method can be used to compute cash flows from operations. SAS-43 (Omnibus Statement on Auditing Standards) concludes that changes of this nature are not a violation of the consistency standard, and if prior years' financial statements are reclassified to conform to another format, the auditor's report need not refer to the change. SAS-43 considers these changes to be reclassifications.

> **PLANNING AID REMINDER:** APB Opinion No. 20 is not applicable to reclassifications. When a reclassification occurs, prior years' financial statements should be reclassified so that all statements are comparable. However, the reclassifications, if significant, should be disclosed in the financial statements or footnotes thereto.

Changing to an acceptable accounting principle

A change from an unacceptable accounting principle to a generally accepted accounting principle is considered to be a correction of an error in financial statements of a prior period. Prior-period errors in financial statements are corrected by restatement of the prior years' financial statements that are presented on a comparative basis with the current year's statements. The nature of the error and the effect of its correction on income before extraordinary items, net income, and the related per-share data must be fully disclosed in the period the error is discovered and corrected.

When there has been a change from an unacceptable accounting principle to an acceptable accounting principle, a paragraph, similar to the one illustrated below, would be added to the standard auditor's report after the opinion paragraph.

> As discussed in Note X to the financial statements, in 20X5 the Company changed from an unacceptable method of accounting for depreciation to an acceptable method. The change in accounting principles has been accounted for as a correction of an error and prior years' financial statements have been restated.

Correction of an error

A correction of an error that arises from circumstances other than a change from an unacceptable accounting principle to an acceptable principle is not an accounting change. For this reason, the auditor's report does not refer to a consistency violation in the year the error is discovered and corrected.

> **PLANNING AID REMINDER:** If the auditor has previously reported on the prior years' financial statements that are being corrected, standards established by SAS-1, AU Section 561 (Subsequent Discovery of Facts Existing at the Date of the Auditor's Report) should be observed.

Change in an accounting estimate

APB Opinion No. 20 concludes that a change in an accounting estimate must be accounted for prospectively. Thus, the effect of a change in an accounting estimate is accounted for (1) in the period of change, if the change affects only that period (for example, a change that affects the allowance for doubtful accounts), or (2) in the period of change and in future periods, if the change affects both periods (for example, a change in the remaining life of a depreciable asset). If the auditor is satisfied that the change in an accounting estimate is reasonable, the auditor's report is not qualified or otherwise modified.

Change in an accounting principle inseparable from a change in estimate

A change in an accounting estimate caused in part or entirely by a change in an accounting principle must be reported as a change in an accounting estimate. Although such a change is reported as a change in accounting estimate, it also involves a change in accounting principle for which the auditor's report must be expanded. In this case, an explanatory paragraph must be added to the auditor's report in which the accounting change is described; however, the opinion paragraph is unqualified, with no reference to the explanatory paragraph.

Change in the reporting entity

SAS-88 notes that a change in a reporting entity generally results from a "transaction or event, such as a pooling of interests, or the creation, cessation, or complete or partial purchase or disposition of a subsidiary or other business unit" and includes the following examples:

- Consolidated or combined financial statements are presented in the current year, but individual financial statements were presented in the previous year.

- Consolidated financial statements for the current year do not include the same subsidiaries that were used to prepare the previous year's consolidated financial statements.

- Combined financial statements for the current year do not include the same companies that were used to prepare the previous year's combined financial statements.

A change in a reporting entity, such as the ones described above, does not require the inclusion of an explanatory paragraph about a consistency violation in the auditor's report.

> **PLANNING AID REMINDER:** A change in a reporting entity that does not result from a transaction or event must be included in an explanatory paragraph.

Pooling of interests

APB-20 (Accounting Changes) requires that a pooling of interests be accounted for by restating all prior years' financial statements that are presented on a comparative basis. If those financial statements are not restated, the auditor must issue either a qualified opinion or adverse option on the consolidated financial statements. Under this reporting format there is no need to include an additional paragraph that addresses the consistency issue.

Substantially different transactions or events

An accounting principle may be changed when transactions or events have a material effect on the financial statements. An accounting change of this nature is not a violation of the consistency standard, and therefore the auditor's report is not modified. For example, a company may account for transactions on a cash basis because the affect on the financial statements is considered immaterial; however, in a subsequent year, the volume of transactions may increase, resulting in the need to adopt an accrual method. The adoption of the accrual method is not considered a change in an accounting principle.

In addition, when an accounting principle is changed to account for transactions or events that are clearly different from previous transactions or events, the accounting change is not a violation of the consistency standard.

Change that may have a material effect in the future

As noted earlier, the auditor's report is not modified when the effect of a change in an accounting principle is immaterial. If it is expected that the change may have a material effect on future financial statements, that expectation should be disclosed in a note to the financial statements; however, there is no need to refer to the change in accounting principle in the auditor's report in the current or future years.

SECTION 431

ADEQUACY OF DISCLOSURES IN FINANCIAL STATEMENTS

Authoritative Pronouncements

SAS-32—Adequacy of Disclosures in Financial Statements

Overview

Adequate disclosure in financial statements is a broad concept and encompasses many factors including the following items:

- The format of the financial statements
- The arrangement of items in the financial statements
- The specific content of items in the financial statements
- Notes to the financial statements
- Terminology used in the financial statements
- Classification of items in the financial statements

The auditor must use professional judgment to determine whether the disclosure in the financial statements is adequate. If the auditor concludes that adequate disclosure has not been achieved, the auditor's report should be qualified or an adverse opinion should be expressed. If practicable, the omitted disclosure should be included in the auditor's report. *Practicable* means that "the information is reasonably obtainable from management's accounts and records and providing the information in his report does not require the auditor to assume the position of a preparer of financial information."

> **ENGAGEMENT STRATEGY:** An auditor may assist management in the preparation of its financial statements, including the preparation of notes. However, under this circumstance the financial statements and the accompanying notes are the representations of management and there is no need for the auditor to modify the audit report.
>
> **RISK ASSESSMENT POINT:** The auditor should not make information obtained during the engagement available to other parties without the consent of management, unless the information is required to be disclosed or presented in order for the

financial statements to be prepared in accordance with generally accepted accounting principles.

EXHIBIT AU 431-1—CHECKLIST DISCLOSURE QUESTIONNAIRE

Use the following checklist to identify possible disclosure deficiencies in the client's financial statements.

The checklist is only a guide, and professional judgment should be exercised to determine whether financial statements satisfy the adequate disclosure criterion.

Initial and date each procedure as it is completed. If the question is not relevant to this engagement, place "N/A" (not applicable) in the space provided for an initial.

Client Name: _____

Date of Financial Statements: _____

QUESTION		SOURCE OF DISCLOSURE	Initials	Date	Workpaper Reference
• Did the client make a change in an accounting principle during the year?	___YES ___NO	APB-20 (Accounting Changes), par. 17, 21, 33, 35, 37, and 38	___	___	___
• Does the client adequately disclose accounting policies?	___YES ___NO	APB-22 (Disclosure of Accounting Polices), par. 12	___	___	___
• Did the client acquire another business during the year that was accounted for as a business combination?	___YES ___NO	APB-16 (Business Combinations), par. 56, 64, 65, 95, and 96	___	___	___
• Does the client present a cash flow statement?	___YES ___NO	FAS-95 (Statement of Cash Flows), par. 29 and 32	___	___	___

§431 • Adequacy of Disclosures in Financial Statements

QUESTION		SOURCE OF DISCLOSURE	Initials	Date	Workpaper Reference
• Do the financial statements include other comprehensive income components?	__YES __NO	FAS-130 (Reporting Comprehensive Income), par. 14, 20, and 26			
• Does the client prepare consolidated financial statements?	__YES __NO	ARB-51 (Consolidated Financial Statements), par. 5			
• Does the client's operations expose it to contingencies, risks, and uncertainties?	__YES __NO	FAS-5 (Accounting for Contingencies), par. 9, 10, 11, 12, and 17; SOP 94-6 (Disclosure of Certain Significant Risk and Uncertainties), par. 10, 11, 13, 16, 22, and 24			
• Does the client properly identify current assets and current liabilities?	__YES __NO	ARB-43 (Restatement and Revision of Accounting Research Bulletins), Chapters 4 and 3A; FAS-12 (Accounting for Certain Marketable Securities), par. 12 and 15; APB-22 (Disclosure of Accounting Policies), par. 13			
• Does the client own capital assets?	__YES __NO	APB-12 (Omnibus Opinion—1967) par. 5; APB-20			

QUESTION		SOURCE OF DISCLOSURE	Initials	Date	Workpaper Reference
		(Accounting Changes), par. 24			
• Is the client a development stage enterprise?	___YES ___NO	FAS-7 (Accounting and Reporting by Development Stage Enterprises), par. 12 and 13; FAS-7 Interpretation (Applying FASB Statement No. 7 in Financial Statements of Established Operating Enterprises), par. 5			
• Does the client present Earnings Per Share information?	___YES ___NO	FAS-128 (Earnings per Share), par. 40 and 41			
• Does the client account for one or more investments using the equity method?	___YES ___NO	APB-18 (The Equity Method of Accounting for Investments in Common Stock), par. 20 and footnote 13			
• Did the client extinguish debt early?	___YES ___NO	FAS-4 (Reporting Gains and Losses from Extinguishment of Debt), par. 9			
• Does the client invest in financial instruments?	___YES ___NO	FAS-133 (Accounting for Derivative Instruments and Hedging Activities)			

§431 • Adequacy of Disclosures in Financial Statements

QUESTION		SOURCE OF DISCLOSURE	Initials	Date	Workpaper Reference
• Does the client engage in foreign operations or exchange transactions?	__YES __NO	FAS-52 (Foreign Currency Translation), par. 30, 31, and 32; FAS-94 (Consolidation of All Majority-Owned Subsidiaries), footnote 1	_____	_____	_____
• Does the client engage in futures transactions?	__YES __NO	FAS-80 (Accounting for Futures Contracts), par. 12	_____	_____	_____
• Does the client have any governmental contracts?	__YES __NO	ARB-43 (Restatement and Revision of Accounting Research Bulletins), Chapters 11A, 11B, and 11C; FAS-30 (Accounting for Tax Benefits Related to U.K. Tax Legislation Concerning Stock Relief), par. 6	_____	_____	_____
• Does the client have impaired loans?	__YES __NO	FAS-118 (Accounting by Creditors for Impairment of a Loan—Income Recognition and Disclosure), par. 6i	_____	_____	_____
• Does the client have impaired long-lived assets?	__YES __NO	FAS-121 (Accounting for the Impairment of Long-Lived Assets and			

QUESTION		SOURCE OF DISCLOSURE	Initials	Date	Workpaper Reference
		for Long-Lived Assets to Be Disposed Of), par. 13 and 19			
• Does the client have deferred tax accounts?	___YES ___NO	FAS-109 (Accounting for Income Taxes), par. 43, 44, 45, 46, and 48			
• Does the client have intangible assets?	___YES ___NO	APB-17 (Intangible Assets), par. 30 and 31			
• Does the client have interest that is subject to capitalization?	___YES ___NO	FAS-34 (Capitalization of Interest Cost), par. 21			
• Does the client have receivables and payables that carry explicit or implicit interest rates?	___YES ___NO	APB-21 (Interest on Receivables and Payables), par. 16			
• Does the client report on an interim basis?	___YES ___NO	APB-28 (Interim Financial Reporting), par. 22, 29, and 31			
• Does the client have inventory?	___YES ___NO	APB-22 (Disclosure of Accounting Policies), par. 12; ARB-43 (Restatement and Revision of Accounting Research Bulletins), Chapter 4			
• Does the client have investment tax credits?	___YES ___NO	APB-4 (Accounting for the "Investment Credit"), par. 11;			

§431 • Adequacy of Disclosures in Financial Statements

QUESTION	SOURCE OF DISCLOSURE		Initials	Date	Workpaper Reference
		FAS-109 (Accounting for Income Taxes), par. 45			
• Does the client have investments in debt and equity securities?	___YES ___NO	FAS-115 (Accounting for Certain Investments in Debt and Equity Securities), par. 19, 20, 21, and 22			
• Does the client have capital lease agreements?	___YES ___NO	FAS-13 (Accounting for Leases), par. 16, 23a, 23b, 29, and 47; FAS-91 (Accounting for Nonrefundable Fees and Costs Associated with Originating or Acquiring Loans and Initial Direct Costs of Leases), par. 25d			
• Does the client have transfers of financial assets whereby it has some continuing involvement?	___YES ___NO	FAS-140 (Accounting for Transfers and Servicing of Financial Assets and Extinguishments of Liabilities), par. 17			
• Does the client have long-term construction contracts?	___YES ___NO	ARB-45 (Long-Term Construction-Type Contracts), par. 15			
• Does the client have long-term obligations and commitments?	___YES ___NO	FAS-47 (Disclosure of Long-Term Obligations), par. 7, 8, and 10			

QUESTION	SOURCE OF DISCLOSURE	Initials	Date	Workpaper Reference
• Has the client settled a liability by transferring assets to the creditor or otherwise obtained an unconditional release or set aside assets that are dedicated to eventually settling a liability?	___YES ___NO FAS-140 (Accounting for Transfers and Servicing of Financial Assets and Extinguishments of Liabilities), par. 17			
• Does the client engage in nonmonetary transactions?	___YES ___NO APB-29 (Accounting for Nonmonetary Transactions), par. 28			
• Does the client have pension and other postretirement benefit plans?	___YES ___NO FAS-132 (Employers' Disclosures about Pensions and Other Postretirement Benefits), par. 5 and 8			
• Has the client gone through a quasi-reorganization?	___YES ___NO ARB-46 (Discontinuance of Dating Earned Surplus), par. 1 and 2			
• Does the client have related party transactions?	___YES ___NO FAS-57 (Related Party Disclosures), par. 2 and 4			
• Has the client incurred research and development costs?	___YES ___NO FAS-2 (Reporting for Research and Development Costs), par. 11 and 13			

§431 • Adequacy of Disclosures in Financial Statements

QUESTION		SOURCE OF DISCLOSURE	Initials	Date	Workpaper Reference
• Has the client disposed of a business segment?	__YES __NO	APB-30 (Reporting the Results of Operations—Reporting the Effects of Disposal of a Segment of a Business, and Extraordinary, Unusual, and Infrequently Occurring Events and Transactions), par. 18			
• Does the client have to disclose segment information?	__YES __NO	FAS-131 (Disclosures about Segments of an Enterprise and Related Information), par. 26, 27, 28, 31, 32, 33, and 37			
• Does the client have outstanding equity shares with various restrictions and rights?	__YES __NO	FAS-129 (Disclosure of Information about Capital Structure), par. 4, 56, 7, and 8			
• Does the client have stock option plans?	__YES __NO	ARB-43 (Restatement and Revision of Accounting Research Bulletins), Chapter 13b; FAS-123 (Accounting for Stock-Based Compensation), par. 45, 46, 47, and 48			

QUESTION	SOURCE OF DISCLOSURE	Initials	Date	Workpaper Reference
• Has the client been involved in a troubled debt restructuring?	___YES ___NO FAS-15 (Accounting by Debtors and Creditors for Troubled Debt Restructurings), par. 20, 25, 26, 40, and 41	_____	_____	_____
• Has the FASB issued recent disclosure requirements that should be made by the client?	___YES ___NO			

EXHIBIT AU 431-2—ENGAGEMENT PROGRAM FOR SOP 94-6

Use the following procedures as a guide for implementing the guidance established by SOP 94-6 (Disclosure of Certain Significant Risks and Uncertainties). The program is only a guide, and professional judgment should be exercised to determine how the standards established in SOP 94-6 should be observed.

Initial and date each procedure as it is completed. If the procedure is not relevant to this engagement, place "N/A" (not applicable) in the space provided for an initial.

Client Name: _____

Date of Financial Statements: _____

	Initials	Date	Workpaper Reference
1. Has the client made appropriate disclosures for estimates that have the following characteristics?	_____	_____	_____

§431 • Adequacy of Disclosures in Financial Statements 335

	Initials	Date	Workpaper Reference

- It is at least reasonably possible that the estimate of the effect on the financial statements of a condition, situation, or set of circumstances that existed at the balance sheet date will change in the near term due to one or more future confirming events. _____ _____ _____
- The effect of the change would have a material effect on the financial statements. _____ _____ _____

2. Have estimates that require disclosure based on the standards established by FAS-5 or another pronouncement been described by the client as being at least reasonably possible that a change in the estimate will occur in the near term? _____ _____ _____

3. If an estimate does not require disclosure under FAS-5 but the estimate meets the standards described in question 1 above, has the client made the following disclosures related to the estimate?

   - Disclosure concerning the nature of the estimate _____ _____ _____
   - Disclosure indicating that it is reasonably possible that a change in the estimate will occur in the near term _____ _____ _____

4. Other comments: _____
_____
_____

Reviewed by: _____
Date: _____

SECTION 435

SEGMENT INFORMATION

FAS-14 (Financial Reporting for Segments of a Business Enterprise) provided guidance for the reporting of segment information for certain companies, and SAS-21 (Segment Information) provided guidance for the audit of segment information. In June 1997, FAS-131 (CT S20) (Disclosures about Segments of an Enterprise and Related Information) superseded FAS-14, and because the audit guidance provided by SAS-21 was inappropriate for the standards established by FAS-131, SAS-21 was rescinded. Audit guidance for segment information is now covered by an Auditing Interpretation (August 1998) titled "Applying Auditing Procedures to Segment Disclosures in Financial Statements," which is discussed in AU Section 326 (Evidential Matter).

AU 500

The Fourth Standard of Reporting

Section 504: Association with Financial Statements 339

Section 508: Reports on Audited Financial Statements 346

Section 530: Dating of the Independent Auditor's Report 381

Section 532: Restricting the Use of an Auditor's Report 384

Section 534: Reporting on Financial Statements Prepared
for Use in Other Countries...392

Section 543: Part of Audit Performed by Other Independent
Auditors 398

Section 544: Lack of Conformity with Generally Accepted
Accounting Principles 406

Section 550: Other Information in Documents Containing
Audited Financial Statements 408

Section 551: Reporting on Information Accompanying the Basic
Financial Statements in Auditor-Submitted Documents 411

Section 552: Reporting on Condensed Financial Statements
and Selected Financial Data 415

Section 558: Required Supplementary Information 419

Section 560: Subsequent Events 426

Section 561: Subsequent Discovery of Facts Existing at the
Date of the Auditor's Report 432

SECTION 504

ASSOCIATION WITH FINANCIAL STATEMENTS

Authoritative Pronouncements

SAS-26—Association with Financial Statements

Auditing Interpretation (November 1979)—Annual Report Disclosure of Unaudited Fourth Quarter Interim Data

Auditing Interpretation (November 1979)—Auditor's Identification with Condensed Financial Data

Auditing Interpretation (November 1979)—Applicability of Guidance on Reporting When Not Independent

Overview

The fourth reporting standard establishes very definite reporting obligations when an auditor is associated with financial statements. SAS-26 (Association with Financial Statements) describes the meaning of "association" when the client is a public entity or a nonpublic entity whose financial statements are audited. Reporting requirements for a nonpublic entity whose financial statements are unaudited are established by Statements on Standards for Accounting and Review Services (SSARS). An auditor is associated with financial statements under the following circumstances:

- The accountant agrees to the use of his or her name in a report or similar document that contains the financial statements.

- The accountant submits to the client or third parties financial statements that the accountant has prepared or has assisted in preparing. (Whether the accountant's name appears on the financial statements is irrelevant.)

The Auditing Interpretation (November 1979) titled "Auditor's Identification with Condensed Financial Data" concludes that an accountant is not associated with *condensed* financial data published by a financial reporting service even when the accountant is identified by the service as being the entity's auditor.

ENGAGEMENT STRATEGY: SAS-26 refers specifically to financial statements and is not applicable to data presented in an alternative format. Although SAS-26 does not define the meaning of "financial statement," SAS-62 (Special Reports) states that financial statements would include information that purports to describe the assets and obligations of an organization or the changes of the assets and obligations over a period of time. In addition, SAS-62 recognizes that financial statements encompass those prepared in accordance with GAAP as well as those that reflect a comprehensive basis of accounting other than GAAP. Finally, SAS-26 states that a tax return prepared solely for a tax authority is beyond the scope of SAS-26.

PLANNING AID REMINDER: The Auditing Interpretation (November 1979) titled "Annual Report Disclosure of Unaudited Fourth Quarter Interim Data" notes that the auditor is not required to audit interim information unless specifically engaged to do so.

Promulgated Reporting Checklist

The auditor may be associated with certain financial statements that have not been audited or reviewed, as follows:

____ Unaudited financial statements of a public entity

____ Unaudited financial statements prepared on a comprehensive basis of accounting

____ Unaudited financial statements arising because the auditor is not independent

____ Unaudited financial statements presented on a comparative basis with audited financial statements

____ Unaudited financial statements that require a modified disclaimer

Analysis and Application of Reporting Standards

Unaudited financial statements of a public entity

An accountant who is associated with the financial statements of a public entity whose financial statements have not been audited or reviewed should issue a disclaimer of opinion on the unaudited financial statements. The disclaimer may be placed directly on the unaudited financial statements, or it may be expressed in the accountant's report that accompanies the financial

§ 504 • Association with Financial Statements 341

statements. Exhibit AU 504-1 provides an example of a disclaimer that accompanies the unaudited financial statements:

> **PLANNING AID REMINDER:** When the accountant issues a disclaimer of opinion under this circumstance, the accountant is not required to perform any procedures except to read the financial statements for obvious material misstatements. If the accountant has performed other procedures, those procedures should not be referred to in the disclaimer of opinion.

If the accountant becomes aware that a public company is going to use his or her name in a client-prepared document that contains financial statements that have not been audited or reviewed, the accountant should request that his name not be used in the document or that the financial statements be marked as "unaudited" and that the document contain a notation that the accountant does not express an opinion on the financial statements.

> **RISK ASSESSMENT POINT:** If the client refuses the accountant's request, the client should be informed that it does not have permission to use the accountant's name in the document and the accountant should consider what other steps may be appropriate, including seeking the advice of legal counsel.

> **ENGAGEMENT STRATEGY:** A disclaimer of opinion should not include negative assurances unless specifically allowed by standards established by the American Institute of Certified Public Accountants. (For example, see AU Section 634, Letters for Underwriters and Certain Other Requesting Parties.)

Unaudited financial statements prepared on a comprehensive basis of accounting

An accountant may be associated with financial statements of a public entity whose financial statements are prepared on a comprehensive basis of accounting other than generally accepted accounting principles. Under this circumstance, the accountant should follow the guidance provided in the previous Section, except the disclaimer should be appropriately modified to reflect the guidance established by SAS-62 (AU 623) (Special Reports).

Exhibit AU 504-2 presents an example of a disclaimer that accompanies unaudited financial statements prepared on a comprehensive basis of accounting other than generally accepted accounting principles.

> **PLANNING AID REMINDER:** Financial statements that are prepared on a comprehensive basis of accounting other than generally accepted accounting principles must include a note that describes the basis of presentation and how it differs from gen-

erally accepted accounting principles. The monetary effects of the differences between the two bases of accounting need not be included in the note.

Unaudited financial statements arising because the auditor is not independent

When an accountant is not independent but is associated with a client's financial statements, the accountant should disclaim an opinion on the financial statements. The reason for the lack of independence should not be disclosed. If the accountant has performed any procedures with respect to the financial statements, those procedures should not be disclosed in the accountant's report.

Exhibit AU 504-3 presents an example of a disclaimer that arises from the accountant's lack of independence.

> **ENGAGEMENT STRATEGY:** If the client is a nonpublic company, the financial statements must be compiled or reviewed based on the standards established by Statements on Standards for Accounting and Review Services.

The Auditing Interpretation (November 1979) titled "Applicability of Guidance on Reporting When Not Independent" notes that the accountant must use professional judgment to determine when independence has been impaired with respect to unaudited financial statements. The Interpretation notes further that the same factors should be used to make that determination that are used to make the judgment when the financial statements have been audited.

Unaudited financial statements are presented on a comparative basis with audited financial statements

Unaudited financial statements may be presented on a comparative basis with audited financial statements that are included in a document filed with the Securities and Exchange Commission (SEC). Under this circumstance, the unaudited financial statements must clearly be marked as "unaudited."

When unaudited financial statements are presented on a comparative basis with audited financial statements in other circumstances (not part of a filing with the SEC), the unaudited financial statements must again be clearly marked as "unaudited" and either of the following must be observed:

- The report on the prior period should be reissued.

- The report on the current period should be expanded to include a separate paragraph that describes the responsibility assumed for the financial statements of the prior period.

When the current-period financial statements are unaudited and the prior-period financial statements are audited and a separate paragraph is included in the current report, the separate paragraph should include the following:

- A statement that the prior-period financial statements were unaudited
- The date of the previous report
- The type of opinion previously expressed on the prior-period financial statements (if the opinion is other than unqualified, the reason for modifying the previous report must be described)
- A statement that no auditing procedures were performed after the date of the prior-year financial statements

When the current-period financial statements are audited and the prior-period financial statements are unaudited and a separate paragraph is included in the current report, the separate paragraph should include the following:

- A statement of the type of service performed in the previous year
- The report date of the previous service
- A description of any modifications to the previous year's report
- A statement that the service performed was less than an audit and did not provide a basis for expressing an opinion on the financial statements
- If the client is a public entity, a disclaimer of opinion on the prior-year financial statements

When the client is a nonpublic entity, the separate paragraph should include a description of either a compilation (see Exhibit AU 504-4) or a review (see Exhibit AU 504-5).

Unaudited financial statements that require a modified disclaimer

When an accountant issues a disclaimer of opinion on unaudited financial statements, the accountant may be aware that the financial statements are not consistent with generally accepted accounting principles. Under this circumstance, the accountant should modify the disclaimer of opinion by doing the following:

- Describing the departure from generally accepted accounting principles
- If practicable, describing the effect of the departure on the financial statements or including the required disclosure in his or her report

- If the effects on the financial statements are not reasonably determinable or it is unreasonable to make the appropriate disclosures, stating so in the report

 > **ENGAGEMENT STRATEGY:** If the client will not agree to the modification of the disclaimer of opinion, the accountant should refuse to be associated with the financial statements and, if appropriate, should withdraw from the engagement.

Practitioner's Aids

EXHIBIT AU 504-1—DISCLAIMER OF OPINION ON UNAUDITED FINANCIAL STATEMENTS

The accompanying balance sheet of Bluefield Company as of December 31, 20X5, and the related statements of income, retained earnings, and cash flows for the year then ended were not audited by us and, accordingly, we do not express an opinion on them.

EXHIBIT AU 504-2—DISCLAIMER OF OPINION ON UNAUDITED FINANCIAL STATEMENTS THAT ARE PREPARED ON A COMPREHENSIVE BASIS OF ACCOUNTING OTHER THAN GENERALLY ACCEPTED ACCOUNTING PRINCIPLES

The accompanying statement of assets and liabilities, resulting from cash transactions of Bluefield Company as of December 31, 20X5, and the related statement of revenues collected and expenses paid during the year then ended were not audited by us and, accordingly, we do not express an opinion on them.

EXHIBIT AU 504-3—DISCLAIMER OF OPINION ON UNAUDITED FINANCIAL STATEMENTS BECAUSE THE ACCOUNTANT IS NOT INDEPENDENT

We are not independent with respect to Bluefield Company, and the accompanying balance sheet as of December 31, 20X5, and the related statements of income, retained earnings, and cash flows for the year then ended were not audited by us and, accordingly, we do not express an opinion on them.

EXHIBIT AU 504-4—DESCRIPTION OF A COMPILATION IN A SEPARATE PARAGRAPH WHEN REPORTING ON AUDITED AND UNAUDITED FINANCIAL STATEMENTS IN COMPARATIVE FORM

The 20X5 financial statements were compiled by us, and our report thereon, dated February 14, 20X6, stated that we did not audit or review those financial statements and, accordingly, express no opinion or other form of assurance on them.

EXHIBIT AU 504-5—DESCRIPTION OF A REVIEW IN A SEPARATE PARAGRAPH WHEN REPORTING ON AUDITED AND UNAUDITED FINANCIAL STATEMENTS IN COMPARATIVE FORM

The 20X5 financial statements were reviewed by us, and our report thereon, dated February 14, 20X6, stated that we were not aware of any material modifications that should be made to those statements for them to be in conformity with accounting principles generally accepted in the United States. However, a review is substantially less in scope than an audit and does not provide a basis for the expression of an opinion on the financial statements taken as a whole.

SECTION 508

REPORTS ON AUDITED FINANCIAL STATEMENTS

Authoritative Pronouncements

SAS-58—Reports on Audited Financial Statements

SAS-93—Omnibus Statement on Auditing Standards—2000

Auditing Interpretation (July 1975)—Report of an Outside Inventory-Taking Firm as an Alternative Procedure for Observing Inventories

Auditing Interpretation (January 1989)—Reference in Auditor's Standard Report to Management's Report

Auditing Interpretation (February 1997)—Reporting on Financial Statements Prepared on a Liquidation Basis of Accounting

Overview

The format of the standard auditor's report is mandated by the following four standards:

1. The report shall state whether the financial statements are presented in accordance with generally accepted accounting principles.

2. The report shall identify those circumstances in which such principles have not been consistently observed in the current period in relation to the preceding period.

3. Informative disclosures in the financial statements are to be regarded as adequate unless otherwise stated in the report.

4. The report shall contain either an expression of opinion regarding the financial statements, taken as a whole, or an assertion to the effect that an opinion cannot be expressed. When an overall opinion cannot be expressed, the reasons therefor must be stated. In all cases where an auditor's name is associated with financial statements, the report must contain a clear-cut indication of the character of the auditor's examination, if any, and the degree of responsibility the auditor is taking.

SAS-58 (Reports on Audited Financial Statements) concludes that the standard auditor's report should include the following:

- A title that includes the word "independent"

- A statement that the financial statements identified in the report were audited

- A statement that the financial statements are the responsibility of the entity's management and that the auditor's responsibility is to express an opinion on the financial statements based on the audit
- A statement that the audit was conducted in accordance with generally accepted auditing standards and an identification of the country of origin of those standards [for example, auditing standards generally accepted in the United States of America or U.S. generally accepted auditing standards (GAAS)]
- A statement that generally accepted auditing standards require that the auditor plan and perform the audit to obtain reasonable assurance about whether the financial statements are free of material misstatement
- A statement that the audit included:
  — An examination of evidence supporting the amounts and disclosures in the financial statements on a test basis
  — An assessment of the accounting principles used and significant estimates made by management
  — An evaluation of the overall financial statement presentation
- A statement that the auditor believes that the audit provides a reasonable basis for his or her opinion
- An opinion of whether the financial statements present fairly, in all material respects, the financial position of the entity as of the balance sheet date and the results of its operations and its cash flows for the period then ended in conformity with generally accepted accounting principles (GAAP), and the opinion should include an identification of the country of origin of those accounting principles [for example, accounting principles generally accepted in the United States of American or U.S. generally accepted accounting principles (GAAP)]
- A manual or printed signature of the auditor's firm
- The date of the audit report

The body of the standard auditor's report should include an introductory paragraph, a scope paragraph, and an opinion paragraph. In the introductory paragraph, the auditor (1) states that an audit has been performed and (2) describes the responsibility assumed by the entity's management and the auditor with respect to the financial statements.

In the scope paragraph, the auditor states that generally accepted auditing standards were observed in the performance of the audit and briefly describes the audit. In the concluding sentence of the scope paragraph, the auditor states that the audit has provided a reasonable basis for expressing an opinion on the financial statements.

In the opinion paragraph, the auditor states that the financial statements present fairly, in all material respects, the entity's financial position, results of operations, and cash flows. The auditor also states that the financial statements are presented in accordance with generally accepted accounting principles; however, the auditor does not refer to the consistent application of accounting principles.

> **OBSERVATION:** For a discussion of the meaning of the phrase "present fairly," see SAS-69 (The Meaning of "Present Fairly in Conformity with Generally Accepted Accounting Principles"). SAS-69 is discussed in AU Section 411.

Exhibit AU 508-1 following is an example of the standard auditor's report.

EXHIBIT AU 508-1—STANDARD AUDITOR'S REPORT

Independent Auditor's Report

Penney and Nichols, CPAs
45789 Beachwood Drive
Centerville, New Jersey 08000

Board of Directors and Stockholders
X Company

We have audited the accompanying balance sheet of X Company as of December 31, 20X5, and the related statements of income, retained earnings, and cash flows for the year then ended. These financial statements are the responsibility of the Company's management. Our responsibility is to express an opinion on these financial statements based on our audit.

We conducted our audit in accordance with auditing standards generally accepted in the United States of America. Those standards require that we plan and perform the audit to obtain reasonable assurance about whether the financial statements are free of material misstatement. An audit includes examining, on a test basis, evidence supporting the amounts and disclosures in the financial statements. An audit also includes assessing the accounting principles used and significant estimates made by management, as well as evaluating the overall financial statement presentation. We believe that our audit provides a reasonable basis for our opinion.

§ 508 • Reports on Audited Financial Statements

In our opinion, the financial statements referred to above present fairly, in all material respects, the financial position of X Company as of December 31, 20X5, and the results of its operations and its cash flows for the year then ended in conformity with accounting principles generally accepted in the United States of America.

[*Report Date*]

[*Signature*]

OBSERVATION: The audit reports presented in this chapter assume that the entity does not have other *comprehensive income* components as defined by FAS-130 (Reporting Comprehensive Income). If the entity has such components and presents a statement of comprehensive income, the first line in each report would refer to "the accompanying balance sheet of X Company as of December 31, 20X5, and the related statements of income, comprehensive income, retained earnings, and cash flows for the year then ended."

The report is dated to coincide with the completion of fieldwork. Generally, the auditor is not required to perform audit procedures after the report date. The report is signed by a firm's partner (or sole proprietor), which legally binds the CPA firm to the assertions made in the report.

The auditor's report may be addressed to the client, its board of directors, or its stockholders. For an unincorporated client, the report may be addressed to the partners or the sole proprietor. When an audit is performed at the request of a party other than the management or owners of the audited entity, the report should be addressed to the party that requested the audit.

The standard report illustrated above is referred to as an unqualified report. SAS-69 (AU 411) states that when an unqualified report is issued, the auditor makes the following assurances:

- That accounting principles selected by the client have general acceptance
- That accounting principles are appropriate for the client
- That disclosures, such as financial statement notes, are adequate to enable the user to use, understand, and interpret the financial statements
- That data presented in the financial statements are classified and summarized in a reasonable manner
- That underlying events and transactions, within a range of acceptable limits, are reflected in the financial statements

RISK ASSESSMENT POINT: The Auditing Interpretation (January 1989) titled "Reference in Auditor's Standard Report to Management's Report" concludes that when an annual shareholders' report or other client-prepared document that includes audited financial statements contains a statement that management is responsibility for the financial statements, the auditor's report should not modify the standard audit report by referring to management's report. Such a modification could imply that the auditor is making assurances about various statements contained in the management report.

Reporting on comprehensive income

FAS-130 describes "comprehensive income" as net income plus other comprehensive income components. The components of other comprehensive income include "revenues, expenses, gains, and losses that under generally accepted accounting principles are included in comprehensive income but excluded from net income." The components of other comprehensive income include items that have the appearance of nominal accounts (income statement accounts) but are currently reported as part of owners' equity (either as an increase or decrease). Specifically, other comprehensive income components include the provision for the "minimum pension liability" identified in FAS-87 (Employers' Accounting for Pension Plans), unrealized gains and losses on investments classified as part of the available-for-sale portfolio identified in FAS-115 (Accounting for Certain Investments in Debt and Equity Securities), the valuation of certain hedge contracts reported at fair value as required by FAS-115, and foreign currency translation adjustments as described by FAS-52 (Foreign Currency Translation).

The language of the standard auditor's report must be changed slightly when comprehensive income is presented depending upon how comprehensive income is presented in the client's financial statements. Although FAS-130 does not require a specific presentation format, the following presentations would be acceptable:

- A separate statement of comprehensive income
- A combined statement of income and comprehensive income
- A statement of change in equity (that includes comprehensive income)

Separate statement of comprehensive income

A separate statement of comprehensive income would include net income and other comprehensive income components. Under this circumstance, the report must be modified to include reference to the separate statement. Presented below is the language of a standard auditor's report for financial statements that include a separate statement of comprehensive income.

> We have audited the accompanying balance sheet of X Company as of December 31, 20X5, and the related statements of income, comprehensive income, retained earnings, and cash flows for the year then ended. These financial statements are the responsibility of the Company's management. Our responsibility is to express an opinion on these financial statements based on our audit.
>
> We conducted our audit in accordance with auditing standards generally accepted in the United States of America. Those standards require that we plan and perform the audit to obtain reasonable assurance about whether the financial statements are free of material misstatement. An audit includes examining, on a test basis, evidence supporting the amounts and disclosures in the financial statements. An audit also includes assessing the accounting principles used and significant estimates made by management, as well as evaluating the overall financial statement presentation. We believe that our audit provides a reasonable basis for our opinion.
>
> In our opinion, the financial statements referred to above present fairly, in all material respects, the financial position of X Company as of December 31, 20X5, and the results of its operations and its cash flows for the year then ended in conformity with accounting principles generally accepted in the United States of America.

Combined statement of income and comprehensive income

A combined statement of income and comprehensive income would include net income and other comprehensive income components, all included in a single financial statement. Under this circumstance, the audit report must be changed so that the reference is to the combined financial statement. The following illustrates an audit report on financial statements that include a combined statement of income and comprehensive income.

> We have audited the accompanying balance sheet of X Company as of December 31, 20X5, and the related statements of combined income and comprehensive income, retained earnings, and cash flows for the year then ended. These financial statements are the responsibility of the Company's management. Our responsibility is to express an opinion on these financial statements based on our audit.

We conducted our audit in accordance with auditing standards generally accepted in the United States of America. Those standards require that we plan and perform the audit to obtain reasonable assurance about whether the financial statements are free of material misstatement. An audit includes examining, on a test basis, evidence supporting the amounts and disclosures in the financial statements. An audit also includes assessing the accounting principles used and significant estimates made by management, as well as evaluating the overall financial statement presentation. We believe that our audit provides a reasonable basis for our opinion.

In our opinion, the financial statements referred to above present fairly, in all material respects, the financial position of X Company as of December 31, 20X5, and the results of its operations and its cash flows for the year then ended in conformity with accounting principles generally accepted in the United States of America.

Statement of change in equity (that includes comprehensive income)

In some instances the components of other comprehensive income may be included in the statement of change in equity, which includes a separate column that reconciles the beginning and ending balances of the equity (permanent) account that tracks the changes in other components of comprehensive income. Under this circumstance, the audit report must be changed so that there is a reference to the statement of change in equity. The following report illustrates a standard audit report on financial statements that include a statement of change in equity.

We have audited the accompanying balance sheet of X Company as of December 31, 20X5, and the related statements of income, retained earnings, change in equity, and cash flows for the year then ended. These financial statements are the responsibility of the Company's management. Our responsibility is to express an opinion on these financial statements based on our audit.

We conducted our audit in accordance with auditing standards generally accepted in the United States of America. Those standards require that we plan and perform the audit to obtain reasonable assurance about whether the financial statements are free of material misstatement. An audit includes examining, on a test basis, evidence supporting the amounts and disclosures in the financial statements. An audit also includes assessing the

§ 508 • Reports on Audited Financial Statements   353

accounting principles used and significant estimates made by management, as well as evaluating the overall financial statement presentation. We believe that our audit provides a reasonable basis for our opinion.

In our opinion, the financial statements referred to above present fairly, in all material respects, the financial position of X Company as of December 31, 20X5, and the results of its operations and its cash flows for the year then ended in conformity with accounting principles generally accepted in the United States of America.

Promulgated Reporting Standards Checklist

The auditor's report may be modified due to one of the following circumstances:

_____ There is a departure from generally accepted accounting principles (GAAP).

_____ There is a departure from an accounting principle promulgated by an authoritative body designated by the AICPA to promulgate such principles, and the auditor agrees with the departure.

_____ Informative disclosures in the financial statements are not reasonably adequate.

_____ There is a change from an unacceptable accounting principle to an acceptable accounting principle.

_____ There is an inappropriate treatment in the accounting for a change in an accounting principle.

_____ Management has not provided reasonable justification for a change in accounting principles.

_____ Sufficient competent evidential matter has not been collected.

_____ There are other scope limitations.

_____ The reporting engagement is limited (e.g., a report on the balance sheet only).

_____ There are uncertainties related to going concern.

_____ An event, condition, or transaction affecting the financial statements is emphasized.

_____ The auditor is not independent with respect to the financial statements.

_____ There is a piecemeal opinion (prohibited).

_____ There are negative assurances (prohibited).

_____ The auditor reports on comparative financial statements.

Analysis and Application of Reporting Standards

There is a departure from GAAP

Generally accepted accounting principles include promulgated rules, as well as unwritten rules that have gained acceptance through general usage. When a client has not observed generally accepted accounting principles, the auditor must decide whether to issue an unqualified, a qualified, or an adverse opinion. The selection of the appropriate opinion depends on the materiality of the departure, the effects of the departure, and the number of accounts affected by the departure. An unqualified opinion can be issued if the departure is not significant to the fair presentation of the financial statements. If the departure affects the fairness of the financial statements but overall the statements can be relied on, a qualified opinion can be issued. On the other hand, when the departure is so significant that the financial statements should not be relied on, an adverse opinion must be issued.

When a qualified or adverse opinion is issued, an explanatory paragraph must describe the departure and its effects, if determinable, on the financial statements. If a qualified opinion is issued, the opinion paragraph should specifically refer to the explanatory paragraph as illustrated in Exhibit AU 508-2.

If the auditor concludes that an adverse opinion is to be issued, language similar to that shown in Exhibit AU 508-3 would be used in the opinion paragraph.

> **RISK ASSESSMENT POINT:** If practicable, an auditor should provide information required by GAAP that has not been disclosed in the financial statements, unless the omission of the information from the auditor's report is recognized as appropriate by another SAS. "Practicable" means that the required information is reasonably obtainable from management's accounts and records and that by providing the information, the auditor is not required to assume the position of preparer of the financial information.

§508 • **Reports on Audited Financial Statements**

The above guidance also applies to those situations in which the auditor expresses a qualified or an adverse opinion because of a departure from GAAP that is not related to disclosure.

When generally accepted accounting principles have not been used to prepare the financial statements, a note to the financial statements may describe the nature and effects of the departure. Rather than repeat this information in an explanation paragraph, the auditor's report may incorporate the information in the note by reference. For example, the explanatory paragraph could read as follows:

> As described more fully in Note 12 to the financial statements, the Company reports all of its sales on the installment method for financial accounting purposes and on its tax return. In our opinion, generally accepted accounting principles require that sales be reported on the accrual basis with an appropriate provision for deferred taxes.

The opinion paragraph (either a qualified or an adverse opinion) would refer to the deviation described in the explanation.

> **ENGAGEMENT STRATEGY:** An auditor may incorporate the information in a note to the financial statements into the auditor's report by reference; however, the auditor must be careful that matters in the note that are inconsistent with the auditor's opinion are not also incorporated. For example, the note may attempt to justify the departure from generally accepted accounting principles in a manner that is inappropriate or misleading. Under this circumstance, it would be advisable to not make reference to the note and to simply repeat the relevant information in the explanatory paragraph.

There is a departure from an accounting principle promulgated by an authoritative body designated by the AICPA to promulgate such principles, and the auditor agrees with the departure

Generally accepted accounting principles include written as well as unwritten accounting principles, methods, and procedures. Rule 203 of the AICPA Code of Professional Conduct states:

> A member shall not (1) express an opinion or state affirmatively that the financial statements or other financial data of any entity are presented in conformity with generally accepted accounting principles or (2) state that he or she is not aware of any material modifications that should be made to such statements or data in order for them to be in conformity with generally accepted ac-

counting principles, if such statements or data contain any departure from an accounting principle promulgated by bodies designated by Council to establish such principles that has a material effect on the statements or data taken as a whole. If, however, the statements or data contain such a departure and the member can demonstrate that due to unusual circumstances the financial statements or data would otherwise have been misleading, the member can comply with the rule by describing the departure, its approximate effects, if practicable, and the reasons why compliance with the principle would result in a misleading statement.

The AICPA Council has adopted resolutions designating the Financial Accounting Standards Board (FASB) and the Governmental Accounting Standards Board (GASB) as having the authority to promulgate accounting standards for commercial enterprises and governmental entities, respectively.

When an accounting principle is promulgated, there is a chance that strict interpretation and application of the rule may in some cases result in misleading financial statements. To prevent this situation, Rule 203 permits a client to use an alternative method. If the auditor agrees with the client's conclusion that the use of a promulgated rule would result in misleading financial statements, he or she may issue an unqualified opinion. However, an explanatory paragraph must be included in the standard report in which the nature, effect, and reason for the departure from the promulgated rule are described. The introductory, scope, and opinion paragraphs are not modified, and no reference is made to the explanatory paragraph in the opinion paragraph.

> **RISK ASSESSMENT POINT:** Although Rule 203 may be needed to provide flexibility in the application of accounting principles, the rule must be used with a great deal of caution. When the rule is used, the auditor is, in effect, promulgating an accounting rule for a specific client, which is a heavy responsibility to undertake. Not surprisingly, there are very few examples where Rule 203 has been employed concerning the adaptation of different accounting methods.

Informative disclosures in the financial statements are not reasonably adequate

The third standard of reporting states that informative disclosures in the financial statements are assumed sufficient unless specifically noted otherwise in the auditor's report. Informative disclosure includes the format and

§508 • Reports on Audited Financial Statements

content of the financial statements, all related notes, terminology, account classification, parenthetical comments, and the degree of detail in the statements and related notes. In general, the financial information should not be abbreviated to the extent that informative disclosures are not communicated. On the other hand, the informative disclosures should not be detailed to the extent that they may be misunderstood.

Information not adequately disclosed in the financial statements should be disclosed in an explanatory paragraph, if practical, when (1) informative disclosures are not considered adequate, (2) the report must be qualified, or (3) an adverse opinion is issued. SAS-32 (AU 431) (Adequacy of Disclosure of Financial Statements) defines "practical" to mean that (1) the information can be obtained from management's records and (2) the auditor's efforts in gathering the information do not constitute the actual preparation of the financial information. Thus, the auditor is not expected to actually prepare basic financial statements or any other financial information in an effort to include such data in the report. SAS-58 specifically states that when a client does not include a statement of cash flows, the auditor is not required to prepare and present such a statement in the report. However, an explanatory paragraph in the auditor's report must clearly state that the client has declined to include a statement of cash flows and that such a statement is required by GAAP. When such a statement is not presented in the financial statements, the auditor's report must be qualified. In all cases, when the auditor issues a qualified or adverse opinion, the explanatory paragraph in the report must be referred to in the opinion paragraph of the report.

Exhibit AU 508-4 illustrates an auditor's report that is qualified because the client did not present a statement of cash flows.

> **OBSERVATION:** The modification of an audit report because of a violation of the consistency standard is discussed in AU Section 420.

There is a change from an unacceptable accounting principle to an acceptable accounting principle

A newly adopted accounting principle must be evaluated to determine if it has general acceptance. If the auditor concludes that the accounting principle is not generally accepted, a decision must be made about whether a qualified opinion or an adverse opinion must be issued based on the deviation from generally accepted accounting principles. An explanatory paragraph(s), similar to the one presented below, should immediately precede the opinion (qualified or adverse) paragraph.

> During 20X5, the Company changed its method of valuing land held for investment from the cost method to the appraisal

method. The increase resulting from the reevaluation amounted to $500,000 and is presented as an increase to stockholders' equity (appraisal capital). In our opinion, the newly adopted accounting principle (appraisal method) is not in conformity with generally accepted accounting principles.

There is no need to add an explanatory paragraph on consistency, because the change in accounting principle has been described adequately in the explanatory paragraph that discusses the selection of an unacceptable accounting principle.

For the years following the adoption of the unacceptable accounting principle, the auditor should continue to express the qualified or adverse opinion on the financial statements for the year in which the change was made. In addition, the auditor must determine whether the effects of applying an unacceptable accounting principle also require the modification of opinion(s) on subsequent financial statements.

There is an inappropriate treatment in the accounting for a change in an accounting principle

APB Opinion No. 20 (Accounting Changes) provides standards for accounting for changes in accounting principles. A change in an accounting principle usually results in a cumulative-effect adjustment or a retroactive restatement of prior years' financial statements. If the standards established by APB Opinion No. 20 are not observed, the auditor must decide whether the auditor's report should be modified because of a deviation from generally accepted accounting principles. If it is concluded that the report should be modified, a paragraph similar to the one illustrated below should immediately precede the opinion (qualified or adverse) paragraph:

> During 20X5, the Company changed its method of accounting for depreciation, as described in Note X to the financial statements. The effects of the change to the new method were accounted for on a prospective basis. In our opinion, the change was not accounted for in accordance with generally accepted accounting principles in that the change should have resulted in a cumulative-effect adjustment being charged to the income statement. If the change had been accounted for as a cumulative-effect adjustment, net income would be decreased $70,000, and earnings per share would be decreased $.50. Additionally, net property, plant, and equipment would be decreased $100,000, and deferred income tax assets would be increased $30,000.

§508 • Reports on Audited Financial Statements

For the years following the incorrect treatment in accounting for the accounting change, the auditor should continue to express the qualified or adverse opinion on the financial statements for the year in which the change was made. If the accounting for the change in an accounting principle was accounted for prospectively when a cumulative-effect adjustment or a restatement of prior years' financial statements was appropriate, subsequent financial statements should be evaluated to determine whether a qualified or adverse opinion is appropriate.

Management has not provided reasonable justification for a change in accounting principles

Once an accounting principle is adopted, the principle should not be changed unless it can be demonstrated that another accounting principle is preferable as well as acceptable. If management does not adequately justify the change in accounting principles, the auditor should determine whether the report should be modified. If the auditor concludes that the report should be modified, a paragraph similar to the one presented below should immediately precede the opinion paragraph.

> During 20X5, the Company changed its method of accounting for amortization, as described in Note X to the financial statements. In previous years, the Company used an accelerated amortization method but has now changed to the straight-line method. Although the straight-line method of amortization is in conformity with generally accepted accounting principles, in our opinion the Company has not provided reasonable justification for making this change as required by generally accepted accounting principles.

There is no need to add an explanatory paragraph on consistency, because the change in accounting principle has been described adequately in the explanatory paragraph that discusses the lack of reasonable justification for making the change in accounting principles.

> **RISK ASSESSMENT POINT:** SAS-58 does not discuss whether a lack of reasonable justification for an accounting change could lead to an adverse opinion. Under most, if not all, circumstances, it would be difficult to argue that an adverse opinion should be expressed.

For the years following the adoption of the new accounting principle, the auditor should continue to express the qualified opinion on the financial statements for the year in which the change was adopted. However, it is not appropriate to express a qualified opinion on subsequent financial statements, since the newly adopted accounting principle is a generally accepted accounting principle.

Sufficient competent evidential matter has not been collected

The third standard of fieldwork requires that the auditor's opinion be based on sufficient competent evidential matter. If adequate evidence is not collected, a scope limitation occurs. In this case, the auditor should express a qualified opinion or issue a disclaimer of opinion on the financial statements. A scope limitation may result from circumstances of the engagement or restrictions imposed by the client. The significance of the restriction depends on the number of accounts affected by the scope limitation and their potential impact on the financial statements.

> **ENGAGEMENT STRATEGY:** SAS-58 notes that when significant scope limitations are imposed by the client, the auditor generally should express a disclaimer of opinion on the financial statements.

When an auditor concludes that a qualified opinion should be expressed, there is no change in the introductory paragraph; however, the auditor modifies the scope paragraph by referring to the scope limitation that is described in an explanatory paragraph. The explanatory paragraph should contain a description of the nature of the scope limitation and the accounts involved. The description of the scope limitation should not be incorporated in the auditor's report by reference to a note to the financial statement, because the auditor, not the client, is responsible for the description of the scope limitation. Finally, the opinion paragraph should refer to the explanatory paragraph as the basis for the qualification and should contain the phrase "except for" in describing the qualification. This type of report is illustrated in Exhibit AU 508-5.

If the scope limitation requires the expression of a disclaimer of opinion, the format illustrated in Exhibit AU 508-6 should be used.

In addition, the second paragraph of the standard report is omitted and an explanatory paragraph is added to describe the scope limitation. If the auditor is aware of any departures from generally accepted accounting principles, these deficiencies should also be described in another separate explanatory paragraph. The opinion paragraph should refer to the explanatory paragraph that describes the scope limitation and also should state that an opinion is not expressed on the financial statements.

Typical scope limitations include an inability to (1) observe the physical inventory, (2) confirm receivables, or (3) obtain financial statements related

§508 • Reports on Audited Financial Statements

to an investment in another (investee) company. If the auditor is able to obtain sufficient competent evidential matter through alternative audit procedures (such as the review of subsequent cash receipts when a receivable is not confirmed), there is no scope limitation and the three-paragraph (unqualified) report should be issued.

> **PLANNING AID REMINDER:** SAS-58 reiterates the point that although alternative procedures may be used when the auditor cannot observe the physical inventory count, "it will always be necessary for the auditor to make, or observe, some physical counts of the inventory and apply appropriate tests of intervening transactions."

> **RISK ASSESSMENT POINT:** The Auditing Interpretation on evidential matter (March 1981) titled "The Effect of an Inability to Obtain Evidential Matter Relating to Income Tax Accruals" requires the auditor to disclaim an opinion on the financial statements if the client limits the auditor's access to tax accrual documentation and to the appropriate client personnel responsible for the tax calculation.

There are other scope limitations

When notes to the financial statements include unaudited information, the audit approach used depends on whether the information is essential to the fair presentation of the financial statements. If the information is considered essential to fair presentation, the auditor must perform procedures to determine whether the information is fairly presented. When the auditor is unable to apply the procedures considered necessary, a qualified opinion or a disclaimer of opinion should be expressed.

If the information is not considered essential for fair presentation of the financial statements, the disclosures may be "identified as unaudited or as not covered by the auditor's report." However, if the information is based on a subsequent event that occurs after the completion of fieldwork but before the financial statements are issued, the auditor must do one of the following:

- Dual-date the report
- Date the report as of the subsequent event
- Extend procedures to enable the auditor to review all subsequent events to the extended date of the report

> **ENGAGEMENT STRATEGY:** In the above circumstances, the auditor cannot accept the labeling of the subsequent event as "unaudited."

> **PLANNING AID REMINDER:** Some companies are in the business of counting, recording, and pricing inventories. The Auditing Interpretation (July 1975) titled "Report of an Outside Inventory-Taking Firm as an Alternative Procedure for Observing Inventories" concludes that the auditor's responsibility for the count and other tasks performed by an inventory-taking company is similar to the responsibility for tasks normally performed directly by the client. Therefore, the auditor should (1) review the client's inventory-counting program, (2) make or observe a test of physical counts, (3) make appropriate mathematical checks, and (4) test the valuation of the inventory.

The reporting engagement is limited (e.g., a report on the balance sheet only)

An auditor may be engaged to audit one or more, but not all, of the financial statements. This type of engagement is not considered a limitation of the scope of an engagement. It is instead described as a limited reporting engagement. Of course, no scope limitation exists if the auditor is unrestricted in the performance of audit procedures considered necessary under the circumstances.

In a limited reporting engagement, the auditor's report is modified so that only the financial statement(s) audited is identified. An example of a limited report on a balance sheet is presented in Exhibit AU 508-7.

> **ENGAGEMENT STRATEGY:** In a limited reporting engagement, the auditor must employ procedures to determine whether accounting principles have been applied consistently with those used in the previous year. If the consistency standard has been violated, an explanatory paragraph should be added to the auditor's report (after the opinion paragraph). An unqualified opinion, however, is expressed on the financial statement(s).

There are uncertainties related to going concern

During the preparation of financial statements, a client must make a variety of accounting estimates, such as the estimated useful life of depreciable assets, a provision for doubtful accounts receivable, and an accrual for a loss contingency. In most instances, the auditor is able to collect sufficient competent evidence to support the reasonableness of accounting estimates. In this case, the auditor's standard report is not modified.

FAS-5 (CT C59) (Accounting for Contingencies) provides accounting and reporting standards applicable to one type of uncertainty, namely, loss contingencies. A loss contingency is defined as "an existing condition, situation, or set of circumstances involving uncertainty as to possible loss to an enterprise that will ultimately be resolved when one or more future events

§ 508 • Reports on Audited Financial Statements

occur or fail to occur." Furthermore, the following classifications are used to categorize loss contingencies:

- *Probable*—The future event or events are likely to occur.
- *Reasonably possible*—The chance of the future event or events occurring is more than remote but less than likely.
- *Remote*—The chance of the future event or events occurring is slight.

> **ENGAGEMENT STRATEGY:** FAS-5 is not applicable to all uncertainties; however, the Statement provides the only broad guidance in this area and may be used as a general frame of reference when evaluating other uncertainties. Additional guidance is established by SOP 94-6 (Disclosure of Certain Significant Risks and Uncertainties).

The accounting and reporting standards for loss contingencies are summarized in Exhibit AU 508-8.

EXHIBIT AU 508-8—ACCOUNTING AND REPORTING STANDARDS FOR LOSS CONTINGENCIES

Characteristics of Loss Contingency	*Presentation in the Financial Statements*
Probable and a reasonable estimate (or range) of the loss can be made	Accrual of loss contingency
Probable but no reasonable estimate of the loss can be made	Disclosure of loss contingency
Reasonable estimate of the loss can be made, but the loss is less than probable but more than remote	Disclosure of loss contingency
Remote likelihood of occurrence	No accrual or disclosure

> **ENGAGEMENT STRATEGY:** With the issuance of SAS-79 (Amendments to Statements on Auditing Standards No. 58, "Reports on Audited Financial Statements"), the Auditing Standards Board no longer requires that an audit report be modified when uncertainties exist, assuming the accounting and reporting standards established by FAS-5 have been observed.
>
> **PLANNING AID REMINDER:** Matters of uncertainty should not be confused with scope limitations and deviations from gener-

ally accepted accounting principles. A scope limitation arises when evidential matter exists with respect to the uncertainty but had not been made available to the auditor. A deviation from generally accepted accounting principles occurs when (1) the uncertainty is not adequately disclosed, (2) an inappropriate accounting principle is used, or (3) an unreasonable accounting estimate is made. Scope limitations may lead to the expression of a qualified opinion or a disclaimer of opinion. Deviations from generally accepted accounting principles may lead to a qualified opinion or an adverse opinion.

An event, condition, or transaction affecting the financial statements is emphasized

Although reporting standards and rules are very detailed, it would be difficult to promulgate rules to provide guidance in every reporting situation. To provide some reporting flexibility, the auditor's report may emphasize a matter without qualifying the opinion. SAS-58 presents the following as matters that could be emphasized:

- The entity reported on is a component of a larger entity.
- There have been significant transactions with a related party.
- A significant subsequent event has taken place.
- Comparability of financial statements has been affected by the accounting treatment of an event or transaction.

When the auditor decides to emphasize a matter, the auditing standards do not specify the placement of the emphasis paragraph, but they do state that the introductory, scope, and opinion paragraphs should not refer to the explanatory paragraph. An unqualified opinion should be expressed. An example of an explanatory paragraph that emphasizes a matter is presented below.

> Company X, a wholly owned subsidiary of Z Company, sells 15% of its output to Z Company. As described more fully in Note Y to the financial statements, these intercompany sales are based on negotiated prices between the Company and Z Company, at approximate market prices that exist within the industry.
>
> **PLANNING AID REMINDER:** When an explanatory paragraph contains more information than the related financial statement disclosure, the auditor should consider whether the financial statements have been prepared in accordance with GAAP (inadequate disclosure).

§ 508 • **Reports on Audited Financial Statements** 365

The auditor is not independent with respect to the financial statements

The second general standard requires that the auditor be independent. Many of the relationships that should be avoided in order not to impair independence or not to suggest the loss of independence in the eyes of others are established by the Code of Professional Conduct. When the independent auditor concludes that he or she is no longer independent, a disclaimer of opinion must be expressed. Under these circumstances, no introductory, scope, or explanatory paragraphs are included in the auditor's report. The disclaimer of opinion should simply state that the auditor is not independent and that no opinion is expressed on the financial statements. The reason for the lack of independence must not be described in the auditor's report.

An example of a disclaimer of an opinion because the auditor is not independent is illustrated below.

> We are not independent with respect to X Company, and the accompanying balance sheet as of December 31, 20X5, and the related statements of income, retained earnings, and cash flows for the year then ended were not audited by us and, accordingly, we do not express an opinion on them.

When the auditor is not independent, and the client is a nonpublic entity, a review report cannot be issued. A compilation report may be issued if the standards established by Statements on Standards for Accounting and Review Services (SSARS) are observed.

There is a piecemeal opinion (prohibited)

When an adverse opinion or a disclaimer of opinion is expressed, the auditor is prohibited from issuing a piecemeal opinion on some items that appear in the financial statements.

There are negative assurances (prohibited)

When an auditor expresses a disclaimer of opinion on the financial statements, the disclaimer should not be contradicted by a negative assurance. A negative assurance implies that the financial statements, or other financial information, may be in accordance with generally accepted accounting principles, since nothing to the contrary was discovered during the engagement.

The auditor reports on comparative financial statements

Most financial statements are presented on a comparative basis. SAS-58 requires that prior-year financial statements presented with the current year be reported on by the continuing auditor or, when appropriate, by the predecessor auditor. When all financial statements presented have been audited by the same accounting firm, the introductory, scope, and opinion paragraphs refer to and report on all the financial statements. This simply means that plural terms are substituted for singular terms, so that reference will be made to balance sheets, income statements, and so forth. An example of an auditor's report that covers comparative statements for two years is illustrated in Exhibit AU 508-9.

If one or more of the financial statements presented on a comparative basis require that the auditor's report be modified, the normal report modification should be applied. For example, the prior year's financial statements may be presented in accordance with GAAP and the current year's financial statements may not be presented in accordance with GAAP. In this event, (1) the introductory paragraph refers to both the current and the prior years' financial statements, (2) an explanatory paragraph is added that contains an explanation of the deviation from GAAP in the current year's financial statements, and (3) the opinion paragraph contains an unqualified opinion on the prior year's financial statements and a qualified opinion (with reference to the explanatory paragraph) on the current year's financial statements.

Exhibit AU 508-10 is an example of an auditor's report with different opinions on the comparative financial statements. In this example, the auditor's opinion on the prior year's income statement is qualified because of a departure from generally accepted accounting principles, but an unqualified opinion is expressed on the current year's financial statements.

Updated opinion different from previous opinion

When a continuing auditor repeats a previous opinion on a prior year's financial statements, it is referred to as updating the report. Updating means that the auditor has considered the appropriateness of the prior opinion in the context of the results of the current engagement. Thus, it must be determined whether the prior opinion is still applicable to the prior financial statements. If it is concluded that the prior opinion is still appropriate, the reporting guidelines applicable to comparative financial statements discussed above are followed.

If the auditor believes the prior opinion is not appropriate, the current report (which covers both years) must include an explanatory paragraph stating why a different opinion on the prior financial statements is being expressed. The explanatory paragraph must disclose (1) that the updated opinion is different from the prior original opinion, (2) the reason the opinion is being revised, (3) the type of opinion previously issued, and (4) the date of the prior audit report. If the revised prior-year opinion is not unqualified, the current report must include an additional explanatory paragraph describing the deficiency.

When an explanatory paragraph is added because of a change in the opinion expressed on a previous year's financial statements, the introductory, scope, and opinion paragraphs would not refer to the explanatory paragraph and an unqualified opinion would be expressed on both years' financial statements (assuming that unqualified opinions are appropriate under the circumstances). An example of the explanatory paragraph is presented below.

> In our report dated February 18, 20X8, we expressed an opinion that the 20X7 statement of income did not fairly present the results of operations in conformity with generally accepted accounting principles because a net provision for loss on abandonment of equipment had been presented as an extraordinary charge against earnings for 20X7. As described in Note X, the Company has changed its presentation of the net provision by revising the 20X7 statement of income so that the statement is now presented in accordance with generally accepted accounting principles. Accordingly, our present opinion on the 20X7 financial statements, as presented herein, is different from that expressed in our previous report.

Reporting by predecessor auditor

In most circumstances, a predecessor auditor will be in a position to "reissue" the report. Reissuance is different from updating a report, in that the predecessor auditor is not in a position to evaluate his or her opinion in the context of the current year's examination. However, before reissuing the report, the predecessor auditor is required to (1) read and compare the current year's financial statements with the prior year's financial statements and (2) obtain a representation letter from the successor auditor. The representation letter should state whether current conditions have any effect on the prior year's opinion. If the predecessor auditor concludes, on the basis of these limited procedures, that the prior year's opinion is still appropriate, the prior year's report is reissued as it was originally, including the same original report date. If the predecessor auditor concludes that the prior year's opinion is no longer appropriate, he or she may issue a revised report. In an explanatory paragraph, the predecessor auditor must fully describe the type of original opinion issued and the reason for changing the opinion. The reissued report should be dual-dated, showing the original report date and the revised report date. Language such as the following should be used: "March 3, 20X5, except for Note 12 as to which the date is February 26, 20X6." (It is important to remember that an auditor is responsible for material subsequent events up to the date appearing on the report.)

If the predecessor auditor's report is omitted from the current year's comparative financial statements, the successor auditor must modify the introductory paragraph of the current report. The introductory paragraph should state that the prior-year financial statements were audited by another CPA, also noting the type of opinion expressed and the date of the report. If the predecessor's report was not unqualified, the reason for the modification must also be explained. The successor auditor's opinion paragraph refers only to the current year's financial statements.

> **ENGAGEMENT STRATEGY:** Based on the standards established by SAS-70, the successor auditor's report should not refer to an uncertainty explanatory paragraph included in the predecessor's report.

Exhibit AU 508-11 provides an example of a successor auditor's report in which the predecessor auditor's report is not presented.

> **RISK ASSESSMENT POINT:** Reference to the predecessor auditor's name is prohibited in the successor auditor's report except when the predecessor auditor's practice has been acquired by or merged into the practice of the successor auditor.

If the prior year's financial statements have been restated, the introductory paragraph of the successor auditor's report should state that the predecessor auditor reported on the previous year's financial statements before they were restated. When the successor auditor has been engaged to audit the restatement adjustments, and has applied sufficient procedures to determine that the adjustments are appropriate, the following paragraph may be added to the successor auditor's report.

> We also audited the adjustments described in Note X that were applied to restate the 20X4 financial statements. In our opinion, such adjustments are appropriate and have been properly applied.

Reporting when predecessor auditor has ceased operations

Reporting complications arise when financial statements of a prior period have been reported on by a predecessor auditor that has ceased operations. In 1991, the Auditing Standards Division provided guidance under this circumstance by issuing a Notice to Practitioners titled "Audit, Review, and Compilation Considerations When a Predecessor Accountant Has Ceased Operations."

> **OBSERVATION:** A Notice to Practitioners is nonauthoritative guidance prepared by the AICPA staff in consultation with members of the Auditing Standards Board. Notices are generally published in the AICPA publication *CPA LETTER*. Notices to Practitioners are not approved, disapproved, or otherwise acted on by a senior technical committee of the AICPA.

Reports on audited financial statements presented with prior-period financial statements audited by a predecessor auditor that has ceased operations

When prior-period financial statements have been audited by a predecessor auditor that has ceased operations, the reporting requirements depend on (1) whether the financial statements have been restated and (2) whether the financial statements are filed with the SEC.

When prior-period financial statements have not been restated, the successor auditor should add the following to the introductory paragraph of the current year's audit report:

- State that the prior-period financial statements were audited by another auditor that has ceased operations
- Disclose the date of the predecessor auditor's report
- Disclose the type of report issued by the predecessor auditor
- If the predecessor auditor's report was other than a standard report, explain the basis for modification

The name of the predecessor auditor should not be referred to in the successor auditor's report.

It should be noted that the information described above should be included in the successor auditor's introductory paragraph even when the predecessor auditor's report is reprinted and presented with the current auditor's report. Reprinting a previous audit report is not the same as reissuing a report.

When prior-period financial statements have been restated, the successor auditor should add the same information to the introductory paragraph as is required when the statements have not been restated and, in addition, should state that the predecessor auditor reported on the financial statements before restatement. When the successor auditor's engagement encompasses the restatement adjustments that apply to the prior-period financial statements, the following paragraph may be added to the end of the current-period audit report:

We also audited the adjustments described in Note X that were applied to restate the 20X1 financial statements. In our opinion, such adjustments are appropriate and have been properly applied.

A successor auditor may believe that financial statements audited by a predecessor auditor that has ceased operations could be materially misstated. Under this circumstance the successor auditor should inform management of the apparent problem and request that management determine whether the financial statements are materially misstated. Management, as part of its investigation, may find it helpful to discuss the matter with the previous engagement partner of the defunct CPA firm. If management concludes that the financial statements are materially misstated, it should convey that information to the individual(s) responsible for concluding the operations of the predecessor firm. Also, the successor auditor should consider whether management action is necessary so that the misstated financial statements will not be relied on in the future. If management does not respond to the problem in a satisfactory manner, the successor auditor should inform the audit committee (or equivalent party) of the matter. If the audit committee does not respond in an appropriate manner, the successor auditor should consider withdrawing from the engagement. Actions contemplated by the auditor should be discussed with legal counsel.

> **PLANNING AID REMINDER:** In planning audit procedures to determine the reasonableness of restatement adjustments, the successor auditor should recognize that the predecessor auditor will be unable to observe the standards established by SAS-1, AU Section 561 (Subsequent Discovery of Facts Existing at the Date of the Auditor's Report).

When the successor auditor does not perform sufficient procedures to determine the reasonableness of restatement adjustments, the restatement adjustments should be designated as unaudited in the notes to the financial statements.

When the prior-period financial statements are filed with the SEC, the introductory paragraph of the successor auditor's report on the current-period financial statements should be expanded as explained above. The predecessor auditor's report should be reprinted, but in place of a manual signature, a statement similar to the following should be reproduced:

> The report that appears below is a copy of the report issued by the company's previous independent auditor, [name of CPA firm]. That firm has discontinued performing auditing and accounting services.

If appropriate, the above statement should be expanded to note that the predecessor firm has filed for protection from creditors under the U.S. Bankruptcy Code, and the date of the filing should be disclosed.

Reports on audited financial statements of a nonpublic entity presented with prior-period financial statements compiled or reviewed by a predecessor accountant that has ceased operations

When prior-period financial statements of a nonpublic company have been compiled or reviewed by a predecessor accountant that has ceased operations and those financial statements are presented with the current-period audited financial statements, the format of the successor auditor's report depends on whether the prior-period financial statements have been restated.

If prior-period financial statements have not been restated, a separate paragraph, similar to the ones illustrated below, should be added to the successor auditor's report.

> [Prior Financial Statements Compiled:]
>
> The 20X5 financial statements were compiled by other accountants who have ceased operations, and their report thereon, dated February 12, 20X6, stated they did not audit or review those financial statements and, accordingly, express no opinion or other form of assurance on them.
>
> [Prior Financial Statements Reviewed:]
>
> The 20X5 financial statements were reviewed by other accountants who have ceased operations, and their report thereon, dated February 12, 20X6, stated they were not aware of any material modifications that should be made to those statements for them to be in conformity with generally accepted accounting principles. However, a review is substantially less in scope than an audit and does not provide a basis for the expression of an opinion on the financial statements taken as a whole.

If the prior-period reports were other than standard compilation and review reports, the paragraphs illustrated above should be expanded to include the basis for modification.

If the prior-period financial statements have been restated, those statements should be compiled, reviewed, or audited and an appropriate report should be issued.

If the successor auditor believes that financial statements compiled or reviewed by a predecessor auditor that has ceased operations could be materially misstated, the successor auditor should inform management of the apparent problem and request that management determine whether the financial statements are materially misstated. Management, as part of its investigation, may find it helpful to discuss the matter with the previous engagement partner of the defunct CPA firm. If management concludes that the financial statements are materially misstated, it should convey that information to the individual(s) responsible for concluding the operations of the predecessor firm. Also, the successor auditor should consider whether management action is necessary so that the misstated financial statements will not be relied on in the future. If management does not respond to the problem in a satisfactory manner, the successor auditor should inform the audit committee (or equivalent party) of the matter. If the audit committee does not respond in an appropriate manner, the successor auditor should consider withdrawing from the engagement. Actions contemplated by the auditor should be discussed with legal counsel.

Reports on compiled or reviewed financial statements presented with prior-period financial statements compiled, reviewed, or audited by a predecessor accountant that has ceased operations

When prior-period financial statements of a company have been compiled, reviewed, or audited by a predecessor accountant that has ceased operations and those financial statements are presented with the current-period compiled or reviewed financial statements, the format of the successor accountant's report depends on whether prior-period financial statements have been restated.

If prior-period financial statements have been compiled or reviewed and have not been restated, a separate paragraph, similar to the ones illustrated below, should be added to the successor accountant's report:

> [Prior Financial Statements Compiled:]
>
> The 20X5 financial statements of X Company were compiled by other accountants who have ceased operations and whose report dated February 12, 20X6, stated that they did not express an opinion or any other form of assurance on those statements.
>
> [Prior Financial Statements Reviewed:]
>
> The 20X5 financial statements of X Company were reviewed by other accountants who have ceased operations and whose report dated February 12, 20X6, stated that they were not aware of any material modifications that should be made to those statements in order for them to be in conformity with generally accepted accounting principles.

§ 508 • Reports on Audited Financial Statements

If prior-period financial statements have been audited and have not been restated, a separate paragraph, similar to the one presented below, should be added to the successor accountant's report:

> The financial statements for the year ended December 31, 20X5, were audited by other accountants who have ceased operations. They expressed an unqualified opinion on the financial statements in their report dated February 12, 20X6, but they have not performed any auditing procedures since that date.

If the prior year's auditor's report was other than unqualified, the above paragraph should be expanded to describe the basis for the report modification.

If the prior-period financial statements have been restated, those financial statements should be compiled, reviewed, or audited, and the successor accountant should issue an appropriate report.

> **PLANNING AID REMINDER:** When the successor accountant believes that prior-period financial statements should be revised but the predecessor accountant has ceased operations, the successor accountant should suggest that the client notify "the party responsible for winding up the affairs of the predecessor firm" of the matter. If the client refuses to make the communication or if the reaction by the client's predecessor accountant is unsatisfactory, the successor accountant should discuss the matter with legal counsel.

Practitioner's Aids

The following exhibits are presented in this section:

- Exhibit AU 508-2—Qualified Auditor's Report
- Exhibit AU 508-3—Adverse Auditor's Report
- Exhibit AU 508-4—Qualified Auditor's Report Because Statement of Cash Flow Is Omitted
- Exhibit AU 508-5—Qualified Auditor's Report Because of a Scope Limitation
- Exhibit AU 508-6—Disclaimer Report
- Exhibit AU 508-7—Auditor's Report Only on the Balance Sheet
- Exhibit AU 508-9—Auditor's Report on Comparative Financial Statements

- Exhibit AU 508-10—Auditor's Report on Comparative Financial Statements with Different Opinions
- Exhibit AU 508-11—Auditor's Report When a Predecessor Auditor's Report Is Not Presented

EXHIBIT AU 508-2—QUALIFIED AUDITOR'S REPORT

We have audited the accompanying balance sheet of X Company as of December 31, 20X5, and the related statements of income, retained earnings, and cash flows for the year then ended. These financial statements are the responsibility of the Company's management. Our responsibility is to express an opinion on these financial statements based on our audit.

We conducted our audit in accordance with auditing standards generally accepted in the United States of America. Those standards require that we plan and perform the audit to obtain reasonable assurance about whether the financial statements are free of material misstatement. An audit includes examining, on a test basis, evidence supporting the amounts and disclosures in the financial statements. An audit also includes assessing the accounting principles used and significant estimates made by management, as well as evaluating the overall financial statement presentation. We believe that our audit provides a reasonable basis for our opinion.

As more fully described in Note 12 to the financial statements, a net provision for loss on abandonment of certain property of $800,000 after related income taxes has been presented as an extraordinary charge against earnings for 20X5. In our opinion, generally accepted accounting principles require that the gross amount of such provision be included in the determination of income before income taxes and that the per-share amount of the provisions ($.75) not be separately presented in the statement of income.

In our opinion, except for the effect of the matter described in the preceding paragraph on the statement of income, the financial statements referred to above present fairly, in all material respects, the financial position of X Company as of December 31, 20X5, and the results of its operations and its cash flows for the year then ended in conformity with accounting principles generally accepted in the United States of America.

EXHIBIT AU 508-3—ADVERSE AUDITOR'S REPORT

We have audited the accompanying balance sheet of X Company as of December 31, 20X5, and the related statements of income, retained earnings, and cash flows for the year then ended. These financial statements are the responsibility of the Company's management. Our responsibility is to express an opinion on these financial statements based on our audit.

We conducted our audit in accordance with auditing standards generally accepted in the United States of America. Those standards require that we plan and perform the audit to obtain reasonable assurance about whether the financial statements are free of material misstatement. An audit includes examining, on a test basis, evidence supporting the amounts and disclosures in the financial statements. An audit also includes assessing the accounting principles used and significant estimates made by management, as well as evaluating the overall financial statement presentation. We believe that our audit provides a reasonable basis for our opinion.

As disclosed in Note 12 to the financial statements, the Company reports all of its sales on the installment method for financial accounting purposes and on its tax return. In our opinion, generally accepted accounting principles require that sales be reported on the accrual basis with an appropriate provision for deferred taxes. As a result of these departures from generally accepted accounting principles, gross profit on sales is understated by $123,456 and income tax expense is understated by $14,222. The total effect of these departures on retained earnings is $109,234, which results in an increase in earnings per share of $1.42.

In our opinion, because of the effects of the matters discussed in the preceding paragraphs, the financial statements referred to above do not present fairly, in conformity with accounting principles generally accepted in the United States of America, the financial position of X Company as of December 31, 20X5, or the result of its operations or its cash flows for the year then ended.

EXHIBIT AU 508-4— QUALIFIED AUDITOR'S REPORT BECAUSE STATEMENT OF CASH FLOW IS OMITTED

We have audited the accompanying balance sheet of X Company as of December 31, 20X5, and the related statements of income and retained earnings for the year then ended. These financial statements are the responsibility of the Company's management. Our responsibility is to express an opinion on these financial statements based on our audit.

We conducted our audit in accordance with auditing standards generally accepted in the United States of America. Those standards require that we plan and perform the audit to obtain reasonable assurance about whether the financial statements are free of material misstatement. An audit includes examining, on a test basis, evidence supporting the amounts and disclosures in the financial statements. An audit also includes assessing the accounting principles used and significant estimates made by management, as well as evaluating the overall financial statement presentation. We believe that our audit provides a reasonable basis for our opinion.

The Company did not present a statement of cash flows for the year ended December 31, 20X5. Presentation of such statement summarizing the Company's operating, investing, and financing activities is required by generally accepted accounting principles.

In our opinion, except that the omission of a statement of cash flows results in an incomplete presentation as explained in the preceding paragraph, the financial statements referred to above present fairly, in all material respects, the financial position of X Company as of December 31, 20X5, and the results of its operations for the year then ended in conformity with accounting principles generally accepted in the United States of America.

EXHIBIT AU 508-5—QUALIFIED AUDITOR'S REPORT BECAUSE OF A SCOPE LIMITATION

We have audited the accompanying balance sheet of X Company as of December 31, 20X5, and the related statements of income, retained earnings, and cash flows for the year then ended. These financial statements are the responsibility of the Company's management. Our responsibility is to express an opinion on these financial statements based on our audit.

Except as discussed in the following paragraph, we conducted our audit in accordance with auditing standards generally accepted in the United States of America. Those standards require that we plan and perform the audit to obtain reasonable assurance about whether the financial statements are free of material misstatement. An audit includes examining, on a test basis, evidence supporting the amounts and disclosures in the financial statements. An audit also includes assessing the accounting principles used and significant estimates made by management, as well as evaluating the overall financial statement presentation. We believe that our audit provides a reasonable basis for our opinion.

We were not able to confirm accounts receivable as of December 31, 20X5, stated at $500,000. The receivables were principally due from agencies of the U.S. government. In addition, we were unable to determine the validity of the accounts through the use of alternative procedures.

In our opinion, except for the effects of such adjustment, if any, as might have been determined to be necessary had we been able to determine the validity of accounts receivable, the financial statements referred to in the first paragraph above present fairly, in all material respects, the financial position of X Company as of December 31, 20X5, and the results of its operations and its cash flows for the year then ended in conformity with accounting principles generally accepted in the United States of America.

EXHIBIT AU 508-6—DISCLAIMER REPORT

We were engaged to audit the accompanying balance sheet of X Company as of December 31, 20X5, and the related statements of income, retained earnings, and cash flows for the year then ended. These financial statements are the responsibility of the Company's management.

No physical inventory was taken for merchandise held for sale by the Company as of December 31, 20X4, or December 31, 20X5, and inventory quantities are stated in the accompanying financial statements at $150,000 and $400,000, respectively.

Since the Company did not take physical inventories and we were not able to apply alternative auditing procedures to satisfy ourselves as to inventory quantities, the scope of our work was not sufficient to enable us to express, and we do not express, an opinion on the financial statements referred to above.

EXHIBIT AU 508-7—AUDITOR'S REPORT ONLY ON THE BALANCE SHEET

We have audited the accompanying balance sheet of X Company as of December 31, 20X5. This financial statement is the responsibility of the Company's management. Our responsibility is to express an opinion on this financial statement based on our audit.

We conducted our audit in accordance with auditing standards generally accepted in the United States of America. Those standards require that we plan and perform the audit to obtain reasonable assurance about whether the balance sheet is free of material misstatement. An audit includes examining, on a test basis, evidence supporting the amounts and disclosures in the balance sheet. An audit also includes assessing the accounting principles used and significant estimates made by management, as well as evaluating the overall balance sheet presentation. We believe that our audit provides a reasonable basis for our opinion.

In our opinion, the balance sheet referred to above presents fairly, in all material respects, the financial position of X Company as of December 31, 20X5, in conformity with accounting principles generally accepted in the United States of America.

EXHIBIT AU 508-9—AUDITOR'S REPORT ON COMPARATIVE FINANCIAL STATEMENTS

We have audited the accompanying balance sheets of X Company as of December 31, 20X5 and 20X4, and the related statements of income, retained earnings, and cash flows for the years then ended. These financial statements are the responsibility of the Company's management. Our responsibility is to express an opinion on these financial statements based on our audits.

We conducted our audits in accordance with auditing standards generally accepted in the United States of America. Those standards require that we plan and perform the audit to obtain reasonable assurance about whether the financial statements are free of material misstatement. An audit includes examining, on a test basis, evidence supporting the amounts and disclosures in the financial statements. An audit also includes assessing the accounting principles used and significant estimates made by management, as well as evaluating the overall financial statement presentation. We believe that our audits provide a reasonable basis for our opinion.

In our opinion, the financial statements referred to above present fairly, in all material respects, the financial position of X Company as of December 31, 20X5 and 20X4, and the results of its operations and its cash flows for the years then ended in conformity with accounting principles generally accepted in the United States of America.

EXHIBIT AU 508-10—AUDITOR'S REPORT ON COMPARATIVE FINANCIAL STATEMENTS WITH DIFFERENT OPINIONS

We have audited the accompanying balance sheets of X Company as of December 31, 20X5 and 20X4, and the related statements of income, retained earnings, and cash flows for the years then ended. These financial statements are the responsibility of the Company's management. Our responsibility is to express an opinion on these financial statements based on our audits.

We conducted our audits in accordance with auditing standards generally accepted in the United States of America. Those standards require that we plan and perform the audit to obtain reasonable assurance about whether the financial statements are free of material misstatement. An audit includes examining, on a test basis, evidence supporting the amounts and disclosures in the financial statements. An audit also includes assessing the accounting principles used and significant estimates made by management, as well as evaluating the overall financial statement presentation. We believe that our audits provide a reasonable basis for our opinion.

As more fully described in Note 7 to the financial statements, a net provision for loss on abandonment of equipment of $14,000,000 after related income taxes has been presented as an extraordinary charge against earnings for 20X4. In our opinion, generally accepted accounting principles require that the gross amount of such provision be part of the determination of income from operations before taxes and that the per-share amount of the provision not be separately presented in the statement of income.

In our opinion, except for the effects of the matter described in the previous paragraph on the 20X4 statement of income, the financial statements referred to above present fairly, in all material respects, the financial position of X Company as of December 31, 20X5 and 20X4, and the results of its operations and its cash flows for the years then ended in conformity with accounting principles generally accepted in the United States of America.

EXHIBIT AU 508-11—AUDITOR'S REPORT WHEN A PREDECESSOR AUDITOR'S REPORT IS NOT PRESENTED

We have audited the balance sheet of X Company as of December 31, 20X5, and the related statements of income, retained earnings, and cash flows for the year then ended. These financial statements are the responsibility of the Company's management. Our responsibility is to express an opinion on these financial statements based on our audit. The financial statements of X Company as of December 31, 20X4, were audited by other auditors whose report, dated February 18, 20X5, expressed an unqualified opinion on those statements.

We conducted our audit in accordance with auditing standards generally accepted in the United States of America. Those standards require that we plan and perform the audit to obtain reasonable assurance about whether the financial statements are free of material misstatement. An audit includes examining, on a test basis, evidence supporting the amounts and disclosures in the financial statements. An audit also includes assessing the accounting principles used and significant estimates made by management, as well as evaluating the overall financial statement presentation. We believe that our audit provides a reasonable basis for our opinion.

In our opinion, the 20X5 financial statements referred to above present fairly, in all material respects, the financial position of X Company as of December 31, 20X5, and the results of its operations and its cash flows for the year then ended in conformity with accounting principles generally accepted in the United States of America.

SECTION 530

DATING OF THE INDEPENDENT AUDITOR'S REPORT

Authoritative Pronouncements

SAS-1—Codification of Auditing Standards and Procedures (Section 530, Dating of the Independent Auditor's Report)

Overview

Under most circumstances the audit report should be dated as of the last day of fieldwork, and the auditor has no responsibility to perform audit procedures subsequent to the audit report date except under the following circumstances:

- Events occurring after completion of fieldwork but before the issuance of the audit report
- Reissuance of the audit report

Events occurring after completion of fieldwork but before the issuance of the audit report

AU Section 560 identifies subsequent events that occur after the client's balance sheet date but require that (1) the financial statements be adjusted or (2) the event be disclosed in the financial statements.

Events that require adjustment

When a subsequent event that requires adjustment occurs after the date of the audit report but before the financial statements have been issued (and the auditor becomes aware of the event), the financial statements should be appropriately adjusted or the auditor should not issue an unqualified opinion on the financial statements. When an adjustment is made and the event is not otherwise disclosed in the financial statements, the date of the audit report should be based on the last day of fieldwork. If the client refuses to make the appropriate adjustment or if the adjustment is made and the event is disclosed in the financial statements, the auditor should date the report in either one of the two following methods.

Dual-dating method Under this approach, the report is dated based on the last day of fieldwork and an exception similar to the following is noted in the report date:

March 3, 20X5, except for Note X, for which the date is March 15, 20X5.

If the auditor dual-dates the report, his or her responsibility is limited to the specific subsequent event and not to other subsequent events that may occur between the two dates (March 3 and March 15).

Single-dating method Under this approach, a single report date (the date that refers to the subsequent event) is used; however, using a single report date means that the auditor's responsibility for all subsequent events extends to the date identified with the specific subsequent event (March 15 in this example).

> **PLANNING AID REMINDER:** When the single-dating method is used, the auditor should follow the guidance established by AU Section 560 with respect to subsequent events.

Events that require disclosure

When a subsequent event that requires disclosure occurs after the date of the audit report but before the financial statements have been issued (and the auditor becomes aware of the event), the financial statements should include the appropriate disclosure or the auditor should not issue an unqualified opinion on the financial statements. When the appropriate disclosure is made, the audit report should be dated using the dual-dating method or the single-dating method, as described above.

Reissuance of the audit report

An auditor may be requested to reissue the original audit report under a number of circumstances, such as the following:

- Subsequent annual reports are filed with the Securities and Exchange Commission or other regulatory agency.
- Subsequent documents are submitted to the client or other parties.
- The client requests that the auditor submit additional copies of the original audit report.

Generally, the auditor has no responsibility to perform audit procedures subsequent to the original engagement and should use the original audit report date except under certain circumstances. For example, the auditor may have become aware of a subsequent event that requires that the original financial statements be adjusted or that the event be disclosed in the financial

§530 • Dating of the Independent Auditor's Report 383

statements as required by AU Section 560. In this instance, the reissued financial statement should not be adjusted unless the circumstances satisfy the conditions for a prior-period adjustment. Furthermore, the auditor should follow the guidance described above (single-dating or dual-dating) to determine how the reissued audit report should be dated.

If the subsequent event occurred between the original report date and the date of the reissued financial statements and the event requires only financial statement disclosure, the event may be disclosed in separate note to the financial statements with the following caption:

> Event (Unaudited) Subsequent to the Date of the Independent Auditor's Report

Under this circumstance, the original audit report date should be used in the reissued audit report.

> **PLANNING AID REMINDER:** Additional guidance for dating the auditor's report can be found in Section 711 (Filings Under Federal Securities Statutes), which addresses the audit report included in a registration statement filed under the Securities Act of 1933, and in AU Section 508 (Reports on Audited Financial Statements), which provides guidance for a predecessor auditor.

SECTION 532

RESTRICTING THE USE OF AN AUDITOR'S REPORT

Authoritative Pronouncements

SAS-87—Restricting the Use of an Auditor's Report

Overview

Generally, when an auditor reports on financial statements that are prepared in conformity with generally accepted accounting principles (GAAP) or an other comprehensive basis of accounting (OCBOA) other than GAAP, the distribution of the audit report is not limited (general-use reports). However, under certain conditions the auditor's report may be intended for specified parties (restricted-use reports), in which case the last paragraph of the report should describe the restriction using language such as the following:

> This report is intended solely for the information and use of [*the specified parties*] and is not intended to be and should not be used by anyone other than these specified parties.

> **RISK ASSESSMENT POINT:** The client, rather than the auditor, controls the actual distribution of an auditor's report. However, it is advised that the auditor inform the client that nonspecified parties should not receive a restricted-use report, even when the restricted-use report is included in a document that contains a separate general-use report. The auditor may want to formalize this understanding as part of the terms of the engagement. When restricted-use reports are filed with a regulatory agency, they may become public based on statute or regulatory requirements.

> **PLANNING AID REMINDER:** The specified parties may be listed in the report or may be referred to in a list of specified parties included elsewhere in the document that includes the auditor's report. When the engagement is covered by guidance established by U.S. Office of Management and Budget (OMB) Circular A-123 and "Audits of States, Local Governments and Non-Profit Organizations," the specified parties can simply be described as "federal awarding agencies and pass-through entities."

> **PLANNING AID REMINDER:** When the auditor issues a single report that covers both general-use and restricted-use situa-

tions, the single report must be restricted. However, when a document includes both a separate restricted-use report and a general-use report, there is no need to restrict the use of the general-use report.

The reporting guidance provided by AU Section 532 does not apply to the following situations:

- SAS-70—Service Organizations (see AU Section 324)
- SAS-72—Letters for Underwriters and Certain Other Requesting Parties (see AU Section 634)

Promulgated Reporting Standards Checklist

The auditor's report should be restricted for distribution in the following circumstances:

_____ The basis-of-reporting criteria are contained in contractual agreements, or regulatory provisions are not GAAP or OCBOA.

_____ The scope of the engagement is based on agreed-upon procedures.

_____ The report is a by-product of an audit of a client's financial statements.

> **ENGAGEMENT STRATEGY:** When the above situations are encountered, the auditor must issue a restricted-use report. The auditor is not prohibited from restricting the distribution of reports that are not listed above.

Analysis and Application of Reporting Standards

The basis of reporting criteria are contained in contractual agreements, or regulatory provisions are not GAAP or OCBOA.

A CPA may accept an engagement whereby the subject matter or presentation is based on measurement or disclosure criteria contained in a contractual agreement or regulatory provisions that do not conform to GAAP or OCBOA. For example, SAS-62 (AU 623) (Special Reports) notes that an auditor may be requested to report on special-purpose financial statements that have been prepared to satisfy a contractual agreement or governmental regulatory requirements. SAS-62 (AU 623) identifies the following as types of special-purpose financial statement presentations:

- A special-purpose financial presentation prepared in compliance with a contractual agreement or regulatory provision that does not constitute a complete presentation of the entity's assets, liabilities, revenues, and expenses but is otherwise prepared in conformity with GAAP or OCBOA
- A special-purpose financial presentation (may be a complete set of financial statements or a single financial statement) prepared on a basis of accounting prescribed in an agreement that does not result in a presentation in conformity with GAAP or another comprehensive basis of accounting

Because of the nature of these engagements, the auditor should prepare a restricted-use report.

Exhibit AU 532-1 illustrates a report on a statement of assets sold and liabilities transferred to comply with a contractual agreement. Exhibit AU 532-2 illustrates a report on financial statements prepared pursuant to a loan agreement that results in a presentation not in conformity with GAAP or OCBOA.

> **PLANNING AID REMINDER:** For a discussion of the guidance established by SAS-62, see AU Section 623.

During or subsequent to an engagement directed to reporting on subject matter or presentations based on measurement or disclosure criteria contained in contractual agreements or regulatory provisions, the auditor may be asked to add other specified parties that may use the report. The auditor may agree to this request, but should consider why the parties are being added. If the auditor agrees to add the other parties, an acknowledgment (usually in writing) should be obtained from these parties affirming that they understand the nature of the engagement, the measurement or disclosure criteria used, and the nature of the report. If the parties are added after the report has been issued, the auditor may reissue a revised report (using the original report date) or may acknowledge in a separate communication that the other parties have been added as specified parties (the communication should note that no additional procedures were performed after the date of the original report).

> **PLANNING AID REMINDER:** AU Section 622 contains additional guidance for adding specified parties to a restricted-use report.

The scope of the engagement is based on agreed-upon procedures

A CPA may accept an engagement wherein a specified party accepts responsibility for the sufficiency of the procedures performed. For example,

§532 • Restricting the Use of an Auditor's Report

SAS-75 (AU 622) provides guidance for agreed-upon procedures (AUP) engagements related to specified elements, accounts, or items of a financial statement. Exhibit AU 532-3 illustrates an AUP engagement report on specified elements, accounts, or items of a financial statement.

> **PLANNING AID REMINDER:** For a discussion of the guidance established by SAS-75, see AU Section 622. For a discussion of guidance for agreed-upon procedures in an attestation engagement, see AT Section 600.

The report is a by-product of an audit of a client's financial statements

In some instances the auditor may audit a client's financial statements and as a by-product report separately on matters that came to his or her attention during the audit engagement. Examples of this reporting circumstance are discussed in the following promulgations:

- SAS-60—Communication of Internal Control Related Matters Noted in an Audit (see AU Section 325)
- SAS-61—Communication with Audit Committees (see AU Section 380)
- SAS-62—Special Reports (paragraphs 19–21) (see AU Section 623)

> **ENGAGEMENT STRATEGY:** A by-product report may be issued in other engagements conducted in accordance with generally accepted auditing standards, such as an engagement to express an opinion on a specified element, account, or item in a financial statement.

Because the report on the above-listed Statements on Auditing Standards is a by-product of the audit of the client's financial statements, the auditor should issue a restricted-use report on these matters. AU Section 532 of the AICPA standards specifically notes that the restricted-use report for these matters should be distributed to the following parties only:

- The entity's audit committee
- The entity's board of directors
- The entity's management and others within the organization
- Specified regulatory agencies
- Parties to the contract or agreement for reports on compliance with aspects of the contractual agreement

Practitioner's Aids

EXHIBIT AU 532-1—RESTRICTED AUDIT REPORT ON SPECIAL-PURPOSE FINANCIAL STATEMENT PRESENTATION

We have audited the accompanying statement of net assets sold of X Company as of July 15, 20X7. This statement of net assets sold is the responsibility of X Company's management. Our responsibility is to express an opinion on the statement of net assets sold based on our audit.

We conducted our audit in accordance with auditing standards generally accepted in the United States of America. Those standards require that we plan and perform the audit to obtain reasonable assurance about whether the statement of net assets sold is free of material misstatement. An audit includes examining, on a test basis, evidence supporting the amounts and disclosures in the statement. An audit also includes assessing the accounting principles used and significant estimates made by management, as well as evaluating the overall presentation of the statement of net assets sold. We believe that our audit provides a reasonable basis for our opinion.

The accompanying statement was prepared to present the net assets of X Company sold to Z Company pursuant to the purchase agreement described in Note 1, and is not intended to be a complete presentation of X Company's assets and liabilities.

In our opinion, the accompanying statement of net assets sold presents fairly, in all material respects, the net assets of X Company as of July 15, 20X7, sold pursuant to the purchase agreement referred to in Note 1, in conformity with accounting principles generally accepted in the United States of America.

This report is intended solely for the information and use of the boards of directors and managements of X Company and Z Company and is not intended to be and should not be used by anyone other than these specified parties.

EXHIBIT AU 532-2—RESTRICTED AUDIT REPORT ON FINANCIAL STATEMENTS PREPARED PURSUANT TO A LOAN AGREEMENT

We have audited the special-purpose statement of assets and liabilities of X Company as of December 31, 20X7 and 20X8, and the related special-purpose statements of revenues and expenses and cash flows for the years then ended. These financial statements are the responsibility of the Company's management. Our responsibility is to express an opinion on these financial statements based on our audits.

We conducted our audits in accordance with auditing standards generally accepted in the United States of America. Those standards require that we plan and perform the audit to obtain reasonable assurance about whether the financial statements are free of material misstatement. An audit includes examining, on a test basis, evidence supporting the amounts and disclosures in the financial statements. An audit also includes assessing the accounting principles used and significant estimates made by management, as well as evaluating the overall financial statement presentation. We believe that our audits provide a reasonable basis for our opinion.

The accompanying special-purpose financial statements were prepared for the purpose of complying with Section A of a loan agreement between the Company and the First State Bank as discussed in Note 1, and are not intended to be a presentation in conformity with accounting principles generally accepted in the United States of America.

In our opinion, the special-purpose financial statements referred to above present fairly, in all material respects, the assets and liabilities of X Company as of December 31, 20X7 and 20X8, and the revenues, expenses, and cash flows for the years then ended, on the basis of accounting described in Note 1.

This report is intended solely for the information and use of the boards of directors and managements of X Company and the First State Bank and is not intended to be and should not be used by anyone other than these specified parties.

EXHIBIT AU 532-3—RESTRICTED AUDIT REPORT ON SPECIFIED ACCOUNTS OF A FINANCIAL STATEMENT

We have performed the procedures enumerated below, which were agreed to by the Board of Directors of X Company, solely to assist you with respect to the evaluation of inventory and property, plant, and equipment of Y Company as part of the proposed acquisition of Y Company by X Company. This engagement to apply agreed-upon procedures was performed in accordance with standards established by the American Institute of Certified Public Accountants. The sufficiency of the procedures is solely the responsibility of the specified users of the report. Consequently, we make no representation regarding the sufficiency of the procedures described below either for the purpose for which this report has been requested or for any other purpose.

The agreed-upon procedures that were performed and the related findings are as follows:

Inventory

1. We obtained the inventory summarization as of December 31, 20X7, and traced 20% of the quantities listed on the summarization to the inventory tags used by Y Company during its physical count on December 31, 20X7.

   We found no differences between the quantities on the inventory summarization and the quantities on the inventory tags.

2. For 1 out of 10 line items on the inventory summarization, we traced the inventory cost per unit listed to vendor invoices for purchases made during the last quarter of 20X7.

   We found no differences between the cost listed on the inventory summarization and vendor invoices for purchases made during the last quarter of 20X7.

3. We added the inventory summarization and compared the total with the total unaudited balance ($2,000,000) in the general ledger account as of December 31, 20X7.

   We found no difference between the total inventory amount we computed and the balance in the general ledger account.

4. For all inventory line items on the inventory summarization that exceeded $10,000, we recomputed their extended value by multiplying the number of units by the cost per unit.

   We found no errors as the result of this procedure.

Property, Plant, and Equipment

1. We obtained a computer printout of assets classified as property, plant, and equipment having an unaudited balance of $3,500,000 as of December 31, 20X7, which we added and traced to the appropriate general ledger accounts.

   We found no differences between the amounts per the computer printout and the appropriate general ledger account balances.

2. We physically inspected approximately 30% of the assets (based on the original cost of the asset as shown on the computer printout) listed on the computer printout and traced the property identification number, which appeared on each, to the appropriate ledger card contained in the computerized plant ledger.

   We found no differences between the identification number that appeared on each asset and the corresponding number included in the plant ledger cards.

We were not engaged to and did not perform an audit, the objective of which would be the expression of an opinion on the specified elements, accounts, or items. Accordingly, we do not express such an opinion. Had we been engaged to perform additional procedures, other matters might have come to our attention that would have been reported to you.

This report is intended solely for the use of the Board of Directors of X Company and is not intended to be and should not be used by anyone other than these specified parties.

SECTION 534

REPORTING ON FINANCIAL STATEMENTS PREPARED FOR USE IN OTHER COUNTRIES

Authoritative Pronouncements

SAS-51—Reporting on Financial Statements Prepared for Use in Other Countries

Auditing Interpretation (May 1996)—Financial Statement for General Use Only Outside of the U.S. in Accordance with International Accounting Standards and International Standards on Auditing

Overview

A U.S. practicing auditor may be engaged by a U.S. entity to report on financial statements that are intended to be used outside the United States and that are to be prepared in conformity with accounting principles generally accepted in another country. Guidance for reporting on such financial statements is provided by SAS-51 (Reporting on Financial Statements Prepared for Use in Other Countries). For the purposes of SAS-51, a "U.S. entity" is one that is either organized or domiciled in the United States.

An auditor should have a clear understanding of the purpose and uses of financial statements that are prepared in conformity with accounting principles of another country. The auditor should obtain management's written representations before reporting on such statements. When using the standard report of another country instead of the U.S.-style auditor's standard report, an auditor must determine whether he or she is exposed to any additional legal responsibilities.

Promulgated Procedures Checklist

The auditor should perform the following procedures when reporting on financial statements prepared for use in another country:

_____ Observe the general standards and the standards of fieldwork established by the U.S. Auditing Standards Board.

_____ Consider whether foreign auditing standards must be observed.

_____ Prepare an appropriate audit report.

Analysis and Application of Procedures

Observe the general standards and the standards of fieldwork established by the U.S. Auditing Standards Board

Before reporting on financial statements prepared in accordance with accounting principles of another country, the auditor must consider which auditing standards are applicable in the engagement. In some engagements, an auditor may be required to follow both U.S. generally accepted auditing standards (GAAS) and auditing standards established by a foreign country.

In reporting on financial statements prepared in accordance with accounting principles of another country, the auditor must observe the three general standards and the three fieldwork standards that are part of U.S. generally accepted auditing standards. In this event, the auditor is also required to comply with all related SASs and SAS Interpretations.

Consider whether foreign auditing standards must be observed

When the auditor is required to comply with auditing standards of another country, both those standards and U.S. generally accepted auditing standards must be observed during the engagement. Thus, some audit procedures will be employed to comply with U.S. GAAS, whereas other audit procedures will be performed to satisfy auditing standards of the foreign country.

Prepare an appropriate audit report

The reporting standards that must be observed in the preparation of the auditor's report on financial statements prepared in accordance with accounting principles of another country are dependent on the purpose of the financial statements. These purposes may be classified as (1) foreign GAAP/foreign use, (2) dual statements (foreign GAAP/U.S. GAAP), and (3) foreign GAAP/general U.S. distribution. Each of these purposes is discussed below.

Foreign GAAP/foreign use

When financial statements of a U.S. entity that are prepared in accordance with accounting principles of another country are to be used exclusively outside the United States, the auditor may use either the U.S.-style standard auditor's report or the standard auditor's report of the foreign country.

The auditor should observe the following reporting standards when deciding to use a U.S.-style standard auditor's report for financial statements prepared in accordance with accounting principles of a foreign country:

- The report must use the word "independent" in the title.
- The report must state that the financial statements were audited.
- The report must refer to the note to the financial statements that discloses the basis of presentation, including the nationality of the accounting principles.
- The report must state that the financial statements are the responsibility of management and that the auditor's responsibility is to express an opinion on them.
- The report must state that the audit was conducted in accordance with U.S. generally accepted auditing standards (and if applicable, the auditing standards of the foreign country).
- The report must state that U.S. standards require the auditor to plan and perform the audit to obtain a reasonable assurance on whether the financial statements are free of material misstatement.
- The report must state that an audit includes (1) examining, on a test basis, evidence supporting the amounts and disclosures in the financial statements; (2) assessing the accounting principles used and significant estimates made by management; and (3) evaluating the overall financial statement presentation.
- The report must state that the auditor believes that the audit provides a reasonable basis for his or her opinion.
- The report must state an opinion on the financial statements with respect to the basis of accounting described. (If the financial statements are not fairly presented, the opinion should be modified appropriately and should refer to a separate paragraph that describes the deficiency.)
- If there is an inconsistent application of the basis of accounting described, the report must contain a separate paragraph that explains the deficiency and the opinion must refer to the note that describes the inconsistency.

An example of a U.S.-style standard auditor's report is presented in Exhibit AU 534-1.

The standard report should be modified when the auditor concludes that the financial statements are not fairly presented in accordance with the basis of accounting described in the note. When the report is modified, a separate paragraph should contain a description of the accounting deficiency. The opinion paragraph should refer to the additional paragraph as the basis of the modification and should contain the appropriate opinion on the financial statements (qualified or adverse).

Rather than use the U.S.-style standard auditor's report, the auditor may use the standard auditor's report of the foreign country, provided two conditions are met. First, the standard report of the foreign country must be the same report that would have been issued by auditors of the foreign country under the same circumstances. Second, the auditor must understand the assertions made in the standard auditor's report of the foreign country, and it is appropriate for the auditor to take the responsibility for those assertions. With respect to the latter condition, it must be recognized that the assertions in the standard auditor's report of another country may be different from those in the U.S.-style standard auditor's report.

The fundamental assertion in the U.S.-style standard auditor's report is that the financial statements are prepared in accordance with generally accepted accounting principles. On the other hand, a foreign country's standard auditor's report may imply or state that the financial statements are prepared in compliance with existing statutory regulations. Thus, before issuing a foreign country's standard auditor's report, the U.S. auditor must fully understand the auditing standards, accounting principles, and laws that are applicable in the foreign country. To gain the appropriate understanding, the U.S. auditor may need to consult with auditors who are familiar with the auditing standards, accounting principles, and laws of the particular foreign country.

When the U.S. practicing auditor concludes that it is appropriate to issue the foreign country's standard auditor's report, the reporting standards of the foreign country should be observed.

Dual statements (foreign GAAP/U.S. GAAP)

One set of financial statements may be prepared in accordance with U.S. generally accepted accounting principles (GAAP) and a second set in accordance with accounting principles acceptable in a foreign country, to provide relevant information to users in both countries. For the financial statements presented in accordance with U.S. generally accepted accounting principles, the auditor should observe the Statements on Auditing Standards issued by the American Institute of Certified Public Accountants (AICPA) Auditing Standards Board in preparing the auditor's report. For the financial statements prepared in accordance with accounting principles acceptable in a foreign country and to be used outside of the United States, the auditor may prepare the U.S.-style standard auditor's report, which was described earlier, or may use the standard report of another country.

Some confusion may arise when the same financial statements of a U.S. entity are prepared on two different accounting bases. SAS-51 suggests that to reduce the possibility of a misunderstanding, one or both of the audit reports should contain a statement advising the reader of the other audit report, which has been issued on the same financial statements but is based on the accepted accounting principles of another country. The auditor's report also may refer to the note to the financial statements, if presented, that describes the significant differences between the two bases of accounting. An example of the auditor's reference to such a note is as follows:

> We also have reported separately on the financial statements of Company X for the same period presented in accordance with accounting principles generally accepted in [*insert name of foreign country*]. The significant differences between the accounting principles accepted in [*insert name of foreign country*] and those generally accepted in the United States are summarized in Note 1.

Foreign GAAP/general U.S. distribution

Financial statements prepared in accordance with accepted accounting principles of a foreign country may be intended for more than a limited distribution in the United States. When the auditor is asked to report on this type of financial statement, there are two acceptable reporting formats.

First, reporting guidance established by SAS-58 (AU 508) (Reports on Audited Financial Statements) should be followed for the U.S.-distributed financial statements. Thus, significant departures from U.S. generally accepted accounting principles, if any, would result in an expression of a qualified opinion or an adverse opinion. The auditor may include an additional paragraph in the standard report to express an opinion on whether the financial statements also are presented in conformity with the accepted accounting principles of another country.

Second, the auditor may present two reports: (1) either the U.S.-style auditor's report or the foreign country's standard report for foreign distribution (see earlier discussion for a description of these reports) and (2) an audit report based on SAS-58 (AU 508), as described in the previous paragraph for U.S. distribution.

> **RISK ASSESSMENT POINT:** SAS-51 does not preclude the limited distribution of financial statements to users within the United States who deal directly with the U.S. entity, as long as the users can discuss with the U.S. entity the significance of the differences between U.S. accounting principles and the foreign accounting principles that were used to prepare the financial statements.
>
> **PLANNING AID REMINDER:** The Auditing Interpretation (May 1996) titled "Financial Statements for General Use Only Outside of the United States in Accordance with International Ac-

counting Standards and International Standards on Auditing" concludes that an auditor may audit financial statements of a U.S. entity that presents its financial statements in accordance with International Accounting Standards for general use only outside of the U.S. Under this circumstance, the U.S. auditor must observe the guidance established by SAS-51.

Practitioner's Aids

Exhibit AU 534-1 is an example of a U.S.-style standard auditor's report.

EXHIBIT AU 534-1—U.S.-STYLE STANDARD AUDITOR'S REPORT

We have audited the accompanying balance sheet of X Company as of December 31, 20X5, and the related statements of income, retained earnings, and cash flows for the year then ended, which, as described in Note X, have been prepared on the basis of accounting principles generally accepted in [*insert name of foreign country*]. These financial statements are the responsibility of the Company's management. Our responsibility is to express an opinion on these financial statements based on our audit.

We conducted our audit in accordance with auditing standards generally accepted in the United States of America. U.S. standards require that we plan and perform the audit to obtain reasonable assurance about whether the financial statements are free of material misstatement. An audit includes examining, on a test basis, evidence supporting the amounts and disclosures in the financial statements. An audit also includes assessing the accounting principles used and significant estimates made by management, as well as evaluating the overall financial statement presentation. We believe that our audit provides a reasonable basis for our opinion.

In our opinion, the financial statements referred to above present fairly, in all material respects, the financial position of X Company as of December 31, 20X5, and the results of its operations and its cash flows for the year then ended in conformity with accounting principles generally accepted in [*insert name of foreign country*].

SECTION 543

PART OF AUDIT PERFORMED BY OTHER INDEPENDENT AUDITORS

Authoritative Pronouncements

SAS-1—Codification of Auditing Standards and Procedures (Section 543, Part of Audit Performed by Other Independent Auditors)

Auditing Interpretation (April 1979)—Inquiries of the Principal Auditor by the Other Auditor

Auditing Interpretation (April 1979)—Form of Inquiries of the Principal Auditor Made by the Other Auditor

Auditing Interpretation (April 1979)—Form of Principal Auditor's Response to Inquiries from Other Auditors

Auditing Interpretation (April 1979)—Procedures of the Principal Auditor

Auditing Interpretation (December 1981)—Application of Additional Procedures Concerning the Audit Performed by the Other Auditor

Auditing Interpretation (November 1996)—Specific Procedures Performed by the Other Auditor at the Principal Auditor's Request

Overview

An auditor must decide whether to make reference to the report of another auditor when part of the examination is made by another auditor. When part of an examination, such as the audit of a subsidiary, has been performed by another auditor, the principal auditor must decide whether that participation permits him or her to act as the principal auditor. If it does, the auditor must decide whether or not reference should be made to the other auditor. This decision is a matter of professional judgment and should be based on the materiality of the portions examined by each auditor. After a decision is reached about who is the principal auditor, the principal auditor must decide whether to refer to the other auditor in the report or to assume sole responsibility for the report. However, regardless of the decision of the principal auditor, the other auditor remains responsible for his or her own work and report.

Promulgated Procedures Checklist

The auditor should perform the following procedures when part of the work in an audit engagement is performed by another independent auditor:

§543 • Part of Audit Performed by Other Independent Auditors

_____ Perform basic audit procedures irrespective of whether the work of the other auditor is to be referred to in the report.

_____ Consider performing additional procedures when the work of the other auditor is not referred to in the report.

_____ Prepare an appropriate audit report.

Analysis and Application of Procedures

Perform basic audit procedures irrespective of whether the work of the other auditor is to be referred to in the report

Whether the principal auditor decides to make reference to another auditor or not, the following basic audit procedures must be performed:

- Determine the professional reputation and standing of the other auditor.
- Obtain a representation from the other auditor that he or she is independent of the client.
- Notify the other auditor that his or her audited financial statements may be included in the consolidated or combined financial statements reported on by the principal auditor.
- Notify the other auditor that his or her report may be relied on and, if appropriate, referred to by the principal auditor.
- Determine whether the other auditor is familiar with generally accepted accounting principles (GAAP) and generally accepted auditing standards (GAAS) and whether he or she uses these standards in engagements and the resulting reports.
- If necessary, determine whether the other auditor is familiar with SEC reporting practices.
- Notify the other auditor that there may be a review of adjusting and eliminating intercompany transactions.

> **PLANNING AID REMINDER:** The Auditing Interpretation (April 1979) titled "Inquiries of the Principal Auditor by the Other Auditor" states that it may be necessary for the other auditor to make inquiries of the principal auditor. For example, inquiry may be appropriate when the other auditor is making inquiries concerning related parties. In addition, the other auditor may make inquiries of the principal auditor about any matter considered significant to his or her examination. Usually the inquiry

should be made in writing and should note that the response should be made in writing. Also, the inquiry should specify the date by which the principal auditor should respond. The principal auditor should identify what stage of completion the examination is in as of the date of the reply. Also, the principal auditor should state that all the information requested by the other auditor would not necessarily be revealed by procedures used by the principal auditor. The principal auditor is not required to perform any procedures directed toward identifying matters that would not affect his or her own audit.

If the principal auditor concludes that the report of the other auditor cannot be relied on, a scope limitation exists and a qualified opinion or a disclaimer of opinion should be expressed.

Consider performing additional procedures when the work of the other auditor is not referred to in the report

When the principal auditor decides not to refer to the report of another auditor, it may be appropriate for the principal auditor to perform one or more of the following procedures:

- Visit the other auditor and discuss the audit procedures the other auditor employed and the results that auditor obtained during the engagement.
- Review the other auditor's audit program.
- Review the other auditor's workpapers.
- Consider whether instructions should be given to the other auditor as to the scope of work.
- Consider whether the principal auditor should discuss relevant matters directly with personnel of the consolidating or combining entity and/or should perform additional tests.

RISK ASSESSMENT POINT: The Auditing Interpretation (December 1981) of AU Section 542 of SAS-1, titled "Application of Additional Procedures Concerning the Audit Performed by the Other Auditor," states that a principal auditor who decides not to make reference to the audit of another auditor may consider various factors when determining whether to apply procedures to obtain information about the adequacy of the other auditor's examination. One factor that may be taken into consideration involves knowledge of the other auditor's quality control policies and procedures that provide the other auditor with reasonable assurance of conformity with GAAS. Other factors that may be considered are (1) past experience with the other auditor, (2) the materiality of the financial statements examined by the other auditor in relationship to the combined or consolidated financial statements, (3) the degree of control exercised by the principal auditor over the work performed by the other auditor, and (4) the results of audit procedures performed by the principal auditor that suggest that the other auditor may have to perform additional procedures.

Generally, an auditor decides not to refer to another auditor when (1) the other auditor is an associate or correspondent, (2) the principal auditor actually engages the other auditor, or (3) the financial statements examined by the other auditor are immaterial in relation to the consolidated or combined group.

Prepare an appropriate audit report

Reporting when reference is made

If the principal auditor decides to refer to the other auditor's examination, the report should, in both the scope and opinion paragraphs, clearly indicate the degree of responsibility and the portions of the financial statements examined by each. (This may be expressed in percentages, total assets, total revenue, or other appropriate criteria.) In addition, the principal auditor may name the other auditor only with his or her express permission.

Reference to another auditor by the principal auditor does not constitute a qualification of opinion but, rather, a description of responsibility between the two auditors.

If the other auditor's opinion is qualified, the principal auditor must decide whether the subject of the qualification is material in relation to the consolidated statements. If the principal auditor decides that it is not, the principal auditor does not need to refer to the qualification in the report.

> **RISK ASSESSMENT POINT:** Another Interpretation (November 1996) of AU Section 543, titled "Specific Procedures Performed by the Other Auditor at the Principal Auditor's Request," states that when a principal auditor requests that the other auditor perform specific procedures, the principal auditor is responsible for determining the extent of the procedures to be performed.

When the principal auditor decides to refer to the report of another auditor, the basic audit procedures described previously must be performed.

ENGAGEMENT STRATEGY: An auditor is placed in the role of principal auditor when a long-term investment is accounted for by the equity method. Furthermore, an auditor may be placed in the role of principal auditor even if the cost method is used to account for a long-term investment. The latter circumstance may arise when the work of the other auditor constitutes a major element of evidence with respect to the investment account. Presumably, this occurs when there is some question about whether there has been a permanent impairment in the carrying value of the investment.

Reporting by successor auditor for a pooling of interests

When a pooling of interests occurs, the previous year's (or years') financial statements should be restated to incorporate the financial statements of all of the entities involved in the business combination. Subsequent to the pooling of the entities, an auditor may be requested to report on the previous year's restated (consolidated) financial statements; however, the auditor may not have audited all of the financial statements that form the basis for the restatement. Under this circumstance, the auditor must decide whether he or she has audited a sufficient part of the prior year's restated financial statements and therefore is in a position to report as principal auditor on the restated financial statements of the previous year. If the auditor concludes that it is appropriate to serve as principal auditor, the guidance discussed earlier with respect to formulating and expressing opinions based on another auditor's report should be observed.

In some circumstances the auditor may conclude that it is not possible to serve as principal auditor with respect to the restated financial statements. In this case, SAS-64 (AU 341, AU 508, AU 543) (Omnibus Statement on Auditing Standards—1990) concludes that the auditor (reporting on the current year's financial statements of the consolidated entity) may express an opinion limited to the combining of the prior year's financial statements. An example of an additional paragraph that may be added to the auditor's opinion on the current year's financial statements is illustrated below.

> We previously audited and reported on the consolidated balance sheet of X Company as of December 31, 20X4, and the related consolidated statements of income and cash flows for the year then ended, prior to their restatement for the 20X5 pooling of interests. The contribution of X Company and its subsidiaries to total assets, revenues, and net income represented 65%, 68%, and 70% of the respective restated totals. Separate financial statements of the other companies included in the 20X4 restated consolidated balance sheet and consolidated statements of in-

come and cash flows were audited and reported on separately by other auditors. We also audited the combination of the accompanying consolidated balance sheets and consolidated statements of income and cash flows for the year ended December 31, 20X4, after restatement for the 20X5 pooling of interests. In our opinion, such consolidated statements have been properly combined on the basis described in Note A of the notes to the consolidated financial statements.

Practitioner's Aids

Exhibit AU 543-1 illustrates an auditor's report where reference is made to the work of another auditor. Exhibit AU 543-2 is an example of the other auditor's inquiry of the principal auditor. Exhibit AU 543-3 is an example of the principal auditor's response to inquiries from the other auditor.

EXHIBIT AU 543-1—REFERENCE TO THE WORK OF ANOTHER AUDITOR IN THE AUDIT REPORT

We have audited the consolidated balance sheet of X Company as of December 31, 20X5, and the related consolidated statements of income, retained earnings, and cash flows for the year then ended. These financial statements are the responsibility of the Company's management. Our responsibility is to express an opinion on these financial statements based on our audit. We did not examine the financial statements of Z Company, a consolidated subsidiary whose statements reflect total assets and revenues constituting 15% and 12%, respectively, of the related consolidated totals. Those statements were audited by other auditors whose report has been furnished to us, and our opinion, insofar as it relates to the amounts included for Z Company, is based solely on the report of the other auditors.

We conducted our audit in accordance with auditing standards generally accepted in the United States of America. Those standards require that we plan and perform the audit to obtain reasonable assurance about whether the financial statements are free of material misstatement. An audit includes examining, on a test basis, evidence supporting the amounts and disclosures in the financial statements. An audit also includes assessing the accounting principles used and significant estimates made by management, as well as evaluating the overall financial statement presentation. We believe that our audit and the report of other auditors provide a reasonable basis for our opinion.

In our opinion, based on our audit and the report of other auditors, the consolidated financial statements referred to above present fairly, in all material respects, the financial position of X Company as of December 31, 20X5, and the results of its operations and its cash flows for the year then ended in conformity with accounting principles generally accepted in the United States of America.

EXHIBIT AU 543-2—EXAMPLE OF INQUIRY BY THE OTHER AUDITOR DIRECTED TO THE PRINCIPAL AUDITOR

We are auditing the financial statements of [*name of client*] as of [*date*] and for the [*period of audit*] for the purpose of expressing an opinion as to whether the financial statements present fairly, in all material respects, the financial position, results of operations, and cash flows of [*name of client*] in conformity with generally accepted accounting principles.

A draft of the financial statements referred to above and a draft of our report are enclosed solely to aid you in responding to this inquiry. Please provide us [*in writing/orally*] with the following information in connection with your current examination of the consolidated financial statement of [*name of parent company*]:

1. Transactions or other matters (including adjustment made during consolidation or contemplated at the date of your reply) that have come to your attention that you believe require adjustment to or disclose in the financial statement of [*name of client*] being audited by us.

2. Any limitation on the scope of your audit that is related to the financial statements of [*name of client*] being audited by us, or that limits your ability to provide us with the information requested in this inquiry.

Please make your response as of a date near [expected date of the other auditor's report].

EXHIBIT AU 543-3—EXAMPLE OF PRINCIPAL AUDIT'S RESPONSE TO INQUIRY MADE BY OTHER AUDITOR

This letter is furnished to you in response to your request that we provide you with certain information in connection with your audit of the financial statement of [*name of component*], a [*subsidiary, division, branch or investment*] of Parent Company for the year ended [*date*].

We are in the process of performing an audit of the consolidated financial statements of Parent Company for the year ended [*date*] [*but have not completed our work as of this date*]. The objective of our audit is to enable us to express an opinion on the consolidated financial statements of Parent Company, and, accordingly, we have performed no procedures directed toward identifying matters that would not affect our audit or our report. However, solely for the purpose of responding to your inquiry, we have read the draft of the financial statement of [*name of component*] as of [*date*] and for the [*period of audit*] and the draft of your report on them, included with your inquiry dated [*date of inquiry*].

Based solely on the work we have performed [*to date*] in connection with our audit of the consolidated financial statements, which would not necessarily reveal all or any of the matters covered in your inquiry, we advise you that:

1. No transactions or other matters (including adjustment made during consolidation or contemplated at this date) have come to our attention that we believe require adjustment to or disclosure in the financial statements of [*name of component*] being audited by you.

2. No limitation has been placed by Parent Company on the scope of our audit that, to our knowledge, is related to the financial statements of [*name of component*] being audited by you, that has limited our ability to provide you with the information requested in your inquiry.

RISK ASSESSMENT POINT: The Auditing Interpretation (April 1979) titled "Procedures of the Principal Auditor" concludes that the above response should be made by the auditor "with final responsibility for the engagement," and that auditor should perform steps considered reasonable under the circumstance to respond in an appropriate manner to the request made by the other auditor. If relevant information is discovered after the principal auditor has responded to the request but before the completion of the audit, the other auditor should be informed of the new information. If the principal auditor discovers information relevant to the other auditor's request after a response has been sent, the guidance established by AU Section 561 (Subsequent Discovery of Facts Existing at the Date of the Auditor's Report) should be followed.

SECTION 544

LACK OF CONFORMITY WITH GENERALLY ACCEPTED ACCOUNTING PRINCIPLES

Authoritative Pronouncements

SAS-1—Codification of Auditing Standards and Procedures (Section 544, Lack of Conformity with Generally Accepted Accounting Principles)

Overview

Generally accepted accounting principles apply to all commercial enterprises, including those enterprises whose accounting practices are established by a governmental agency. For example, insurance companies must file financial statements with the appropriate state insurance commissioner and must observe the accounting and reporting standards established by that state's commissioner.

When financial statements of these enterprises are prepared for purposes other than for filing with the regulatory agency that establishes the accounting and reporting principles, those statements must follow generally accepted accounting principles as defined in SAS-69 (AU 411) (The Meaning of "Present Fairly in Conformity with Generally Accepted Accounting Principles"). If the regulated enterprise does not revise the general-purpose financial statements to conform to the accounting standards established by SAS-69 (AU 411), the auditor must determine whether a qualified opinion or an adverse opinion must be expressed on the financial statements. SAS-1 notes that when an adverse opinion is expressed, the auditor's report may be accompanied by an opinion on a supplementary presentation that is consistent with generally accepted accounting principles.

> **PLANNING AID REMINDER:** The auditor may follow the reporting standards established by SAS-62 (Special Reports) in order to report on financial statements that are prepared in accordance with regulatory accounting standards and that are to be used only to satisfy the filing requirement established by the governmental regulatory authority.

In some instances the enterprise's financial statements, prepared on regulatory accounting standards, may have to be filed "in presentations for distribution in other than filings with the entity's regulatory agency." If the auditor is requested to express an opinion on the financial statements under this circumstance, the guidance established by SAS-58 (AU 508) (Reports on Audited Financial Statements) must be observed, and any material differences with generally accepted accounting principles would require that a qualified opinion or an adverse opinion be expressed. The auditor's report should include an additional paragraph stating whether the financial statements are prepared in accordance with the regulatory accounting standards.

SECTION 550

OTHER INFORMATION IN DOCUMENTS CONTAINING AUDITED FINANCIAL STATEMENTS

Authoritative Pronouncements

SAS-8—Other Information in Documents Containing Audited Financial Statements

Auditing Interpretation (May 1994)—Report by Management on the Internal Control Structure Over Financial Reporting

Auditing Interpretation (May 1994)—Other References by Management to Internal Control Over Financial Reporting, Including References to the Independent Auditor

Auditing Interpretation (March 1997)—Other Information in Electronic Sites Containing Audited Financial Statements

Overview

The auditor's report may be included in a document that contains other information. For example, a company's annual report may include a message from the chief executive officer and descriptions of operations and future plans, as well as a variety of charts and graphs accompanied by explanations.

SAS-8 (Other Information in Documents Containing Audited Financial Statements) establishes the review and reporting responsibilities of the independent auditor with respect to other information in (1) annual reports sent to holders of securities, (2) annual reports sent to charitable or philanthropic organizations, (3) annual reports filed with the SEC as required by the Securities Exchange Act of 1934, and (4) other documents reviewed by the auditor at the client's request.

Although not required to audit the other information, the auditor must read it to determine whether—compared with the information presented in the financial statements—there is (1) a material inconsistency or (2) a material misstatement of fact.

> **PLANNING AID REMINDER:** The Auditing Interpretation (May 1994) titled "Report by Management on the Internal Control Structure Over Financial Reporting" concludes that if the auditor is engaged to report on other information related to management's assertions about the effectiveness of the client's

internal control over financial reporting, the standards established by Statements on Standards for Attestation Engagements (SSAEs) must be followed. The Auditing Interpretation (May 1994) titled "Other References by Management to Internal Control Over Financial Reporting, Including References to the Independent Auditor" concludes that if the auditor is not engaged to report on other information related to management's assertions about the effectiveness of the client's internal control over financial reporting, the procedures established by SAS-8 must be followed.

Promulgated Procedures Checklist

The auditor should perform the following procedures on other data and information in a document containing audited financial statements:

_____ Determine whether there is a material inconsistency in the other data and information.

_____ Determine whether there is a material misstatement of fact in the other data and information.

Analysis and Application of Procedures

Determine whether there is a material inconsistency in the other data and information

In determining whether there is a material inconsistency, the auditor should compare other information in the document to the audited financial statements. For example, the president's letter may refer to sales for the current year, and the auditor should simply verify that the sales figure in the president's letter agrees with the sales amount reported on the income statement.

When a material inconsistency is discovered, the auditor must determine which information is correct. If it is concluded that the client's other information is incorrect and the client refuses to change the other information, the auditor may choose to (1) withdraw from the engagement, (2) refuse to allow the client to include the auditor's report in the document, or (3) report on the material inconsistency. If the auditor decides to report on the material inconsistency, an explanatory paragraph containing a description of the inconsistency would be included; however, the opinion paragraph is unqualified and makes no reference to the explanatory paragraph. The rationale for this is that the auditor's opinion is limited to the information that was audited in accordance with generally accepted auditing standards.

Determine whether there is a material misstatement of fact in the other data and information

It is more difficult to identify a material misstatement of fact in an annual report, because the nature of much of the other information will be nonaccounting and beyond the expertise of the auditor. SAS-8 simply states that judgment should be used, and that the auditor may consider (1) notifying the client in writing of the apparent material misstatement and (2) seeking legal advice concerning other steps to be taken.

> **RISK ASSESSMENT POINT:** SAS-8 is vague in this area of material misstatement, because it relies on the auditor's limited expertise in relation to the other information. In other words, the auditor must proceed with caution. However, if the auditor discovers a material misstatement of fact and the client refuses to change the other information but the auditor still issues a report, it may be wise for the auditor to follow the reporting format prescribed when a material inconsistency is encountered.

> **PLANNING AID REMINDER:** The Auditing Interpretation (March 1997) titled "Other Information in Electronic Sites Containing Audited Financial Statements" notes that audited financial statements may be included on the client's Web site or other similar electronic presentations and those electronic locations may include other information. The Interpretation concludes that the other information contained in the electronic presentation is not subject to the standards established by SAS-8.

SECTION 551

REPORTING ON INFORMATION ACCOMPANYING THE BASIC FINANCIAL STATEMENTS IN AUDITOR-SUBMITTED DOCUMENTS

Authoritative Pronouncements

SAS-29—Reporting on Information Accompanying the Basic Financial Statements in Auditor-Submitted Documents

Overview

SAS-29 is applicable to auditor-submitted documents that contain information accompanying basic financial statements.

Auditor-submitted documents may contain information outside the basic financial statements, such as statistical data concerning operating ratios and trends, historical financial summaries, descriptions of auditing procedures, and nonaccounting data. The auditor must report on the additional information contained in the auditor-submitted document. The report should clearly identify the additional information and should state that the information is not a required part of the basic financial statements and is presented as additional data for the user. The report should also state that the purpose of the examination is to form an opinion on the financial statements taken as a whole. Finally, the report should either disclaim an opinion on the additional information or note that information is fairly stated in relation to the financial statements taken as a whole.

> **RISK ASSESSMENT POINT:** The auditor's reporting responsibilities for client-prepared documents (for example, an annual report) and auditor-submitted documents (for example, a document bound in the CPA firm's cover) differ. In a client-prepared document, other information (that is, information other than the financial statements, related notes, and required supplementary information) included in the document is not referred to in the auditor's report. In an auditor-submitted document, the auditor must disclaim an opinion on the other information, unless he or she has been engaged to audit it, and has done so.

Promulgated Procedures Checklist

The auditor should apply the following procedures for reporting on information accompanying the basic financial statement in auditor-submitted documents:

_____ Report on the additional information.

_____ Report on consolidating or combining information if such information is presented.

_____ Report on supplementary information.

Analysis and Application of Procedures

Report on the additional information

The auditor's opinion on the additional information may be incorporated in the standard report or may appear in a separate opinion elsewhere in the auditor-submitted document. The following illustrates a paragraph added to the standard auditor's report applicable to additional information in an auditor-submitted document.

> Our audit was made for the purpose of forming an opinion on the basic financial statements taken as a whole. The accompanying information on pages 14 through 16 is presented for purposes of additional analysis and is not a required part of the basic financial statements. Such information has been subjected to the procedures applied in the audit of the basic financial statements and, in our opinion, is fairly stated in all material respects in relation to the basic financial statements taken as a whole.

If the auditor concludes that the additional information is materially misstated, the report should be modified or the auditor should not agree to include the information in the auditor-submitted document.

> **ENGAGEMENT STRATEGY:** The auditor-submitted document may contain nonaccounting information that the auditor cannot verify. Under these circumstances, the auditor should issue a disclaimer of opinion. On the other hand, auditing procedures may be described as additional information. These procedures should be separated from other information, and care must be taken so that the additional information does not contradict or otherwise detract from the scope paragraph of the report.

Report on consolidating or combining information if such information is presented

Auditor-submitted documents may contain consolidated or combined financial statements supplemented by consolidating or combining information.

§551 • Information Accompanying the Basic Financial Statements 413

When the additional information has not been separately audited, an explanatory paragraph should state that (1) the purpose of the audit was to form an opinion on the financial statements taken as a whole, (2) the consolidating information is presented as additional data, and (3) the consolidating information is fairly stated in all material respects in relation to the consolidated financial statements.

The following is an example of a paragraph added to the standard auditor's report that is applicable to consolidating or combining information included in an auditor-submitted document.

> Our audit was made for the purpose of forming an opinion on the consolidated financial statements taken as a whole. The consolidating information is presented for purposes of additional analysis of the consolidated financial statements rather than to present the financial position, results of operations, and cash flows of the individual companies. The consolidated information has been subjected to the procedures applied in the audit of the consolidated financial statements and, in our opinion, is fairly stated in all material respects in relation to the consolidated financial statements taken as a whole.
>
> > **PLANNING AID REMINDER:** SAS-29 does not provide the auditor with the option to disclaim an opinion on the consolidating information. This is reasonable, because an opinion on the consolidated financial statements could not be formed if the consolidating information were not subjected to appropriate auditing procedures.

Report on supplementary information

When an auditor-submitted document includes supplementary information required by the Financial Accounting Standards Board (FASB) or the Government Accounting Standards Board (GASB), and the engagement did not include the audit of the supplementary information, the auditor should disclaim an opinion on the supplementary information. The following is an example of a disclaimer of opinion on required supplementary information included in an auditor-submitted document:

> The [*identify the supplementary information*] on page XX is not a required part of the basic financial statements but is supplementary information required by the [Financial Accounting Standards Board/Governmental Accounting Standards Board]. We have applied certain limited procedures, which consisted principally of inquiries of management regarding the methods of measurement and presentation of the supplementary infor-

mation. However, we did not audit the information and express no opinion on it.

An explanatory paragraph applicable to required supplementary information included in an auditor-submitted document should be added to the standard auditor's report under the following conditions:

- Required supplementary information is omitted.
- Measurement or presentation of the required supplementary information deviates from guidelines established by the FASB or GASB.
- The auditor is unable to apply the limited procedures to the required supplementary information.
- The auditor has substantial doubt about whether the required supplementary information conforms to established guidelines.

Under these circumstances, the auditor should add an explanatory paragraph similar to the ones discussed in AU Section 558.

SECTION 552

REPORTING ON CONDENSED FINANCIAL STATEMENTS AND SELECTED FINANCIAL DATA

Authoritative Pronouncements

SAS-42—Reporting on Condensed Financial Statements and Selected Financial Data

Overview

SAS-42 (Reporting on Condensed Financial Statements and Selected Financial Data) is applicable to reports on condensed financial statements or selected financial data that are derived from audited financial statements and that appear in a client-prepared document. Specifically, the reporting guidelines established by SAS-42 relate to the following:

- Condensed financial statements that are derived from audited financial statements of a public entity that is required to file, at least annually, complete financial statements with a regulatory agency
- Selected financial data that are derived from audited financial statements of a public or nonpublic entity and presented in a document containing audited financial statements or incorporated by reference to information filed with a regulatory agency

> **ENGAGEMENT STRATEGY:** If the condensed financial information or selected financial data are presented in an auditor-submitted document, SAS-29 (Reporting on Information Accompanying the Basic Financial Statements in Auditor-Submitted Documents) should be followed.

Promulgated Procedures Checklist

The auditor should report on condensed financial statements and selected financial data by observing the following guidelines:

____ Express an opinion on condensed financial statements.

____ Express an opinion on selected financial data.

Analysis and Application of Procedures

Express an opinion on condensed financial statements

The very nature of condensed financial statements is that they are presented in less detail than conventional financial statements. For this reason, they do not fairly present the financial position or results of operation of an entity. When an auditor is engaged to report on condensed financial statements derived from audited financial statements of a public entity, the auditor should observe the following reporting guidelines in preparing the auditor's report:

- State that the complete financial statements have been audited.
- Disclose the date of the auditor's report on the complete financial statements.
- Describe the type of opinion expressed. If the opinion was other than unqualified, explain the nature of and reason for the modification.
- State whether the condensed information is fairly stated in relation to the audited financial statements from which the information was extracted.

The following paragraph illustrates an auditor's report on condensed financial statements that reflects the reporting guidelines described previously:

> We have audited, in accordance with auditing standards generally accepted in the United States of America, the consolidated balance sheet of B Company and its subsidiaries as of December 31, 20X5, and the related consoli-dated statements of income, retained earnings, and cash flows for the year then ended (not presented herein), and in our report dated February 12, 20X6, we expressed an unqualified opinion on those consolidated financial statements.

In our opinion, the information set forth in the accompanying condensed consolidated financial statements is fairly stated in all material respects in relation to the consolidated financial statements from which it has been derived.

> **RISK ASSESSMENT POINT:** When the condensed financial statements are presented with financial statements of a subsequent interim period and the auditor's review report on the interim financial statements, the auditor is considered to be associated with the condensed financial statements. Under this

§552 • Condensed Financial Statements and Selected Data 417

circumstance, the auditor would add an additional paragraph, similar to the one described above, to the review report to cover the condensed financial statements.

Express an opinion on selected financial data

Selected financial data for a public or nonpublic company may be presented, along with audited financial statements, in a client-prepared document. For example, some reports filed with the SEC must contain selected financial data for a five-year period. The auditor is not required to audit this data, but, as required by SAS-8 (AU 550) (Other Information in Documents Containing Audited Financial Statements), the auditor must read the data for possible material inconsistencies between it and the audited financial statements.

> **PLANNING AID REMINDER:** SAS-8 is not applicable to filings under the Securities Act of 1933. SAS-37 (Filings under Federal Securities Statutes) provides guidance for filings under the Securities Act of 1933.

Selected financial data are not an integral part of the basic financial statements of a public or nonpublic company and, as noted above, may not be audited. Under certain circumstances, the auditor may be asked or required to examine the supplementary information. In this case, the report should observe the following guidelines:

- State that the complete financial statements have been audited.
- Describe the type of opinion expressed. If the opinion was other than unqualified, explain the nature of and reason for the modification.
- State whether the selected financial data are fairly stated in relation to the audited financial statements from which the data were derived.
- If appropriate, identify the statements that were audited by another CPA firm, but express no opinion on the selected data derived from those financial statements.

The auditor may meet these reporting requirements by adding an additional paragraph to the standard auditor's report. For example, the following explanatory paragraph is applicable to the audited (comparative) financial statements for 20X4 and 20X5 and the selected financial data from 20X1 through 20X5.

> We previously audited, in accordance with generally accepted auditing standards, the consolidated balance sheets as of De-

cember 31, 20X3, 20X2, and 20X1 and the related consolidated statements of income, retained earnings, and cash flows for the years ended December 31, 20X3, 20X2, and 20X1 (none of which are presented herein); we expressed unqualified opinions on those consolidated financial statements. In our opinion, the information set forth in the selected financial data for each of the five years in the period ended December 31, 20X5, appearing on pages 18 through 22, is fairly stated in all material respects in relation to the consolidated financial statements from which it has been derived.

ENGAGEMENT STRATEGY: The auditor should report only on the data derived from the audited financial statements. For example, if nonaccounting data are presented, such as number of employees, the auditor should specifically identify the data to which the report is applicable.

SECTION 558

REQUIRED SUPPLEMENTARY INFORMATION

Authoritative Pronouncements

SAS-52—Omnibus Statement on Auditing Standards—1987 (Requirement Supplementary Information)

Auditing Interpretation (February 1989)—Supplementary Oil and Gas Information

Overview

The Financial Accounting Standards Board (FASB) and Government Accounting Standards Board (GASB) have the authority to promulgate accounting and reporting standards, including required supplementary information. Although required supplementary information is not part of the basic financial statements, certain entities that the FASB or GASB have designated must disclose such information. The required supplementary information is considered to be an essential part of the financial report for these designated entities. While, this information does not have to be audited, certain limited procedures established by SAS-52 must be applied.

> **OBSERVATION:** The auditor also may be required to perform certain procedures on information as prescribed in an AICPA Audit Guide. For example, the Audit and Accounting Guide titled *Common Interest Realty Associations* requires presentation of unaudited supplementary information about the funding of future major repairs and replacements of common property by these types of entities. It also sets forth procedures for the auditor to perform on this information.

> **OBSERVATION:** SAS-52 is not applicable when the engagement includes the audit of the required supplementary information.

Promulgated Procedures Checklist

The auditor should perform the following procedures with respect to required supplementary information.

_____ Perform the minimum procedures to supplementary information included in audited financial statements.

_____ Perform certain procedures for required supplementary oil and gas reserve information.

_____ Identify those circumstances under which the audit report should be modified.

Analysis and Application of Procedures

Perform the minimum procedures to supplementary information included in audited financial statements

The auditor should apply the following procedures to supplementary information that an entity is required to include in its financial report:

- Make inquiries of management concerning the methods used to prepare the required supplementary information, such as the following:

  — Is the information measured and presented as required?

  — Have measurement methods and presentation formats changed from those used in the previous year?

  — What significant assumptions or interpretations are used to measure or present the information?

- Determine the required supplementary information's consistency with:

  — Answers to the inquiries received from management.

  — Audited financial statements.

  — Knowledge obtained as part of the audit of the financial statements.

- Determine whether written representations about the required supplementary information should be obtained from management.

- Apply other procedures, if any, that have been specified by other SASs, SAS Interpretations, Audit and Accounting Guides, or Statements of Position.

- Make additional inquiries if the application of procedures listed above raises questions about the measurement or presentation of the required supplementary information.

When an entity voluntarily includes supplementary information that is required for other entities, the auditor must observe the procedures established by SAS-52, except in the following circumstances:

§558 • Required Supplementary Information

- The entity has indicated in the financial report that the auditor has not applied limited procedures to the supplementary information.
- The auditor's report includes an explanatory paragraph that disclaims an opinion on the supplementary information. The explanatory paragraph would read as follows:

> The [*identify the supplementary information*] on page X [*or in Note X*] is not a required part of the basic financial statements, and we did not audit or apply limited procedures to such information and do not express any assurance on such information.

> **PLANNING AID REMINDER:** If the auditor does not apply the limited procedures as required by SAS-52 to the voluntary presentation of the supplementary information, the standards established by SAS-8 must be observed.

Perform certain procedures for required supplementary oil and gas reserve information

FAS-19 (CT Oi5) (Financial Accounting and Reporting by Oil and Gas Producing Companies), as amended by FAS-25 (CT Oi5) (Suspension of Certain Accounting Requirements for Oil and Gas Producing Companies), requires that certain disclosures concerning oil and gas reserves and changes in the reserves be disclosed as information supplementary to the financial statements. This supplementary information is subject to the basic audit procedures established by SAS-52 and to the additional audit procedures established by SAS-45 (AU 313, AU 334), as follows:

- Determine the client's understanding of these factors:

  — *Data used to compute reserve quantity information*—The auditor should make inquiries of management concerning reserve quantity information, which includes (1) quantities of proved oil and gas reserves owned net of interests of others, (2) reserves that are attributable to consolidated subsidiaries, (3) reserves that are attributable to investees (on a proportional basis), and (4) reserves related to royalty interests owned.

  — *Separate disclosure of sources of reserves*—The auditor should make inquiries of management concerning separate disclosures such as (1) share of oil and gas produced from royalty interests for which reserve quantity information is not available, (2) reserves related to agreements with governments or authorities where the entity participates in the operations or serves as producer, (3) reserves that are attributable to investees (on a proportional basis), (4) information that may affect reserve quantities such as subsequent events or significant uncertainties, (5) whether reserves are located in entity's home country, and (6) disclosure that certain governments restrict the disclosure of reserve information or require that the information include other than proved reserves.

— *Factors used to compute the standardized measure of discounted future net cash flows*—The auditor should make inquiries of management concerning such factors.

- Determine if the client personnel who estimated reserves are appropriately qualified. (For example, the Society of Petroleum Engineers has prepared "Standards Pertaining to the Estimation and Auditing of Oil and Gas Reserve Information," which indicates the normal qualifications of a reserve estimator.)

- Compare recent production with reserve estimates for properties that have significant production or significant reserve quantities, and inquire about disproportionate ratios.

- Compare reserve information for supplementary information to information used to compute depletion and amortization, and investigate any differences.

- Inquire about methods and bases used to compute reserve information and whether they are documented and current.

- Inquire about methods used to calculate the standardized measure of discounted future net cash flows.

When the auditor is not certain that the oil and gas reserve information is presented in accordance with established guidelines, a paragraph similar to the following should be added to the auditor's report.

> The oil and gas reserve information is not a required part of the basic financial statements, and we did not audit and do not express an opinion on such information. However, we have applied certain limited procedures prescribed by professional standards that raised doubts that we were unable to resolve regarding whether material modifications should be made to the information for it to conform with guidelines established by the Financial Accounting Standards Board.

The auditor may expand the above paragraph to include the reasons that led to the questions about the presentation of the reserve information.

§ 558 • Required Supplementary Information

Identify those circumstances under which the audit report should be modified

An explanatory paragraph applicable to required supplementary information should not be added to the standard auditor's report except in the following circumstances:

- Required supplementary information is omitted.
- Measurement or presentation of the required supplementary information deviates from guidelines established by FASB or GASB.
- The auditor is unable to apply the limited procedures to the required supplementary information.
- The auditor has substantial doubt about whether the required supplementary information conforms to established guidelines.

Required supplementary information is omitted

When the supplementary information required by FASB or GASB is omitted from the financial statements, the auditor should add an explanatory paragraph to the standard report after the opinion paragraph. The introductory, scope, and opinion paragraphs should not refer to the explanatory paragraph, and an unqualified opinion should be expressed on the basic financial statements. An explanatory paragraph that is appropriate when required supplementary information is omitted is illustrated below:

> The [*name of company or governmental entity*] has not presented [*describe supplementary information required by FASB or GASB*] that the [Financial Accounting Standards Board/ Governmental Accounting Standards Board] has determined is necessary to supplement, although not required to be part of, the basic financial statements.

Deviation in measurement or presentation of required supplementary information

When the required supplementary information is not prepared or presented as prescribed, an explanatory paragraph should be added to the standard report. An example of such an explanatory paragraph is presented below.

> The [*specifically identify the supplementary information*] on page XX is not a required part of the basic financial statements, and we did not audit and do not express an opinion on such in-

formation. However, we have applied certain limited procedures, which consist principally of inquiries of management regarding the methods of measurement and presentation of the supplementary information. As a result of such limited procedures, we believe that [*specifically identify the supplementary information*] is not in conformity with guidelines established by the [Financial Accounting Standards Board/Governmental Accounting Standards Board] because [*describe the material departures from FASB or GASB guidelines*].

Limited procedures not applied to required supplementary information

When the auditor is not able or is not allowed to apply limited procedures to the required supplementary information, an explanatory paragraph should be added to the standard report. An example for an explanatory paragraph of this nature is as follows:

> The [*specifically identify the supplementary information*] on page XX is not a required part of the basic financial statements, and we did not audit and do not express an opinion on such information. Further, we were unable to apply to the information certain procedures prescribed by professional standards, because [*describe reasons*].
>
> **RISK ASSESSMENT POINT:** Even though the auditor was unable to apply the limited procedures, the auditor may be aware of deviations from the measurement or presentation of the supplementary required information. These deviations also should be described in an explanatory paragraph.

Substantial doubt about conformance of required supplementary information

When the auditor has applied the limited procedures to the required supplementary information but is unable to resolve substantial doubts about the measurement or presentation of the information, an explanatory paragraph should be added to the standard report. The following is an example of an explanatory paragraph appropriate under this circumstance:

> The [*specifically identify the supplementary information*] on page XX is not a required part of the basic financial statements, and we did not audit and do not express an opinion on such information. However, we have applied certain limited procedures prescribed by professional standards that raised doubts

that we were unable to resolve regarding whether material modifications should be made to the information for it to conform with guidelines established by the [Financial Accounting Standards Board/Governmental Accounting Standards Board].

RISK ASSESSMENT POINT: The auditor should consider including in the explanatory paragraph the reasons the substantial doubts were not resolved.

SECTION 560

SUBSEQUENT EVENTS

Authoritative Pronouncements

SAS-1—Codification of Auditing Standards and Procedures (Section 560, Subsequent Events)

Overview

The auditor is responsible for collecting evidential matter pertaining to events that occur subsequent to the balance sheet date. Generally, the responsibility for identifying significant subsequent events continues through the date of the auditor's report, which is the last date of fieldwork. Subsequent events may affect the financial statements in two ways. First, the event may provide the basis for an adjusting entry at the date of the balance sheet. This occurs when the subsequent event affects the valuation of any account as of the balance sheet date. Second, the event may not affect the valuations at the balance sheet date, because the event is not associated with assets or liabilities that existed at the balance sheet date. For this reason, the subsequent event does not require an accrual adjustment, but it is likely to be disclosed in the financial statements.

> **ENGAGEMENT STRATEGY:** It is sometimes difficult to classify a subsequent event, because usually there is an informational lag period between the date the auditor becomes aware of the event and the actual identification of the economic event that affects the valuation of an account. For example, during the subsequent-event period, a competitor may announce a new product that places a client's product at a significant disadvantage and probably requires an inventory writedown. Although the product announcement occurred after the balance sheet date, it is likely that the technological breakthrough occurred on or before the balance sheet date. Of course, it becomes a little speculative to try to pinpoint the economic event, because the client and the auditor probably have limited information. For this reason, SAS-1 concludes that subsequent events that affect the realization of receivables and inventories and the settlement of estimated liabilities generally require an adjustment to the financial statements.

Promulgated Procedures Checklist

The auditor should use the following approach to identify and account for subsequent events that occur after the end of the client's fiscal year:

_____ Employ appropriate procedures to identify relevant subsequent events.

_____ Determine whether the subsequent event requires an audit adjustment.

_____ Determine whether the subsequent event requires disclosure in the financial statements.

Analysis and Application of Procedures

Employ appropriate procedures to identify relevant subsequent events

Audit procedures must be employed to obtain evidential matter associated with all subsequent events. These audit procedures may be classified as those associated with other phases of the audit engagement and those specifically designed to identify subsequent events. In many parts of the engagement, audit procedures call for the auditor to determine whether an account is presented in accordance with generally accepted accounting principles (GAAP) by reviewing subsequent events. For example, cash collected on account subsequent to the balance sheet date is associated with subsequent events, but it provides evidence to support the collectibility of accounts receivable as of the balance sheet date. However, SAS-1 identifies the following audit procedures that the auditor should perform in order to specifically identify possible subsequent events that may require an accrual adjustment or disclosure in the financial statements.

- Inquire of and discuss with members of management who have financial accounting responsibility whether:
  — Any material contingent liabilities or commitments existed at the date of the balance sheet or shortly thereafter.
  — Any significant change in owners' equity, long-term debt, or working capital has occurred since the balance sheet date.
  — Any material adjustments have been made during the subsequent period.

- Inquire of and discuss with members of management who have financial accounting responsibility the status of items that were accounted for in the financial statements on the basis of tentative or preliminary data.
- Read the available minutes of stockholders, directors, and other committee meetings during the subsequent period.
- Obtain from client's legal counsel a description and evaluation of any impending litigation, claims, and contingent liabilities.
- Obtain a letter of representation from management (usually the chief financial officer) regarding any events occurring during the subsequent period that require adjustment to or disclosure in the financial statements.
- Follow any other procedures that are deemed appropriate depending on the results of the procedures described above.

> **RISK ASSESSMENT POINT:** SAS-58 (Reports on Audited Financial Statements) states that a note on a subsequent event that contains unaudited information, pro forma calculations, or other similar disclosures should not be labeled as "unaudited."

Determine whether the subsequent event requires an audit adjustment

As noted earlier, SAS-1 describes two types of subsequent events. The first type relates to "events that provide additional evidence with respect to conditions that existed at the date of the balance sheet and affect the estimates inherent in the process of preparing financial statements." Evidence available to the auditor before the issuance of the financial statements should be used to evaluate estimates used by management. The auditor evaluates these estimates in light of subsequent events by making inquiries of management and having a current knowledge of the technological factors that affect the client's operations.

Determine whether the subsequent event requires disclosure in the financial statements

The second type of subsequent event relates to "events that provide evidence with respect to conditions that did not exist at the date of the balance sheet being reported on but arose subsequent to that date." An example of this type of subsequent event would be fire or flood damages to property, plant, and equipment that occurred after the date of the balance sheet. The auditor may discover this type of subsequent event by reviewing the minutes of the board of directors' meetings after the balance sheet date, making inquiries of management, and obtaining written representations from management.

PLANNING AID REMINDER: Examples of subsequent events that do not require an accrual adjustment are the issuance of additional capital stock or losses resulting from fire or flood after the balance sheet date. The second type of subsequent event is usually disclosed in a note to the financial statements. If the event is material, however, it may be more appropriate to show the effects of the subsequent event in the form of pro forma financial statements supplementary to the financial statements. The pro forma statement is presented as if the subsequent event had occurred on the last day of the period being audited.

Practitioner's Aids

Exhibit AU 560-1 illustrates an audit program for subsequent events.

EXHIBIT AU 560-1—SUBSEQUENT EVENTS
AUDIT PROGRAM

Use the following procedures as a guide to identify subsequent events that occur after the date of the financial statements but before the date of our audit report. The audit program is only a guide, and professional judgment should be exercised to determine how the procedures should be modified by revising procedures listed or adding procedures to the audit program.

Initial and date each procedure as it is completed. If the procedure is not relevant to this particular review engagement, place "N/A" (not applicable) in the space provided for an initial.

Client Name: _____

Date of Financial Statements: _____

Date of Fieldwork: _____

	Initials	Date	Workpaper Reference
1. Inquire of and discuss with appropriate management personnel whether any material contingent liabilities or commitments existed at the date of the balance sheet or shortly thereafter.	_____	_____	_____

	Initials	Date	Workpaper Reference

2. Inquire of and discuss with appropriate management personnel whether any significant change in owners' equity, long-term debt, or working capital has occurred since the date of the balance sheet.

3. Inquire of and discuss with appropriate management personnel whether any material adjustments have been made during the subsequent period

4. Inquire of and discuss with appropriate management personnel the status of items that were accounted for in the financial statements on the basis of tentative or preliminary data.

5. Read the latest minutes of stockholders', directors', and other committee meetings that occurred during the subsequent period.

6. Obtain from the client's legal counsel a description and evaluation of any impending litigation, claims, and contingent liabilities.

7. Obtain a letter of representation from management regarding any events occurring during the subsequent period that require adjustment or disclosure.

8. Read the latest interim financial statements and compare them to (a) the year-end financial statements and (b) the interim financial information for the previous year.

9. Review journal entries made after the end of the year for unusual amounts, unusual activity, or other unusual characteristics.

10. Determine whether the client is considering changing any of its accounting policies or procedures.

§560 • Subsequent Events

	Initials	Date	Workpaper Reference
11. Perform any other procedures deemed appropriate depending on the results of the procedures described above.	_____	_____	_____

Reviewed by: _____

Date: _____

SECTION 561

SUBSEQUENT DISCOVERY OF FACTS EXISTING AT THE DATE OF THE AUDITOR'S REPORT

Authoritative Pronouncements

SAS-1—Codification of Auditing Standards and Procedures (Section 561, Subsequent Discovery of Facts Existing at the Date of the Auditor's Report)

Auditing Interpretation (February 1989)—Auditor Association with Subsequently Discovered Information When the Auditor Has Resigned or Been Discharged

Overview

Although the auditor is not required to continue auditing after the date of the report, in some instances he or she discovers facts after the report date that could impact the audited financial statements. The discovery of such facts may occur when the auditor performs interim audit work or other nonaudit service for the client.

Promulgated Procedures Checklist

The auditor should perform the following procedures with respect to discovery of facts existing at the date of the auditor's report:

_____ Determine whether the discovered facts are relevant to the audited financial statements.

_____ If the discovered facts are considered relevant, take appropriate measures with respect to the audited financial statements.

_____ If the client does not cooperate with the auditor's conclusions and proposed remedies, notify the client's board of directors.

_____ If the client refuses to cooperate, communicate the problem with appropriate parties.

Analysis and Application of Procedures

Determine whether the discovered facts are relevant to the audited financial statements

If the auditor becomes aware (1) of material information that would have affected the report and (2) that persons are currently relying, or are likely to rely, on the financial statements covered by the report, the auditor should contact the client and discuss the matter with appropriate management personnel.

If the discovered facts are considered relevant, the auditor should take appropriate measures with respect to the audited financial statements

After appropriate discussion, if both the client and the auditor agree that the discovered facts are relevant to the audited financial statements, the auditor and client should take the following steps:

- The client should issue revised financial statements, and the auditor should issue a new report as soon as practical, describing the reasons for revision.
- If financial statements, accompanied by an auditor's report for a subsequent period, are to be issued imminently, the auditor may make the necessary disclosures and revisions therein.
- The client should be advised to discuss the new disclosures or revisions with the Securities and Exchange Commission (SEC), stock exchanges, and appropriate regulatory agencies where applicable.
- The auditor must satisfy himself or herself that the client has taken appropriate steps.

If the client does not cooperate with the auditor's conclusions and proposed remedies, the client's board of directors should be notified

If the client refuses to proceed as outlined above, the auditor should notify each member of the client's board of directors that (1) the client has refused and (2) in the absence of disclosure by the client, to prevent further reliance on the report and the financial statements the auditor will take the following additional steps:

- Notify any regulatory agencies involved, if applicable, that the report should no longer be relied on.

- Notify persons known to be relying, or likely to rely, on the financial statements that the auditor's report should no longer be relied on.

These notifications should contain the following:

- A description of the effects of the newly discovered information on the auditor's report and on the financial statements
- The most precise and factual information available about the financial statement misstatement

If the client refuses to cooperate, the auditor should communicate the problem with appropriate parties

In those circumstances where the client refuses to cooperate and, as a result, the auditor is unable to conduct an adequate investigation of the new information, the auditor's notifications need state only that new information has come to his or her attention and that if the new information is correct, the report should no longer be relied on or be associated with the financial statements.

> **RISK ASSESSMENT POINT:** The auditor must use professional judgment in the circumstances described above. Consultation with legal counsel usually is advisable.

> **ENGAGEMENT STRATEGY:** The Auditing Interpretation (February 1989) titled "Auditor Association with Subsequently Discovered Information When the Auditor Has Resigned or Been Discharged" concludes that the auditor's responsibility to investigate whether subsequently discovered information existed at the date of the auditor's report does not change even when the auditor has resigned or been discharged from the engagement.

Practitioner's Aids

EXHIBIT AU 561-1—DISCOVERY OF FACTS AFTER THE DATE OF THE REPORT

Use the following procedures, which are adapted from guidance found in SAS-1, AU Section 561 (Subsequent Discovery of Facts Existing at the Date of the Auditor's Report), as a guide for evaluating the discovery of facts after the date of the report. The program is only

§561 • Subsequent Discovery of Facts

a guide, and professional judgment should be exercised to determine how the guidance established in the auditing standard should be adapted to a particular engagement.

Initial and date each procedure as it is completed. If the procedure is not relevant to this engagement, place "N/A" (not applicable) in the space provided for an initial.

Client Name: _____

Date of Financial Statements: _____

	Initials	Date	Workpaper Reference

1. Determine whether the discovered facts are relevant to the financial statements by considering the following factors: _____ _____ _____

- The report would have been affected if the CPA had known the information at the date of the audit report, _____ _____ _____

- The matter would have been reflected in the financial statements, and _____ _____ _____

- The CPA believes that there are third-party users relying on or likely to rely on the financial statements who would attach importance to the subsequently discovered information. _____ _____ _____

2. If the conditions described in 1 above exist, advise the client to inform third-party users currently relying or likely to rely on the financial statements, following the general guidance: _____ _____ _____

- When the effects of the subsequently discovered information can be determined quickly, and the issuance of more current financial statements is not imminent, revised financial statements and a revised report should be issued. (Both the financial statements and the report should describe the reason for the revision.) _____ _____ _____

	Initials	Date	Workpaper Reference

- When the issuance of more recent financial statements is imminent, the disclosure of the revision can be made in the more recent financial statements; the earlier financial statements need not be reissued. _____ _____ _____

- When the effects of the subsequently discovered information cannot be determined without a prolonged investigation, third-party users who are currently relying or likely to rely on the financial statements and the associated report should be notified not to rely on them and should be informed that a revised financial statement and report will be issued when an investigation is completed. _____ _____ _____

3. If the client refuses to make appropriate disclosures to third-party users, inform each member of the board of directors of the refusal. _____ _____ _____

4. If the board of directors is notified but appropriate disclosures to third-party users still are not made, discuss the matter with legal counsel. _____ _____ _____

5. If it appears there are or will be third-party users who will rely on the financial statements, consider the following: _____ _____ _____

- Notify the client that the CPA's report should no longer be associated with the client's financial statements. _____ _____ _____

- Notify regulatory agencies having jurisdiction over the client that the CPA's report should no longer be associated with the client's financial statements. _____ _____ _____

- To the extent practical, the CPA should notify each third-party user known to be relying on the financial statements that the report should no longer be associated with them. _____ _____ _____

	Initials	Date	Workpaper Reference

6. If the matters have been satisfactorily investigated and the subsequent information considered reliable, disclosures to regulatory authorities and third-party users should include the following: _____ _____ _____

- The nature of the subsequently acquired information and the effects on the financial statements. _____ _____ _____
- The effects of the subsequently acquired information on the CPA's report, if the information had been known to him or her at the date of the report and had not been reflected in the financial statements. _____ _____ _____

7. If a satisfactory investigation is not conducted, make the following disclosure to regulatory authorities and third-party users: _____ _____ _____

- Describe the general nature of the problem (specific details are not required). _____ _____ _____
- State that the effects of the problem cannot be substantiated because the client did not cooperate in the investigation of the matter. _____ _____ _____
- State that if the information is correct, the CPA believes the report should no longer be associated with the client's financial statements. No disclosure should be made unless the CPA believes that the financial statements are likely to be misleading and that his or her audit engagement should not be associated with them. _____ _____ _____

8. Other engagement procedures: _____
_____
_____

Reviewed by: _____

Date: _____

AU 600

Other Types of Reports

Section 622 (Withdrawn): Engagements to Apply Agreed-Upon Procedures to Specified Elements, Accounts, or Items of a Financial Statement 441

Section 623: Special Reports 442

Section 625: Reports on the Application of Accounting Principles 465

Section 634: Letters for Underwriters and Certain Other Requesting Parties 471

SECTION 622 (WITHDRAWN)

ENGAGEMENTS TO APPLY AGREED-UPON PROCEDURES TO SPECIFIED ELEMENTS, ACCOUNTS, OR ITEMS OF A FINANCIAL STATEMENT

SAS-93 (Omnibus Statement on Auditing Standards—2000) withdraws Section 622, which was based on SAS-75 (Engagements to Apply Agreed-Upon Procedures to Specified Elements, Accounts, or Items of a Financial Statement) and Auditing Interpretation (November 1997—Applying Agreed-Upon Procedures to All, or Substantially All, of the Elements, Accounts, or Items of a Financial Statement). Now all agreed-upon procedures engagements must be performed to satisfy the standards established by the Statements on Standards for Attestation Engagements (SSAE). Guidance for the performance of an agreed-upon procedures engagement is found in the chapter titled "Agreed-Upon Procedures Engagements" (AT Section 201).

SECTION 623

SPECIAL REPORTS

Authoritative Pronouncements

SAS-62—Special Reports

Auditing Interpretation (February 1999)—Auditor's Reports on Property and Liability Insurance Companies' Loss Reserves

Auditing Interpretation (February 1999)—Reports on the Financial Statements Included in Internal Revenue Form 990

Auditing Interpretation (February 1999)—Reporting on Current-Value Financial Statements That Supplement Historical-Cost Financial Statements in a General-Use Presentation of Real Estate Entities

Auditing Interpretation (February 1999)—Reporting on a Special-Purpose Financial Statement That Results in an Incomplete Presentation but Is Otherwise in Conformity with GAAP

Auditing Interpretation (January 1998)—Evaluating the Adequacy of Disclosure in Financial Statements Prepared on the Cash, Modified Cash, or Income Tax Basis of Accounting

Auditing Interpretation (February 1997)—Evaluation of the Appropriateness of Informative Disclosures in Insurance Enterprises' Financial Statements Prepared on a Statutory Basis

Overview

An auditor may be engaged to report on financial statements that are prepared on a comprehensive basis that is not GAAP or information presentations that do not constitute a set of financial statements. These reporting situations are discussed in this Section.

Promulgated Procedures Checklist

The auditor may issue a special report in any one of the following five broad categories:

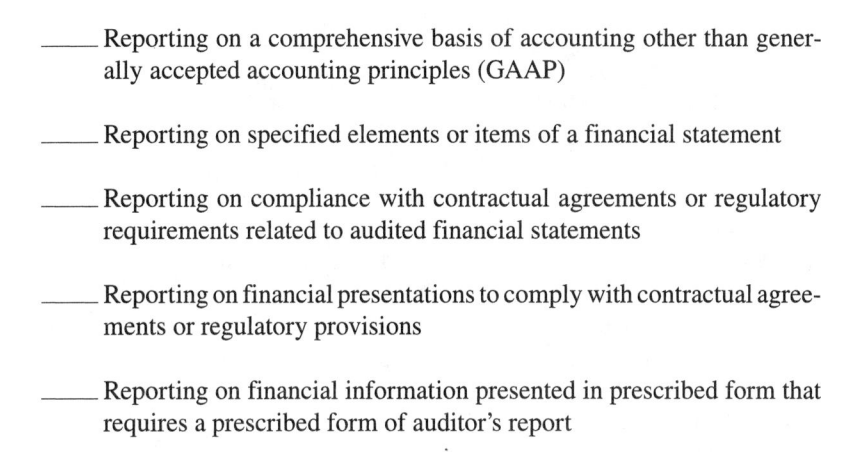

_____ Reporting on a comprehensive basis of accounting other than generally accepted accounting principles (GAAP)

_____ Reporting on specified elements or items of a financial statement

_____ Reporting on compliance with contractual agreements or regulatory requirements related to audited financial statements

_____ Reporting on financial presentations to comply with contractual agreements or regulatory provisions

_____ Reporting on financial information presented in prescribed form that requires a prescribed form of auditor's report

Analysis and Application of Procedures

Reporting on a comprehensive basis of accounting other than GAAP

Financial statements may be issued by all types of entities or segments of entities, including commercial enterprises, not-for-profit organizations, individuals, estates, and governmental units. SAS-62 defines a "financial statement" as a "presentation of financial data, including accompanying notes, derived from accounting records that are intended to communicate an entity's economic resources or obligations at a point in time or the changes therein for a period of time in conformity with a comprehensive basis of accounting." For reporting purposes, SAS-62 considers a "financial statement" to consist of a statement of (1) financial position (balance sheet), (2) income or operations, (3) retained earnings, (4) cash flows, (5) changes in owners' equity, (6) assets and liabilities (excludes owners' equity accounts), (7) revenues and expenses, (8) summary of operations, (9) operations by product lines, and (10) cash receipts and disbursements. This broad definition does not restrict financial statements to those that are prepared in accordance with GAAP. Thus, an entity may prepare and issue a financial statement based on a comprehensive basis of accounting other than GAAP.

When financial statements based on an other comprehensive basis of accounting (OCBOA) are prepared, the accountant should determine whether the financial statements are properly labeled. Care must be taken in titling financial statements so that a reader of the statements will not infer that the financial statements are prepared in accordance with GAAP.

The earlier definition of "financial statement" referred to a presentation of financial data that intends to communicate an entity's economic resources or obligations in accordance with generally accepted accounting principles or a comprehensive basis of accounting other than generally accepted accounting principles. When GAAP-based financial statements are presented, such a statement is referred to as a balance sheet or a statement of financial position. When OCBOA-based financial statements are presented, it would be inappropriate to refer to the statement as a balance sheet or a statement of financial position. Instead, for example, if the financial statements are prepared on a modified cash basis, the title might be "Statement of Assets and Liabilities—Modified Cash Basis." If the financial statements are prepared on a regulatory accounting basis an appropriate name would be "Balance Sheet—Regulatory Accounting Basis."

The definitions of "financial statement" in Statement on Standards for Accounting and Review Services (SSARS) No. 1 (Compilation and Review of Financial Statements) and SAS-62 refer to presenting financial data related to changes in an entity's economic resources and obligations. When GAAP-based financial statements are presented, they are referred to as an income statement or a statement of operations. When OCBOA-based financial statements are presented, more appropriate names may be "Statement of Cash Receipts and Disbursements" (for a cash-based financial statement) and "Statement of Revenues and Expenses—Income Tax Basis" (for a tax-based financial statement).

A financial statement or presentation should be clearly and accurately titled. If the auditor concludes that a financial statement or presentation is not properly titled, an explanatory paragraph should be added to the auditor's special report, and the opinion on the statement or presentation should be qualified.

> **PLANNING AID REMINDER:** Under SAS-58 (Reports on Audited Financial Statements), if an auditor is requested to report on only one financial statement from a set of financial statements, there is no scope limitation of the audit. Under SAS-58, this type of engagement is classified as a limited reporting engagement.

Under the provisions of SAS-62, a comprehensive basis of accounting other than generally accepted accounting principles is restricted to the following.

- A basis of accounting that the reporting entity uses to comply with the requirements or financial reporting provisions of a governmental regulatory agency to whose jurisdiction the entity is subject

- A basis of accounting that the reporting entity uses or expects to use to file its income tax return for the period covered by the financial statements

- The cash receipts and disbursements basis of accounting, and modifications of the cash basis having substantial support, such as recording depreciation on fixed assets or accruing income taxes

- A definite set of criteria having substantial support that is applied to all material items appearing in financial statements, such as the price-level basis of accounting

> **PLANNING AID REMINDER:** The Auditing Interpretation (February 1999) of SAS-62 titled "Reporting on Current-Value Financial Statements That Supplement Historical-Cost Financial Statements in a General-Use Presentation of Real Estate Entities" concludes that an engagement to report on current-value financial statements that supplement historical-cost financial statements of a real estate entity may be accepted only if (1) the current-value financial statements are based on measurement and disclosure criteria that are reasonable and (2) the current-value financial statements are reliable (competent persons using the same criteria would arrive at similar financial statements that are not materially different from one another).

If an entity reports on a comprehensive basis of accounting not listed above, the concepts established in SAS-69 (AU 411) (The Meaning of "Present Fairly in Conformity with Generally Accepted Accounting Principles" should be used to determine whether the special-basis financial statements are presented in a manner that results in a material deviation from GAAP. If the deviation(s) from GAAP is considered to be material, the auditor should observe the reporting standards established by SAS-58 (AU 508) when preparing the auditor's special report. That is, the auditor should express a qualified or an adverse opinion on the financial statements.

Adequate disclosure

Generally accepted auditing standards are applicable to the audit of financial statements prepared in conformity with an other comprehensive basis of accounting. Thus, the auditor must consider the third reporting standard (adequate informative disclosures).

In determining whether financial statements prepared in conformity with an other comprehensive basis of accounting satisfy the adequate disclosure criterion, the auditor should consider the following concepts established in SAS-69 (AU 411):

- The accounting principles selected and applied should have general acceptance.

- The accounting principles should be appropriate in the circumstances.
- The financial statements, including the related notes, should be informative of matters that may affect their use, understanding, and interpretation.
- The information presented in the financial statements should be classified and summarized in a reasonable manner; that is, it should be neither too detailed nor too condensed.
- The financial statements should reflect the underlying events and transactions (in a manner that satisfies the purpose of the financial statements) within a range of acceptable limits; that is, limits that are reasonable and practicable to attain in financial statements.

The notes to the financial statements should include a summary of significant accounting policies to describe the basis of presentation and how the presentation differs from a presentation that conforms with GAAP.

> **ENGAGEMENT STRATEGY:** The Auditing Interpretation (January 1998) titled "Evaluating the Adequacy of Disclosure in Financial Statements Prepared on the Cash, Modified Cash, or Income Tax Basis of Accounting" discusses the requirement established by AU Section 623 that OCBOA-based financial statements contain a summary of significant accounting policies that explains the basis of presentation and how that basis differs from generally accepted accounting principles. The Interpretation concludes that the disclosure may be brief, using language such as "The accompanying financial statements present financial statements results on the accrual basis of accounting used for federal income tax reporting." In addition, only the primary differences between GAAP and the tax basis need be included in the disclosure. Quantifying the differences is not necessary.

Finally, items that are presented as part of a financial statement prepared in conformity with an other comprehensive basis of accounting and are similar to items that would be presented as part of GAAP-based financial statements should include related disclosures that would be similar to disclosures that would appear in the GAAP-based financial statements. For example, if long-term debt is presented in financial statements prepared on a modified cash basis, information related to the terms, maturity, description, and restrictions of long-term debt must be disclosed.

> **ENGAGEMENT STRATEGY:** There is no comprehensive list of minimum disclosures for OCBOA-based financial statements. Professional judgment must be used to determine whether the

basic concept of adequate disclosure has been achieved in the OCBOA-based financial statements.

ENGAGEMENT STRATEGY: Another Interpretation (February 1997) of SAS-62, titled "Evaluation of the Appropriateness of Informative Disclosures in Insurance Enterprises' Financial Statements Prepared on a Statutory Basis," states that the auditor should use the same analysis that is used in the evaluation of GAAP-based financial statements to determine whether financial statements based on accounting standards established by insurance regulators (statutory basis) satisfy the criterion of informative disclosure required by the third standard of reporting. Insurance companies should follow GAAP when preparing general-purpose financial statements and should follow appropriate accounting procedures established by each state's insurance department when preparing statutory financial statements.

Reporting standards

The title of the special auditor's report should include the word "independent." In addition, the report should have a manual or printed signature and be dated based on the completion date of fieldwork.

SAS-62 requires that a four-paragraph format be used in the standard special report. The content of each paragraph is described below.

- Introductory paragraph

  — State that the financial statements identified in the report were audited.

  — State that the financial statements are the responsibility of company's management and that the auditor is responsible for expressing an opinion on the financial statements based on the audit.

- Scope paragraph

  — State that the audit was conducted in accordance with generally accepted auditing standards (GAAS).

  — State that GAAS require that the auditor plan and perform the audit to obtain reasonable assurance about whether the financial statements are free of material misstatement.

  — State that an audit includes examining, on a test basis, evidence supporting the amounts and disclosures in the financial statements.

  — State that an audit includes assessing the accounting principles used and significant estimates made by management.

- — State that an audit includes evaluating the overall financial statement presentation.
- — State that the auditor believes that his or her audit provides a reasonable basis for the opinion.
- Presentation basis paragraph
  - — State the basis of presentation and refer to the note to the financial statements that describes the basis.
  - — State that the basis of presentation is a comprehensive basis of accounting other than generally accepted accounting principles.
- Opinion paragraph
  - — Express an opinion on whether the financial statements are presented fairly, in all material respects, in conformity with the basis of accounting described.

When the auditor is reporting on financial statements that are prepared in conformity with accounting procedures established by a governmental regulatory agency, an additional paragraph should be included in the standard special auditor's report. The additional paragraph should state that the use of the report is for those within the entity or for filing with the regulatory agency. This additional paragraph should be included even though by law or regulation the report is part of the public record.

> **PLANNING AID REMINDER:** When financial statements that are prepared on a regulatory basis of accounting are to be generally distributed, the standard report form, as established by SAS-58, should be modified for departures from generally accepted accounting principles. The standard report may include an additional paragraph that expresses an opinion on whether the financial statements are presented in conformity with the regulatory basis of accounting.

Exhibit AU 623-1 presents an example of a special auditor's report on financial statements prepared on the cash basis.

Reporting on specified elements or items of a financial statement

An auditor may be engaged to report on a specified element(s), account(s), or item(s) of a financial statement. Even though an engagement of this nature is limited in its scope, generally accepted auditing standards must be satisfied.

ENGAGEMENT STRATEGY: The first reporting standard would not be applicable if the element, account, or item is presented on a basis other than GAAP. The other basis of accounting should not be confused with a comprehensive basis of accounting discussed earlier. For example, the other basis of accounting could be derived from a clause contained in a contract.

An engagement to express an opinion on an element, account, or item of a financial statement may be conducted as part of the audit of the financial statements or may be undertaken as a separate engagement. The basis for materiality in the limited-scope audit is the specific element, account, or item being reported on, and for this reason, generally a more detailed audit of the element, account, or item would be conducted.

PLANNING AID REMINDER: Although the engagement may be limited to reporting on a specified element, account, or item of a financial statement, the scope of the audit includes all related matters and, if appropriate, other related accounts. For example, an engagement to report on accounts receivable requires that the credit sales system and the cash receipts system as part of the entity's internal control be considered.

ENGAGEMENT STRATEGY: SAS-62 concludes that "if a specified element, account, or item is, or is based on, an entity's net income or stockholders' equity or the equivalent thereof, the auditor should have audited the complete financial statements to express an opinion on the specified element, account, or item."

Reporting standards

The following format should be used in the preparation of the standard special auditor's report on a specified element, account, or item of a financial statement.

- Introductory paragraph

  — State that the specified element, account, or item identified in the report was audited.

  — State, if applicable, that the audit was made in conjunction with the audit of the entity's financial statements. (Also disclose the date of the auditor's report and describe any departure from the standard auditor's report on the financial statement if the basis for the departure is considered relevant to the evaluation of the specified element, account, or item.)

- State that the specified element, account, or item is the responsibility of the company's management and that the auditor is responsible for expressing an opinion on the specified element, account, or item based on the audit.

- Scope paragraph
  - State that the audit was conducted in accordance with GAAS.
  - State that GAAS require that the auditor plan and perform the audit to obtain reasonable assurance about whether the specified element, account, or item is free of material misstatement.
  - State that an audit includes examining, on a test basis, evidence supporting the amounts and disclosures in the presentation of the specified element, account, or item.
  - State that an audit includes assessing the accounting principles used and significant estimates made by management.
  - State that an audit includes evaluating the overall presentation of the specified element, account, or item.
  - State that the auditor believes that the audit provides a reasonable basis for his or her opinion.

- Presentation basis paragraph
  - State the basis on which the specified element, account, or item is presented and, when applicable, any agreement specifying such basis if the presentation is not prepared in conformity with GAAP. (If the basis of presentation is an other comprehensive basis of accounting, state so. Alternatively, the description contained in this paragraph may be incorporated into the introductory paragraph.)

- Opinion paragraph
  - Express an opinion on whether the specified element, account, or item is fairly presented, in all material respects, in conformity with the basis of accounting described.
  - If not presented fairly on the basis of accounting described or if the scope of the engagement has been limited, an explanatory paragraph preceding the opinion paragraph should state all substantive reasons for the above conclusions. The opinion paragraph should include modifying language and a reference to the explanatory paragraph(s).

When the auditor is reporting on a specified element, account, or item to satisfy a contract or agreement, and the information is not presented on a GAAP basis or an other comprehensive basis of accounting, an additional paragraph should be included in the standard special auditor's report. The additional paragraph should state that the distribution of the report is restricted solely to those that are parties to the contract or agreement. When the auditor is reporting on an element, account, or item that is presented on an other comprehensive basis of accounting prescribed by a governmental regulatory agency, an additional paragraph should disclose that the distribution of the report is restricted solely to those within the entity and for filing with the regulatory agency. This additional paragraph should be included even though by law or regulation the report is part of the public record.

An additional paragraph may be added to the standard special auditor's report that describes the scope of the engagement in greater detail. SAS-62 permits an additional paragraph of this nature; however, the additional paragraph must be a separate paragraph and should not be merged into the standard scope paragraph described above.

Exhibit AU 623-2 presents an example of a special auditor's report on accounts receivable.

SAS-62 concludes that a potential conflict exists when the auditor has expressed an adverse opinion or has disclaimed an opinion on the entity's basic financial statements, but has been requested to express an opinion on an element(s), account(s), or item(s) that is part of the basic financial statements. Under this circumstance, an opinion on the element, account, or item can be expressed only when the information being reported on does not constitute a major portion of the financial statement(s). To do otherwise would constitute a piecemeal opinion, which is prohibited by SAS-58 (AU 508). If the auditor decides to express an opinion on an element, account, or item, that report should be presented separately from the report on the entity's basic financial statements.

> **PLANNING AID REMINDER:** In some engagements, an auditor may be requested to perform agreed-upon procedures encompassing only a portion of an entity's financial statements. Guidance for this type of service is provided in SAS-75 (Engagements to Apply Agreed-Upon Procedures to Specified Elements, Accounts, or Items of a Financial Statement).

> **PLANNING AID REMINDER:** The Auditing Interpretation (February 1999) titled "Auditor's Reports on Property and Liability Insurance Companies' Loss Reserves" notes that the auditor should follow the guidance established by AU Section 623 (paragraphs 11–18) when he or she is requested to express an opinion on a company's loss and loss adjustment expense reserves and on the schedule of liabilities for losses and loss adjustment expenses that accompany the auditor's report on the financial statements filed by property and liability insurance companies with state regulatory agencies.

Reporting on compliance with contractual agreements or regulatory requirements related to audited financial statements

Financial statement users, such as banks and regulatory agencies, may request that an entity's auditor specifically state whether the entity has observed a particular contract clause or administrative regulation. For example, a loan agreement may require that the entity's working capital be not less than a certain dollar amount. If the entity's financial statements are audited and the clause or regulation is subject to verification, the auditor may issue a negative assurance in an auditor's special report with respect to the contractual clause or regulation.

> **PLANNING AID REMINDER:** If the regulatory requirement is to be tested to determine compliance with laws and regulations consistent with *Government Auditing Standards* (the Yellow Book), the guidance established by SAS-74 (Compliance Auditing Considerations in Audits of Governmental Entities and Recipients of Governmental Financial Assistance) must be observed.

The negative assurance on matters contained in contractual agreements or regulatory requirements must have been related to the audit of the entity's basic financial statements. If an adverse opinion or disclaimer of opinion was expressed on the basic financial statements, a negative assurance on matters contained in contractual agreements or regulatory requirements should not be given.

> **PLANNING AID REMINDER:** If the matter for which the auditor is providing the assurance has not been subject to audit as part of the audit of the entity's basic financial statements, guidance established in Statement on Standards for Attestation Engagements (SSAE) No. 3 (Compliance Attestation) should be followed.

Reporting standards

The negative assurance on the matter specified in the contractual agreement or regulatory requirement may be expressed in a separate report or added to the auditor's report on the basic financial statements.

Separate report

The title of the special auditor's report on matters contained in contractual agreements or regulatory requirements should include the word "indepen-

§623 • Special Reports   453

dent." Also, the report should have a manual or printed signature and should be dated based on the completion date of fieldwork for the basic financial statements.

The separate report should be formatted in the manner described below.

- Introductory paragraph
  - State that the financial statements were audited in accordance with GAAS, include the date of the auditor's report on the audited financial statements, and, if applicable, disclose any departure from the standard auditor's report on the audited financial statements.

- Limited assurance paragraph
  - Identify the specific covenant or paragraphs of the agreement.
  - Provide a negative assurance on the aspects of the contractual agreement or regulatory requirements insofar as they relate to accounting matters.
  - State that the negative assurance is being given in connection with the audit of the financial statements.
  - State that the audit was not directed primarily toward obtaining knowledge regarding compliance with the contractual agreement or regulatory provision.

- Explanatory paragraph
  - Describe significant interpretations, if any, and their sources, that have been made by the entity's management relating to the contractual agreement or regulatory provision.

- Distribution paragraph
  - State that the distribution of the report is restricted to those within the entity and the parties to the contract or agreement or for filing with the regulatory agency.

Exhibit AU 623-3 presents an example of a (separate) auditor's special report expressing a negative assurance on whether certain terms of a debt agreement have been observed.

Report added to standard report

The negative assurance on compliance with aspects of contractual agreements or regulatory requirements may be expressed in the auditor's report on the entity's basic financial statements. Under this reporting circumstance, three additional paragraphs, as described below, may need to be added to the standard (three-paragraph) auditor's report after the opinion paragraph.

- Fourth paragraph
  - Identify the specific covenant or paragraphs of the agreement.
  - Provide a negative assurance on the aspects of the contractual agreement or regulatory requirements insofar as they relate to accounting matters. Note that the negative assurance is being given in connection with the audit of the financial statements.
  - State that the audit was not directed primarily toward obtaining knowledge regarding compliance with the contractual agreement or regulatory provisions.
- Fifth paragraph
  - Describe significant interpretations, if any, and their sources, that the entity's management has made relating to the contractual agreement or regulatory provision.
- Sixth paragraph
  - State that the distribution of the report is restricted to those within the entity and the parties to the contract or agreement or for filing with the regulatory agency.

Reporting on financial presentations to comply with contractual agreements or regulatory provisions

An auditor may be requested to report on special-purpose financial statements that have been prepared to satisfy a contractual agreement or governmental regulatory requirements. SAS-62 identifies the following as types of special-purpose financial statement presentations:

> a. A special-purpose financial presentation prepared in compliance with a contractual agreement or regulatory provision that does not constitute a complete presentation of the entity's assets, liabilities, revenues and expenses, but is otherwise prepared in conformity with GAAP or another comprehensive basis of accounting.
>
> b. A special-purpose financial presentation (may be a complete set of financial statements or a single financial statement) prepared on a basis of accounting prescribed in an agreement that does not result in a presentation in conformity with GAAP or another comprehensive basis of accounting.

These special-purpose financial presentations are discussed below.

Incomplete presentations

Because of a contractual agreement or regulatory provision, an entity may be required to prepare a financial statement that is incomplete but nonetheless presents financial information that is prepared in accordance with GAAP or an other comprehensive basis of accounting. For example, an entity may be required by contract to present a statement of net assets sold as of a specific date. SAS-62 concludes that these presentations constitute a financial statement even though the presentations are incomplete, and accordingly, an auditor can express an opinion on incomplete financial presentations.

> **RISK ASSESSMENT POINT:** The Auditing Interpretation (February 1999) of SAS-62 titled "Reporting on a Special-Purpose Financial Statement That Results in an Incomplete Presentation But Is Otherwise in Conformity with Generally Accepted Accounting Principles" concludes that an offering memorandum is not considered a "contractual agreement" as defined by SAS-62. However, an agreement between a client and a third party to prepare financial statements using a special-purpose presentation format is a "contractual agreement" as defined by SAS-62.

In the conduct of an engagement related to incomplete financial presentations, the basis for determining materiality should be the incomplete financial presentation taken as a whole. The presentation should omit only information that is not pertinent to satisfying the contractual agreement or regulatory provision. Information that is presented as part of the incomplete financial presentation and that is similar to information that would be presented as part of GAAP-based financial statements should include related disclosures that would be similar to disclosures that would appear in the GAAP-based financial statements. Finally, the incomplete financial presentation should be titled in a manner that would not suggest that the presentation is a complete financial statement.

Reporting standards

The title of the special auditor's report should include the word "independent," and the report should have a manual or printed signature. The report should be dated based on the completion date of fieldwork.

The format shown below should be used to prepare a special auditor's report on incomplete financial presentations.

- Introductory paragraph
  - State that the financial statements identified in the report were audited.
  - State that the financial statements are the responsibility of the company's management and that the auditor is responsible for expressing an opinion on the financial statements based on the audit.
- Scope paragraph
  - State that the audit was conducted in accordance with GAAS.
  - State that GAAS require that the auditor plan and perform the audit to obtain reasonable assurance about whether the financial statements are free of material misstatement.
  - State that an audit includes examining, on a test basis, evidence supporting the amounts and disclosures in the financial statements.
  - State that an audit includes assessing the accounting principles used and significant estimates made by management.
  - State that an audit includes evaluating the overall financial statement presentation.
  - State that the auditor believes that the audit provides a reasonable basis for his or her opinion.
- Presentation basis paragraph
  - Explain what the presentation is intended to present and refer to the note to the special-purpose financial statements that describes the basis of presentation.
  - If the basis of presentation is in conformity with GAAP, state that the presentation is not intended to be a complete presentation of the entity's assets, liabilities, revenue, and expenses.
  - If the basis of presentation is an other comprehensive basis of accounting, state that the basis of presentation is a comprehensive basis of accounting other than GAAP and that it is not intended to be a complete presentation of the entity's assets, liabilities, revenues, and expenses on the basis described.
- Opinion paragraph
  - Express an opinion on whether the information is fairly presented, in all material respects.
  - State that the presentation is intended to present the information in conformity with GAAP or an other comprehensive basis of accounting.

- Distribution paragraph

  — State that the report is restricted to those within the entity, to the parties to the contract or agreement, for filing with a regulatory agency, or to those with whom the entity is negotiating directly. (A distribution paragraph is not necessary when the financial information must be filed with a regulatory agency and is to be included in a document that is distributed to the general public.)

Exhibit AU 623-4 presents an example of a report on a statement of assets sold and liabilities transferred to comply with a contractual agreement.

Presentation not in accordance with GAAP or OCBOA

The terms of a contract may require an entity to prepare financial statements that are in accordance with neither GAAP nor an other comprehensive basis of accounting. For example, an entity may be required to prepare financial statements that use unacceptable methods to value various accounts and transactions. The auditor may be requested to express an opinion on financial statements of this type, but it should be emphasized that this type of engagement is not the same as the engagement described earlier.

Reporting standards The title of the special auditor's report should include the word "independent," and the report should have a manual or printed signature. The report should be dated based on the completion date of fieldwork.

The following format should be used to prepare a special auditor's report on financial statements prepared on a basis of accounting prescribed in an agreement that results in a presentation that is not in conformity with GAAP or OCBOA.

- Introductory paragraph

  — State that the special-purpose financial statements identified in the report were audited.

  — State that the financial statements are the responsibility of the company's management and that the auditor is responsible for expressing an opinion on the financial statements based on the audit.

- Scope paragraph

  — State that the audit was conducted in accordance with GAAS.

  — State that GAAS require that the auditor plan and perform the audit to obtain reasonable assurance about whether the financial statements are free of material misstatement.

- State that an audit includes examining, on a test basis, evidence supporting the amounts and disclosures in the financial statements.

- State that an audit includes assessing the accounting principles used and significant estimates made by management.

- State that an audit includes evaluating the overall financial statement presentation.

- State that the auditor believes that the audit provides a reasonable basis for his or her opinion.

• Presentation basis paragraph

- Explain what the presentation is intended to present, and refer to the note to the special-purpose financial statements that describes the basis of presentation.

- State that the presentation is not intended to be a presentation in conformity with GAAP.

• Explanatory paragraph

- Describe significant interpretations, if any—and their sources—that the entity's management have made relating to the contractual agreement.

• Opinion paragraph

- Express an opinion on whether the information is fairly presented, in all material respects, on the basis of accounting specified. If the information is not presented fairly on the basis of accounting described or if the scope of the engagement has been limited, an explanatory paragraph preceding the opinion paragraph should disclose all substantive reasons for the above conclusions. The opinion paragraph should include modifying language and a reference to the explanatory paragraph(s).

• Distribution paragraph

- State that the report is restricted to those within the entity, to the parties to the contract or agreement, for filing with a regulatory agency, or to those with whom the entity is negotiating directly.

Exhibit AU 623-5 presents an example of a special auditor's report on financial statements prepared pursuant to a loan agreement that results in a presentation not in conformity with GAAP or an OCBOA.

§623 • Special Reports

Reporting on financial information presented in prescribed form that requires a prescribed form of auditor's report

An entity may be required to file financial information on a form supplied or approved by a governmental agency, institution, or other authority. In addition, an auditor may be engaged to express an opinion on the information in the form, and the wording of the auditor's report may also be part of the prescribed form. For example, a state agency may require certain not-for-profit entities to submit periodic financial reports on prescribed forms. Before signing the prescribed report, the auditor must be careful to protect him- or herself from making inappropriate statements in the report.

Under some circumstances, the auditor may be able to sign the prescribed report by modifying the report language in the form. If a significant amount of rewording is necessary, it may be more appropriate for the auditor to attach a separate auditor's report. The auditor can find guidance for writing a separate report by following the reporting formats on financial statements prepared in accordance with a comprehensive basis of accounting other than GAAP.

> **PLANNING AID REMINDER:** The Interpretation (February 1999) of SAS-62 titled "Reports on the Financial Statements Included in Internal Revenue Form 990" states that a special report situation may arise when a charitable organization presents its financial statements in a manner consistent with Internal Revenue Form 990 (Return of Organizations Exempt from Income Tax). These financial statements may be submitted to state and federal regulatory authorities. When the presentation materially departs from GAAP and the financial statements are intended solely for filing with a regulatory agency, a special report following the reporting format established for statements prepared on a comprehensive basis of accounting other than GAAP may be followed. When the presentation materially departs from GAAP and there is public distribution of the report, reporting requirements established by SAS-62 are not applicable. In this situation, the auditor must observe SAS-58 by issuing a qualified or adverse opinion on the financial statements.

Modifications to the standard auditor's special report

When an auditor concludes that an unqualified opinion is not applicable, the special auditor's report should be appropriately modified. If the deficiency is related to accounting principles used to prepare the financial presentation, the modification to the report should include an explanatory paragraph(s) that describes the deficiency, and the opinion paragraph should refer to the explanatory paragraph as the basis for the qualified or adverse opinion. On the other hand, if the deficiency is related to the scope of the audit engagement, an explanatory paragraph(s) should be added to the special auditor's report, and the opinion paragraph should refer to the explanatory paragraph as the basis for the qualified opinion or disclaimer of opinion. Under both circumstances (accounting deficiency and scope deficiency), the explanatory paragraph should precede the opinion paragraph.

In addition to modifications to the special auditor's report arising from accounting and scope deficiencies, the report should be modified under the following circumstances:

- There is a lack of consistent application of accounting principles.
- Substantial doubt exists about the entity's ability to continue as a going concern.
- Part of the audit was conducted by another auditor.
- The auditor expresses an opinion on the financial presentation that is different from the one expressed in a previous engagement on the same presentation.
- A matter is to be emphasized.

When an entity changes its basis of accounting from GAAP to a comprehensive basis of accounting other than GAAP, in the year of change the matter should not be treated as a consistency violation. Nonetheless, it may be appropriate to include an additional paragraph that discloses that a different basis of accounting was used to prepare financial statements in previous periods or that the entity has also prepared another report that uses generally accepted accounting principles as the basis of accounting.

In addition, when financial statements are prepared on a tax basis, a change in the tax laws would not constitute a violation of the consistency standard; however, it may be appropriate to disclose the matter in the financial statements.

Practitioner's Aids

The following exhibits are presented in this Section:

- Exhibit AU 623-1—Special Report on Cash-Based Financial Statements
- Exhibit AU 623-2—Special Report on an Account in a Financial Statement

§623 • Special Reports   461

- Exhibit AU 623-3—Special Report on Whether Certain Terms of a Debt Agreement Have Been Observed
- Exhibit AU 623-4—Special Report on a Statement of Assets Sold and Liabilities Transferred
- Exhibit AU 623-5—Special Report on Financial Statements Prepared Pursuant to a Loan Agreement

EXHIBIT AU 623-1—SPECIAL REPORT ON CASH-BASED FINANCIAL STATEMENTS

We have audited the accompanying statements of assets and liabilities arising from cash transactions of X Company as of December 31, 20X5 and 20X4, and the related statements of revenues collected and expenses paid for the years then ended. These financial statements are the responsibility of the Company's management. Our responsibility is to express an opinion on these financial statements based on our audits.

We conducted our audits in accordance with auditing standards generally accepted in the United States of America. Those standards require that we plan and perform the audit to obtain reasonable assurance about whether the financial statements are free of material misstatement. An audit includes examining, on a test basis, evidence supporting the amounts and disclosures in the financial statements. An audit also includes assessing the accounting principles used and significant estimates made by management, as well as evaluating the overall financial statement presentation. We believe that our audits provide a reasonable basis for our opinion.

As described in Note X, these financial statements were prepared on the basis of cash receipts and disbursements, which is a comprehensive basis of accounting other than generally accepted accounting principles.

In our opinion, the financial statements referred to above present fairly, in all material respects, the assets and liabilities arising from cash transactions of X Company as of December 31, 20X5 and 20X4, and its revenues collected and expenses paid during the years then ended, on the basis of accounting described in Note X.

EXHIBIT AU-623-2—SPECIAL REPORT ON AN ACCOUNT IN A FINANCIAL STATEMENT

We have audited the accompanying schedule of accounts receivable of X Company as of December 31, 20X5. This schedule is the responsibility of the Company's management. Our responsibility is to express an opinion on this schedule based on our audit.

We conducted our audit in accordance with generally accepted auditing standards. Those standards require that we plan and perform the audit to obtain reasonable assurance about whether the schedule of accounts receivable is free of material misstatement. An audit includes examining, on a test basis, evidence supporting the amounts and disclosures in the schedule of accounts receivable. An audit also includes assessing the accounting principles used and significant estimates made by management, as well as evaluating the overall schedule presentation. We believe that our audit provides a reasonable basis for our opinion.

In our opinion, the schedule of accounts receivable referred to above presents fairly, in all material respects, the accounts receivable of X Company as of December 31, 20X5, in conformity with generally accepted accounting principles.

EXHIBIT AU 623-3—SPECIAL REPORT ON WHETHER CERTAIN TERMS OF A DEBT AGREEMENT HAVE BEEN OBSERVED

We have audited, in accordance with generally accepted auditing standards, the balance sheet of X Company as of December 31, 20X5, and the related statements of income, retained earnings, and cash flows for the year then ended, and have issued our report thereon dated February 20, 20X6.

In connection with our audit, nothing came to our attention that caused us to believe that the Company failed to comply with the terms, covenants, provisions, or conditions of the restrictive terms of the loan agreement (dated March 4, 20X0), as explained in Section A of the agreement with First State Bank insofar as they relate to accounting matters. However, our audit was not directed primarily toward obtaining knowledge of such noncompliance.

This report is intended solely for the information and use of the boards of directors and managements of X Company and First State Bank and is not intended to be and should not be used by anyone other than these specified parties.

EXHIBIT AU 623-4—SPECIAL REPORT ON A STATEMENT OF ASSETS SOLD AND LIABILITIES TRANSFERRED

We have audited the accompanying statement of net assets sold of X Company as of July 15, 20X5. This statement of net assets sold is the responsibility of X Company's management. Our responsibility is to express an opinion on the statement of net assets sold based on our audit.

We conducted our audit in accordance with generally accepted auditing standards. Those standards require that we plan and perform the audit to obtain reasonable assurance about whether the statement of net assets sold is free of material misstatement. An audit includes examining, on a test basis, evidence supporting the amounts and disclosures in the statement. An audit also includes assessing the accounting principles used and significant estimates made by management, as well as evaluating the overall presentation of the statement of net assets sold. We believe that our audit provides a reasonable basis for our opinion.

The accompanying statement was prepared to present the net assets of X Company sold to Z Company pursuant to the purchase agreement described in Note 1, and is not intended to be a complete presentation of X Company's assets and liabilities.

In our opinion, the accompanying statement of net assets sold presents fairly, in all material respects, the net assets of X Company as of July 15, 20X5, sold pursuant to the purchase agreement referred to in Note 1, in conformity with generally accepted accounting principles.

This report is intended solely for the information and use of the boards of directors and managements of X Company and Z Company and is not intended to be and should not be used by anyone other than these specified parties.

EXHIBIT AU 623-5—SPECIAL REPORT ON FINANCIAL STATEMENTS PREPARED PURSUANT TO A LOAN AGREEMENT

We have audited the special-purpose statement of assets and liabilities of X Company as of December 31, 20X5 and 20X4, and the related special-purpose statements of revenues and expenses and cash flows for the years then ended. These financial statements are the responsibility of the Company's management. Our responsibility is to express an opinion on these financial statements based on our audits.

We conducted our audits in accordance with generally accepted auditing standards. Those standards require that we plan and perform the audit to obtain reasonable assurance about whether the financial statements are free of material misstatement. An audit includes examining, on a test basis, evidence supporting the amounts and disclosures in the financial statements. An audit also includes assessing the accounting principles used and significant estimates made by management, as well as evaluating the overall financial statement presentation. We believe that our audits provide a reasonable basis for our opinion.

The accompanying special-purpose financial statements were prepared for the purpose of complying with Section A of a loan agreement between the Company and the First State Bank as discussed in Note 1, and are not intended to be a presentation in conformity with generally accepted accounting principles.

In our opinion, the special-purpose financial statements referred to above present fairly, in all material respects, the assets and liabilities of X Company as of December 31, 20X5 and 20X4, and the revenues, expenses, and cash flows for the years then ended, on the basis of accounting described in Note 1.

This report is intended solely for the information and use of the boards of directors and managements of X Company and the First State Bank and is not and should not be used for anyone other than these specified parties.

SECTION 625

REPORTS ON THE APPLICATION OF ACCOUNTING PRINCIPLES

Authoritative Pronouncements

SAS-50—Reports on the Application of Accounting Principles

Overview

Accountants are often requested to give an informal opinion on how a transaction should or could be accounted for or what type of opinion would be appropriate for a particular set of financial statements. Requests of this nature are frequently associated with prospective clients who are "shopping for an opinion." Unfortunately, such requests have resulted in a significant amount of adverse publicity for the accounting profession.

To provide some guidance in this sensitive area, in 1986 the Auditing Standards Board issued SAS-50 (Reports on the Application of Accounting Principles). The scope of SAS-50 is not limited to shopping for opinions, but also includes written reports and oral advice rendered by a reporting accountant in public practice to principals in the transaction, other accountants, and intermediaries. "Intermediaries" are parties who advise principals and may include such professionals as lawyers and bankers.

SAS-50 covers the following circumstances, irrespective of whether the request is associated with a proposal to obtain a new client:

- Written reports

  — *Specific transactions*—Determining the applicability of accounting principles to specified transactions that are either completed or proposed

  — *Specific entity's financial statements*—Determining the appropriate opinion that may be expressed on a specified entity's financial statements

  — *Hypothetical transactions*—Determining for an intermediary the applicability of accounting principles to facts or circumstances that are not related to a particular principal

- Oral advice

  — *Specific transactions*—Determining the applicability of accounting principles to specified transactions that are either completed or proposed

— *Specific entity's financial statements*—Determining the appropriate opinion that may be expressed on a specified entity's financial statements

Situations involving oral advice are covered by SAS-50 only when the reporting accountant believes that the advice will constitute an important part in the principal's ultimate decision.

> **RISK ASSESSMENT POINT:** Clearly, the Auditing Standards Board expanded the scope of SAS-50 to include oral advice so that the reporting accountant could not circumvent professional standards simply by not preparing a written report.

The standards established in SAS-50 are not applicable to situations in which:

- A continuing accountant is engaged to report on financial statements.
- An accountant is engaged to assist in litigation involving accounting questions.
- An accountant is engaged to provide expert testimony in litigation involving accounting questions.
- An accountant in public practice gives professional advice to another accountant in public practice.
- An accountant-prepared communication (such as a newsletter, an article, or a speech) on an accounting matter is not intended as advice on the applicability of accounting principles to specific transactions or the type of opinion that may be expressed on a specific entity's financial statements.

Promulgated Procedures Checklist

The auditor should follow the following performance standards when reporting on the application of accounting principles:

_____ The auditor must be adequately trained and proficient.

_____ Due professional care must be observed in the conduct of the engagement.

_____ The engagement must be planned and assistants adequately supervised.

___ Sufficient information must be accumulated.

___ Reporting standards must be followed in the preparation of the report.

Analysis and Application of Procedures

The auditor must be adequately trained and proficient

The first performance standard is similar to the first general standard of generally accepted auditing standards, which is discussed in AU Section 210 of this book.

Due professional care must be observed in the conduct of the engagement

The second performance standard is similar to the third general standard of generally accepted auditing standards, which is discussed in AU Section 230 of this book.

The engagement must be planned and assistants must be adequately supervised

The third performance standard is similar to the first standard of fieldwork of generally accepted auditing standards, which is discussed in AU Section 311 of this book.

Sufficient information must be accumulated

Before the applicability of an accounting principle can be evaluated, the reporting accountant must accumulate sufficient information that provides a reasonable basis for drawing a conclusion with respect to the accounting principle. To make this determination, the accountant should obtain an adequate understanding of the transactions. Once the transactions are understood, the accountant should identify those accounting principles that could be used to account for the transactions. The identification of acceptable accounting principles should be guided by SAS-69 (AU 411) (The Meaning of "Present Fairly in Conformity with Generally Accepted Accounting Principles" in the Independent Auditor's Report). SAS-69 is discussed in AU Section 411 of this book.

> **RISK ASSESSMENT POINT:** If the applicability of a specific accounting principle is unclear after the accountant has reviewed

the professional literature identified in SAS-69, it may be appropriate to consult with other experts or perform additional research to identify a precedent or analogous situation that could be used to support the application of the specific accounting principle.

In addition, the reporting accountant should contact the continuing accountant when the special engagement involves (1) the evaluation of the applicability of accounting principles for specific transactions or the type of opinion to be expressed on a specific entity's financial statements and (2) a request for the service by a principal or an intermediary acting for a principal. The reporting accountant should inform the principal or the intermediary of the importance of communicating with the continuing accountant. SAS-50 lists the following as examples of information that the accountant may obtain from communicating with the continuing accountant:

- The form and substance of certain transactions
- Management's previous accounting for similar transactions
- Any disagreement(s) between management and the continuing accountant with respect to the transactions or statements in question
- Identification of the continuing accountant's solution to the applicability of accounting principles or the appropriate opinion that should be expressed on the financial statements

PLANNING AID REMINDER: The reporting accountant should ask the principal for permission to contact the continuing accountant, and the principal should authorize the continuing accountant to respond fully to any inquiries the reporting accountant makes. With respect to the responsibilities of the continuing accountant, SAS-50 concludes that the continuing accountant's responsibilities are similar to those of a predecessor auditor as described in SAS-84 (Communications Between Predecessor and Successor Auditors).

Reporting standards must be followed in the preparation of the report

SAS-50 identifies the following as reporting standards that the reporting accountant ordinarily should observe by when preparing a written report on the applicability of accounting principles:

- Brief description of the nature of the engagement and a statement that the engagement was performed in accordance with standards established by the AICPA

- Description of transactions; a statement of the relevant facts, circumstances, and assumptions; and a statement about the source of the information (Principals to specific transactions should be identified, and hypothetical transactions should be described using generic references such as "Company X.")

- Statement describing the appropriate accounting principles to be applied or the type of opinion that may be rendered on the entity's financial statements, and if appropriate, a description of the reasons for the reporting accountant's conclusion

- Statement that the responsibility for the proper accounting treatment rests with the preparers of the financial statements, who should consult with their continuing accountants

- Statement that any difference in the facts, circumstances, or assumptions presented may change the report

> **ENGAGEMENT STRATEGY:** The reporting standards just listed are applicable to written reports prepared by the accountant. As noted earlier, the accountant may provide oral advice on specific transactions or a specific entity's financial statements. SAS-50 provides no reporting standards for oral advice, but footnote 4 of SAS-50 states that the reporting standards for written reports may provide useful guidance for presenting oral advice.

The accountant's report should be addressed to the principal or intermediary in the transaction. The accountant's report may be divided into the following four sections: (1) introduction; (2) description of transactions, facts, or circumstances; (3) appropriate accounting principles or opinion to be expressed; and (4) concluding comments. Generally, the first and fourth sections will contain a single paragraph, which for the most part will have a standard format. The second and third sections will be unique to the specific accounting issue being raised.

Exhibit AU 625-1 presents an example of an accountant's report from SAS-50 that covers the applicability of accounting principles.

Practitioner's Aids

Exhibit AU 625-1 is an example of an accountant's report on the applicability of accounting principles and is based on the report standards established by SAS-50.

EXHIBIT AU 625-1—ACCOUNTANT'S REPORT ON THE APPLICABILITY OF ACCOUNTING PRINCIPLES

[Introduction:]

We have been engaged to report on the appropriate application of generally accepted accounting principles to the specific transactions described below. This report is being issued to Company X for assistance in evaluating accounting principles for the described specific transactions. Our engagement has been conducted in accordance with standards established by the American Institute of Certified Public Accountants.

[Description of Transactions:]

The facts, circumstances, and assumptions relevant to the specific transactions as provided to us by the management of Company X are as follows: [*Describe transactions being evaluated.*]

[Appropriate Accounting Principles:]

[*Include discussion of accounting principles being evaluated.*]

[Concluding Comments:]

The ultimate responsibility for the decision on the appropriate application of generally accepted accounting principles for actual transactions rests with the preparers of financial statements, who should consult with their continuing accountants. Our judgment on the appropriate application of generally accepted accounting principles for the described specific transactions is based solely on the facts provided to us as described above; should these facts and circumstances differ, our conclusion may change.

SECTION 634

LETTERS FOR UNDERWRITERS AND CERTAIN OTHER REQUESTING PARTIES

Authoritative Pronouncements

SAS-72—Letters for Underwriters and Certain Other Requesting Parties

SAS-76—Amendments to Statement on Auditing Standards No. 72, Letters for Underwriters and Certain Other Requesting Parties

Auditing Interpretation (June 1993)—Letters to Directors Relating to Annual Reports on Form 10-K

Auditing Interpretation (August 1998)—Commenting in a Comfort Letter on Quantitative Disclosures About Market Risk Made in Accordance with Item 305 of Regulations S-K

Overview

SAS-72 (Letters for Underwriters and Certain Other Requesting Parties), as amended by SAS-86 (AU 634) (Amendment to Statement on Auditing Standards No. 72, Letters for Underwriters and Certain Other Requesting Parties), provides guidance to accountants in performing engagements to provide (1) letters to underwriters in conjunction with filings with the Securities and Exchange Commission (SEC) under the Securities Act of 1933 (the 1933 Act) and (2) letters to a requesting party in conjunction with other securities offerings.

SAS-72 supersedes SAS-49 (Letters for Underwriters). SAS-49 was issued in 1984, before the issuance of Statements on Standards for Attestation Engagements (Attestation Standards; Financial Forecasts and Projections; and Reporting on Pro Forma Financial Information). Therefore, the guidance and examples pertaining to letters (commonly referred to as "comfort letters") issued to underwriters and certain other parties (referred to hereafter as "requesting parties") had to be revised to reflect the issuance of these standards. Furthermore, since SAS-49 was issued, accountants have been requested to issue comfort letters to parties other than underwriters and in connection with securities offerings other than those registered under the Act. SAS-72 provides guidance on those parties to whom accountants may provide comfort letters.

> **PLANNING AID REMINDER:** The Auditing Interpretation (April 1981, revised June 1993) of SAS-72 titled "Letters to Directors

Relating to Annual Reports on Form 10-K" concludes that the auditor may perform some services requested by the board of directors relating to the annual reports on Form 10-K (9634.01–.09).

Applicability of Statement on Auditing Standards No. 72

As part of the registration of securities under the 1933 Act, underwriters of the securities often ask an accountant to provide them with a comfort letter. The comfort letter is not a requirement of the 1933 Act and is not included in the registration statement. However, underwriters request it to assist them in discharging their duty of reasonable investigation and to help establish their affirmative defense under Section 11 of the 1933 Act (often referred to as "Section 11 investigation" or "due diligence"). Therefore, obtaining the accountant's comfort letter is one of many activities that underwriters undertake to respond to the liability imposed on them under Section 11 of the 1933 Act.

> **RISK ASSESSMENT POINT:** SAS-72 states that the accountant may address the comfort letter to parties other than a named underwriter only when (1) the requesting party has a statutory due diligence defense under Section 11 of the 1933 Act and (2) legal counsel for the requesting party issues a written legal opinion to the accountant explicitly stating that such party has a statutory due diligence defense under Section 11 of the 1933 Act. If the requesting party cannot provide such a legal opinion letter from its counsel, the accountant should obtain a representation letter, as described below, from the requesting party.

SAS-72 states that the accountant may also provide comfort letters to other requesting parties, in addition to underwriters, in the following situations only if the representation letter described below is obtained:

- To a broker-dealer or other financial intermediary in connection with the following types of securities offerings:

  — For foreign offerings (e.g., Regulation S, Eurodollar, and other offshore offerings)

  — For transactions that are exempt from the registration requirements of Section 5 of the 1933 Act, including those pursuant to Regulation A, Regulation D, and Rule 144A

  — For offerings of securities issued or backed by governmental, municipal, banking, tax-exempt, or other entities that are exempt from registration under the 1933 Act

§634 • Letters for Underwriters and Certain Other Parties 473

- To a buyer or a seller, or both, in connection with acquisition transactions involving an exchange of stock (e.g., Form S-4 or merger proxy situation)

A comfort letter (or alternative letter, described below) should be prepared only for parties referred to in paragraphs 3–5 of SAS-72. If another party requests a letter, the standards established by SAS-72 and SAS-76 do not apply. However, the accountant may accept an engagement that satisfies the standards established by either SAS-75 (AU 622) (Engagements to Apply Agreed-Upon Procedures to Specified Elements, Accounts, or Items of a Financial Statement) or SSAE-4 (Agreed-Upon Procedures Engagements).

SAS-76 (Amendments to Statement on Auditing Standards No. 72 on Letters for Underwriters) concludes that when a party specifically identified in paragraphs 3–5 of SAS-72 (other than an underwriter of a party with a due diligence defense based on Section 11 of the 1933 Act) requests a comfort letter *but does not provide the representations established by paragraphs 6 and 7 of SAS-72*, the accountant should not provide a comfort letter. However, the accountant may provide an alternative letter that does not include a negative assurance on the financial statements or specified elements, accounts, or items of those statements. In addition, the alternative letter should state the following:

- That the accountant had no responsibility for determining the procedures enumerated in the letter

- That the enumerated procedures do not constitute an audit of the financial statements

- That the enumerated procedures should not substitute for additional inquiries or procedures that the party may perform as part of considering the proposed offering

- That the letter is solely for the other party's information and should not be used for any other purpose

- That the accountant has no responsibility for updating the letter for events that may occur after the cut-off date

The guidance established by SAS-72 that applies to performing procedures related to a comfort letter also should apply to the procedures referred to in the alternative letter.

> **RISK ASSESSMENT POINT:** The Auditing Interpretation (August 1998) titled "Commenting in a Comfort Letter on Quantitative Disclosures About Market Risk Made in Accordance with Item

305 of Regulations S-K" concludes that the auditor should not offer positive or negative assurances on information related to Item 305 of Regulation S-K.

Required representation letter

The required representation letter from the requesting parties identified above should (1) be addressed to the accountant and signed by the requesting party and (2) include a statement that the review process to be applied by the requesting party is substantially consistent with the due diligence review process that would be performed pursuant to the 1933 Act. Exhibit AU 634-1 illustrates a representation letter as would be found in SAS-72.

If a nonunderwriter requests a comfort letter in connection with a securities offering registered pursuant to the 1933 Act, the second and third sentences of the representation letter should be revised as follows:

> This review process, applied to the information relating to the issuer, is substantially consistent with the due diligence review process that an underwriter would perform in connection with this placement of securities. We are knowledgeable with respect to the due diligence review process that an underwriter would perform in connection with a placement of securities registered pursuant to the Securities Act of 1933.
>
> **RISK ASSESSMENT POINT:** When the requesting party has provided the accountant with a representation letter regarding its due diligence review process as described above, the accountant should make reference to those representations in the comfort letter.

General guidance

Although SAS-72 provides guidance on comfort letters issued in various types of securities transactions, it generally addresses comfort letters issued in connection with securities offerings registered pursuant to the 1933 Act. Accordingly, guidance provided in SAS-72 with respect to comments made in comfort letters on compliance with SEC rules and regulations (e.g., Regulation S-X or S-K) generally applies when securities offerings are registered pursuant to the 1933 Act.

Scope of comfort procedures

The scope and conclusions in the comfort letter should be guided, wherever possible, by the pertinent sections of the underwriting agreement. There-

§634 • **Letters for Underwriters and Certain Other Parties**

fore, the accountant should obtain a draft copy of the underwriting agreement and review it at the earliest practicable date.

In requiring comfort letters from accountants, underwriters are seeking assistance in performing a reasonable investigation of data (unaudited financial information and other data) on the authority of an expert. Unfortunately, what constitutes a reasonable investigation of unaudited data sufficient to satisfy an underwriter's purpose has never been authoritatively established. Therefore, it is only the underwriter who can determine the amount of work sufficient to satisfy his or her due diligence requirement. Accordingly, accountants are willing to carry out procedures that will aid underwriters in discharging their responsibility for exercising due diligence, but cannot furnish any assurance on whether those procedures are sufficient for the underwriter's purpose.

To ensure that the accountant's professional responsibility is understood, the accountant should meet with the underwriter and the client and explain the typical procedures (as discussed later in this section) employed as a basis for the issuance of a comfort letter. SAS-72 states that the accountant should accompany any such discussion of procedures with a clear statement that the accountant cannot furnish any assurance regarding the sufficiency of the procedures and should include a statement to that effect in the comfort letter. Paragraph 4 of the sample comfort letter in this section illustrates this requirement.

Promulgated Procedures Checklist

The auditor should perform the following procedures with respect to letters for underwriters and certain other requesting parties:

_____ Prepare a draft letter to the underwriter.

_____ Obtain a copy of the draft comfort letter from other accountants.

_____ Based on the circumstances of the engagement, prepare an appropriate comfort letter.

Analysis and Application of Procedures

Prepare a draft letter to the underwriter

After receiving a draft of the underwriting agreement or being informed of its contents, the accountant should furnish the underwriter with a draft of the proposed comfort letter that responds to the underwriting agreement. This practice offers the underwriter and the client the opportunity to review the draft letter and discuss with the accountant the procedures expected to be performed. The accountant should not make statements about performing, or imply that he or she will perform, the procedures he or she considers necessary in the circumstances, as this may lead to a misunderstanding about the accountant's responsibility for the sufficiency of the procedures for the underwriter's purposes.

To further emphasize the point that the underwriter and not the accountant is responsible for the sufficiency of the comfort procedures, SAS-72 indicates that the accountant may include a legend or a concluding paragraph on the draft letter to the underwriter to address its functions and limitations. SAS-72 contains the following example of such a paragraph:

> This draft is furnished solely for the purpose of indicating the form of letter that we would expect to be able to furnish [*name of underwriter*] in response to their request, the matters expected to be covered in the letter, and the nature of the procedures that we would expect to carry out with respect to such matters. On the basis of our discussions with [*name of underwriter*], it is our understanding that the procedures outlined in this draft letter are those they wish us to follow. Unless [*name of underwriter*] informs us otherwise, we shall assume that there are no additional procedures they wish us to follow. The text of the letter itself will depend, of course, on the results of the procedures, which we would not expect to complete until shortly before the letter is given and in no event before the cut-off date indicated therein.

In the absence of any discussions with the underwriter, the accountant should outline in the draft letter those procedures specified in the underwriting agreement that he or she is willing to perform. In this situation, the second sentence above should be revised as follows:

> In the absence of any discussions with [*name of underwriter*], we have set out in this draft letter those procedures referred to in the draft underwriting agreement (of which we have been furnished a copy) that we are willing to follow.

Obtain a copy of the draft comfort letter from other accountants

SAS-72 indicates that comfort letters are sometimes requested from more than one accountant (e.g., in connection with registration statements to be used in the subsequent sale of shares issued in recently effected mergers or from predecessor auditors). The principal accountant should obtain a copy of the draft comfort letter written by the other accountant.

There also may be situations in which a registration statement includes the report of more than one accountant on financial statements included therein—for example, if a significant subsidiary or division is audited by other accountants. In that event, SAS-72 indicates that

- The principal accountant should read the comfort letter the other accountant has prepared. Such comfort letter should include statements similar to those contained in the principal accountant's comfort letter, including representations about the accountant's independence.
- The principal accountant should make the following comments in his or her comfort letter: (1) that the principal accountant has read the comfort letter prepared by the other accountant and (2) that procedures performed by the principal accountant relate only to the financial statements audited by the principal accountant and the consolidated financial statements.

Shelf registrations

A shelf registration statement enables an entity to register securities under the 1933 Act and then issue these securities over a period of time. At the effective date of the registration statement, an underwriter or lead underwriter may not have been named, although the accountant may have been asked to issue a comfort letter. SAS-72 indicates that since only the underwriter can determine the appropriate procedures to be performed with respect to the accountant's comfort letter, the accountant should not agree to issue a comfort letter to the client, to the counsel for the underwriter group (when a lead underwriter has not been named), or to an unspecified party such as "any or all underwriters to be selected." However, the accountant may issue a draft comfort letter to the client or the legal counsel representing the underwriter group, based on the actual procedures the accountant has performed. In this circumstance, the accountant should include a legend or a paragraph in the draft comfort letter addressing the letter's functions and limitations. The following is an example of such a paragraph as illustrated in SAS-72:

> This draft describes the procedures that we have performed and represents a letter we would be prepared to sign as of the effective date of the registration statement if the managing underwriter had been chosen at that date and had requested such a letter. On the basis of our discussions with [*name of client or legal counsel*], the procedures set forth are similar to those that experience indicates that underwriters often request in such circum-

stances. The text of the final letter will depend, of course, on whether the managing underwriter who is selected requests that other procedures be performed to meet his or her needs and whether the managing underwriter requests that any of the procedures be updated to the date of issuance of the signed letter.

Based on the circumstances of the engagement, prepare an appropriate comfort letter

The contents of comfort letters vary depending on the specific circumstances of the individual engagement. However, a comfort letter typically includes the following:

1. *Date*—The comfort letter usually is dated on or shortly before the effective date of the registration statement.
2. *Addressee*—The comfort letter usually is addressed to the parties to whom the accountant is giving assurance (e.g., the client and the underwriter).
3. *Introductory paragraph*—This paragraph typically refers to the accountant's report on the audited financial statements and related schedules included or incorporated by reference in the registration statement.
4. *Independence*—The comfort letter typically makes a brief statement regarding the accountant's independence.
5. *Compliance with SEC requirements*—When the underwriting agreement requests the accountant to comment on compliance with SEC requirements, the accountant should add a paragraph in the comfort letter to that effect.
6. *Comments on information other than audited financial statements.*
7. *Comments on tables, statistics, and other financial data.*
8. *Concluding paragraph*—To avoid misunderstanding by the requesting party, the comfort letter typically includes a paragraph about its purpose and intended use.
9. *Disclosure of subsequently discovered matters.*

Date

Ordinarily, the comfort letter is dated on or shortly before the effective date of the registration statement. Usually the underwriting agreement specifies the date to which the procedures described in the letter are to relate. This

§634 • Letters for Underwriters and Certain Other Parties 479

date, commonly referred to as the cutoff date, is customarily within five business days before the effective date of the registration statement.

> **RISK ASSESSMENT POINT:** SAS-72 indicates that the comfort letter should state that the procedures described therein do not cover the intervening period from the cutoff date to the date of the letter.

Underwriters also sometimes require that an additional comfort letter be issued and dated at or shortly before the closing date on which the entity or selling shareholders deliver the securities to the underwriter in exchange for the proceeds of the offering. SAS-72 does not prohibit the accountant from furnishing both of these letters. However, when both are required, the accountant should carry out the specified procedures as of the cut-off date of each letter.

Addressee

SAS-72 states that the accountant should not address or give the comfort letter to any parties other than the client, the named underwriter, the broker-dealer, the financial intermediary, or the buyer or seller, or both, in connection with acquisition transactions as discussed above.

Introductory paragraph

Although not required, it is customary, and desirable according to SAS-72, for the accountant to include an introductory paragraph in the comfort letter that describes which financial statements are included in the registration statement the accountant has audited. The following is an example of such a paragraph as illustrated in SAS-72:

> We have audited the [*identify the financial statements and financial statement schedules*] included [*incorporated by reference*] in the registration statement (no. 33-00000) on Form X filed by the company under the Securities Act of 1933 (the Act); our reports with respect thereto are also included [*incorporated by reference*] in that registration statement. The registration statement, as amended as of [*date*], is herein referred to as the registration statement.
>
> **RISK ASSESSMENT POINT:** Occasionally, underwriters will request that the accountant's opinion on the financial statements contained in the registration statement be repeated in the comfort letter. There does not appear any valid reason to do so,

and it should not be done; also, the accountant should not give negative assurance regarding his or her report. Furthermore, the accountant should not give negative assurance with respect to financial statements and schedules that have been audited and are reported on in the registration statement by other accountants.

Modified introductory paragraph

The introductory paragraph of the accountant's comfort letter should be modified when the accountant's report on audited financial statements and related schedules included in the registration statement contains the following material:

- An explanatory paragraph or emphasis-of-matter paragraph
- A qualified opinion on the financial statements

In these instances, the introductory paragraph should be modified to refer to and discuss such matters.

Reference to other reports in the introductory paragraph The accountant may have previously reported on any of the following:

- Condensed financial statements derived from audited financial statements, in accordance with SAS-42 (AU 552) (Reporting on Condensed Financial Statements and Selected Financial Data)
- Selected financial data, in accordance with SAS-42 (AU 552)
- Interim financial information, in accordance with SAS-71 (AU 722) (Interim Financial Information)
- Pro forma financial information, in accordance with Statement on Standards for Attestation Engagements [Reporting on Pro Forma Financial Information (AT 401)]
- A financial forecast, in accordance with SSAE-1 (AT 301)
- Management's discussion and analysis (MD&A)

In these situations, in the introductory paragraph of the comfort letter the accountant may refer to the previously issued reports. However, these reports should not be repeated in the comfort letter; nor should the accountant otherwise imply that he or she is reporting as of the date of the comfort letter or is assuming responsibility for the sufficiency of the procedures for the underwriter's purposes.

Independence

In conjunction with SEC filings, the underwriting agreement customarily requests that the accountant represent in the comfort letter that he or she is independent. A simple statement, such as the one shown below, suffices:

> We are independent certified public accountants with respect to [*name of client*], within the meaning of the Act and the applicable published rules and regulations thereunder.

In a non-SEC filing, a statement such as the one shown below suffices:

> We are independent certified public accountants with respect to [*name of client*], under Rule 101 of the AICPA Code of Professional Conduct and its interpretations and rulings.

SAS-72 indicates that the accountants for previously nonaffiliated companies recently acquired by the registrant would not be required to have been independent with respect to the company whose shares are being registered. In this situation, the statement regarding independence should be modified, as shown below:

> As of [*date of the accountant's most recent report on the financial statements of the client*] and during the period covered by the financial statements on which we reported, we were independent certified public accountants with respect to [*name of client*] within the meaning of the Act and the applicable published rules and regulations thereunder.

Compliance with SEC requirements

Usually, the underwriting agreement requests that the accountant comment on whether the financial statements comply with SEC requirements. The accountant may do so in the comfort letter by adding a paragraph like the one shown below:

> In our opinion [*include phrase "except as disclosed in the registration statement," if applicable*], the [*identify the financial statements and financial statement schedules*] audited by us and included [*incorporated by reference*] in the registration statement comply as to form in all material respects with the applicable accounting requirements of the Act and the related published rules and regulations.

If there is a material departure from the pertinent published SEC requirements, the accountant should disclose such departure in the comfort letter. Normally, representatives of the SEC will have agreed to such a departure. The following is an example of wording to be used in the comfort letter when the SEC has agreed to a departure from its published accounting requirements:

> In our opinion [*include phrase "except as disclosed in the registration statement," if applicable*], the [*identify the financial statements and financial statement schedules*] audited by us and included [*incorporated by reference*] in the registration statement comply as to form in all material respects with the applicable accounting requirements of the Act and the related published rules and regulations; however, as agreed to by representatives of the SEC, separate financial statements and financial statement schedules of ABC Company (an equity investee) as required by rule 3-09 of Regulation S-X have been omitted.

> **RISK ASSESSMENT POINT:** SAS-72 states that if departures from pertinent published SEC requirements either are not disclosed in the registration statement or have not been agreed to by representatives of the SEC, the accountant should carefully consider whether to consent to the use of the accountant's report in the registration statement.

Commenting in comfort letter on information other than audited financial statements

The accountant's comfort letter often refers to information other than audited financial statements. The accountant's comments in the letter generally pertain to:

- Unaudited condensed interim financial information
- Capsule financial information
- Pro forma financial information
- Financial forecasts
- Changes in capital stock, increases in long-term debt, and decreases in other specified financial statement items

As discussed above, the comfort letter should refer to the agreed-upon procedures, with the following exception: When the accountant has been asked to provide negative assurance on interim financial information or capsule financial information, the accountant does not need to specify the procedures involved in a SAS-71 (AU 722) review. The accountant should make no comments or suggestions that he or she has applied procedures that the accountant considered necessary for the underwriter's purposes. Terms or comments that are subjective and unclear (e.g., "general review," "limited review," "reconcile," "check," and "test") should not be used in describing the accountant's work, unless the procedures implied by these terms are described in the comfort letter.

Notwithstanding the above, SAS-72 states that the accountant should not comment in a comfort letter on certain unaudited financial information unless the accountant has obtained knowledge of the client's internal controls as they relate to the preparation of both annual and interim financial information. Such knowledge of internal controls is ordinarily acquired when the accountant audits the entity's financial statements. If the accountant has not acquired such knowledge, the accountant should perform the necessary procedures to obtain that knowledge in order to make the required comments in the comfort letter. This knowledge of internal controls is required when the accountant is requested to comment in a comfort letter on the following:

- Unaudited condensed interim financial information
- Capsule financial information
- A financial forecast when historical financial statements provide a basis for one or more significant assumptions for the forecast
- Changes in capital stock, increases in long-term debt, and decreases in selected financial statement items

> **ENGAGEMENT STRATEGY:** SAS-86 concludes that an auditor should not use the comment letter to comment on "compliance as to form of MD&A with rules and regulations adopted by the SEC." However, an auditor may accept an engagement to examine or review MD&A based on the guidance established by Statements on Standards for Attestation Engagements.

Unaudited condensed interim financial information The comfort letter should (1) identify the unaudited condensed interim financial information and (2) state that the accountant has not audited such information in accordance with generally accepted auditing standards and, therefore, does not express an opinion on such information. (Paragraph 3 of the sample comfort letter at the end of this Section illustrates this requirement.)

The accountant's comments in the comfort letter regarding unaudited condensed interim financial information should provide negative assurance on whether:

1. Any material modifications should be made to such information for it to be in conformity with generally accepted accounting principles.

2. Such information complies as to form in all material respects with the applicable accounting requirements of the 1933 Act and the related rules and regulations. [Paragraph 5(a) of the sample comfort letter at the end of this Section illustrates this requirement.]

The accountant may provide such negative assurance in the comfort letter only when he or she has conducted a review of such information in accordance with SAS-71 (AU 722). In this case, the accountant may:

1. State in the comfort letter that he or she has performed the procedures identified in SAS-71 (AU 722). [Paragraph 4(a)(i) of the sample comfort letter at the end of this Section illustrates this requirement.]

2. If the accountant has issued a report on the review of the interim financial information, mention that fact in the comfort letter. In this case, the accountant should attach the review report to the comfort letter, unless the review report is already included or incorporated by reference in the registration statement.

If a review in accordance with SAS-71 (AU 722) has not been conducted, the accountant may not provide negative assurance in the comfort letter regarding the interim financial information. (The accountant is limited to reporting the procedures performed and results obtained.) (SAS-72, example O in the appendix, illustrates the wording in this case.)

Capsule financial information A registration statement may contain capsule financial information (i.e., unaudited summarized interim information for periods subsequent to the date of the audited financial statements and for the corresponding period of the prior year or the date of the unaudited condensed interim financial information). The accountant may express a negative assurance on whether such capsule financial information conforms with generally accepted accounting principles and comment on whether the dollar amounts were determined on a basis substantially consistent with corresponding amounts in the audited financial statements only if both of the following conditions are met:

1. The capsule financial information meets the minimum reporting requirements established in paragraph 30 of APB Opinion No. 28 (Interim Financial Reporting).

2. The accountant has performed a SAS-71 (AU 722) review of the financial statements underlying the capsule financial information.

§634 • Letters for Underwriters and Certain Other Parties

If the minimum reporting requirements in 1. above are not met, the accountant may provide only negative assurance on whether the dollar amounts were determined on a basis substantially consistent with corresponding amounts in the audited financial statements, as long as the accountant has performed a SAS-71 (AU 722) review.

> **ENGAGEMENT STRATEGY:** If the accountant determines that a negative assurance cannot be given because the conditions discussed above are not met, the accountant is limited to reporting in the comfort letter the procedures performed and the results obtained.

Pro forma financial information In a comfort letter, the accountant should not give negative assurance on (1) pro forma financial information, (2) the application of pro forma adjustments to historical amounts, (3) the compilation of pro forma financial information, or (4) whether the pro forma financial information complies as to form in all material respects with the applicable accounting requirements of rule 11-02 of Regulation S-X unless one of the following conditions is met:

1. The accountant has performed an audit of the entity's annual financial statements (or a significant part of a business combination) and has obtained an appropriate level of knowledge of its accounting and financial reporting practices.

2. The accountant has performed a SAS-71 (AU 722) review of the entity's interim financial statements to which the pro forma adjustments were applied.

If the conditions indicated above are not met, the accountant's comments in the comfort letter are limited to the procedures performed and results obtained. (Example O in the appendix to SAS-72 illustrates the wording in this case.)

Financial forecasts SAS-72 states that to perform agreed-upon procedures and comment in the comfort letter on a financial forecast, the accountant should:

1. Obtain knowledge of the entity's internal controls as they relate to the preparation of annual and interim financial statements, as discussed earlier.

2. Perform the procedures required for a compilation of a forecast, as prescribed in Appendix B of SSAE-1.

3. Follow the guidance in paragraphs 16 and 17 of SSAE-1 regarding reporting on the compilation of the financial forecast, and attach the report to the comfort letter.

> **RISK ASSESSMENT POINT:** If the forecast is included in the registration statement, the forecast must be accompanied by an indication that the accountant has not examined the forecast and, therefore, does not express an opinion on it. If the accountant has issued a compilation report on the forecast in connection with the comfort letter, the accountant's report need not be included in the registration statement.

The accountant may not give negative assurance in the comfort letter on the procedures performed in connection with a financial forecast. Furthermore, the accountant may not give negative assurance on the forecast's compliance with rule 11-03 of Regulation S-X unless the accountant has performed an examination of the forecast in accordance with Financial Forecasts and Projections. (Examples E and O in the appendix to SAS-72 provide illustrations of the accountant's wording in a comfort letter in connection with financial forecasts.)

Subsequent changes The underwriter usually will ask the accountant to comment in the comfort letter on changes in certain financial statement items during a period (commonly referred to as the change period) subsequent to that of the latest financial statements included, or incorporated by reference, in the registration statement. These comments usually relate to (1) changes in capital stock, (2) increases in long-term debt, (3) decreases in net current assets, (4) decreases in stockholders' equity, (5) decreases in net sales, and (6) decreases in total and per-share amounts of income before extraordinary items and of net income.

> **RISK ASSESSMENT POINT:** The accountant should base his or her comments solely on the limited procedures performed with respect to the period between the date of the latest financial statements made available and the cut-off date (i.e., the date to which the procedures described in the comfort letter are to relate). These procedures usually are limited to inquiries of company officials and the reading of minutes, which should be made clear in the comfort letter. (Paragraph 6 of the sample comfort letter at the end of this Section illustrates this requirement.)

The accountant may, on the underwriter's request, provide negative assurance in the comfort letter on subsequent changes in specified financial statement items as of any date that is less than 135 days from the end of the most recent period for which the accountant has performed an audit or a SAS-71 (AU 722) review. (Paragraphs 5b and 6 of the sample comfort letter at the end of this Section illustrate appropriate wording for expressing such negative assurance when there have been no subsequent changes. Example M in the appendix to SAS-72 provides illustrations of appropriate wording when there have been subsequent changes.)

If the underwriter requests negative assurance with respect to subsequent changes as of any date that is 135 days or more after to the end of the most recent period for which the accountant has performed an audit or a SAS-71 (AU 722) review, the accountant may not provide such negative assurance. In this case, the accountant's comments in the comfort letter are limited to the procedures performed and results obtained. (Example O in the appendix to SAS-72 illustrates the wording in this case.)

> **RISK ASSESSMENT POINT:** In the comfort letter the accountant should use the terms "change," "increase," and "decrease" rather than "adverse change." The term "adverse change" implies that the accountant is making a judgment about the change, which might be misinterpreted by the underwriter.

Some subsequent changes may be disclosed in the registration statement and need not be repeated in the comfort letter. Under this circumstance, the accountant should use the phrase "except for changes, increases, or decreases that the registration statement discloses have occurred or may occur" in the comfort letter. [Paragraph 5b(i) of the sample comfort letter at the end of this Section illustrates wording that would be appropriate when the accountant is making such a statement.]

The change period, which ends on the cutoff date, ordinarily begins (1) immediately after the date of the latest balance sheet in the registration statement, for balance sheet items, and (2) immediately after the latest period for which such items are presented in the registration statement, for income statement items. If the underwriter requests the use of a different change period, the accountant may use the period requested. To avoid any misunderstanding about the change period and the date of the financial statements used in comparison, both dates should be identified in the comfort letter in both the draft and the final form of the letter.

When more than one accountant is involved in the audit of the financial statements of the entity, and the principal accountant has obtained a copy of the comfort letter of the other accountant that does not disclose matters that affect the negative assurance given, the principal accountant should make appropriate modifications to the comfort letter commenting on subsequent changes. The modifications consist of an addition to paragraph 4, a substitute for the applicable part of paragraph 5, and an addition to the last sentence of paragraph 6 of the sample comfort letter at the end of this Section.

4c. We have read the letter dated [*date*] of [*the other accountants*] with regard to [*the related company*].

5. Nothing came to our attention as a result of the foregoing procedures (which, so far as [*the related company*] is concerned, consisted solely of reading the letter referred to in 4c), however, that caused us to believe that . . .

6. On the basis of these inquiries and our reading of the minutes and the letter dated [*date*] of [*the other accountants*] with regard to [*the related company*], as described in 4, nothing came to our attention that caused us to believe that there was any such change, increase, or decrease, except in all instances for changes, increases, or decreases that the registration statement discloses have occurred or may occur.

Tables, statistics, and other financial information

The comfort letter may refer to tables, statistics, and other financial information in the registration statement only if the accountant has the expertise to make a competent statement on them. Therefore, comments in the comfort letter regarding such information should be limited to the following categories:

- Information that is expressed in dollars, or percentages derived from dollar amounts, and that has been obtained from accounting records that are subject to internal controls of the company's accounting system

- Information that has been derived directly from such accounting records by analysis or computation

- Quantitative information that has been obtained from an accounting record if the information is of a type that is subject to the same controls as the dollar amounts

The accountant should not comment in the comfort letter on tables, statistics, and other financial information relating to an unaudited period unless the accountant has obtained a knowledge of the client's internal control.

The registration statement may include certain financial information to comply with specific requirements of Regulation S-K, such as the following items:

- Item 301, "Selected Financial Data"

- Item 302, "Supplementary Financial Information"

- Item 402, "Executive Compensation"
- Item 503(d), "Ratio of Earnings to Fixed Charges"

The accountant is limited to providing negative assurance on conformity of the information presented in the registration statement with the disclosure requirements of Regulation S-K. The accountant may provide such negative assurance only if the following conditions are met:

1. The information presented is derived from the accounting records subject to the internal control policies and procedures of the entity's accounting system, or has been derived directly from such accounting records by analysis or computation.
2. The information presented can be evaluated against reasonable criteria that have been established by the SEC.

The accountant should describe in the comfort letter the procedures and related findings with respect to the other financial information. The accountant should use specific, unambiguous language—such as page numbers or paragraph numbers—in the comfort letter when referring to the other information being commented on. If applicable, the accountant should comment on the acceptability of the allocation methods the client used in computing such other financial information. The accountant should not use the phrase "presents fairly" when commenting on tables, statistics, and other financial information, since this phrase relates to presentations of financial statements. (Appropriate ways of expressing comments on tables, statistics, and other financial information addressing these points are illustrated in examples F, G, and H in the appendix to SAS-72.)

Concluding paragraph

The comfort letter ordinarily concludes with a paragraph describing the purpose and intended use of the letter, including a statement that it is strictly for the use of the addressees and the underwriter. (Paragraph 7 of the sample comfort letter at the end of this Section illustrates appropriate wording for a concluding paragraph.)

Disclosure of subsequentlky discovered matters

When the accountant discovers matters (e.g., decreases or changes in specified items not disclosed in the registration statement) that may require mention in the final comfort letter, the accountant should discuss them with the client so that appropriate consideration is given to whether disclosure should be made in the registration statement. The accountant should inform the client that if such disclosure is not made, such matters will be mentioned in the comfort letter. Also, the accountant should recommend that the client promptly inform the underwriter of the matters the accountant has discovered.

A variety of sample comfort letters is found in the appendix to SAS-72. Exhibit AU 634-2 is a typical comfort letter that has been extracted from that appendix (Example A: Typical Comfort Letter).

Practitioner's Aids

Exhibit AU 634-1 is an example of a required representation letter as illustrated in SAS-72. Exhibit AU 634-2 is an example of a sample comfort letter as illustrated in the appendix to SAS-72.

EXHIBIT AU 634-1—REPRESENTATION LETTER FROM REQUESTING PARTIES

Dear ABC Accountants:

[*Name of financial intermediary*], as principal or agent, in the placement of [*identify securities*] to be issued by [*name of issuer*], will be reviewing certain information relating to [*issuer*] that will be included [*incorporated by reference*] in the document [*if appropriate, the document should be identified*], which may be delivered to investors and utilized by them as a basis for their investment decision. This review process, applied to the information relating to the issuer, is [will be] substantially consistent with the due diligence review process that we would perform if this placement of securities [*or issuance of securities in an acquisition transaction*] were being registered pursuant to the Securities Act of 1933 (the Act). We are knowledgeable with respect to the due diligence review process that would be performed if this placement of securities were being registered pursuant to the Act. We hereby request that you deliver to us a "comfort" letter concerning the financial statements of the issuer and certain statistical and other data included in the offering document. We will contact you to identify the procedures we wish you to follow and the form we wish the comfort letter to take.

Very truly yours,

[*Name of financial intermediary*]

EXHIBIT AU 634-2—SAMPLE COMFORT LETTER

June 28, 20X6

[*Addressee*]

Dear Sirs:

We have audited the consolidated balance sheets of the Blank Company, Inc. (the company) and subsidiaries as of December 31, 20X5 and 20X4, and the consolidated statements of income, retained earnings (stockholders' equity), and cash flows for each of the three years in the period ended December 31, 20X5, and the related financial statement schedules all included in the registration statement (no. 33-00000) on Form S-1 filed by the company under the Securities Act of 1933 (the Act); our reports with respect thereto are also included in that registration statement.[1] The registration statement, as amended on June 28, 20X6, is herein referred to as the registration statement.[2] In connection with the registration statement:

1. We are independent certified public accountants with respect to the company within the meaning of the Act and the applicable published rules and regulations thereunder.

2. In our opinion [*include the phrase "except as disclosed in the registration statement," if applicable*], the consolidated financial statements and financial statement schedules audited by us and included in the registration statement comply as to form in all material respects with the applicable accounting requirements of the Act and the related published rules and regulations.

3. We have not audited any financial statements of the company as of any date or for any period subsequent to December 31, 20X5; although we have conducted an audit for the year ended December 31, 20X5, the purpose (and therefore the scope) of the audit was to enable us to express our opinion on the consolidated financial statements as of December 31, 20X5, and for the year then ended, but not on the financial statements for any interim period within that year. Therefore, we are unable to and do not express any opinion on the unaudited condensed consolidated balance sheet as of March 31, 20X6, and the unaudited condensed consolidated statements of income, retained earnings (stockholders' equity), and cash flows for the three-month periods ended March 31, 20X6 and 20X5, included in the registration statement, or on the financial position, results of operations, or cash flows as of any date or for any period subsequent to December 31, 20X5.

4. For purposes of this letter we have read the 20X6 minutes of meetings of the stockholders, the board of directors, and [include other appropriate committees, if any] of the company and its subsidiaries as set forth in the minute books at June 23, 20X6, officials of the company having advised us that the minutes of all such meetings[3] through that date were set forth therein; we have carried out other procedures to June 23, 20X6, as follows (our work did not extend to the period from June 24, 20X6, to June 28, 20X6, inclusive):

   a. With respect to the three-month periods ended March 31, 20X6 and 20X5, we have:

      (i) Performed the procedures specified by the American Institute of Certified Public Accountants for a review of interim financial information as described in SAS No. 71, Interim Financial Information, on the unaudited condensed consolidated balance sheet as of March 31, 20X6, and unaudited condensed consolidated statements of income, retained earnings (stockholders' equity), and cash flows for the three-month periods ended March 31, 20X6 and 20X5, included in the registration statement.

      (ii) Inquired of certain officials of the company who have responsibility for financial and accounting matters whether the unaudited condensed consolidated financial statements referred to in a(i) comply as to form in all material respects with the applicable accounting requirements of the Act and the related published rules and regulations.

   b. With respect to the period from April 1, 20X6, to May 31, 20X6, we have:

      (i) Read the unaudited consolidated financial statements[4] of the company and subsidiaries for April and May of both 20X5 and 20X6 furnished us by the company, officials of the company having advised that no such financial statements as of any date or for any period subsequent to May 31, 20X6, were available.

      (ii) Inquired of certain officials of the company who have responsibility for financial and accounting matters whether the unaudited consolidated financial statements referred to in b(i) are stated on a basis substantially consistent with that of the audited consolidated financial statements included in the registration statement.

   The foregoing procedures do not constitute an audit conducted in accordance with generally accepted auditing standards. Also, they would not necessarily reveal matters of significance with respect to the comments in the following paragraph. Accordingly, we make no representations regarding the sufficiency of the foregoing procedures for your purposes.

5. Nothing came to our attention as a result of the foregoing procedures, however, that caused us to believe that:

   a. (i) Any material modifications should be made to the unaudited condensed consolidated financial statements described in 4a(i), included in the registration statement, for them to be in conformity with generally accepted accounting principles.[6]

   (ii) The unaudited condensed consolidated financial statements described in 4a(i) do not comply as to form in all material respects with the applicable accounting requirements of the Act and the related published rules and regulations.

   b. (i) At May 31, 20X6, there was any change in the capital stock, increase in long-term debt, or decrease in consolidated net current assets or stockholder's equity of the consolidated companies as compared with amounts shown in the March 31, 20X6, unaudited condensed consolidated balance sheet included in the registration statement, or

   (ii) for the period from April 1, 20X6, to May 31, 20X6, there were any decreases, as compared to the corresponding period in the preceding year, in consolidated net sales or in the total or per-share amounts of income before extraordinary items or of net income, except in all instances for changes, increases, or decreases that the registration statement discloses have occurred or may occur.

6. As mentioned in 4b, company officials have advised us that no consolidated financial statements as of any date or for any period subsequent to May 31, 20X6, are available; accordingly, the procedures carried out by us with respect to changes in financial statement items after May 31, 20X6, have, of necessity, been even more limited than those with respect to the periods referred to in 4. We have inquired of certain officials of the company who have responsibility for financial and accounting matters whether (a) at June 23, 20X6, there was any change in the capital stock, increase in long-term debt or any decreases in consolidated net current assets or stockholders' equity of the consolidated companies as compared with amounts shown on the March 31, 20X6, unaudited condensed consolidated balance sheet included in the registration

statement or (b) for the period from April 1, 20X6, to June 23, 20X6, there were any decreases, as compared with the corresponding period in the preceding year, in consolidated net sales or in the total or per-share amounts of income before extraordinary items or of net income. On the basis of these inquiries and our reading of the minutes as described in 4, nothing came to our attention that caused us to believe that there was any such change, increase, or decrease, except in all instances for changes, increases, or decreases that the registration statement discloses have occurred or may occur.

7. This letter is solely for the information of the addressees and to assist the underwriters in conducting and documenting their investigation of the affairs of the company in connection with the offering of the securities covered by the registration statement, and it is not to be used, circulated, quoted, or otherwise referred to within or without the underwriting group for any purpose, including but not limited to the registration, purchase, or sale of securities, nor is it to be filed with or referred to in whole or in part in the registration statement or any other document, except that reference may be made to it in the underwriting agreement or in any list of closing documents pertaining to the offering of the securities covered by the registration statement.

---

[1] The example includes financial statements required by SEC regulations to be included in the filing. If additional financial information is covered by the comfort letter, appropriate modifications should be made.

[2] The example assumes that the accountants have not previously reported on the interim financial information. If the accountants have previously reported on the interim financial information, they may refer to that fact in the introductory paragraph of the comfort letter as follows:

> Also, we have reviewed the unaudited condensed consolidated financial statements as of March 31, 20X6 and 20X5, and for the three-month periods then ended, as indicated in our report dated May 15, 20X6, which is included (incorporated by reference) in the registration statement.

The report may be attached to the comfort letter (see paragraph 28 of SAS-72). The accountants may agree to comment in the comfort letter on whether the interim financial information complies as to form in all material respects with the applicable accounting requirements of the published rules and regulations of the SEC.

[3] The accountants should discuss with the secretary those meetings for which minutes have not been approved. The letter should be modified to identify specifically the unapproved minutes of meetings that the accountants have discussed with the secretary.

§634 • **Letters for Underwriters and Certain Other Parties** 495

[4] If the interim financial information is incomplete, a sentence similar to the following should be added: "The financial information for April and May is incomplete in that it omits the statements of cash flows and other disclosures."

[5] If there has been a change in accounting principle during the interim period, a reference to that change should be included therein.

[6] SAS-71 (AU 722) does not require the accountants to modify the report on a review of interim financial information for a lack of consistency in the application of accounting principles provided that the interim financial information appropriately discloses such matters.

NOTE TO EXHIBIT AU 634-2: This letter assumes the following circumstances: The prospectus (Part I of the registration statement) includes audited consolidated balance sheets as of December 31, 20X5 and 20X4, and audited consolidated statements of income, retained earnings (stockholders' equity), and cash flows for each of the three years in the period ended December 31, 20X5. Part I also includes an unaudited condensed consolidated balance sheet as of March 31, 20X6, and unaudited condensed consolidated statements of income, retained earnings (stockholders' equity), and cash flows for the three-month periods ended March 31, 20X6 and 20X5, reviewed in accordance with SAS-71 (AU 722) but not previously reported on by the accountants. Part II of the registration statement includes audited consolidated financial statement schedules for the three years ended December 31, 20X5. The cutoff date is June 23, 20X6, and the letter is dated June 28, 20X6. The effective date is June 28, 20X6. Each of the comments in the letter is in response to a requirement of the underwriting agreement. For purposes of this example, the income statement items of the current interim period are to be compared with those of the corresponding period of the preceding year.

AU 700
Special Topics

Section 711: Filings under Federal Securities Statutes 499

Section 722: Interim Financial Information 505

SECTION 711

FILINGS UNDER FEDERAL SECURITIES STATUTES

Authoritative Pronouncements

SAS-37—Filings Under Federal Securities Statutes

Auditing Interpretation (May 1983)—Subsequent Events Procedures for Shelf Registration Statements Updated After the Original Effective Date

Auditing Interpretation (June 1992)—Consenting to the Use of an Audit Report in an Offering Document in Securities Offerings Other Than One Registered Under the Securities Act of 1993

Auditing Interpretation (March 1995)—Consenting to Be Named as an Expert in an Offering Document in Connection with Securities Offerings Other Than Those Registered Under the Securities Act of 1933

Overview

SAS-37 (Filings Under Federal Securities Statutes) provides guidance for the accountant whose report, based on a review of interim financial information, is presented or incorporated by reference in a filing under the Securities Act of 1933. SAS-37 also provides guidance for the auditor and accountant in the area of subsequent events that occur after filings with the Securities and Exchange Commission (SEC).

SAS-37 states that generally an accountant's responsibility for filings under federal securities statutes is no different from the accountant's responsibility in any other reporting engagement. However, the Securities Act of 1933 and its related rules and regulations contain specific duties and responsibilities for any expert whose report or valuation is used as part of a registration statement filed with the SEC. An accountant's report on a review of interim financial information is not a report under the existing rules of the SEC. If an accountant's report is based on a review of interim financial information, the SEC requires that any reference to such a report in any filing with the SEC contain a statement that the report is not a report on part of the registration statement under Sections 7 and 11 of the Securities Act of 1933. Thus, an accountant's report on a review of interim financial information is exempt under Sections 7 and 11 of the Securities Act of 1933. Section 11(a) is one of the most important sections of the Act, in specifying the duties and responsibilities of an auditor or an accountant.

> Section 11(a): If any part of a registration statement that becomes effective contains an untrue statement of a material fact

or omits a material fact required in order to make the statement not misleading, any person acquiring such security may either at law or at equity sue:

1. Every person who signed the registration statement
2. Every person who was a director or partner
3. Every accountant, engineer, or appraiser, or any other expert professional
4. Every underwriter with respect to such securities

Although an accountant's report based on a review of interim financial information is exempt from Sections 7 and 11 of the Securities Act of 1933, an auditor's report on an examination of financial statements that is made in accordance with generally accepted auditing standards is not exempt.

A registration statement is effective on the twentieth day after filing, or after filing of the last amendment to the registration statement. The independent auditor's statutory duties and responsibilities for his or her reports, other than those based on an interim review of financial information, do not cease until the effective date of the registration statement. Thus, an auditor must perform certain audit procedures to include the period from the date of the financial statements covered by the report through the effective date of the registration statement. This is called the "subsequent-events period." To complete a review of subsequent events, the auditor must arrange for the client to keep him or her informed of the progress of the registration statement. In the subsequent-events period, the auditor should employ the same audit procedures used to identify subsequent events in regular audited statements.

Promulgated Procedures Checklist

The auditor should perform the following procedures related to filings under federal securities statutes:

_____ Perform standard subsequent review procedures.

_____ Perform subsequent review procedures specifically related to filings under federal securities statutes.

_____ Determine whether unaudited financial information incorporated through reference is appropriate.

_____ Review documents filed with the SEC.

Analysis and Application of Procedures

Perform standard subsequent review procedures

The auditor should perform the same procedures typically performed as part of the review for subsequent events related to the audit engagement. These procedures are discussed in AU Section 560.

Perform subsequent review procedures specifically related to filings under federal securities statutes

In addition to the usual audit procedures for the subsequent-events period, the auditor should perform the following additional procedures:

1. Read the entire prospectus and the pertinent parts of the registration statement thoroughly.

2. Make inquiries of responsible executives of the client regarding any financial and accounting matters of a material nature that may have occurred during the subsequent-events period.

3. Obtain client representation letters covering any subsequent events that have a material effect on the audited financial statements.

A predecessor auditor whose report for a prior period appears in a filing with the SEC is responsible for subsequent events from the date of the financial statements covered in the prior-period report to the effective date of the registration statement that materially relate to the prior-period financial statements. The predecessor auditor should perform the following procedures:

1. Read the pertinent portions of the prospectus and registration statement carefully.

2. Obtain a representation letter from the current auditor on whether anything of a material nature came to his or her attention during the examination, including subsequent events, for which the predecessor auditor is required to disclose or make an adjustment.

3. If adjustments or disclosures are discovered that affect the prior-period financial statements, the predecessor auditor needs to be satisfied about what procedures are necessary under the circumstances. Thus, the predecessor auditor may need to make inquiries and perform certain audit procedures in order to be satisfied.

If the client refuses to make adjustments or disclosures for subsequent events as deemed necessary by the auditor, the auditor should follow the procedures promulgated for Subsequent Discovery of Facts Existing at the Date of the Auditor's Report. These procedures are discussed in AU Section 561.

> **PLANNING AID REMINDER:** The Auditing Interpretation (May 1983) of SAS-37 titled "Subsequent-Events Procedures for Shelf Registration Statements Updated After the Original Effective Date" states that an auditor must perform subsequent-events procedures as described in SAS-37, paragraphs 10 and 11, with respect to filing a single shelf registration statement that permits companies to register a designated amount of securities for continuous or delayed offering when (1) a posteffective amendment to the shelf registration statement is filed pursuant to Item 512(a) of Regulation S-K or (2) a 1934 Act filing that includes or amends audited financial statements is incorporated by reference into the shelf registration statement.

> **RISK ASSESSMENT POINT:** Another Interpretation (March 1995) of SAS-37 titled "Consenting to Be Named as an Expert in an Offering Document in Connection with Securities Offerings Other Than Those Registered Under the Securities Act of 1933" states that the auditor should *not* consent to be named, or referred to, as an expert with respect to a securities offering other than those registered under the Securities Act of 1933. Another Interpretation (June1992), "Consenting to the Use of an Audit Report in an Offering Document in Securities Offerings Other Than One Registered Under the Securities Act of 1993," states that an auditor may consent to the use of his or her audit report in an offering document other than the one registered under the Securities Act of 1933.

When subsequent events or subsequently discovered facts come to the auditor's attention, standards established by AU Section 560 (Subsequent Events) and AU Section 561 (Subsequent Discovery of Facts Existing at the Date of the Auditor's Report) should be observed.

Determine whether unaudited financial information incorporated through reference is appropriate

If unaudited financial statements or unaudited interim financial statements are presented or incorporated by reference in a filing with the SEC, and if the accountant subsequently determines that such statements are not in conformity with generally accepted accounting principles, the accountant must

§711 • Filings under Federal Securities Statutes   503

insist that the client make the appropriate disclosures or revisions. If the client refuses to make the appropriate changes, the accountant should consider withholding consent to the use of the report on the client's audited financial statements, if any, for filings with the SEC. The accountant should also seek the advice of legal counsel.

Review documents filed with the SEC

Usually, a prospectus contains an expert section that includes the names of the experts whose reports or valuations are included in the registration statement. An important procedure that the auditor or accountant should perform is to read all the pertinent sections of the prospectus, the registration statement, and any other documents filed with the SEC. No document filed with the SEC should imply that the independent auditor actually prepared the financial statements on which the report is based. Financial statements are prepared by, and are direct representations of, the management of an enterprise. The auditor or accountant should read the relevant sections of filings made to the SEC carefully to make sure that they contain no indication of responsibility for the financial statement greater than what was actually intended.

Practitioner's Aids

Exhibit AU 711-1, which is reproduced from SAS-37, illustrates acceptable wording to be included in a registration statement that describes the status of the accountant's review report that was part of the 10-Q filing and is now incorporated in the registration statement through reference.

EXHIBIT AU 711-1—DESCRIPTION OF STATUS OF REVIEW REPORT INCORPORATED THROUGH REFERENCE IN A REGISTRATION STATEMENT

The consolidated balance sheet as of December 31, 20X2 and 20X1, and the consolidated statements of income, retained earnings, and cash flows for each of the three years in the period ended December 31, 20X2, incorporated by reference in this prospectus, have been included herein in reliance on the report of _____ independent public accountants, given on the authority of that firm as experts in auditing and accounting.

With respect to the unaudited interim financial information for the periods ended March 31, 20X3 and 20X2, incorporated by reference in this prospectus, the independent public accountants have reported that they have applied limited procedures in accordance with professional standards for a review of such information. However, their separate report included in the company's quarterly report on Form 10-Q for the quarter ended March 31, 20X3, and incorporated by reference herein, states that they did not audit and they do not express an opinion on that interim financial information. Accordingly, the degree of reliance on their report on such information should be restricted in light of the limited nature of the review procedure applied. The accountants are not subject to the liability provisions of Section 11 of the Securities Act of 1933 for their report on the unaudited interim financial information, because that report is not a "report" or a "part" of the registration statement prepared or certified by the accountants within the meaning of Sections 7 and 11 of the Act.

SECTION 722

INTERIM FINANCIAL INFORMATION

Authoritative Pronouncements

SAS-71—Interim Financial Information

SAS-90—Audit Committee Communications

Overview

Interim financial information may be issued on a monthly or a quarterly basis or at any other interval deemed appropriate by the client or a regulatory authority. SAS-71 (Interim Financial Information) notes that an interim period also includes data or information issued for a twelve-month period ending on a date other than the client's normal year-end date. Interim financial information may be presented alone or may be included in a note to the audited financial statements. SAS-71 was issued to provide guidance for public companies for the review of interim financial information when (1) the information is presented alone as a separate financial statement(s), (2) the information is presented alone as summarized interim financial data, or (3) the information accompanies or is included in a note to the audited financial statements of a public or nonpublic entity. SAS-71 also establishes certain communications that are required when the accountant assists in preparing interim financial information or performs procedures thereon that are less than a review.

> **PLANNING AID REMINDER:** SAS-71 is applicable to interim financial information that is to be reviewed. Interim financial statements may be audited, in which case the auditor would follow generally accepted auditing standards. The special accounting practices and modifications established by Accounting Principles Board (APB) Opinion No. 28 (Interim Financial Reporting) and Financial Accounting Standards Board Interpretation (FIN) No. 18 (Accounting for Income Taxes in Interim Periods) should be followed in the preparation of the interim financial statements, with one exception. APB Opinion No. 28 states that the gross-profit method can be used to determine inventories at the interim date. If the interim financial statements are audited, the auditor would have to observe the inventory at or near the date of the interim statements.

Responsibility and function of the accountant

The purpose of an audit is to determine whether the financial statements are presented fairly in accordance with generally accepted accounting principles. A review of interim financial information differs significantly from an audit of financial information, because a review does not include the collection of corroborative evidence through the performance of typical substantive audit tests. Basically, the review of interim financial information consists of the performance of certain inquiries and analytical procedures. For these reasons, a review provides limited assurance on the interim financial information.

SAS-71 states that the purpose of a review is to provide the accountant with a basis for reporting whether material modifications are necessary for the interim financial information to be in conformity with generally accepted accounting principles (GAAP). The accountant acquires the basis for reporting by applying the standards for a review of interim financial information in accordance with SAS-71. The accountant issues a report containing an expression of limited assurance that, on the basis of the review, he or she is not aware of any material modification that should be made to the interim financial information for it to be in conformity with GAAP.

Pre-engagement planning

Rule 201 of the Code of Professional Conduct states, in part, that a professional service engagement must be adequately planned and supervised. The Code defines professional services as one or more types of services performed in the practice of public accounting. Thus, Rule 201 is applicable to a review of interim financial information.

In most instances, the auditor's review of interim financial information will be a continuation of a professional relationship that has included the audit of the prior period's annual financial statements. For this reason, much of the pre-engagement planning will be an extension of the audit engagement, which is discussed in AU Section 311.

Generally accepted auditing standards

SAS-71 notes that the purpose of a review of interim financial information differs significantly from the purpose of an audit of financial statements in accordance with generally accepted auditing standards. As noted earlier, a review of interim financial information does not provide a basis for the auditor to express an opinion on the interim information, because not all generally accepted auditing standards are followed. The nonobservance of GAAS is reflected in the scope paragraph of the report on a review of interim financial information.

General standards

Two of the general standards are concerned with technical training and due professional care. Rule 201 of the Code of Professional Conduct applies to services performed by a member in the practice of public accounting. This rule specifically states that a member shall (1) undertake only those engagements that he or she or the firm can reasonably expect to complete with professional competence and (2) exercise due professional care in the performance of an engagement. The third general standard of generally accepted auditing standards deals with independence. Once again, the Code of Professional Conduct extends the concept of independence to all other services performed by a member in public practice. Rule 201 states that members shall not subordinate their judgment to others or knowingly misrepresent facts.

Standards of fieldwork

The first standard of fieldwork is concerned with planning and supervision. Once again, Rule 201 extends these concepts to the review of interim financial information by requiring that all engagements performed by a member in public practice be adequately planned and supervised. Of course, planning a review is different from planning an audit engagement. The second standard of fieldwork deals with a client's internal control. SAS-71 requires that the accountant have a sufficient knowledge of the internal controls that relate to the preparation of annual and interim financial information, in order to:

- Identify types of potential material misstatements in the interim financial information and consider the likelihood of their occurrence.

- Select the inquiries and analytical procedures that will provide the accountant with a basis for reporting whether material modifications should be made in order for such information to conform with generally accepted accounting principles.

Finally, the third standard of fieldwork is concerned with the collection and evaluation of sufficient competent evidential matter.

SAS-71 does not require the auditor to collect evidence be to a degree that would allow the auditor to form an opinion on the interim financial information. However, SAS-71 does require that certain review procedures, mainly inquiry and analytical procedures, be emphasized before the accountant can issue a review report. In addition, Rule 201 of the Code of Professional Conduct requires that sufficient relevant data be obtained to afford a reasonable basis for the conclusions the accountant draws.

Standards of reporting

The first and third standards of reporting deal with accounting principles and adequate disclosure, respectively. Although the accountant does not express an opinion on the reviewed interim financial information, known departures from GAAP or inadequate disclosures would require that the accountant modify the review report. The fourth reporting standard is concerned with the accountant's expression of an opinion on the financial statements taken as a whole. Although SAS-71 does not provide a basis for the expression of an opinion on the interim financial information, it does require that a negative assurance and a disclaimer of opinion be expressed. The second reporting standard is concerned with the consistent application of accounting principles.

Promulgated Procedures Checklist

The auditor should perform the following procedures when reporting on interim financial information:

_____ Consider preparing an engagement letter.

_____ Determine whether accounting principles are appropriate for interim reporting.

_____ Adequately plan the interim engagement.

_____ Obtain a sufficient knowledge of internal controls.

_____ Obtain appropriate evidence related to the interim engagement.

_____ Prepare an appropriate accountant's report on the interim information.

Analysis and Application of Procedures

Consider preparing an engagement letter

SAS-71 states that the auditor should make sure that the client understands the nature of a review engagement and the type of report that the accountant will issue. Ideally, the nature of the engagement should be documented in a separate engagement letter or as part of the audit engagement letter. The letter should include (1) a general description of procedures the accountant will employ, (2) an explanation that the engagement will not be conducted in accordance with generally accepted auditing standards, (3) a description

§722 • **Interim Financial Information** 509

of the review report that the accountant will issue, and (4) a statement that management is responsible for the financial information.

An example of an engagement letter is presented in Exhibit AU 722-1 below.

Determine whether accounting principles are appropriate for interim reporting

In Opinion No. 28, the APB concluded that interim financial statements generally should be based on the accounting principles and practices used by an enterprise in the preparation of its latest annual financial statements. The APB recognized that certain accounting practices should be modified when they are applied to interim financial data.

Each interim period must be viewed as an integral part of the annual period, and accounting principles and reporting practices should be based on those principles and practices that were used in the preparation of the latest annual reports of the entity, unless there has been a change in an accounting principle.

The accounting and reporting on the results of operations for interim financial statements are discussed in the following paragraphs.

Revenues are recognized as earned using the same methods as those used in the preparation of the company's annual financial statements.

As closely as possible, product costs are determined in a manner similar to the methods used to prepare the company's annual financial statement. The following exceptions apply to the valuation of inventory:

- Companies using the gross-profit method to determine interim inventory costs, or other methods different from those used for annual inventory valuation, should disclose the method used at the interim date and any material difference from the reconciliation with the annual physical inventory.

- A liquidation of a base-period LIFO (last in, first out) inventory at an interim date that apparently will be replaced by the end of the annual period should be valued at the expected cost of replacement. Cost of sales for the interim period should include the expected cost of replacement and not the cost of the base-period LIFO inventory.

- Inventory losses from market declines should be included in the interim period in which they occur, and gains in subsequent interim periods should be recognized in such interim periods but should not exceed the losses included in prior interim periods.

- Inventory and product costs computed by the use of a standard cost accounting system should be determined by the same procedures used at the end of a fiscal year. Variances from standard costs that are expected to be eliminated by the end of the fiscal year need not be included in interim-period statements.

Other costs and expenses should be charged or allocated to produce a fair presentation of the results of operation, cash flows, and financial position for all interim periods. The following should apply in accounting for other costs and expenses:

- The general rule in preparing interim-period financial statements is that costs and expenses that clearly benefit more than one period should be properly allocated to the periods affected. This procedure should be consistently applied.
- Companies that have material seasonal revenue variations must avoid the possibility that interim-period financial statements become misleading. Disclosure of material seasonal revenue variations should be made in the interim-period financial statements. It is desirable also to disclose results for a full year, ending at the interim date.
- Unusual and infrequent transactions that are material and are not designated as extraordinary items, such as the effects of a disposal of a segment of a business, should be reported separately in the interim periods in which they occur.
- All other pertinent information, such as accounting changes, contingencies, seasonal results, and purchase or pooling transactions, should be disclosed to provide the necessary information for the proper understanding of the interim financial statements.

Interim reports should not contain arbitrary amounts of costs or expenses. Estimates should be reasonable and should be based on all available information applied consistently from period to period. An effective tax rate is used for income tax provision in interim periods.

Material contingencies and other uncertainties that exist at an interim date must be disclosed in interim reports in the same manner as that required for annual reports. However, contingencies and uncertainties at an interim date should be evaluated in relation to the annual report. The disclosure for such items must be repeated in every interim report and annual report until the contingency is resolved or becomes immaterial.

Reporting accounting changes—interim periods

The cumulative effect of an accounting change is always included in net income of the first interim period, regardless of in which interim period during the year the accounting change occurs. If the accounting change occurs in other than the first interim period, the current-period and prior-period interim statements should be restated to reflect the newly adopted accounting principle. However, the cumulative effect of the change in an accounting principle is included only in the net income of the first interim period.

When the cumulative effect of a change in an accounting principle cannot be determined, the pro forma amounts cannot be computed. In this event, the cumulative effect and pro forma amounts are omitted. However, the amount of the effect of adopting the new accounting principle and its per-share data for each interim period and year-to-date amounts must be disclosed in a footnote to the financial statements, along with the reasons for omitting the cumulative effect and pro forma information.

Publicly traded companies that do not issue separate fourth-quarter reports must disclose in a note to their annual reports any effect of an accounting change made during the fourth quarter. This is similar to other disclosure requirements of publicly traded companies that do not issue fourth-quarter interim reports.

The following disclosure concerning a cumulative-effect type accounting change should be made in interim financial reports:

1. The nature and justification of the change should be made in the interim period in which the new accounting principle is adopted.

2. The effects of the accounting change on income from continuing operations, net income, and related per share data for both, should be made:

   — In the interim period in which the change is made

   — In each, if any, prior interim period

   — In each, if any, restated prior interim period

   — In year-to-date and in last-twelve-months-to-date financial reports that include the adoption of a new accounting principle

   — In interim financial reports of the fiscal year, subsequent to the interim period in which the accounting change was adopted

3. The pro forma effects of the accounting change on income from continuing operations, net income, and related per-share data should be made:

   — For the interim period in which the change is made

   — For any interim period of prior fiscal years for which financial information is presented

   — In year-to-date and last-twelve-months-to-date financial reports that include the adoption of a new accounting principle

If no interim periods of prior fiscal years are presented, note disclosure for the corresponding interim period of the immediate fiscal year in which the accounting change occurred should be made for actual and pro forma income from continuing operations, net income, and related per share data.

Summarized interim financial statements

Publicly traded companies reporting summarized financial information at interim dates should include the following minimum information:

1. Gross revenues, provision for income taxes, extraordinary items, effects of accounting changes (principle or practice), and net income
2. Primary and fully diluted earnings-per-share data
3. Material seasonal variations of revenues, costs, or expenses
4. Contingent items and effects of the disposal of a segment of a business
5. Material cash flows

Summarized interim financial statements based on these minimum disclosures do not constitute a fair presentation of financial position and results of operations in conformity with GAAP.

In the event that fourth-quarter results are not issued separately, the annual report of a public company should include disclosures for the fourth quarter on the aggregate effect of material year-end adjustments and infrequently occurring items, extraordinary items, and disposal of business segments that occurred in the fourth quarter.

When summarized interim financial information is not presented by a public company, significant changes in liquid assets, working capital, long-term liabilities, and stockholders' equity should be disclosed and disseminated to the public.

Adequately plan the interim engagement

In most instances, the review of interim financial information likely would be an extension of the audit engagement. When the auditor has previously audited the annual financial statements of the client for the immediately preceding year, the audit engagement should provide a basis for the review of subsequent interim financial information. SAS-71 specifically notes that knowledge of the client's internal control includes the five component elements. (See AU Section 319 for a list of the components.) SAS-71 requires that when the accountant has not audited the preceding year's financial statements, he or she must nonetheless obtain a sufficient knowledge of the client's internal control that relates to the preparation of annual and interim financial information.

Part of planning an engagement for the review of interim financial information should include evaluating any new accounting standard and how it might affect the client's interim financial information. For example, the issuance of a pronouncement by the Financial Accounting Standards Board (FASB) that prohibits the capitalization of costs that previously could be deferred should alert the accountant that there may be changes in the interrelationship of accounting information. Moreover, such action by the FASB would require that the accountant ask the client how the new pronouncement affected its accounting system and what specific procedures it has adopted to ensure the observance of the new accounting rule. Of course, the accountant should be aware of special accounting principles or practices, if any, that are unique to the client's industry or transactions.

Adequate planning of a review of interim financial information must include consideration of the degree of centralization of the client's accounting function. If the client has multiple locations but the general accounting is performed only at one central location, there would be no need to visit the other locations. When a significant amount of information is processed at multiple locations, however, the accountant must select review procedures and apply them at both the central accounting location and other locations. In some instances, other accountants may review the other locations. Under this circumstance, the accountant may be placed in the position of a principal accountant and must evaluate and coordinate the work of the other accountants and decide whether to refer to the work of the other accountants in the interim review report. Relationships and procedures associated with an audit engagement involving a principal auditor and other auditors are discussed in AU Section 326. These guidelines are applicable to a principal accountant in a review of interim financial information.

Planning of the interim review is affected by the very nature of interim financial data. Interim financial information is typically released to interested parties more quickly than is audited information. SAS-71 notes that some review procedures may be performed before the end of the interim period to increase the likelihood that the interim review will be completed on a timely basis. Performing some review procedures early in the engagement also may help the accountant identify problems that can be addressed earlier in the engagement.

Generally, interim review engagements will encompass periods that eventually will be audited. The procedures normally used in the review of interim financial information may be modified because of the use of procedures performed in conjunction with the audit of financial statements. For example, an engagement may include the review of interim data for each of the first three quarters of a year and the audit of the annual financial statements. Preliminary work for the audit engagement may reduce the need for the accountant to perform certain procedures for the second-quarter and third-quarter interim financial statement reviews.

Obtain a sufficient knowledge of internal controls

SAS-71 requires the accountant to obtain a sufficient knowledge of the client's internal controls that relate to the preparation of annual and interim financial information. However, in most interim review engagements, the accountant would have audited the preceding year's annual financial statements, which would have included an assessment of the client's internal controls. During a subsequent interim review, the accountant should ask the client whether there have been any significant changes in internal control, and should evaluate changes to determine whether they may affect the client's ability to prepare interim financial information in accordance with generally accepted accounting principles.

In a first-time engagement with a new client, an accountant who has been engaged to perform a review of interim financial information cannot be expected to understand the client's internal controls. SAS-71 requires that the accountant possess adequate knowledge and understanding of the client's accounting and reporting practices and internal controls. Thus, in a new engagement the accountant must develop an understanding or the client's internal control.

With respect to internal control, the accountant's inquiries should be structured to determine whether there have been changes in control since the completion of the preceding audit engagement and to identify controls for interim financial reporting that differ from controls used for annual financial reporting. Interim financial reporting procedures may differ from annual reporting procedures because (1) it is usually necessary to use more estimates at the interim date and (2) accounts at an interim date may be affected by forecasts of results for the entire year. The accountant must evaluate these procedures to determine whether they are appropriate for the preparation of interim financial data. If the accountant concludes that there are reportable conditions in internal control as it applies to the preparation of interim data, the implications for the engagement should be considered. In some instances, these conditions may be viewed as a restriction on the scope of the engagement, and the accountant may decide not to issue an interim review report or not to permit his or her name to be used in a written communication containing the interim financial information. The accountant should notify senior management and the client's board of directors or audit committee of reportable conditions in internal controls that are used to prepare interim financial data, and the accountant may make suggestions to the client for improving the controls.

§722 • Interim Financial Information

Obtain appropriate evidence related to the interim engagement

A review of interim financial information does not include tests of the accounting records or the collection of corroborating evidential matter through the use of audit procedures such as confirmation, observation, and inspection. For the most part, an interim review consists of inquiries and analytical procedures. These procedures are directed toward significant accounting matters that could affect interim financial information. SAS-71 lists the following analytical procedures that normally would be employed:

- Through inquiries, obtain information about the following:
  — Internal controls for both annual and interim financial information
  — Significant changes in internal controls since the audit or review of the most recent financial statements

- Apply the following analytical procedures to interim financial information:
  — Compare the current-period interim financial information to the previous-period interim financial information.
  — Evaluate the plausibility of relationships among interim financial information and, where relevant, nonfinancial information.
  — Compare recorded amounts (or related ratios) to expectations.

  > **ENGAGEMENT STRATEGY:** When performing analytical procedures for interim financial information, the auditor may find the guidance established in SAS-56 (Analytical Procedures) and SAS-57 (Auditing Accounting Estimates) useful.

- To identify matters that may affect the interim financial information, read the minutes of meetings of (1) stockholders, (2) the board of directors, and (3) committees of the board of directors.

- Considering the information gathered through inquiry and analytical procedures, read the interim financial information to determine whether it conforms to generally accepted accounting principles.

- If appropriate, obtain review reports from other accountants who have been engaged to review the interim financial information of significant affiliates, for example, subsidiaries or other investees.

- Through inquiry of officers and other accounting or financial executives, determine the following:
  — Whether interim financial information has been prepared in accordance with generally accepted accounting principles

- Changes in accounting principles or practices
- Changes in business activities
- Responses to questions that have arisen from the application of other interim analytical procedures
- Events that have occurred after the date of the interim financial information but have an effect on the information

• Obtain written representation from the client. See SAS-85 (Management Representations) for guidance on what matters may be contained in the representation letter.

In a review of interim financial information, the accountant does not need to send audit inquiry letters to a client's attorney unless information comes to the accountant's attention that leads him or her to believe that the accounting for litigation, claims, or assessments pertaining to unaudited interim information departs from GAAP.

A review of interim financial information is not necessarily limited to the performance of the procedures described above. Other information that comes to the accountant's attention may provide a basis for additional inquiries. For example, if the accountant becomes aware that the client has significantly changed its product warranties, this change must be discussed with appropriate client personnel to determine its effect on the presentation of the interim data. In addition, the results of inquiries and analytical procedures may suggest to the accountant that the interim financial information may not conform to generally accepted accounting principles. In this case, the accountant should use whatever procedures he or she deems appropriate to resolve the questions that are raised.

> **PLANNING AID REMINDER:** The technique of inquiry and analytical procedures is considered relatively weak with respect to the criteria of obtaining competent evidential matter. However, these analytical procedures are not performed in isolation. The procedures can be performed successfully only if the accountant has (1) a thorough knowledge of the client's accounting and financial reporting practices and (2) a thorough understanding of the client's internal control.

The analytical procedures applied and the results of these procedures must be adequately documented in the workpapers. SAS-41 (AU 339) (Working Papers) notes that workpapers should aid in the conduct and review of an engagement and should provide adequate support for the conclusions the accountant reaches. SAS-71 does not contain specific suggestions about the content of workpapers for an interim financial information review.

§722 • Interim Financial Information

Communication with the audit committee

If the accountant believes that the interim financial information filed or to be filed with the specified regulatory agency is probably materially misstated, the accountant should discuss the matter with the appropriate level of the client's management. If, after being notified, management does not respond in a timely and appropriate manner, the accountant should bring the matter to the attention of the client's audit committee (or equivalent body). The communication with the audit committee may be written or oral; however, if oral communication is used, the communication should be documented in the workpapers.

If the audit committee does not respond in a timely and appropriate manner, SAS-71 concludes that the accountant should consider the following courses of action:

- Resign from the interim financial information engagement.
- Resign from the related audit engagement.

When selecting a course of action, the accountant should consider consulting with legal counsel.

Other matters that should be communicated to the audit committee include the following:

- Fraudulent acts discovered during the engagement, except those that are clearly inconsequential
- Illegal acts discovered during the engagement, except those that are clearly inconsequential
- Reportable conditions discovered

During the performance of the required procedures in a review of interim financial information, the CPA may discover matters that should be communicated to the client's audit committee. (These matters are discussed in AU Section 380, "Communication with Audit Committees.") The CPA should communicate these matters to the client's audit committee or should take appropriate steps to determine that the matters have been communicated to the committee.

In part, AU Section 380 requires that an auditor that has an SEC client should make judgments, as part of the audit engagement, about the quality of an entity's accounting principles used to prepare the annual, audited financial statements. However, a review of interim financial information is not the same as an audit engagement, and the CPA's judgments in a review engagement with respect to judgments about the quality of accounting principles used by the client would "generally be limited to the impact of significant events, transactions and change in accounting estimates" considered by the CPA in performing the review procedures.

> **PLANNING AID REMINDER:** When the CPA has conducted the review before the client's filing of the interim financial information with the SEC (or some other regulatory authority), matters discovered as part of the review that relate to required communications established by AU Section 380 should be communicated to the audit committee (or at least its chair) and an appropriate member of management. When the communication cannot be made prior to the filing, it should be made as soon as practicable under the circumstances.

Prepare an appropriate accountant's report on the interim information

Interim financial information may be presented in a set of separate financial statements, or it may accompany the audited financial statements. The way the accountant reports on the interim financial information depends on the method used to present the information.

The accountant cannot allow his or her name to be included in a written communication containing the information unless a review has been performed. The accountant's review report may be addressed to the client, its board of directors, or its stockholders, and usually it should be dated as of the date of the completion of the review. The standard review report itself should:

- Include a title that uses the word "independent."
- Identify the interim information subject to review.
- State that the information is the responsibility of management.
- State that the review was performed in accordance with standards established by the American Institute of Certified Public Accountants (AICPA).
- Describe the nature of review procedures.
- State that the scope of a review is substantially less than that of an audit in accordance with generally accepted auditing standards (GAAS), the objective of which is an expression of an opinion on the information.
- Disclaim an opinion on the information.
- State that nothing came to the accountant's attention that would suggest that the information needs to be modified in order for it to be in accordance with GAAP (limited assurance).

§722 • Interim Financial Information

The date of the auditor's report should be based on the completion date of the engagement, and each page of the interim financial information should be clearly marked "unaudited." Finally, the report should carry the manual or printed signature of the CPA firm.

Exhibit AU 722-2 presents an example of a review report that incorporates the requirements listed in the preceding paragraph.

When the interim financial information is presented on a comparative basis with that of the corresponding previous period and the accountant has reviewed the previous period, the accountant should report on the prior period.

Modifications to the standard review report

As with an auditor's report on audited financial statements, circumstances may arise that require the modification of the standard review report. However, because of the nature of a report on the review of interim financial information, the modifications are unique. They are summarized below.

Scope modification

An accountant may not be able to perform appropriate procedures for the review of interim financial information. Nonperformance of these procedures may result from an inadequate accounting system, client-imposed restrictions, or reportable conditions in the internal control. When the scope of the review is restricted, the accountant should not issue a review report or let his or her name be included in a written communication that contains the interim financial information.

> **RISK ASSESSMENT POINT:** SAS-71 does not establish a review report format that would be equivalent to a disclaimer of opinion or a qualified opinion on annual financial statements when the scope of the review has been significantly limited.

Using the work of another accountant

When an accountant has served as the principal auditor in the audit of a client's annual financial statements, it is likely that the accountant will be in a similar position with respect to reporting on a subsequent interim financial period(s). Under these circumstances, the accountant must decide whether to refer to the work performed by any other accountant. When the principal accountant decides to refer to the work of another accountant, the scope paragraph and negative assurance paragraph should clearly indicate the division of responsibility. The scope paragraph should disclose the magnitude of the portion of the interim financial information reviewed by the other accountant. The magnitude may be described by reference to one or more of the following: total assets, total revenues, or other appropriate criteria, whichever most clearly indicates the portion of the interim financial information reviewed by the other accountant. Dollar amounts or percentages may be used to describe the magnitude of the work performed by the other accountant. Reference to the work of another accountant is not a qualification but rather an indication of the division of responsibility between all the accountants involved in the review.

> **PLANNING AID REMINDER:** When an interim review engagement involves the use of another accountant, guidance established in SAS-1, AU Section 543 (Part of Audit Performed by Other Independent Auditors), should be followed.

Exhibit AU 722-3 illustrates a review report with reference by the principal accountant to the report of another accountant.

GAAP modification

During the review, an accountant may discover that the interim financial information is materially affected by a departure from generally accepted accounting principles. When this occurs, an explanatory paragraph should be added to the review report. The explanatory paragraph should describe the nature of the departure from GAAP and, if practical, the effects of the departure on the interim financial information. The last paragraph (limited assurance paragraph) must refer to the departure from GAAP described in the explanatory paragraph.

When a review report is modified because of a departure from generally accepted accounting principles, paragraphs similar to the ones presented below are added to the first two paragraphs of the standard review report.

> Based on information supplied to us by management, we believe that the company has excluded a net provision for loss or abandonment of certain properties that should be reported as a loss in order to conform with generally accepted accounting principles. This information indicates that if the loss had been recognized at March 31, 20X5, net income and earnings per share would have been decreased by $450,000 and $.17, respectively.
>
> Based on our review, with the exception of the matter described in the preceding paragraph, we are not aware of any material modifications that should be made to the accompanying finan-

cial statements [information] for them [it] to be in conformity with generally accepted accounting principles.

Inadequate disclosure modification

What constitutes adequate disclosure for interim financial information is not as well defined as disclosures required in annual audited financial statements. In Opinion No. 28, the APB adopted the philosophy that users of summarized interim financial data will have read the latest published annual report and that the limited interim data will be evaluated in that context.

When the accountant concludes that interim financial information does not contain adequate disclosures, the review report should be modified. The accountant should add to the review report an explanatory paragraph in which he or she describes the nature of the information that has not been disclosed. If practicable, the description should contain all the information necessary to achieve adequate disclosure. The final paragraph of the review report should refer to the explanatory paragraph, and a qualified limited assurance should be expressed. When a review report is modified because of inadequate disclosures in the interim financial information, paragraphs similar to the following are to be added to the first two paragraphs of the standard review report:

> Management has informed us that on April 10, 20X1, the Company issued debentures in the amount of $2,500,000 for the purpose of financing the construction of a new research and development facility. The debentures were placed with a consortium of private investors. The interim financial information failed to disclose this matter, which we believe is required to be disclosed in conformity with generally accepted accounting principles.
>
> On the basis of our review, with the exception of the matter described in the preceding paragraph, we are not aware of any material modifications that should be made to the accompanying financial statements [information] for them [it] to be in conformity with generally accepted accounting principles.

Going-concern modification

SAS-71 states that, normally, substantial doubt about the entity's ability to continue as a going concern would not require the accountant to modify the report, provided the appropriate disclosures were made in the interim financial information. Apparently this position is taken because the accountant is not expressing an opinion on the interim financial information.

Inconsistency modification

A change in the application of accounting principles affecting an interim period will not result in a modification of the standard review report if the inconsistency is appropriately disclosed. If an inconsistency is not appropriately disclosed in the interim financial information, the accountant's report would have to be modified on the basis of inadequate disclosure.

If the newly adopted accounting principle is not generally accepted, the review report must be modified in the same manner as it would be for a departure from GAAP.

Subsequent events

Ordinarily the review report is dated as of the date of completion of the review of interim financial information. However, three circumstances may lead to a departure from this dating practice when a subsequent event occurs after the date of the interim review but before the report is issued. These three circumstances are summarized as follows:

- The subsequent event results in an adjustment to the interim financial information, and the event is disclosed.

- The subsequent event is disclosed in a note to the supplementary information.

- A subsequent event is not properly accounted for (that is, an adjustment is not made or the event is not disclosed), and the review report is modified because of this departure from GAAP.

When any one of these three circumstances occurs, the accountant must dual-date the interim review report. A dual-dating might read: "April 12, 20X5, except for Note B, as to which date is April 22, 20X5." Alternatively, the accountant may use the single date on which the subsequent event was discovered. In the example, that date is April 22. It should be remembered that when the later date is used, the accountant's responsibilities with respect to other subsequent events extend to that date.

Responsibilities after the report date

An accountant has no responsibility to continue investigating interim financial information after the date of the accountant's report.

Nonetheless, the accountant should *not* ignore the subsequent discovery of facts that existed at the date of the report and that may have had an effect on the accountant's report. SAS-71 does not provide specific guidance for this circumstance, but it recommends that the accountant consider the standards established in SAS-1, AU Section 561 (Subsequent Discovery of Facts Existing at the Date of the Auditor's Report).

Reports on interim financial information accompanying audited financial statements

Certain public companies must disclose selected quarterly financial data in their annual reports or other documents that contain audited financial statements and are filed with the SEC. These disclosures are considered supplementary information and are not a required part of the basic financial statements. Each page of the supplementary information must be clearly marked as "unaudited." The accountant should apply the interim review procedures on the supplementary information that were described earlier in this Section. When the accountant has reviewed the interim financial information, usually no reference is made to the interim review in the auditor's report on the audited financial statements. The reason for not referring to the review or to the interim financial information is that it is considered supplementary information and is not needed in order for the annual financial statements to be presented in accordance with generally accepted accounting principles.

Companies that are not required to disclose the mandated SEC quarterly information may voluntarily choose to disclose this information along with their audited financial statements. Under these circumstances, the auditor must review the supplementary data using the interim review procedures described earlier in this Section, unless the company indicates that the data have not been reviewed or unless the auditor expands the standard audit report by noting that the supplementary data have not been reviewed.

The auditor's report on the annual financial statements must be modified if the client does not present the quarterly financial data required by the SEC. Under these circumstances, an additional paragraph is included in the three-paragraph standard audit report. It might read as follows:

> The Company has not presented the selected quarterly financial data, specified by item 302(a) of Regulation S-K, which the Securities and Exchange Commission requires as supplementary information to the basic financial statements.

When the quarterly financial information is included but the auditor has not reviewed the information, the additional paragraph to the standard audit report might be worded in the following manner.

> The selected quarterly financial data on page X contain information that we did not audit, and accordingly, we do not express

an opinion on that data. We attempted, but were unable, to review the quarterly data in accordance with standards established by the American Institute of Certified Public Accountants, because we believe that the company's system for preparing interim financial information does not provide an adequate basis to enable us to complete such a review.

When the interim information is not presented or a review of the interim information is not made, the inclusion of an additional paragraph does not provide the basis for a qualified opinion on the audited financial statements. Therefore, the opinion paragraph contains no reference to the additional paragraph on the selected quarterly financial data.

In addition, the standard auditor's report should be modified under the following conditions:

- Interim financial information included in a note to the audited financial statements has been reviewed but has not been clearly marked as "unaudited."
- Quarterly information voluntarily presented has not been reviewed, and the information has not been marked as "not reviewed."
- The interim financial information does not appear to be presented in accordance with generally accepted accounting principles, and the auditor's separate review report, which refers to the departure, is not presented with the information.
- The client notes that a review was made of the interim information but fails to state that a review is substantially less than an audit, and the accountant's separate review report is not presented with the information.

Although these circumstances would lead to an expansion of the auditor's standard report on the annual financial statements, they are not a basis for the expression of a qualified opinion.

Practitioner's Aids

The following exhibits are presented below.

- Exhibit AU 722-1—Engagement Letter for a Review of Interim Financial Information
- Exhibit AU 722-2—Accountant's Report on Interim Financial Information

- Exhibit AU 722-3—Review Report with Reference to the Work of Another Accountant

EXHIBIT AU 722-1—ENGAGEMENT LETTER FOR A REVIEW OF INTERIM FINANCIAL INFORMATION

X Company

[*Address*]

Annually, we consider it necessary to confirm our understanding of the terms and objectives of our engagement and the limitations on the services we will provide.

Our objectives will be to perform the following services:

We will review the income statement of X Company for the three-month and six-month periods ending June 30, 20X5, in accordance with standards established by the American Institute of Certified Public Accountants. We will not perform an audit of such interim financial statements, the objective of which is the expression of an opinion regarding the financial statements taken as a whole. Accordingly, we will not express such an opinion on them. Our report on the financial statement for each quarter is presently expected to read as follows:

We have reviewed the accompanying income statements of X Company as of June 30, 20X5, for the three-month and six-month periods then ended. These financial statements [information] are [is] the responsibility of the company's management.

We conducted our review in accordance with standards established by the American Institute of Certified Public Accountants. A review of interim financial information consists principally of applying analytical procedures to financial data and making inquiries of persons responsible for financial and accounting matters. It is substantially less in scope than an audit conducted in accordance with generally accepted auditing standards, the objective of which is the expression of an opinion regarding the financial statements taken as a whole. Accordingly, we do not express such an opinion.

Based on our review, we are not aware of any material modifications that should be made to the accompanying financial statements [information] for them [it] to be in conformity with generally accepted accounting principles.

Although we will review the financial information, your company's management is responsible for the financial information.

If, for any reason, we are unable to complete our review of your interim financial statements, we will not issue a report on such statements as a result of this engagement.

Our engagement cannot be relied on to disclose all errors, fraud, or illegal acts, including fraud or defalcations, that may exist. However, we will inform the appropriate level of management of any material errors that come to our attention and any fraud or illegal acts that come to our attention, unless they are clearly inconsequential.

Fees for the above services at our standard rates, together with any out-of-pocket costs, will be billed as the work progresses. Our invoices are payable on presentation.

We shall be pleased to discuss the services we are to provide you at any time. If you are in agreement with the foregoing, we request that you please sign the copy of this letter in the space provided below and return it to us.

Yours very truly,

[*Signature of accountant*]

Acknowledged:

X Company

[*Officer*]

[*Date*]

EXHIBIT AU 722-2—ACCOUNTANT'S REPORT ON INTERIM FINANCIAL INFORMATION

X Company
Stockholders and Board of Directors

We have reviewed the accompanying [describe the statements or information reviewed] of X Company as of June 30, 20X5, and for the three-month and six-month periods then ended. These financial statements [information] are [is] the responsibility of the company's management.

We conducted our review in accordance with standards established by the American Institute of Certified Public Accountants. A review of interim financial information consists principally of applying analytical procedures to financial data and making inquiries of persons responsible for financial and accounting matters. It is substantially less in scope than an audit conducted in accordance with generally accepted auditing standards, the objective of which is the expression of an opinion regarding the financial statements taken as a whole. Accordingly, we do not express such an opinion.

Based on our review, we are not aware of any material modifications that should be made to the accompanying financial statements [information] for them [it] to be in conformity with generally accepted accounting principles.

July 29, 20X5

[*Signature of accountant*]

EXHIBIT AU 722-3—REVIEW REPORT WITH REFERENCE TO THE WORK OF ANOTHER ACCOUNTANT

We have reviewed the accompanying [*describe statements or information reviewed*] of X Company and consolidated subsidiaries as of June 30, 20X5, and for the three-month and six-month periods then ended. These financial statements [information] are [is] the responsibility of the company's management.

We were furnished with the report of other accountants on their review of the interim financial information of Y Subsidiary, whose total assets as of June 30, 20X5, and whose revenues for the three-month and six-month periods then ended, constituted 25%, 10%, and 15%, respectively, of the related consolidated totals.

We conducted our review in accordance with standards established by the American Institute of Certified Public Accountants. A review of interim financial information consists principally of applying analytical procedures to financial data and making inquiries of persons responsible for financial and accounting matters. It is substantially less in scope than an audit conducted in accordance with generally accepted auditing standards, the objective of which is the expression of an opinion regarding the financial statements taken as a whole. Accordingly, we do not express such an opinion.

Based on our review and the report of other accountants, we are not aware of any material modifications that should be made to the accompanying financial statements [information] for them [it] to be in conformity with generally accepted accounting principles.

July 29, 20X5

[*Signature of accountant*]

AU 800
Compliance Auditing

Section 801: Compliance Auditing Considerations in Audits of Governmental Entities and Recipients of Governmental Financial Assistance 531

SECTION 801

COMPLIANCE AUDITING CONSIDERATIONS IN AUDITS OF GOVERNMENTAL ENTITIES AND RECIPIENTS OF GOVERNMENTAL FINANCIAL ASSISTANCE

Authoritative Pronouncements

SAS-74—Compliance Auditing Considerations in Audits of Governmental Entities and Recipients of Governmental Financial Assistance

Overview

SAS-74 addresses issues related to the audits of governmental entities and of entities that receive governmental support.

Promulgated Procedures Checklist

Appropriate audit procedures depend upon whether the audit relates to a governmental entity or to an entity that receives governmental support.

Analysis and Application of Procedures

Audits of governmental entities

As in every engagement, the auditor should consider all significant and relevant factors when planning and conducting an audit. Because of the nature of a governmental entity, an auditor should be aware of (1) laws and regulations that have a direct and material effect on the financial statements and (2) risk factors that are unique to a governmental reporting entity.

A governmental entity is subject to a variety of laws and regulations that do not apply to a commercial enterprise. For example, financial reporting requirements that a governmental entity must observe may be established by a law or regulation. More specifically, some governmental entities are required to establish separate funds to account for activities specified by a statute.

SAS-74 concludes that an auditor should obtain an understanding of laws and regulations that could have a possible direct and material effect on the financial statements. This requirement should be viewed in the context that the auditor is not a lawyer and that the management of the governmental entity is responsible for the preparation of the financial statements. Thus, the audit approach should include an assessment of management's identification of laws and regulations that may affect the financial statements. To achieve these audit objectives (understanding and assessment), the auditor may adopt the following procedures:

- Using prior-year audits, identify relevant laws and regulations.

- Discuss relevant laws and regulations with appropriate officials, including the entity's legal counsel and chief financial officer.

- Obtain written representations that (l) management is responsible for complying with laws and regulations that may have a direct and material effect on the financial statements and (2) management has identified and disclosed to the auditors all such laws and regulations.

- Review the relevant portions of any directly related agreements, such as those related to grants and loans.

- Review minutes of the entity's legislative body to identify laws and regulations that may be of concern to the auditor.

- Contact relevant oversight units, such as the state auditor, to determine which laws and regulations (including statutes and uniform reporting requirements) apply to the reporting entity.

- Contact program administrators of governmental entities that provided grants to the reporting entity for identification of terms of grants.

- Review compliance requirements compiled by state societies of CPAs or associations of governments.

- Review information about compliance requirements, such as the information included in OMB's Compliance Supplement for Single Audits of State and Local Governments; Compliance Supplement for Audits of Institutions of Higher Learning and Other Non-Profit Institutions; the Catalog of Federal Domestic Assistance, issued by the Government Printing Office; and state and local policies and procedures.

An integral part of an audit is the assessment of audit risk at the financial statement level and at the account balance or transaction class level. With respect to the audit of a governmental entity, the auditor must consider the effect that the possibility of violations of laws and regulations has on audit risk. Similarly, the auditor must consider a governmental entity's internal control in assessing control risk from the perspective that laws and regulations may be violated in such a manner that the financial statements of the entity would be materially affected. While SAS-74 does not attempt to construct a comprehensive audit program with respect to the consideration of a governmental entity's internal control and its observance of laws and regulations, several factors would be relevant to the auditor's investigation:

- Management's awareness or lack of awareness of applicable laws and regulations
- Entity policy regarding such matters as acceptable operating practice and codes of conduct
- Assignment of responsibility and delegation of authority to deal with such matters as organizational goals and objectives, operating functions, and regulatory requirements

In conducting compliance audit requirements described in SAS-74, the auditor should follow all applicable Statements on Auditing Standards, including SAS-41 (AU 339) (Working Papers), SAS-55 (AU 319) (Consideration of Internal Control in a Financial Statement Audit), and SAS-60 (AU 325) (Communication of Internal Control Structure Related Matters Noted in an Audit).

Audits of entities that receive governmental support

A governmental entity may provide a variety of financial support to other governmental entities, not-for-profit organizations, and commercial enterprises. The recipient of the financial support may be subject to laws and regulations that, if violated, may have a direct and material effect on the recipient entity's financial statements. SAS-74 notes that laws and regulations of this nature may involve the following restrictions and requirements:

- General requirements that involve national policy and that apply to all or most federal financial assistance programs, and
- Specific requirements that apply to a particular federal program and that generally arise from statutory requirements and regulations.

The auditor of an entity that receives financial aid from a governmental entity and is subject to laws and regulations that may have a direct and material effect on its financial statements should follow the guidelines discussed above (see section above titled "Audits of Governmental Entities").

AU 900
Special Reports of the Committee on Auditing Procedure

Section 901: Public Warehouses—Controls and Auditing
 Procedures for Goods Held 537

SECTION 901

PUBLIC WAREHOUSES—CONTROLS AND AUDITING PROCEDURES FOR GOODS HELD

Authoritative Pronouncements

SAS-1—Codification of Auditing Standards and Procedures (Section 901, Public Warehouses—Controls and Auditing Procedures for Goods Held)

Overview

Generally, the direct confirmation of the inventory held by outside custodians provides sufficient evidence to validate the existence and ownership of the inventory. However, if the inventory held by outside custodians is significant in relation to current assets and total assets, the auditor must supplement the confirmation by performing the following procedures:

- Discuss with the client (owner of the goods) the client's control procedures in investigating the warehouseman, including tests of related evidential matter.

- Whenever practical and reasonable, observe the warehouseman's or client's count of goods.

- If warehouse receipts have been pledged as collateral, confirm details with the lenders to the extent the auditor deems necessary.

- Obtain an independent auditor's report on the warehouseman's control procedures relevant to custody of goods and, if applicable, pledge receipts; or apply alternative procedures at the warehouse to gain reasonable assurance that information received from the warehouseman is reliable [SAS-43 (Omnibus Statement on Auditing Standards)].

Although these procedures are required by generally accepted auditing standards (GAAS), when the inventory of the auditor's client is held by a public warehouse, the public warehouse's auditor must also be concerned with the inventories owned by others but held by the public warehouse. In a special report issued by the Committee on Auditing Procedures (predecessor of the Auditing Standards Board) and incorporated as part of SAS-1 (Codification of Auditing Standards and Procedures), the following recommendations were made:

- Study and evaluate the system relating to the goods held for others.
- Test the system described above.
- Test the warehouse's accountability for recorded outstanding warehouse receipts.
- Observe physical counts whenever practical and reasonable.
- Confirm accountability with owners of the goods to the extent deemed necessary.
- Follow other audit procedures considered appropriate in the circumstances.

AT SECTION

Statements on Standards for Attestation Engagements

AT Section 101: Attest Engagements 541

AT Section 201: Agreed-Upon Procedures Engagements 563

AT Section 301: Financial Forecasts and Projections 571

AT Section 401: Reporting on Pro Forma Financial Information......595

AT Section 501: Reporting on an Entity's Internal Control Over
  Financial Reporting 605

AT Section 601: Compliance Attestation 620

AT Section 701: Management's Discussion and Analysis 635

For the latest information, refer to the *Miller GAAS Update Service* and the Miller GAAS Library, at http://www.MillerSeries.com.

AT SECTION 101

ATTEST ENGAGEMENTS

Authoritative Pronouncements

SSAE-10—Attestation Standards: Revision and Recodification (Chapter 1)

OBSERVATION: SSAE-10 supersedes SSAE-1 through SSAE-9.

SSAE Interpretation (August 1987)—Defense Industry Questionnaire on Business Ethics and Conduct

SSAE Interpretation (February 1992)—Responding to Requests for Reports on Matters Relating to Solvency

SSAE Interpretation (July 1990)—Applicability of Attestation Standards to Litigation Services

SSAE Interpretation (May 1996)—Providing Access to or Photocopies of Working Papers to a Regulator

Overview

Before standards for attest engagements (or attestation engagements) were promulgated, the professional standards did not specifically address certain types of auditing and accounting engagements. For example, there were no professional standards for engagements to report on (1) descriptions of computer software; (2) compliance with statutory, regulatory, and contractual requirements; (3) investment performance statistics; and (4) nonfinancial information supplementary to financial statements. These and other auditing and accounting engagements that are not addressed by other existing professional standards may be covered by the standards for attest engagements.

Statements on Standards for Attestation Engagements (SSAE) establish attestation standards that must be satisfied by an auditor when he or she is "engaged to issue or does issue an examination, a review, or an agreed-upon procedures report on subject matter, or an assertion about the subject matter (the assertion), that is the responsibility of another party" except in the following circumstances:

- Engagements performed in accordance with Statements on Auditing Standards (SASs)

- Engagements performed in accordance with Statements on Standards for Accounting and Review Services (SSARSs)

- Engagements performed in accordance with Statements on Standards for Consulting Services (SSCS)
- Engagements in which the auditor is the client's advocate (such as tax disputes with the Internal Revenue Service)
- Engagements to prepare tax returns or give tax advice

As suggested in the above definition, in an attest engagement subject to SSAE standards the auditor reports on subject matter or an assertion. SSAE-10 notes that the subject matter of an attest engagement can be varied and can include the following:

- Provide an assurance on historical or prospective performance or condition, such as historical financial information, perspective financial information, and backlog data.
- Provide an assurance on physical characteristics, such as the number of square feet in a building.
- Provide an assurance on historical events, such as the price of commodities on a specified date.
- Provide an assurance on analytical material, such as break-even analysis.
- Provide an assurance on systems and processes, such as internal controls.
- Provide an assurance on compliance with established procedures, such as laws and regulations.

On the other hand, when the attest engagement deals with issuing a report on an "assertion about the subject matter," the auditor is concerned with whether the assertion is based on or in conformity with the criteria selected.

In an examination or a review attest engagement, the auditor should obtain a written assertion. The written assertion could be communicated to the auditor in a variety of ways, including as a representation letter addressed to the auditor or a declaration on a related schedule.

> **OBSERVATION:** When a written assertion is not obtained, an auditor can report on the subject matter as explained later.

The responsible party in an attest engagement is "the person or persons, either as individuals or representatives of the entity, responsible for the subject matter." The auditor cannot be the "responsible party" even when the auditor has obtained information to help the responsible party to understand the nature of the written assertion. SSAE-10 points out that the responsible party must "accept responsibility for its assertion and the subject matter and must not base its assertion solely on the practitioner's procedures." In fact, the auditor can accept an SSAE engagement only if one of the following conditions is satisfied:

> The party wishing to engage the practitioner is responsible for the subject matter, or has a reasonable basis for providing a written assertion about the subject matter if the nature of the subject matter is such that a responsible party does not otherwise exist.
>
> The party wishing to engage the practitioner is not responsible for the subject mater but is able to provide the practitioner, or have a third party who is responsible for the subject matter provide the practitioner, with evidence of the third party's responsibility for the subject matter.
>
>> **PLANNING AID REMINDER:** The Interpretation (July 1990) titled "Applicability of Attestation Standards to Litigation Services" concludes that attestation standards apply only to litigation service engagements in which an auditor "is engaged to issue or does issue an examination, a review, or an agreed-upon procedures report on subject matter, or an assertion about the subject matter, that is the responsibility of another party."
>>
>> **PLANNING AID REMINDER:** The Interpretation (August 1987) of SSAE-1 titled "Defense Industry Questionnaire on Business Ethics and Conduct" states that Statements on Standards for Attestation Engagements apply to an engagement in which a practitioner has been requested to express a written conclusion on a defense contractor's Statement of Responses to the Defense Industry Questionnaire on Business Ethics and Conduct and the additional attached questionnaire and responses.

EXAMINATIONS AND REVIEWS

Due to the nature of attest engagements, SSAE standards require that the CPA establish an understanding of the engagement with the client. That understanding between the CPA and the client (preferably in writing) should include (1) the objectives of the engagement, (2) management's responsibilities with respect to the presentation, (3) the CPA's responsibilities, and (4) limitations of the attest engagement.

> **OBSERVATION:** The balance of this chapter discusses the general standards, fieldwork standards, and reporting standards in the context of an examination attest engagement and a review attest engagement. These standards also apply to agreed-upon procedures engagements, which is the subject matter of the following chapter.

Promulgated Procedures Checklist

The auditor should perform the following procedures in an attest engagement:

____ Preplan the attest engagement.

____ Plan the attest engagement.

____ Obtain sufficient evidence depending on the nature of the attest engagement.

____ Prepare an appropriate report on the results of the attest engagement.

____ Prepare appropriate workpapers.

Analysis and Application of Procedures

Preplan the attest engagement

Pre-engagement planning is an essential element of all professional engagements a CPA performs. The practitioner must determine whether the attest engagement will include an examination, a review, or the application of agreed-upon procedures. In addition, the practitioner must determine whether to accept or reject the attest engagement. The pre-engagement planning phase of an attest engagement is based on the first five general standards for attest engagements, which are discussed below.

General Standard No. 1—Training and Proficiency

The first general attestation standard states that "the engagement shall be performed by a practitioner having adequate technical training and proficiency in the attest function." Adequate technical training is a combination of an appropriate educational background and extensive practical experience. A CPA with adequate technical training should be competent enough to obtain and evaluate the necessary evidence to determine whether or not another party's written assertions are supportable. The CPA can develop proficiency only by applying knowledge he or she has gained in an actual attest engagement.

> **ENGAGEMENT STRATEGY:** Unlike the first standard of generally accepted auditing standards, the first general attestation standard does not refer to the auditor's technical training and proficiency. The scope of the attestation function described in the SSAE standards goes beyond the boundaries of financial reporting.

AT § 101 • Attest Engagements

General Standard No. 2—Knowledge of Assertion

The second general attestation standard concludes that "the engagement shall be performed by a practitioner having adequate knowledge of the subject matter." Although it can be assumed that a CPA is familiar with financial reporting standards, it cannot be assumed that a CPA is familiar with the procedures and concepts of all attest engagements. Thus, before a CPA accepts an attest engagement, he or she should have an adequate understanding of the nature of the written assertion(s). Obviously, a CPA cannot express an opinion on the written assertions unless he or she has a certain level of expertise relating to the nature of the assertions.

The knowledge required to perform an attest engagement may be obtained through a variety of sources, including formal courses and professional experience. Under some circumstances, the CPA does not have to master a portion of the expertise but may obtain it through the use of specialists [SAS-73 (AU 336) (Using the Work of a Specialist)]. When a CPA decides to use the work of a specialist, he or she must have a sufficient understanding of the subject matter to explain the objectives of the engagement to the specialist. The CPA must also be able to evaluate the work of the specialist to determine whether the objectives of the engagement have been achieved.

General Standard No. 3—Suitable and Available Criteria

Not all engagements provide a basis for attestation. The third general standard requires that the auditor "perform the engagement only if he or she has reason to believe that the subject matter is capable of evaluation against criteria that are suitable and available to users."

The fundamental element in the engagement is the existence of reasonable criteria that provide the basis for the written assertions. In an audit engagement, the reasonable criteria are generally accepted accounting principles (GAAP), which in turn provide a reasonable basis for the preparation of financial statements. Because of the diversity of attest engagements, there is no single set of reasonable criteria for all such engagements. However, SSAE standards note that criteria are considered to be suitable only if they have the following characteristics:

- Objective (free from bias)
- Measurable (provide a reasonable basis for the consistent measurement of the subject matter)
- Complete (no relevant factors that would alter a conclusion are omitted)
- Relevant (related to the subject matter)

There is no single source of criteria for the various attest engagements, and the auditor must use professional judgment to determine whether a specific set of criteria is suitable to a particular subject matter.

> **PLANNING AID REMINDER:** Criteria may be established by an appropriate professional group that follows due process or they may be established by a client or other parties or groups that do not follow due process procedures. In all cases the auditor must use the four criteria listed above to determine the suitability of criteria established for the attest engagement. An engagement should not be accepted "when the criteria are so subjective or vague that reasonably consistent measurements, qualitative or quantitative, of subject matter cannot ordinarily be obtained."
>
> **RISK ASSESSMENT POINT:** In some engagements the appropriateness of criteria may apply only to parties who have participated in the establishment of the criteria or that have a particular level or type of expertise. In these circumstances the auditor should restrict the use of the engagement report.
>
> **ENGAGEMENT STRATEGY:** The suitability of criteria is determined without regard to the type of attest engagement. For example, if criteria are considered to be unsuitable for an examination attest engagement, they are also unsuitable for a review attest engagement.

Finally, SSAE standards require that criteria be available to users under at least one of the following circumstances:

- The criteria are publicly available.
- The criteria are clearly presented in the presentation of the subject matter or the assertion.
- The criteria are clearly presented in the auditor's report.
- The criteria are commonly understood and are not unique to the attest engagement.
- The criteria are available only to the specified parties (and therefore the availability of auditor's report is restricted).

General Standard No. 4—Independence

The fourth general attestation standard requires that a CPA be independent in fact as well as in appearance. Independence in fact is a mental state of mind wherein a CPA is impartial in determining the reliability of assertions made in the written communication. In reaching a conclusion, a CPA favors neither the asserter nor the user of the information. Independence in appearance means that the CPA should avoid situations or relationships that may suggest to an outside party that the CPA is not independent.

General Standard No. 5—Due Care

The fifth general attestation standard requires that the CPA exercise due professional care in conducting an attest engagement. The CPA achieves due professional care by observing the two standards of fieldwork and the four reporting standards. For a CPA to agree to perform an attest engagement implies that the practitioner has a level of expertise that is possessed by other CPAs who perform similar services. Upon accepting the engagement, the CPA is expected to perform the engagement and exercise those skills to a degree expected by a reasonable person. However, this does not imply that the CPA's judgment is infallible or that he or she can be expected to fill the role of a guarantor of information contained in written reports. If the practitioner is not negligent in the execution of the engagement and conducts him- or herself in an honest manner, the due care standard generally will be satisfied.

Plan the attest engagement

Critical elements of every professional engagement include planning and supervision. The importance of these elements is recognized in the first standard of fieldwork, which states that an attest engagement should be adequately planned and that assistants, if any, should be properly supervised.

Fieldwork Standard No. 1—Planning and Supervision

Planning allows the practitioner to develop a strategy for conducting an attest engagement. Adequate planning matches the objectives of the attest engagement with the specific procedures that must be performed to achieve the objectives. Each engagement plan is unique, because it is based on the specific characteristics of a particular engagement. SSAE standards identify the following as factors that should be considered by the auditor in planning an attest engagement:

- The criteria that are the basis for the engagement
- Preliminary judgments about attestation risk and materiality related to the engagement.
- The likelihood of revision or adjustment of items within the assertion or the nature of the subject matter
- Possible conditions that may require that attestation procedures be modified or extended

- The nature of the attestation report that is expected to be issued by the auditor

In addition, an understanding with the client should be established and should include the following elements:

- The objectives of the attest engagement
- The responsibilities of management with respect to the attest engagement
- The responsibility of the auditor with respect to the attest engagement
- The limitations of the attest engagement

If an appropriate understanding with the client cannot be reached, the auditor should refuse the attest engagement.

> **RISK ASSESSMENT POINT:** The understanding with the client should be documented in the work papers, preferably through a written communication with the client (an engagement letter).

Obtain sufficient evidence depending on the nature of the attest engagement

The second standard of fieldwork requires that the auditor obtain sufficient evidence as a reasonable basis for the conclusion expressed in the attest report.

Fieldwork Standard No. 2—Sufficient Evidence

There are a variety of attest procedures that may be used to obtain evidential matter. The selection of specific procedures to be employed in a specific attest engagement is based on professional judgment. In addition, SSAE standards provide the following guidelines:

- Evidence obtained from independent sources outside an entity provides greater assurance of an assertion's reliability than does evidence secured solely from within the entity.
- Information obtained through the practitioner's direct personal knowledge (such as through physical examination, observation, computation, operating tests, or inspection) is more persuasive than information not obtained through the practitioner's personal knowledge.
- Assertions developed under effective internal controls are more reliable than those developed under ineffective internal controls.

The above guidelines are concerned with the quality of the evidential matter that is obtained in an attest engagement, but the CPA must also be concerned with the quantity of the evidential matter. Here again, professional judgment must ultimately be used to identify what constitutes sufficient evidence in an attest engagement. In addition, SSAE standards provide that the practitioner should consider the following items in determining the sufficiency of evidential matter:

- Nature and materiality of the information in the presentation of the assertions taken as a whole
- Likelihood of misstatements
- Knowledge obtained during current and previous engagements
- Practitioner's competence in the subject matter of the assertion
- Extent to which the information is affected by the asserter's judgment
- Inadequacies in the assertions' underlying data

The quality of evidence and the sufficiency of evidence must be determined in the context of the specific type of attest engagement. As described earlier, an attest engagement may be an examination engagement, a review engagement, or an agreed-upon procedures engagement.

Examination engagement Attest procedures must be selected so that the quality and quantity of evidence obtained is sufficient to reduce the attestation risk (probability of not discovering materially misstated assertions) to a low level. Of course, the overall attestation risk cannot be quantified, but the CPA must exercise professional judgment in order to assess inherent risk and control risk and must establish an appropriate level of detection risk. The practitioner has little influence, if any, on the levels of inherent risk and control risk in an attest engagement. However, the practitioner can influence the level of detection risk through the selection of attest procedures. The generalized relationships in Exhibit AT 101-1 can be used to establish an acceptable level of detection risk.

EXHIBIT AT 101-1—ACCEPTABLE LEVEL OF DETECTION RISK

Assessment Risk	Effect on Detection Risk Level
Inherent risk is assessed to be relatively high.	Detection risk should be established at a relatively low level.
Inherent risk is assessed to be relatively low.	Detection risk should be established at a relatively high level.

Assessment Risk	Effect on Detection Risk Level
Control risk is assessed to be relatively high.	Detection risk should be established at a relatively low level.
Control risk is assessed to be relatively low.	Detection risk should be established at a relatively high level.

After considering inherent risk, control risk, and detection risk, the practitioner should attempt to achieve a low level of attestation risk. In an examination engagement, the practitioner can achieve a low level of attestation risk by relying on search and verification procedures, such as physical observation, confirmation, and inspection, in addition to inquiry and analytical procedures.

Review engagement The level of assurance the practitioner provides in a review engagement is not as great as the level of assurance he or she provides in an examination engagement. In a review engagement, the auditor expresses a limited assurance, whereas in an examination engagement, the practitioner expresses a positive assurance on the assertions. For this reason, the level of attestation risk that must be achieved in a review engagement is a moderate level, rather than a low level. On the basis of the interrelationship of inherent risk, control risk, and detection risk, the practitioner selects attest procedures that will result in an overall moderate level of attestation risk.

Generally, in a review engagement, the CPA limits attest procedures to inquiry and analytical procedures, in much the same manner as an accountant would in the conduct of a review of historical financial statements. This is not to suggest that other attest procedures, such as search and verification procedures, are not appropriate under some circumstances. For example, Exhibit AT 101-2 presents circumstances that may be encountered in a review engagement and the effects of the circumstances on attest procedures.

EXHIBIT AT 101-2—CIRCUMSTANCES ENCOUNTERED IN REVIEW ENGAGEMENTS AND THEIR EFFECTS ON ATTEST PROCEDURES

Circumstance	*Effects of Circumstance on Attest Procedures Used in a Review Engagement*
Inquiry and analytical procedures cannot be performed.	Use other attest procedures to achieve a level of assurance that

Circumstance	Effects of Circumstance on Attest Procedures Used in a Review Engagement
	would have been achieved if the inquiry and analytical procedures had been performed.
Inquiry and analytical procedures are considered to be inefficient.	Use other attest procedures that are more efficient to achieve a level of assurance that would have been achieved if the less efficient inquiry and analytical procedures had been performed.
Inquiry and analytical procedures are employed, but results suggest that assertions may be incorrect or incomplete.	Use additional attest procedures to the extent deemed necessary to remove doubts about the accuracy or completeness of assertions.

ENGAGEMENT STRATEGY: The Attestation Interpretation (May 1996) titled "Providing Access to or Photocopies of Working Papers to a Regulator" notes that the guidance provided in the Auditing Interpretation (July 1994) (see the discussion in AU Section 339) for audit engagements also applies to attest engagements.

SSAE standards conclude that an auditor should consider obtaining a representation letter from the responsible party in both an examination engagement and a review engagement. To some extent the content of the representation letter will be unique to the nature of the subject matter, but elements of the letter may include the following:

- Acknowledgment of responsibility for the subject matter and, when applicable, the assertion
- Acknowledgement of responsibility for selecting the criteria
- Acknowledgement of responsibility for the appropriateness of the criteria (when the responsible party is the client)
- The assertion about the subject matter
- Representation that all known matters contradicting the assertion have been made available to the auditor

- Representation that communications from regulatory agencies related to the subject matter have been made available to the auditor
- Statement that all relevant records have been made available to the auditor
- Statement that material subsequent events related to the subject matter have been communicated to the auditor

> **ENGAGEMENT STRATEGY:** In an attest engagement in which the client is the responsible party the client will ordinarily be capable of providing the auditor with a written assertion about the subject matter. If the client does not provide a written assertion, the auditor should (1) modify the engagement report because of the client-imposed scope limitation in an examination engagement, or (2) withdraw from a review engagement. However, when a party other than the client is the responsible party and that party does not provide a written assertion, SSAE standards point out that the auditor "may be able to conclude that he or she has sufficient evidence to form a conclusion about the subject matter."

Prepare an appropriate report on the results of the attest engagement

Although the nature of attest engagements is varied, there are four reporting standards that must be observed in the preparation of the auditor's report.

Reporting Standard No. 1—Character of Engagement

The first reporting standard requires that the assertions being reported on and the character of the engagement be referred to clearly in the practitioner's report on the attest engagement. The examination or review report should provide an assurance on the subject matter or the assertion, describe the nature and scope of the engagement, and identify the professional standards that apply to the engagement.

Reporting Standard No. 2—Conclusions

SSAE standards require that the engagement report state the auditor's conclusion "about the subject matter or the assertion in relation to the criteria against which the subject matter was evaluated."

The nature and scope of the attest engagement should enable the auditor to draw a conclusion about whether there are material omissions or misstatements with respect to the subject matter or assertion. Professional judgment must be exercised to identify material misstatements. An item is considered material if a user of the information would be influenced by its omission or misstatement. Materiality is expressed in relative (percentage) terms rather than absolute (dollar) terms.

In an examination engagement, the auditor's report should express a positive conclusion about whether the presentation of assertions is in accordance with the established or stated criteria. The practitioner may expand the report by adding paragraphs that emphasize certain matters relating to the attest engagement or the presentation of assertions. This type of report modification does not result in a qualified opinion, and the opinion paragraph of the report should not refer to the emphasized matters.

Circumstances that may lead to the expression of an opinion that is not unqualified are discussed later in this chapter under the section on "Reporting Standard No. 3."

When a review engagement is completed, the auditor's report expresses negative assurance on the subject matter or assertion. In addition to negative assurance, the report should state that the scope of a review is narrower than that of an examination, and it should disclaim a positive opinion on the presentation. The practitioner may expand the report by adding paragraphs that emphasize certain matters relating to the attest engagement. Other circumstances that may lead to the modification of a review report are discussed later in this section under the discussion of "Reporting Standard No. 3."

Reporting Standard No. 3—Significant Reservations

The third reporting standard is unique in that it explicitly requires that the attest report include all significant reservations the auditor has with respect to the engagement, the subject matter and, if applicable, the assertions. When attestation standards have not been satisfied and the practitioner has significant reservations, an unqualified conclusion should not be expressed in the examination report or the review report. Significant reservations may be categorized as scope deficiencies and engagement reservations.

Scope deficiencies   The second standard of fieldwork requires that sufficient evidence be obtained to support the auditor's report. When significant reservations exist because of the limited scope of the attest engagement, the auditor should qualify or disclaim any assurance on the presentation of assertions or withdraw from the engagement.

Scope limitations may arise if all necessary or alternative procedures (examination and review engagements) cannot be performed because of the circumstances surrounding the engagement or because of restrictions imposed by the client. Generally, if the client imposes restrictions, the auditor should withdraw from the engagement and issue no report or should disclaim any assurance on the presentation.

When the scope limitation is caused by the practitioner's inability to perform attest procedures or express a conclusion on the presentation of assertions, the significance of the restrictions determines whether a qualified conclusion, disclaimer of conclusion, or withdrawal from the engagement is appropriate. Specifically, the actions the auditor should take depend on the following factors:

- Nature and magnitude of the scope restrictions
- Significance of restrictions to the presentation of assertions
- Nature of the service being performed (examination or review)

If the practitioner concludes that a qualified conclusion or disclaimer of conclusion should be expressed, the basis for the qualification or disclaimer must be described in the practitioner's report.

Engagement reservations The auditor may have reservations about the subject matter or the assertion concerning conformity of the subject matter with the criteria, which includes the adequacy of related disclosures. The nature of a reservation can relate to "the measurement, form arrangement, content or underlying judgments and assumptions applicable to the subject matter or assertion and its appended notes." Professional judgment must be exercised to determine whether the reservation results in a qualified or adverse opinion in an examination engagement or a modified conclusion in a review engagement.

> **PLANNING AID REMINDER:** According to the Interpretation (February 1988) of SSAE-1 titled "Responding to Requests for Reports on Matters Relating to Solvency," an accountant should provide no level of assurance, through an audit, a review, or an agreed-upon procedures engagement, that an entity (1) is not insolvent at the time debt is incurred or would not be rendered insolvent thereby, (2) does not have unusually small capital, or (3) has the ability to pay its debt as the debt matures. These and similar situations are referred to as matters relating to solvency.
>
> **ENGAGEMENT STRATEGY:** Although an accountant cannot provide assurance about matters relating to solvency, he or she can provide other services, such as the audit or review of the historical financial statements, the examination or review of pro forma financial information, or the examination or compilation of prospective financial information.

AT §101 • Attest Engagements

Reporting Standard No. 4—Restricted Distribution

The fourth standard of reporting requires that the engagement report specifically note that the report is restricted to specified parties under the following conditions:

- When the criteria used to evaluate the subject matter are determined by the practitioner to be appropriate only for a limited number of parties who either participated in their establishment or can be presumed to have an adequate understanding of the criteria
- When the criteria used to evaluate the subject matter are available only to specified parties
- When reporting on subject matter and a written assertion has not been provided by the responsible party
- When the report is on an attest engagement to apply agreed-upon procedures to the subject matter

When a restricted report is issued, that report should include the following points:

- A statement noting that the report is "intended solely for the information and use of the specified parties"
- Identification of the specified parties
- A statement that the report "is not intended to be and should not be used by anyone other than the specified parties"

Prepare appropriate workpapers

The work performed and the conclusions reached by the auditor should be adequately documented in the workpapers.

> **RISK ASSESSMENT POINT:** Workpapers are the property of the accountant, and he or she should establish appropriate procedures to protect the confidentiality of the information. Workpapers should be retained for a period that meets the legal requirements for and the needs of the accountant.

In general, the SSAE states that workpapers must demonstrate that Fieldwork Standards No. 1 (Adequate Planning and Supervision) and No. 2 (Sufficient Evidential Matter) were satisfied. Workpapers may include memoranda, engagement programs, and letters of confirmation and representation; however, the type of workpapers the auditor will prepare will depend on the circumstances of the engagement.

APPENDIX—ATTESTATION STANDARDS AND CONSULTING ENGAGEMENTS

An auditor may accept a consulting service engagement that includes an attest service as described in AT Section 101. The practitioner should perform the two separate phases of the single engagement by observing Statements on Standards for Consulting Services (SSCS) for the consulting phase of the engagement and Statements on Standards for Attestation Engagements (SSAE) for the attest phase. The auditor should explain to the client the difference between the two services and should obtain the client's agreement that the attest service should be performed in accordance with professional standards. The agreement that an attest service is to be performed should be documented in the consulting engagement letter.

Practitioner's Aids

The following practitioner's aids are based on illustrations provided in SSAE-10.

- Exhibit AT 101-3—Checklist for an examination report on a subject matter
- Exhibit AT 101-4—Checklist for an examination report on an assertion
- Exhibit AT 101-5—Checklist for a review report on a subject matter
- Exhibit AT 101-6—Checklist for a review report on an assertion
- Exhibit AT 101-7—Examination Report—Subject Matter
- Exhibit AT 101-8—Examination Report—Assertion
- Exhibit AT 101-9—Review Report—Subject Matter
- Exhibit AT 101-10—Review Report—Assertion (Restricted Distribution)

EXHIBIT AT 101-3—CHECKLIST FOR AN EXAMINATION REPORT ON A SUBJECT MATTER

An examination report on a subject matter should include the following:

- ❑ A title that includes the word "independent"
- ❑ An identification of the subject matter and the responsible party
- ❑ A statement that the subject matter is the responsibility of the responsible party

- ❏ A statement that the practitioner's responsibility is to express an opinion on the subject matter based on his or her examination

- ❏ A statement that the examination was conducted in accordance with attestation standards established by the American Institute of Certified Public Accountants and, accordingly, included procedures that the practitioner considered necessary in the circumstances

- ❏ A statement that the practitioner believes the examination provides a reasonable basis for his or her opinion

- ❏ The practitioner's opinion on whether the subject mater is based on (or in conformity with) the criteria in all material respects

- ❏ A statement restricting the use of the report to specified parties, if applicable

- ❏ The manual or printed signature of the practitioner's firm

- ❏ The date of the examination report

EXHIBIT AT 101-4—CHECKLIST FOR AN EXAMINATION REPORT ON AN ASSERTION

An examination report on an assertion should include the following:

- ❏ A title that includes the word "independent"

- ❏ An identification of the assertion and the responsible party (If the assertion is not included in the practitioner's report, the first paragraph of the report should also contain a statement of the assertion.)

- ❏ A statement that the assertion is the responsibility of the responsible party

- ❏ A statement that the practitioner's responsibility is to express an opinion on the assertion based on his or her examination

- ❏ A statement that the examination was conducted in accordance with attestation standards established by the American Institute of Certified Public Accountants and, accordingly, included procedures that the practitioner considered necessary in the circumstances

- ❏ A statement that the practitioner believes the examination provides a reasonable basis for his or her opinion

- ❏ The practitioner's opinion on whether the assertion is presented (or fairly stated), in all material respects, based on the criteria

- ❏ A statement restricting the use of the report to specified parties, if applicable
- ❏ The manual or printed signature of the practitioner's firm
- ❏ The date of the examination report

EXHIBIT AT 101-5—CHECKLIST FOR A REVIEW REPORT ON A SUBJECT MATTER

A review report on a subject matter should include the following:

- ❏ A title that includes the word "independent"
- ❏ An identification of the subject matter and the responsible party
- ❏ A statement that the subject matter is the responsibility of the responsible party
- ❏ A statement that the review was conducted in accordance with attestation standards established by the American Institute of Certified Public Accountants
- ❏ A statement that a review is substantially less in scope than an examination, the objective of which is an expression of an opinion on the subject matter, and accordingly, no such opinion is expressed in the review
- ❏ A statement about whether the practitioner is aware of any material modifications that should be made to the subject matter in order for it to be based on (or in conformity with), in all material respects, the criteria, other than those modifications, if any, indicated in his or her report
- ❏ A statement restricting the use of the report to specified parties, if applicable
- ❏ The manual or printed signature of the auditor's firm
- ❏ The date of the review report

EXHIBIT AT 101-6—CHECKLIST FOR A REVIEW REPORT ON AN ASSERTION

A review report on an assertion should include the following:

- ❏ A title that includes the word "independent"
- ❏ An identification of the assertion and the responsible party (if the assertion is not included in the practitioner's report, the first

paragraph of the report should also contain a statement of the assertion.)

- A statement that the assertion is the responsibility of the responsible party
- A statement that the review was conducted in accordance with attestation standards established by the American Institute of Certified Public Accountants
- A statement that a review is substantially less in scope than an examination, the objective of which is an expression of opinion on the subject matter, and accordingly, no such opinion is expressed in the review
- A statement about whether the practitioner is aware of any material modifications that should be made to the assertion in order for it to be presented (or fairly stated), in all material respects, based on (or in conformity with) the criteria, other than those modifications, if any, indicated in his or her report
- A statement restricting the use of the report to specified parties, if applicable
- The manual or printed signature of the practitioner's firm
- The date of the review report

EXHIBIT AT 101-7—EXAMINATION REPORT—SUBJECT MATTER

Independent Accountant's Report

We have examined the [identify the subject matter—for example, the accompanying schedule of investment returns of XYZ Company for the year ended December 31, 20X5]. XYZ Company's management is responsible for the schedule of investment returns. Our responsibility is to express an opinion based on our examination.

Our examination was conducted in accordance with attestation standards established by the American Institute of Certified Public Accountant and, accordingly, included examining, on a test basis, evidence supporting [identify the subject matter—for example, XYZ Company's schedule of investment return] and performing such other procedures as we considered necessary in the circumstances. We believe that our examination provides a reasonable basis for our opinion.

[Additional paragraph(s) may be added to emphasize certain matters relating to the attest engagement or the subject matter.]

In our opinion, the schedule referred to above presents, in all material respects, [*identify the subject matter—for example, the investment returns of XYZ Company for the year ended December 31, 20X5*] based on [*identify criteria—for example, the ABC criteria set for in Note 1*].

[*Signature*]

[*Date*]

EXHIBIT AT 101-8—EXAMINATION REPORT—ASSERTION

Independent Accountant's Report

We have examined management's assertion that [*identify the assertion—for example, the accompany schedule of investment return of XYZ Company for the year ended December 31, 20X5*] *is presented in accordance with ABC criteria set for in Note 1.* XYZ Company's management is responsible for the assertion. Our responsibility is to express an opinion on the assertion based on our examination.

Our examination was conducted in accordance with attestation standards established by the American Institute of Certified Public Accountants and, accordingly, included examining, on a test basis, evidence supporting management's assertion and performing such other procedures as we considered necessary in the circumstances. We believe that our examination provides a reasonable basis for our opinion.

[*Additional paragraph(s) may be added to emphasize certain matters relating to the attest engagement or the assertion.*]

In our opinion, management's assertion referred to above is fairly stated, in all material respects, based on [*identify established or stated criteria—for example, the ABC criteria set forth in Note 1*].

[*Signature*]

[*Date*]

EXHIBIT AT 101-9—REVIEW REPORT—SUBJECT MATTER

Independent Accountant's Report

We have reviewed the [*identify the subject matter—for example, the accompanying schedule of investment returns of XYZ Company for the year ended December 31, 20X5]*. XYZ Company's management is responsible for the schedule of investment returns.

Our review was conducted in accordance with attestation standards established by the American Institute of Certified Public Accountants. A review is substantially less in scope than an examination, the objective of which is the expression of an opinion on [*identify the subject matter—for example, XYA Company's schedule of investment returns*]. Accordingly, we do not express such an opinion.

[*Additional paragraph(s) may be added to emphasize certain matters relating to the attest engagement or the subject matter.*]

Based on our review, nothing came to our attention that caused us to believe that the [*identify the subject matter—for example, schedule of investment returns of XYZ Company for he year ended December 31, 20X5*] is not presented, in all material respects, in conformity with [*identify the criteria—for example, the ABC criteria set forth in Note 1*].

[*Signature*]

[*Date*]

EXHIBIT AT 101-10—REVIEW REPORT—ASSERTION (RESTRICTED DISTRIBUTION)

Independent Accountant's Report

We have reviewed management's assertion that [*identify the assertion—for example, the accompanying schedule of investment returns of XYZ Company for the year ended December 31, 20X5*] *is presented in accordance with the ABC criteria referred to in Note 1.* XYZ Company's management is responsible for the assertion.

Our review was conducted in accordance with attestation standards established by the American Institute of Certified Public Accountants. A review is substantially less in scope than an examination, the objective of which is the expression of an opinion on management's assertion. Accordingly, we do not express such an opinion.

[*Additional paragraph(s) may be added to emphasize certain matters relating to the attest engagement or the assertion.*]

Based on our review, nothing came to our attention that caused us to believe that management's assertion referred to above is not fairly stated, in all material respects, based on [*identify the criteria—for example, the ABC criteria referred to in the investment management agreement between XYZ Company and DEF Investment Managers, Ltd., dated November 15, 20X1*].

This report is intended solely for the information and use of XYZ Company and [*identify other specified parties—for example, DEF Investment Managers, Ltd.,*] and is not intended to be and should not be used by anyone other than these specified parties.

[*Signature*]

[*Date*]

AT SECTION 201

AGREED-UPON PROCEDURES ENGAGEMENTS

Authoritative Pronouncements

SSAE-10—Attestation Standards: Revision and Recodification (Chapter 2)

Overview

An auditor should observe the Statements on Standards for Attestation Engagement (SSAE) standards when performing an agreed-upon procedures (AUP) engagement except in the following circumstances:

- Engagements in which an auditor reports on specified compliance requirements based solely on an audit of financial statements, as addressed in paragraphs 19 through 21 of SAS-62 (AU 623) (Special Reports).
- Engagements for which the objective is to report in accordance with SAS-74 (AU 801) (Compliance Auditing Considerations in Audits of Governmental Entities and Recipients of Governmental Financial Assistance), unless the terms of the engagement specify that the engagement be performed pursuant to the SSAEs
- Engagements covered by paragraph 58 of SAS-70 (AU 324) (Service Organizations, as amended), when the service auditor is requested to apply substantive procedures to user transactions or assets at the service organization and he or she makes specific reference in his or her service auditor's report to having carried out designated procedures (However, SSAE standards for agreed-upon procedures apply when the service auditor provides a separate report on the performance of agreed-upon procedures in an attestation engagement.)
- Engagements covered by SAS-72 (AU 634) (Letters for Underwriters and Certain Other Requesting Parties, as amended)
- Engagements that would not be considered as subject to SSAE standards as described in the chapter titled "Attest Engagements" [see the previous chapter (AT 101)]

In an AUP engagement the auditor issues a report after performing specific procedures on the subject matter, the procedures having been agreed to by the auditor and the specified party. In this engagement, the specified procedures can vary greatly, but the specified party is responsible for determining the sufficiency of the procedures. For this reason, the use of the auditor's report must be restricted to the specified party or parties.

The general, fieldwork, and reporting standards for attestation engagements, as discussed in the previous chapter (AT 101), must be observed in an AUP engagement.

Promulgated Procedures Checklist

The auditor should perform the following procedures with respect to AUP engagements:

- Determine whether pre-engagement conditions exist.
- Perform appropriate engagement procedures.
- Prepare an appropriate report based on the scope of the engagement.

Analysis and Application of Procedures

Determine whether pre-engagement conditions exist

Before the accountant accepts an AUP engagement based on a written assertion, SSAE standards require that the following conditions be satisfied:

- The auditor must be independent.
- There must be an agreement between the auditor and the specified party on which procedures are to be performed.
- The specified party must take responsibility for the sufficiency of the agreed-upon procedures.
- The subject matter must be subject to reasonably consistent measurement.
- There must be an agreement between the auditor and specified party on the criteria to be used for determining the findings.
- The application of the agreed-upon procedures is expected to result in reasonably consistent findings using the criteria agreed upon.
- There is an expectation that evidential matter exists that will provide a reasonable basis for expressing the auditor's findings.
- There is an agreement between the auditor and the specified party with respect to materiality, where applicable.
- The use of the auditor's report is restricted.

AT §201 • Agreed-Upon Procedures Engagements

In addition to the above requirements, SSAE standards require that one of the following conditions exist:

- The party wishing to engage the auditor is responsible for the subject matter, or has a reasonable basis for providing a written assertion about the subject matter when the nature of the subject matter is such that a responsible party does not otherwise exist.

- The party wishing to engage the auditor is not responsible for the subject matter but is able to provide the auditor, or have a third party who is responsible for the subject matter provide the auditor with evidence of the third party's responsibility for the subject matter.

> **PLANNING AID REMINDER:** When the AUP engagement relates to prospective financial information, a summary of significant assumptions must be included in the prospective financial statements.

Identification and sufficiency of procedures

Generally the auditor should communicate directly with the specified party to determine which procedures are to be performed and to make it clear that the specified party is responsible for the sufficiency of the procedures. SSAE standards note that when the auditor is unable to communicate directly with the specified party, procedures such as the following should be employed:

- Compare the procedures to be applied to written requirements established by the specified party.

- Discuss with a representative of the specified party the procedures to be employed.

- Review relevant contracts or correspondence from the specified party.

Understanding with the client

The terms of the AUP engagement should be understood by the auditor and ideally should be expressed in an engagement letter. SSAE standards note that items that may be appropriate for the engagement letter include the following:

- Description of the engagement

- Identification of the subject matter (or the related assertion), the criteria used, and the responsible party

- An acknowledgment by the specified party with respect to the responsibility for the sufficiency of the agreed-upon procedures
- The auditor responsibilities
- Reference to attestation standards established by the AICPA
- Enumerating the agreed-upon procedures
- Description of disclaimers expected to be part of the auditor's report
- The restricted nature of the auditor's report
- Assistance expected to be provided to the auditor
- The work of a specialist, if any
- Materiality thresholds

> **RISK ASSESSMENT POINT:** In an AUP engagement the auditor assumes the risk that (1) misapplication of the procedures might result in inappropriate findings being reported and (2) appropriate findings might not be reported or might be reported inaccurately.

Perform appropriate engagement procedures

Specified users, not the auditor, are responsible for the nature, timing, and extent of agreed-upon procedures; however, the auditor must have an adequate knowledge of the specific subject matter to which the agreed-upon procedures will be applied.

The specific procedures to be employed in an AUP engagement are dependent upon the nature of the engagement; however, in general the auditor must "obtain evidential matter from applying the agreed-upon procedures to provide a reasonable basis for the findings or findings expressed in his or her report, but need not perform additional procedures outside the scope of the engagement to gather additional evidential matter." SSAE standards identify the following as appropriate procedures in an AUP engagement:

- Executing a sampling application after agreeing on relevant parameters
- Inspecting specified documents evidencing certain types of transactions or detailed attributes thereof
- Confirming specific information with third parties
- Comparing documents, schedules, or analyses with certain specified attributes

AT §201 • Agreed-Upon Procedures Engagements

- Performing specific procedures on work performed by others (including the work of internal auditors)
- Performing mathematical computations

On the other hand, the following would be inappropriate procedures in an AUP engagement:

- Merely reading the work performed by others solely to describe their findings
- Evaluating the competency or objectivity of another party
- Obtaining an understanding about a particular subject
- Interpreting documents outside the scope of the practitioner's professional expertise

Use of a specialist

In some AUP engagements it is appropriate for an auditor to use the work of a specialist; however, the auditor and the specified party should explicitly agree to that use. The auditor's report should explain the work performed by the specialist.

> **PLANNING AID REMINDER:** As one of the agreed-upon procedures, the auditor may agree to apply procedures to the work product created by a specialist. This approach is not considered the "use of a specialist" in the context of an AUP engagement. SSAE standards note that the auditor should not agree to simply read a specialist's report "solely to describe or repeat the findings, or take responsibility for all or a portion of any procedures performed by a specialist or the specialist's work product."

Use of an internal auditor or other personnel

The auditor is responsible for performing the agreed-upon procedures, but he or she may use internal auditors or other personnel to accumulate data and perform other similar procedures. In addition, the auditor may agree to perform procedures on information included in an internal auditor's working papers; however, SSAE standards point out that the following would be inappropriate:

- Agree to simply read an internal auditor's report for the sole purpose of describing the findings in the engagement report

- Prepare an engagement report in a manner that suggests that the auditor and the internal auditor share responsibility for the performance of the agreed-upon procedures

Prepare an appropriate report based on the scope of the engagement

Based on the performance of the agreed-upon procedures, the auditor should formulate the findings that are to be expressed in his or her report. The findings should be expressed in a manner that is clear and unambiguous. The report may also include explanatory language such as an explanation of sampling risk and descriptions of controls.

> **RISK ASSESSMENT POINT:** SSAE standards prohibit the auditor from expressing a negative assurance about the subject matter or the assertion.

Practitioner's Aids

The following practitioner's aids are based on illustrations provided in SSAE-10.

- Exhibit AT 201-1—Checklist for an AUP report
- Exhibit AT 201-2—AUP Engagement Report

EXHIBIT AT 201-1— CHECKLIST FOR AN AUP REPORT

An AUP report should include the following:

- ❑ A title that includes the word "independent"
- ❑ An identification of the specified party
- ❑ An identification of the subject matter (or the written assertion) and the character of the engagement
- ❑ An identification of the responsible party and a statement that the subject matter is the responsibility of the responsible party
- ❑ A statement that the procedures were agreed to by the specified party
- ❑ A statement that the AUP engagement was conducted in accordance with attestation standards established by the American Institute of Certified Public Accountants

- ❏ A statement that the specified party is solely responsible for sufficiency of the agreed-upon procedures; furthermore, the statement should disclaim any responsibility for the sufficiency of the procedures
- ❏ List the procedures performed and related findings
- ❏ Description of materiality thresholds, where applicable
- ❏ A statement that the auditor was not engaged to and did not conduct an examination of the subject matter, the objective of which would be the expression of an opinion, a disclaimer of opinion on the subject matter, and a statement that if the auditor had performed additional procedures, other matters might have come to his or her attention that would have been reported
- ❏ A statement restricting the use of the report to specified parties
- ❏ Reservations or restrictions related to procedures or findings, if applicable
- ❏ A description of the assistance provided by a specialist, if applicable
- ❏ The manual or printed signature of the practitioner's firm
- ❏ The date of the AUP report

PLANNING AID REMINDER: When the AUP engagement concerns prospective financial information, the guidance established in the chapter titled "Financial Forecast and Projections" (AT 301) should be observed in preparing an agreed-upon procedures report for prospective financial information.

EXHIBIT AT 201-2—AUP ENGAGEMENT REPORT

Independent Accountant's Report on Applying Agreed-Upon Procedures

To the Audit Committees and Managements of ABC Inc. and XYZ Fund:

We have performed the procedures enumerated below, which were agreed to by the audit committees and managements of ABC Inc. and XYZ Fund, solely to assist you in evaluating the accompanying Statement of Investment Performance Statistics of XYZ Fund (prepared in accordance with the criteria specified therein) for the year ended December 31, 20X1. XYZ Fund's management is responsible for the statement of investment performance statistics. This agreed-upon procedures engagement was conducted in accordance with attestation standards established by the American Institute of Certified Public Accountants. The sufficiency of these procedures is solely the responsibility of those parties specified in this report. Consequently, we make no representation regarding the sufficiency of the procedures described below either for the purpose for which this report has been requested or for any other purpose.

[Include paragraphs to enumerate procedures and findings.]

We were not engaged to, and did not conduct, an examination, the objective of which would be to express of an opinion on the accompanying Statement of Investment Performance Statistics of XYZ Fund. Accordingly, we do not express such an opinion. Had we performed additional procedures, other matters might have come to our attention that would have been reported to you.

This report is intended solely for the information and use of the audit committees and managements of ABC Inc. and XYZ Fund, and is not intended to be, and should not be, used by anyone other than these specified parties.

[Signature]

[Date]

AT SECTION 301

FINANCIAL FORECASTS AND PROJECTIONS

Authoritative Pronouncements

SSAE-10—Attestation Standards: Revision and Recodification (Chapter 3)

Overview

A prospective financial statement is either a financial forecast or a financial projection that reflects an entity's expected statement of financial position, results of operations, statement of cash flows, and summaries of significant assumptions and accounting policies. A prospective financial statement is based on expected future economic conditions that represent the best knowledge and belief of the person or persons responsible for the underlying assumptions in the forecast or projection. A prospective financial statement is a financial forecast or projection that covers a period of time that is partially but not completely expired or a period of time wholly in the future. Financial statements that cover an expired period of time are not considered prospective financial statements).

> **ENGAGEMENT STRATEGY:** Pro forma financial statements attempt to reflect the effects of a possible transaction or event on historical financial statements. Pro forma financial statements are not considered to be prospective financial statements. Pro forma financial information is discussed in the chapter titled "Reporting on Pro Forma Financial Information" (AT 401).

The person or persons who establish the underlying assumptions for the prospective financial statements are referred to in the attestation standards as the "responsible party" or "responsible parties." As a rule, the responsible party for a prospective financial statement is the management of an enterprise, but it may be a prospective buyer or some other outsider. An auditor who is engaged to report on prospective financial statements may assist the responsible party in identifying assumptions and gathering information for the forecast or projection. However, all of the underlying assumptions and the preparation and presentation of the prospective financial statements are the responsibility of the responsible party. Thus, the term *preparation of prospective financial statements* should not be used in the accountant's report or in any other correspondence relating to the engagement.

Under the attestation standards, an accountant who is engaged to report on prospective financial statements must determine whether such statements are intended for general use or for limited use. Prospective financial statements that are issued for general use are those that are intended to be used by parties that are not negotiating directly with the responsible party. Since the parties not negotiating directly are generally unable to make direct inquiries about the prospective financial statements, the most useful presentation for them is one that reflects the responsible party's best knowledge and belief of the expected results. Thus, only a financial forecast is appropriate for general use.

Prospective financial statements that are issued for limited use are those that are intended to be used only by the responsible party and those parties negotiating directly with the responsible party. Since the parties are negotiating directly and are able to make direct inquiries of the responsible party, either a financial forecast or a financial projection is appropriate for limited use.

A financial forecast reflects an entity's expected statement of financial position, results of operations, and statement of cash flows, based on the responsible party's assumptions of the conditions that are expected to exist during the forecast period and the course of action that is expected to be taken if the expected conditions materialize. A financial projection reflects an entity's expected statement of financial position, results of operations, and statement of cash flows, based on the responsible party's assumptions of the conditions that will exist during the projection period if one or more hypothetical assumptions occur and the course of action that will be taken if the hypothetical assumptions materialize. Thus, a financial forecast is based on expected future economic conditions and the course of action to be taken if the expected conditions materialize, whereas a financial projection is based on expected future economic conditions that will exist if one or more hypothetical assumptions occur and the course of action that will be taken if the hypothetical assumptions materialize.

A prospective financial statement may be prepared as a single set of estimates or as a range of estimates. To facilitate comparisons, prospective financial statements should be presented in the same format as that used for historical financial statements. The attestation standards require the following minimum presentation standards for prospective financial statements:

1. Sales or gross revenues
2. Gross profit or cost of sales
3. Unusual or infrequently occurring items
4. Provision for income taxes
5. Discontinued operations or extraordinary items
6. Income from continuing operations

AT §301 • Financial Forecasts and Projections

7. Net income
8. Basic and diluted earnings per share
9. Significant changes in financial position
10. Description of what the responsible party intends the prospective financial statements to present, a statement that assumptions are based on information about circumstances and conditions existing at the time the prospective information was prepared, and a caveat that the prospective results might be achieved
11. Summary of significant assumptions
12. Summary of significant accounting policies

Types of Engagements

An auditor can accept the following engagements for prospective financial statements:

- Review engagement
- Compilation engagement
- Agreed-upon procedures engagement

> **RISK ASSESSMENT POINT:** SSAE standards require that an auditor must perform one of the three types of engagement for prospective financial statements when the auditor "(a) submits, to his or her client or others, prospective financial statements that he or she has assembled, or assisted in assembling, that are or reasonably might be expected to be used by another (third) party or (b) reports on prospective financial statements that are, or reasonably might be expected, to be used by another (third) party."

EXAMINATION ENGAGEMENT

The purpose of an examination of prospective financial statements is to express an opinion on whether the statements are presented in conformity with American Institute of Certified Public Accountants (AICPA) guidelines and to determine whether the responsible party's assumptions provide a reasonable basis for the preparation of the prospective financial statements.

> **RISK ASSESSMENT POINT:** For financial projections, the accountant must determine whether the given hypothetical assumptions provide a reasonable basis for the responsible party's presentation.

Materiality is a highly subjective factor that the auditor must consider in the examination of prospective financial statements in the same manner as he or she would do in the evaluation of historical financial statements. Because of the higher degree of uncertainty associated with prospective financial statements, prospective financial information cannot be expected to be as precise as historical financial information. Thus, the range or reasonableness for evaluating prospective financial information is broader than the range an auditor would use to evaluate historical financial information.

> **RISK ASSESSMENT POINT:** An examination of prospective financial statements must observe the general, fieldwork, and reporting standards for an attestation engagement as described in the chapter titled "Attestation Engagements" (AT 101).

Promulgated Procedures Checklist

The auditor should perform the following procedures in an examination engagement for prospective financial statements:

- Establish an understanding with the responsible party
- Plan the examination engagement
- Obtain sufficient evidence to provide a reasonable basis for the report
- Obtain sufficient evidence concerning the reasonableness of assumptions
- Obtain sufficient evidence concerning the preparation and presentation of the prospective financial statements
- Prepare an appropriate report on the prospective financial statements

Analysis and Application of Procedures

Establish an understanding with the responsible party

The auditor should establish an understanding with the responsible party that includes (1) the objective of the engagement, (2) the responsibilities of the responsible party, (3) the auditor's responsibilities, and (4) limitations of the examination engagement. This understanding should be documented in the working papers, preferably through written communication with the responsible party.

> **PLANNING AID REMINDER:** When the client and the responsible party are not the same, the understanding must encompass the client as well as the responsible party.

AT §301 • Financial Forecasts and Projections

Plan the examination engagement

SSAE standards identify the following as some of the factors that are important in the proper planning of an examination engagement:

- Accounting principles to be used and the type of presentation
- The level of attestation risk related to the engagement
- Initial assessment of materiality
- Elements of the prospective financial statements that are likely to require revision
- Conditions that could change the nature, timing, or extent of examination procedures
- Understanding of the entity's business environment
- The responsible party's experience in preparing prospective financial statements
- The period of time covered by the prospective financial statements
- The process used to develop the prospective financial statements
- Understanding key factors (such as costs of production; competitiveness of markets; pace of technology within the industry; and past patterns of revenues, costs, and management policies) that will affect the prospective financial statements

Obtain sufficient evidence to provide a reasonable basis for the report

In an examination of prospective financial statements the auditor must collect sufficient evidential matter "to restrict attestation risk to a level that is, in his or her professional judgment, appropriate for the level of assurance that may be imparted by his or her examination report." The Statements on Standards for Attestation Engagements (SSAE) standards describe the purpose of an examination of prospective financial statements as follows:

> The practitioner provides assurance only about whether the prospective financial statements are presented in conformity with AICPA presentation guidelines and whether the assumptions provide a reasonable basis for management's forecast, or a reasonable basis for management's projection given the hypothetical assumptions.

There is no single list of engagement procedures that must be executed by the auditor in an examination of prospective financial statements; however, the SSAE standards point out that the following factors should be considered in determining the extent of examination procedures:

- The nature and materiality of the item under examination in relationship to the prospective financial statements taken as a whole
- The likelihood of misstatement
- Existing evidence obtained during the current engagement as well as previous engagements
- The competency of the responsible party in the preparation of prospective financial statements
- The degree to which the prospective financial statements are affected by judgments made by the responsible party
- The adequacy of the data that supports the prospective financial statements

Obtain sufficient evidence concerning the reasonableness of assumptions

Evidence must be collected to determine if assumptions used in the preparation of the prospective financial statements are reasonable.

Financial forecasts

The SSAE standards conclude that in a financial forecast engagement the auditor can be satisfied with respect to the reasonableness of assumptions made by the responsible party if the examination procedures lead to the following conclusions:

- The responsible party has explicitly identified all factors expected to materially affect the operations of the entity during the prospective period and has developed appropriate assumptions with respect to such factors.
- The assumptions are suitably supported.

Financial projections

The SSAE standards conclude that in a financial projection engagement (given the hypothetical assumptions) the auditor can be satisfied with respect to the reasonableness of assumptions made by the responsible party if the examination procedures lead to the following conclusions:

- The responsible party has explicitly identified all factors that would materially affect the operations of the entity during the prospective period if the hypothetical assumptions were to materialize and developed appropriate assumptions with respect to such factors.

- The other assumptions are suitably supported given the hypothetical assumptions.

> **ENGAGEMENT STRATEGY:** In determining whether assumptions are suitably supported in a financial forecast the auditor must be able to conclude that "the preponderance of information supports each significant assumption." For a financial projection, the auditor must be satisfied that the assumptions provide a reasonable basis for the projection, given the hypothetical assumptions. In a financial projection engagement the auditor does not have to obtain support for the hypothetical assumptions.

The determination of whether there is a preponderance of information is highly subjective and does not suggest that a particular outcome is the only outcome that will actually occur. The auditor's conclusion must be concerned with whether assumptions provide a reasonable basis for the preparation of the prospective financial statements. The following should be considered when determining whether there is suitable support for assumptions:

- Have sufficient pertinent sources of information about the assumptions been considered? Examples of external sources the accountant might consider are government publications, industry publications, economic forecasts, existing or proposed legislation, and reports of changing technology. Examples of internal sources are budgets, labor agreements, patents, royalty agreements and records, sales backlog records, debt agreements, and actions of the board of directors involving entity plans.

- Are the assumptions consistent with the sources from which they are derived?

- Are the assumptions consistent with each other?

- Are the historical financial information and other data used in developing the assumptions sufficiently reliable for that purpose? Reliability can be assessed by inquiry and analytical and other procedures, some of which may have been completed in past examinations or reviews of the historical financial statements. If historical financial statements have been prepared for an expired part of the prospective period, the accountant should consider the historical data in relation to the prospective results for the same period, where applicable. If the prospective financial statements incorporate such historical financial results and that period is significant to the presentation, the accountant should make a review of the historical information in conformity with the applicable standards.

- Are the historical financial information and other data used in developing the assumptions comparable over the periods specified? Were the effects of any lack of comparability considered in developing the assumptions?
- Are the logical arguments or theory, considered with the data supporting the assumptions, reasonable?

Obtain sufficient evidence concerning the preparation and presentation of the prospective financial statements

With respect to the evaluation of the preparation and presentation of prospective financial statements, the accountant should collect evidence to satisfy him- or herself that:

- Suitably supported assumptions are reflected in the statements.
- Computations to convert the assumptions to dollar values are mathematically correct.
- Assumptions are internally consistent.
- Generally accepted accounting principles used in the preparation of the prospective financial statements are the same principles (1) used in the latest historical financial statements and (2) expected to be used in the historical financial statements that will cover the same reporting period as the prospective financial statements (for financial projections the accounting principles should be consistent with the purpose of the presentation).
- Prospective financial statements are presented in accordance with AICPA guidelines.
- Assumptions have been adequately disclosed based on AICPA presentation guidelines.

Written representations should be obtained from the responsible party with respect to the prospective financial statements.

Prepare an appropriate report on the prospective financial statements

SSAE standards require that an examination report on prospective financial statements include the following:

- A title that includes the word "independent"
- An identification of the prospective financial statements presented

AT §301 • Financial Forecasts and Projections

- An identification of the responsible party and a statement that the prospective financial statements are the responsibility of the responsible party
- A statement that the auditor's responsibility is to express an opinion on the prospective financial statements
- A statement that the examination of the prospective financial statements was made in accordance with AICPA standards, and included such procedures as considered necessary by the auditor
- A statement that the auditor believes that the examination provides a reasonable basis for the opinion expressed
- The auditor's opinion that the prospective financial statements are presented in conformity with AICPA presentation guidelines and that the underlying assumptions provide a reasonable basis for the forecast or a reasonable basis for the projection, given the hypothetical assumptions
- A caveat that the prospective results might not be achieved
- A statement that the auditor assumes no responsibility to update the report for events and circumstances occurring after the date of the report
- Identification of the purpose of the prospective financial statements (for a projection only)
- Statement that restricts the distribution of the report (for a projection only)
- The manual or printed signature of the auditor's firm
- The date of the examination report

Exhibit AT 301-1 is an example taken from SSAE-10 of a standard report on an examination of a forecast.

EXHIBIT AT 301-1—STANDARD REPORT ON AN EXAMINATION OF A FORECAST

Independent Accountant's Report

We have examined the accompanying forecasted balance sheet, statements of income, retained earnings, and cash flows of XYZ Company as of December 31, 20X5, and for the year then ending. XYZ Company's management is responsible for the forecast. Our responsibility is to express an opinion on the forecast based on our examination.

Our examination was conducted in accordance with attestation standards established by the American Institute of Certified Public Accountants and, accordingly, included such procedures as we considered necessary to evaluate both the assumptions used by management and the preparation and presentation of the forecast. We believe that our examination provides a reasonable basis for our opinion.

In our opinion, the accompanying forecast is presented in conformity with guidelines for presentation of a forecast established by the American Institute of Certified Public Accountants, and the underlying assumptions provide a reasonable basis for management's forecast. However, there will usually be differences between the forecasted and actual results, because events and circumstances frequently do not occur as expected, and those differences may be material. We have no responsibility to update this report for events and circumstance occurring after the date of this report.

[*Signature*]

[*Date*]

Exhibit AT 301-2 is an example taken from SSAE-10 of a standard report on an examination of a projection.

EXHIBIT AT 301-2 — STANDARD REPORT ON AN EXAMINATION OF A PROJECTION

Independent Accountant's Report

We have examined the accompanying projected balance sheet, statements of income, retained earnings, and cash flows of XYZ Company as of December 31, 20X5, and for the year then ending. XYZ Company's management is responsible for the projection, which was prepared for [*state special purpose, for example, "the purpose of negotiating a loan to expand XYA Company's plant"*]. Our responsibility is to express an opinion on the projection based on our examination.

Our examination was conducted in accordance with attestation standards established by the American Institute of Certified Public Accountants and, accordingly, included such procedures as we considered necessary to evaluate both the assumptions used by management and the preparation and presentation of the projection. We believe that our examination provides a reasonable basis for our opinion.

In our opinion, the accompanying projection is presented in conformity with guidelines for presentation of a projection established by the American Institute of Certified Public Accountants, and the underlying assumptions provide a reasonable basis for management's projection [*describe the hypothetical assumption, for example, "assuming the granting of the requested loan for the purpose of expanding XYZ Company's plant as described in the summary of significant assumptions."*] However, even if [*describe hypothetical assumption, for example, "the loan is granted and the plant is expanded"*], there will usually be differences between the projected and actual results, because events and circumstances frequently do not occur as expected, and those differences may be material. We have no responsibility to update this report for events and circumstance occurring after the date of this report.

The accompanying projection and this report are intended solely for the information and use of [*identify specified parties, for example, "XYZ Company and DEF National Bank"*] and is not intended to be and should not be used by anyone other than these specified parties.

[*Signature*]

[*Date*]

Modifications of the examination report

An auditor may encounter a variety of circumstances that might require that the standard report on prospective financial statements be modified. The following summarizes these modifications.

Departure from presentation guidelines

An auditor may conclude that AICPA presentation guidelines have not been followed in the preparation or presentation of the prospective financial statements. When the deviations are considered to be material, either a qualified opinion or an adverse opinion should be expressed. If the auditor decides to modify the opinion, an explanatory paragraph(s) should be included in the report in which the deviations are described. When a qualified opinion is expressed, the opinion paragraph should refer to the explanatory paragraph and use the qualifying language "except for." When an adverse opinion is expressed, the accountant should refer to the deviations described in the explanatory paragraph and state that the prospective financial statements are not presented in accordance with AICPA presentation guidelines.

If the presentation deficiency results from the entity's nondisclosure of significant assumptions, the accountant should express an adverse opinion and describe the omitted assumptions.

Lack of reasonable basis

An auditor should express an adverse opinion on the prospective financial statements when a significant assumption does (or assumptions do) not provide a reasonable basis for a forecast [or, given the hypothetical assumptions, a significant assumption does (or assumptions do) not provide a reasonable basis for a projection].

Scope limitation

A disclaimer of opinion should be expressed when procedures that the accountant considers necessary cannot be performed. The report should describe the nature of the scope limitation in an explanatory paragraph.

Use of another auditor

When another auditor is involved in the engagement and reports on his or her portion of the examination, the principal auditor must decide whether or not to make reference to the work of the other auditor.

Emphasis of a matter

An auditor may emphasize a specific item or event in his or her report and still express an unqualified opinion on the prospective financial statements. The item or event that is emphasized should be described in a separate paragraph of the auditor's report, but the opinion paragraph should make no reference to the item or event emphasized.

Comparative information

Historical financial statements or summarizations of such statements may be included in the document that contains the prospective financial statements or that summarizes the prospective financial information. The auditor's report on the prospective financial statements should include a reference to the historical financial statements, as follows:

> The historical financial statements for the year ended December 31, 20X5, and our report thereon are set forth on pages XX through XX of this document.

Larger engagement

The examination of prospective financial statements may be only a part of a larger engagement. For example, a feasibility study may include the examination of prospective financial statements. When an auditor reports on the expanded engagement, the report should be tailored to fit the complete nature of the engagement.

COMPILATION ENGAGEMENT

A compilation of prospective financial statements does not provide a basis for the auditor to express an opinion on the financial statements. When a compilation report is issued, the auditor gives no assurance that AICPA presentation guidelines have been followed or that assumptions used in the preparation of the statements are reasonable. The accountant should not compile prospective financial statements that exclude a summary of significant assumptions. In addition, a compilation engagement is inappropriate when a financial projection does not identify the hypothetical assumptions that are used or fails to describe the limitation of the usefulness of the presentation.

A compilation of prospective financial statements must satisfy the following standards:

- The engagement must be performed by a person having adequate technical training and proficiency to compile prospective financial statements.
- Due professional care should be exercised in the performance of the engagement and the preparation of the report.
- The work should be adequately planned and assistants, if any, should be properly supervised.
- Appropriate compilation procedures should be performed as a basis for reporting on the compiled prospective financial statements.

> **PLANNING AID REMINDER:** SSAE standards note that a compilation may include the "assembling, to the extent necessary, the prospective financial statements based on the responsible party's assumptions."

Promulgated Procedures Checklist

The auditor should perform the following procedures in a compilation engagement for prospective financial statements:

- Establish an understanding with the responsible party
- Make inquiries about accounting principles
- Make inquiries about key factors and assumptions
- Identify significant assumptions
- Consider the internal consistency of assumptions
- Test the mathematical accuracy of computations
- Read the prospective financial statements
- Inquire about historical transactions
- Obtain written representations from the responsible party
- Consider extended engagement procedures
- Prepare an appropriate report on the prospective financial statements

Analysis and Application of Procedures

Establish an understanding with the responsible party

The auditor should establish an understanding with the responsible party that includes (1) the objective of the engagement, (2) the responsibilities of the responsible party, (3) the auditor's responsibilities, and (4) limitations of the compilation engagement. This understanding should be documented in the working papers, preferably through written communication with the responsible party.

Make inquiries about accounting principles

SSAE standards require the auditor to make the following inquiries about the accounting principles used in the preparation of the prospective financial statements:

- For existing entities, compare the accounting principles used to those used in the preparation of previous historical financial statements and inquire whether such principles are the same as those expected to be used in the historical financial statements covering the prospective period.

- For entities to be formed or for entities formed that have not commenced operations, compare specialized industry accounting principles used, if any, to those typically used in the industry. Inquire whether the accounting principles used for the prospective financial statements are those that are expected to be used when, or if, the entity commences operations.

Make inquiries about key factors and assumptions

The auditor should make inquiries of the responsible party concerning key factors and assumptions used to prepare the prospective financial statements. Key factors include such items as the entity's sales, production, service, and financing activities.

Identify significant assumptions

SSAE standards require that the auditor "list, or obtain a list of, the responsible party's significant assumptions providing the basis for the prospective financial statements. Consider whether there are any obvious omissions in light of the key factors on which the prospective results of the entity appear to depend."

Consider the internal consistency of assumptions

The auditor should read the assumptions established by the responsible party and consider whether they are internally consistent.

Test the mathematical accuracy of computations

Part of the compilation procedures should include testing the mathematical accuracy of translating assumptions into prospective financial statements.

Read the prospective financial statements

SSAE standards require that the auditor read the prospective financial statements, including the summary of significant assumptions, and consider whether:

- The statements, including the disclosures of assumptions and accounting policies, appear to be presented in conformity with the AICPA presentation guidelines for prospective financial statements.

- The statements, including the summary of significant assumptions, appear to be appropriate in relation to the auditor's knowledge of the entity, the industry in which the entity operates, and (1) for a financial forecast, the expected conditions and course of action in the prospective period and (2) for a financial projection, the purpose of the presentation.

Inquire about historical transactions

In some instances a significant part of the period covered by the prospective financial statements will have expired. Under this circumstance the auditor should make inquires about the results of operations or significant portions of the operations (such as sales volume) and significant cash flows. The auditor should consider the effects of these historical transactions on the prospective financial statements. When historical financial statements have been prepared for an expired portion of the period, the auditor should read those financial statements and consider the results in relation to the prospective financial statements.

Obtain written representations from the responsible party

The auditor should obtain written representations about the prospective financial statements, including assumptions upon which they are made. For a financial forecast, SSAE standards require that the written representations include the following statements:

- The financial forecast presents, to the best of the responsible party's knowledge and belief, the expected financial position, results of operations, and cash flows.
- The financial forecast reflects the responsible party's judgment, based on present circumstances, of the expected conditions and its expected course of action.
- The financial forecast is presented in conformity with guidelines for presentation of a forecast established by the AICPA.
- The assumptions on which the forecast is based are reasonable.
- To the best of the responsible party's knowledge and belief, the item or items subject to the assumptions are expected to actually fall within the range and that the range was not selected in a biased or misleading manner (applies only when the financial forecast contains a range).

For a financial projection SSAE standards require that the written representations include the following:

- State that the financial projection presents, to the best of the responsible party's knowledge and belief, the expected financial position, results of operations, and cash flows for the projection period given the hypothetical assumptions.
- State that the financial projection reflects the responsible party's judgment, based on present circumstances, of expected conditions and its expected course of action given the occurrence of the hypothetical events.
- Identify the hypothetical assumptions and describe the limitations on the usefulness of the presentations.

AT §301 • Financial Forecasts and Projections

- State that the assumptions are appropriate.
- Indicate if the hypothetical assumptions are improbable.
- State that to the best of the responsible party's knowledge and belief, given the hypothetical assumptions, the item or items subject to the assumptions are expected to actually fall within the range and that the range was not selected in a biased or misleading manner (applies only when the financial projection contains a range).
- State that the financial projection is presented to conform with the guidelines for presentation of a projection established by the AICPA.

Consider extended engagement procedures

If, after completing the compilation procedures, the auditor concludes that certain information is incomplete or inappropriate, the client should be requested to make proper revisions. If the financial information is not properly revised, generally the auditor should withdraw from the engagement.

> **ENGAGEMENT STRATEGY:** The omission of disclosures (except for those related to significant assumptions) does not require that the auditor withdraw from the engagement.

Prepare an appropriate report on the prospective financial statements

SSAE standards require that a compilation report on prospective financial statements include the following:

- An identification of the prospective financial statements presented
- A statement that the auditor has compiled the prospective financial statements in accordance with attestation standards established by the AICPA
- A statement that that a compilation is limited in scope and does not enable the auditor to express an opinion or any other form of assurance on the statement or assumptions
- A caveat that the prospective results might not be achieved
- A statement that the auditor assumes no responsibility to update the report for events and circumstances occurring after the date of the report
- The manual or printed signature of the practitioner's firm
- The date of the compilation report

Exhibit AT 301-3 is an example taken from SSAE-10 of a standard report on a compilation of a financial statement forecast.

EXHIBIT AT 301-3—STANDARD REPORT ON A COMPILATION OF A FINANCIAL STATEMENT FORECAST

We have compiled the accompanying forecasted balance sheet, statements of income, retained earnings, and cash flows of XYZ Company as of December 31, 20X5, and for the year then ending, in accordance with attestation standards established by the American Institute of Certified Public Accountants.

A compilation is limited to presenting in the form of a forecast information that is the representation of management and does not include evaluation of the support for the assumptions underlying the forecast. We have not examined the forecast and, accordingly, do not express an opinion or any other form of assurance on the accompanying statements or assumptions. Furthermore, there will usually be differences between the forecasted and actual results, because events and circumstances frequently do not occur as expected, and those differences may be material. We have no responsibility to update this report for events and circumstances occurring after the date of this report.

[*Signature*]

[*Date*]

Exhibit AT 301-4 is an example taken from SSAE-10 of a standard report on a compilation of projected financial statements.

EXHIBIT AT 301-4—STANDARD REPORT ON A COMPILATION OF PROJECTED FINANCIAL STATEMENTS

We have compiled the accompanying projected balance sheet, statements of income, retained earnings, and cash flows of XYZ Company as of December 31, 20X5, and for the year then ending, in accordance with attestation standards established by the American Institute of Certified Public Accountants. The accompanying projection was prepared for [*state special purpose, for example, "the purpose of negotiating a loan to expand XYZ Company's plant"*].

A compilation is limited to presenting in the form of a projection information that is the representation of management and does not include evaluation of the support for the assumptions underlying the projection. We have not examined the projections, and accordingly, do not express an opinion or any other form of assurance on the accompanying statements or assumptions. Furthermore, even if [*describe hypothetical assumption, for example, "the loan is granted and the plan is expanded"*], there will usually be differences between the projected and actual results, because events and circumstances frequently do not occur as expected, and those differences may be material. We have no responsibility to update this report for events and circumstances occurring after the date of this report.

The accompanying projection and this report are intended solely for the information and use of [*identify specified parties, for example, "XYZ Company and DEF Bank"*] and is not intended to be and should not be used by anyone other than these specified parties.

[*Signature*]

[*Date*]

Modifications of the examination report

The compilation report should be modified when prospective financial statements are presented on a comprehensive basis of accounting other than generally accepted accounting principles (GAAP) and the basis of accounting is not disclosed in the prospective financial statements.

> **RISK ASSESSMENT POINT:** An auditor may compile prospective financial statements that have presentation deficiencies or omit disclosures (except those related to the disclosure of significant assumptions) provided that (1) the deficiencies or omissions are presented in the auditor's report and (2) to the auditor's knowledge the responsible party did not create the presentation deficiencies or omissions with the intent to deceive those who are expected to use the prospective financial statements.

AGREED-UPON PROCEDURES ENGAGEMENT

When an auditor accepts an agreed-upon procedures (AUP) engagement related to prospective financial statements the general, fieldwork, and reporting standards discussed in the chapter titled "Attestation Standards" (AT 101) and the guidance discussed in the chapter titled "Agreed-Upon Procedures Engagements" (AT 201) must be observed. In addition, SSAE standards conclude that an AUP engagement on prospective financial statements can be accepted only if all of the following conditions are satisfied:

- The auditor is independent.
- The auditor and the specified party agree to the procedures to be performed.
- The specified party accepts responsibility for the sufficiency of the agreed-upon procedures.
- A summary of significant assumptions is included in the prospective financial statements.
- The prospective financial statements "are subject to reasonably consistent evaluation against criteria that are suitable and available to the specified parties.
- The auditor and the specified party agree to the criteria to be used in determining the findings.
- The procedures agreed to are expected to create reasonably consistent findings based on the criteria used.
- Evidential matter related to the engagement is expected to exist in order to provide a reasonable basis for expressing the findings in the auditor's report.
- The auditor and the specified party agree to material limits (where applicable).
- The report is to be restricted to use only by the specified party.

Promulgated Procedures Checklist

The auditor should perform the following procedures with respect to AUP engagements:

- Determine whether pre-engagement conditions exist.
- Perform appropriate engagement procedures.
- Prepare an appropriate report based on the scope of the engagement.

Analysis and Application of Procedures

Determine whether pre-engagement conditions exist

This procedure is discussed in the chapter titled "Attestation Engagements" (AT 101).

AT §301 • Financial Forecasts and Projections

Perform appropriate engagement procedures

This procedure is discussed in the chapter titled "Attestation Engagements" (AT 101).

Prepare an appropriate report based on the scope of the engagement

SSAE standards require that an AUP report on prospective financial statements include the following:

- A title that includes the word "independent"
- An identification of the specified party
- Reference to the prospective financial statements and the character of the engagement
- A statement that the procedures performed were agreed to by the specified party
- An identification of the responsible party
- A statement that the prospective financial statements are the responsibility of the responsible party
- A statement that the engagement was conducted in accordance with attestation standards established by the American Institute of Certified Public Accountants
- A statement that the sufficiency of the procedures is the sole responsibility of the specified parties
- Disclaim responsibility for the sufficiency of the procedures
- List the agreed-upon procedures and related findings
- Describe the agreed-upon materiality limits (where applicable)
- A statement that the auditor was not engaged to examine the prospective financial statements
- Disclaim an opinion on the prospective financial statements
- A statement restricting the use of the auditor's report
- If applicable, reservations or restrictions concerning procedures or findings
- A caveat that the prospective results might not be achieved
- A statement that the auditor is not responsible to update the report for events or circumstances that have occurred after the date of the report

- If applicable, a description of the nature of work performed by specialist
- The manual or printed signature of the auditor's firm
- The date of the review report

Exhibit AT 301-5 is an example taken from SSAE-10 of a report on an AUP engagement for prospective financial statements.

EXHIBIT AT 301-5—REPORT ON AN AUP ENGAGEMENT FOR PROSPECTIVE FINANCIAL STATEMENTS

Independent Accountant's Report on Applying Agreed-Upon Procedures

Board of Directors—XYZ Corporation

Board of Directors—ABC Company

At your request, we have performed certain agreed-upon procedures, as enumerated below, with respect to the forecasted balance sheet and the related forecasted statements of income, retained earnings, and cash flows of DEF Company, a subsidiary of ABC Company, as of December 31, 20X5, and for the year then ending. These procedures, which were agreed to by the Boards of Directors of XYZ Corporation and ABC Company, were performed solely to assist you in evaluating the forecast in connection with the proposed sale of DEF Company to XYZ Corporation. DEF Company's management is responsible for the forecast.

This agreed-upon procedures engagement was conducted in accordance with attestation standards established by the American Institute of Certified Public Accountants. The sufficiency of these procedures is solely the responsibility of the specified parties. Consequently, we make no representation regarding the sufficiency of the procedures described below either for the purpose for which this report has been requested or for any other purpose.

[*Include paragraphs to enumerate procedures and findings.*]

We were not engaged to and did not conduct an examination, the objective of which would be the expression of an opinion on the accompanying prospective financial statements. Accordingly, we do not express an opinion on whether the prospective financial statements are presented in conformity with AICPA presentation guidelines or on whether the underlying assumptions provide a reasonable basis for the presentation. Had we performed additional procedures, other matters might have come to our attention that would have been reported to you. Furthermore, there will usually be differences between the forecasted and actual results, because events and circumstances frequently do not occur as expected, and those differences may be material. We have no responsibility to update this report for events and circumstances occurring after the date of this report.

This report is intended solely for the information and use of the Boards of Directors of ABC Company and XYZ Corporation and is not intended to be and should not be used by anyone other than these specified parties.

[*Signature*]

[*Date*]

PARTIAL PRESENTATIONS

When prospective financial statements exclude one or more of the minimum presentation guidelines established by the AICPA (as discussed earlier in this chapter), the information is considered a "partial presentation." Due to the limited nature of a partial presentation, the auditor's report should be restricted to the specified party who will be negotiating directly with the responsible party.

SSAE standards do not establish specific engagement procedures that should be used in partial presentation engagement because of the limited content of the presentation. However, the standards do point out that the auditor "may find it necessary for the scope of the examination or compilation of some partial presentations to be similar to that for the examination or compilation of a presentation of prospective financial statements."

> **RISK ASSESSMENT POINT:** The auditor should carefully consider the interrelationship of elements, accounts, and items in complete financial statements to determine whether all key factors have been considered and all significant assumptions have been disclosed by the responsible party in the partial presentation.

OTHER INFORMATION

In some instances an auditor may compile, review, or audit historical financial statements that are included in an auditor-submitted document that also includes prospective financial statements. Under this circumstance the prospective financial statements must be examined, compiled, or subjected to agreed-upon procedures, except when all of the following conditions exist:

- The prospective financial statements are identified as a "budget."
- The budgetary period covered by the prospective financial statements does not extend beyond the end of the current fiscal year.
- The budget is presented with interim historical financial statements for the current year.

> **ENGAGEMENT STRATEGY:** When the budgetary exception applies as described above, the auditor should report on the "budget" and (1) state that the auditor did not examine or compile the budget and (2) disclaim an opinion or any assurance on the budget. The budget may exclude the summary of significant assumptions and accounting polices if the auditor believes the omission was not made to mislead those reasonably expected to use the budget: however, the omission must be referred to in the auditor's report.

When the prospective financial statements are included in a client-prepared document that includes compiled, reviewed, or audited financial statements, the auditor should not agree to the use of his or her name except under one of the following circumstances:

- The auditor has examined, compiled or applied agreed-upon procedures to the prospective financial statements and the related report is included in the document.
- The prospective financial statements are accompanied by an indication by either the responsible party or the auditor that the auditor has performed no service with respect to the prospective financial statements and takes no responsibility for them.
- The prospective financial statements have been examined, compiled or subjected to agreed-upon procedures by another auditor and that auditor's report is included in the document.

> **PLANNING AID REMINDER:** When the auditor has not examined, reviewed, or applied agree-upon procedures to the prospective financial statements, the standards discussed in SAS-8 (Other Information in Documents Containing Audited Financial Statements) must be followed.

AT SECTION 401

REPORTING ON PRO FORMA FINANCIAL INFORMATION

Authoritative Pronouncements

SSAE-10—Attestation Standards: Revision and Recodification (Chapter 4)

Overview

Pro forma financial information reflects the effects of applying significant assumptions, such as a proposed transaction, to an enterprise's historical financial statements or information. The more common uses of pro forma financial information include showing the effects of transactions such as a business combination, change in capitalization, change in form of business organization, proposed sale or purchase, or the disposition of a significant segment of a business. When pro forma financial information is presented, the following should be observed:

- Pro forma financial information should be labeled to distinguish it from historical financial information.
- The transactions or events that are being integrated into the historical financial information should be clearly described.
- The historical financial information that is the basis for the pro forma financial information should be clearly identified.
- The assumptions used by management in constructing the pro forma financial information should be clearly identified.
- Any significant uncertainties related to management's assumptions should be clearly identified.
- A clear indication must be made that the pro forma financial information should be read in conjunction with the related historical financial information.
- It must be clearly indicated that the pro forma financial information is not necessarily indicative of what would have occurred had the transaction taken place at an earlier date.

> **ENGAGEMENT STRATEGY:** Reporting on pro forma financial information does not apply to post-balance-sheet events or transactions that are included in historical financial statements for the purposes of a more meaningful presentation (for example,

revision of earnings per share for a stock split or the revision of debt maturities).

PLANNING AID REMINDER: The general and fieldwork standards described in the chapter titled "Attestation Engagements" should be observed in a pro form financial information engagement.

An auditor may accept an engagement to examine or review pro forma financial information if all of the following conditions exist:

- The document that includes the pro forma financial information also includes (or incorporates by reference) the most recent historical financial statements [if pro forma financial information is presented for an interim period, the document must also include (or incorporate by reference) the historical interim financial information that covers the same period as the pro form presentation].
- The historical financial statements that are the basis for the pro forma financial information must have been audited or reviewed.
- The auditor must have an adequate level of knowledge of the accounting and financial reporting practices of the reporting entity.

PLANNING AID REMINDER: An auditor has an appropriate level of knowledge of the reporting entity when he or she has audited or reviewed the entity's historical financial statements. In a proposed business combination the auditor must have an appropriate level of knowledge of the two entities involved in the transaction. SSAE standards note that "if another practitioner has performed such an audit or review, the need by a practitioner reporting on the pro forma financial information for an understanding of the entity's accounting and financial reporting is not diminished, and that practitioner should consider whether, under the particular circumstances, he or she can acquire sufficient knowledge of these matters to perform the procedures necessary to report on the pro forma financial information."

PLANNING AID REMINDER: The type of pro forma financial information engagement that an accountant can accept depends on the type of service performed on the related historical financial statements. That is, an audit of the pro forma financial information can be performed only when the historical financial statements have been audited. Only a review of the pro forma financial information can be performed when the historical financial statements have been reviewed only. The rationale for these guidelines is that the level of assurance that can be made for pro forma financial information can be no

AT §401 • Reporting on Pro Forma Financial Information

higher than the level of assurance the accountant made with respect to the historical financial statements.

The objectives, as stated in the Statements on Standards for Attestation Engagements (SSAE) standards, of an examination (reasonable assurance) and a review (negative assurance) of pro forma financial information are presented in Exhibit AT 401-1.

EXHIBIT AT 401-1— OBJECTIVES OF EXAMINATIONS AND REVIEWS OF PRO FORMA FINANCIAL INFORMATION

	Examination Engagement	**Review Engagement**
Management's assumptions	They provide a reasonable basis for presenting the significant effects directly attributable to the underlying transaction (or event)	No information came to the auditor's attention during the engagement to suggest they do not provide a reasonable basis for presenting the significant effects directly attributable to the underlying transaction (or event)
Related pro forma adjustments	They give appropriate effect to those assumptions	No information came to the auditor's attention during the engagement to sugest they do not give appropriate effect to those assumptions
The pro forma column	It reflects the proper application of those adjustments to the historical financial statements	No information came to the auditor's attention during the engagement to suggest it does not reflect the proper application of those adjustments to the historical financial statements

Promulgated Procedures Checklist

As noted earlier, the starting point for a pro forma engagement is the historical financial statements, which have been audited or reviewed by the auditor. In addition to those procedures, the auditor should perform the following procedures in an examination or review of pro forma financial information:

- Obtain an understanding of the underlying transaction (or event)
- Obtain a level of knowledge of each constituent part of the combined entity in a business combination
- Discuss the assumptions made by management
- Evaluate the completeness of the pro forma adjustments
- Obtain sufficient evidence to support the pro forma adjustments
- Evaluate the presentation and consistency of assumptions
- Test the mathematical accuracy of the pro forma adjustments
- Obtain written representation from management
- Read the pro forma financial information
- Prepare an appropriate report on the pro forma financial information

Analysis and Application of Procedures

Obtain an understanding of the underlying transaction (or event)

The auditor must understand the nature of the transaction that is the basis for converting the historical financial statements into pro forma financial information. Obtaining this understanding could include the reading of contracts and agreements between the parties involved in the transaction and by making inquiries of appropriate management personnel.

Obtain a level of knowledge of each constituent part of the combined entity in a business combination

As noted earlier in this section, the performance of a pro forma financial information engagement is based on the assumption that the auditor has an adequate understanding of the parties involved in a business combination or a proposed combination. Generally, this knowledge already exists because the auditor would have audited or reviewed the financial statements of the parties involved in the combination. However, if the auditor has not audited or reviewed one of the parties to the combination, the SSAE standards note that an adequate level of knowledge may be obtained by "communicating with other practitioners who have audited or reviewed the historical financial information on which the pro forma financial statements is based."

Discuss the assumptions made by management

The auditor should discuss the significant assumptions made by management to integrate the transaction into the historical financial statements in order to create the pro forma financial information.

Evaluate the completeness of the pro forma adjustments

Once the assumptions made by management are understood, the auditor should determine whether all significant pro forma adjustments directly related to the transaction have been made to the historical financial statements.

Obtain sufficient evidence to support the pro forma adjustments

Professional judgment must be used to determine what constitutes sufficient evidential matter for each pro forma adjustment. For example, the auditor may obtain appraisal reports to support the assignment of fair values in a purchase transaction or review debt agreements.

> **ENGAGEMENT STRATEGY:** Generally, a greater level of evidential matter is required in an examination than in a review engagement.

Evaluate the presentation and consistency of assumptions

Generally a variety of assumptions are necessary in order to provide a basis for the creation of pro forma financial information. SSAE standards require that the auditor "evaluate whether management's assumptions that underlie the pro forma adjustments are presented in a sufficiently clear and comprehensive manner." In addition, the auditor should determine whether the pro forma adjustments are internally consistent and properly reflect the data used to create them.

Test the mathematical accuracy of the pro forma adjustments

The auditor should test the mathematical accuracy of the pro forma adjustments and the conversion of the historical column to the pro forma column.

Obtain written representation from management

As part of the pro forma financial information engagement, the following written representations should be obtained from management:

- Management takes responsibility for the assumptions.
- Assumptions provide a reasonable basis for presenting the effects of the transaction or event.
- The pro forma adjustments are based on these assumptions.
- The pro forma financial information reflects the pro forma adjustments.
- Significant effects related to the transaction or event are appropriately disclosed in the pro forma financial information.

Read the pro forma financial information

Based on the auditor's knowledge of the entities involved in the transaction and the understanding of the transaction itself, the pro forma financial information should be read to determine if:

- They properly describe the transaction or event, pro forma adjustments, significant assumptions, and significant uncertainties.
- They properly identify the sources of the historical financial information that serves as the basis for the pro forma financial information.

Prepare an appropriate report on the pro forma financial information

The reporting guidelines in Exhibit AT 401-2 should be followed in the preparation of an examination/review of pro forma financial information.

EXHIBIT AT 401-2—REPORTING GUIDELINES FOR PREPARATION/REVIEW OF PRO FORMA FINANCIAL INFORMATION

Guideiines for an Examination	Guidelines for a Review
Title that includes the word "independent"	Title that includes the word "independent"
Identification of the pro forma financial information	Identification of the pro forma financial information

AT §401 • Reporting on Pro Forma Financial Information

Guidelines for an Examination	Guidelines for a Review
Reference to the historical financial statements that are the basis for the preparation of the pro forma financial information and state that they were audited (if the report was modified, the modification should be described)	Reference to the historical financial statements that are the basis for the preparation of the pro forma financial information and state that they were audited or reviewed (if the report was modified, the modification should be described)
Identification of the responsible party and state that the responsible party is responsible for the presentation	Identification of the responsible party and state that the responsible party is responsible for the presentation
Statement that the auditor's responsibility is to express an opinion on the information based on the results of the engagement	
Statement that the examination was made in accordance with AICPA standards, and included such procedures as considered necessary by the auditor	Statement that the review was made in accordance with AICPA standards
Statement that the auditor believes that the examination provides a reasonable basis for the opinion expressed	Statement that a review is substantially less in scope than an examination, the objective of which is an expression of opinion on the pro forma financial information, and accordingly, no such opinion is expressed
Separate paragraph that explains the objective and limitations of pro forma financial information	Separate paragraph that explains the objective and limitations of pro forma financial information
Opinion as to whether management's assumptions provide a reasonable basis for	Conclusion as to whether any information came to the auditor's attentions to cause him or her to

Guidelines for an Examination	Guidelines for a Review
presenting the significant effects of the transaction, whether the pro forma adjustments areappropriate, and whether the pro forma column properly reflects the adjustments.	believe that management's assumptions do not provide a reasonable basis for presenting the significant effects of the transaction, whether the pro forma adjustments are appropriate and whether the pro forma column properly reflects the adjustments
Manual or printed signature of the auditor's firm	Manual or printed signature of the auditor's firm
Date of the examination report	Date of the review report

RISK ASSESSMENT POINT: The auditor may decide that the use of the report may be restricted, in which case an appropriate paragraph would be added to the examination/review report.

Exhibit AT 401-3 is an example taken from SSAE-10 of an examination report on pro forma financial information.

EXHIBIT AT 401-3—EXAMINATION REPORT ON PRO FORMA FINANCIAL INFORMATION

Independent Accountant's Report

We have examined the pro forma adjustments reflecting the transaction (or event) described in Note 1 and the application of those adjustments to the historical amounts in the accompanying pro forma condensed balance sheet of X Company as of December 31, 20X1, and the pro forma condensed statement of income for the year then ended. The historical condensed financial statements are derived from the historical financial statements of X company, which were audited by us, and of Y Company, which were audited by other accountants, appearing elsewhere herein (or incorporated by reference). Such pro forma adjustments are based on management's assumptions described in Note 2. X Company's management is responsible for the pro forma financial information. Our responsibility is to express an opinion on the pro forma financial information based on our examination.

Our examination was conducted in accordance with attestation standards established by the American Institute of Certified Public Accountants and, accordingly, included such procedures as we considered necessary in the circumstances. We believe that our examination provides a reasonable basis for our opinion.

The objective of this pro forma financial information is to show what the significant effects on the historical financial information might have been had the transaction (or event) occurred at an earlier date. However, the pro forma condensed financial statements are not necessarily indicative of the results of operations or related effects on financial position that would have been attained had the above-mention transaction (or event) actually occurred earlier.

In our opinion, management's assumptions provide a reasonable basis for presenting the significant effects directly attributable to the above-mentioned transaction (or event) described in Note 1, the related pro forma adjustments give appropriate effect to those assumptions, and the pro forma column reflects the proper application of those adjustments to the historical financial statement amounts in the pro forma condensed balance sheet as of December 31, 20X1, and the pro forma condensed statement of income for the year then ended.

[*Signature*]

[*Date*]

Exhibit AT 401-4 is an example taken from SSAE-10 of a review report on pro forma financial information.

EXHIBIT AT 401-4—REVIEW REPORT ON PRO FORMA FINANCIAL INFORMATION

Independent Accountant's Report

We have reviewed the pro forma adjustments reflecting the transaction (or event) described in Note 1 and the application of those adjustments to the historical amounts in the accompanying pro forma condensed balance sheet of X Company as of March 31, 20X2, and the pro forma condensed statement of income for the three months then ended. These historical condensed financial statements are derived from the historical unaudited financial statements of X Company, which were reviewed by us, and of Y Company, which were reviewed by other accountants, appearing elsewhere herein (or incorporated by reference). Such pro forma adjustments are based on management's assumptions as described in Note 2. X Company's management is responsible for the pro forma financial information

Our review was conducted in accordance with attestation standards established by the American Institute of Certified Public Accountants. A review is substantially less in scope than an examination, the objective of which is the expression of an opinion on management's assumptions, the pro forma adjustments and the application of those adjustments to historical financial information. Accordingly, we do not express such an opinion.

The objective of this pro forma financial information is to show what the significant effects on the historical financial information might have been had the transaction (or event) occurred at an earlier date. However, the pro forma condensed financial statements are not necessarily indicative of the results of operations or related effects on financial position that would have been attained had the above-mentioned transaction (or event) actually occurred earlier.

Based on our review, nothing came to our attention that causes us to believe that management's assumptions do not provide a reasonable basis for presenting the significant effects directly attributable to the above-mentioned transaction (or event) described in Note 1, that the related pro forma adjustments do not give appropriate effect to those assumptions, or that the pro forma column does not reflect the proper application of those adjustments to the historical financial statement amounts in the pro forma condensed balance sheet as of March 31, 20X2, and the pro forma condensed statement of income for the three months then ended.

[*Signature*]

[*Date*]

AT SECTION 501

REPORTING ON AN ENTITY'S INTERNAL CONTROL OVER FINANCIAL REPORTING

Authoritative Pronouncements

SSAE-10—Attestation Standards: Revision and Recodification (Chapter 5)

SSAE Interpretation (February 1997)—Pre-Award Surveys

Overview

The basic concepts of an internal control and its assessment are discussed in Section 319. Guidance for reporting on internal control is established by the Statements on Standards for Attestation Engagements (SSAE) standards and is discussed in this section.

An auditor may accept an engagement to report on a client's internal control only if the following conditions are satisfied:

- The responsible party accepts responsibility for the effectiveness of the internal control.

- The responsible party evaluates the effectiveness of the entity's internal control based on control criteria.

- Sufficient evidential matter is available (or can be developed) to substantiate the responsible party's evaluation of its internal control.

- The responsible party presents a written assertion in a separate report that will accompany the auditor's report or in a representation letter about the effectiveness of its internal control.

There is no specific language that management must use in its assertion about the effectiveness of its internal control; management must decide what language is appropriate. However, SSAE standards provide the following as two examples that could be used:

> management's assertion that XYZ Company maintained an effective internal control over financial reporting as of September 30, 20X5

> management's assertion that XYZ Company's internal control over financial reporting as of September 30, 20X5, is sufficient to meet the stated objectives

RISK ASSESSMENT POINT: Although management decides how to phrase its assertion, standards caution that the assertion should not be so subjective that different auditors would not necessarily agree on the assertion. For example, it may be inappropriate for the auditor to report on management's assertion that its internal control is "extremely strong."

PLANNING AID REMINDER: SSAE standards note that the responsible party in the context of an internal control engagement is management personnel who "accept responsibility for the effectiveness of the entity's internal control."

Although the auditor is engaged to report on management's assertion about its internal control, management is responsible for designing and maintaining an effective control structure. In addition, management is free to evaluate its internal control without the involvement of the auditor.

ENGAGEMENT STRATEGY: A company's management is responsible for defining the components that make up its internal control. Management may accept the five components (control environment, risk assessment, control activities, information and communication, and monitoring) established by the Committee of Sponsoring Organizations of the Treadway Commission (COSO); however, if management selects other components to make up its internal control, the five components established by COSO might be irrelevant.

ENGAGEMENT STRATEGY: The effectiveness of internal controls can be determined only when appropriate evidence is available (or can be created) for the auditor to evaluate. For example, when internal controls are not well documented or when supporting documentation is not maintained, the auditor might not be able to form an opinion on management's assertion about the effectiveness of its internal controls.

EXAMINATION ENGAGEMENT

The purpose of an examination engagement that reports on an entity's internal control over financial reporting is to express an opinion on (1) the effectiveness of the entity's internal control, in all material respects, based on the control criteria or (2) whether the responsible party's written assertion about the effectiveness of internal control is fairly stated, in all material respects, based on the control criteria. In order to express an opinion concerning the effectiveness of its internal control, the auditor must collect sufficient evidence that supports the opinion.

AT §501 • Reporting on an Entity's Internal Control

PLANNING AID REMINDER: The opinion expressed is based on management's assertion or the internal controls taken as a whole, and it is not directed to a specific control policy or procedure or to the separate components of internal control.

Promulgated Procedures Checklist

The auditor should perform the following procedures when reporting on a client's internal control over financial reporting:

- Plan the engagement.
- Understand the client's internal control.
- Evaluate the design of internal control.
- Test and evaluate operational effectiveness of internal controls.
- Obtain written representations from the responsible party.
- Prepare an appropriate report on the entity's (client's) internal control.

Analysis and Application of Procedures

Plan the engagement

Proper planning of the engagement requires that the auditor consider a number of factors that may be relevant to forming an opinion related to the client's internal control. SSAE standards list the following as some of the factors that may be relevant to planning the engagement:

- Industry characteristics, such as economic conditions, rate of technological change, extent and nature of governmental regulation, and financial reporting practices
- Understanding of the internal control based on other services (such as the audit of the financial statements) that the auditor may have performed
- Characteristics of the client, such as its organizational and financial structure
- Nature and extent of changes in the client's operations or internal control
- Manner by which the responsible party evaluates its internal control
- Preliminary judgments, such as materiality thresholds and inherent risk

- Assessment and evaluations of other relevant factors that are basic to determining what constitutes a material weakness in the internal control
- Existence of documentation that is relevant to the evaluation of internal control
- Nature and significance of specific internal controls established to achieve control criteria objectives
- Initial evaluations concerning the effectiveness of the internal control

An effective internal audit function can be an important element in internal control. When assessing the role of the internal audit function, the auditor should rely on the general guidance established in SAS-65 (AU 322) (The Auditor's Consideration of the Internal Audit Function in an Audit of Financial Statements).

In addition, the planning of the engagement will be affected by whether the client has multiple locations. If there are multiple locations, the auditor must determine whether the internal control is essentially the same at each location. SSAE standards state that the auditor should consider the following factors in determining whether it is necessary to understand and test controls at each location:

- The degree of similarity of operations at each location
- The degree of similarity of internal control features at each location
- The degree to which central records are maintained
- The effectiveness of control environment policies and procedures over each location (especially the ability to exercise direct control over persons in authority at each location)
- The nature and magnitude of transactions executed at each location and the amount of assets held at each location

One additional factor that the auditor should consider when planning the engagement is the extent to which the internal control is documented. The selection of methods used to document the structure is a managerial decision based on the size and complexity of the operations, and it may include documentation methods such as policy manuals, memoranda, flowcharts, questionnaires, and accounting manuals. These methods should document the relationship between internal controls and the control objectives.

> **ENGAGEMENT STRATEGY:** Although management is responsible for the documentation of its internal control, the auditor may be engaged to help management identify the methods they are using to document the controls.

Understand the client's internal control

The auditor should obtain an understanding of the client's internal control. The understanding is generally obtained in a manner similar to the internal control phase of an audit engagement. That is, the auditor generally makes appropriate inquiries, inspects documents, and observes activities.

Evaluate the design of internal control

The auditor should obtain an understanding of the policies and procedures for each component of an internal control. The components of the internal control over financial reporting are discussed in Section 319.

Test and evaluate operational effectiveness of internal controls

After evaluating the effectiveness of internal control policies and procedures, the auditor must test those policies and procedures. The tests should be designed to determine (1) how the policy or procedure was applied, (2) whether the policy or procedure was applied consistently, and (3) who applied the policy or procedure. The auditor can make these determinations by applying a variety of examination procedures, including inquiry, inspection of documents, observation of activities, and reapplication or reperformance of internal control procedures.

The extent to which examination procedures should be performed is a matter of professional judgment. Generally, the nature, timing, and extent of tests of operating effectiveness are based on the preliminary assessment of the client's control environment. Specific factors that the auditor may consider in determining what constitutes sufficient evidential matter include the following:

- The nature of the policy or procedure
- The significance of a policy or procedure in achieving the objectives of the control criteria
- The nature and extent of tests of operating effectiveness that the client performs

In addition, the appropriate level of sufficient evidential matter should be related to the risk of noncompliance with a control policy or procedure. SSAE standards note that the auditor may assess the risk by considering the following:

- The degree to which the volume or nature of transactions has changed
- Changes, if any, in controls the client employs

- The extent to which the effectiveness of a control relies on another control
- Changes in personnel who are an important part of performing or monitoring a control
- Whether the control is manual or computerized
- The complexity of the control
- Whether more than one control achieves a specific objective

As stated earlier, a client may perform various tests of the operational effectiveness of its internal control. The auditor must decide to what extent, if at all, he or she should rely on the work performed by client personnel when drawing a conclusion about the client's internal control. If the auditor plans to rely to some degree on the work performed by client personnel, it may be appropriate for the auditor to corroborate the tests performed internally. Obviously, the auditor would place more reliance on work he or she performs him- or herself than on tests performed by the client. Finally, the auditor must make fundamental judgments about the testing process. For example, it would be inappropriate for the client to decide what constitutes sufficient evidence or a material weakness.

The auditor must decide over what period of time the test procedures should be applied. The nature of the control being tested will, to some extent, determine the period over which the control should be tested. For example, some procedures are performed only periodically (e.g., controls over the preparation of interim financial statements and the physical inventory count), while other controls are continuous (e.g., controls over payroll transactions).

> **ENGAGEMENT STRATEGY:** An auditor may be engaged to express an opinion on management's assertion about its internal control for a period of time. For example, the operating year could be used. If management's assertion is stated to encompass a period of time rather than as of a particular date, the auditor must modify the examination approach accordingly.

Management may have changed internal controls before the date of its assertion about the effectiveness of the internal control. There is no need for the auditor to consider the previous controls if the newly adopted controls have been operational long enough for the auditor to assess their effectiveness.

> **ENGAGEMENT STRATEGY:** When management's assertion about its internal control relates to the preparation of interim financial information, the auditor should perform tests of con-

AT §501 • Reporting on an Entity's Internal Control 611

trols related to interim reporting objectives for one or more of the interim periods.

Obtain written representations from the responsible party

In an engagement to report on an entity's internal control over financial reporting, management should provide the auditor with the following written representations:

- A statement that responsibility for establishing and maintaining internal control is that of the responsible party

- A statement that the responsible party has performed an evaluation of the effectiveness of internal control based on control criteria (control criteria should be specified)

- A statement that the responsible party's assertion about the effectiveness of internal control is based on the control criteria as of a specified date

- A statement that the responsible party has communicated to the auditor all significant deficiencies in the design or operation of internal control that could adversely affect the entity's ability to record, process, summarize, and report financial data consistent with the assertions of management in the financial statements, and that the responsible party has identified those weaknesses that it believes to be material

- A statement that the responsible party has described any material fraud and any other fraud that involves management or other employees who have a significant role in the entity's internal control, even though the fraud is not material

- A statement that, subsequent to the date of the report, there were no events, changes in internal control, or occurrences of other factors that might significantly affect internal control

Prepare an appropriate report on the entity's internal control

In an engagement to report on an entity's internal control over financial reporting, the auditor may report in either of the following ways:

- Report directly on the entity's effectiveness of internal control

- Report on the responsible party's written assertion concerning the effectiveness of internal control

The reporting guidelines in Exhibit AT 501-1 should be followed in the preparation of report on internal control.

EXHIBIT AT 501-1—REPORTING GUIDELINES FOR PREPARATION OF AN EXAMINATION REPORT ON AN ENTITY'S INTERNAL CONTROL OR A RESPONSIBLE PARTY'S WRITTEN ASSERTION

Standards For Reporting Directly on The Entity's Effectiveness of Internal Control	**Standards For Reporting on The Responsible Party's Written Assertion Concerning the Effectiveness of Internal Control**
Title that includes the word "independent"	Title that includes the word "independent"
Identification of subject matter (internal control) and the responsible party	Identification of the written assertion concerning the effectiveness of internal control
Statement that the responsible party is responsible for the effectiveness of internal control over financial reporting	Statement that the responsible party is responsible for the written assertion concerning the effectiveness of internal control over financial reporting
Statement that the auditor's responsibility is to express an opinion on the effectiveness of internal control based on the results of the engagement	Statement that the auditor's responsibility is to express an opinion on the written assertion based on the results of the engagement
Statement that the examination was made in accordance with AICPA standards, and included such procedures as considered necessary by the auditor	Statement that the examination was made in accordance with AICPA standards, and included such procedures as considered necessary by the auditor
Statement that the auditor believes that the examination provides a reasonable basis for the opinion expressed	Statement that the auditor believes that the examination provides a reasonable basis for the opinion expressed
Separate paragraph describing the inherent limitations of internal control, along with a warning	Separate paragraph describing the inherent limitations of internal control, along with a warning

Standards For Reporting Directly on The Entity's Effectiveness of Internal Control	Standards For Reporting on The Responsible Party's Written Assertion Concerning the Effectiveness of Internal Control
that the effectiveness of the internal control may be inadequate for future periods	that the effectiveness of the internal control may be inadequate for future periods
An opinion on whether the entity has maintained, in all material respects, effective internal control as of a specified date based on the control criteria	An opinion on whether the written assertion is fairly stated as of a specified date, in all material respects, based on the control criteria
When appropriate, a statement restricting the use of the report	When appropriate, a statement restricting the use of the report
Manual or printed signature of the auditor's firm	Manual or printed signature of the auditor's firm
Date of the examination report	Date of the examination report

RISK ASSESSMENT POINT: SSAE standards (fourth reporting standard) require that the auditor restrict the use of the report when the criteria used to evaluate internal control over financial reporting are (1) determined by the auditor to be appropriate only for a limited number of parties who either participated in their establishment or can be presumed to have an adequate understanding of the criteria or (2) available only to specified parties.

Exhibit AT 501-2 is an example taken from SSAE-10 of an examination on the effectiveness of an entity's internal control over financial reporting.

EXHIBIT AT 501-2—EXAMINATION ON THE EFFECTIVENESS OF AN ENTITY'S INTERNAL CONTROL OVER FINANCIAL REPORTING

Independent Accountant's Report

We have examined the effectiveness of W Company's internal control over financial reporting as of December 31, 20X5, based on [*identify criteria*]. W Company's management is responsible for maintaining effective internal control over financial reporting. Our responsibly is to express an opinion on the effectiveness of internal control based on our examination.

Our examination was conducted in accordance with attestation standards established by the American Institute of Certified Public Accountants and, accordingly, included obtaining an understanding of internal control over financial reporting, testing, and evaluating the design and operating effectiveness of internal control, and performing such other procedures as we considered necessary in the circumstances. We believe that our examination provides a reasonable basis for our opinion.

Because of inherent limitations in any internal control, misstatements due to error or fraud may occur and not be detected. Also, projections of any evaluation of internal control over financial reporting to future periods are subject to the risk that the internal control may become inadequate because of changes in conditions, or that the degree of compliance with the policies or procedures may deteriorate.

In our opinion, W Company maintained, in all material respects, effective internal control over financial reporting as of December 31, 20X5, based on [*identify criteria*].

[*Signature*]

[*Date*]

Exhibit AT 501-3 is an example taken from SSAE-10 of an examination on the written assertion on the effectiveness of an entity's internal control over financial reporting.

EXHIBIT AT 501-3—EXAMINATION ON THE WRITTEN ASSERTION ON THE EFFECTIVENESS OF AN ENTITY'S INTERNAL CONTROL OVER FINANCIAL REPORTING

Independent Accountant's Report

We have examined management's assertion, included in the accompanying [*title of management report*], that W Company maintained effective internal control over financial reporting as of December 31, 20X5, based on [*identify criteria*]. W Company's management is responsible for maintaining effective internal control over financial reporting. Our responsibly is to express an opinion on management's assertion based on our examination.

Our examination was conducted in accordance with attestation standards established by the American Institute of Certified Public Accountants and, accordingly, included obtaining an understanding of internal control over financial reporting, testing, and evaluating the design and operating effectiveness of internal control, and performing such other procedures as we considered necessary in the circumstances. We believe that our examination provides a reasonable basis for our opinion.

Because of inherent limitations in any internal control, misstatements due to error or fraud may occur and not be detected. Also, projections of any evaluation of internal control over financial reporting to future periods are subject to the risk that the internal control may become inadequate because of changes in conditions, or that the degree of compliance with the policies or procedures may deteriorate.

In our opinion, management's assertion that W Company maintained effective internal control over financial reporting as of December 31, 20X5 is fairly stated, in all material respects, based on [*identify criteria*].

[*Signature*]

[*Date*]

Report modifications

SSAE standards conclude that the auditor may modify the standard report (on either a direct opinion on internal control or on a written assertion on internal control) if any of the following circumstances exist:

- Material weakness
- Scope limitation
- Reference to another examination report
- Subsequent event
- Segment of internal control
- Report limited to suitability of design
- Regulatory control criteria not based on due process

Material weakness

SAS-60 (AU 325) (Communication of Internal Control Matters Noted in an Audit) provides the following two definitions for the types of deficiencies the auditor may discover when evaluating an entity's internal control.

> *Reportable condition*—Matters coming to an auditor's attention that represent significant deficiencies in the design or operation of internal control that could adversely affect the entity's ability to record, process, summarize, and report financial data consistent with the assertions of management in the financial statements.
>
> *Material weakness*—Condition in which the design or operation of one or more of the internal control elements does not reduce to a relatively low level the risk that errors or fraud in amounts that would be material in relation to the financial statements may occur and not be detected within a timely period by employees in the normal course of performing their assigned functions.
>
> **RISK ASSESSMENT POINT:** It should be noted that a material weakness is always a reportable condition, but a reportable condition may or may not be severe enough for the management or the auditor to consider it a material weakness.

When a material weakness is discovered, SSAE standards point out that the auditor should report directly on the effectiveness of internal control rather than on the written assertion. The auditor's report should be modified depending on "the weakness and its effect on the achievement of the objectives of the control criteria."

Scope limitation

When significant examination procedures deemed necessary to achieve the standard of sufficient evidence cannot be performed, the auditor must decide whether to issue a qualified examination report, express a disclaimer of opinion, or withdraw from the engagement

Reference to another examination report

If internal control components of the entity are examined by other auditors, an auditor may still report on the entity's internal control over financial reporting. Under this circumstance, the auditor must decide whether or not to serve as the principal auditor and, if he or she serves as principal auditor, whether to refer to the work of the other auditor in the examination report. Specific guidance for making these determinations is discussed in Section 326 and is based on AU Section 543 (Part of Audit Performed by Other Independent Auditors). Although the guidance is discussed in the context of an audit of financial statements, SSAE standards conclude that the general guidance is also applicable to the examination of management's assertion about its internal control.

Subsequent event

After the date of management's assertion about its internal control but before the date of the examination report, there may have been changes in policies, procedures, or other factors that may have a significant effect on the entity's internal control. SSAE standards conclude that to determine whether such changes have occurred, the auditor should determine whether the following reports were issued subsequent to the date of the examination report, and, if so, he or she should read them:

- Other reports issued by independent auditor(s) that identify reportable conditions or material weaknesses
- Relevant reports issued by internal auditors
- Reports on the client's internal control issued by regulatory agencies
- Information generated through other professional engagements that relates to the effectiveness of the client's internal control

When the auditor identifies a subsequent event that appears to significantly affect the entity's internal control as of the date specified in the assertion, the auditor should report directly on the effectiveness of internal control by expressing a qualified or adverse opinion.

Segment of internal control

An auditor may be engaged to report on a segment of an entity's internal control. For example, the scope of the engagement may include only the operations of a branch office or controls over cash disbursements. Under such circumstances, the auditor should use the examination procedures established by SSAE standards (as discussed earlier in this section) and modify the examination report so that it is consistent with the scope of the engagement.

Report limited to suitability of design

Management may have designed internal control but not put the system into practice. For example, controls may have been designed for a newly organized component that has yet to start operations, or the controls may have been designed for a unit that is subject to regulatory approval (for example, approval by a casino regulatory authority). In this type of engagement, the auditor's report should be modified to reflect the nature of the scope of the engagement.

Regulatory control criteria not based on due process

A regulatory agency may develop control criteria that must be followed by entities that are subject to its oversight. When a regulatory agency establishes control criteria, SSAE standards present the following two definitions of material weakness:

- A condition in which the design or operation of one or more of the specific internal control components does not reduce to a relatively low level the risk that errors or fraud in amounts that would be material in relation to the applicable grant or program might occur and not be detected on a timely basis by employees in the normal course of performing their assigned functions

- A condition in which the lack of conformity with the regulatory agency's criteria is material in accordance with any guidelines for determining materiality that are included in such criteria

If the control criteria are not developed through due process, the use of the auditor's report should be restricted.

Audit of financial statements

When the financial statements of an entity are audited, the second standard of fieldwork requires that the auditor obtain a sufficient understanding of the client's internal control in order to plan the engagement and to design the nature, timing, and extent of audit procedures. SAS-55 (AU 319) (Consideration of the Internal Control in a Financial Statement Audit) provides guidance for the implementation of the second standard of fieldwork.

Both the reporting on an entity's internal control over financial reporting and the audit of a client's financial statements require an understanding of internal control. However, SSAE standards conclude that "an auditor's consideration of internal control in a financial statement audit is more limited than that of a practitioner engaged to examine the effectiveness of the entity's internal control." Nonetheless, when the auditor performs both types of engagements for the same client, the results of an internal control evaluation performed in one engagement may be used in the other engagements.

Foreign Corrupt Practices Act

SSAE standards note that the reporting on an entity's internal control over financial reporting does not indicate that the client is in compliance with the Foreign Corrupt Practices Act of 1977.

Pre-Award Surveys

A client may be requested to prepare or file a pre-award survey (assertion) as part of applying for a governmental grant or contract. The assertion may be concerned with the effectiveness of the design of part or all of a client's internal control, and it may require the client's auditor to report on the assertion. An Attestation Interpretation (February 1997) concludes that the auditor's consideration of the client's internal control as part of the audit of its financial statements is not a basis for reporting on the assertion included in the pre-award survey.

In order to report on the client's assertion concerning its internal control, the auditor must perform an examination or an agreed-upon procedures (AUP) engagement based on the SSAE standards.

The auditor cannot sign a form prescribed by a governmental agency that relates to the assertion the client made regarding its internal control unless the auditor has performed an examination or an AUP engagement. Additionally, the auditor must read the prescribed form carefully to make sure it conforms to professional standards related to reporting on an entity's assertion about its internal control.

Additionally, a client may be requested by the governmental agency to file a pre-award survey (assertion) about its ability to establish an appropriately designed internal control, along with its auditor's report on the assertion. The Attestation Interpretation concludes that an auditor cannot report an assertion concerning such ability, because for such a statement "there are no suitable criteria for evaluating the entity's ability to establish suitably designed internal control." The governmental agency may be willing to accept a consulting (nonattest) engagement, however, in which case the auditor's report may include the following statements:

- A statement that the practitioner is unable to perform an attest engagement on the entity's ability to establish suitably designed internal control, because there are no suitable criteria for evaluating the entity's ability to do so
- A description of the nature in scope of the auditor's services
- The auditor's findings

AT SECTION 601

COMPLIANCE ATTESTATION

Authoritative Pronouncements

SSAE-10—Attestation Standards: Revision and Recodification (Chapter 6)

Overview

The Statements on Standards for Attestation Engagements (SSAE) standards provide guidance for an engagement in which the auditor either (1) reports on the client's compliance with requirements of specified laws, regulations, rules, contracts, or grants (referred to as compliance with specified requirements) or (2) reports on the effectiveness of the client's internal control over compliance with specified requirements.

> **PLANNING AID REMINDER:** When an auditor is engaged to report on compliance with specified requirements, the general, fieldwork, and reporting standards discussed in the chapter titled "Attestation Engagements" should be observed, along with the standards established in this chapter.

Although the standards discussed in this chapter are concerned with engagements related to compliance with specified requirements, the guidance does not apply to the following engagements:

- Audits of financial statements that are subject to generally accepted auditing standards (GAAS)

- Certain audit reports on specified compliance requirements based solely on the audit of financial statements [see paragraphs 19 through 21 of SAS-62 (AU 623) (Special Reports)]

- Reports on engagements that are subject to the standards established by SAS-74 (AU 801) (Compliance Auditing Considerations in Audits of Governmental Entities and Recipients of Governmental Financial Assistance), unless the terms of the engagement specifically require the type of attest report discussed in this chapter

- Engagements subject to SAS-72 (AU 634) (Letters for Underwriters and Certain Other Requesting Parties)

- Report engagements related to a broker or dealer's internal control as required by Rule 17a-5 of the Securities Exchange Act of 1934

AT §601 • Compliance Attestation

A compliance attestation engagement can take either the form of an agreed-upon procedures engagement or an examination.

AGREED-UPON PROCEDURES ENGAGEMENT

SSAE standards state the purpose of an agreed-upon procedures (AUP) compliance attestation engagement is "to present specific findings to assist users in evaluating an entity's compliance with specified requirements or the effectiveness of an entity's internal control over compliance based on procedures agreed upon by the users of the report." An auditor may accept an AUP compliance attestation engagement if both of the following conditions are satisfied:

- The responsible party accepts responsibility for compliance with the specified requirements and the effectiveness of the internal control over compliance.
- The responsible party evaluates compliance with the specified requirements or the effectiveness of the internal control over compliance.

Engagement Procedures

An AUP engagement must satisfy the standards established in this chapter as well as the guidance discussed in the chapter titled "Agreed-Upon Procedures Engagements" (AT 201).

As part of he AUP engagement, SSAE standards require that the auditor obtain an understanding of the specified compliance requirements by considering the following:

- Laws, regulations, rules, contracts, and grants that relate to the compliance requirements
- Experienced gained from previous engagement and regulatory reports
- Inquiries made of appropriate management personnel
- Inquiries made of external parties such as specialists and regulators

Reporting Guidance

The auditor's AUP report should include the following items:

- A title that includes the word "independent"
- An identification of the specified party
- An identification of the subject matter (or the written assertion) and the character of the engagement

- An identification of the responsible party and a statement that the subject matter is the responsibility of the responsible party
- A statement that the procedures were agreed to by the specified party and they were performed to assist the specified party in evaluating compliance with the specified requirements or the effectiveness of internal control over compliance
- A statement that the AUP engagement was conducted in accordance with attestation standards established by the American Institute of Certified Public Accountants
- A statement that the specified party is solely responsible for the sufficiency of the agreed-upon procedures and disclaim any responsibility for the sufficiency of the procedures
- List of the procedures performed and related findings
- Description of materiality thresholds, where applicable
- A statement that the auditor was not engaged to and did not conduct an examination of the compliance with specified requirements (or the effectiveness of internal control over compliance), a disclaimer of opinion, and a statement that if the auditor had performed additional procedures, other matters might have come to his or her attention that would have been reported
- A statement restricting the use of the report to specified parties
- Reservations or restrictions related to procedures or findings, if applicable
- A description of the assistance provided by a specialist, if applicable
- The manual or printed signature of the auditor's firm
- The date of the AUP report

Exhibit AT 601-1 is an example taken from SSAE-10 of an AUP engagement on an entity's compliance with specified requirements.

EXHIBIT AT 601-1—AUP REPORT ON AN ENTITY'S COMPLIANCE WITH SPECIFIED REQUIREMENTS

Independent Accountant's Report on Applying Agreed-Upon Procedures

We have performed the procedures enumerated below, which were agreed to by the [*identify specify parties*], solely to assist the specified parties in evaluating [*name of entity*]'s compliance with [*list specified requirements*] during the [*period*] ended [*date*]. Management is responsible for [*name of entity*]'s compliance with those requirements.

This agreed-upon procedures engagement was conducted in accordance with attestation standards established by the American Institute of Certified Public Accountants. The sufficiency of these procedures is solely the responsibility of those parties specified in this report. Consequently, we make no representation regarding the sufficiency of the procedures described below either for the purpose for which this report has been requested or for any other purpose.

[*Include paragraphs to enumerate procedures and findings.*]

We were not engaged to and did not conduct an examination, the objective of which would be the expression of an opinion on compliance. Accordingly, we do not express such an opinion. Had we performed additional procedures, other matters might have come to our attention that would have been reported to you.

This report is intended solely for the information and use of [*list or refer to specified parties*] and is not intended to be and should not be used by anyone other than these specified parties.

[*Signature*]

[*Date*]

EXAMINATION ENGAGEMENT

SSAE standards state that the purpose of an examination engagement is "to express an opinion on an entity's compliance (or assertion related thereto), based on the specified criteria." An auditor may accept an examination compliance attestation engagement if all of the following conditions are satisfied:

- The responsible party accepts responsibility for compliance with the specified requirements and the effectiveness of the internal control over compliance.

- The responsible party evaluates compliance with the specified requirements.

- Sufficient evidential matter exists or could be developed to support the responsible party's evaluation.

Promulgated Procedures Checklist

The auditor should perform the following procedures in an examination engagement:

- Obtain an understanding of compliance requirements.
- Plan the examination engagement.
- Consider relevant internal control components.
- Obtain sufficient evidential matter.
- Consider subsequent events.
- Obtain written representations from the client.
- Prepare an appropriate compliance report.

Analysis and Application of Procedures

Obtain an understanding of compliance requirements

Since the scope of compliance attestation is broad and the standards can be applied to a variety of circumstances, it is difficult to generalize about the auditor's knowledge of compliance requirements. Basically, the auditor must develop an understanding of the specified compliance requirements. SSAE standards identify the following as sources of information that can provide the auditor with an adequate understanding:

- Specific laws, regulations, rules, contracts, and grants on which the specified requirements are based
- Experience developed from previous similar examination engagements
- Information contained in relevant regulatory reports
- Conversations with management personnel concerning the specified requirements
- Conversations with external parties, including regulatory authorities and specialists in the area

Plan the examination engagement

One of the fundamental components of a compliance attestation engagement is the assessment of attestation risk, defined as follows:

AT §601 • Compliance Attestation

The risk that the practitioner may unknowingly fail to modify appropriately his or her opinion on management's assertion.

When the auditor offers an opinion on an entity's compliance with specified requirements, there is always a chance that the opinion will be incorrect. Simply stated, it is impossible for the auditor to reduce the attestation risk to zero because, for example, sampling methods must be used, judgments must be made, and management personnel can collude to deceive the auditor.

To assess attestation risk, the auditor must consider (1) inherent risk, (2) control risk, and (3) detection risk.

"Inherent risk" relates to the fundamental characteristics of the entity. These characteristics provide the background or context in which a particular activity is performed. Not surprisingly, the auditor uses a significant degree of professional judgment in assessing inherent risk.

While there is no comprehensive list of factors that contribute to inherent risk, SSAE standards note that some of the factors that the auditor may consider can be found in paragraphs 10 through 12 of SAS-82 (AU 316) (Consideration of Fraud in a Financial Statement Audit). In addition, SSAE standards list the following as other factors that should be considered in assessing inherent risk:

- Level of complexity of specified compliance requirements
- Period of time that the entity has been subject to the specified compliance requirements
- Auditor's prior experience with the entity's compliance with the specified requirements
- Possible ramifications of lack of compliance with the specified requirements

"Control risk" refers to the probability that material deviations from specified compliance requirements exist. Thus, the design of the client internal control with respect to specified requirements will have an impact on the level of control risk. Control risk, like inherent risk, cannot be changed by the auditor. In general, the stronger the internal control for specified requirements, the more likely it is that material compliance deviations will be prevented or detected by the system on a timely basis. Thus, the auditor must carefully assess control risk at a level that accurately reflects the internal control policies and procedures that have been adopted by the client. (Of course, the auditor can make recommendations for improving the system, which may affect future engagements.)

As referred to earlier, the auditor's assessment of the internal control over compliance with specified requirements is based on obtaining an understanding of relevant internal control policies and procedures.

"Detection risk" is the risk that an auditor's procedures will lead to the conclusion that material deviations from specified requirements do not exist when in fact such deviations do exist. During the planning phase of the engagement, the auditor should consider inherent risk, control risk, and detection risk and select an examination strategy that will result in a low level of attestation risk once the engagement is complete. There is an inverse relationship between the auditor's assessment of inherent risk and control risk and the level of detection risk. If the inherent risk and control risk are higher, the auditor should establish a lower level of detection risk. The level of detection risk established has a direct effect on the design of the nature, timing, and extent of compliance tests performed.

From a broad perspective, the concept of materiality in a compliance attestation engagement is similar to its role in an audit of financial statements. Immaterial deviations [from generally accepted accounting principles (GAAP) or from established or agreed-upon criteria] will generally exist in both types of engagements, but it is unreasonable to direct the focus of the engagements to immaterial items.

Although the concept of materiality applies to both types of engagements, it is probably more difficult to apply the concept in a compliance attestation engagement. First, because the engagement can be directed to a variety of specified requirements, it is very difficult to generalize about the examination approach. Second, the specified requirements may or may not be quantifiable in monetary terms. Third, there has been little research, if any, into what the focal point should be for determining materiality in a compliance attestation engagement. SSAE standards provide little guidance for determining materiality, except to state that the following may affect the determination of materiality:

- The nature of management's assertion and the compliance requirements, which may or may not be quantifiable in monetary terms
- The nature and frequency of noncompliance identified with appropriate consideration of sampling risk
- Qualitative considerations, including the needs and expectations of the report's users

> **RISK ASSESSMENT POINT:** Some compliance attestation engagements require the auditor to prepare a supplemental report identifying all or certain deviations discovered. Any threshold guidance established for reporting items in the sup-

plemental report should not have an effect on the auditor's determination of a materiality threshold for the primary examination report.

In many engagements, the operations of the entity will encompass two or more locations. As part of the planning of the compliance attestation engagement, the auditor should decide whether the internal control policies and procedures at all of the locations or some of the locations should be considered. SSAE standards point out that the auditor should consider factors such as the following when determining the scope of the engagement with respect to the component units:

- The degree to which the specified requirements apply to each component
- The assessment of materiality in the context of each component's operations
- The degree to which records are processed at each component
- The effectiveness of control environment policies and procedures over each component's operations
- The similarities of operations among components

Consider relevant internal control components

The auditor should obtain an understanding of the relevant internal control policies and procedures related to the entity's ability to comply with the specified requirements. This understanding enables the auditor to plan the engagement properly and determine the planned assessed level of control risk. At this point, the auditor should have developed insight into the strengths and weaknesses of the internal control by identifying the processing steps and procedures that are (1) most likely to enhance the occurrence of material noncompliance and (2) most likely to reduce the likelihood that material noncompliance will occur.

ENGAGEMENT STRATEGY: The consideration of the internal control in a compliance attestation engagement is very similar to the consideration of the internal control in an audit of financial statements. In an audit of financial statements, the auditor (1) obtains an understanding of internal control, (2) determines the planned assessed level of control risk, (3) generally performs tests of controls, and (4) designs substantive tests based on the assessed level of control risk. In a compliance attestation engagement, the auditor (1) obtains an understanding of internal control, (2) determines the planned assessed level of control risk, (3) generally performs tests of controls, and (4) designs compliance tests based on the assessed level of control risk. Thus, the only difference is that in a compliance attestation engagement the auditor performs tests of compliance rather than substantive tests as the final step.

The understanding of internal control may be obtained by performing such procedures as (1) making inquiries of appropriate client personnel, (2) inspecting relevant documents and records, (3) observing the entity's relevant activities and operations, and (4) if applicable, reviewing workpapers from the previous engagement(s). The understanding of internal control includes an analytical phase and a corroborative phase. In the analytical phase, the auditor's responsibility is to gain an understanding of relevant internal controls. In the corroborative phase (tests of controls), the auditor must determine the effectiveness of the design of internal controls and the operations of the relevant internal controls.

The evidential matter obtained through these and other examination procedures should provide the auditor with a basis for the design of tests of compliance. SSAE standards specifically note that the nature and extent of tests of compliance procedures may be affected by a variety of factors, including the following:

- The newness and complexity of the specified requirements
- The auditor's experience with the client's relevant internal control based on previous engagements
- The nature of the specified compliance requirements
- The characteristics of the client
- The assessment as to what constitutes material noncompliance

> **PLANNING AID REMINDER:** During the engagement, the auditor may discover noncompliance that is considered "significant" but not material. Under this circumstance, guidance established by SAS-60 (Communication of Internal Control Related Matters Noted in an Audit) should be considered.

> **PLANNING AID REMINDER:** If the auditor decides that the work of a specialist is required in a compliance attestation engagement, the guidance established by SAS-73 (Using the Work of a Specialist) should be observed. If the auditor decides to consider a client's internal audit function, the guidance established by SAS-65 (The Auditor's Consideration of the Internal Audit Function in an Audit of Financial Statements) should be observed.

AT §601 • Compliance Attestation

Obtain sufficient evidential matter

Based on the assessed level of control risk, which is the final phase in the development of an understanding of the client's internal control, the auditor must perform tests of compliance. The extent to which these tests should be performed is a matter of professional judgment and in general an auditor should follow the guidance established in SAS-39 (AU 350) (Audit Sampling).

> **PLANNING AID REMINDER:** If the client is subject to regulatory requirements, the engagement approach should include "reviewing reports of significant examinations and related communications between regulatory agencies and the entity and, when appropriate, making inquiries of the regulatory agencies, including inquiries about examinations in progress."

Consider subsequent events

SSAE standards identify two types of subsequent events that the auditor should consider in the compliance attestation engagement. The first type of subsequent event provides additional information about the entity's compliance during the period covered by engagement. In a manner similar to the approach used in an audit of financial statements, the auditor should perform, between the end of the period covered by the engagement and the date of the report, specific subsequent-event procedures to evaluate the appropriateness of management's assertions. While there is no comprehensive list of subsequent audit procedures, SSAE standards list the following as examples:

- Review relevant internal audit reports that have been issued during the subsequent period.
- Determine whether relevant reports by other practitioners have been issued during the subsequent period.
- Consider whether relevant subsequent events have been discovered due to the conduct of other professional engagements for the client.
- Consider reports on the entity's noncompliance issued by regulatory agencies during the subsequent period.

The second type of subsequent events relates to noncompliance events that actually occur between the end of the period covered by the engagement and the date of the report. While the scope of the engagement focuses on the period covered by the engagement, the auditor must nonetheless take into consideration subsequent noncompliance events that could have implications for the effectiveness of internal control in operations for the period covered by the auditor's report. SSAE standards conclude that if the noncompliance is significant, it may be appropriate for the auditor to describe the event in the auditor's report.

Obtain written representations from the client

The auditor should obtain written representations from management concerning an examination to express an opinion on compliance with specified requirements. SSAE standards conclude that appropriate management personnel should make the following representations:

- State that the responsible party is responsible for complying with the specified requirements.
- State that the responsible party is responsible for establishing and maintaining effective internal control with respect to compliance with specified requirements.
- State that the responsible party has evaluated the entity's compliance with specified requirements.
- State the responsible party's assertion about compliance with the specified requirements or about the effectiveness of internal controls, based on the stated or established criteria.
- State that the responsible party has informed the auditor of all known noncompliance.
- State that the responsible party has made available to the auditor all documentation relevant to the engagement.
- State the responsible party's interpretation of any specified requirements that have alternative interpretations.
- State that the responsible party has communicated to the auditor all communications from regulatory agencies, internal auditors, and other auditors concerning possible noncompliance, including communications received up to the date of the auditor's report.
- State that the responsible party has informed the auditor of any noncompliance that occurred from the date covered by the engagement through the date of the auditor's report.

Prepare an appropriate compliance report

Once the auditor has obtained sufficient evidence, the auditor states an opinion on the entity's compliance with the specified internal controls.

In a compliance attestation engagement to report on specified controls, the auditor may report in either of the following ways:

AT §601 • Compliance Attestation

- Report directly on the entity's compliance with the specified controls.
- Report on the responsible party's written assertion concerning compliance with the specified controls.

The reporting guidelines in Exhibit AT 601-2 should be followed in the preparation of a compliance report.

EXHIBIT AT 601-2—REPORTING GUIDELINES FOR PREPARATION OF AN EXAMINATION/REVIEW OF PRO FORMA FINANCIAL INFORMATION

Guidance For Reporting Directly on The Specified Controls	Guidance For Reporting on The Responsible Party's Written Assertion Concerning the Specified Controls
Title that includes the word "independent"	Title that includes the word "independent"
Identification of specified compliance requirements, including the period covered, and the responsible party	Identification of specified compliance requirements, including the period covered, and the responsible party
Statement that management is responsible for compliance with the specified requirements	Statement that management is responsible for compliance with the specified requirements
Statement that the auditor's responsibly is to express an opinion on the compliance with specified requirements	Statement that the auditor's responsibly is to express an opinion on the responsible party's assertion on compliance with specified requirements
Statement that the examination was performed in accordance with attestation standards established by the AICPA, a brief description of the nature of the examination, and a statement that the auditor believes that the examination provided a reasonable basis for the opinion expressed should be included	Statement that the examination was performed in accordance with attestation standards established by the AICPA, a brief description of the nature of the examination, and a statement that the auditor believes that the examination provided a reasonable basis for the opinion expressed should be included

Guidance For Reporting Directly on The Specified Controls	Guidance For Reporting on The Responsible Party's Written Assertion Concerning the Specified Controls
Statement that the auditor's examination did not make a legal determination with respect to compliance with specified requirements should be included.	Statement that the auditor's examination did not make a legal determination with respect to compliance with specified requirements should be included.
An opinion on the compliance with specified requirements	An opinion on whether the responsible party's assertions about compliance is fairly stated in all material respects based on the specified criteria
Statement restricting the use of the report, when appropriate	Statement restricting the use of the report, when appropriate
Manual or printed signature of the auditor's firm	Manual or printed signature of the auditor's firm
Date of the examination report	Date of the examination report

RISK ASSESSMENT POINT: SSAE standards (fourth reporting standard) require that the auditor restrict the use of the report when the criteria used in the examination are (1) determined by the auditor to be appropriate only for a limited number of parties who either participated in their establishment or can be presumed to have an adequate understanding of the criteria or (2) available only to specified parties.

Exhibit AT 601-3 is an example taken from SSAE-10 of an examination on the compliance with specified requirements.

EXHIBIT AT 601-3—EXAMINATION ON THE COMPLIANCE WITH SPECIFIED REQUIREMENTS

Independent Accountant's Report

We have examined [*name of entity*] compliance with [*list specified compliance requirements*] during the [*period*] ended [*date*]. Management is responsible for [*name of entity*]'s compliance with those requirements. Our responsibility is to express an opinion on [*name of entity*]'s compliance based on our examination.

Our examination was conducted in accordance with attestation standards established by the American Institute of Certified Public Accountants and, accordingly, included examining, on a test basis, evidence about [*name of entity*]'s compliance with those requirements and performing such other procedures as we considered necessary in the circumstances. We believe that our examination provides a reasonable basis for our opinion. Our examination does not provide a legal determination of [*name of entity*]'s compliance with specified requirements.

In our opinion, [*name of entity*] complies, in all material respects, with the aforementioned requirements for the year ended December 31, 20X5.

[*Signature*]

[*Date*]

Exhibit AT 601-4 is an example taken from SSAE-10 of an examination on management's assertion concerning compliance with specified requirements.

EXHIBIT AT 601-4—EXAMINATION ON MANAGEMENT'S ASSERTION CONCERNING COMPLIANCE WITH SPECIFIED REQUIREMENTS

Independent Accountant's Report

We have examined management's assertion, included in the accompanying [*title of management report*], that [*name of entity*] complied with [*list specified compliance requirements*] during the [*period*] ended [*date*]. Management is responsible for [*name of entity*]'s compliance with those requirements. Our responsibility is to express an opinion on [*name of entity*]'s compliance based on our examination.

Our examination was conducted in accordance with attestation standards established by the American Institute of Certified Public Accountants and, accordingly, included examining, on a test basis, evidence about [*name of entity*]'s compliance with those requirements and performing such other procedures as we considered necessary in the circumstances. We believe that our examination provides a reasonable basis for our opinion. Our examination does not provide a legal determination of [*name of entity*]'s compliance with specified requirements.

In our opinion, management's assertion that [*name of entity*] complied with the aforementioned requirements during the [*period*] ended [*date*] is fairly stated, in all material respects.

[*Signature*]

[*Date*]

In some instances it is necessary to interpret the specified requirements established by laws, regulations, rules, contracts, or grants. If the examination report (on either the separate management report or the representation letter) is based on significant interpretations, the auditor may add an additional paragraph to the report explaining the nature of the interpretation and its source.

SSAE standards note that it may be necessary to modify the examination report for the following reasons:

- Material noncompliance with specified requirements exists. (During the examination, the auditor may discover a noncompliance that he or she believes has a material effect on the entity's compliance with the specified requirements. Under this circumstance the auditor should report on the entity's specified compliance requirements and not on the responsible party's assertion.)

- Scope of the engagement has been restricted. [When there is a restriction in the scope of the engagement, the auditor should report in a manner described in the chapter titled "Attestation Engagements" (AT 101).]

- Reference is made to the work of another auditor. [When the work of another auditor is used as the basis for reporting on the client's compliance with specified requirements, the auditor should report in a manner described in the chapter titled "Reporting on an Entity's Internal Control Over Financial Reporting." (AT 501)]

AT SECTION 701

MANAGEMENT'S DISCUSSION AND ANALYSIS

Authoritative Pronouncements

SSAE-10—Attestation Standards: Revision and Recodification (Chapter 7)

Overview

An auditor may be engaged to examine or review management's discussion and analysis (MD&A) (a written assertion) that is presented to conform to the rules and regulations adopted by the Securities and Exchange Commission (SEC). This service is considered an attestation engagement subject to the standards established in the Statements on Standards for Attestation Engagements (SSAE) standards. Under these standards the auditor may perform either an examination or review of MD&A. Examinations and reviews should satisfy the general, fieldwork, and reporting standard discussed in the chapter titled "Attestation Engagements" (AT 101), as well as the guidance discussed in this chapter.

> **ENGAGEMENT STRATEGY:** An auditor may perform an agreed-upon procedures engagement on MD&A if the standards established in the chapter titled "Agreed-Upon Procedures Engagements" are observed.

EXAMINATION ENGAGEMENT

SSAE standards conclude that the objective of an examination of MD&A information is for the auditor to express an opinion on the information taken as a whole by reporting on the following:

- Whether the presentation includes, in all material respects, the required elements of the rules and regulations adopted by the SEC
- Whether the historical financial amounts have been accurately derived, in all material respects, from the entity's financial statements
- Whether the underlying information, determinations, estimates, and assumptions of the entity provide a reasonable basis for the disclosures contained therein

An auditor may examine a MD&A presentation in order to express an opinion on the presentation if (1) the auditor has audited at least the latest financial statements to which the MD&A information pertains and (2) either the auditor or a predecessor auditor has audited the prior years' financial statements to which the MD&A information pertains.

When a predecessor auditor has audited one or more of the financial statements for the period covered by the MD&A information, the successor auditor must determine whether it is possible to "acquire sufficient knowledge of the business and of the entity's accounting and financial reporting practices for such period" so that the following can be satisfied:

- The types of potential material misstatements in MD&A can be identified and the likelihood of their occurrence can be determined.

- Procedures can be performed that will provide the auditor with a basis for expressing an opinion on whether the MD&A presentation includes, in all material respects, the required elements of the rules and regulations adopted by the SEC.

- Procedures can be performed that will provide the auditor with a basis for expressing an opinion on the MD&A presentation with respect to whether the historical financial amounts have been accurately derived, in all material respects, from the entity's financial statements for such a period.

- Procedures can be performed that will provide the auditor with a basis for expressing an opinion on whether the underlying information, determinations, estimates, and assumptions of the entity provide a reasonable basis for the disclosures contained therein.

The auditor examining the MD&A information may decide to review the workpapers (for the financial statement audit and the examination or review of MD&A information) of the predecessor auditor; however, the review of the predecessor auditor's workpapers alone does not provide a basis sufficient to express an opinion on the MD&A information that applies to the periods for which the predecessor auditor was involved. The results of the review of the predecessor auditor's workpapers should be used to determine the nature, extent, and timing of the examination engagement procedures (which are discussed below) with respect to the MD&A information covered by the work of the predecessor auditor. In addition, the auditor should "make inquiries of the predecessor auditor and management as to audit adjustments proposed by the predecessor auditor that were not recorded in the financial statements."

> **PLANNING AID REMINDER:** The auditor should follow the standards established by SAS-84 (AU 315) (Communications Between Predecessor and Successor Auditors) to determine

whether to accept an audit engagement with respect to the financial statements. When the requested engagement also encompasses the examination of MD&A information, the successor auditor should expand the inquiries directed to the predecessor auditor so that they include questions concerning the previous MD&A engagement. If the successor auditor is requested to examine the MD&A information after being engaged to audit the client's financial statements, the successor auditor should review the predecessor auditor's workpapers related to the previous MD&A engagement.

Promulgated Procedures Checklist

The auditor should plan and execute the MD&A engagement in order to determine, with reasonable assurance, whether any material misstatements in the MD&A information will be identified. SSAE standards require that, in order to achieve this objective, the auditor perform the following procedures during the engagement:

- Plan the engagement.
- Obtain an understanding of MD&A requirements.
- Obtain an understanding of the client's methods used to prepare MD&A information.
- Consider relevant portions of the entity's internal control applicable to the preparation of MD&A.
- Obtain sufficient evidence, including testing for completeness.
- Consider the effect of events subsequent to the balance-sheet date.
- Obtain written representations from management.
- Prepare an appropriate examination report.

Analysis and Application of Procedures

Plan the engagement

In an examination engagement, the auditor must collect evidence sufficient to limit attestation risk to an "appropriate low level." The components of attestation risk in an examination are similar to those that are related to an audit of financial statements, and they are described by the SSAE standards as follows:

Inherent risk—The susceptibility of an assertion within MD&A to become a material misstatement, assuming that there are no related controls (inherent risk varies depending on the nature of each assertion included in the MD&A information)

Control risk—The risk that a material misstatement that could occur in an assertion within MD&A will not be prevented or detected on a timely basis by the entity's controls (some control risk will always exist because of the inherent limitations of any internal control)

Detection risk—The risk that the practitioner will not detect a material misstatement that exists in an assertion with MD&A (the establishment of an acceptable level of detection risk is related to the auditor's assessment of inherent risk and control risk)

The foregoing risk factors should be integrated into the planning phase of the engagement by taking into consideration the following factors:

- The anticipated level of attestation risk related to assertions embodied in the MD&A presentation
- Preliminary judgments about materiality levels for attest purposes
- The items within the MD&A presentation that are likely to require revision or adjustment
- Conditions that may require extension or modification of attest procedures

The focus of the examination of MD&A information is the assertions (explicit or implicit) that are included in the client's MD&A presentation. There are four broad assertions:

1. *Occurrence assertion:* The occurrence assertion is concerned with whether transactions included in the MD&A information actually occurred during the period covered by the presentation.

2. *Consistency assertion:* The consistency assertion focuses on whether the information in the MD&A presentation is consistent with information included in the financial statements and related financial records. The assertion is also concerned with whether nonfinancial data have been "accurately derived from related records."

3. *Completeness assertion:* The completeness assertion is concerned with whether descriptions of transactions and events included in MD&A in-

AT §701 • Management's Discussion and Analysis

formation are sufficient to adequately reflect the entity's financial condition, changes in financial condition, results of operations, and material commitments for capital resources. This assertion also requires that relevant "known events, transactions, conditions, trends, demands, commitments, or uncertainties" that will or may affect these transactions and events be properly presented in the MD&A information.

4. *Presentation and disclosure assertion:* The presentation and disclosure assertion focuses on the proper classification, description, and disclosure of information included in the MD&A presentation.

> **ENGAGEMENT STRATEGY:** The assertions listed above are similar to the assertions that the auditor is concerned with when the client's financial statements are audited. These latter assertions are discussed in Section 326 of this book. However, the examination of assertions related to a MD&A engagement is limited to the assertions described in the SSAE standards [not the assertions described in SAS-31 (AU 326) (Evidential Matter)]. For example, if a client asserts that revenues increased due to a strengthening of the dollar relative to other foreign currencies, the auditor should determine the completeness of that assertion, but he or she would not be concerned with the completeness of the assertion related to total revenues. This latter assertion would have been evaluated as part of the audit of the entity's financial statements.

The auditor must use professional judgment to determine the specific planning strategy to be used in a particular MD&A engagement; however, SSAE standards note that planning should consider factors such as the following:

- Industry characteristics (such as economic conditions, accounting principles, and legal considerations)
- An understanding of the client's internal control (and recent changes thereto) with respect to the preparation of MD&A information that may have been obtained during the audit of the entity's financial statements
- Specific characteristics of the entity (such as business form, capital structure, and distribution systems)
- The type of relevant information provided to external parties (such as press releases and presentations to financial analysts)
- The approach the client used to analyze operating activities (such as budgeted versus actual result comparisons) and the types of reports pre-

sented to its board of directors to keep the board members informed of day-to-day operations as well as long-range planning strategies
- Management's familiarity with MD&A rules and regulations
- The purpose of the MD&A information, if the entity is nonpublic
- Initial judgments about materiality, inherent risk, and factors related to MD&A internal controls
- Fraud risk factors and other relevant conditions identified as part of the audit of the entity's latest financial statements
- The client's documentation to support MD&A information
- The possible need for a specialist due to the complexity of the material included in the MD&A information [when a specialist is required, the guidance established by SAS-73 (AU 336) (Using the Work of a Specialist) may be followed]
- The existence of an internal audit function [when an internal audit function exists, the guidance established by SAS-65 (AU 322) (The Auditor's Consideration of the Internal Audit Function in an Audit of Financial Statements) may be followed]

In addition, the auditor should take into consideration the results of auditing the client's financial statements. For example, the planning of the MD&A engagement may be affected by such matters as the type of audit adjustment proposed and the types of misstatements identified. If the auditor's report on the client's financial statements is other than unqualified, that fact may have an impact on the planning of the MD&A engagement.

> **ENGAGEMENT STRATEGY:** When the auditor has not previously examined MD&A information for the client, the auditor should obtain an understanding of the internal controls relative to the preparation of the MD&A information for the previous year(s).

Often public companies will consist of various subsidiaries, branches, and other operating entities. SSAE standards note that the auditor should consider factors such as the following in order to determine the procedures to be applied to a particular operating component.

- The significance of each component for the MD&A information taken as a whole
- The degree to which centralized records are maintained
- The effectiveness of controls over the various operating components

AT §701 • Management's Discussion and Analysis

- The activities conducted at an operating component location
- The similarity of activities and related internal controls at each operating component

Obtain an understanding of MD&A requirements

The auditor must develop an understanding of the MD&A rules and regulations adopted by the SEC. These rules and regulations are established in the following SEC publications and related Interpretations:

- Item 303 of Regulation S-K
- Item 303 of Regulation S-B
- Item 9 of Form 20-F

> **PLANNING AID REMINDER:** The SEC rules and regulations listed above establish "reasonable criteria" as required by General Standard No. 3. The auditor should also be familiar with any additional rules and regulations that the SEC may subsequently issue.

Obtain an understanding of the client's methods used to prepare MD&A information

For developing the MD&A information, the client should have established procedures (similar in concept to its established procedures for the preparation of its financial statements) that conform to the rules and regulations established by the SEC. The auditor should obtain from the client a description (oral or written) of the procedures the client used to prepare the MD&A information. The description should include such matters as the following:

- The sources of the information
- The manner in which the information is obtained
- The factors that management considered relevant in determining the materiality of information
- The identification of any changes in procedures

Consider the relevant portions of the entity's internal control applicable to the preparation of MD&A

The auditor must consider the client's internal controls that relate to its preparation of MD&A information in much the same manner as the auditor evaluates internal controls in the audit of an entity's financial statements. In order to satisfy the SSAE standards, the auditor should follow the steps listed below when considering internal controls in an examination of MD&A information:

Step 1: Obtain an understanding of the client's internal controls.

Step 2: Assess the control risk.

Step 3: Perform tests of controls (when control risk is assessed at a level less than the maximum level).

Step 4: Determine the nature, timing, and extent of substantive tests.

Step 5: Document the assessment of control risk.

Step 1

In all examination engagements, the auditor must adequately understand those controls relevant to the client's preparation of MD&A information. Relevant controls are concerned with the recording, processing, summarizing, and reporting of financial and nonfinancial data consistent with the assertions embodied in the MD&A presentation. Thus, the auditor needs to understand internal controls that increase the likelihood that the MD&A information will be prepared in accordance with rules and regulations established by the SEC.

The auditor generally obtains an understanding of the entity's internal controls that relate to the MD&A presentation by employing the following procedures:

- Making appropriate inquiries of client personnel
- Inspecting relevant entity documents
- Observing relevant control activities

Step 2

Once the auditor has obtained an understanding of the client's internal control, it is possible to assess the level of control risk for a particular engagement. The auditor should have documented the system and, based on that documentation, identified potential misstatements (including material omissions of MD&A information). The assessment of the level of control risk provides the auditor with a general strategy for planning the remaining internal control evaluation. If the auditor believes the internal control is well designed, the level of control risk will be assessed at a relatively low level for a given assertion. On the other hand, if the internal control appears to be poorly designed, the level of control risk will be assessed at a maximum level.

AT §701 • Management's Discussion and Analysis

Step 3

In order to assess control risk at a relatively low level, the auditor must perform tests of controls. Tests of controls are used to determine the effectiveness of (1) the design of internal controls and (2) operations of internal controls that relate to the preparation of the MD&A information in accordance with the rules and regulations established by the SEC. For example, if the MD&A information includes statistics, such as the average net sales per square foot of retail space, the auditor must test the internal controls related to how this information is accumulated and reported.

Step 4

Based on his or her assessment of inherent risk and assessment of control risk resulting from the understanding of the entity's internal control and perhaps tests of control (if control risk is assessed at a level less than the maximum), the auditor determines an acceptable level of detection risk. Detection risk is the risk that the auditor will not detect a material misstatement in an assertion that is included or that should be included in the MD&A presentation. The establishment of a level of acceptable detection risk is used as a basis for determining the nature, timing, and extent of substantive tests.

Step 5

The assessment of control risk for a particular assertion (or group of assertions related to a component of the MD&A presentation) must be documented. The assessment must be related to the results of obtaining an understanding of the client's relevant internal controls and, perhaps, to the performance of tests of controls. SSAE standards note that "the form and extent of this documentation is influenced by the size and complexity of the entity, as well as the nature of the entity's control applicable to the preparation of MD&A."

Obtain sufficient evidence (including testing completeness)

In order to obtain sufficient evidence to allow the auditor to offer a reasonable assurance on the client's presentation of MD&A information, SSAE standards require the auditor to perform the following procedures:

- Read the MD&A and compare the content with the audited financial statements for consistency; compare financial amounts to the audited financial statements and related accounting records and analyses; and recompute the increases, decreases, and percentages disclosed.

- Compare nonfinancial amounts to the audited financial statements, if applicable, or to other records (see the discussion below for nonfinancial data).
- Consider whether the explanations in MD&A are consistent with the information obtained during the audit; through inquiry (including inquiry of officers and other executives having responsibility for operational areas) and inspection of client records, investigate further those explanations that cannot be substantiated by information in the audit workpapers.
- Examine internally generated documents (for example, variance analyses and business plans or programs) and externally generated documents (for example, correspondence, contracts, or loan agreements) in support of the existence, occurrence, or expected occurrence of events, transactions, conditions, trends, demands, commitments, or uncertainties disclosed in the MD&A.
- Obtain available prospective financial information (for example, budgets; sales forecasts; forecasts of labor, overhead, and materials cost; capital expenditure requests; and financial forecasts and projections) and compare such information to forward-looking MD&A disclosures. Ask management about the procedures used to prepare the prospective financial information. Evaluate whether the underlying information, determinations, estimates, and assumptions of the entity provide a reasonable basis for the MD&A disclosures of events, transactions, conditions, trends, demands, commitments, or uncertainties.
- Consider obtaining available prospective financial information relating to prior periods and comparing actual results with forecasted and projected amounts.
- Ask officers and other executives who have responsibility for operational areas (such as sales, marketing, and production) and financial and accounting matters about their plans and expectations for the future that could affect the entity's liquidity and capital resources.
- Consider obtaining external information concerning industry trends, inflation, and changing prices and comparing the related MD&A disclosures with such information.
- Compare the information in MD&A with the rules and regulations adopted by the SEC, and consider whether the presentation includes the required elements of such rules and regulations.
- Read the minutes of meetings to date of the board of directors and other significant committees to identify matters that may affect MD&A; consider whether such matters are appropriately addressed in MD&A.

- Ask officers about the entity's prior experience with the SEC and the extent of comments received upon review of documents by the SEC; read correspondence between the entity and the SEC with respect to such review, if any.

- Obtain public communications (for example, press releases and quarterly reports) and the related supporting documentation dealing with historical and future results; consider whether MD&A is consistent with such communications.

- Consider obtaining other types of publicly available information (for example, analyst reports and news articles); compare the MD&A presentation with such information.

Nonfinancial data

MD&A information may include a variety of nonfinancial data, such as number of customers, backorders, and capacity utilization rates. SSAE standards note that the auditor must determine whether the definitions used by management for such nonfinancial data are reasonable for the particular disclosure in the MD&A and whether there are reasonable criteria for the measurement. If nonfinancial data have such characteristics, the auditor should apply appropriate examination procedures, taking into consideration the materiality of the data in relationship to the MD&A information taken as a whole and the assessed level of control risk.

Testing completeness

The information (especially explanations) included in MD&A does not arise simply from the client's observance of SEC rules and regulations. As part of the test of completeness, the auditor should consider whether "the MD&A discloses matters that could significantly impact future financial condition and results of operations of the entity by considering information that he or she obtained through the following:

- As the result of the audit of the entity's financial statements
- Through inquiries of the client's personnel with respect to current events, conditions, economic changes, commitments, and uncertainties that are unique to the client or to the industry in which it operates
- By the application of other engagement procedures

> **RISK ASSESSMENT POINT:** SSAE standards note that if the MD&A engagement is characterized by a high level of inherent risk, it may be appropriate for the auditor to expand the en-

gagement by performing extended procedures, including additional inquiries of client personnel and examining additional documentation.

Consider the effect of events subsequent to the balance sheet date

The auditor should consider events that may have an effect on the MD&A presentation but occur after the period covered by the MD&A information and prior to the issuance of the examination report. Relevant events would be those that have a material impact on the client's financial condition (including liquidity and capital resources), changes in financial conditions, results of operations, and material commitments for capital resources. Attestation standards require that the MD&A presentation disclose subsequent events or matters such as the following:

- Items that are expected to have a material effect on (1) net sales or revenues and (2) income from continuing operations

- Items that are expected to have a material effect on the entity's liquidity

- Items that are expected to have a material effect on the entity's capital resources

- Items that are expected to have an impact on the entity in a manner that would distort reported financial information that is used as a basis for indicating future financial condition or operating results

The identification of subsequent events may require that the MD&A presentation be adjusted or that additional disclosures be included in the material.

> **ENGAGEMENT STRATEGY:** SSAE standards note that when MD&A information is included in a 1933 Securities Act document (or incorporated through reference), examination procedures must be extended to the filing date or "as close to it as is reasonable and practicable in the circumstances." This time extension also applies when the examination report is included in a 1933 Securities Act document.

Generally the auditor's fieldwork extends beyond the date of the auditor's report on the client's financial statements. For this reason SSAE standards (as part of the consideration of the possible occurrence of subsequent events) requires that the auditor perform the following procedures:

- Read available minutes of meetings of stockholders, the board of directors, and other appropriate committees; for meetings whose minutes are not available, inquire about matters dealt with at the meetings.

- Read the latest available interim financial statements for periods subsequent to the date of the auditor's report and compare them with the financial statements for the periods covered by the MD&A. Discuss with officers and other executives who have responsibility for operational, financial, and accounting matters (limited where appropriate to major locations) such matters as the following:

    —Whether the interim financial statements have been prepared on the same basis as the audited financial statements

    —Whether any significant changes took place in the entity's operations, liquidity, or capital resource in the subsequent period

    —The current status of items in the financial statements for which the MD&A has been prepared that were accounted for on the basis of tentative, preliminary, or inconclusive data

    —Whether any unusual adjustments were made during the period from the balance sheet date to the date of inquiry

- Make inquiries of members of senior management about the current status of matters concerning litigation, claims, and assessments identified during the audit of the financial statements and about any new matters or unfavorable developments. Consider obtaining updated legal letters from legal counsel.

- Consider whether any changes have occurred in economic conditions or in the industry that could have a significant effect on the entity.

- Obtain written representations from appropriate officials about whether any events occurred subsequent to the latest balance sheet date that would require disclosure in the MD&A.

- Make additional inquiries or perform other procedures considered necessary and appropriate to address questions that arise in carrying out the foregoing procedures, inquiries, and discussions.

Obtain written representations from management

Attest standards require that an auditor obtain written representations from the client in an MD&A examination (and a review) engagement. The purpose of written representations is to confirm oral representations made by management during the engagement and to reduce the likelihood of misunderstandings between the client and the auditor. The written representations may be documented in a client representation letter. Although no comprehensive list of items exists that must be included in a client representation letter (or other form of written communication), SSAE standards identify the following as items that management should include:

- Acknowledgment that management is responsible for the preparation of the MD&A information and that it has prepared the information in accordance with the rules and regulations established by the SEC
- A statement that the historical financial amounts have been accurately derived from the client's financial statements and are reflected in the MD&A presentation
- An affirmation of the belief that the underlying information, determinations, estimates, and assumptions provide a reasonable basis for the MD&A presentation
- A statement that all significant documentation that relates to the compliance with the SEC rules and regulations has been made available
- Confirmation that complete minutes of all meetings of stockholders, the board of directors, and committees of directors have been made available
- A statement about whether the client (if it is a public entity) has received relevant communications from the SEC
- A statement about whether events subsequent to the latest balance sheet date and required disclosure in the MD&A presentation have occurred
- A statement about whether forward-looking information is included in MD&A information and, if it is included, whether the following is also true:
  — The forward-looking information is based on the client's best estimate of expected events and operations and is consistent with budgets, forecasts, or operating plans prepared for such periods.
  — The same accounting principles used in the preparation of the financial statements were used to prepare the MD&A presentation.
  — The latest versions of budgets, forecasts, or operating plans have been provided, and the auditor has been informed of any anticipated changes or modifications to such information that could affect the disclosures contained in the MD&A presentation.
- A statement that, if voluntary information is included and subject to the SEC rules and regulations, such voluntary information has been prepared in accordance with the SEC rules and regulations
- A statement that, if pro forma information is included in the MD&A information, the following is also true:
  — The client is responsible for establishing the assumptions upon which the pro forma adjustments are based.
  — The client believes that the assumptions used provide a reasonable basis for the pro forma adjustments, and the pro forma column accu-

rately reflects the application of the adjustments to the historical financial statements.

— The pro forma information appropriately discloses the significant effects directly attributable to the transaction or event that is the basis for the pro forma adjustments.

> **ENGAGEMENT STRATEGY:** The guidance established in SAS-85 (Management Representations) should be followed to determine the date of the representations and who should sign the representations. When a client refuses to provide the auditor with appropriate written representations, the auditor should not issue an unqualified opinion on the MD&A information but rather should decide whether a qualified opinion, a disclaimer of opinion, or withdrawal from the engagement is appropriate. (If the engagement is a review, the auditor should generally withdraw from the engagement.) The fact that a client will not provide an appropriate written representation may suggest that the auditor should not rely on other representations the client has made.

> **RISK ASSESSMENT POINT:** When a client provides written representation concerning a matter but does not allow the auditor to apply appropriate examination procedures to the matter, the auditor should express a qualified opinion or a disclaimer of an opinion or should withdraw from the engagement.

Prepare an appropriate examination report

Based on the results of applying examination procedures, the auditor should form an opinion on the MD&A presentation. The report must be accompanied by the financial statements covered by the MD&A information, the auditor's report(s) on those financial statements, and the MD&A presentation itself.

> **ENGAGEMENT STRATEGY:** When the client is a nonpublic company, a written statement should be included in the MD&A information pointing out that the information has been prepared in accordance with rules and regulations established by the SEC. A separate written assertion should accompany the MD&A presentation or such assertion should be included in a representation letter obtained from the client.

The examination report should include the following items:

- A title that includes the word "independent"
- An identification of the MD&A presentation, including the period that is covered

- A statement that management is responsible for the preparation of the MD&A pursuant to the rules and regulations adopted by the SEC, and a statement that the practitioner's responsibility is to express an opinion on the presentation based on his or her examination
- A reference to the auditor's report on the related financial statements and, if the report was other than a standard report, the substantive reasons why
- A statement that the examination was made in accordance with attestation standards established by the American Institute of Certified Public Accountants (AICPA), and a description of the scope of an examination of MD&A
- A statement that the practitioner believes the examination provides a reasonable basis for the opinion given
- A paragraph stating the following:
  — That the preparation of MD&A requires management to interpret the criteria, make determinations as to the relevancy of information to be included, and make estimates and assumptions that affect reported information
  — That actual results in the future may differ materially from management's present assessment of information regarding the estimated future impact of transactions and events that have occurred or are expected to occur, expected sources of liquidity and capital resources, operating trends, commitments, and uncertainties
- If the entity is a nonpublic entity, a statement that, although the entity is not subject to the rules and regulations of the SEC, the MD&A presentation is intended to be a presentation in accordance with the rules and regulations adopted by the SEC
- The practitioner's opinion on the following:
  —Whether the presentation includes, in all material respects, the required elements of the rules and regulations adopted by the SEC
  —Whether the historical financial amounts have been accurately derived, in all material respects, from the entity's financial statements
  —Whether the underlying information, determinations, estimates, and assumptions of the entity provide a reasonable basis for the disclosures contained therein
- The manual or printed signature of the auditor's firm
- The date of the examination report

Exhibit AT 701-1 is an example taken from SSAE-10 of an examination report on an entity's MD&A presentation.

EXHIBIT AT 701-1—EXAMINATION REPORT ON AN ENTITY'S MD&A PRESENTATION

We have examined XYZ Company's Management's Discussion and Analysis taken as a whole, including [*incorporated by reference*] in the Company's [*insert description of registration statement or document*]. Management is responsible for the preparation of the Company's Management's Discussion and Analysis, pursuant to the rules and regulations adopted by the Securities and Exchange Commission. Our responsibility is to express an opinion on the presentation based on our examination. We have audited, in accordance with auditing standards generally accepted in the United States of America, the financial statements of XYZ Company as of December 31, 20X5 and 20X4, and for each of the years in the three-year period ending December 31, 20X5. In our report dated [*month*] XX, 20X6, we expressed an unqualified opinion on those financial statements.

Our examination of Management's Discussion and Analysis was made in accordance with attestation standards established by the American Institute of Certified Public Accountants and, accordingly, included examining, on a test basis, evidence supporting the historical amounts and disclosures in the presentation. An examination also includes assessing the significant determinations made by management as to the relevancy of information to be included and the estimates and assumptions that affect reported information. We believe that our examination provides a reasonable basis for our opinion.

The preparation of Management's Discussion and Analysis requires management to interpret the criteria, make determinations as to the relevancy of information to be included, and make estimates and assumptions that affect reported information. Management's Discussion and Analysis includes information regarding the estimated future impact of transactions and events that have occurred or are expected to occur, expected sources of liquidity and capital resources, operating trends, commitments, and uncertainties. Actual results in the future may differ materially from management's present assessment of this information because events and circumstances frequently do not occur as expected.

In our opinion, the Company's presentation of Management's Discussion and Analysis includes, in all material respects, the required elements of the rules and regulations adopted by the Securities and Exchange Commission; the historical financial amounts included therein have been accurately derived, in all material respects, from the Company's financial statements; and the underlying information, determinations, estimates, and assumptions of the Company provide a reasonable basis for the disclosures contained therein.

[*Signature*]

[*Date*]

The standard examination report on MD&A presentations may be modified for the following reasons:

- A material element as required by SEC rules and regulations is omitted from the presentation (a qualified or adverse opinion should be expressed).

- Historical financial amounts have not been accurately derived (in all material respects) from the client financial statements (a qualified or adverse opinion should be expressed).

- Underlying information, determinations, estimates, and assumptions used by the client do not provide the auditor a reasonable basis on which to prepare the MD&A presentation (a qualified or adverse opinion should be expressed).

- The auditor is unable to perform procedures deemed appropriate for the MD&A engagement (a qualified opinion or a disclaimer of opinion should be expressed, or the auditor should withdraw from the engagement).

- The auditor decided to refer to the work of another auditor.

- The auditor has been engaged to examine the client MD&A presentation after it has been filed with the SEC.

- The auditor has decided to emphasize a matter.

REVIEW ENGAGEMENT

SSAE standards conclude that the objective of a review of MD&A information is for the auditor to report on whether any information came to his or her attention to cause him or her to believe that:

- The MD&A presentation does not include, in all material respects, the required elements of the rules and regulations adopted by the SEC.

- The historical financial amounts included therein have not been accurately derived, in all material respects, from the entity's financial statements.

- The underlying information, determinations, estimates, and assumptions of the entity do not provide a reasonable basis for the disclosures contained therein.

An auditor may review a MD&A presentation if (1) the auditor has audited at least the latest financial statements to which the MD&A information pertains and (2) either the auditor or a predecessor auditor has audited the prior years' financial statements to which the MD&A information pertains.

When a predecessor auditor has audited one or more of the financial statements for the period covered by the MD&A information, the successor auditor must determine whether it is possible to "acquire sufficient knowledge of the business and of the entity's accounting and financial reporting practices for such period" so that the following can be satisfied:

- The types of potential material misstatements in MD&A can be identified and the likelihood of their occurrence can be determined.

- Procedures can be performed that will provide the auditor with a basis for determining whether any information obtained in the engagement suggests that

    — The MD&A information excludes required material.

    — The historical financial amounts included in the MD&A information have not been derived from the historical financial statements.

    — The underlying information, determinations, estimates, and assumptions of the entity do not provide a reasonable basis for the disclosures included in the MD&A presentation.

Promulgated Procedures Checklist

The auditor should plan and execute the MD&A engagement in order to provide limited assurance that the material misstatements in the MD&A information will be identified. According to SSAE standards, to achieve this objective the auditor should perform the following:

- Plan the engagement.
- Obtain an understanding of MD&A requirements.
- Obtain an understanding of the client's methods used to prepare MD&A information.

- Consider relevant portions of the entity's internal control applicable to the preparation of MD&A.
- Apply analytical procedures and make inquires of management and other appropriate personnel.
- Consider the effect of events subsequent to the balance sheet date.
- Obtain written representations from management.
- Prepare an appropriate review report.

Analysis and Application of Procedures

Plan the engagement

The auditor must use professional judgment to determine the specific planning strategy to be used in a particular MD&A engagement; however, SSAE standards note that in planning the review engagement, the auditor should consider factors such as the following:

- Industry characteristics (such as economic conditions, accounting principles, and legal considerations)
- Specific characteristics of the entity (such as business form, capital structure, and distribution systems)
- Relevant information provided to external parties (such as press releases and presentations to financial analysts)
- Management's familiarity with MD&A rules and regulations
- The purpose of the MD&A information, if the entity is nonpublic
- Matters identified during the audit or review of the client financial statements that may provide insight into the preparation and reporting of MD&A information
- Matters identified during the examination or review concerning the prior years' MD&A presentations
- Initial judgments about materiality levels
- Items that are either relatively complex or subjective that provide a basis for assertions in the MD&A information
- The existence of an internal audit function and the degree to which the function was involved in the verification of MD&A information

AT §701 • Management's Discussion and Analysis

Consider relevant portions of the entity's internal control applicable to the preparation of MD&A

SSAE standards conclude that as a basis for performing appropriate analytical procedures and inquiries of client personnel, the auditor must develop an adequate understanding of the client's internal controls related to its preparation and presentation of MD&A information. While the standards do not provide specific guidance as to how this is to be accomplished, the auditor's knowledge of internal controls must be sufficient to accomplish the following:

- Identification of types of potential misstatements in MD&A, including types of material omissions, and consideration of the likelihood of their occurrence

- Selection of the inquiries and analytical procedures that will provide a basis for reporting whether any information causes the practitioner to believe the following:

  —That the MD&A presentation does not include, in all material respects, the required elements of the rules and regulations adopted by the SEC, or that the historical financial amounts included therein have not been accurately derived, in all material respects, from the entity's financial statements

  —That the underlying information, determinations, estimates, and assumptions of the entity do not provide a reasonable basis for the disclosures contained therein

Apply analytical procedures and make inquiries of management and other appropriate personnel

The auditor should apply a variety of analytical procedures and make specific inquiries of client personnel. The results of these procedures should be evaluated in the context of the auditor's understanding of other relevant information that he or she knows. While there is not a specific list of analytical procedures and inquiries that should be performed in a review engagement, SSAE standards point out that generally the auditor should employ the following procedures:

- Compare information in the MD&A presentation with the audited financial statement and related accounting records and analyses.

- Recompute decreases, increases, and percentage changes relative to financial amounts included in or derived from the financial statements.

- Compare nonfinancial amounts in the MD&A presentation with audited amounts in the financial statements, if appropriate, or in other records.
- Inquire about the types of records that support the nonfinancial amounts, and determine the existence of the records.
- Determine whether the nonfinancial information is relevant to users and is clearly defined in the MD&A information, and inquire about whether the definition of nonfinancial information was consistently applied.
- Consider whether explanations included in the MD&A presentation are consistent with information obtained as part of the audit of the client's financial statements, and direct any related inquiries to appropriate personnel.
- Compare prospective financial information (such as budgets) to forward-looking information included in the MD&A presentation.
- Make inquiries of relevant personnel concerning procedures used to develop prospective financial information and forward-looking information.
- Consider whether information obtained suggests that underlying information, determinations, estimates, and assumptions of the entity do not provide a reasonable basis for the disclosures of trends, demands, commitments, events, or uncertainties.
- Make inquiries of appropriate operational personnel (such as production and marketing) and financial personnel as to plans that could have an effect on the client's liquidity and capital resources.
- Determine whether the MD&A presentation includes disclosures required by the SEC.
- Consider whether the MD&A presentation properly reflects any relevant matters discussed in the minutes of meetings of the board of directors and other significant committees.
- Make inquiries about the experience the client has had with the SEC relative to MD&A presentations made in previous years, and read any correspondence between the client and the SEC relative to these matters.
- Make inquiries concerning the nature of public communications that include historical and future results. Determine whether those communications are consistent with the MD&A presentation.

While a review engagement is characterized by the use of analytical procedures and inquiries of management personnel, the auditor should use whatever procedures he or she deems appropriate (including corroborative procedures) if it appears that the MD&A presentation is "incomplete or contains inaccuracies or is otherwise unsatisfactory."

> **ENGAGEMENT STRATEGY:** The auditor might find the general guidance for the application of analytical procedures in SAS-56 (Analytical Procedures) helpful in applying the procedures to a review of MD&A information.

Obtain an understanding of MD&A requirements

In order to develop an understanding of MD&A requirements established by the SEC for a review engagement, the auditor should follow the guidance discussed earlier for an examination engagement.

Obtain an understanding the client's methods used to prepare MD&A information

In a review engagement, in order to develop an understanding of the client's methods used to create MD&A information, the auditor should follow the guidance discussed earlier for an examination engagement.

Consider the effect of events subsequent to the balance-sheet date

In order to consider the effect of an event occurring subsequent to the balance sheet date in a review engagement, the auditor should follow the guidance discussed earlier for the occurrence of this situation in an examination engagement.

Obtain written representations from management

In a review engagement, the auditor should obtain written representations similar to those obtained in an examination engagement, as discussed earlier. However, when the client refuses to provide the auditor with appropriate written representations in a review engagement, the auditor should withdraw from the engagement.

Prepare an appropriate review report

Based on the results of applying review procedures, the auditor should consider which report would be appropriate to issue on the MD&A presentation. However, the report must be accompanied by the financial statements covered by the MD&A information, the auditor's report(s) on those financial statements, and the MD&A presentation.

ENGAGEMENT STRATEGY: When the client is a public company and the MD&A presentation covers an interim period, the presentation should be accompanied by (1) the related interim financial statements and the review report applicable to the MD&A presentation and (2) the most recent comparative financial statements and the related MD&A presentation. (The information may be included by reference to filings with the SEC.)

RISK ASSESSMENT POINT: When the client is a nonpublic company, there should be a statement that the MD&A information has been prepared in accordance with rules and regulations established by the SEC. The statement may be included the MD&A presentation itself or presented as a separate statement that accompanies the MD&A presentation. If the presentation for a nonpublic company relates to an interim period, the MD&A presentation should be accompanied by (1) the entity's most recent annual MD&A presentation and the related examination or review report and (2) the related interim financial statements and the most recent financial statements.

The review report should include the following items:

- A title that includes the word "independent"

- An identification of the MD&A presentation, including the period covered

- A statement that management is responsible for preparing the MD&A pursuant to the rules and regulations adopted by the SEC

- A reference to the auditor's report on the related financial statements and, if the report was other than a standard report, the substantive reasons for it

- A statement that the review was made in accordance with attestation standards established by the AICPA

- A description of the procedures for a review of MD&A

- A statement that a review of MD&A is substantially less in scope than an examination, the objective of which is an expression of opinion regarding the MD&A presentation and that, accordingly, no such opinion is expressed

- A paragraph stating the following:

  —That the preparation of MD&A requires management to interpret the criteria, make determinations as to the relevancy of information to be included, and make estimates and assumptions that affect reported information

—That future results may differ materially from management's present assessment of information regarding the estimated future impact of transactions and events that have occurred or are expected to occur, expected sources of liquidity and capital, operating trends, commitments, and uncertainties

- If the entity is a nonpublic entity, a statement that, although the entity is not subject to the rules and regulations of the SEC, the MD&A presentation is intended to be a presentation in accordance with the rules and regulations adopted by the SEC
- A statement about whether any information came to the practitioner's attention that caused him or her to believe any of the following:

   —That the presentation does not include, in all material respects, the required elements of the rules and regulations adopted by the SEC

   —That the historical financial amounts have not been accurately derived, in all material respects, from the entity's financial statements

   —That the underlying information, determinations, estimates, and assumptions of the entity do not provide a reasonable basis for the disclosures contained therein

- If the entity is a public entity or nonpublic entity that is making an offering of securities to the public, a statement restricting the use of the report to specified parties
- The manual or printed signature of the auditor's firm
- The date of the review report

Exhibit AT 701-2 is an example taken from SSAE-10 of a report for a review engagement on an entity's MD&A presentation.

EXHIBIT AT 701-2—REVIEW REPORT ON AN ENTITY'S MD&A PRESENTATION

Independent Accountant's Report

We have reviewed XYZ Company's Management's Discussion and Analysis taken as a whole, including [*incorporated by reference*] in the Company's [*insert description of registration statement or document*]. Management is responsible for the preparation of the Company's Management's Discussion and Analysis pursuant to the rules and regulations adopted by the Securities and Exchange Commission. We have audited, in accordance with auditing standards generally accepted in the United States of America, the financial Statements of

XYZ Company as of December 31, 20X5 and 20X4, and for each year in the three-year period ended December 31, 20X5, and in our report date [*month*] XX, 20X6, we expressed an unqualified opinion on those financial statements.

We conducted our review of Management's Discussion and Analysis in accordance with attestation standards established by the American Institute of Certified Public Accounts. A review of Management's Discussion and Analysis consists principally of applying analytical procedures and making inquiries of persons responsible for financial, accounting, and operating matters. It is substantially less in scope than an examination, the objective of which is the expression of an opinion on the presentation. Accordingly, we do not express such an opinion.

The preparation of Management's Discussion and Analysis requires management to interpret the criteria, make determinations as to the relevancy of information to be included, and make estimates and assumptions that affect reported information. Management's Discussion and Analysis includes information regarding the estimated future impact of transactions and events that have occurred or are expected to occur, expected sources of liquidity and capital resources, operating trends, commitments, and uncertainties. Actual results in the future may differ materially from management's present assessment of this information because events and circumstances frequently do not occur as expected.

Based on our review, nothing came to our attention that caused us to believe that the Company's presentation of Management's Discussion and Analysis does not include, in all material respects, the required elements of the rules and regulations adopted by the Securities and Exchange Commission, that the historical financial amounts included therein have not been accurately derived, in all material respects, from the Company's financial statements, or that the underlying information, determinations, estimates and assumptions of the Company do not provide a reasonable basis for the disclosures contained therein.

The report is intended solely for the information and use of [*list or refer to specified parties*] and is not intended to be and should not be used by anyone other than the specified parties.

[*Signature*]

[*Date*]

The standard review report on MD&A presentations may be modified for the following reasons:

- A material element as required by SEC rules and regulations is omitted from the presentation (modify the review report by describing the omission).
- Historical financial amounts have not been accurately derived (modify the review report by describing the misstated information).
- Underlying information, determinations, estimates, and assumptions used by the client do not provide a reasonable basis upon which to prepare the MD&A presentation (modify the review report by describing the deficiency).
- The auditor decides to emphasize a matter with respect to the MD&A presentation (a standard review report is issued with an explanatory paragraph describing the nature of the matter emphasized).

The auditor's review report may also be modified when another auditor has examined or reviewed (and issued a separate report on) MD&A information for a component that represents a significant part of the overall financial statements. Under this circumstance the principal auditor's report should refer to the work of the other auditor as a basis for offering the limited assurance on the MD&A presentation. When the other auditor has not issued a separate report on the (component) MD&A presentation, there should be no reference to the work of the other auditor in the review report on the MD&A presentation. (This does not mean that the principal auditor cannot refer in the review report to the fact that a component's financial statements were audited by another auditor.)

RISK ASSESSMENT POINT: When the auditor is unable to perform appropriate review procedures or the client is unwilling to provide appropriate written representations, the auditor should not issue a review report on the MD&A presentation.

OTHER ISSUES

Combined Reporting

An auditor may be engaged to report on the results of (1) an examination on an MD&A presentation related to the latest annual financial statements and (2) a review of an MD&A presentation on interim financial information for a period that is subsequent to the date of the annual financial statements. When the two engagements are "completed at the same time," the auditor can issue a single report that incorporates both a separate examination format and a separate review format (except that the explanatory paragraph in the review report is omitted).

> **ENGAGEMENT STRATEGY:** In some instances the client may prepare a combined MD&A presentation for an annual period and an interim period. SSAE standards note that if the discussion of liquidity and capital resources applies only as of the most recent interim period (not as of the date of the annual financial statements), the auditor is "limited to performing the highest level of service that is provided with respect to the historical financial statements of any of the periods covered by the MD&A presentation." Thus, if annual financial statements are audited and the interim financial statements are reviewed, the combined MD&A presentation can be reviewed but cannot be examined.

Engagement of the auditor subsequent to filing of MD&A presentation

Public companies are required to report significant subsequent events on Form 8-K, on Form 10-Q, or in a registration statement. They are not required to modify previously filed MD&A presentations for the occurrence of subsequent events. If the auditor is engaged to examine or review an MD&A presentation after the document has been filed, the auditor should consider whether subsequent events have been reported in Form 8-K or Form 10-K or in a registration statement, rather than whether the MD&A presentation has been modified to reflect the subsequent event. However, under this circumstance the following sentence should be added to the opinion paragraph in an examination engagement and to the concluding paragraph in a review engagement:

> The accompanying Management's Discussion and Analysis does not consider events that have occurred subsequent to [*month*] XX, 20X9, the date as of which it was filed with the Securities and Exchange Commission.
>
> **RISK ASSESSMENT POINT:** If the client has not notified the SEC of a material subsequent event, the auditor should express a qualified or adverse opinion on the MD&A presentation in a examination engagement (or in a review engagement appropriately modifying the review report), assuming that the auditor concludes that it is appropriate to issue a report on the MD&A information. This circumstance may occur when the

SEC filing has not yet been completed but management intends to make the appropriate filing on a timely basis. However, if the subsequent event is not disclosed in a proper manner, the auditor must decide whether to withdraw from both the MD&A engagement and the audit engagement.

Communicating with the Client's Audit Committee

Under the following circumstances (assuming the client refuses to correct the deficiency), the auditor should communicate the deficiency to the entity's audit committee (or others with equivalent authority):

- Material inconsistencies exist between the MD&A presentation and other information included in the document containing the MD&A material.
- Material inconsistencies exist between the MD&A presentation and the historical financial statements.
- Material omissions are made in the MD&A presentation.
- Material misstatements of facts are made in the MD&A presentation.

AR Section

Statements on Standards for Accounting and Review Services

AR Section 100: Compilation and Review of Financial
    Statements 667

AR Section 200: Reporting on Comparative Financial
    Statements 762

AR Section 300: Compilation Reports on Financial Statements
    in Certain Prescribed Forms 776

AR Section 400: Communications between Predecessor and
    Successor Accountants 779

AR Section 600: Reporting on Personal Financial Statements
    Included in Written Personal Financial Plans 782

For the latest information, refer to the *Miller GAAS Update Service* and the Miller GAAS Library, at http://www.MillerSeries.com.

AR SECTION 100

COMPILATION AND REVIEW OF FINANCIAL STATEMENTS

Authoritative Pronouncements

SSARS-1—Compilation and Review of Financial Statements

SSARS-7—Omnibus Statement on Standards for Accounting and Review Services—1992

SSARS-8—Amendments to Statement on Standards for Accounting and Review Services No. 1, Compilation and Review of Financial Statements—2000

SSARS Interpretation 1—Omission of Disclosures in Reviewed Financial Statements (December 1979)

SSARS Interpretation 2—Financial Statements Included in SEC Filings (December 1979)

SSARS Interpretation 3—Reporting on the Highest Level of Service (December 1979)

SSARS Interpretation 4—Discovery of Information After the Date of Accountant's Report (November 1980)

SSARS Interpretation 5—Planning and Supervision (August 1981)

SSARS Interpretation 6—Withdrawal from Compilation or Review Engagements (August 1981)

SSARS Interpretation 7—Reporting When There Are Significant Departures from Generally Accepted Accounting Principles (August 1981)

SSARS Interpretation 8—Reports on Specified Elements, Accounts, or Items of a Financial Statement (November 1981, amended November 1988)

SSARS Interpretation 9—Reporting When Management Has Elected to Omit Substantially All Disclosures (May 1982)

SSARS Interpretation 10—Reporting on Tax Returns (November 1982)

SSARS Interpretation 11—Reporting on Uncertainties (December 1982)

SSARS Interpretation 12—Reporting on a Comprehensive Basis of Accounting Other than Generally Accepted Accounting Principles (December 1982)

SSARS Interpretation 13—Additional Procedures (March 1983)

SSARS Interpretation 14—Reporting on Financial Statements when the Scope of the Accountant's Procedures Has Been Restricted (April 1984; withdrawn April 1990)

SSARS Interpretation 15—Differentiating a Financial Statement Presentation from a Trial Balance (September 1990)

SSARS Interpretation 16—withdrawn by issuance of SSARS-7

SSARS Interpretation 17—Submitting Draft Financial Statements (September 1990)

SSARS Interpretation 18—Special-Purpose Financial Presentations to Comply with Contractual Agreements or Regulatory Provisions (September 1990)

SSARS Interpretation 19—Reporting When Financial Statements Contain a Departure from Promulgated Accounting Principles That Prevent the Financial Statements from Being Misleading (February 1991)

SSARS Interpretation 20—Applicability of Statements on Standards for Accounting and Review Services to Litigation Services (May 1991)

Overview

Statements on Standards for Accounting and Review Services (SSARS) cover two different levels of service that an accountant can provide for unaudited financial statements of nonpublic entities. The first level of service is referred to as a compilation. The accountant's report on a compilation includes a statement that an audit or a review was not performed and no opinion or other assurance is expressed on the accompanying financial statements. The second level of service is called a review. The accountant's report on a review includes a statement of limited assurance that the financial statements are in accordance with generally accepted accounting principles (GAAP) or an other comprehensive basis of accounting.

Engagements under SSARS standards are directed to nonpublic entities, as defined in the pronouncements. SSARS-1 (Compilation and Review of Financial Statements) defines a "nonpublic entity" as (1) one whose securities are not traded in a public market or (2) one that has not filed with a regulatory agency for the purpose of selling any of its securities in a public market. A subsidiary, a corporate joint venture, or any other entity controlled by a nonpublic entity is also considered a nonpublic entity. SSARS-1 defines a "financial statement" as a presentation of financial information for the purpose of communicating the resources or obligations of an entity at a specific time, or communicating the changes in such resources or obligations during a time period, in accordance with GAAP or another comprehensive basis of accounting. A financial presentation includes all accompanying notes, but the scope of SSARS-1 does not include financial forecasts, projections, or similar presentations.

A financial presentation may consist of a single financial statement (e.g., a balance sheet, an income statement, a statement of cash flows, a statement of cash receipts and cash disbursements, a statement of assets and liabilities, or a statement of operations by product lines). An accountant may issue a compilation or review report on one financial statement, such as a balance sheet, and not issue a report on other related statements, such as the statement of income or the statement of retained earnings.

> **PLANNING AID REMINDER:** The SSARS Interpretation (November 1981) titled "Reports on Specified Elements, Accounts, or Items of a Financial Statement" states that SSARS-1 is not applicable to an engagement wherein the accountant reports on presentations of specified elements, accounts, or items of a financial statement, because such presentations do not constitute financial statements. The SSARS Interpretation notes that SAS-62 (Special Reports), SAS-75 (Engagements to Apply Agreed-Upon Procedures to Specified Elements, Accounts, or Items of a Financial Statement), and related Interpretations provide guidance for when the engagement is intended to result in (1) an expression of an opinion on specified elements, accounts, or items of a financial statement or (2) the application of agreed-upon procedures to specified elements, accounts, or items of a financial statement.

An "other comprehensive basis of accounting" is defined in SAS-62 (AU 623) as a basis to which at least one of the following applies:

1. The accounting basis is used to comply with the requirements or financial reporting provisions of a government agency.

2. The accounting basis is used to file income tax returns.

3. The cash receipts and disbursements basis or the modified accrual basis is used.

4. The accounting basis has substantial support, such as price-level accounting.

Both SSARS-1 and SAS-62 (AU 623) identify the following as examples of financial statements:

- Balance sheet
- Statement of income

- Statement of cash flows
- Statement of changes in owners' equity
- Statement of assets and liabilities (with or without owners' equity accounts)
- Statement of revenue and expenses
- Summary of operations
- Statement of operations by product lines
- Statement of cash receipts and disbursements

SSARS apply to those situations in which the accountant is associated with a financial statement presentation. The standards established by SSARS do not have to be observed when the accountant prepares or assists in the preparation of a client's trial balance. The SSARS Interpretation (September 1990) titled "Differentiating a Financial Statement Presentation from a Trial Balance" points out that the accountant should consider the following factors in differentiating a financial statement presentation from a trial balance:

- Generally, a financial statement requires the grouping of similar accounts or transactions with corresponding subtotals and totals, and the netting of contra accounts, whereas a trial balance presentation is limited to displaying accounts in a debit/credit format.
- Generally, financial statements use titles that relate to financial position, results of operations, or presentation of cash flows, whereas a trial balance presentation uses titles such as "trial balance," "adjusted trial balance," and "listing of general ledger accounts."
- Financial statements are formatted to show mathematical relationships, such as Assets = Liabilities + Owners' Equity, and Revenues − Expenses = Net income, whereas a trial balance is formatted to show that Debits = Credits.
- The activity statement shows the net results of operations for a period (net income, revenues in excess of expenditures, etc.), whereas a trial balance makes no attempt to disclose results of operations.
- Generally, the statement of financial position shows assets in order of liquidity and liabilities in order of maturity, whereas a trial balance presents accounts in the order in which they appear in the general ledger.
- A set of financial statements demonstrates the articulation of the individual financial statements in that the results of operations are added to

or subtracted from retained earnings, whereas in a trial balance no such articulation is attempted.

Services that certified public accountants (CPAs) provide that are other than compilation, review, or audit services are considered "other accounting services." Examples are (1) adjusting and closing books, (2) consulting on financial matters, (3) preparing tax returns, and (4) providing automated bookkeeping or data processing services. Other accounting services may not include the preparation or issuance of financial statements. Other accounting services may be performed prior to or concurrently with an engagement to compile or review financial statements.

All types of financial statements may be compiled or reviewed and may be for any type of business organization, including an estate, a trust, or an individual. The financial statements may reflect the operations of not-for-profit organizations, governments, governmental agencies, or other entities that prepare their financial statements using a comprehensive basis of accounting other than GAAP. Whenever the term "GAAP" is used in connection with compilation or review, its meaning also includes "an other comprehensive basis of accounting." As mentioned previously, compilation and review standards are not applicable to forecasts, projections, or similar financial presentations, or to financial information included in tax returns.

> **PLANNING AID REMINDER:** The SSARS Interpretation (November 1982) titled "Reporting on Tax Returns" states that an accountant may, at the client's request, compile or review financial information contained in tax returns or Form 5500 (Return of Employee Benefit Plan).

Services to a nonpublic client could include year-end examination in accordance with generally accepted auditing standards (GAAS), quarterly reviews (interim), monthly compilations (other than quarter or year end), tax return preparation, and other accounting services. Each of these is a separate service that may be rendered to a single client. The results accomplished by each service are significantly different from the results accomplished in any one of the other services. The performance of one service may overlap that of one or more of the other services, but each service has a different purpose and intended result. The purpose and intended result of each service should be clear to the accountant and the client and documented in the workpapers. Information that the accountant obtains while performing other accounting services may help the accountant complete the compilation or review service. If an engagement to perform accounting services for a client does not include compilation or review services, the accountant may not issue a report on unaudited financial statements if the client is a nonpublic company.

RISK ASSESSMENT POINT: The SSARS Interpretation (May 1991) titled "Applicability of Statements on Standards for Accounting and Review Services to Litigation Services" states that SSARS standards do not apply to financial statements submitted as part of a litigation or regulatory dispute before a trier of fact (1) if the accountant is functioning as an expert witness, (2) if the accountant's service involves being a trier of fact or acting for one, (3) if the work performed is to be subject to challenge by each party to the dispute, or (4) if the work performed is to be used exclusively as part of the dispute and becomes part of the attorney's work. (A "trier of fact" means a court, regulatory body, or governmental authority; their agents; a grand jury; or an arbitrator or mediator.)

Submission of Financial Statements

The CPA cannot submit financial statements to a nonpublic client or other parties unless those financial statements have been either compiled or reviewed. SSARS-1 (as amended by SSARS-8) establishes the following definition of submission of financial statements:

> Presenting to a client or third parties financial statements that the accountant has prepared either manually or through the use of computer software.

Based on the definition, at a minimum, a compilation must be performed by the CPA when both (1) the CPA presents financial statements to the client or a third party and (2) the CPA has prepared the financial statements. Unfortunately, SSARS-8 does not define what it means to present financial statements or what it means to prepare financial statements. The AICPA believes that it is the responsibility of each CPA to apply the definition of "submission of financial statements" to each engagement and then determine whether a compilation engagement, at a minimum, must be performed.

Although SSARS-8 does not define the preparation of financial statements, the *Compilation and Review Alert 2000/01* provides the following broad guidance:

- Bookkeeping services such as preparing, adjusting, and correcting entries is not the same as preparing financial statements.
- Preparing financial statements includes the use of "your knowledge, education, and experience to create financial statements that would not have existed otherwise."

Of course the degree of actions taken by the CPA are just as important as the actual services performed. For example, if a CPA prepares a single adjusting entry in order to complete the financial statements, that should generally not be construed to be the preparation of financial statements. However, if the CPA prepared all of the adjusting entries, it is likely that most CPAs would conclude that those actions would mean that the CPA has prepared the financial statements in the context of the guidance established by SSARS-8.

Responsibility and function of the accountant

In a compilation or review engagement, the accountant must comply with the general standards set forth in Rule 201 of the Code of Professional Conduct. The general standards are as follows:

> A member shall comply with the following standards and with any interpretations thereof by bodies designated by Council.
>
> A. Professional Competence. Undertake only those professional services that the member or the member's firm can reasonably expect to be completed with professional competence.
>
> B. Due Professional Care. Exercise due professional care in the performance of professional services.
>
> C. Planning and Supervision. Adequately plan and supervise the performance of professional services.
>
> D. Sufficient Relevant Data. Obtain sufficient relevant data to afford a reasonable basis for conclusions or recommendations in relation to any professional services performed.
>
> **PLANNING AID REMINDER:** The SSARS Interpretation (August 1981) titled "Planning and Supervision" states that Statements on Auditing Standards do not govern a compilation or review engagement of a nonpublic entity. However, accountants may still wish to consider a Statement on Auditing Standards [such as SAS-22 (Planning and Supervision)], or other textbooks and articles when they need guidance on planning and supervising a compilation or review engagement.

The degree of responsibility that the accountant takes on in a compilation or review must be clearly defined in a written report. An accountant may not issue a report on unaudited financial statements of a nonpublic entity unless he or she has complied with the applicable standards for a compilation or a review. The procedures, standards, and reporting obligations for a compilation or review are quite specific and are discussed in detail later in this chapter.

It is well established in accounting literature that the accuracy and fairness of financial statements are the responsibility of the management of the entity. Thus, the management of an entity is directly responsible for the design and proper implementation of effective internal control.

Independence

SSARS-1 does not require accountants to be independent on compilation engagements. Thus, accountants may issue compilation reports for entities of which they are not independent, provided that the report includes an additional paragraph stating that the accountant is not independent. The reason for the lack of independence, however, cannot be stated. Accountants must be independent for review engagements, or they may not issue reports on the review. Accountants should be guided by Rule 101 of the Code of Professional Conduct in determining whether they are independent.

Before accepting a review engagement, the accounting firm should make inquiries of its staff to determine whether there are any relationships with the client that might impair the firm's independence. For example, a member of the firm's staff in the office performing the engagement may have a relative who is a key employee of the prospective client.

Engagement letters

The use of engagement letters has long been encouraged. Most CPA firms, large and small, use them for all engagements, including those for write-up or other services. The engagement letter should clearly set forth the nature and limitations, if any, of the engagement. A carefully prepared engagement letter will considerably reduce the possibility of a misunderstanding with a client. Compilation and review standards require accountants to establish an understanding with their clients about the services to be performed. SSARS-1 states a preference that the understanding be in writing and cover at least the following:

- A description of the specific compilation and/or review services to be performed
- A description of the report expected to be rendered upon completion of the engagement and a caveat that if the accountant is unable to complete the compilation or a review, no report will be issued
- An explanation of the limitations of the engagement, including:
  — That the engagement cannot be relied on to disclose errors, irregularities (fraud), or illegal acts

— That the accountant will bring to the attention of management any material errors, irregularities (fraud), or illegal acts that are discovered during the engagement, unless they are clearly inconsequential

- A detailed description of any other accounting services to be performed

> **OBSERVATION:** The engagement letter content for a management-use-only compilation engagement is described later in this chapter.

If financial statements that omit substantially all disclosures and/or the statement of cash flows are to be compiled, an additional paragraph to the compilation report disclosing such omissions should be included in the engagement letter.

At the outset of an engagement the accountant may know that a departure, or departures, from GAAP exists. In this event, it may be appropriate to include in the engagement letter information to the effect that a modified report will be issued reflecting the departure(s) from GAAP, instead of the standard compilation or review report. This procedure should eliminate any misunderstanding about what type of report the client will receive when the engagement is completed.

The engagement letter should represent the understanding and agreement between the accountant and the client, and it may include information on the accountant's fee.

Generally accepted accounting principles

Generally accepted accounting principles apply to reviews, compilations, and audits. There is no special (limited) set of accounting rules that applies only to reviews and compilations.

> **PLANNING AID REMINDER:** The SSARS Interpretation (September 1990) titled "Special-Purpose Financial Presentations to Comply with Contractual Agreements or Regulatory Provisions" states that an accountant may conduct a review or a compilation of special-purpose financial presentations that (1) comply with a contractual agreement or regulatory provision and in so doing are incomplete but are otherwise in accordance with GAAP or OCBOA or (2) are not in accordance with GAAP or OCBOA because the basis of accounting is prescribed by a contractual agreement or regulatory provision. Reports on special-purpose financial presentations should be expanded to explain the purpose of the presentation and to note that the distribution of the accountant's report is restricted.

Generally accepted auditing standards

Compliance with GAAS is necessary in an audit engagement. GAAS are concerned with the professional qualities and judgment of the independent auditor in the performance of an audit and in the issuance of the audit report. Statements on Auditing Standards (SASs) are issued as Interpretations of GAAS and may also provide guidance to the accountant who performs services in connection with the unaudited financial statements of a public company. Statements on Quality Control Standards (SQCSs) cover all aspects of auditing or accounting and review services. Thus, they are applicable to compilation and review engagements as well as audit engagements.

Compilation and Review Alert—1999/2000 reiterates the basic concept that while the guidance found in generally accepted auditing standards and their related interpretations (SASs) do not have to be observed in a compilation or review engagement, that guidance may be helpful in some engagements. Exhibit AR 100-1 summarizes auditing standards that must be observed in compilation and review engagements.

EXHIBIT AR 100-1—AUDITING STANDARDS THAT MUST BE OBSERVED IN COMPILATION AND REVIEW ENGAGEMENTS

Auditing Standard	Applicability to Compilation and Review Engagements (with Reference to Codification of Statements on Auditing Standards and This Text)
• SAS-26: Association with Financial Statements report.	Observe guidance for determining when a successor CPA is allowed to reference the work of the predecessor CPA in the current (See AU Section 504.14–504.17.)
• SAS-50: Reports on the Application of Accounting Principles	Observe guidance when the CPA has not been engaged to report on an entity's financial statements but has been requested to provide written advice (1) on the application of accounting principles to specific transactions, (2) on the type of report that may be rendered on a client's financial statements, or (3) to intermediaries about the application of accounting principles. (See AU Section 625.)

AR § 100 • Compilation and Review of Financial Statements

Auditing Standard	Applicability to Compilation and Review Engagements (with Reference to Codification of Statements on Auditing Standards and This Text)
• SAS-58: Reports on Audited Financial Statements	Observe guidance when the CPA reports on comparative financial statements that omits required disclosures and the previous year's report was either qualified or an adverse or disclaimer of opinion was expressed.
• SAS-59: The Auditor's Consideration of an Entity's Ability to Continue as a Going Concern	Observe guidance when the CPA is evaluating the client's disclosure related to the going concern assumption. (See AU Section 341.)
• SAS-62: Special Reports	Observe guidance for determining what is a comprehensive basis of accounting other than GAAP. (See AU Section 623.10.)
• SAS-69: The Meaning of "Present Fairly in Conformity with Generally Accepted Accounting Principles"	Observe guidance for determining what constitutes GAAP for commercial enterprises, not-for-profit organizations, and state and local governments. (See AU Section 411.)
• SAS-75: Engagement to Apply Agreed-upon Procedures in Specified Elements, Accounts or Items of a Financial Statement	Observe guidance when the CPA is providing an assurance on elements, items, or accounts of a financial statement. (Note: A compilation or review report cannot be issued on these engagements.) (See AU Section 622.)

SSARS are issued to provide guidance to accountants concerning the standards and procedures applicable to the compilation or review of nonpublic entities.

In a compilation or review engagement, the accountant must first comply with the four general standards of Rule 201 of the Code of Professional

Conduct. These are (1) professional competence, (2) due professional care, (3) planning and supervision, and (4) sufficient relevant data.

> **ENGAGEMENT STRATEGY:** The SSARS Interpretation (December 1979) titled "Financial Statements Included in SEC Filings" states that an accountant, after considering all relevant facts, may conclude that he or she should follow Statements on Auditing Standards for guidance (instead of issuing a compilation or review report) where nonpublic companies are required to file unaudited financial statements with the SEC (for example, in issuing common stock to an ESOP or in the sale of limited partnership units).

Planning the engagement

The general standards of the profession require planning and supervision of a compilation or review engagement. Unfortunately, no promulgated pronouncements have been issued on this topic. A thorough discussion of planning and supervision is included in *Miller Compilations & Reviews*.

Probably the best method of planning and supervising a compilation engagement or a review engagement is to create a written work program tailored to the specific engagement.

As mentioned previously, no official pronouncements have been issued for supervising a compilation or a review engagement. However, much can be extracted from SAS-22 (AU 311) (Planning and Supervision)—which was issued for audit engagements—and applied to compilation and review engagements. The following discussion is based on SAS-22 (AU 311).

An accountant is required by the general standards of the profession (Rule 201) to adequately plan and supervise a compilation or review engagement. Planning and supervision usually necessitate (1) preparing a written work program, (2) obtaining knowledge of the client's business activities, and (3) dealing with differences that may arise between accountants involved in the engagement. Planning and supervision constitute a continuous function that lasts throughout the entire engagement, and the in-charge accountant may delegate it to other personnel.

More often than not, the accountant with final responsibility for the engagement will require that assistants help accomplish the objectives of the engagement. Controlling and directing the efforts of the assistants are integral parts of supervising. The supervising accountant must obtain assurance that the assistants are following the planned procedures.

Both the quality and the quantity of supervision are important. The extent of supervision depends on the qualifications of the assistants and the complexity of the work or subject matter. The supervisor must be kept constantly informed of new developments and significant problems that arise during the engagement. Also, the supervisor usually is charged with the responsibility of evaluating the quality and quantity of work performed by assistants.

A disagreement may arise between the supervisor and the assistants during the engagement. If the difference is not resolved, it should be appropriately documented in the workpapers of the engagement. In this event, the basis for final resolution of the disagreement should also be documented.

A time and personnel budget should be established and maintained for all but very small engagements. The budget should reflect the estimated time allocated to each item on the work program for the engagement. It should also reflect the type and grade of personnel assigned to the engagement. This budget should be carefully planned to allow the proper time and personnel for each facet of the engagement. More important, after the budget is carefully planned, it must be properly supervised in order to avoid significant variances with the actual results. The client should be informed when actual time on an engagement is significantly exceeding the budgeted time. Clients can become quite upset when faced with a much higher professional fee than was estimated, and the accountant's relationship with the client may suffer irreparable damage. Thus, the time and personnel budget, like all other aspects of an engagement, must be carefully planned and supervised.

Consideration of internal control

The objective of a review of financial statements is substantially different from the objective of a compilation of financial statements. In a review, the accountant performs inquiries and analytical procedures to provide a reasonable basis for expressing limited assurance that no material modifications need to be made to the financial statements in order for them to be in conformity with generally accepted accounting principles. In a compilation, the accountant's report includes a statement that he or she did not audit or review the financial statements and does not express any opinion or other form of assurance on them. Thus, a compilation is considered to be a lower level of service than a review.

The objective of a review also differs substantially from the objective of an audit of financial statements performed in accordance with generally accepted auditing standards. In an audit, the objective is to provide a reasonable basis for the auditor to express an opinion on the financial statements taken as a whole. The auditor obtains a reasonable basis for expressing an opinion by assessing internal controls, by testing controls, and by performing substantive tests of the accounting records.

In a compilation of financial statements, the accountant has no basis for expressing any opinion or other form of limited assurance. In a review, the accountant has a limited basis for expressing limited assurance that the financial statements substantially conform to GAAP. In an audit, the auditor is able to form a reasonable basis for expressing an opinion on the financial statements taken as a whole. One reason the auditor can express an opinion is that in an audit of financial statements an assessment of the internal controls over financial reporting is mandatory. In a compilation or a review, however, an assessment of internal controls is not required.

Compilation and review reporting obligations

The accountant's report communicates the extent of the responsibility being assumed, or the disclaimer of any responsibility, with respect to financial statements that the accountant is associated with. Compilation and review standards require that an accountant issue a report whenever financial statements of a nonpublic entity have been compiled or reviewed in compliance with standards for such services. Further, an accountant may not issue any report on unaudited financial statements of a nonpublic entity, and may not submit such financial statements to clients or others, unless the accountant has complied with standards for a compilation or a review. Under certain circumstances the CPA may be able to accept an engagement whereby compiled financial statements are not distributed to third parties. This type of compilation engagement is described later in this chapter under the heading "Management-Use-Only Compilation Engagements."

> **RISK ASSESSMENT POINT:** The SSARS Interpretation (September 1990) titled "Submitting Draft Financial Statements" states that the accountant should not submit draft financial statements if the accountant does not plan to complete the compilation or review engagement in a manner consistent with SSARS. When the accountant plans to complete the engagement in accordance with SSARS, draft financial statements may be submitted, but each page of the financial statements should be labeled "Working Draft" or some similar terminology. A draft of the accountant's anticipated report need not accompany the draft financial statements. The Interpretation notes that if the accountant originally intended to complete the engagement and submitted draft financial statements to the client but did not subsequently complete the engagement, it may be appropriate to document in the workpapers the reason for not completing the engagement.

Pencil copies of financial statements prepared solely for internal use of management by the accountant should include an appropriate compilation or review report. Moreover, financial statements or information completed on prescribed forms, such as those requested by regulatory and credit agencies, may not be prepared and issued unless the accountant (auditor) attaches to the prescribed form a compilation, review, or audit report.

> **RISK ASSESSMENT POINT:** The SSARS Interpretation (December 1979) titled "Reporting on the Highest Level of Service" states that if an accountant has both compiled and reviewed a client's financial statements for a review engagement, only the review report should be issued. However, if the accountant had been engaged only to perform a compilation, then the auditor is not obligated to issue the review report, unless the client decides to upgrade the engagement to a review.

If an accountant is engaged to compile interim-period financial statements and also to review the financial statements for another period that ends on the same date, the accountant may issue both reports.

All financial statements prepared under a comprehensive basis of accounting other than GAAP must include adequate disclosure describing the basis of accounting used. If the basis is not disclosed in a footnote or on each page of the financial statements, then it must be disclosed in the accountant's compilation or review report.

Association with financial statements

An accountant's name should not be used in a document that includes a nonpublic client's unaudited financial statements, unless the accountant performs a compilation or a review and prepares an appropriate report to accompany the financial statements. Alternatively, unaudited financial statements that have not been reviewed or compiled may include the name of the accountant if the client indicates the following on the financial statements:

- The accountant did not compile or review the financial statements.
- The accountant assumes no responsibility for the statements.

This notation may appear on each financial statement or on a separate page as a preface to the financial statements.

Reference to accountant's report

Each page of compiled or reviewed financial statements should be marked (1) "See accountant's compilation report" or (2) "See accountant's review report." If both compilation and review services are involved, the reference might state "See accountant's report."

Dating of accountant's report

Reports should be dated at the time substantially all the compilation or review procedures are completed in the field. That date may be prior to the accounting firm's supervisory review of the accountant's work. However, if the quality control review results in significant additional work to be performed at the client's premises, it may be appropriate to change the report date. Dual-dating may be used, when necessary, for a compilation report or a review report. The need for dual-dating arises when information disclosed in a note to the financial statements is of a date that is different from the date of the accountant's report. In other words, the accountant's report may refer to one date for most of the financial statement content and to one or more different dates for other specific items in the financial statements. For example, an accountant's report may be dated May 31, 20X8, except for footnote 10, which is dated June 15, 20X9.

If an accountant discovers that his or her name has been used without consent in connection with unaudited financial statements, the accountant should take whatever action is necessary to prevent the further use of his or her name. That may require consulting with legal counsel.

Withdrawing from an engagement

An accountant may decide to withdraw from an engagement before the engagement is completed. Withdrawing from an engagement may expose the accountant to legal liability, and for this reason it generally is prudent to consult legal counsel. SSARS-1 specifically states that the accountant should withdraw from an engagement under the following circumstances:

- The accountant is not independent and the client requires reviewed financial statements.
- The scope of the engagement has substantial limitations.
- The client has not allowed the accountant to correspond with its legal counsel or has not signed the client representation letter and is requesting a reduction in the level of services the accountant was to offer (either from an audit to a review or from a review to a compilation).
- The accountant is aware of client-supplied information that is "incorrect, incomplete, or otherwise unsatisfactory," and the client has refused or is unable to provide revised information.
- The accountant believes that disclosures were omitted for the purpose of misleading users.

- The accountant has not (or cannot) obtain sufficient knowledge of the client's business or industry as required for a compilation engagement.
- The financial statements contain departures from GAAP that cannot be adequately communicated to users in the modified accountant's report.

Change in the level of an engagement

During, but before the completion of, an engagement, a client may ask to change the level of service the accountant is performing. If the request for change in services is from a lower level to a higher level—for example, from a review to an audit or from a compilation to a review—no problem arises. A problem does arise, however, when the change is to a level of service lower than that which was being provided. The client may request a change to a lower level of service for many different reasons; for example:

- An audit or a review may no longer be required or may no longer be applicable, because of a change in circumstances.
- The client may have misunderstood the type of service that was being rendered or may not be aware of the other levels of service that the accountant can render.
- The client or others may impose a restriction on the scope of the examination.

Before agreeing to change to a lower level of service, the accountant must carefully consider the client's reason for the change and all other factors related to the change. Elimination of the requirement for an audit or a review or a misunderstanding about the type of services the accountant can provide would ordinarily be considered a reasonable basis for the accountant to accept a change in the engagement. However, a restriction on the scope of the examination should be evaluated for the possibility that information affected by the scope restriction may be incorrect, incomplete, or otherwise unsatisfactory. The restriction may preclude the accountant from issuing a review report or compilation report because he or she may be unable to satisfy the standards established by Statements on Standards for Accounting and Review Services (SSARS). Moreover, the accountant may consider the restrictions so severe that a review or compilation report cannot be issued.

In an audit engagement, if the client prohibits the accountant from obtaining information from the client's legal counsel, the accountant ordinarily should not issue a compilation report or review report on the financial statements. If in an audit or review engagement the client refuses to provide a client representation letter, the accountant should not issue a review report (when stepping down from an audit) on the financial statements and generally should not issue a compilation report (when stepping down from a review) on the financial statements.

If in the accountant's judgment a change to a lower level of service is acceptable, the accountant should perform the service in accordance with the standards applicable to the changed engagement. The accountant should make no mention in the report of the original engagement, any procedures accomplished for the original engagement, or any scope limitation that resulted in the changed service.

TYPES OF COMPILATION ENGAGEMENTS

SSARS-1 was amended by SSARS-8 to allow for the performance of a (1) traditional compilation engagement and (2) management-use-only compilation engagement, which are described in the *Compilation and Review Alert 2000/01* as follows:

- *Traditional compilation*—the CPA performs a compilation and issues a compilation report when he or she has been (1) engaged to compile and report on the financial statements or (2) when the CPA reasonably expects the financial statements to be used by a third party.

- *Management-use-only compilation*—the CPA performs a compilation, does not issue a compilation report, and does not reasonably expect the financial statements to be used by a third party.

Because of the nature of the management-use-only compilation the CPA should be cautious in performing this service. *Compilation and Review Alert 2000/01* notes that the issues that should be considered by the CPA in making this determination includes the following:

- *Needs of third parties*—Does a third party (for example, a bank) need compiled financial statements on a regular basis?

- *Information that might bear on the integrity of management*—Has information come to the CPA's attention that gives him or her reason to doubt the integrity of management?

- *Past experience with management*—Have past experiences on other engagements been positive?

- *Independence considerations*—The CPA may have to consider carefully the independence implications of being closely involved with management-use-only financial statements.

- *Cost/benefit considerations*—Can you perform the engagement at a reasonable cost to the client versus the benefit over a traditional compilation engagement?

- *Risk management considerations*—Some practitioners perceive this engagement as more risk than a traditional compilation (which offers the additional protection of the compilation report).

COMPILATION ENGAGEMENTS—TRADITIONAL

A compilation of financial statements is an accounting service in which an accountant prepares, or assists in preparing, financial statements without expressing any assurance that the statements are accurate and complete or are in conformity with GAAP. A compilation engagement may involve compiling and reporting on one financial statement, such as the balance sheet or a statement of income, and not on the other related financial statements, if those statements are not presented. As with audited financial statements, this limited reporting objective is not considered a scope limitation. It may also involve financial statements that omit the statement of cash flows and substantially all disclosures required by GAAP.

The accountant may actually prepare the financial statements, and the client could rely on the accountant's competence to see that they are appropriate and proper for the industry involved. This situation requires that the financial statements and all significant decisions made in preparing them be reviewed in detail with the client so that the client understands them as much as possible. In this manner, the client should be willing to accept the responsibility that the financial statements are the representations of management and not of the accountant. Compilation engagements may be undertaken for:

- Organizations for which the accountant is also writing up or adjusting the books and/or preparing tax returns
- Closely held organizations needing only limited outside credit
- Interim periods of a company's fiscal year with quarterly and/or year-end periods that are reviewed or audited

Promulgated Procedures Checklist

The CPA should perform the following procedures in a compilation engagement:

_____ Develop an understanding of the client

_____ Consider whether the client needs other accounting services

_____ Read the financial statements

_____ Consider whether additional procedures are needed in the engagement

_____ Consider obtaining a client representation letter

_____ Prepare an appropriate compilation report

Analysis and Application of Procedures

Develop an understanding of the client

The CPA should possess an adequate level of knowledge of the accounting principles and practices of the client's industry—to enable the accountant to compile financial statements in the form that is appropriate for the industry—and a general understanding of the client's business, including:

- Business transactions
- Form of accounting records
- Stated qualifications of accounting staff
- Accounting basis used to prepare statements
- Form and content of financial statements

An understanding of the client can be obtained through:

1. Experience with the client:
   a. Services in prior years (audits, preparation of tax returns and unaudited financial statements, consulting on various financial matters)
   b. Other accounting services being performed along with the engagement to compile financial statements, such as adjusting the books or preparing a working trial balance
2. Inquiry of responsible client personnel: The inquiries may be limited in that their intent is to obtain information on the broad characteristics of the five areas deemed necessary for adequate understanding. At the same time, however, they should be of sufficient scope that the accountant will understand the client well enough to read the financial statements as a knowledgeable professional and be able to assess the following:

a. Whether the statements are in the appropriate form for the client and the industry in which it operates

b. Whether all necessary disclosures have been made

c. Whether accounting principles appear to have been properly applied

d. Whether the relationship of information in the financial statements corresponds with the accountant's understanding of the client's business transactions

The level of understanding an accountant should achieve in the course of a compilation is not as deep as is required for a review or an audit. It does not, for example, include a review of the client's internal control.

Consider whether the client needs other accounting services

On the basis of the accountant's general knowledge of the client's business, the accountant should consider the need to perform other accounting services. (Such services may be limited to consulting on a specific accounting matter or may involve adjusting all or many of the significant accounts in the general ledger.) The need for such services may result from the accountant discovering, for example, that:

- The accounting records are inadequate.
- The accounting or bookkeeping personnel do not possess sufficient abilities or experience.
- The accounting basis used to maintain the books is incorrect.
- The information to be disclosed in the financial statements is not available.

Read the financial statements

After the accountant has obtained the required knowledge of the client and the industry in which the client operates, has completed any other accounting services deemed ßnecessary, and has prepared the financial statements, he or she should read the financial statements.

Reading the financial statements is one of the more important procedures in a compilation engagement. The accountant must apply all the knowledge and understanding previously obtained and must use his or her professional expertise effectively. Some of the questions the accountant must answer are these:

- Do the financial statements appear to be in the proper form and complete?
- Do the financial statements appear to be free from obvious material errors?
- Are all necessary disclosures made in reasonable detail?

Any information that the accountant is aware of, from any source, should be considered for possible indications that the financial statements may be inaccurate, incomplete, or otherwise unsatisfactory.

Financial statements that may be inaccurate or incomplete

Compilation standards do not require the accountant to perform any procedures to verify, corroborate, or review information supplied by the entity. However, the accountant may make inquiries or perform other procedures in the course of rendering other accounting services.

The accountant may discover—through inquiries, completion of other procedures, knowledge from prior engagements, and reading of the financial statements—information that is inaccurate, incomplete, or otherwise unsatisfactory. Compilation standards then require the accountant to obtain additional or revised information. However, the accountant is not required to verify, corroborate, or substantiate any additional or revised information received. If the entity refuses to provide the accountant with the requested additional or revised information, the accountant should withdraw from the compilation engagement. When an accountant is in the above situation, he or she should consider the need for consulting legal counsel.

Consider whether additional procedures are needed in the engagement

When an accountant has reason to suspect that the client's information, records, or statements may be inaccurate or incomplete, he or she must perform other accounting services unless the client agrees to correct the deficiencies that are impeding the completion of the accountant's engagement. If a client objects to any procedures that the accountant has deemed necessary, the accountant should consider withdrawing from the engagement. Additional procedures are simply extra procedures, not specifically required by applicable compilation or review standards, that an accountant may perform to assure a given set of facts or transactions.

Additional procedures should not be described in the compilation report. There is no prohibition against the accountant performing procedures of a review or an audit nature in order to verify or corroborate any information. However, such additional procedures should not be so expansive that a review, or even an audit, is in substance performed.

RISK ASSESSMENT POINT: The SSARS Interpretation (March 1983) titled "Additional Procedures" states that when an accountant performs auditing procedures such as the confirmation of receivables or the observation of inventories, the nature of the engagement is not changed from a compilation engagement or review engagement to an audit engagement. The accountant is free to perform those additional procedures he or she deems necessary under the circumstances. However, the accountant should be careful that others do not interpret the additional procedures as being part of an audit. For example, if information is confirmed with third parties, the confirmation may state that the information is sought as part of a compilation engagement and not as part of the audit of the client's financial statements.

Consider obtaining a client representation letter

Compilation standards do not require that client representations be obtained. However, because of the very limited procedures required for a compilation and the possibility of misunderstandings on accounting information, having obtained a client representation letter may be useful, especially when the client does not understand that the financial statements are its responsibility.

Prepare an appropriate compilation report

The accountant's report, which should accompany financial statements that have been compiled, but not reviewed or audited, should state that:

1. A compilation has been performed.

2. A compilation is limited to presenting information that is the representation of management or owners in the form of financial statements.

3. The accountant has not audited or reviewed the statements and expresses no opinion or any assurance on them.

The compilation report should make no reference to GAAP or to its consistent application. Furthermore, any additional procedures that may have been performed should not be described in the accountant's report.

The following is the recommended form for an accountant's report on a compilation of financial statements:

> We have compiled the accompanying balance sheet of ABC Company as of December 31, 20XX, and the related statements of income, retained earnings, and cash flows for the year then

ended, in accordance with Statements on Standards for Accounting and Review Services issued by the American Institute of Certified Public Accountants.

A compilation is limited to presenting in the form of financial statements information that is the representation of management. We have not audited or reviewed the accompanying financial statements and, accordingly, do not express an opinion or any other form of assurance on them.

Compilation report modifications

An accountant's report on a compilation of financial statements may have to be modified under some circumstances. The following circumstances may require a modification of the accountant's compilation report:

- Substantial omission of disclosures
- Accountant not independent
- Departure from GAAP
- Inadequate disclosure
- Uncertainty and going concern
- Inconsistency
- Comprehensive basis of accounting other than GAAP

Substantial omission of disclosures

If the client requests it, the accountant may compile financial statements that omit substantially all disclosures required by GAAP. Such disclosures include those often found in the body of the financial statements, such as:

- Inventories by type (raw materials, work in process, finished goods)
- Property by major classes
- Capital stock authorized, issued, and outstanding

Required disclosures may be omitted only if the accountant believes that the omissions are not intended to mislead any persons who may reasonably be expected to use the financial statements. If the required disclosures are omitted, the accountant's compilation report must clearly indicate the omissions.

RISK ASSESSMENT POINT: The SSARS Interpretation (August 1981) titled "Withdrawal from Compilation or Review Engagement" states that if the accountant concludes that a client's departures from GAAP are intended to mislead users of the financial statements, the accountant should withdraw from the engagement.

The accountant must evaluate carefully the reasons for the omission of required disclosures. Management's apparent reasons for the omissions and the intended purpose of the financial statements must be included in the accountant's evaluation.

If the financial statements include some notes and the accountant has concluded that required disclosures may be omitted, the notes should be labeled "Selected information—substantially all disclosures required by generally accepted accounting principles are not included." The compilation report also should be modified by the addition of a third paragraph disclosing the omissions.

A similar situation arises when the statement of cash flows is omitted from a presentation that includes a balance sheet, a statement of income, and a statement of retained earnings. Under GAAP, a statement of cash flows is a required statement, and reference to such omission must be made in the accountant's compilation report. The following is the recommended third paragraph that should be added to the accountant's compilation report when disclosures and/or a statement of cash flows is omitted:

> Management has elected to omit substantially all the disclosures (and the statement of cash flows) required by generally accepted accounting principles. If the omitted disclosures were included in the financial statements, they might influence the user's conclusions about the Company's financial position, results of operations, and cash flows. Accordingly, these financial statements are not designed for those who are not informed about such matters.

If only the statement of cash flows is omitted, the third paragraph should read:

> A statement of cash flows for the year ended December 31, 20XX, has not been presented. Generally accepted accounting principles require that such a statement be presented when financial statements purport to present financial position and results of operations.

RISK ASSESSMENT POINT: The SSARS Interpretation (November 1980) titled "Reporting on Financial Statements That Previously Did Not Omit Substantially All Disclosures" states that if financial statements that omit substantially all disclosures are compiled from financial statements the accountant had previously audited, the report on the newly issued comparative compiled financial statements should indicate whether the accountant's opinion is qualified, adverse, or disclaimed, and the principal reasons for such opinion. Similarly, if the accountant issued a modified compilation or review report on financial statements that previously did not omit disclosures, the newly issued comparative compilation report should include a discussion of any modifications.

RISK ASSESSMENT POINT: The SSARS Interpretation (May 1982) titled "Reporting When Management Has Elected to Omit Substantially All Disclosures" encourages the use of the phrase "management has elected to omit substantially all of the disclosures" to make it obvious that it was management's decision, rather than the accountant's decision, to omit the required information. Other phrases may be used if the report clearly indicates that management has made the decision to omit the information. However, the phrase "the financial statements do not include substantially all of the disclosures" should *not* be used.

Accountant not independent

An accountant who is not independent with respect to an entity may compile financial statements for such an entity and issue a compilation report thereon. In this circumstance, the accountant adds the following statement to the standard compilation report: "We are not independent with respect to Company X."

Departure from GAAP

During any type of engagement, the accountant may become aware that the financial statements are not in conformity with GAAP, which require adequate disclosure. The omission of substantially all disclosures and/or the statement of cash flows, although such omissions constitute a departure from GAAP, is permitted in a compilation because of the special disclosure provisions. In any other departure from GAAP, however, the accountant should recommend that the financial statements be revised to conform to GAAP. If the client does not agree to revise the financial statements, the accountant must consider whether to modify the compilation report or to with-

AR § 100 • Compilation and Review of Financial Statements 693

draw from the engagement and provide no further services to the client regarding the financial statements. In this event, it may be advisable for the accountant to consult with legal counsel.

If the accountant decides that a modification to the compilation report is adequate to disclose the departure from GAAP, the report should be modified in the following manner:

- The second paragraph of the standard compilation report should be expanded to include a statement that the accountant has become aware of a departure or departures from GAAP.

- The departure or departures should be described in a separate paragraph.

- The effects of the departure or departures on the financial statements should be disclosed—if such effects are known because of determination by management or because of procedures completed by the accountant. If the effects are not known, the accountant is not required to determine them. The accountant must, however, include a statement in the compilation report that the effects of the departure or departures have not been determined.

The following is an example of an accountant's compilation report that has been modified to disclose a departure from GAAP:

> We have compiled the accompanying balance sheet of ABC Company as of December 31, 20XX, and the related statements of income, retained earnings, and cash flows for the year then ended, in accordance with Statements on Standards for Accounting and Review Services issued by the American Institute of Certified Public Accountants.
>
> A compilation is limited to presenting in the form of financial statements information that is the representation of management. We have not audited or reviewed the accompanying financial statements and, accordingly, do not express an opinion or any other form of assurance on them. However, we did become aware of a departure from generally accepted accounting principles that is described in the following paragraph.
>
> As disclosed in note X to the financial statements, generally accepted accounting principles require that land and building be stated at cost. Management has informed us that the Company has stated its land and building at appraised value and that, if generally accepted accounting principles had been followed, the land and building accounts and stockholders' equity would have been decreased by $800,000.

Inadequate disclosure

Generally accepted accounting principles require that adequate disclosure be made of all pertinent information. Thus, inadequate disclosure is a departure from GAAP, and the same modification rules apply.

Uncertainty and going concern

GAAP require that significant uncertainties be disclosed in the financial statements. Thus, an undisclosed uncertainty requires a modification of the accountant's compilation report in the same manner as that of a departure from GAAP.

> **PLANNING AID REMINDER:** The SSARS Interpretation (December 1982) titled "Reporting on Uncertainties" states that SAS-59 (The Auditor's Consideration of an Entity's Ability to Continue as a Going Concern) should be used as a guide when the accountant is evaluating the disclosure of an uncertainty in compiled or reviewed financial statements. The Interpretation also notes that compiled financial statements may omit substantially all of the disclosures required by GAAP, including a disclosure of an uncertainty, no matter how significant the uncertainty may be. However, the phrase "substantial doubt about the entity's ability to continue as a going concern" (as illustrated in SAS-59) should be used only in an audit report and not in a review report or compilation report that refers to the going-concern uncertainty (emphasis of a matter).

Inconsistency

A violation of the consistency standard does not require modification of the accountant's standard compilation report if the accounting change is properly accounted for and disclosed in the financial statements. However, the accountant is free to emphasize in a separate paragraph that an accounting change has occurred.

Comprehensive basis of accounting other than GAAP

A compilation of financial statements may be presented on a comprehensive basis of accounting other than GAAP. The basis of the accounting used must be disclosed in the financial statements. If the basis of accounting other than GAAP is not disclosed in the financial statements, the accountant must modify the compilation report to include the disclosure of the basis of accounting used. The modification of the accountant's report is accomplished in the same manner as that for substantial omission of disclosures, which was discussed earlier in this Section.

The SSARS Interpretation (December 1982) titled "Reporting on a Comprehensive Basis of Accounting Other Than Generally Accepted Accounting Principles" states that when compiled financial statements are prepared on a comprehensive basis other than GAAP and omit substantially all disclosures, the following paragraph should be added to the standard compilation report:

> The financial statements have been prepared on the accounting basis [*describe accounting basis*], which is a comprehensive basis of accounting other than generally accepted accounting principles.

Emphasis of a matter

Regardless of the quality and quantity of disclosures for uncertainties, inconsistencies, and other disclosures, the accountant may deem it advisable to emphasize a particular matter in the compilation report.

Subsequent discovery of facts existing at date of accountant's report

Standards for compilation services do not include any obligation that the accountant perform procedures after the date of the compilation report. However, the accountant may become aware of information subsequent to the date of the report that may cause doubt about the accuracy or completeness of the information previously received from the client. If the new information is accurate and would have caused the accountant to modify the report or to recommend adjustments to the financial statements, the accountant should look to GAAS for guidance. Under GAAS, this situation is covered by AU Section 561 (Subsequent Discovery of Facts Existing at the Date of the Auditor's Report) of SAS-1 (Codification of Auditing Standards and Procedures). In applying this guidance, the accountant must keep in mind the different objectives of an audit and a compilation engagement. Because of possible legal implications, the accountant also should consider consulting with legal counsel.

> **ENGAGEMENT STRATEGY:** The SSARS Interpretation (November 1980) titled "Discovery of Information After the Date of the Accountant's Report" states that if the accountant knows that the financial statements should be revised because of the discovery of information after the date of the report, the accountant should follow the general guidance established by SAS-1, AU Section 561.

Supplementary information

In many cases, financial statements reported on by accountants will include supplementary information, such as:

- Details of balance sheet accounts, such as aging of accounts receivable or inventory by product lines
- Details of cost of sales and/or operating expenses
- Sales analysis

Supplementary information that is not part of the client's basic financial statements may be compiled, depending on the requirements of the engagement as specified in the engagement letter or on the understanding with the client. When the client has requested that the supplementary information be compiled, the accountant should clearly indicate in the compilation report that the information has been part of the engagement. Alternatively, the accountant can issue a separate compilation report on the supplementary information.

When the engagement does not include compiling supplementary information, there should be no chance that readers of the financial statements will misunderstand the responsibility of the accountant. Misunderstanding may be avoided by (1) the client clearly stating (in a preamble to the supplementary information) that the accountant has not compiled the supplementary information or (2) the accountant adding a separate paragraph stating that the supplementary information has not been compiled.

COMPILATION ENGAGEMENTS—MANAGEMENT USE ONLY

SSARS-8 addresses some of the issues related to the perceived need for financial statements that are not distributed externally. One issue was addressed by creating a new reporting method (called "management use only") when a compilation engagement is performed. As explained here, the same procedures are used in a management-use-only compilation as in a traditional compilation engagement except a compilation report is not issued.

The Meaning of Third Parties

A management-use-only compilation engagement (communication but no compilation report) can only be performed when the CPA "submits financial statements to a client that are not reasonably expected to be used by a third party." SSARS-8 defines a third party as follows:

All parties except for members of management who are generally knowledgeable and understand the nature of the procedures applied and the basis of accounting and assumptions used in the preparation of the financial statements.

The CPA's determination of whether the financial statements are not reasonably expected to be used by a third party is simply based on the representation by management that third parties will not use the financial statements. The CPA can accept that representation unless the he or she has obtained information that suggests otherwise.

The definition of a third party established by SSARS-8 is by exception. That is, all parties are considered to be third parties (including members of management) except when (1) they are members of management and (2) they have sufficient expertise to understand the unique nature of the management-use-only compilation engagement and the accounting basis used to prepare the financial statements. In determining who may be a member of management the following description found in FAS-57 (T R36) (Related Parties) is useful:

> Persons who are responsible for achieving the objectives of the enterprise and who have the authority to establish policies and make decisions by which those objectives are to be pursued. Management normally includes members of the board of directors, the chief executive officer, chief operating officer, vice presidents in charge of principal business functions (such as sales, administration, or finance), and other persons who perform similar policymaking functions. Persons without formal titles also may be members of management.

The CPA has no responsibility to determine whether the client has actually restricted the distribution of management-use-only financial statements to the appropriate individuals. For this reason, the CPA may wish to emphasize the importance of the limited distribution of the financial statements by requiring the engagement letter to state explicitly that if management needs to distribute financial statements to third parties, that will require a separate service.

If the CPA becomes aware that the client has unintentionally provided the financial statements to third parties (as defined in SSARS-8), the client should be instructed to obtain the financial statements from those inappropriate parties. If the client complies with this request, no further action is necessary. On the other hand, if the client does not retrieve the financial statements or if the client intentionally provides the financial statements to third parties, the CPA should seek legal advice in determining whether third parties should be informed that the financial statements are not for third-party use.

Promulgated Procedures Checklist

When an accountant accepts a management-use-only compilation engagement, the following procedures (which are found in paragraphs 5 and 7 through 10 of SSARS-1) must be performed:

- Develop an understanding with the client.
- Acquire an adequate understanding of the accounting principles and practices of the client's industry.
- Develop a general understanding of the nature of the client's business transactions.
- Develop a general understanding of the stated qualifications of the client's accounting personnel.
- Develop a general understanding of the accounting basis used to prepare the client's financial statements.
- Develop a general understanding of the form and content of the client's financial statements.
- Consider whether other professional services are needed in order to complete the compilation engagement.
- Read the financial statements.
- On the basis of information collected by using other compilation procedures and information that otherwise has come to your attention, consider whether additional or revised information must be obtained.
- Prepare an engagement letter (method of reporting on financial statements).

The procedures listed above are the same as those that must be performed in a traditional compilation (that is, the engagement where a compilation report is issued). These procedures are discussed earlier in this chapter and are not discussed here except for how their application differs in a management-use-only compilation engagement.

Develop an understanding with the client

When a management-use-only compilation is performed the CPA does not issue a compilation report but, rather, "communicates" with the client. This written communication takes the form of an engagement letter, which is more fully discussed later in this chapter (see the section titled "Standard Engagement Letter").

> **OBSERVATION:** An engagement letter is not required in a traditional compilation engagement; however, it is advisable to obtain one. Whether or not an engagement letter is obtained in a traditional compilation engagement, the CPA must nonetheless develop an understanding with the client.

Consider whether additional or revised information must be obtained

In a traditional compilation engagement, when the CPA concludes that the client has provided information that is "incorrect, incomplete, or otherwise unsatisfactory," the CPA must obtain revised or additional information. However, in a management-use-only compilation, it may not be necessary to obtain the revised or additional information if the CPA concludes that management may "have the requisite knowledge of the business to put the information in the proper context."

Prepare an engagement letter (method of reporting on financial statements)

When a management-use-only compilation engagement is completed, the CPA does not issue a compilation report. The communication of the nature of the engagement is provided to the client through an engagement letter that includes the following:

- Description of the nature and limitations of the services provided

- Statement that a compilation is limited to presenting in the form of financial statements information that is the representation of management

- Statement that the financial statements have not been audited or reviewed

- Statement that no opinion or any other form of assurance on the financial statements will be provided

- Acknowledgement that management has knowledge about the nature of the procedures applied and the basis of accounting and assumptions used in the preparation of the financial statements

- Acknowledgement of management's representation and agreement that the financial statements will not be used by third parties

- Statement that the engagement cannot be relied upon to disclose errors, fraud, or illegal acts

Exhibit AR100-2 illustrates an engagement letter that includes the understanding between the CPA and the client in a management-use-only compilation engagement.

EXHIBIT AR 100-2—ENGAGEMENT LETTER—COMPILATION OF FINANCIAL STATEMENTS NOT INTENDED FOR THIRD PARTY USE

Mr. Randall G. Calfee, President
Bluefield Company,
Bluefield, NJ 08000

Dear Mr. Calfee:

This letter is to confirm our understanding of the terms and objectives of our engagement and the nature and limitations of the services we will provide.

We will perform the following services:

1. We will compile, from information you provide, the [*monthly, quarterly, or other frequency*] financial statements of Bluefield Company for the year 20X5. A compilation is limited to presenting in the form of financial statements information that is the representation of management. We will not audit or review the financial statements and, accordingly, will not express an opinion or any other form of assurance on them. The financial statements will not be accompanied by a report.

Based upon our discussion with you, these statements are for management's use only and are not intended for third-party use.

Material departures from generally accepted accounting principles (GAAP) or other comprehensive basis of accounting (OCBOA) may exist and the effects of those departures, if any, on the financial statements may not be disclosed. In addition, substantially all disclosures required by GAAP or OCBOA may be omitted. [*The CPA may wish to identify known departures.*] Notwithstanding these limitations, you represent that you have knowledge about the nature of the procedures applied and the basis of accounting and assumptions used in the preparation of the financial statements that allows you to place the financial information in the proper context. Further, you represent and agree that the use of the financial statements will be limited to members of management with similar knowledge.

The financial statements are intended solely for the information and use of [*include specified members of management*] and are not intended to be and should not be used by any other party [*optional*].

2. We will also [*discussion of other services—optional*].

Our engagement cannot be relied upon to disclose errors, fraud, or illegal acts that may exist. However, we will inform the appropriate level of management of any material errors that come to our attention and any fraud or illegal acts that come to our attention unless they are clearly inconsequential.

In view of the limitations described above, you agree not to take or assist in any action seeking to hold us liable for damages due to any deficiency in the financial statements we prepare and you agree to hold us harmless from any liability and related legal costs arising from any third-party use of the financial statements in contravention of the terms of this agreement [*optional*].

Our fee for these services [*fill in*].

Should you require financial statements for third-party use, we would be pleased to discuss with you the requested level of service. Such engagement would be considered separate and not deemed to be part of the services described in this engagement letter.

If the foregoing is in accordance with our understanding, please sign the copy of the letter in the space provided and return it to us.

Sincerely,

[*Signature of CPA*]

Accepted and agreed to:
Bluefield Company

_____   _____

[*Signature and Title*]   [*Date*]

Note: SSARS-8 points out that some CPAs prefer not to obtain an acknowledgement from the client, in which case the last paragraph of the foregoing letter would be omitted. In that case, the first sentence to the engagement letter may read "This letter sets forth our understanding of the terms and objectives of our engagement . . ."

> **OBSERVATION:** Although it is not required by SSARS-8, it is preferable to have the engagement letter signed by management and returned to the CPA.

In some instances, the CPA may want to restrict the use of the financial statements to specifically named individuals. In that case, the engagement letter can include wording such as "the financial statements are intended solely for the information and use of [*name the individuals*], and are not intended to be and should not be used by any other party."

> **OBSERVATION:** The engagement letter may cover more than one period; however, it is advisable to update the engagement letter on an annual basis.

Standard engagement letter modifications

Although the engagement letter is not a report, there are certain matters related to the engagement that should be communicated to the reader (certain management personnel as discussed earlier). The modification circumstances include the following:

- Lack of independence
- Departures from GAAP or OCBOA
- Omission of substantially all disclosures
- Reference to supplementary information

Lack of independence

A management-use-only compilation engagement can be accepted when the CPA is not independent; however, the CPA's lack of independence should be disclosed in the engagement letter. The reason for the lack of independence should not be explained in the letter. When the CPA is not independent the following sentence is added to the standard engagement letter:

> I (we) am (are) not independent with respect to Bluefield Company.
>
> **OBSERVATION:** The CPA cannot report in anyway on reviewed financial statements when he or she is not independent. The standards established by SSARS-8 apply only to compilation engagements, not review engagements.
>
> **OBSERVATION:** SSARS-1 notes that the determination of independence is a matter of professional judgment. The CPA should

use the guidelines on independence provided by the AICPA Code of Professional Conduct Rule 101 (Independence), Interpretations of Rule 101, and Ethics Rulings on Independence. Also a CPA must be aware of any additional independence rules that may be established by his or her state board of accountancy, state CPA society, or relevant regulatory agencies.

Departures from GAAP or OCBOA

If the CPA believes that the financial statements may have material departures from GAAP or OCBOA, the standard engagement letter may be modified to warn the reader of this possibility. This can be accomplished by adding the following sentence to the letter:

> Material departures from generally accepted accounting principles [other comprehensive basis of accounting] may exist and the effects of those departures, if any, on the financial statements may not be disclosed.

SSARS-8 does not require in a management-use-only compilation engagement that every known material departure be identified in the engagement letter.

Compilation and Review Alert 2000/01 points out that there is no need to identify in the engagement letter the specific basis used to prepare the financial statements. The management-use-only compilation engagement is based on the assumption that the user(s) have participated in determining which basis or presentation best suits his or her needs. Thus, the financial statement presentation could be based on GAAP, OCBOA, or presumably on any other basis of accounting deemed appropriate by the intended users.

> **OBSERVATION:** Generally the CPA must be careful to use the appropriate financial statement headings depending on the basis of accounting used to prepare the financial statements. For example, the title "Income Statement" would be appropriate for a GAAP-based financial statements but not a cash-based activity statement. However, *Compilation and Review Alert 2000/01* notes that in a for management-use-only compilation engagement "[because of the] restricted nature of these financial statements, strict adherence to proper titles is not always necessary."

Omission of substantially all disclosures

A client may prepare the financial statements that are intended for management use only and omit substantially all disclosures. In this circumstance, the CPA may modify the standard engagement letter and alert the reader to the omissions by including the following sentence in the letter.

> Substantially all disclosures (and the statement of comprehensive income and statement of cash flows) required by generally accepted accounting principles (or an other comprehensive basis of accounting) may be omitted.

Reference to supplementary information

Management-use-only financial statements may be accompanied by supplementary information that is not part of the financial statements. For example, those financial statements may be accompanied by charts, tables, and additional information for a particular line item in the financial statements. Under this circumstance, the CPA should modify the standard engagement letter to explain the level of responsibility taken with respect to the supplementary information. This can be accomplished by adding the following sentence to the engagement letter:

> The other data accompanying the financial statements are presented only for supplementary analysis purposes and were compiled from information that is the representation of management, without audit or review, and we do not express an opinion or any other form of assurance on such data.

Comparative financial statements

A CPA may prepare a report on comparative financial statements when the previous year's financial statements were subject to a management-use-only compilation; however, the current compilation report must cover both years of the engagement.

Notations on financial statements

SSARS-8 requires that each page of the financial statements include a legend that identifies the restricted nature of the financial statements. *Compilation and Review Alert 2000/01* identifies the following as examples that could be used to satisfy this requirement:

- Restricted for management's use only.

- Solely for the information and use of the management of Bluefield Company and is not intended to be and should not be used by any other party.

- These financial statements are for use by management only and should not be relied upon by others. These statements may contain material departures from generally accepted accounting principles and the effects of those departures, if any, are not disclosed.
- Restricted for management use only—not for external distribution.

> **OBSERVATION:** The legend placed on the financial statements should not suggest that the financial statements are "for internal use." They are more restrictive than internal-use financial statements.

Applicability of management-use financial statements to business enterprises

A management-use-only compilation engagement can be accepted for business organizations (corporations, partnerships, joint ventures, etc.) and other organizations if the financial statements are not subject to public examination. For example, a management-use-only compilation engagement would not be appropriate for governmental entities, because the entity's management cannot legally restrict the distribution of the financial statements. On the other hand, it would be appropriate to accept a management-use-only engagement for the compilation of personal financial statements where the individual is the only intended user, assuming that the individual is "generally knowledgeable and understands the nature of the procedures applied and the basis of accounting and assumptions used in the preparation of the financial statements."

Change to a different engagement

A CPA may be initially engaged to perform a traditional compilation engagement and then be requested to change to a management-use-only engagement. The CPA may change to the latter type of engagement if he or she believes that the request is reasonable. In addition, the CPA must reasonably expect that the financial statements will not be used by a third party.

In some instances the CPA may accept and/or perform a management-use-only compilation engagement and then later be requested to perform a different service (i.e., traditional compilation, review, or audit). There is no restriction on accepting the new engagement; however, this is a new service and the previous engagement letter for the management-use-only compilation engagement would not apply. Also, the new engagement must be performed in a manner to satisfy the appropriate professional standards established by either the SSARS series or the SAS series.

Compilation of interim financial statements

A CPA may perform a management-use-only compilation engagement for interim financial statements and then at the end of the year perform a traditional compilation engagement on the annual financial statements. However, the year-end engagement is considered a separate engagement and the performance and reporting standards established by SSARS-1 must be observed.

Draft financial statements

During the course of a management-use-only compilation engagement appropriate management personnel (not third parties) may ask the CPA to submit a draft of the financial statements compiled. The CPA may submit such a draft as long as the performance standards listed earlier in this chapter have been completed and each page of the financial statements carries a legend (as discussed earlier) indicating the restricted nature of the financial statements.

REVIEW OF ENGAGEMENTS

A review is a level of service higher than a compilation because it results in an expression of limited assurance. The limited assurance is contained in a report by the accountant stating that he or she is not aware of any material modifications that should be made to the financial statements in order for them to be in conformity with GAAP. The accountant must perform sufficient inquiry and analytical procedures to give a reasonable basis for that conclusion. These inquiries and analytical procedures are the major difference between a review and a compilation.

A review is a level of service lower than an audit of financial statements. It does not provide a basis for expressing an opinion under GAAS, because it does not require many of the significant procedures required in an audit.

A review engagement may involve reporting on all the basic financial statements or on only one financial statement, such as a balance sheet or a statement of income. A review may not include reporting on financial statements that omit substantially all disclosures required by GAAP, unless such omissions are completely disclosed in the accountant's report. This obviously is not a practical alternative.

Promulgated Procedures Checklist

The CPA should perform the following procedures in a review engagement:

    _____ Develop knowledge of the client's accounting principles and practices.

AR §100 • Compilation and Review of Financial Statements

_____ Develop knowledge of the client's business.

_____ Perform appropriate inquiries and analytical procedures.

_____ Consider performing additional review procedures.

_____ Document procedures performed in the review engagement.

_____ Read the financial statements.

_____ Obtain a client representation letter.

_____ Prepare an appropriate review report.

Analysis and Application of Procedures

Develop knowledge of the client's accounting principles and practices

The accountant should possess a level of knowledge of the accounting principles and practices of the industry in which the client operates. The level of knowledge of accounting principles should be sufficient enough to provide the accountant with a reasonable basis to express limited assurance that no material modifications are needed to have financial statements conform to GAAP or to an other comprehensive basis of accounting.

Develop knowledge of the client's business

The accountant should posses an understanding of the following characteristics of a client's business:

1. Organization
2. Operating characteristics (including types of product or services, method of production or acquisition of products sold, method of distributing products or rendering services, operating locations and compensation method)
3. Nature of its assets, liabilities, revenues, and expenses
4. Material transactions with related parties

The knowledge and understanding should be of such a level that the accountant's inquiry and analytical procedures will provide a reasonable basis for expressing the limited assurance that is the ultimate goal of a review engagement.

The required level of understanding of a client's business may be obtained by:

- Previous or current experience in providing the client services such as audits, of tax return preparation, compiling of financial statements, and consultation on various financial matters
- Inquiry of client personnel
- Previous or current experience with other entities in the same industry as the client

Perform appropriate inquiries and analytical procedures

Inquiries should be directed at persons in the client's organization at sufficiently high levels to obtain reasonable assurance that the responses are proper and adequate. They should be tailored to each engagement and should cover all the following:

- Accounting principles and practices used and the method of applying them
- Procedures for recording, classifying, and summarizing transactions and for accumulating information for disclosure in footnotes
- Actions authorized by stockholders, board of directors, committees of the board, or other management groups

Inquiries also should be directed to officers responsible for financial and accounting matters concerning these questions: (1) Have the financial statements been prepared in conformity with GAAP? (2) Have the accounting principles and practices been consistently applied? (3) Have there been changes in business activities? (4) Have any events occurred subsequent to the date of the financial statements? Further, any questions that have come up in performing the review should be directed to these officers.

The accountant must use professional judgment to determine the extent of inquiries required, and the inquiries must be sufficiently comprehensive to cover all significant amounts and matters. When determining the extent and type of inquiries, the accountant should consider the following items:

- Nature and significance of an item
- Probability of misstatement

- Extent to which management's judgment enters into the determination of a particular item
- Knowledge obtained during a previous or the current engagement
- Qualifications of accounting personnel
- Deficiencies in financial data or the accounting system

Analytical procedures to be performed for the purpose of a review should be designed to detect relationships and individual items that appear to be unusual and therefore subject to inquiries addressed to responsible individuals. Additional procedures may involve the following: comparison of current-period financial statements with those for comparable prior period(s) and with budgets or forecast of anticipated results (if available), and the study of financial statements to isolate items that do not conform to their predictable pattern on the basis of prior experience. Examples of some of the elements in financial statements that would be expected to conform to a predictable relationship are:

- Sales and accounts receivable
- Sales and cost of sales
- Interest expense and debt
- Sales and commissions and freight out
- Depreciation and property (also maintenance and repairs)

Moreover, the accountant should consider adjustments made to the financial statements in previous periods, because they may affect his or her judgment on the results of other analytical procedures. In addition, the accountant should consider whether similar adjustments should be made during the current period.

Review procedures also require that the accountant read the financial statements to determine whether they are in conformity with GAAP.

Consider performing additional review procedures

The performance of a review does not provide assurance that the accountant will become aware of all significant matters, nor does it provide assurance that inaccuracies or the omission of necessary disclosures will come to his or her attention. However, any information that the accountant becomes aware of during a review, regardless of its source, that casts doubt on the accuracy or completeness of the financial statements must be resolved. In order to issue the report with limited assurance, the accountant should perform any additional procedures he or she deems necessary. Such other procedures may include:

- Further inquiry of responsible persons
- Other accounting services
- Consultation with the client on matters such as the proper accounting principles to be applied in recording transactions or the proper treatment of transactions for tax purposes

Degree of corroborative evidence

When the CPA concludes that additional review procedures should be performed, the circumstances surrounding the questionable information should dictate the degree of corroborative evidence that should be collected. In general, the decision to collect additional evidence does not mean that the level of assurance for a particular item has increased from that of a review engagement (limited assurance) to that of an audit engagement (reasonable assurance). For example, if the CPA is concerned with the nature of a large, nontrade notes receivable that is presented as a current asset, it does not mean that the CPA must confirm the receivable with the outside party. An appropriate explanation by the client may satisfy the CPA that the note is properly classified in the balance sheet. On the other hand, the CPA, because of the circumstances of the particular engagement, may employ extended review procedures that would normally be considered more rigorous than those related to a typical audit engagement.

Incomplete review

There can be no scope limitation on a review. The accountant must be free to perform whatever procedures he or she deems necessary, and those procedures must be accomplished or the review will be incomplete. An incomplete review will preclude an accountant from issuing a review report. The circumstances may be such that the accountant also will be precluded from issuing a compilation report. Information an accountant obtains during the performance of an incomplete review cannot be ignored if the engagement is reduced to a compilation. Knowledge of possible inaccuracies or inadequate disclosures, such as inadequate allowance for doubtful accounts or nondisclosure of significant contingencies, must be resolved to the accountant's satisfaction. If some items are not properly adjusted or disclosed, the accountant should consider matters discussed below in the section titled "Departures from GAAP." In deciding whether or not a review report or a compilation report may be issued, the accountant should consider matters covered below in the section titled "Change in Engagement."

Document procedures performed in the review engagement

The workpapers should be adequate to support the report issued. They should include:

1. Descriptions of all inquiries and analytical procedures employed, including any additional procedures deemed necessary, and summaries of the information and conclusions derived from such procedures
2. Unusual matters disclosed by the procedures or brought to the accountant's attention and their subsequent resolution

The accountant may have acquired significant knowledge of the client's affairs, because of past experience with the client or because of other accounting services rendered, to allow for reduction of some of the inquiry procedures. The reasons for such reductions should be clearly set forth in the workpapers.

Read the financial statements

For a discussion of what the CPA should be looking for when reading a client's financial statements, refer to the related discussion in the compilation section of this chapter.

Obtain a client representation letter

A client's representation letter must be obtained for each review engagement. Such letters should be signed by the client's chief executive and chief financial officer or by the owners of the entity.

> **RISK ASSESSMENT POINT:** The accountant must obtain a representation letter for each review engagement that results in the issuance of a review report. For example, if the accountant reviews and reports on quarterly interim financial statements, he or she must obtain a representation letter for each of the four separate and distinct review engagements.

Prepare an appropriate review report

The accountant's report on a review of financial statements should contain the following statements:

1. A review has been performed in accordance with Statements on Standards for Accounting and Review Services issued by the American Institute of Certified Public Accountants.
2. All of the information in the financial statements is the representation of the management or owners of the entity.
3. A review consists principally of inquiries and analytical procedures.
4. A review is substantially less in scope than an audit, and no opinion is expressed.
5. On the basis of a review, the accountant is not aware of any material modifications that should be made to the financial statements in order for them to be in conformity with GAAP, except for those modifications, if any, described in the report.

Any additional procedures that may have been performed should not be described in the accountant's review report, and no reference should be made to GAAP or to its consistent application.

The following is the recommended form for an accountant's report on a review of financial statements.

> We have reviewed the accompanying balance sheet of ABC, Inc., as of December 31, 20XX, and the related statements of income, retained earnings, and cash flows for the year then ended, in accordance with Statements on Standards for Accounting and Review Services issued by the American Institute of Certified Public Accountants. All information included in these financial statements is the representation of ABC, Inc.
>
> A review consists principally of inquiries of company personnel and analytical procedures applied to financial data. It is substantially less in scope than an examination in accordance with generally accepted auditing standards, the objective of which is the expression of an opinion regarding the financial statements taken as a whole. Accordingly, we do not express such an opinion.
>
> On the basis of our review, we are not aware of any material modifications that should be made to the accompanying financial statements in order for them to be in conformity with generally accepted accounting principles.

Incomplete review

A review report may not be issued if the review procedures deemed necessary by the accountant have not been completed to his or her satisfaction. In such situations, there is no adequate basis for expressing the limited assurance contemplated by a review. Moreover, the circumstances may be such that the accountant may not issue a compilation report. Information the accountant obtains during the performance of an incomplete review cannot be ignored if the engagement is reduced to a compilation.

When determining whether to issue a compilation report where a review is incomplete, the accountant should consider the same points that would be considered when an engagement were changed from a higher service level to a lower service level.

Review standards require that an accountant perform whatever additional procedures deemed necessary under the circumstances. Additional procedures may include corresponding with the client's legal counsel or confirming balances and transactions. If the client will not agree to such correspondence or will not sign a representation letter, there is a scope limitation, which usually is considered to be of such significance that the accountant should not issue a review report.

Accountant's independence

An accountant who is not independent of a client may not issue a review report on the financial statements of that client.

Rule 101 of the AICPA's Code of Professional Conduct states, "A member in public practice shall be independent in the performance of professional services as required by standards promulgated by bodies designated by Council." Since no opinion is expressed in a compilation report, the requirement that the accountant be independent does not apply. However, in a review report the accountant is providing negative assurance, and Rule 101 of the Code of Professional Conduct applies.

Review report modifications

Under some circumstances, an accountant's report on a review of financial statements may have to be modified. The following circumstances may or may not require a modification of the accountant's review report:

1. Departure from GAAP
2. Inadequate disclosure
3. Uncertainty
4. Inconsistency
5. Comprehensive basis of accounting other than GAAP

Departure from GAAP During a review of financial statements, the accountant may become aware of a departure from GAAP. In this case the accountant should recommend that the financial statements be appropriately revised to conform with GAAP. If the client does not agree to revise the financial statements, the accountant must consider whether to modify the review report or to withdraw from the engagement. If the accountant decides to withdraw from the engagement, it may be advisable for him or her to consult with legal counsel.

> **PLANNING AID REMINDER:** The SSARS Interpretation (February 1991) titled "Reporting When Financial Statements Contain a Departure from Promulgated Accounting Principles That Prevent the Financial Statements from Being Misleading" concludes that Rule 203 of the Code of Professional Conduct applies to review engagements; however, Rule 203 does not apply to compilation engagements. Rule 203 of the Code of Professional Conduct permits in audit engagements the use of methods other than GAAP when adhering to GAAP may cause the financial statements to be misleading. Rule 203 must be applied with a great deal of caution.

If the accountant decides that a modification to the review report is sufficient to disclose the departure from GAAP, the report should read as follows:

> We have reviewed the accompanying balance sheet of ABC, Inc., as of October 31, 20XX, and the related statements of income, retained earnings, and cash flows for the year then ended, in accordance with Statements on Standards for Accounting and Review Services issued by the American Institute of Certified Public Accountants. All information included in these financial statements is the representation of the management of ABC, Inc.
>
> A review consists principally of inquiries of company personnel and analytical procedures applied to financial data. It is substantially less in scope than an examination in accordance with generally accepted auditing standards, the objective of which is the expression of an opinion regarding the financial statements taken as a whole. Accordingly, we do not express such an opinion.
>
> Based on our review, with the exception of the matter described in the following paragraph, we are not aware of any material modifications that should be made to the accompanying financial statements in order for them to be in conformity with generally accepted accounting principles.
>
> As disclosed in Note X to the financial statements, generally accepted accounting principles require that inventory cost con-

sist of material, labor, and overhead. Management has informed us that the inventory of finished goods in the accompanying financial statements is stated at material and direct labor cost only. The effects of this departure from generally accepted accounting principles on financial position, results of operations, and cash flows have not been determined by management.

> **RISK ASSESSMENT POINT:** The SSARS Interpretation (December 1979) titled "Omission of Disclosures in Reviewed Financial Statements" states that if the client declines to include substantially all the required disclosures in reviewed financial statements, the accountant should not accept an engagement to review the financial statements.

Inadequate disclosure GAAP require that adequate disclosure be made of all pertinent information. Inadequate disclosure in a review of financial information is a departure from GAAP, and the same modification rules apply as for a departure from GAAP.

Uncertainty GAAP require that significant uncertainties be disclosed appropriately in the financial statements. If the uncertainties are appropriately disclosed in the financial statements, the accountant's review report does not have to be modified. However, if an uncertainty is not appropriately disclosed in the financial statements, the accountant's review report must be modified in the same manner as that for a departure from GAAP.

Inconsistency A violation of the consistency standard does not require modification of the accountant's standard review report if the accounting change is properly accounted for and disclosed in the financial statements. However, the accountant is free to emphasize in a separate paragraph that an accounting change has occurred.

Comprehensive basis of accounting other than GAAP A review of financial statements may be presented on a comprehensive basis of accounting other than GAAP. However, the basis of accounting used must be clearly disclosed in the financial statements. If the basis of accounting other than GAAP is not clearly disclosed in the financial statements, the accountant must modify the review report to include disclosure of the basis of accounting that is used.

Emphasis of a matter

The accountant may conclude that a particular item or matter should be emphasized in a separate paragraph of the review report.

> **PLANNING AID REMINDER:** The SSARS Interpretation (August 1981) titled "Reporting When There Are Significant Departures from Generally Accepted Accounting Principles" notes that a CPA may add a paragraph *emphasizing* the limitations of the financial statements because of the departure from GAAP.

Inadequacy of report modification

The deficiencies in the financial statements, taken as a whole, may be so significant that the accountant concludes that modification of the report would be inadequate. Under these circumstances, the accountant has little choice but to withdraw from the engagement and to consider consulting with legal counsel.

Subsequent discovery of facts existing at date of accountant's report

Standards for review services do not include any obligation for the accountant to perform any procedures after the date of the review report. However, the accountant may become aware of information subsequent to the date of the report that confirms that the financial statements are inaccurate or incomplete, and the review report should be modified. Under these circumstances, the accountant should refer to AU Section 561 (Subsequent Discovery of Facts Existing at the Date of the Auditor's Report) of SAS-1 for guidance.

> **ENGAGEMENT STRATEGY:** The SSARS Interpretation (November 1980) titled "Discovery of Information After the Date of the Accountant's Report" states that if the accountant knows that the financial statements should be revised because of discovery of information after the date of the report, the accountant should follow the general guidance established by SAS-1, AU Section 561.

Supplementary information

Basic financial statements include descriptions of accounting policies, notes, and additional material specifically identified as part of the basic financial statements. All information that is part of the client's basic financial statements must be either compiled or reviewed according to SSARS.

Information that is not part of the client's basic financial statements may be reviewed or compiled—depending on the requirements of the review engagement as specified in the engagement letter, or based on the understanding with the client.

Supplementary information compiled or reviewed When the client has requested that the supplementary information be compiled or reviewed, the accountant should follow the appropriate compilation or review procedures.

If the supplementary information has been compiled, the accountant's report should clearly state this in the first paragraph of the compilation report. Alternatively, the accountant can issue a separate compilation report on the supplementary information.

If the supplementary information has been reviewed, the accountant may state this in the review report or issue a separate report on the supplementary information. In either case, the accountant's review report should state the following:

- That the review was made primarily for the purpose of expressing limited assurance that there are no material modifications that should be made to the financial statements in order for them to be in conformity with GAAP.

- That the other data accompanying the financial statements are presented only for supplementary analysis and have been subjected to the inquiry and analytical procedures applied in the review of the basic financial statements, and the accountant is not aware of any material modifications that should be made to this data.

Supplementary information not compiled or reviewed When the engagement does not include a compilation or review of the supplementary information, the accountant does not have a responsibility to compile or review the information. To reasonably ensure that the role of the accountant is not misunderstood with respect to the supplementary information, the accountant may (1) have the client clearly state (as a preface to the supplementary information) that the supplementary information has not been compiled or reviewed by the accountant or (2) add a separate paragraph stating that the supplementary information has not been compiled or reviewed.

Practitioner's Aids

EXHIBIT AR 100-3—ENGAGEMENT LETTER IN A NONCONTINUING COMPILATION ENGAGEMENT

[*Client Name*]
[*Company Name and Address*]

Dear [*Client*]:

This letter is to confirm our understanding of the terms and objectives of our engagement and the nature and limitations of the services we will provide.

We will perform the following services:

1. We will compile, from information you provide, the balance sheet as of December 31, 20X8, and related statements of income, retained earnings, and cash flows of [Company] for the year then ended. We will not audit or review such financial statements. Our report on the 20X8 financial statements of [Company] is currently expected to read as follows:

> We have compiled the accompanying balance sheet of [Company] as of December 31, 20X8, and the related statements of income, retained earnings, and cash flows for the year then ended, in accordance with Statements on Standards for Accounting and Review Services issued by the American Institute of Certified Public Accountants.
>
> A compilation is limited to presenting in the form of financial statements information that is the representation of management. We have not audited or reviewed the accompanying financial statements and, accordingly, do not express an opinion or any other form of assurance on them.

If, for any reason, we are unable to complete the compilation of your financial statements, we will not issue a compilation report on such statements as a result of this engagement.

Our engagement cannot be relied upon to disclose errors, irregularities, or illegal acts, including fraud or defalcations, that may exist. However, we will inform the appropriate level of management of any material errors that come to our attention and any irregularities or illegal acts that come to our attention, unless they are clearly inconsequential.

As we discussed with you, it is our understanding that the accountants who compiled [Company]'s 20X7 financial statements will reissue their report. Furthermore, we understand that we are authorized to communicate with the predecessor accountant to discuss matters relevant to the current compilation and to inspect working papers that may facilitate the performance of the current engagement. In addition, we will supply a preliminary draft of the comparative 20X7 and 20X8 financial statements and our report to the predecessor accountants to assist them in reissuing their report. If, during our current engagement, matters come to our attention that either affect the 20X7 financial statements or the compilation report on those statements, we will communicate such matters to the predecessor accountant.

2. We will also prepare the state and federal income tax returns for [Company] for the year ended December 31, 20X8.

Our fee for these services will be based upon the number of hours required by the staff assigned to complete the engagement. In accordance with our recent discussion we believe that the engagement fee will not exceed $12,000. However, if we encounter unexpected circumstances that require us to devote more staff time to the engagement than anticipated, we will discuss the matter with you.

We look forward to a long relationship with your company and we are available to discuss the contents of this letter or other professional services you may desire.

If the foregoing is in accordance with your understanding, please sign the copy of this letter in the space provided and return it to us.

Sincerely,

ACKNOWLEDGED:

[Company]

[Signature of President]

[Date]

EXHIBIT AR 100-4—STANDARD REVIEW ENGAGEMENT LETTER

[Client Name]
[Company Name and Address]

Dear [Client]:

This letter is to confirm our understanding of the terms and objectives of our engagement and the nature and the limitations of the services we will provide.

We will perform the following services:

1. We will review the balance sheet of [Company] as of December 31, 20X8, and the related statements of income, retained earnings, and cash flows for the year then ended, in accordance with Statements on Standards for Accounting and Review Services issued by the American Institute of Certified Public Accountants.

Our review will consist primarily of inquiries of company personnel and analytical procedures applied to financial data, and we will require a representation letter from management. A review does not contemplate obtaining an understanding of the internal control structure or assessing control risk, tests of accounting records, and responses to inquiries by obtaining corroborating evidential matter, and certain other procedures ordinarily performed during an audit. Thus, a review does not provide assurance that we will become aware of all significant matters that would be disclosed in an audit. Our engagement cannot be relied upon to disclose errors, irregularities, or illegal acts, including fraud or defalcations, that may exist. However, we will inform the appropriate level of management of any material errors that come to our attention and any irregularities or illegal acts that come to our attention, unless they are clearly inconsequential. We will not perform an audit of such financial statements, the objective of which is the expression of an opinion regarding the financial statements taken as a whole, and accordingly, we will not express such an opinion on them.

In addition, we will update our review report on the 20X7 financial statements. Our review report on the comparative financial statements of [Company] for 20X8 and 20X7 is currently expected to read as follows:

> We have reviewed the accompanying balance sheets of [Company] as of December 31, 20X8 and 20X7, and the related statements of income, retained earnings, and cash flows for the years then ended, in accordance with Statements on Standards for Accounting and Review Services issued by the American Institute of Certified Public Accountants. All information included in these financial statements is the representation of the management of [Company].
>
> A review consists principally of inquiries of company personnel and analytical procedures applied to financial data. It is substantially less in scope than an audit in accordance with generally accepted auditing standards, the objective of which is the expression of an opinion regarding the financial statements taken as a whole. Accordingly, we do not express such an opinion.
>
> Based on our review, we are not aware of any material modifications that should be made to the accompanying financial statements in order for them to be in conformity with generally accepted accounting principles.

If, for any reason, we are unable to complete the review of your financial statements, we will not issue a review report on such statements as a result of this engagement

2. We will also prepare the state and federal income tax returns for [Company] for the year ended December 31, 20X8.

Our fee for these services will be based on the number of hours required by the staff assigned to complete the engagement. In accordance with our recent discussion, we believe that the engagement fee will not exceed $20,000. However, if we encounter unexpected circumstances that require us to devote more staff hours to the engagement than estimated, we will discuss the matter with you.

We look forward to a continued relationship with your company, and we are available to discuss the contents of this letter or other professional services you may desire.

If the foregoing is in accordance with your understanding, please sign the copy of this letter in the space provided and return it to us.

Sincerely,

ACKNOWLEDGED:

[*Company*]

[*Signature of President*]

[*Date*]

EXHIBIT AR 100-5—ENGAGEMENT LETTER IN A NONCONTINUING REVIEW ENGAGEMENT

[*Client Name*]
[*Company Name and Address*]

Dear [*Client*]:

This letter is to confirm our understanding of the terms and objectives of our engagement and the nature and the limitations of the services we will provide.

We will perform the following services:

1. We will review the balance sheet of [*Company*] as of December 31, 20X8, and the related statements of income, retained earnings, and cash flows for the year then ended, in accordance with Statements on Standards for Accounting and Review Services issued by the American Institute of Certified Public Accountants.

Our review will consist primarily of inquiries of company personnel and analytical procedures applied to financial data, and we will require a representation letter from management. A review does not contemplate obtaining an understanding of the internal control structure or assessing control risk, tests of accounting records and responses to inquiries by obtaining corroborating evidential matter, and certain other procedures ordinarily performed during an audit. Thus, a review does not provide assurance that we will become aware of all significant matters that would be disclosed in an audit. Our engagement cannot be relied upon to disclose errors, irregularities, or illegal acts, including fraud or defalcations, that may exist. However, we will inform the appropriate level of management of any material errors that come to our attention and any irregularities or illegal acts that come to our attention, unless they are clearly inconsequential. We will not perform an audit of such financial statements, the objective of which is the expression of an opinion regarding the financial statements taken as a whole, and accordingly, we will not express such an opinion on them.

Our review report on the financial statements of [*Company*] for 20X8 is currently expected to read as follows:

> We have reviewed the accompanying balance sheet of [*Company*] as of December 31, 20X8, and the related statements of income, retained earnings, and cash flows for the year then ended, in accordance with Statements on Standards for Accounting and Review Services issued by the American Institute of Certified Public Accountants. All information included in these financial statements is the representation of the management of [*Company*].
>
> A review consists principally of inquiries of company personnel and analytical procedures applied to financial data. It is substantially less in scope than an audit in accordance with generally accepted auditing standards, the objective of which is the expression of an opinion regarding the financial statements taken as a whole. Accordingly, we do not express such an opinion.
>
> Based on our review, we are not aware of any material modifications that should be made to the accompanying financial statements in order for them to be in conformity with generally accepted accounting principles.

If, for any reason, we are unable to complete the review of your financial statements, we will not issue a review report on such statements as a result of this engagement.

As we discussed with you, it is our understanding that the accountants who reviewed [*Company*]'s 20X7 financial statements will reissue their report. Furthermore, we understand that we are authorized to communicate with the predecessor accountant to discuss matters relevant to the current review and to inspect workpapers that may facilitate the performance of the current engagement. In addition, we will supply a preliminary draft of the comparative 20X7 and 20X8 financial statements and our preliminary review report to the predecessor accountants to assist them in reissuing their report. If during our current engagement, matters come to our attention that affect either the 20X7 financial statements or the review report on those statements, we will communicate such matters to the predecessor accountant.

2. We will also prepare the state and federal income tax returns for [*Company*] for the year ended December 31, 20X8.

Our fee for these services will be based on the number of hours required by the staff assigned to complete the engagement. In accordance with our recent discussion, we believe that the engagement fee will not exceed $30,000. However, if we encounter unexpected circumstances that require us to devote more staff hours to the engagement than estimated, we will discuss the matter with you.

We look forward to a continued relationship with your company, and we are available to discuss the contents of this letter or other professional services you may desire.

If the foregoing is in accordance with your understanding, please sign the copy of this letter in the space provided and return it to us.

Sincerely,

ACKNOWLEDGED:

[*Company*]

[*Signature of President*]

[*Date*]

EXHIBIT AR 100-6 — CLIENT REPRESENTATION LETTER FOR A COMPILATION ENGAGEMENT

[*CPA Name*]
[*CPA Firm Name and Address*]

Dear [*CPA*]:

In connection with your compilation of the balance sheet of [*Company*] as of [*Date*], and the related statements of income, retained earnings, and cash flows for the year then ended, we confirm to the best of our knowledge and belief that there are no material modifications that should be made to the financial statements in order for them to be in conformity with generally accepted accounting principles. Furthermore, we confirm the following representations, which we made to you during your compilation of the financial statements:

- The nature of the company's business transactions has been accurately described to you.
- The description of the company's accounting records and related data fairly represent the accounting system used during the period of your compilation engagement.
- The description of the stated qualifications of the company's accounting personnel is accurate and complete.
- The company's financial statements are prepared in accordance with generally accepted accounting principles.
- The assertions that are reflected in the financial statements are supported by the accounting records and underlying accounting data.
- The company's accounting principles, and the practices and methods followed in applying them, are as disclosed in the financial statements.
- The financial statements reflect adequate disclosures as required by generally accepted accounting principles.
- We have advised you of all actions taken at meetings of stockholders, board of directors, and committees of the board of directors that may affect the financial statements.
- We have responded fully to all inquiries made to us by you during your compilation engagement.

[*Signature of Chief Executive Officer*]   [*Date*]

[*Signature of Chief Financial Officer*]   [*Date*]

EXHIBIT AR 100-7— CLIENT REPRESENTATION LETTER FOR A REVIEW ENGAGEMENT

[*Client Name*]
[*Address*]

Dear [*Client*]:

In connection with your review of the balance sheet of [*Company*] as of [*Date*], and the related statements of income, retained earnings, and cash flows for the year then ended, for the purpose of expressing limited assurance that there are no material modifications that should be made to the statements in order for them to be in conformity with generally accepted accounting principles, we confirm, to the best of our knowledge and belief, the following representations made to you during your review.

1. The financial statements referred to above present the financial position, results of operations, and cash flows of [*Company*] in conformity with generally accepted accounting principles. In that connection, we specifically confirm that:

    a. The company's accounting principles, and the practices and methods followed in applying them are as disclosed in the financial statements.

    b. There have been no changes during the year ended [*Date*] in the company's accounting principles and practices.

    c. We have no plans or intentions that may materially affect the carrying amounts or classification of assets and liabilities.

    d. There are no material transactions that have not been properly reflected in the financial statements.

    e. There are no material losses (such as from obsolete inventory or purchase or sales commitments) that have not been properly accrued or disclosed in the financial statements.

    f. There are no violations or possible violations of laws or regulations whose effects should be considered for disclosure in the financial statements or as a basis for recording a loss contingency, and there are no other material liabilities or gain or loss contingencies that are required to be accrued or disclosed. Also, there are no unasserted claims or assessments that our lawyer has advised us are probable of assertion that must be disclosed in accordance with Financial Accounting Standards Board (FASB) Statement No. 5 (Section C59), Accounting for Contingencies.

    g. The company has satisfactory title to all owned assets, and there are no liens or encumbrances on such assets, nor has any asset been pledged, except as disclosed in the financial statements.

    h. There are no related-party transactions, including sales, purchases, loans, transfers, leasing arrangements, and guarantees, and amounts receivable from or payable to related parties that have not been properly disclosed in the financial statements.

i. We have complied with all aspects of contractual agreements that would have a material effect on the financial statement in the event of noncompliance.

j. To the best of our knowledge and belief, no events have occurred subsequent to the balance-sheet date and through the date of this letter that would require adjustment to our disclosure in the financial statements.

k. We have no knowledge of concentrations existing at the date of the financial statements that make the entity vulnerable to the risk of a near-term severe impact that have not been properly disclosed in the financial statements. We understand that concentrations refer to volumes of business, revenues, available sources of supply, or markets or geographic areas for which events could occur that would significantly disrupt normal finances within the next year.

l. Management has identified all significant estimates used in the preparation of the financial statements.

2. We have advised you of all actions taken at meetings of stockholders, the board of directors, and committees of the board of directors (or other similar bodies, as applicable) that may affect the financial statements.

3. We have responded fully to all inquiries made to us by you during your review.

EXHIBIT AR 100-8—CLIENT REPRESENTATION LETTER FOR A REVIEW ENGAGEMENT (ALTERNATIVE ILLUSTRATION)

[*Client Name*]
[*Address*]

Dear [*Client*]:

In connection with your review of the balance sheet of [*Company*] as of [*Date*], and the related statements of income, retained earnings, and cash flows for the year then ended, for the purpose of expressing limited assurance that there are no material modifications that should be made to the statements in order for them to be in conformity with generally accepted accounting principles, we confirm, to the best of our knowledge and belief, the following representations made to you during your review.

1. The financial statements referred to above present the financial position, results of operations, and cash flows of [*Company*] in conformity with generally accepted accounting principles. We are responsible for the fair presentation of the financial statements of position, results of operations, and cash flows of [*Company*] in conformity with generally accepted accounting principles. However, because of our limited expertise with generally accepted accounting principles, including financial statement disclosure, we have engaged you to advise us in fulfilling that responsibility. In that connections, we specifically confirm that:

   a. The company's accounting principles, and the practices and methods followed in applying them are as disclosed in the financial statements.

   b. There have been no changes during the year ended [*Date*] in the company's accounting principles and practices.

   c. We have no plans or intentions that may materially affect the carrying amounts or classification of assets and liabilities.

   d. There are no material transactions that have not been properly reflected in the financial statements.

   e. There are no material losses (such as from obsolete inventory or purchase or sales commitments) that have not been properly accrued or disclosed in the financial statements.

   f. There are no violations or possible violations of laws or regulations whose effects should be considered for disclosure in the financial statements or as a basis for recording a loss contingency, and there are no other material liabilities or gain or loss contingencies that are required to be accrued or disclosed. Also, there are no unasserted claims or assessments that our lawyer has advised us are probable of assertion that must be disclosed in accordance with Financial Accounting Standards Board (FASB) Statement No. 5 (AC Section C59), Accounting for Contingencies.

   g. The company has satisfactory title to all owned assets, and there are no liens or encumbrances on such assets, nor has any asset been pledged, except as disclosed in the financial statements.

   h. There are no related-party transactions, including sales, purchases, loans, transfers, leasing arrangements, and guarantees, and amounts receivable from or payable to related parties that have not been properly disclosed in the financial statements.

   i. We have complied with all aspects of contractual agreements that would have a material effect on the financial statement in the event of noncompliance.

j. To the best of our knowledge and belief, no events have occurred subsequent to the balance-sheet date and through the date of this letter that would require adjustment to our disclosure in the financial statements.

k. We have no knowledge of concentrations existing at the date of the financial statements that make the entity vulnerable to the risk of a near-term severe impact that have not been properly disclosed in the financial statements. We understand that concentrations refer to volumes of business, revenues, available sources of supply, or markets or geographic areas for which events could occur that would significantly disrupt normal finances within the next year.

l. Management has identified all significant estimates used in the preparation of the financial statements.

2. We have advised you of all actions taken at meetings of stockholders, the board of directors, and committees of the board of directors (or other similar bodies, as applicable) that may affect the financial statements.

3. We have responded fully to all inquiries made to us by you during your review.

[*Signature of Chief Executive Officer*]   [*Date*]

[*Signature of Chief Financial Officer*]   [*Date*]

EXHIBIT AR 100-9—COMPILATION PROGRAM —CONTINUING ENGAGEMENT

Use the following procedures as a guide for performing a continuing compilation engagement. The compilation program is only a guide, and professional judgment should be exercised to determine how the procedures should be modified by revising or adding procedures to the compilation program.

Initial and date each procedure as it is completed. If the procedure is not relevant to this particular compilation engagement, place "N/A" (not applicable) in the space provided for an initial and cross-reference the omitted procedure to another workpaper that explains why the procedure was omitted.

AR §100 • Compilation and Review of Financial Statements 729

Client Name: _____

Date of Financial Statements: _____

| | *Initials* | *Date* | *Workpaper Reference* |

1. Acquire an adequate understanding of the accounting principles and practices of the client's industry.   _____ _____ _____

2. Develop a general understanding of the nature of the client's business transactions.   _____ _____ _____

3. Develop a general understanding of the stated qualifications of the client's accounting personnel.   _____ _____ _____

4. Develop a general understanding of the accounting basis used to prepare the client's financial statements.   _____ _____ _____

5. Develop a general understanding of the form and content of the client's financial statements.   _____ _____ _____

6. Consider whether other professional services are needed in order to complete the compilation engagement.   _____ _____ _____

7. Read the financial statements.   _____ _____ _____

8. On the basis of information collected by using other compilation procedures and/or information that otherwise has come to our attention, consider whether additional or revised information must be obtained.   _____ _____ _____

9. Other compilation procedures used: _____

_____

_____

Reviewed By: _____

Date: _____

EXHIBIT AR 100-10—COMPILATION PROGRAM —NONCONTINUING ENGAGEMENT

Use the following procedures as a guide for performing a noncontinuing compilation engagement. The compilation program is only a guide, and professional judgment should be exercised to determine how the procedures should be modified by revising procedures listed or adding procedures to the compilation program.

Initial and date each procedure as it is completed. If the procedure is not relevant to this particular compilation engagement, place "N/A" (not applicable) in the space provided for an initial.

Client Name: _____

Date of Financial Statements: _____

	Initials	Date	Workpaper Reference
1. Evaluate communications with the predecessor CPA related to the acceptance of the engagement for possible effect on the current compilation engagement.	_____	_____	_____
2. Evaluate communications with the predecessor CPA not related to the acceptance of the compilation engagement for possible effect on the current compilation engagement.	_____	_____	_____
3. Consider reviewing predecessor CPA's workpapers.	_____	_____	_____
4. Acquire an adequate understanding of accounting principles and practices of the client's industry.	_____	_____	_____
5. Develop a general understanding of the nature of the client's business transactions.	_____	_____	_____

AR §100 • Compilation and Review of Financial Statements

	Initials	Date	*Workpaper Reference*

6. Develop a general understanding of the form of the client's accounting records. _____ _____ _____

7. Develop a general understanding of the stated qualifications of accounting personnel. _____ _____ _____

8. Develop a general understanding of the accounting basis used to prepare the client's financial statements. _____ _____ _____

9. Develop a general understanding of the form and content of the client's financial statements. _____ _____ _____

10. Consider whether other professional services are needed in order to complete the compilation engagement. _____ _____ _____

11. Read the financial statements. _____ _____ _____

12. On the basis of information collected using other compilation procedures and/or information that otherwise has come to our attention, consider whether additional or revised information must be obtained. _____ _____ _____

13. Other compilation procedures: _____

_____

_____

Reviewed By: _____

Date: _____

EXHIBIT AR 100-11—REVIEW PROGRAM —CONTINUING ENGAGEMENT

Use the following procedures as a guide for performing a continuing review engagement. The review program is only a guide, and professional judgment should be exercised to determine how the procedures should be modified by revising procedures listed or adding procedures to the review program.

Initial and date each procedure as it is completed. If the procedure is not relevant to this particular review engagement, place "N/A" (not applicable) in the space provided for an initial.

Client Name: _____

Date of Financial Statements: _____

Date of Fieldwork: _____

	Initials	Date	*Workpaper Reference*

1. Acquire an adequate understanding of accounting principles and practices of the client's industry and methods of applying them.

2. Develop an understanding of the client's organization.

3. Develop an understanding of the client's operating characteristics.

4. Develop an understanding of the nature of the client's assets, liabilities, revenues, and expenses.

5. Make inquiries concerning the client's accounting principles, practices, and methods.

6. Make inquiries concerning the client's procedures for recording, classifying, and summarizing transactions and accumulating information for disclosure in the financial statements.

7. Make inquiries concerning actions taken at meetings of stockholders, board of directors, or other meetings that may affect the financial statements.

	Initials	Date	*Workpaper Reference*

8. Make inquiries concerning the consistent application of GAAP. _____ _____ _____

9. Make inquiries concerning changes in the client's business activities or accounting principles and the implication for financial statements. _____ _____ _____

10. Make inquiries concerning occurrence of subsequent events that may have a material effect on the financial statements. _____ _____ _____

11. Apply analytical procedures to identify relationships and individual items that appear to be unusual. _____ _____ _____

12. Consider whether other professional services are needed before starting the review engagement. _____ _____ _____

13. If appropriate, obtain reports from other accountants. _____ _____ _____

14. Consider whether other review procedures should be performed on the basis of the results of performing the minimum review procedures. _____ _____ _____

15. Read the financial statements to consider if they conform with GAAP. _____ _____ _____

16. Obtain a client representation letter. _____ _____ _____

17. Other review procedures: _____

_____

_____

Reviewed By: _____

Date: _____

EXHIBIT AR 100-12—REVIEW PROGRAM —NONCONTINUING ENGAGEMENT

Use the following procedures as a guide for performing a noncontinuing review engagement. The review program is only a guide, and professional judgment should be exercised to determine how the procedures should be modified by revising or adding procedures to the review program.

Initial and date each procedure as it is completed. If a procedure is not relevant to this particular review engagement, place "N/A" (not applicable) in the space provided for an initial.

Client Name: _____

Date of Financial Statements: _____

Date of Fieldwork: _____

	Initials	Date	Workpaper Reference
1. Obtain the client's permission to communicate with the predecessor CPA.	___	___	___
2. Consider whether communications with the predecessor CPA related to the acceptance of the engagement have an effect on the current review engagement.	___	___	___
3. Consider whether communications with the predecessor CPA not related to the acceptance of the review engagement have an effect on the current review engagement.	___	___	___
4. Consider reviewing the predecessor CPA's workpapers.	___	___	___
5. Acquire an adequate understanding of the client's industry-specific accounting principles and practices and the methods of applying them.	___	___	___
6. Develop an understanding of the client's organization.	___	___	___

	Initials	Date	Workpaper Reference

7. Develop an understanding of the client's operating characteristics.

8. Develop an understanding of the nature of the client's assets, liabilities, revenues, and expenses.

9. Make inquiries concerning the client's accounting principles, practices, and methods.

10. Make inquiries concerning the client's procedures for recording, classifying, and summarizing transactions and accumulating information for disclosure in the financial statements.

11. Make inquiries concerning actions taken at meetings of stockholders, board of directors, or other groups that may affect the financial statements.

12. Make inquiries concerning the consistent application of GAAP.

13. Make inquiries concerning changes in the client's business activities or accounting principles and the implications of those changes for the financial statements.

14. Make inquiries concerning the occurrence of subsequent events that may have a material effect on the financial statements.

15. Apply analytical procedures to identify relationships and individual items that appear to be unusual.

16. If appropriate, obtain reports from other accountants.

	Initials	Date	Workpaper Reference

17. Consider whether other professional services are needed in order to execute the review engagement. _____ _____ _____

18. Consider whether other review procedures should be performed on the basis of the results of performing the minimum review procedures. _____ _____ _____

19. Read the financial statements.

20. Obtain a client representation letter.

21. Other review procedures: _____

_____

_____

Reviewed By:

Date:

_____

EXHIBIT AR 100-13—REVIEW QUESTIONNAIRE CHECKLIST—CONTINUING ENGAGEMENT

Use the following checklist as a guide for performing review procedures in a continuing engagement. The checklist is only a guide, and professional judgment should be exercised to determine how the checklist should be modified by revising questions listed or adding questions to the checklist where appropriate.

Initial and date each question as it is considered. If the question is not relevant to this particular review engagement, place "N/A" (not applicable) in the space provided for an initial. If the answer to the question is "no" or if additional explanation is needed with respect to a question, provide a proper cross-reference to another workpaper.

Client Name: _____

Date of Financial Statements: _____

	Initials	Date	Workpaper Reference

1. Have we acquired an adequate understanding of specialized accounting principles and practices of the client's industry by: _____ _____ _____

    - Reviewing relevant AICPA Accounting/Audit Guides? _____ _____ _____

    - Reviewing financial statements of other entities in the same industry? _____ _____ _____

    - Consulting with other individuals familiar with accounting practices in the specialized industry? _____ _____ _____

    - Reading periodicals, textbooks, and other publications? _____ _____ _____

    - Performing other procedures? _____ _____ _____

2. Have we developed an understanding of the client's organization, including: _____ _____ _____

    - The form of business organization? _____ _____ _____

    - The history of the client? _____ _____ _____

    - The principals involved in the organizational chart or similar analysis? _____ _____ _____

    - Other relevant matters? _____ _____ _____

3. Have we developed an understanding of the client's operating characteristics, including: _____ _____ _____

    - An understanding of the client's products and services? _____ _____ _____

    - Identification of operating locations? _____ _____ _____

    - An understanding of production methods? _____ _____ _____

    - Other operating characteristics? _____ _____ _____

4. Have we developed an understanding of the nature of the client's assets, liabilities, revenues, and expenses by: _____ _____ _____

	Initials	Date	Workpaper Reference

- Reviewing the client's chart of accounts? _____ _____ _____
- Reviewing the previous year's financial statements? _____ _____ _____
- Considering the relationships between specific accounts and the nature of the client's business? _____ _____ _____
- Performing other procedures? _____ _____ _____

5. Have we made inquiries concerning accounting principles, practices, and methods? _____ _____ _____

6. Have we made inquiries concerning the accounting procedures used by the client, including: _____ _____ _____
   - Recording transactions? _____ _____ _____
   - Classifying transactions? _____ _____ _____
   - Summarizing transactions? _____ _____ _____
   - Accumulating information for making disclosures in the financial statements? _____ _____ _____
   - Other accounting procedures? _____ _____ _____

7. Have we made inquiries concerning the effect on the financial statements due to actions taken at meetings of: _____ _____ _____
   - Stockholders? _____ _____ _____
   - The board of directors? _____ _____ _____
   - Other committees? _____ _____ _____

8. If there were changes in the application of accounting principles: _____ _____ _____
   - Did the change in accounting principle include the adoption of another acceptable accounting principle? _____ _____ _____
   - Was the change properly justified? _____ _____ _____

AR §100 • Compilation and Review of Financial Statements

	Initials	Date	Workpaper Reference

- Were the effects of the change presented in the financial statements, including adequate disclosure, in a manner consistent with APB-20? _____ _____ _____

- Were there other matters that we took into consideration? _____ _____ _____

9. Have we made inquiries concerning changes in the client's business activities that may require the adoption of different accounting principles, and have we considered the implication of this change for the financial statements? _____ _____ _____

10. Have we made inquiries concerning the occurrence of events subsequent to the date of the financial statements that may require: _____ _____ _____

    - Adjustments to the financial statements? _____ _____ _____

    - Disclosures in the financial statements? _____ _____ _____

11. Have we performed analytical procedures, including: _____ _____ _____

    - Comparing current financial statements with comparable prior period(s)? _____ _____ _____

    - Comparing current financial statements with anticipated results? _____ _____ _____

    - Studying financial statement elements and expected relationships? _____ _____ _____

    - Other analytical procedures? _____ _____ _____

12. Have we considered whether other professional services are needed in order to complete the review engagement, including: _____ _____ _____

    - Preparing a working trial balance? _____ _____ _____

    - Preparing adjusting journal entries? _____ _____ _____

	Initials	Date	Workpaper Reference

- Consulting matters fundamental to the preparation of acceptable financial statements? _____ _____ _____
- Preparing tax returns? _____ _____ _____
- Providing bookkeeping or data processing services that do not include the generation of financial statements? _____ _____ _____
- Considering other services that may be necessary before a review can be performed? _____ _____ _____

13. Have we obtained reports from other CPA(s) who reported on the financial statements of components of the client-reporting entity? _____ _____ _____

14. Have we read the financial statements to determine whether they appear to be in accordance with GAAP based on the information that has come to our attention? _____ _____ _____

15. Have we obtained a client representation letter? _____ _____ _____

16. Have we used other procedures to resolve questions during the review arrangement? _____ _____ _____

Reviewed By: _____

Date: _____

EXHIBIT AR 100-14—INQUIRY CHECKLIST FOR A REVIEW ENGAGEMENT

Use this checklist to document inquiries made concerning accounting procedures used by the client. The checklist is only a guide, and professional judgment should be exercised to determine how the checklist should be modified by revising questions listed or adding questions where appropriate.

AR §100 • Compilation and Review of Financial Statements

If a question is not relevant to this particular review engagement, place "N/A" (not applicable) in the space provided for a comment. If an additional explanation is needed in response to the question, provide a proper cross-reference to another workpaper. Note the source of the information in the space provided after each question.

Client Name: _____

Date of Financial Statements: _____

Sources of Information: _____

_____

_____

_____

	Yes	No	Date of Inquiry	Comment

CASH

1. Have bank balances been reconciled with book balances? ___ ___ _____ _____

   Source:

2. Have old or unusual reconciling items between bank balances and book balances been reviewed and adjustments made where necessary? ___ ___ _____ _____

   Source:

3. Has a proper cut-off of cash transactions been made? ___ ___ _____ _____

   Source:

4. Are there any restrictions on the availability of cash balances? ___ ___ _____ _____

   Source:

5. Have cash funds been counted and reconciled with control accounts? ___ ___ _____ _____

   Source:

6. Have cash overdrafts been classified as current liabilities? ___ ___ _____ _____

   Source:

	Date of	
Yes No	Inquiry	Comment

7. Have amounts that represent temporary investments been identified and reclassified?

   Source:

INVESTMENTS IN MARKETABLE EQUITY SECURITIES

1. Have investments in marketable equity securities been classified into current and noncurrent portfolios?

   Source:

2. Has an analysis been made to report each portfolio at the lower of cost or market?

   Source:

3. Have adjustments to cost for the current portfolio been reported in the income statement?

   Source:

4. Have adjustments to cost for the noncurrent portfolio been reported as a contra-equity account?

   Source:

5. Has the noncurrent portfolio been evaluated to determine reductions that are other than temporary?

   Source:

6. Have gains or losses from the sale of securities in each portfolio been reported on the income statement?

   Source:

7. Have reclassifications between the two portfolios been made at the lower of cost or market?

   Source:

	Yes	No	Date of Inquiry	Comment

8. Has an analysis been made to accrue dividends declared but not paid at the end of the period?

Source:

INVESTMENTS IN DEBT SECURITIES

1. Have investments in debt securities been classified into current and non-current portfolios?

Source:

2. Has an analysis been made to report the current portfolio at cost or at lower of cost or market?

Source:

3. Has an analysis been made to report the noncurrent portfolio at amortized cost?

Source:

4. In amortizing premiums or discounts related to the noncurrent portfolio, has the effective interest method been used (unless there is no significant difference between that method and the straight-line method)?

Source:

5. Has accrued interest income at the end of the period been analyzed?

Source:

6. Has the current portfolio been evaluated to determine whether reductions below cost are (1) other than temporary or (2) expected to be realized through a sale before the market value recovers to cost?

Source:

	Yes	No	Date of Inquiry	Comment

7. Has the noncurrent portfolio been evaluated to determine whether any reductions are other than temporary?

Source:

8. Have gains or losses from the sale of securities in the two portfolios been reported on the income statement?

Source:

RECEIVABLES

1. Has a reasonable allowance been made for doubtful accounts?

Source:

2. Have receivables considered uncollectible been written off?

Source:

3. If appropriate, has interest been reflected?

Source:

4. Has a proper cut-off of sales transactions been made?

Source:

5. Are there any receivables from employees and related parties?

Source:

6. Are any receivables pledged, discounted, or factored?

Source:

7. Have receivables been properly classified between current and noncurrent?

Source:

8. Have noncurrent receivables been evaluated to determine whether they carry a reasonable interest rate?

Source:

	Yes	No	Date of Inquiry	Comment

INVENTORIES

1. Have inventories been physically counted? (If not, how have inventory quantities been determined?)
   Source:

2. Have general ledger control accounts been adjusted to agree with physical inventories?
   Source:

3. If physical inventories are taken at a date other than the balance sheet date, have appropriate procedures been used to record changes in inventory between the date of the count and the balance sheet date?
   Source:

4. Were consignments in or out considered in taking physical inventories?
   Source:

5. Has inventory been valued using an inventory method consistent with that of the previous period?
   Source:

6. Does inventory cost include material, labor, and overhead where applicable?
   Source:

7. Have writedowns for obsolescence or cost in excess of net realizable value been made?
   Source:

8. Have proper cut-offs of purchases, goods in transit, and returned goods been made?
   Source:

	Yes	No	Date of Inquiry	Comment

9. Are there any inventory encumbrances?

Source:

10. Have there been any exchanges during the period that involve similar items?

Source:

PROPERTY, PLANT, AND EQUIPMENT

1. Have gains or losses on disposal of property or equipment been properly reflected?

Source:

2. Have the criteria for capitalizing property, plant, and equipment been established, and have they been applied during the fiscal period?

Source:

3. Does the repairs and maintenance account only include expenses?

Source:

4. Are property, plant, and equipment stated at cost?

Source:

5. Have depreciation methods been applied in a consistent manner?

Source:

6. Are there any unrecorded additions, retirements, abandonments, sales, or trade-ins?

Source:

7. Does the client have material lease agreements, and have they been properly reflected in the financial statements?

Source:

	Yes	No	Date of Inquiry	Comment

8. Is any property, plant, or equipment mortgaged or otherwise encumbered?

   Source:

9. Have there been any exchanges during the period that involved similar items?

   Source:

PREPAID EXPENSES

1. Have the items included in prepaid expenses been evaluated to determine whether they are appropriately classified as prepayments?

   Source:

2. Has a rational and systematic method been used to amortize prepaid expenses, and has the method been used in a manner consistent with the previous period?

   Source:

INTANGIBLE ASSETS

1. Have the items included in intangible assets been evaluated to determine whether they are appropriately classified as intangible assets?

   Source:

2. Has the straight-line method been used to amortize the cost of the intangible asset, and has the method been used in a manner consistent with the previous period?

   Source:

OTHER ASSETS

1. Have the items included in other assets been evaluated to determine whether they are appropriately classified?

   Source:

	Yes	No	Date of Inquiry	Comment

2. Has each item classified as other assets been accounted for in accordance with GAAP?

   Source:

3. Have any of the other assets been mortgaged or otherwise encumbered?

   Source:

ACCOUNTS AND NOTES PAYABLE AND ACCRUED LIABILITIES

1. Have all significant payables been reflected in the financial statements?

   Source:

2. Have all short-term liabilities been properly classified?

   Source:

3. Have all significant accruals, such as payroll, interest, and provisions for pension and profit-sharing plans, been properly reflected in the financial statements?

   Source:

4. Have any of the liabilities been collateralized?

   Source:

5. Are there any payables to employees and related parties?

   Source:

LONG-TERM LIABILITIES

1. Have the terms and other provisions of long-term liability agreements been properly reflected in the financial statements?

   Source:

	Yes	No	Date of Inquiry	Comment

2. Have liabilities been evaluated to determine whether they are properly classified as noncurrent?

   Source:

3. Has interest expense been properly reflected in the financial statements?

   Source:

4. Has there been compliance with restrictive covenants of loan agreements?

   Source:

5. Have any of the long-term liabilities been collateralized or subordinated?

   Source:

6. Has pension liability been determined in accordance with FAS-87 (including, if applicable, the computation of a minimum liability)?

   Source:

INCOME AND OTHER TAXES

1. Has provision been made for current- and prior-year federal income taxes payable?

   Source:

2. Have any assessments or reassessments been received, and are tax examinations in process?

   Source:

3. Have differences between accounting methods used in the financial statements and those used in the tax return been properly reflected in the financial statements?

   Source:

	Yes	No	Date of Inquiry	Comment

4. Has the income statement been prepared to reflect intraperiod income tax allocation?

Source:

5. Has provision been made for state and local income, franchise, sales, and other taxes payable?

Source:

OTHER LIABILITIES, CONTINGENCIES, AND COMMITMENTS

1. Have the items included in other liabilities been evaluated to determine whether they are properly classified?

Source:

2. Have the items included in other liabilities been evaluated to determine whether they are current or noncurrent?

Source:

3. Are there any contingent liabilities such as discounted notes, drafts, endorsements, warranties, litigation, unsettled asserted claims, and unasserted potential claims?

Source:

4. Are there any material contractual obligations for construction or purchase of real property and equipment and any commitments or options to purchase or sell company securities?

Source:

EQUITY

1. Have changes in equity accounts for the period been properly accounted for and presented in the financial statements?

Source:

	Yes	No	Date of Inquiry	Comment

2. Have all classes of authorized capital stock been identified and properly reflected in the financial statements?

Source:

3. Has the par or stated value of the various classes of stock been identified and properly reflected in the financial statements?

Source:

4. Has there been a reconciliation between the number of outstanding shares of capital stock and subsidiary records?

Source:

5. Have capital stock preferences, if any, been properly disclosed?

Source:

6. Have stock options been granted?

Source:

7. Has the client made any acquisitions of its own capital stock?

Source:

8. Has a determination been made as to whether there are any restrictions on retained earnings or other capital accounts?

Source:

REVENUES AND EXPENSES

1. Has there been a proper cutoff for the recognition of revenues from the sale of major products and services?

Source:

2. Has there been a proper cutoff for the measurement of expenses and purchases of inventory made during the period?

Source:

	Yes	No	Date of Inquiry	Comment

3. Are revenues and expenses properly classified in the financial statements?

    Source:

4. Has an evaluation been made to determine whether the financial statements properly include discontinued operations or items that may be considered extraordinary?

    Source:

OTHER

1. Have there been any material transactions between the client and related parties?

    Source:

2. Have there been evaluations to determine whether there are any material uncertainties?

    Source:

3. Has the status of material uncertainties previously disclosed been evaluated?

    Source:

CONSOLIDATION

1. Have all subsidiaries been evaluated to determine whether they should be included in the consolidated financial statements?

    Source:

2. Have all divisions and branches been included in the client's financial statements?

    Source:

3. Have all intercompany and intracompany accounts and transactions been eliminated?

    Source:

	Yes	No	Date of Inquiry	Comment

4. For intercorporate investments not consolidated, has there been an evaluation as to whether the equity method or the cost method should be used to account for the investment? ___ ___ _____ _____

   Source:

5. Has there been any change in the accounting for an intercorporate investment? ___ ___ _____ _____

   Source:

6. If there were any business combinations during the period, has there been an evaluation to determine whether the purpose method or pooling-of-interests method is appropriate? ___ ___ _____ _____

   Source:

STATEMENT OF CASH FLOWS

1. Has a statement of cash flows been prepared? ___ ___ _____ _____

   Source:

2. Has there been an evaluation to determine whether the focus of the statement should be cash, or cash and cash equivalents? ___ ___ _____ _____

   Source:

3. If the direct method of determining cash flows from operations is not used, has a supplemental reconciliation been included in the financial statement disclosures? ___ ___ _____ _____

   Source:

Prepared By: _____

Reviewed By: _____

Date: _____

EXHIBIT AR 100-15—ANALYTICAL PROCEDURES FOR A REVIEW ENGAGEMENT

Use this form to document the performance of analytical procedures for a review engagement. The form is only a guide, and professional judgment should be exercised to determine how the form should be modified by omitting or adding analytical procedures.

Client Name: _____

Date of Financial Statements: _____

COMPARISON OF CURRENT FINANCIAL STATEMENTS WITH COMPARABLE PRIOR-PERIOD FINANCIAL STATEMENTS

The following ratios were computed:

_____ Using financial data that reflect review adjustments proposed to date.

_____ Using financial data that do not reflect review adjustments.

Formula

LIQUIDITY RATIOS

1. Current ratio
$$\frac{\text{Current Assets}}{\text{Current Liabilities}}$$

2. Acid-test ratio
$$\frac{\text{Quick Assets}}{\text{Current Liabilities}}$$

3. Days' sales in accounts receivable
$$\frac{\text{Average Accounts Receivable} \times 365 \text{ Days}}{\text{Net Credit Sales}}$$

4. Current liabilities to total assets
$$\frac{\text{Current Liabilities}}{\text{Total Assets}}$$

ACTIVITY RATIOS

1. Inventory turnover
$$\frac{\text{Cost of Goods Sold}}{\text{Average Inventory}}$$

	Formula
2. Receivable turnover	$\dfrac{\text{Net Credit Sales}}{\text{Average Accounts Receivable}}$
3. Asset turnover	$\dfrac{\text{Net Sales}}{\text{Average Total Assets}}$
4. Gross profit percentage	$\dfrac{\text{Gross Profit}}{\text{Net Sales}}$

PROFITABILITY RATIOS

1. Bad debt to sales	$\dfrac{\text{Bad Debt Expense}}{\text{Net Sales}}$
2. Rate of return	$\dfrac{\text{Net Income}}{\text{Total Assets}}$
	$\dfrac{\text{Net Income}}{\text{Total Equity}}$
3. Net margin	$\dfrac{\text{Net Income}}{\text{Net Sales}}$

COVERAGE RATIOS

1. Debt to total assets	$\dfrac{\text{Total Debt}}{\text{Total Assets}}$
2. Interest expense to sales	$\dfrac{\text{Interest Expense}}{\text{Net Sales}}$
3. Number of times interest earned	$\dfrac{\text{Income before Interest and Taxes}}{\text{Interest Expenses}}$

OTHER RATIOS

1. Effective tax rate	$\dfrac{\text{Income Taxes}}{\text{Income before Taxes}}$

	Formula
2. Bad debt rate	<u>Allowance for Bad Debts</u> Accounts Receivable
3. Depreciation rate	<u>Depreciation Expense</u> Depreciable Property
4. Accounts payable to purchases	<u>Accounts Payable</u> Purchases
5. Dividend rate	<u>Dividends</u> Common Stock (Par)
6. Interest rate	<u>Interest Expense</u> Average Interest-Bearing Debt
7. Payroll rate	<u>Payroll Expense</u> Net Sales
8. Dividend return	<u>Dividend Income</u> Average Equity Investments
9. Interest income return	<u>Interest Income</u> Average Debt Investments

OTHER

COMPARISON OF CURRENT FINANCIAL STATEMENTS
WITH ANTICIPATED RESULTS

		20XX		
Acct #	Account Name	Actual	Budgeted	Difference
	Cash in bank—name			
	Cash in bank—name			
	Petty cash			
	Cash in bank—payroll			
	Investment marketable equity securities (current)			
	Allowance for decline in market value—marketable equity securities (current)			

		20XX		
Acct #	Account Name	Actual	Budgeted	Difference
	Accounts receivable			
	Allowance for doubtful accounts			
	Other receivables (current)			
	Accrued interest receivable			
	Notes receivable (current)			
	Discount on notes receivable			
	Dividends receivable			
	Inventory (year-end balance)			
	Prepaid insurance			
	Prepaid rent			
	Prepaid advertising			
	Land			
	Buildings			
	Accumulated depreciation—buildings			
	Delivery equipment			
	Accumulated depreciation—delivery equipment			
	Fixtures			
	Accumulated depreciation—fixtures			
	Office equipment			
	Accumulated depreciation—Office equipment			
	Property—capital leases			
	Investment—marketable equity securities (noncurrent)			
	Allowance for decline in market value—marketable equity securities (noncurrent)			

		20XX		
Acct #	Account Name	Actual	Budgeted	Difference
	Deferred bond issuance costs			
	Other receivables (non-current)			
	Investment—convertible bonds			
	Land held for investment			
	Accounts payable			
	Accrued liabilities			
	Payroll taxes and other withholdings			
	Interest payable			
	Notes payable			
	Discounts/premiums—notes payable			
	Obligations—capital leases (current)			
	Dividends payable			
	Income taxes payable			
	Notes payable (noncurrent)			
	Bonds payable			
	Discounts/premiums—bonds payable			
	Obligation—capital leases (noncurrent)			
	Common stock			
	Paid-in capital in excess of par			
	Unappropriated retained earnings			
	Appropriated retained earnings			
	Unrealized loss—marketable equity securities (noncurrent)			

AR §100 • Compilation and Review of Financial Statements

		20XX
Acct #	*Account Name*	*Actual Budgeted Difference*
	Sales	
	Sales returns and allowances	
	Sales discounts	
	Cost of goods sold	
	Purchases	
	Freight-in	
	Bad debt expense	
	Utilities expense	
	Travel expense	
	Advertising expense	
	Delivery expense	
	Miscellaneous expense	
	Insurance expense	
	Rent expense	
	Professional fees expense	
	Salaries and wages expense	
	Payroll taxes expense	
	Depreciation expense—buildings	
	Depreciation expense—delivery equipment	
	Depreciation expense—fixtures	
	Depreciation expense—office equipment	
	Depreciation expense—capital leases	
	Repairs and maintenance expense	
	Miscellaneous income	
	Extraordinary items	
	Dividend income	
	Interest income	
	Interest expense	

		_20XX_
Acct # _Account Name_		_Actual Budgeted Difference_

- Loss/gain on sale of assets
- Unrealized loss—marketable equity securities
- Recovery of market reduction of marketable equity securities (current) recorded in prior years
- Loss on exchange of assets
- Loss due to permanent decline in value of security investments
- Loss/gain on sale of investments
- Income tax expense
- Totals

Prepared By: _____

Reviewed By: _____

STUDY OF FINANCIAL STATEMENT ELEMENTS AND UNEXPECTED RELATIONSHIPS

Unexpected Relationships	_Summary of Analysis_

AR §100 • Compilation and Review of Financial Statements 761

OTHER ANALYTICAL PROCEDURES

Summary of findings: _____

Prepared By: _____

Date:_____

Reviewed By: _____

Date:_____

AR SECTION 200

REPORTING ON COMPARATIVE FINANCIAL STATEMENTS

Authoritative Pronouncements

SSARS-2—Reporting on Comparative Financial Statements

SSARS Interpretation 1—Reporting on Financial Statements That Previously Did Not Omit Substantially All Disclosures (November 1980)

Overview

"Comparative financial statements" are defined as "financial statements of two or more periods presented in columnar form." The periods may be other than annual, such as the three months (quarter) ended March 31, 20X9 (current period), compared to the three months ended March 31, 20X8 (prior period). The statements may cover more than two periods; for example, statements for the five years ended May 31, 20XX. However, each type of financial statement (for example, balance sheet, statement of income) for all periods presented must be on the same page in columnar form. The columns may be in vertical or horizontal format.

When financial statements of more than one period are presented in columnar form, the accountant must report on all periods presented. A *reissued* report is one that has been issued subsequent to the date of the original report but with its original date. A reissued report should be dual-dated if it is revised for specific events. An *updated* report is issued by a continuing accountant and bears the same date as the current report. It may or may not contain the same conclusions reached in the original report, and it should consider information that the accountant becomes aware of during the current engagement.

Financial statements that have been compiled, reviewed, or audited and that are accompanied by appropriate reports may *not* be presented in columnar form with financial statements that are *not* compiled, reviewed, or audited. In such cases, the accountant should advise the client that the report and the accountant's name should not be used in connection with such comparative financial statements. In other words, the accountant may *not* report on client-prepared comparative financial statements containing statements that *were not* compiled, reviewed, or audited and statements that *were* compiled, reviewed, or audited. However, the client-prepared statements may be presented on a separate page of a document that includes, on another separate page of the same document, the accountant's compiled, reviewed, or audited financial statements. In this event, each page of the client-prepared statements must bear a comment that the accountant has not compiled, reviewed, or audited the statements and assumes no responsibility for them.

AR §200 • Reporting on Comparative Financial Statements

Substantially all disclosures may be omitted in compiled financial statements; however, it is inappropriate for an accountant to issue reviewed or audited financial statements that omit substantially all disclosures. Thus, only when all periods are compiled and all periods omit substantially all disclosures can an accountant report on comparative financial statements that omit substantially all disclosures.

Promulgated Procedures Checklist

The structure of the CPA's report on comparative financial statements depends upon the various reporting circumstances that may be encountered in an engagement. The following are some of the more common reporting circumstances:

_____ All periods covered by the financial statements are compiled or reviewed.

_____ The current period's financial statements are reviewed, while the prior period financial statements are compiled.

_____ The current period's financial statements are compiled, while the prior period financial statements are reviewed.

_____ The current or prior period's financial statements are audited, while the other period's financial statements or compiled or reviewed.

_____ There has been a change in the report on the prior period's financial statements.

_____ Other accountants have compiled or reviewed the financial statements of the prior period or periods.

_____ An exception exists on the highest level of service rendered.

_____ The status of the client (public versus nonpublic) has changed.

Analysis and Application of Procedures

All periods covered by the financial statements are compiled or reviewed

When periods presented in comparative financial statements are either all compiled or all reviewed, the continuing accountant should update the report on the prior period, or periods, and issue it as part of the report on the current period. An example of a report on all periods compiled is presented in Exhibit AR 200-1. An example of a report on all periods reviewed is presented in Exhibit AR 200-2.

The current period's financial statements are reviewed, while the prior period financial statements are compiled

When the accountant performs a level of service in the current period that is higher than that performed in the prior period, he or she should update the report on the prior period, or periods, and issue it as the last paragraph of the report on the current period. An example of the standard report in this situation is presented in Exhibit AR 200-3.

The current period's financial statements are compiled, while the prior period financial statements are reviewed

When the accountant performs a level of service in the current period that is lower than that of the prior period, he or she may report on such comparative financial statements by (1) issuing two separate reports, (2) issuing a compilation report on the current period and adding a last paragraph for the prior period, or (3) issuing a combined compilation and review report.

If the accountant elects to issue two separate reports, the current period will be covered in a compilation report. The prior period will be covered in a review report bearing its original date.

If the accountant elects to issue a compilation report with a last paragraph referring to the prior period, certain information must be included. The last paragraph should contain a description of the degree of responsibility the accountant is assuming for the prior period, the date of the accountant's original report, and a statement that the accountant has not performed any procedures in connection with the prior period's review after the date of the prior-period review report. An example of such an additional last paragraph is presented in Exhibit AR 200-4.

The combined report should include the current-period compilation report and the reissued review report for the prior period. The combined report should be dated as of the completion of the current-period compilation engagement. The report should also mention that the accountant has not performed any procedures in connection with the prior-period review report after the date of that report.

The current or prior period's financial statements are audited, while the other period's financial statements or compiled or reviewed

SAS-26 (AU 504) (Association with Financial Statements) provides the reporting standards that should be followed when current-period financial statements are audited and included with prior-period compiled or reviewed financial statements. When the financial statements are those of a nonpublic entity, the accountant's opinion on the current-year audited financial statements should be expanded to include a final separate paragraph describing the compilation or review of the prior-period financial statements. When prior-period financial statements were compiled, the separate paragraph may be worded as follows:

> The 20X8 financial statements were compiled by us, and our report thereon, dated January 31, 20X9, stated that we did not audit or review those financial statements and, accordingly, express no opinion or other form of assurance on them.

When prior-period financial statements were reviewed, the separate paragraph may be worded as follows:

> The 20X8 financial statements were reviewed by us, and our report thereon, dated January 31, 20X9, stated that we were not aware of any material modifications that should be made to those statements for them to be in conformity with generally accepted accounting principles. However, a review is substantially less in scope than an audit and does not provide a basis for the expression of an opinion on the financial statements taken as a whole.

When the prior-period financial statements have been audited, the accountant should issue a compilation report or review report on the current-period financial statements and should either (1) reissue the audit report for the prior period or (2) add a separate paragraph to the current-period compilation or review report describing the responsibility assumed for the prior-period financial statements. The description paragraph should include the date of the prior-period audit report, a statement that the financial statements were previously examined, the type of opinion expressed and whether the opinion was other than unqualified, the substantive reasons for the qualification, and, finally, a statement that no auditing procedures have been performed since the date of the prior-period audit report. An example of this type of paragraph follows:

> The financial statements for the year ended December 31, 20X8, were audited by us (other accountants) and we (they) expressed an unqualified opinion on them in our (their) report dated March 1, 20X9, but we (they) have not performed any auditing procedures since that date.

There has been a change in the report on the prior period's financial statements

Before or during the current-period engagement, a continuing accountant may become aware of information that affects the prior-period report; for example, a modification in the prior-period report to disclose a departure from generally accepted accounting principles (GAAP) may no longer be applicable, or a modification to disclose a departure from GAAP may become necessary. In this event, the accountant's report on the prior-period statements should be expanded to include an additional separate paragraph. This separate paragraph should contain (1) the date of the original report; (2) the reasons for the change in the original report; and (3) if applicable, a statement to the effect that the prior-period financial statements have been changed. Exhibit AR 200-5 provides an example of such an explanatory paragraph.

If the revised report is reissued (issued separately from the report on the current financial statements), it should be dual-dated. The second date should be the date when substantially all the information that resulted in the revision of the report was obtained. This date may be the same date as that used for the current year's report.

Other accountants have compiled or reviewed the financial statements of the prior period or periods

Predecessor accountant reissues unchanged report

The successor accountant should consider the provisions of SSARS-4 (Communication Between Predecessor and Successor Accountants) when communicating with the predecessor accountant (auditor) and when determining the types of communications that are appropriate under the circumstances. SSARS-4 indicates that the successor accountant should obtain the permission of the client before communicating with the predecessor accountant.

A predecessor accountant is not required to reissue a compilation or review report. However, the predecessor accountant may reissue the report on prior-period financial statements, at the client's request, if the accountant makes satisfactory arrangements with the former client and complies with the following provisions before reissuing the report:

1. Evaluates whether the prior-period report is still appropriate by considering (1) the form and style of the report presentation; (2) the effects of any subsequent events; and (3) as a result of changes, whether a modification is required or should be deleted
2. Reads the current-period financial statements and the accompanying accountant's report

3. Compares the prior-period financial statements to previously issued financial statements and the financial statements of the current period
4. Obtains a letter from the current accountant stating that he or she is (is not) aware of any matter that might have a material effect on the prior-period financial statements

If, as a result of the above procedures, the predecessor accountant becomes aware of information that may affect the prior-period report on the financial statements, he or she should perform (1) procedures similar to those that would have been performed if the accountant had been aware of such information during the prior engagement and (2) any other procedures considered necessary under the circumstances. Because of the seriousness of the situation, the procedures may include discussion with the successor accountant and review of pertinent portions of the current-period workpapers. If the predecessor accountant cannot complete the necessary procedures, he or she should not reissue the report on the prior-period financial statements. Under these circumstances, the predecessor accountant may consider the need to consult with legal counsel regarding appropriate action.

> **ENGAGEMENT STRATEGY:** The situation may be such that the predecessor accountant should consider the guidance SAS-1 provides to an auditor when a subsequent discovery of facts exists at the date of the accountant's report.

After performing the required procedures, if the predecessor accountant is not aware of any information that would require restatement or revision of the prior-period report, the predecessor accountant should reissue the report on the former client's request. The reissued report should be dated as it was originally. No reference should be made to any procedures performed, including the representation letter from the successor accountant and the report that the successor accountant will issue on the current period.

Predecessor accountant issues changed report

After following the prescribed procedures, the predecessor accountant may determine that a prior-period report cannot be reissued exactly as it was issued originally. In this event, the prior-period report and/or financial statements should be appropriately revised, and the report should contain a separate explanatory paragraph. The separate explanatory paragraph should disclose (1) the date of the original report and the date of the revised report, if different; (2) all of the substantive reasons for the change to the original report; and (3) if applicable, a statement to the effect that the financial statements of the prior period have been changed. Before issuing a revised report, the predecessor accountant should obtain a written representation from the former client covering the following:

1. Complete details on any newly obtained information and its effect on the prior-period financial statements
2. The former client's understanding, if any, of the effects of the new information on the predecessor's report

Predecessor accountant's report not reissued

A predecessor accountant may decide not to reissue the original prior-period report and not to issue any changed report on the prior period. In this event, the successor accountant should either (1) refer to the report of the predecessor accountant in the current report or (2) compile, review, or audit the prior-period financial statements.

If the predecessor accountant's report is not to be reissued and the successor accountant is not engaged to compile, review, or audit the prior-period financial statements, the successor accountant should expand the report on the current period to include a separate paragraph containing the following information:

1. Without naming the prior-period accountants, a statement that the prior-period financial statements were compiled, reviewed, or audited by other accountants (auditors)
2. The date of the prior-period report
3. A description of the form of disclaimer, limited assurance, or other opinion given in the prior-period report
4. Quotation or description of any modification in the prior-period report and of any matter emphasized in the report

An example of a separate paragraph for a compilation appears in Exhibit AR 200-6. An example of a separate paragraph for a review appears in Exhibit AR 200-7.

The successor accountant may compile, review, or audit prior-period financial statements even though they have already been compiled, reviewed, or audited by the predecessor accountant. This is particularly true when the client wants to upgrade the services of the prior period. Under these circumstances, the successor accountant (auditor) should consider the guidance provided by SSARS-4 or SAS-84 (AU 315) (Communications Between Predecessor and Successor Auditors). The client must give both the predecessor accountant and the successor accountant permission to com-

AR § 200 • Reporting on Comparative Financial Statements   769

municate with each other. The predecessor accountant may provide information that may affect the successor accountant's decision to accept the engagement. In addition to making specific inquiries of the predecessor accountant, the successor accountant may have an opportunity to review the predecessor accountant's workpapers for the prior period.

Considerations when the predecessor accountant has ceased operations

When the accountant presents a compilation or review report with a compilation, review, or audit report of a prior period, and the prior-period report was prepared by a predecessor accountant that has ceased operations, the successor auditor should follow the Notice to Practitioners titled "Audit, Review, and Compilation Considerations When a Predecessor Accountant Has Ceased Operations," which the American Institute of Certified Public Accountants (AICPA) issued in February 1991. This Notice is discussed in AU Section 508.

> **RISK ASSESSMENT POINT:** The Notice to Practitioners recommends that when the successor accountant believes that prior-period financial statements should be revised but the predecessor accountant has ceased operations, the successor accountant should suggest that the client notify "the party responsible for winding up the affairs of the predecessor firm" of the matter. If the client refuses to make the communication or if the reaction by the client's predecessor accountant is unsatisfactory, the successor accountant should discuss the matter with legal counsel. A Notice to Practitioners is nonauthoritative guidance prepared by the AICPA staff in consultation with members of the Auditing Standards Board and the Accounting and Review Services Committee. Notices generally are published in the AICPA's newsletter *The CPA Letter*. They are not approved, disapproved, or otherwise acted on by a senior technical committee of the AICPA.

An exception exists on the highest level of service rendered

SSARS-1 requires that the accountant report on the highest level of service rendered. For example, when a compilation is performed followed by a review of the same set of financial statements, the review report should be issued. An exception occurs, however, when the prior-period financial statements *do not* omit substantially all disclosures required by GAAP and the current-period financial statements *do* omit these disclosures. In this instance, the current period must be a compilation engagement, because when financial statements omit substantially all the disclosures required by GAAP, the accountant can only issue a compilation report. It is inappropriate for an accountant to issue a review report or an audit report on financial statements that omit substantially all disclosures. Thus, only when *all* periods are *compiled* and *all* periods omit substantially all disclosures can an accountant report on comparative financial statements that omit substantially all disclosures.

However, a situation may arise where the accountant has issued compiled financial statements that omit substantially all disclosures for the current period but issued a review report in the prior period and the client now requests *comparative* compiled financial statements that omit substantially all disclosures. In order for the financial statements to be comparative, the client must ask the accountant to compile the prior-period statements and omit substantially all disclosures. Although SSARS-1 requires that the accountant issue a report on the highest level of service for the prior period, SSARS-2 provides for an exception. Under SSARS-2, the accountant can reissue a prior-period report on the basis of a lower level of service if the following steps are taken:

1. The accountant must fully comply with all the standards applicable to reporting on compiled financial statements that omit substantially all disclosures.

2. A separate paragraph must be included in the accountant's report that discloses (1) the type of previous services rendered by the accountant in the prior period and (2) the date of the accountant's previous report.

Exhibit AR 200-8 presents an example of the required separate paragraph that is added to the end of the compilation report on the comparative financial statements that omit substantially all disclosures.

The status of the client (public versus nonpublic) has changed

A company is a public or a nonpublic entity according to its status for the current period. If a company is classified as nonpublic for the current period, an accountant can issue a compilation report or review report. If a company is classified as public for the current period, however, the accountant usually cannot issue a compilation report or review report and must follow standards for public companies [generally accepted auditing standards (GAAS)].

A situation may arise where a company is a public entity for the current period and was a nonpublic entity in the prior period. The standards applicable to this situation are those applicable to the current period. Since the company is a public company in the current period, generally accepted auditing standards apply and compilation or review standards do not apply.

Thus, a compilation report or review report issued for the prior period cannot be reissued or referred to in the audit report for the current period.

If a company is a nonpublic entity in the current period and its financial statements are compiled or reviewed, and if the company was a public company in the prior period and its financial statements were audited, the rules for "Current Period Compiled or Reviewed and Prior Period Audited" are used. In this event, the accountant should issue a compilation report or review report on the current period and either (1) reissue the audit report for the prior period or (2) add a separate paragraph to the current-period compilation report or review report describing the responsibility assumed by the accountant for the prior-period financial statements. The description paragraph should include the date of the prior-period report; a statement that the financial statements were previously examined; the type of opinion expressed, and if the opinion was other than unqualified, the substantive reasons for the qualification; and, finally, a statement that no auditing procedures have been performed since the date of the prior-period audit report. Exhibit AR 200-9 presents an example of a report where the current period has been compiled and the prior period has been audited.

If a company is a nonpublic entity in the current period and its financial statements are compiled or reviewed, and if an unaudited disclaimer of opinion was issued in the prior period, the unaudited disclaimer of opinion may not be reissued or referred to in the report on the financial statements for the current period. Under these circumstances, the accountant should comply with the compilation or review standards or should perform an audit on the prior period and report accordingly.

Practitioner's Aids

The following practitioner's aids are presented in this section:

- Exhibit AR 200-1—Report on Comparative Financial Statements Where All Periods Have Been Compiled

- Exhibit AR 200-2—Report on Comparative Financial Statements Where All Periods Have Been Reviewed

- Exhibit AR 200-3—Report on Comparative Financial Statements Where the Current Period Is Reviewed and the Prior Period Is Compiled

- Exhibit AR 200-4—Additional Paragraph to a Compilation Report on the Current Period That Refers to the Prior Period That Had Been Reviewed

- Exhibit AR 200-5—Explanatory Paragraph Added to a Current Report That Refers to a Change in a Previous Report Issued by the Accountant

- Exhibit AR 200-6—Separate Paragraph Added to the Current Report That Refers to the Predecessor Accountant's Compilation Report
- Exhibit AR 200-7—Separate Paragraph Added to the Current Report That Refers to the Predecessor Accountant's Review Report
- Exhibit AR 200-8—Compilation Report on Comparative Financial Statements That Omit Substantially All Disclosures but Where the Prior Year Had Originally Been Reviewed by the Accountant
- Exhibit AR 200-9—Report on Comparative Financial Statements Where the Current Year Is Compiled and the Prior Year Is Audited

EXHIBIT AR 200-1—REPORT ON COMPARATIVE FINANCIAL STATEMENTS WHERE ALL PERIODS HAVE BEEN COMPILED

We have compiled the accompanying balance sheets of ABC Company as of March 31, 20X9 and 20X8, and the related statements of income, retained earnings, and cash flows for the years then ended, in accordance with Statements on Standards for Accounting and Review Services issued by the American Institute of Certified Public Accountants.

A compilation is limited to presenting in the form of financial statements information that is the representation of management. We have not audited or reviewed the accompanying financial statements and, accordingly, do not express an opinion or any other form of assurance on them.

EXHIBIT AR 200-2—REPORT ON COMPARATIVE FINANCIAL STATEMENTS WHERE ALL PERIODS HAVE BEEN REVIEWED

We have reviewed the accompanying balance sheets of ABC Company as of December 31, 20X9 and 20X8, and the related statements of income, retained earnings, and cash flows for the years then ended, in accordance with Statements on Standards for Accounting and Review Services issued by the American Institute of Certified Public Accountants. All information included in these financial statements is the representation of the management of ABC Company.

A review consists principally of inquiries of company personnel and analytical procedures applied to financial data. It is substantially less in scope than an examination in accordance with generally accepted auditing standards, the objective of which is the expression of an opinion regarding the financial statements taken as a whole. Accordingly, we do not express such an opinion.

Based on our reviews, we are not aware of any material modifications that should be made to the accompanying financial statements in order for them to be in conformity with generally accepted accounting principles.

EXHIBIT AR 200-3—REPORT ON COMPARATIVE FINANCIAL STATEMENTS WHERE THE CURRENT PERIOD IS REVIEWED AND THE PRIOR PERIOD IS COMPILED

We have reviewed the accompanying balance sheet of ABC Company as of December 31, 20X9, and the related statements of income, retained earnings, and cash flows for the year then ended, in accordance with Statements on Standards for Accounting and Review Services issued by the American Institute of Certified Public Accountants. All information included in these financial statements is the representation of the management of ABC Company.

A review consists principally of inquiries of company personnel and analytical procedures applied to financial data. It is substantially less in scope than an examination in accordance with generally accepted auditing standards, the objective of which is the expression of an opinion regarding the financial statements taken as a whole. Accordingly, we do not express such an opinion.

Based on our review, we are not aware of any material modifications that should be made to the 20X9 financial statements in order for them to be in conformity with generally accepted accounting principles.

The accompanying 20X8 financial statements of ABC Company were compiled by us. A compilation is limited to presenting in the form of financial statements information that is the representation of management. We have not audited or reviewed the 20X8 financial statements and, accordingly, do not express an opinion or any other form of assurance on them.

EXHIBIT AR 200-4—ADDITIONAL PARAGRAPH TO A COMPILATION REPORT ON THE CURRENT PERIOD THAT REFERS TO THE PRIOR PERIOD THAT HAD BEEN REVIEWED

The accompanying 20X8 financial statements of ABC, Inc., were previously reviewed by me, and my report dated March 1, 20X9, stated that I was not aware of any material modifications that should be made to those statements in order for them to be in conformity with generally accepted accounting principles. I have not performed any procedures in connection with that review engagement after the date of my report on the 20X8 financial statements.

EXHIBIT AR 200-5—EXPLANATORY PARAGRAPH ADDED TO A CURRENT REPORT THAT REFERS TO A CHANGE IN A PREVIOUS REPORT ISSUED BY THE ACCOUNTANT

In my previous review report, dated March 1, 20X9, on the 20X8 financial statements, I referred to a departure from generally accepted accounting principles because the Company carried its land at appraised values. However, as disclosed in note X, the Company has restated its 20X8 financial statements to reflect its land at cost in accordance with generally accepted accounting principles.

EXHIBIT AR 200-6—SEPARATE PARAGRAPH ADDED TO THE CURRENT REPORT THAT REFERS TO THE PREDECESSOR ACCOUNTANT'S COMPILATION REPORT

The 20X8 financial statements of ABC Company were compiled by other accountants whose report, dated February 1, 20X9, stated that they did not express an opinion or any other form of assurance on those statements.

EXHIBIT AR 200-7—SEPARATE PARAGRAPH ADDED TO THE CURRENT REPORT THAT REFERS TO THE PREDECESSOR ACCOUNTANT'S REVIEW REPORT

The 20X8 financial statements of ABC Company were reviewed by other accountants whose report, dated March 1, 20X9, stated that they were not aware of any material modifications that should be made to those statements in order for them to be in conformity with generally accepted accounting principles.

EXHIBIT AR 200-8—COMPILATION REPORT ON COMPARATIVE FINANCIAL STATEMENTS THAT OMIT SUBSTANTIALLY ALL DISCLOSURES BUT WHERE THE PRIOR YEAR HAD ORIGINALLY BEEN REVIEWED BY THE ACCOUNTANT

We have compiled the accompanying balance sheets of ABC Company as of December 31, 20X9 and 20X8, and the related statements of income, retained earnings, and cash flows for the years then ended, in accordance with Statements on Standards for Accounting and Review Services issued by the American Institute of Certified Public Accountants.

A compilation is limited to presenting in the form of financial statements information that is the representation of management. We have not audited or reviewed the accompanying financial statements and, accordingly, do not express an opinion or any other form of assurance on them.

Management has elected to omit substantially all the disclosures required by generally accepted accounting principles. If the omitted disclosures were included in the financial statements, they might influence the user's conclusions about the company's financial position, results of operations, and cash flows. Accordingly, these financial statements are not designed for those who are not informed about such matters.

The accompanying 20X8 financial statements were compiled by us from financial information that did not omit substantially all of the disclosure required by generally accepted accounting principles and that we previously reviewed, as indicated in our report dated March 1, 20X9.

EXHIBIT AR 200-9—REPORT ON COMPARATIVE FINANCIAL STATEMENTS WHERE THE CURRENT YEAR IS COMPILED AND THE PRIOR YEAR IS AUDITED

We have compiled the accompanying balance sheet of ABC Company as of December 31, 20X9, and the related statements of income, retained earnings, and cash flows for the year then ended, in accordance with Statements on Standards for Accounting and Review Services issued by the American Institute of Certified Public Accountants.

A compilation is limited to presenting in the form of financial statements information that is the representation of management. We have not audited or reviewed the accompanying 20X9 financial statements and, accordingly, do not express an opinion or any other form of assurance on them.

The financial statements for the year ended December 31, 20X8, were audited by us (other accountants) and we (they) expressed an unqualified opinion on them in our (their) report dated March 1, 20X9, but we (they) have not performed any auditing procedures since that date.

AR SECTION 300

COMPILATION REPORTS ON FINANCIAL STATEMENTS IN CERTAIN PRESCRIBED FORMS

Authoritative Pronouncements

SSARS-3—Compilation Reports on Financial Statements in Certain Prescribed Forms

SSARS Interpretation 1—Omission of Disclosures in Financial Statements Included in Certain Prescribed Forms (May 1982)

Overview

In December 1981, the American Institute of Certified Public Accountants (AICPA) Accounting and Review Services Committee issued SSARS-3 (Compilation Reports on Financial Statements Included in Certain Prescribed Forms). The purpose of SSARS-3 is to emphasize that the accountant's reporting responsibility extends to the compilation or review of financial statements included in a prescribed form. Also, the Statement provides an alternative report format when the prescribed form or related instructions call for departures from generally accepted accounting principles (GAAP) (or from a comprehensive basis of accounting other than GAAP). Thus, when a prescribed form is designed with material departures from GAAP, the accountant may issue (1) the standard compilation report with a description of the departures from GAAP or (2) the report described in SSARS-3, which makes no reference to the specific departures from GAAP.

Promulgated Procedures Checklist

The CPA should perform the following procedures in determining whether to report on financial statements formatted in certain prescribed forms:

_____ Determine whether the prescribed form is appropriate.

_____ Prepare an appropriate compilation report.

Analysis and Application of Procedures

Determine whether the prescribed form is appropriate

A "prescribed form" is any "standard form designed or adopted by the body to which it is to be submitted." A form designed or adopted by the client is

AR §300 • Compilation Reports on Financial Statements

not considered to be a prescribed form. Prescribed forms include financial statement formats used by industry trade associations, banks, and regulatory authorities.

> **OBSERVATION:** The Robert Morris Associates (association of bank lending officers) and the AICPA have developed a Business Credit Information Package (BCIP) to be used by nonpublic businesses requesting loans from financial institutions. The BCIP includes, among other documents, a prescribed form for the preparation of financial statements that does not require all GAAP disclosures. This form of financial statement presentation falls within the requirements established by SSARS-3.

Prepare an appropriate compilation report

SSARS-3 adopts the basic philosophy that a body that prescribes a form for financial statements has defined the requirements it considers sufficient to meet its informational needs. Thus, except when an audit report or a review report has been requested, the accountant's compilation report need not refer to departures from generally accepted accounting principles (including disclosure). Exhibit AR 300-1 is an example of a compilation report on financial statements included in a prescribed form that specifies measurement principles that do not conform to GAAP.

The SSARS Interpretation (May 1982) titled "Omission of Disclosures in Financial Statements Included in Certain Prescribed Forms" states that in a compilation report on financial statements included in a prescribed form, an accountant may refer to the review report previously issued on the financial statements if the difference between the previously reviewed financial statements and the financial statements included in the prescribed form is limited to the omission of disclosures not required by the form.

The following sentence might be added to the third paragraph presented in Exhibit AR 300-1:

> These financial statements were compiled by us from financial statements for the same period that we previously reviewed, as indicated in our report dated February 12, 20X6.

During the performance of the compilation, the accountant may discover departures from generally accepted accounting principles not sanctioned by the prescribed form or related instructions. Also, the accountant may discover departures from the prescribed format or instructions. In either case, such a departure requires that the accountant modify the compilation report by including a separate paragraph that describes the departure.

Practitioner's Aids

EXHIBIT AR 300-1—COMPILATION REPORT ON FINANCIAL STATEMENTS INCLUDED IN A PRESCRIBED FORM

We have compiled the accompanying balance sheet of X Company as of December 31, 20X8, and the related statements of income, retained earnings, and cash flows for the year then ended included in the accompanying prescribed form in accordance with Statements on Standards for Accounting and Review Services issued by the American Institute of Certified Public Accountants.

Our compilation was limited to the presentation of information that is the representation of management in the form prescribed by the West Virginia Fine Arts Commission. We have not audited or reviewed the financial statements referred to above and, accordingly, do not express an opinion or any other form of assurance on them.

These financial statements (including related disclosures) are presented in accordance with the requirements of the West Virginia Fine Arts Commission, which differ from generally accepted accounting principles. Accordingly, these financial statements are not designed for those who are not informed about such differences.

AR SECTION 400

COMMUNICATIONS BETWEEN PREDECESSOR AND SUCCESSOR ACCOUNTANTS

Authoritative Pronouncements

SSARS-4—Communications Between Predecessor and Successor Accountants

SSARS Interpretation 1—Reports on the Application of Accounting Principles (August 1987)

Overview

In December 1981, the American Institute of Certified Public Accountants (AICPA) Accounting and Review Services Committee issued SSARS-4, "Communications Between Predecessor and Successor Accountants." SSARS-4 does not require that the successor accountant communicate with the predecessor accountant; however, it identifies circumstances that may cause a successor accountant to decide to communicate with the predecessor accountant. SSARS-4 does require that the predecessor accountant respond promptly and fully to the successor accountant's inquiries. The following definitions are established by SSARS-4:

> *Successor accountant*—An accountant who has been invited to make a proposal for an engagement to compile or review financial statements or who has accepted such an engagement.

> *Predecessor accountant*—An accountant who has resigned or who has been notified that his services have been terminated and who, as a minimum, was engaged to compile the financial statements of the entity for the prior year or for a period ended within twelve months of the date of the financial statements to be compiled or reviewed by the successor auditor.

Promulgated Procedures Checklist

The successor accountant should perform the following procedures with respect to communications between the predecessor accountant and the successor accountant:

_____ Consider whether circumstances make it advisable to make inquiries of the predecessor accountant.

_____ Determine whether the predecessor accountant should be advised that prior-period financial statements must be revised.

Analysis and Application of Procedures

Consider whether circumstances make it advisable to make inquiries of the predecessor accountant

Although the successor accountant is not required to make inquiries of the predecessor accountant, circumstances surrounding the engagement may suggest that such inquiries be made. SSARS-4 does not attempt to provide general or specific guidelines for defining which circumstances may suggest a need to communicate with the predecessor accountant, but it lists four examples that may lead the successor accountant to contact the predecessor accountant: (1) frequent changes of accountants, (2) limited information about the client and its principals, (3) existing information that raises questions about the client and its principals, or (4) the change of accountants at a date significantly after the end of the accounting period for which the service is to be provided.

Before the oral or written inquiries are made, the predecessor accountant must obtain the consent of the client, so that the predecessor accountant is not put in the position of violating Rule 301 (Confidential Client Information) of the Code of Professional Conduct. If the client refuses to authorize the successor accountant to communicate with the predecessor accountant, the successor accountant should evaluate the basis for such refusal in deciding whether to accept the engagement. The predecessor accountant is expected to respond promptly and fully to the successor accountant's inquiries—except under unusual circumstances, such as impending litigation with respect to services performed by the predecessor accountant. If the predecessor accountant refuses to respond to the inquiries, he or she should explain to the successor accountant that responses are limited by circumstances.

The following items are identified as typical inquiries that the successor accountant might make:

- Information about the management's or owners' integrity
- Disagreements about accounting matters or the performance of procedures
- The degree of cooperation of management or the owners in providing additional or revised information
- The predecessor accountant's explanation of why there was a change of accountants

Other inquiries

SSARS-4 notes that a successor accountant may wish to make inquiries of the predecessor accountant as a typical part of the acceptance of any engagement, even if circumstances do not suggest that there may be problems with the client's management or its owners. For example, the successor accountant may simply wish to inquire about the adequacy of underlying financial data or about recurring problem areas of the engagement. Again, the predecessor accountant is expected to respond to reasonable requests from the successor accountant. However, the predecessor accountant still must obtain the client's permission to release information to the successor accountant.

The fact that the predecessor accountant has responded to inquiries or has made workpapers available to the successor accountant does not provide a basis for referring to the work of the predecessor accountant in the successor accountant's report. However, the predecessor accountant's report may be used when comparative financial statements are presented. The reporting formats for comparative financial statements when predecessor and successor accountants are involved are discussed above in AR Section 200.

Determine whether the predecessor accountant should be advised that prior-period financial statements must be revised

During the engagement, the accountant may become aware of information that requires the revision of financial statements that the predecessor accountant reported on. Under this circumstance, SSARS-7 requires that the successor accountant request that the client communicate the information to the predecessor accountant.

> **PLANNING AID REMINDER:** Accountants may be asked by entities that are not their clients to give advice on how a transaction should or could be accounted for and what type of opinion or assurance would be appropriate for a particular set of financial statements. In some instances, these requests are made by prospective clients who are shopping for an opinion. To provide guidance in this area, the Auditing Standards Board issued SAS-50 (AU 625) (Reports on the Application of Accounting Principles). The SSARS Interpretation (August 1987) titled "Reports on the Application of Accounting Principles" states that standards established by SAS-50 (AU 625) are applicable to requests related to compilations and reviews as well as audit engagements.

AR SECTION 600

REPORTING ON PERSONAL FINANCIAL STATEMENTS INCLUDED IN WRITTEN PERSONAL FINANCIAL PLANS

Authoritative Pronouncements

SSARS-6—Reporting on Personal Financial Statements Included in Written Personal Financial Plans

SSARS Interpretation 1—Submitting a Personal Financial Plan to a Client's Advisers (May 1991)

Overview

SSARS-1 states that an accountant associated with unaudited financial statements of a nonpublic entity must either compile or review the financial statements. SSARS-6 (Reporting on Personal Financial Statements Included in Written Personal Financial Plans) provides an exception to this general requirement.

Promulgated Procedures Checklist

The accountant should perform the following procedures when reporting on personal financial statements included in written personal financial plans:

_____ Determine whether the standards established by SSARS-1 have to be observed.

_____ Prepare the appropriate report on the financial statements.

Analysis and Application of Procedures

Determine whether the standards established by SSARS-1 have to be observed

When an accountant prepares a written personal financial plan that includes unaudited personal financial statements, the requirements established by SSARS-1 (as amended) do not have to be observed if the following conditions exist:

- An understanding with the client is reached (preferably in writing) that the financial statements (1) will be used only by the client or the client's advisers to develop personal financial goals and objectives and (2) will not be used to obtain credit or for any purpose other than the establishment of goals and objectives related to the financial plan.

- During the engagement, nothing came to the accountant's attention that would suggest that the personal financial statements would be (1) used to obtain credit or (2) used for any purpose other than the establishment of financial goals and objectives for the client.

> **PLANNING AID REMINDER:** The SSARS Interpretation (May 1991) titled "Submitting a Personal Financial Plan to a Client's Advisers" states that actual implementation of the personal financial plan by the client or the client's advisers (investment adviser, attorney, insurance broker, etc.) is part of "developing a client's personal financial goals and objectives."

Prepare the appropriate report on the financial statements

If the accountant concludes that the exemption criteria described above have been satisfied, a written report should be prepared. The accountant's report should include the following comments:

- That the unaudited financial statements were prepared to facilitate the development of the client's personal financial plan

- That the unaudited financial statements may be incomplete or may contain other departures from generally accepted accounting principles and should not be used to obtain credit or for any purpose other than the establishment of the personal financial plan

- That the unaudited financial statements have not been audited, reviewed, or compiled by the accountant

An example of an accountant's report on personal financial statements included in a written personal financial plan is presented in Exhibit AR 600-1.

Each personal financial statement should contain a reference to the accountant's report (such as "See accountant's report").

> **ENGAGEMENT STRATEGY:** Although SSARS-6 provides an exemption to the requirements established by SSARS-1, the accountant is not precluded from observing the standards established by SSARS-1. It should also be noted that when an accountant decides to audit, review, or compile personal financial statements, SOP 82-1 (Accounting and Financial Reporting for Personal Financial Statements) requires that the personal financial statements present assets at their estimated

current values and liabilities at their estimated current amounts at the date of the financial statements when presented in accordance with generally accepted accounting principles (GAAP). However, if the personal financial statements are presented at historical cost, instead of at current value, the presentation constitutes an other comprehensive basis of accounting.

Practitioner's Aids

EXHIBIT AR 600-1—ALTERNATIVE ACCOUNTANT'S REPORT ON PERSONAL FINANCIAL STATEMENTS INCLUDED IN WRITTEN PERSONAL FINANCIAL PLANS

The accompanying Statement of Financial Condition of [name of client], as of December 31, 20X8, was prepared solely to help you develop your personal financial plan. Accordingly, it may be incomplete or contain other departures from generally accepted accounting principles and should not be used to obtain credit or for any purposes other than developing your financial plan. We have not audited, reviewed, or compiled the statement.

Accounting Resources on the Web

The following World Wide Web sites are just a few of the resources on the Internet that are available to practitioners. Because of the constantly changing nature of the Internet, addresses change and new resources become available every day. To find additional resources, use search engines such as HotBot (http://www.hotbot.lycos.com), the Open Directory Project (http://www.dmoz.org), and Yahoo! (http://www.yahoo.com).

AICPA   http://www.aicpa.org

American Accounting Association   http://accounting.rutgers.edu/raw/aaa/

ACCPE   http://www.ACCPE.com

Aspen Publishers   http://www.AspenPublishers.com

Aspen Law & Business   http://www.AspenLawDirect.com

ePace! Software   http://www.ePaceSoftware.com

FASB   http://accounting.rutgers.edu/raw/fasb/

Federal Tax Code Search   http://www.tns.lcs.mit.edu/uscode/

Fedworld   http://www.fedworld.gov

GASB   http://accounting.rutgers.edu/raw/gasb/

General Accounting Office   http://www.gao.gov

International Accounting Standards Board (formerly International Accounting Standards Committee (IASC)]   http://www.iasb.org.uk

Internal Revenue Service   http://www.irs.gov/

Library of Congress   http://www.loc.gov/

Miller Series Online   http://www.MillerSeries.com

Securities and Exchange Commission   http://www.sec.gov

Thomas: Legislative Information   http://thomas.loc.gov

U.S. House of Representatives   http://www.house.gov/

U.S. Office of Management and Budget   http://www.whitehouse.gov/omb/

Cross-Reference

STATEMENTS ON AUDITING STANDARDS (SASs) AND SAS INTERPRETATIONS

ORIGINAL PRONOUNCEMENT	GAAS GUIDE REFERENCE
SAS-1—Codification of Auditing Standards and Procedures	
Responsibilities and Functions of the Independent Auditor	Section 110
• No Interpretations	
Generally Accepted Auditing Standards	Section 150
• No Interpretations	
Nature of the General Standards	Section 201
• No Interpretations	
Training and Proficiency of the Independent Auditor	Section 210
• No Interpretations	
Independence	Section 220
• No Interpretations	
Due Care in the Performance of Work	Section 230
• No Interpretations	
Inventories	Section 331
• No Interpretations	
Adherence to Generally Accepted Accounting Principles	Section 410
• Auditing Interpretation (February 1997)—The Impact of the Auditor's Report of a FASB Statement Prior to the Statement's Effective Date	
Consistency of Application of Generally Accepted Accounting Principles	Section 420

ORIGINAL PRONOUNCEMENT	GAAS GUIDE REFERENCE
• Auditing Interpretation (February 1974)—The Effect of APB Opinion 28 on Consistency	
• Auditing Interpretation (December 1980)—Change in Presentation of Accumulated Benefit Information in the Financial Statements of a Defined Benefit Pension Plan	
• Auditing Interpretation (April 1989)—Impact of the Auditor's Report of LIFO to LIFO Change in Comparative Financial Statements	
• Auditing Interpretation (June 1993)—The Effect of Accounting Changes by an Investee on Consistency	
Dating of the Independent Auditor's Report	Section 530
• No Interpretations	
Part of Audit Performed by Other Independent Auditors	Section 543
• Auditing Interpretation (April 1979)—Inquiries of the Principal Auditor by the Other Auditor	
• Auditing Interpretation (April 1979)—Form of Inquiries of the Principal Auditor Made by the Other Auditor	
• Auditing Interpretation (April 1979)—Form of Principal Auditor's Response to Inquiries from Other Auditors	
• Auditing Interpretation (April 1979)—Procedures of the Principal Auditor	
• Auditing Interpretation (December 1981)—Application of Additional Procedures Concerning the Audit Performed by the Other Auditor	
• Auditing Interpretation (November 1996)—Specific Procedures Performed by the Other Auditor at the Principal Auditor's Request	
Lack of Conformity with Generally Accepted Accounting Principles	Section 544
• No Interpretations	
Subsequent Events	Section 560
• No Interpretations	

Cross-Reference

ORIGINAL PRONOUNCEMENT	GAAS GUIDE REFERENCE
Subsequent Discovery of Facts Existing at the Date of the Auditor's Report	Section 561
• Auditing Interpretation (February 1989)—Auditor Association with Subsequently Discovered Information When the Auditor Has Resigned or Been Discharged	
Public Warehouses—Controls and Auditing Procedures for Goods Held	Section 901
• No Interpretations	
SAS-2—Reports on Audited Financial Statements	Superseded by SAS-58.
SAS-3—The Effects of EDP on the Auditor's Study and Evaluation of Internal Control	Superseded by SAS-48.
SAS-4—Quality Control Considerations for a Firm of Independent Auditors	Superseded by SAS-25.
SAS-5—The Meaning of "Present Fairly in Conformity with Generally Accepted Accounting Principles" in the Independent Auditor's Report	Superseded by SAS-69.
SAS-6—Related Party Transactions	Superseded by SAS-45.
SAS-7—Communications Between Predecessor and Successor Auditors	Superseded by SAS-84.
SAS-8—Other Information in Documents Containing Audited Financial Statements	Section 550
• Auditing Interpretation (May 1994)—Report by Management on the Internal Control Structure Over Financial Reporting	
• Auditing Interpretation (May 1994)—Other References by Management to Internal Control Over Financial Reporting, Including References to the Independent Auditor	
• Auditing Interpretation (March 1997)—Other Information in Electronic Sites Containing Audited Financial Statements	
SAS-9—The Effect of an Internal Audit Function on the Scope of the Independent Auditor's Examination	Superseded by SAS-65.

ORIGINAL PRONOUNCEMENT	GAAS GUIDE REFERENCE
SAS-10—Limited Review of Interim Financial Information	Superseded by SAS-24.
SAS-11—Using the Work of a Specialist	Superseded by SAS-73.
SAS-12—Inquiry of a Client's Lawyer Concerning Litigation, Claims, and Assessments	Section 337

- Auditing Interpretation (March 1977)—Specifying Relevant Date in an Audit Inquiry Letter
- Auditing Interpretation (March 1977)—Relationship Between Date of Lawyer's Response and Auditor's Report
- Auditing Interpretation (March 1977)—Form of Audit Inquiry Letter When Client Represents That No Unasserted Claims and Assessments Exist
- Auditing Interpretation (March 1977)—Documents Subject to Lawyer–Client Privilege
- Auditing Interpretation (June 1983)—Alternative Wording of the Illustrative Audit Inquiry Letter to a Client Lawyer
- Auditing Interpretation (June 1983)—Client Has Not Consulted a Lawyer
- Auditing Interpretation (February 1997)—Assessment of a Lawyer's Evaluation of the Outcome of Litigation
- Auditing Interpretation (June 1983)—Use of the Client's Inside Counsel in the Evaluation of Litigation, Claims, and Assessments
- Auditing Interpretation (February 1990)—Use of Explanatory Language about the Attorney–Client Privilege or the Attorney Work-Product Privilege
- Auditing Interpretation (January 1997)—Use of Explanatory Language Concerning Unasserted Possible Claims or Assessments in Lawyer's Response to Audit Inquiry Letters

SAS-13—Reports on a Limited Review of Interim Financial Information	Superseded by SAS-24.
SAS-14—Special Reports	Superseded by SAS-62.
SAS-15—Reports on Comparative Financial Statements	Superseded by SAS-58.

Cross-Reference

ORIGINAL PRONOUNCEMENT	GAAS GUIDE REFERENCE
SAS-16—The Independent Auditor's Responsibility for the Detection of Errors or Irregularities	Superseded by SAS-53.
SAS-17—Illegal Acts by Clients	Superseded by SAS-54.
SAS-18—Unaudited Replacement Cost Information	Withdrawn
SAS-19—Client Representations	Superseded by SAS-85.
SAS-20—Required Communication of Material Weaknesses in Internal Accounting Control	Superseded by SAS-60.
SAS-21—Segment Information	Rescinded [See Interpretation (August 1998) in Section 326.]
SAS-22—Planning and Supervision	Section 311
• Auditing Interpretation (February 1980)—Communications Between the Auditor and Firm Personnel Responsible for Non-Audit Services	
• Auditing Interpretation (February 1986)—Responsibility of Assistants for the Resolution of Accounting and Auditing Issues	
• Auditing Interpretation (January 1998)—Auditing Considerations for the Year 2000 Issue	Withdrawn
SAS-23—Analytical Review Procedures	Superseded by SAS-56.
SAS-24—Review of Interim Financial Information	Superseded by SAS-36.
SAS-25—The Responsibility of Generally Accepted Auditing Standards to Quality Control Standards	Section 161
• No Interpretations	
SAS-26—Association with Financial Statements	Section 504
• Auditing Interpretation (November 1979)—Annual Report Disclosure of Unaudited Fourth Quarter Interim Data	
• Auditing Interpretation (November 1979)—Auditor's Identification with Condensed Financial Data	
• Auditing Interpretation (November 1979)—Applicability of Guidance on Reporting When Not Independent	

ORIGINAL PRONOUNCEMENT	GAAS GUIDE REFERENCE
SAS-27—Supplementary Information Required by the Financial Accounting Standards Board	Superseded by SAS-52.
SAS-28—Supplementary Information on the Effects of Changing Prices	Superseded by SAS-52.
SAS-29—Reporting on Information Accompanying the Basic Financial Statements in Auditor-Submitted Documents	Section 551
• No Interpretations	
SAS-30—Reporting on Internal Control	Superseded by SSAE-2.
SAS-31—Evidential Matter	Section 326
• Auditing Interpretation (October 1980)—Evidential Matter for an Audit of Interim Financial Statements	
• Auditing Interpretation (March 1981)—The Effect of an Inability to Obtain Evidential Matter Relating to Income Tax Accruals	
• Auditing Interpretation (April 1986)—The Auditor's Consideration of the Completeness Assertion	
• Auditing Interpretation (August 1998)—Applying Auditing Procedures to Segment Disclosures in Financial Statements	
SAS-32—Adequacy of Disclosures in Financial Statements	Section 431
• No Interpretations	
SAS-33—Supplementary Oil and Gas Reserve Information	Superseded by SAS-45.
SAS-34—The Auditor's Considerations When a Question Arises about an Entity's Continued Existence	Superseded by SAS-59.
SAS-35—Special Reports—Applying Agreed-Upon Procedures to Specified Elements, Accounts, or Items of a Financial Statement	Superseded by SAS-75.
SAS-36—Review of or Performing Procedures on Interim Financial Information	Superseded by SAS-71.

Cross-Reference

ORIGINAL PRONOUNCEMENT	GAAS GUIDE REFERENCE
SAS-37—Filings Under Federal Securities Statutes	Section 711
• Auditing Interpretation (May 1983)—Subsequent Events Procedures for Shelf Registration Statements Updated after the Original Effective Date	
• Auditing Interpretation (June 1992)—Consenting to the Use of an Audit Report in an Offering Document in Securities Offerings Other Than One Registered Under the Securities Act of 1993	
• Auditing Interpretation (March 1995)—Consenting to Be Named as an Expert in an Offering Document in Connection with Securities Offerings Other Than Those Registered Under the Securities Act of 1933	
SAS-38—Letters for Underwriters	Superseded by SAS-49.
SAS-39—Audit Sampling	Section 350
• Auditing Interpretation (January 1985)—Audit Sampling: Auditing Interpretations of Section 350—Applicability	
SAS-40—Supplementary Mineral Reserve Information	Superseded by SAS-52.
SAS-41—Working Papers	Section 339
• Auditing Interpretation (June 1996)—Providing Access to, or Photocopies of, Working Papers to a Regulator	
SAS-42—Reporting on Condensed Financial Statements and Selected Financial Data	Section 552
• No Interpretations	
SAS-43—Omnibus Statement on Auditing Standards	Sections 150, 331, 350, 420, and 901
SAS-44—Special-Purpose Reports on Internal Accounting Control at Service Organizations	Superseded by SAS-70.
SAS-45—Omnibus Statement on Auditing Standards—1983	Sections 313 and 334

ORIGINAL PRONOUNCEMENT	GAAS GUIDE REFERENCE
• Auditing Interpretation (April 1979)—Examination of Identified Related Party Transactions with a Component	
• Auditing Interpretation (1979)—Exchange of Information Between the Principal and Other Auditor on Related Parties	
• Auditing Interpretation (May 1986)—The Nature and Extent of Auditing Procedures for Examining Related Party Transactions	
• Auditing Interpretation (May 2000)—Management's and Auditor's Responsibilities With Regard to Related Party Disclosures Prefaced by Terminology Such As "Management Believes That"	
SAS-46—Consideration of Omitted Procedures After the Report Date	Section 390
• No Interpretations	
SAS-47—Audit Risk and Materiality in Conducting an Audit	Section 312
• Auditing Interpretation (December 2000)—The Meaning of the Term Misstatement	
• Auditing Interpretation (December 2000)—Evaluating Differences in Estimates	
• Auditing Interpretation (December 2000)—Quantitative Measures of Materiality in Evaluating Audit Findings	
• Auditing Interpretation (December 2000)—Considering the Qualitative Characteristics of Misstatements	
SAS-48—The Effects of Computer Processing on the Examination of Financial Statements	Sections 311 and 326
SAS-49—Letters for Underwriters	Superseded by SAS-72.
SAS-50—Reports on the Application of Accounting Principles	Section 625
• No Interpretations	
SAS-51—Reporting on Financial Statements Prepared for Use in Other Countries	Section 534
• Auditing Interpretation (May 1996)—Financial Statement for General Use	

Cross-Reference

ORIGINAL PRONOUNCEMENT	GAAS GUIDE REFERENCE
Only Outside of the U.S. in Accordance with International Accounting Standards and International Standards on Auditing	
SAS-52—Omnibus Statement on Auditing Standards—1987 (Requirement Supplementary Information)	Section 558
• Auditing Interpretation (February 1989)—Supplementary Oil and Gas Information	
SAS-53—The Auditor's Responsibility to Detect and Report Errors and Irregularities	Superseded by SAS-82.
SAS-54—Illegal Acts by Clients	Section 317
• Auditing Interpretation (October 1978)—Consideration of the Internal Control Structure in a Financial Statement Audit and the Foreign Corrupt Practices Act	
• Auditing Interpretation (October 1978)—Material Weakness in Internal Control and the Foreign Corrupt Practices Act	
SAS-55—Consideration of Internal Control in a Financial Statement Audit	Section 319
• Auditing Interpretation (January 1998)—Auditing Considerations for the Year 2000 Issue	Withdrawn
SAS-56—Analytical Procedures	Section 329
• No Interpretations	
SAS-57—Auditing Accounting Estimates	Section 342
• Auditing Interpretation (February 1993)—Performance and Reporting Guidance Related to Fair Value Disclosures	
SAS-58—Reports on Audited Financial Statements	Section 508
• Auditing Interpretation (July 1975)—Report of an Outside Inventory-Taking Firm as an Alternative Procedures for Observing Inventories	
• Auditing Interpretation (January 1989)—Reference in Auditor's Standard Report to Management's Report	

ORIGINAL PRONOUNCEMENT	GAAS GUIDE REFERENCE
• Auditing Interpretation (February 1997)—Reporting on Financial Statements Prepared on a Liquidation Basis of Accounting	
SAS-59—The Auditor's Consideration of an Entity's Ability to Continue as a Going Concern	Section 341
• Auditing Interpretation (August 1995)—Elimination of a Going Concern Explanatory Paragraph from a Reissued Report	
• Auditing Interpretation (July 1998)—Effect of the Year 2000 Issue on the Auditor's Consideration of an Entity's Ability to Continue as a Going Concern	Withdrawn
SAS-60—Communication of Internal Control Related Matters Noted in an Audit	Section 325
• Auditing Interpretation (February 1989)—Reporting on the Existence of Material Weaknesses	
• Auditing Interpretation (January 1998)—Auditing Considerations for the Year 2000 Issue	Withdrawn
SAS-61—Communication with Audit Committees	Section 380
• Auditing Interpretation (August 1993)—Applicability of Section 380	
SAS-62— Special Reports	Section 623
• Auditing Interpretation (February 1999)—Auditor's Reports on Property and Liability Insurance Companies' Loss Reserves	
• Auditing Interpretation (February 1999)—Reports on the Financial Statements Included in Internal Revenue Form 990	
• Auditing Interpretation (February 1999)—Reporting on Current-Value Financial Statements That Supplement Historical-Cost Financial Statements in a General-Use Presentation of Real Estate Entities	
• Auditing Interpretation (February 1999)—Reporting on a Special-Purpose Financial Statement That Results in an Incomplete Presentation but Is Otherwise in Conformity with GAAP	

Cross-Reference

ORIGINAL PRONOUNCEMENT	GAAS GUIDE REFERENCE
• Auditing Interpretation (January 1998) —Evaluating the Adequacy of Disclosure in Financial Statements Prepared on the Cash, Modified Cash, or Income Tax Basis of Accounting	
• Auditing Interpretation (February 1997) —Evaluation of the Appropriateness of Informative Disclosures in Insurance Enterprises' Financial Statements Prepared on a Statutory Basis	
SAS-63—Compliance Auditing Applicable to Governmental Entities and Other Recipients of Governmental Financial Assistance	Superseded by SAS-68.
SAS-64—Omnibus Statement on Auditing Standards—1990	Sections 341, 508, and 543
SAS-65—The Auditor's Consider of the Internal Audit Function in an Audit of Financial Statements	Section 322
• No Interpretations	
SAS-66—Communication of Matters About Interim Financial Information Filed or to Be Filed with Specified Regulatory Agencies—An Amendment to SAS No. 36, Review of Interim Financial Information	Superseded by SAS-71.
SAS-67—The Confirmation Process	Section 330
• No Interpretations	
SAS-68—Compliance Auditing Applicable to Governmental Entities and Other Recipients of Governmental Financial Assistance	Superseded by SAS-74.
SAS-69—The Meaning of "Present Fairly in Conformity with Generally Accepted Accounting Principles"	Section 411
• Auditing Interpretation (March 1995)— The Auditor's Consideration of Management's Adoption of Accounting Principles for New Transactions or Events	
SAS-70—Service Organizations	Section 324
• Auditing Interpretation (April 1995)— Describing Tests of Operating Effectiveness and the Results of Such Tests	

ORIGINAL PRONOUNCEMENT	GAAS GUIDE REFERENCE
• Auditing Interpretation (April 1995)—Service Organizations That Use the Services of Other Service Organizations (Subservice Organizations)	
• Auditing Interpretation (March 1998)—Responsibility of Service Organizations and Service Auditors with Respect to Information about the Year 2000 Issue in a Service Organization's Description of Controls	Withdrawn
SAS-71—Interim Financial Information	Section 722
• No Interpretations	
SAS-72—Letters for Underwriters and Certain Other Requesting Parties	Section 634
• Auditing Interpretation (June 1993)—Letters to Directors Relating to Annual Reports on Form 10-K	
• Auditing Interpretation (August 1998)—Commenting in a Comfort Letter on Quantitative Disclosures about Market Risk Made in Accordance with Item 305 of Regulations S-K	
SAS-73—Using the Work of a Specialist	Section 336
• Auditing Interpretation (October 1998)—The Use of Legal Interpretations as Evidential Matter to Support Management's Assertion That a Transfer of Financial Assets Has Met the Isolation Criterion in Paragraph 9(a) of Financial Accounting Standards Board Statement 125	
SAS-74—Compliance Auditing Considerations in Audits of Governmental Entities and Recipients of Governmental Financial Assistance	Section 801
• No Interpretations	
SAS-75—Engagements to Apply Agreed-Upon Procedures to Specified Elements, Accounts, or Items of a Financial Statement	Withdrawn
SAS-76—Amendments to Statement on Auditing Standards No. 72, Letters for Underwriters and Certain Other Requesting Parties	Section 634

Cross-Reference

ORIGINAL PRONOUNCEMENT	GAAS GUIDE REFERENCE
SAS-77—Amendments to Statements on auditing Standards No. 22, "Planning and Supervision," No. 59, "The Auditor's Consideration of an Entity's Ability to Continue as a Going Concern," and No. 62, "Special Reports"	Sections 311, 341, and 623
SAS-78—Consideration of Internal Control in a Financial Statement Audit: An Amendment to SAS-55	Section 319
• No Interpretations	
SAS-79—Amendments to Statement on Auditing Standards No. 58, "Reports on Audited Financial Statements"	Section 508
• No Interpretations	
SAS-80—Amendment to Statement on Auditing Standards No. 31, Evidential Matter	Section 326
• No Interpretations	
SAS-81—Auditing Investments	Superseded by SAS-92
• No Interpretations	
SAS-82—Consideration of Fraud in a Financial Statement Audit	Section 316
• No Interpretations	
SAS-83—Establishing an Understanding with the Client	Section 310
• No Interpretations	
SAS-84—Communications Between Predecessor and Successor Auditors	Section 315
• No Interpretations	
SAS-85—Management Representations	Section 333
• Auditing Interpretation (March 1979)—Management Representations on Violations and Possible Violations of Laws and Regulations	
SAS-86—Amendment to Statement on Auditing Standards No. 72, Letters for Underwriters and Certain Other Requesting Parties	Section 634
• No Interpretations	

ORIGINAL PRONOUNCEMENT	GAAS GUIDE REFERENCE
SAS-87—Restricting the Use of an Auditor's Report	Section 532
• No Interpretations	
SAS-88—Service Organizations and Reporting on Consistency	Sections 324 and 420
• No Interpretations	
SAS-89—Audit Adjustments	Sections 310, 333 and 380
• No Interpretations	
SAS-90—Audit Committee Communications	Sections 380 and 722
• No Interpretations	
SAS-91—Federal GAAP Hierarchy	Section 411
• No Interpretations	
SAS-92—Auditing Derivative Instruments, Hedging Activities, and Investments in Securities	Section 332
• No Interpretations	
SAS-93—Omnibus Statement on Auditing Standards—2000	Sections 315, 508, and 622
• No Interpretations	
SAS-94—The Effect of Information Technology on the Auditor's Consideration of Internal Control in a Financial Statement Audit	Section 319
• No Interpretations	

STATEMENTS ON STANDARDS FOR ACCOUNTING AND REVIEW SERVICES (SSARS) AND SSARS INTERPRETATIONS

ORIGINAL PRONOUNCEMENT	GAAS GUIDE REFERENCE
SSARS-1—Compilation and Review of Financial Statements	AR Section 100
• SSARS Interpretation-1—Omission of Disclosures in Reviewed Financial Statements (December 1979)	

ORIGINAL PRONOUNCEMENT	GAAS GUIDE REFERENCE

- SSARS Interpretation-2—Financial Statements Included in SEC Filings (December 1979)
- SSARS Interpretation-3—Reporting on the Highest Level of Service (December 1979)
- SSARS Interpretation-4—Discovery of Information After the Date of Accountant's Report (November 1980)
- SSARS Interpretation-5—Planning and Supervision (August 1981)
- SSARS Interpretation-6—Withdrawal from Compilation or Review Engagements (August 1981)
- SSARS Interpretation-7—Reporting When There Are Significant Departures from Generally Accepted Accounting Principles (August 1981)
- SSARS Interpretation-8—Reports on Specified Elements, Accounts, or Items of a Financial Statement (November 1981, amended November 1988)
- SSARS Interpretation-9—Reporting When Management Has Elected to Omit Substantially All Disclosures (May 1982)
- SSARS Interpretation-10—Reporting on Tax Returns (November 1982)
- SSARS Interpretation-11—Reporting on Uncertainties (December 1982)
- SSARS Interpretation-12—Reporting on a Comprehensive Basis of Accounting Other than Generally Accepted Accounting Principles (December 1982)
- SSARS Interpretation-13—Additional Procedures (March 1983)
- SSARS Interpretation-14—Reporting on Financial Statements When the Scope of the Accountant's Procedures Has Been Restricted (April 1984, withdrawn April 1990)
- SSARS Interpretation-15—Differentiating a Financial Statement Presentation from a Trial Balance (September 1990)
- SSARS Interpretation-16 (Withdrawn by issuance of SSARS-7.)
- SSARS Interpretation-17—Submitting Draft Financial Statements (September 1990)

ORIGINAL PRONOUNCEMENT	GAAS GUIDE REFERENCE
• SSARS Interpretation-18—Special-Purpose Financial Presentations to Comply with Contractual Agreements or Regulatory Provisions (September 1990)	
• SSARS Interpretation-19—Reporting When Financial Statements Contain a Departure from Promulgated Accounting Principles That Prevent the Financial Statements from Being Misleading (February 1991)	
• SSARS Interpretation-20—Applicability of Statements on Standards for Accounting and Review Services to Litigation Services (May 1991)	
SSARS-2—Reporting on Comparative Financial Statements	AR Section 200
• SSARS Interpretation-1—Reporting on Financial Statements That Previously Did Not Omit Substantially All Disclosures (November 1980)	
SSARS-3—Compilation Reports on Financial Statements Included in Certain Prescribed Forms	AR Section 300
• SSARS Interpretation-1—Omission of Disclosures in Financial Statements Included in Certain Prescribed Forms (May 1982)	
SSARS-4—Communication Between Predecessor and Successor Accountants	AR Section 400
• SSARS Interpretation-1—Reports on the Application of Accounting Principles (August 1987)	
SSARS-5—Reporting on Compiled Financial Statements	Deleted by SSARS-7.
SSARS-6—Reporting on Personal Financial Statements Included in Written Personal Financial Plans	AR Section 600
• SSARS Interpretation-1—Submitting a Personal Financial Plan to a Client's Advisers (May 1991)	
SSARS-7—Omnibus Statement on Standards for Accounting and Review Services—1992	AR Sections 100 and 400
• No Interpretations	

Cross-Reference

ORIGINAL PRONOUNCEMENT	GAAS GUIDE REFERENCE
SSARS-8—Amendments to Statement on Standards for Accounting and Review Services No. 1, Compilation and Review of Financial Statements	AR Section 100

STATEMENTS ON STANDARDS FOR ATTESTATION ENGAGEMENTS (SSAEs) AND SSAE INTERPRETATIONS

ORIGINAL PRONOUNCEMENT	GAAS GUIDE REFERENCE
SSAE-10—Attestation Standards: Revision and Recodification: Chapter 1—Attest Engagements	AT Section 101

- SSAE Interpretation (August 1987)—Defense Industry Questionnaire on Business Ethics and Conduct
- SSAE Interpretation (February 1992)—Responding to Requests for Reports on Matters Relating to Solvency
- SSAE Interpretation (July 1990)—Applicability of Attestation Standards to Litigation Services
- SSAE Interpretation (May 1996)—Providing Access to or Photocopies of Working Papers to a Regulator

SSAE-10—Attestation Standards: Revision and Recodification: Chapter 2—Agreed-Upon Procedures Engagements	AT Section 201

- No Interpretations

SSAE-10—Attestation Standards: Revision and Recodification: Chapter 3—Financial Forecasts and Projections	AT Section 301

- No Interpretations

SSAE-10—Attestation Standards: Revision and Recodification: Chapter 4—Reporting on Pro Forma Financial Information	AT Section 401

- No Interpretations

SSAE-10—Attestation Standards: Revision and Recodification: Chapter 5—Reporting on An Entity's Internal Control Over Financial Reporting	AT Section 501

ORIGINAL PRONOUNCEMENT	GAAS GUIDE REFERENCE
• SSAE Interpretation (February 1997)—Pre-Award Surveys	
SSAE-10—Attestation Standards: Revision and Recodification: Chapter 6—Compliance Attestation	AT Section 601
• No Interpretations	
SSAE-10—Attestation Standards: Revision and Recodification: Chapter 7—Management's Discussion and Analysis	AT Section 701
• Attestation Interpretation (February 1999)—Consideration of the Year 2000 Issue When Examining or Reviewing Management's Discussion and Analysis	Withdrawn

OBSERVATION: SSAE-10 revises and recodifies SSAE-1 through SSAE-9.

Index

A

Accountant. *See also* Auditor; CPA
 communication between predecessor and successor (SSARS-4), 766, 768–769, 780–781
 predecessor, defined, 779
 responsibilities and functions, 673–674
 successor, defined, 779
Accounting
 changes, classification of, 318. *See also* APB Opinion No. 20
 comprehensive basis, 667, 694–695
 deficiencies, 460
 estimates, auditing of. *See* SAS-57
 estimates, change in, 323
 estimates, defined, 248
 hierarchies, 312–317
 liquidation basis, 243, 346
 principles. *See* SAS-50
Accounting and auditing practice, defined, 7
Accounting and Financial Reporting for Certain Investments and for External Investment Pools (GASB-31), 192
Accounting and Financial Reporting for Personal Financial Statements (SOP 82-1), 783–784
Accounting for Certain Investments Held by Not-for-Profit Organizations (FAS-124), 193
Accounting for Certain Investments in Debt and Equity Securities (FAS-115), 193
Accounting for Contingencies. *See* FAS-5
Accounting for Derivative Instruments and Hedging Activities (FAS-133), 192
Accounting for Income Taxes (FAS-109), 217
Accounting for Income Taxes in Interim Periods (FIN-18), 505
Accounting for Transfers and Servicing of Financial Assets and Extinguishments of Liabilities (FAS-125), 221–222
Accounting Trends and Techniques, 313
Accounts receivable
 confirmations, 178–179, 182–184
 defined, 178
Accumulated benefit information, 318, 319
Adequacy of Disclosures in Financial Statements (SAS-32), 325–335, 357
Agreed-Upon Procedures (AUP) Engagements, 386–387. *See also* SAS-75
 compliance attestation, 621–623
 engagement letter, 565–566
 engagement report, 569–570
 financial forecasts and projections, 589–593
 identification and sufficiency of procedures, 565
 negative assurance, 568
 pre-engagement conditions, 564–565
 procedures checklist, 564
 reporting, 568–570
 scope of engagement, 386–387
 SSAE-10 (Attestation Standards: Revision and Recodification), 563–564
 understanding with the client, 565–566
 use of internal auditors or other personnel, 567–568
 use of specialist, 567
AICPA. *See also* Code of Professional Conduct
 Accounting Trends and Techniques, 313

AICPA, *cont.*
auditing standards. *See* Generally Accepted Auditing Standards (GAAS)
Financial Report Survey, 313
guidelines for opinions, 573
restricted-use report distribution, 387
Amendment to Statement on Auditing Standards No. 1, Compilation and Review of Financial Statements (SSARS-8), 667
Amendment to Statement on Auditing Standards No. 31, Evidential Matter (SAS-80), 151, 154
Amendments to Statements on Auditing Standards No. 22, "Planning and Supervision," No. 59, "The Auditor's Consideration of an Entity's Ability to Continue as a Going Concern," and No. 62 "Special Reports" (SAS-77), 32, 243, 245
Amendments to Statements on Auditing Standards No. 58, "Reports on Audited Financial Statements" (SAS-79), 363
Amendments to Statement on Auditing Standards No. 72, Letters for Underwriters and Certain Other Requesting Parties
SAS-76, 471, 472–473
SAS-86, 471, 483
Amendments to Statement on Standards for Attestation Engagements No.1, Attestation Standards (SSASE-5), 541
Analytical Procedures. *See* SAS-56
APB Opinion No. 18 (The Equity Method of Accounting for Investments in Common Stock), 193
APB Opinion No. 20 (Accounting Changes)
change in accounting estimate, 323
change in inventory methods, 321
classification of accounting changes, 318
reclassification, 322
standards for accounting for changes, 358–359
APB Opinion No. 28 (Interim Financial Reporting)
accounting principles, 505, 509
application of GAAP, 321
effect on consistency, 318, 321
interim financial reports, 521
letters to underwriters, 484
Assertion
completeness, 151, 154
financial statement, 49, 103, 115–116, 153–154, 172, 197–199
Assessed risk. *See* Risk assessment
Assessments, unasserted, 223, 230
Assets
misappropriation of, 80, 84–86
transfers and servicing of, 221–222
Assistants
planning the engagement, 36–37, 467
resolution of accounting issues, 32
Association
defined, 339
with financial statements. *See* SAS-26
Assurance
negative. *See* Negative assurance
positive, 550
Attestation Engagements
availability of information, 546
complete information, 545
compliance attestation, 620–634
consulting engagements, 556
CPA's responsibilities, 543
deficiencies, 553–554
defined, 541–542
distribution of reports, 555
due care, 547
evidence, 548–549
examination engagement, 543
independence, 546–547
information criteria characteristics, 545–546
knowledge of assertion of practitioner, 545
materiality, 547

Index

measurable information, 545
objective information, 545
planning, 547–548
pre-engagement planning, 544–547
pro forma financial information, 596
procedures checklist, 544
prospective financial statement examination, 574
reasonable criteria, 545–546, 547
relevant information, 545
reporting, 556–562
reporting standards, 552–555
representation letters, 551–552
reservations, 554
restricted distribution report, 561–562
review engagement, 543, 550–551, 553
risk, 547, 549–550
significant reservations, 553
SSAE-10 (Attestation Standards: Revision and Recodification), 541–543
sufficient evidence, 548–549
suitable criteria, 545–546
training and proficiency of practitioner, 544
workpapers, 555
Attestation standards. *See* specific SSAE
Attestation Standards, Revision and Recodification (SSAE-10). *See* SSAE-10
Attorney. *See* Lawyer
Audit adjustments. *See* SAS-89
Audit committee, communication with
illegal acts by clients, 95–96
interim financial reports, 517–518
internal controls, 142–143, 147
Audit Committee Communications (SAS-90), 297, 298–300 SEC, 297
Audit engagement. *See* Engagement
Audit risk. *See also* Materiality; SAS-47
in audit strategy, 7–8
defined, 48
determination of, in planning audit, 49–66, 50–51
incremental, controlling of, 68–69
Audit Risk and Materiality in Conducting an Audit. *See* SAS-47
Audit Sampling. *See* SAS-39
Auditing Accounting Estimates. *See* SAS-57
Auditing Derivative Instruments, Hedging Activities, and Investments in Securities (SAS-92), 192–193
Auditing Insurance Entities' Loss Reserves (SOP 92-4), 216–217
Auditing Interpretations
(February 1974)—The Effect of APB Opinion 28 on Consistency, 318, 321
(July 1975)—Report of an Outside Inventory-Taking Firm as an Alternative Procedure for Observing Inventories, 346, 362
(March 1977)—Documents Subject to Lawyer-Client Privilege, 223, 225
(March 1977)—Form of Audit Inquiry Letter When Client Represents That No Unasserted Claims and Assessments Exist, 223, 230
(March 1977)—Relationship Between Date of Lawyer's Response and Auditor's Report, 223, 227
(March 1977)—Specifying Relevant Date in an Audit Inquiry Letter, 223, 227
(October 1978)—Consideration of the Internal Control Structure in a Financial Statement Audit and the Foreign Corrupt Practices Act, 91–92, 145
(October 1978)—Material Weakness in Internal Control and the Foreign Corrupt Practices Act, 91, 93
(March 1979)—Management Representations on Violations and Possible Violations of Laws and Regulations, 200, 206

Auditing Interpretations, *cont.*
- (April 1979)—Examination of Identified Related Party Transactions with a Component, 209, 210
- (April 1979)—Exchange of Information Between the Principal and Other Auditor on Related Parties, 209–210
- (April 1979)—Form of Inquiries of the Principal Auditor Made by the Other Auditor, 398, 399–400
- (April 1979)—Form of Principal Auditor's Response to Inquiries from Other Auditors, 398
- (April 1979)—Procedures of the Principal Auditor, 398, 405
- (October 1979)—The Impact on an Auditor's Report of a FASB Statement Prior to the Statement's Effective Date, 309–310
- (November 1979)—Annual Report Disclosure of Unaudited Fourth Quarter Interim Data, 339, 340
- (November 1979)—Applicability of Guidance on Reporting When Not Independent, 339, 342, 344
- (November 1979)—Auditor's Identification with Condensed Financial Data, 339
- (February 1980)—Communications Between the Auditor and Firm Personnel Responsible for Non-Audit Services, 32
- (October 1980)—Evidential Matter for an Audit of Interim Financial Statements, 151
- (December 1980)—Change in Presentation of Accumulated Benefit Information in the Financial Statements of a Defined Benefit Pension Plan, 318, 319
- (March 1981)—The Effect of an Inability to Obtain Evidential Matter Relating to Income Tax Accruals, 151, 155, 361
- (April 1981, revised June 1993)—Letters to Directors Relating to Annual Reports on Form 10-K, 471–472
- (December 1981)—Application of Additional Procedures Concerning the Audit Performed by the Other Auditor, 398, 400–401
- (May 1983)—Subsequent Events Procedures for Shelf Registration Statements Updated After the Original Effective Date, 499, 503
- (June 1983)—Alternative Wording of the Illustrative Audit Inquiry Letter to a Client's Lawyer, 223, 226
- (June 1983)—Assessment of a Lawyer's Evaluation of the Outcome of Litigation, 228
- (June 1983)—Client Has Not Consulted Lawyer, 206, 223, 225
- (June 1983)—Use of the Client's Inside Counsel in the Evaluation of Litigation, Claims, and Assessments, 223, 226
- (December 1984)—Reporting on Financial Statements Prepared on a Liquidation Basis of Accounting, 243
- (January 1985)—Audit Sampling: Auditing Interpretations of Section 350, 256
- (February 1986)—Responsibility of Assistants for the Resolution of Accounting and Auditing Issues, 32
- (April 1986)—The Auditor's Consideration of the Completeness Assertion, 151, 154
- (May 1986)—The Nature and Extent of Auditing Procedures for Examining Related Party Transactions, 209, 211
- (January 1989)—Reference in Auditor's Standard Report to Management's Report, 346, 350

Index

(February 1989)—Auditor Association with Subsequently Discovered Information When the Auditor Has Resigned or Been Discharged, 432, 434
(February 1989)—Reporting on the Existence of Material Weaknesses, 140, 144
(February 1989)—Supplementary Oil and Gas Information, 419
(April 1989)—Impact of the Auditor's Report of FIFO to LIFO Change in Comparative Financial Statements, 318, 321
(February 1990)—Use of Explanatory Language About the Attorney-Client Privilege or the Attorney Work-Product Privilege, 223, 227–228
(June 1992)—Consenting to the Use of an Audit Report in an Offering Document in Securities Offerings Other Than One Registered Under the Securities Act of 1933, 499, 502
(February 1993)—Performance and Reporting Guidance Related to Fair Value Disclosures, 248, 252
(June 1993)—Letters to Directors Relating to Annual Reports on Form 10-K, 471
(June 1993)—The Effect of Accounting Changes by an Investee on Consistency, 318, 319
(August 1993)—Applicability of Section 380, 297, 298
(May 1994)—Other References by Management to Internal Control Over Financial Reporting, Including References to the Independent Auditor, 408
(May 1994)—Report by Management on the Internal Control Structure Over Financial Reporting, 408–409
(July 1994)—Providing Access to or Photocopies of Working Papers to a Regulator, 234, 551
(March 1995)—Consenting to Be Named as an Expert in an Offering Document in Connection with Securities Offerings Other Than Those Registered Under the Securities Act of 1933, 499, 502
(March 1995)—The Auditor's Consideration of Management's Adoption of Accounting Principles for New Transactions or Events, 311, 313
(April 1995)—Describing Tests of Operating Effectiveness and the Results of Such Tests, 124, 136
(April 1995)—Service Organizations That Use the Services of Other Service Organizations (Subservice Organizations), 124, 136
(August 1995)—Eliminating a Going Concern Explanatory Paragraph from a Reissued Report, 238, 245
(May 1996)—Financial Statement for General Use Only Outside of the U.S. in Accordance with International Accounting Standards and International Standards on Auditing, 392, 396–397
(June 1996)—Providing Access to, or Photocopies of, Working Papers to a Regulator, 232
(November 1996)—Specific Procedures Performed by the Other Auditor at the Principal Auditor's Request, 398, 401
(January 1997)—Use of Explanatory Language Concerning Unasserted Possible Claims or Assessments in Lawyer's Response to Audit Inquiry Letters, 223, 226
(February 1997)—Assessment of a Lawyer's Evaluation of the Outcome of Litigation, 223

Auditing Interpretations, *cont.*
(February 1997)—Evaluation of the Appropriateness of Informative Disclosures in Insurance Enterprises' Financial Statements Prepared on a Statutory Basis, 442, 447
(February 1997)—Reporting on Financial Statements Prepared on a Liquidation Basis of Accounting, 346
(February 1997)—The Impact of the Auditor's Report of a FASB Statement Prior to the Statement's Effective Date, 309
(March 1997)—Other Information in Electronic Sites Containing Audited Financial Statements, 408, 410
(November 1997)—Applying Agreed-Upon Procedures to All, or Substantially All, of the Elements, Accounts, or Items of a Financial Statement, 441
(January 1998)—Evaluating the Adequacy of Disclosure in Financial Statements Prepared on the Cash, Modified Cash, or Income Tax Basis of Accounting, 442, 446
(February 1998)—isolation criterion, 222
(August 1998)—Applying Auditing Procedures to Segment Disclosures in Financial Statements, 151–153, 336
(August 1998)—Commenting in a Comfort Letter on Quantitative Disclosures About Market Risk Made in Accordance with Item 305 of Regulations S-K, 471, 473–474
(October 1998)—The Use of Legal Interpretations as Evidential Matter to Support Management's Assertion That a Transfer of Financial Assets Has Met the Isolation Criterion in Paragraph 9(a) of Financial Accounting Standards Board Statement 125, 216
(February 1999)—Auditor's Reports on Property and Liability Insurance Companies' Loss Reserves, 442, 451
(February 1999)—Reporting on a Special-Purpose Financial Statement That Results in an Incomplete Presentation But Is Otherwise in Conformity with GAAP, 442, 455
(February 1999)—Reporting on Current-Value Financial Statements That Supplement Historical-Cost Financial Statements in a General-Use Presentation of Real Estate Entities, 442, 445
(February 1999)—Reports on the Financial Statements Included in Internal Revenue Form 990, 442, 459
(May 2000)—Management's and Auditor's Responsibilities With Regard to Related Party Disclosures Prefaced by Terminology Such As "Management Believes That," 209, 213
(December 2000)—Considering the Qualitative Characteristics of Misstatements, 53–54, 61
(December 2000)—Evaluating Differences in Estimates, 56
(December 2000)—The Meaning of the term Misstatement, 48–49
(December 2000)—Quantitative Measures of Materiality in Evaluating Audit Findings, 52
Auditing Investments, 192–193
Auditor. *See also* Accountant; CPA
form of inquiries of principal auditor by other auditor, 398, 399–400
independent. *See* Auditor, independent
predecessor. *See* Auditor, predecessor

Index

service, 125, 129–136
successor. *See* Auditor, successor
user, 125–129
Auditor, independent. *See also* Independence
  appointment of, 27–31
  disclaimer of opinion due to not being independent, 365
  opinion. *See* Opinion
  part of audit performed by others, 398–405
  prospective financial statements, 578, 591
  responsibilities, 3–4
  training and proficiency of, 14–15, 467, 544
Auditor, predecessor
  communications with successor auditors. *See* SAS-84; SSARS-4
  defined, 72
  MD&A information, 636–637
  reporting after ceasing of operations, 368–373
  reporting by, 367–369, 379–380
  subsequent review procedures under federal securities statutes, 501–502
Auditor, successor
  communications with predecessor auditors, 766–769, 774–775. *See also* SAS-84
  defined, 72
  MD&A information, 636–637
  representation letter, 367–368
Auditor's Consideration of an Entity's Ability to Continue as a Going Concern. *See* SAS-59
Auditor's Consideration of the Internal Audit Function in an Audit of Financial Statements. *See* SAS-65
Auditor's report. *See also* SAS-58; SAS-62
  adverse, 354–355, 374–375
  change in accounting principles, 358–359
  comparative financial statements, 365–373, 378–379, 762–775

  comprehensive income, 350–353
  departure from GAAP, 354–356, 374–375
  disclaimer of opinion due to not being independent, 365
  emphasis paragraph, 364
  example, 348–349
  foreign, 392–397
  format, 346
  informative disclosures, 356–357, 375–376
  inventories, 346, 360–361, 362
  justification for accounting change, 359–360
  limited reporting engagement, 362, 377–378, 444
  loss contingencies, 362–364
  negative assurances. *See* Negative assurance
  piecemeal opinion, 365
  qualified, 354–355, 375–377
  restricting the use of, 384–391
  scope limitations, 360–362, 376–377, 582
  standards checklist, 353–354, 385
  statements to include, 346–347
Audits of States, Local Governments and Non-Profit Organizations, 384
AUP. *See* Agreed-upon procedures (AUP) engagements

B

Benefit pension plan, 318, 319
Business Credit Information Package (BCIP), 777
By-product report, 387

C

Capsule financial information, 484–485
Cash flow statement
  flexibility in preparation of, 321–322
  reporting omission of, 357, 375–376
Circular A-123, 384
Claims and assessments, 230

Classification of Short-Term Obligations Expected to Be Refinanced (FAS-6), 200
Client acceptance and continuance, 9–10
Client Representations. *See* SAS-19
Code of Professional Conduct. *See also* Rules of Conduct
  Rule 101, independence, 17–19, 674, 703, 713
  Rule 201, adequate planning and supervision, 506, 673, 677–678, 678
  Rule 202, compliance, 6
  Rule 203, conformity to GAAP, 355–356, 714
  Rule 301, communication between predecessor and successor auditors, 73, 780
Codification of Auditing Standards and Procedures. *See* SAS-1
Comfort letters. *See also* SAS-72
  addressee, 478, 479
  alternative letter, 473–474
  comments on other information, 478, 482–483
  compliance with SEC requirements, 478, 481–482
  concluding paragraph, 478, 489
  date, 478
  defined, 471
  disclosure of subsequent discoveries, 478, 486–488, 489–490
  draft letters from other accountants, 476–477
  draft of proposed letter, 475–476
  independence of accountant, 478, 481
  introductory paragraph, 478, 479–480
  preparation of, 478–480
  pro forma financial information, 485
  to requesting parties, 472
  sample, 491–495
  scope of, 474–475
Committee of Sponsoring Organizations of the Treadway Commission (COSO), 606
Communication and information. *See* Information and communication between predecessor and successor auditors. *See* SAS-84
Communication of Internal Control Related Matters Noted in an Audit. *See* SAS-60
Communication with Audit Committees. *See* SAS-61
Communications Between Predecessor and Successor Auditors. *See* SAS-84
Compilation and Review Alert-1999/2000, 676
Compilation and Review Alert-2000/01, 672, 684
  departure from OCBOA, 702
  financial statement notes, 704–705
Compilation and Review of Financial Statements. *See* SSARS-1
Compilation Engagements-Management Use Only, 696–706
  change to different engagement, 705
  comparative financial statements, 704
  compilation of interim financial statements, 705
  departures from GAAP, 703
  departures from OCBOA, 703
  develop understanding with client, 698–699
  engagement letter, 698–703
  financial statement drafts, 705
  financial statement notes, 704
  independence, 702–703
  omissions of disclosures, 703–704
  procedure checklist, 698
  supplementary information, 704
  third parties defined, 696–698
  types, 684
Compilation Reports on Financial Statements in Certain Prescribed Forms (SSARS-3), 776–778
Compilation service, 668. *See also* Financial statement compilation
Completeness assertion, 151, 154
Compliance Attestation Engagement
  agreed-upon procedures, 621–623
  AUP report, 622–623

Index

evidential matter, 629
examination engagement, 623
internal controls, 627–628, 681–682
management representations, 629–630
planning the engagement, 624–627
procedures checklist, 624
reporting, 622–623, 660–634
risk, 624–627
SSAE-10 (Attestation Standards: Revision and Recodification), 620–621
subsequent events, 629–630
understanding of compliance requirements, 624
Compliance Auditing Considerations in Audits of Governmental Entities and Recipients of Governmental Financial Assistance. *See* SAS-74
Comprehensive basis of accounting, 667, 694–695. *See also* Other comprehensive basis of accounting
Comprehensive income, 349, 350–353
Computer
effect on financial statement examination, 32, 151
effect on internal controls, 102–103
skills required for audit, 35–36
Confirmation Process. *See* SAS-67
Confirmation requests, 172–179
accounts receivable, 178–179, 182–184
information to confirm, 174
mortgage obligation, 181–182
negative, 173–174, 180
obligation under long-term leases, 180–181
positive, 172–173, 179–180
Consideration of Fraud in a Financial Statement Audit. *See* SAS-82
Consideration of Internal Control in a Financial Statement Audit. *See* SAS-55
Consideration of Omitted Procedures after the Report Date (SAS-46), 303–305

Consistency standards. *See also* Inconsistency
accounting changes by investee, 318, 319
beginning account balances and, 75–76
circumstances for, 319–324
modification of audit report, 357
Contractual agreement, 455
Control, tests. *See* Tests of controls
Control activities
classification of, 99
defined, 97
obtaining understanding of, 105–106
Control criteria, 618
Control environment, 97
elements affecting, 98
obtaining an understanding of, 105
Control risk, 56–57
analytical procedures in planning the engagement, 157–158
assessment of, 195–196
in attestation engagements, 549–550
in compliance attestation engagements, 625–626
defined, 56–57
determination of, 108–109
and fraud risk factors, 87
interrelationship of risk factors, 58
MD&A engagement, 638, 642
in planned assessed level of control risk, 108
service organization, 127–128
tests of controls, 109–113
COSO (Committee of Sponsoring Organizations of the Treadway Commission), 606
CPA. *See also* Accountant; Auditor
examination, 14
independence requirements, 17–19
other accounting services, 671–672
responsibility in attest engagements. *See* Attestation Engagements
when not independent, 342, 344

CPA Letter, Notice to Practitioners, 369, 769

D

Dating of documents, 381–383
   audit inquiry letter, 223, 227
   comfort letter, 478–479
   compilations and reviews, 682
   dual-dating of accountant's report, 682
   dual-dating of auditor's reports, 205, 361, 381–382
   dual-dating of interim review report, 522
   dual-dating of reissued reports, 367, 767
   impact of auditor's report dated prior to statement date, 309–310
   omitted procedures after completion, 303–305
   relationship between lawyer's response and auditor's report, 223, 227
   single-dating, 382, 522
Defense Industry business ethics, 541, 543
Deficiency
   accounting, 460
   MD&A presentations, 663
   reportable condition vs. material weakness, 616
   scope, 460, 553–554
Derivative Instruments, 192
   defined, 192
   substantive procedures, 197–199
   understanding, 193–194
Detection risk, 57–59
   analytical procedures in planning the engagement, 157–158
   in compliance attestation engagements, 549–550, 626
   defined, 57, 114
   interrelationship of risk factors, 58
   MD&A, 638, 643
   in planned assessed level of control risk, 108

Deviation
   defined, 262
   population rate, 266–267, 280
   in sampling, 266–67, 269
Disclaimers
   due to auditor not being independent, 365
   unaudited financial statements, 340–345
Disclosure of Certain Significant Risks and Uncertainties (SOP 94-6), 202
Disclosures about Fair Value of Financial Instruments (FAS-107), 252
Documentation. *See also* Workpapers
   audit results, 89
   control risk, 113
   review of financial statements, 711
   sampling, 273, 280–281
   understanding, 29–31
Due diligence, 472
Due process in control criteria development, 618
Due professional care, 20–24
   application of accounting principles, 467
   in attestation engagements, 547
   professional skepticism, 20–21, 22–24, 86, 175
   reasonable assurance, 21

E

Effectiveness
   of design, 111, 112
   operational, 111–112, 124, 136
Effect of Information Technology on the Auditor's Consideration of Internal Control in a Financial Statement Audit, (SAS-94), 97
Effects of Computer Processing on the Examination of Financial Statements (SAS-48), 32, 151
Employers' Accounting for Pensions (FAS-87), 218
Engagement
   acceptance and continuance of, 9–10
   communication between predeces-

Index

sor and successor auditors. *See* SAS-84
discovered after report date, omission, 304–305
independence requirements, 17–19
letter. *See* Letters, engagement
limited reporting, 362, 377–378, 444
performance, 10
planning. *See* Planning the engagement
prospective financial statement, agreed-upon procedures, 589–593
prospective financial statement, compilation, 583–589
prospective financial statement, examination, 573–583
purpose of, 3
review, analytical procedures, 164–170
scope of, 386–387
Engagements to Apply Agreed-Upon Procedures to Specified Elements, Accounts, or items of a Financial Statement. *See* SAS-75
Environment. *See* Control environment
Equity Method of Accounting for Investments in Common Stock (APB Opinion No. 18), 193
Errors. *See also* Fraud; Material misstatement
defined, 49
material misstatement due to, 51
prior-period, 322
significance in audit, 49
Establishing an Understanding with the Client. *See* SAS-83
Estimates
accounting, auditing of. *See* SAS-57
accounting, change in, 323
accounting, defined, 248
used in determining audit risk, 56, 59–62
Events
new transactions, 311, 313
subsequent, 426–431

Evidence
in attestation engagements, 548–549
in compliance attestation engagement, 629
defined, 256
interim financial statements, 151
MD&A, 643–645
prospective financial statements, 575–576
Evidential matter. *See also* SAS-31; SAS-80
income tax accruals, 151, 155, 361
scope limitations due to insufficient evidence, 360–361, 376–377
sufficient, 152–153
Expectation, analytical procedures, 158
Explanatory paragraph, 367

F

Fair value disclosures, 248, 252
FAS-2 (Qualitative Characteristics of Accounting Information), 48, 299
FAS-5 (Accounting for Contingencies)
accrual of loss contingency, 224
legal assistance in, 15
loss contingencies, 362–364
loss contingency standards, 80
loss from illegal acts, 95
unasserted claims or assessments, 202
FAS-6 (Classification of Short-Term Obligations Expected to Be Refinanced), 200
FAS-13, in-substance purchases, defined, 80
FAS-14 (Financial Reporting for Segments of a Business Enterprise), 152–153, 336. *See also* FAS-131
FAS-19 (Financial Accounting and Reporting by Oil and Gas Producing Companies), 421
FAS-25 (Suspension of Certain Accounting Requirements for Oil and Gas Producing Companies), 421
FAS-52 (Foreign Currency Translation), 350

FAS-57 (Related Party Disclosures), 210
   affiliates of enterprise, 210
   financial statement disclosures, 211, 213–215
FAS-87 (Employers' Accounting for Pensions), 218, 350
FAS-95 (Statement of Cash Flows), 321–322
FAS-107 (Disclosures about Fair Value of Financial Instruments), 252
FAS-109 (Accounting for Income Taxes), 217
FAS-115 (Accounting for Certain Investments in Debt and Equity Securities), 193, 350
FAS-124 (Accounting for Certain Investments Held by Not-for-Profit Organizations), 193
FAS-125 (Accounting for Transfers and Servicing of Financial Assets and Extinguishments of Liabilities), 221–222
FAS-130 (Reporting Comprehensive Income), 349, 350–351
FAS-131 (Disclosures about Segments of an Enterprise and Related Information), 153, 336
FAS-133 (Accounting for Derivative Instruments and Hedging Activities), 192
Fax responses to confirmation requests, 175–176
Federal GAAP hierarchy (SAS-91), 316–317
Fieldwork Standards No. 1 (Adequate Planning and Supervision), 547–548, 555
Fieldwork Standards No. 2 (Sufficient Evidential Matter), 548–549, 555
Filings under Federal Securities Statutes. *See* SAS-37
FIN-18 (Accounting for Income Taxes in Interim Periods), 505
Financial Accounting and Reporting by Oil and Gas Producing Companies (FAS-19), 421

Financial Accounting Standards Board Statements. *See* specific FAS
Financial forecasts and projections
   accounting principles used in preparation, 584
   agreed-upon procedures engagement, 573, 589–593
   assumptions used, 576–578, 585
   comparison to actual financial statements, 582
   compilation engagement, 573, 583–589
   engagement procedures, 591
   establishing an understanding, 574–575, 584
   evidence, 575–576
   examination engagement, 573–583
   historical transactions, 585–586
   limited use, 572
   management representations, 585–586
   materiality, 574
   partial presentations, 593
   planning the examination engagement, 575
   pre-engagement conditions, 590
   presentation standards, 572–573
   procedures checklist, 574, 583–584, 590
   prospective financial statements. *See* Financial statements, prospective
   reporting, 578–583, 587–589, 591–593
   review engagement, 573
   SSAE-10 (Attestation Standards: Revision and Recodification), 571–573
   standards for attestation engagement, 574
Financial Report Survey, 313
Financial Reporting for Segments of a Business Enterprise (FAS-14), 152–153, 336. *See also* FAS-131
Financial statement compilation, 685. *See also* SSARS-1

Index

basis of accounting other than GAAP, 694–695
client representation letter, 689, 723–724
departure from GAAP, 692–693
determine additional procedures are needed, 728
determine other accounting needs, 687
engagement letter, continuing engagement, 728
engagement letter, noncontinuing engagement, 717–719, 730–731
independence of accountant, 692
prescribed forms, 776–777
procedures checklist, 685–686
reading the financial statements, 687–688
report modifications, 690
report omission of disclosures, 691–692
reports, 689–696
subsequent discovery of facts, 695
supplementary information, 696
uncertainty and going concern, 694
understanding the client, 686–687
Financial statement review, 706
additional procedures, 709–711
analytical procedures, 709–710, 754–761
basis of accounting other than GAAP, 715
checklist, continuing engagement, 736–740
checklist, inquiry, 740–753
checklist, procedures, 706–707
client inquiries, 708–709
client representation letter, 711, 724–728
corroborative evidence, 710
departure from GAAP, 714–715
disclosures, 715
documentation, 711
engagement letter, continuing engagement, 731–733
engagement letter, noncontinuing engagement, 721–723, 734–736
engagement letter, standard, 719–721
incomplete, 710–711, 712–713
inconsistency, 715
independence of accountant, 713
obtain knowledge of client's business, 707–708
obtain knowledge of industry accounting practices, 707–708
read the statements, 711
report modifications, 713, 716
reports, 711–717
subsequent discovery of facts, 716
supplementary information, 716
uncertainty, 715
Financial statement(s). *See also* Generally Accepted Accounting Principles; Generally Accepted Auditing Standards
assertions, 49, 103, 115–116, 153–154, 172, 197–199
association with. *See* SAS-26
comparative, auditor reports, 365–373, 377–379. *See also* SSARS-2
compilation. *See* Financial statement compilation
condensed, 339, 412–413, 415–418
current, compared with anticipated results, 166–170
current-value, 442, 445
defined, 443–444, 668
differentiating from a trial balance, 668, 670
draft, 668
electronic, 408, 410
examples, 669–670
fraudulent, 80–90
international, 392–397
material effect of transactions or events, 324
prior period, 369–373
prior-period errors, 322
pro forma. *See* Pro forma financial information
prospective. *See* Financial statements, prospective

Financial statement(s), *cont.*
restricted, 386, 389–391
retroactive restatement, 320–321
special-purpose, 385–386, 388–389, 442, 455, 668, 675
unaudited, 340–345
Financial statements, prospective, 571–572
financial. *See* Financial forecasts and projections
included in comfort letters, 485–486
Foreign Corrupt Practices Act, 91, 92, 93, 145, 619
auditing standards, 393
financial statements prepared for use in, 392–397
foreign GAAP, 393–395, 397
U. S. distribution, 396
Foreign Currency Translation (FAS 52), 350
Form 8-K, 662
Form 10-K, 471–472, 662
Form 10-Q, 662
Form 20-F, 641
Form 990 (Return of Organizations Exempt from Income Tax), 442, 459
Form 5500 (Return of Employee Benefit Plan), 671
Fraud. *See also* Errors
communication of, 89–90
defined, 49
effect on level or assurance, 21
financial reporting, 80–84
in financial statement audit. *See* SAS-82
identification of, 49
material misstatement. *See* Material misstatement
significance in audit, 49

G

GAAP. *See* Generally Accepted Accounting Principles
GAAP, departures
compilation engagements-management use only, 703

GAAS. *See* Generally Accepted Auditing Standards
Gas and oil information, 419, 421–422
GASB-31 (Accounting and Financial Reporting for Certain Investments and for External Investment Pools), 192
General-use reports, 384
Generally Accepted Accounting Principles (GAAP)
adherence to, 309–310
auditor's reporting of departure from, 354–356, 374–375
conformity with, 311–317
departure from, in financial statement compilation, 667, 692–693
departure from, in financial statement review, 714–715
described, 311
deviation from, in work of specialists, 221
foreign, 393–397
industry practice, precedence over, 66
interim financial reports, 509–512, 520–521
lack of conformity with, 406–407
reporting on basis of accounting other than GAAP, 443–448
reports not in accordance with, 457–458, 463–464
reviews and compilations, 675
Generally Accepted Auditing Standards (GAAS)
consistency of application, 318–324
general standards, 4
identification of originating country, 347
interim financial reports, 506–508
standards of fieldwork, 5
standards of reporting, 5–6
Going concern. *See also* Uncertainties
entity's ability to continue, 246–247. *See also* SAS-59
explanatory paragraph, 238, 246
interim financial reports, 521
reporting of uncertainties, 362–364

Index

Government Auditing Standards
   regulatory reporting requirements, 452
   reports on internal control, 143
Governmental entities, audit of. *See* SAS-74

H

Hedging Activities, 192
Highest level of service, reporting on, 667, 681, 769–770

I

Illegal acts. *See also* SAS-54
   defined, 91, 92
   effects on financial statements, 92–93
Immaterial misstatements, 65–66
Income, comprehensive, 349, 350–353
Incomplete presentations, 455
Inconsistency. *See also* Consistency standards
   in appearance, 17
   disclaimer of opinion due to not being independent, 365–366
   engagements requiring, 17–19
   financial statement compilations, 694
   financial statement reviews, 715
   independence, 16–19
   interim financial reports, 522
   lack of, 341–343, 345
   quality control, 9
   rule of conduct, 16–19
Independence
   for compilation engagements, 674
   compilation Engagements-Management Use Only, 702–703
   in fact, 17
   in financial statement compilation, 692
   in financial statement review, 713
   rule of conduct, 674
Independent auditor. *See* Auditor, independent
Information and communication, 98
   internal control, 99–100
   obtaining understanding of, 106
Information technology
   internal controls, 101–102
   understanding internal control, 107–108
Informative disclosures, 356–357
Inherent risk
   analytical procedures in planning the engagement, 157
   assessment of, 194–195
   in attestation engagements, 549–550
   in compliance attestation engagements, 625
   defined, 56
   factors, 56
   interrelationship of risk factors, 58
   MD&A engagement, 638
   in planned assessed level of control risk, 108
Inquiry of a Client's Lawyer Concerning Litigation, Claims, and Assessments. *See* SAS-12
Insurance company loss reserves, 216, 442, 451
Insurance informative disclosures, 442, 447
Integrity of auditors, 9, 17
Intentional misstatements
   auditor's response, 66
   immaterial misstatement, 65–66
Interim financial information, 483–484. *See also* SAS-71
Interim Financial Reporting. *See* APB Opinion No. 28
Intermediaries, 465
Internal audit function. *See* SAS-65
Internal Control Review Engagement
   compilation and review of financial statements, 679–680
   components, 97–98
   criteria, 618
   described, 97
   effect of information technology, 101–102
   effect of internal audit function, 120

Internal Control Review Engagement, *cont.*
  evaluating client's internal controls, 609
  examination report on effectiveness of internal controls, 613–615
  financial statement audits, 618. *See also* SAS-55
  management's representation, 611
  material weakness, 616
  MD&A engagements, 642, 655
  planning the engagement, 607–609
  pre-award survey, 619
  in preparation of interim financial reports, 514
  procedures checklist, 607
  regulatory control criteria, 618
  relevant, 103
  report by management, 408–409
  reporting, 611–618
  risk. *See* Control risk
  scope limitations, 616
  service organizations, 126–127
  SSAE-10 (Attestation Standards: Revision and Recodification), 605–606
  subsequent events, 617
  testing client's internal controls, 609–611
  understanding client's internal controls, 609
  understanding of, in audit, 28
Internal Revenue Service
  Form 990 (Return of Organizations Exempt from Income Tax), 442, 459
International financial statements, 392–397
Inventory
  auditor's observation of physical count, 360–361
  FIFO to LIFO change, 318, 321
  held in public warehouse, 186–187, 190–191, 537
  in interim financial reports, 509–510
  observation procedures, 187–190
  outside inventory-taking firm, 346, 362
  perpetual inventory records, 186
  physical count, 185–186
  reporting changes in methods, 321
  statistical sampling, 186
  substantiation of, 185–187
Investment. *See also* SAS-92
  auditing of, 192–193
  derivative instruments, hedging activities, 192
  government, 193
  long-term, accounting for, 402
Investment Company Act of 1940, 298

L

Lawyer
  audit inquiry letter, 223, 225–227, 228–231
  client has not consulted, 206, 223–224
  evaluation of litigation, 223, 228
  inquiry on litigation, claims, and assessments. *See* SAS-12
  lawyer-client privilege, 223, 225, 227–228
Leases, confirmation of, 180–181
Letters
  alternative, 473–474
  audit inquiry to lawyer, 223, 225–227, 228–231
  client consent and acknowledgment, 79
  comfort letters. *See* Comfort letters
  to directors, 471–472
  engagement. *See* Letters, engagement
  financial statement compilation, client representation, 689, 723–724
  financial statement review, client representation, 711, 724–728
  illustrative audit inquiry, 226
  management representation, 201–208, 586–587, 600, 611, 630, 647–649, 657

Index

predecessor and successor auditor, 78–79
representation. *See* Letters, representation
successor auditor representation, 367–368
for underwriters. *See* SAS-49; SAS-72
updating representation, 205
Letters, engagement
agreed-upon procedures, 565–566
compilation Engagements-Management Use Only, 698–703
financial statement compilations, 674–675, 717–719, 728–731
financial statement reviews, 674–675, 719–723, 731–733, 734–736
interim financial reports, 508–509, 524–526
understanding with the client, 29–31
Letters, representation
attestation engagements, 551–552
compilation engagement, 586–587
management, 201–208, 586–587, 600, 611
from requesting parties, 474, 490
from successor auditor, 367–368
updating, 205
Levels in determining audit risk and materiality
financial statement, 50–55
individual account-balance or class-of-transactions, 54–59
Levels of accounting hierarchies, 314–317
Levels of service
changes in, 683–684
highest level, reporting on, 667, 681, 769–770
review of financial statements, 706
Liabilities, transfers and servicing of, 221–222
Limited reporting engagement, 362, 377–378, 444

Litigation
attestation standards for, 541, 543
SSARS, 668, 672
Loss contingencies
accounting and reporting standards, 363
accrual of, 223
classifications, 363
defined, 362–363
Loss reserve specialist, 216

M

Management Representation Letter, 201–208, 600, 630, 647–649, 657
Management Representations. *See* SAS-85
Management representations on violations, 200, 206
Management's Discussion and Analysis (MD&A)
analytical procedures, 655–657
assertions, 638–639
client's methods used to prepare information, 641, 657
combined reporting, 661–662
communicating deficiencies with audit committee, 663
completeness test of evidence, 645–646
engagement report, 649–652
evidence, 643–645
internal control, 655
nonfinancial data as evidence, 645
other information included, 663
planning the engagement, 637–641, 654
procedures checklist, 637, 653–654
review report, 657–661
risk assessment, 638
subsequent events, 646–647, 657, 663
understanding of requirements, 641, 657
written management representations, 647–649, 657
Material inconsistency, determination of, 409

Material misstatement. *See also* Errors; Fraud; Immaterial misstatements
   aggregating and netting, 64–65
   assessing materiality, 62–64
   determining nateriality, 50–62
   of facts in information, 410
   of financial statements, by predecessor auditor that has ceased operations, 370
   materiality defined, 48
   misappropriation of assets, 80–81, 84–86
   misstatement defined, 48–49
   in previously issued financial statements, 77
   in sampling, 278–280, 287, 291–293
Material noncompliance and uncertainty in compliance attestation engagement, 686
Material weakness, 143–145
   defined, 143, 616
   example, 147–149
   internal control, 616
   internal control and Foreign Corrupt Practices Act, 91–92, 93
   reporting of, 140, 144
Materiality. *See also* Audit risk; Material misstatement; SAS-47
   assessing, 62–64
   in attest engagements, 552–553
   in audit strategy, 7–8
   defined, 48
   determination of, in planning audit, 50–62
   effect on financial statements, 324
   prospective financial statements, 575
   in prospective financial statements, 574
   in sampling, 278
   types of, 63
Meaning of "Present Fairly in Conformity with Generally Accepted Accounting Principles" in the Independent Auditors' Report. *See* SAS-69
Misappropriation of assets, 80–81, 84–86

Misstatement. *See* Material misstatement
Monitoring
   CPA firm's practices, 7–8
   defined, 98
   internal control, 100
   obtaining understanding of, 106–107
   quality control, 9
Mortgage obligation confirmation request, 181–182

N

Negative assurance, 365
   in attest engagements, 550
   in comfort letters, 484, 485, 486–488
   compliance with contracts or regulations, 453–454
   in pro forma financial information reviews, 597
New transactions, accounting principles, 311, 313
Nonpublic entities. *See also* Private-sector
   accountant services, 671–672
   comparative financial statements, 770–771, 775
   defined, 668
   MD&A information, 658, 662
   SSARS standards, 668–669
   use of BCIP, 777
Nonquantitative audit risk, 50–51
Notice to Practitioners, 369, 769
   in regulatory reports, 452
Notice to Practitioners, "Audit, Review, and Compilation Considerations When a Predecessor Accountant Has Ceased Operations" (February 1991), 368, 769

O

Objectivity of auditors, 9, 17
OCBOA. *See also* Other comprehensive basis of accounting
   compilation Engagements-Management Use Only, 703
Oil and gas information, 419, 421–422

Index

OMB Circular A-123, 384
Omitted procedures after the report date, 303–305
Omnibus Statement on Auditing Standards. *See* SAS-43; SAS-45; SAS-52; SAS-64; SAS-93
Operational effectiveness, 111–112, 124, 136
Opinion
    adverse, in auditor's report, 213, 354–355, 374–375
    auditor's, on financial statements, 309
    defined, 49
    disclaimer of, 365
    piecemeal, 365
Other comprehensive basis of accounting (OCBOA), 384, 385–386
    adequate disclosure, 446
    defined, 669
    labeling reports, 443
    reports not in accordance with, 457–458, 463–464
Other Information in Documents Containing Audited Financial Statements. *See* SAS-8

P

Paragraphs in reports
    distribution, 453, 457, 458
    explanatory, 453, 458
    introductory, 447, 449–450, 453, 456, 457
    limited assurance, 453
    opinion, 448, 450, 456, 458
    presentation basis, 448, 450, 456, 458
    scope, 447–448, 450, 456, 457–458
Partial presentations of prospective financial information, 593
Personal financial statements, 782–783
Personnel management
    assignment of personnel in audit engagement, 87
    quality control, 9
Photocopies to regulator, 232, 234, 541

Planning, pre-engagement
    attest engagements, 544–547
    interim financial reports, 506
Planning and Supervision. *See* SAS-22; SSARS Interpretation 5
Planning the engagement, 32
    adequate level of knowledge of business, 35
    analytical procedures, 157–158
    application of accounting principles, 467–470
    assistants' responsibilities, 36–37
    attest engagements, 547–548
    compilations and reviews, 678–679
    compliance attestation, 624–627
    computer skills requirements, 35–36
    continuing engagement checklist, 42–46
    determining risk. *See* SAS-47
    engagement checklist, 37–40
    financial forecasts and projections, 575
    interim financial reports, 512–514
    internal control review, 607–609
    MD&A, 637–641, 654
    preliminary plan memorandum, 30, 34
    procedures checklist, 32–33
    prospective client evaluation form, 40–42
    strategy development, 33–35
    supervision checklist, 46–47
    understanding client's internal controls, 609
    understanding with the client, 548
    written audit program, 34–35
Pooling of interests
    financial statement restatement due to, 323–323, 402–403
    reporting by successor auditor, 402–403
Population selection for sampling, 259–260, 262, 266–267, 274–275
Positive assurance in attest engagement, 550
PPPO report. *See* Report on policies and procedures placed in operation

PPPO/TOE report. *See* Report on controls placed in operation and tests of operating effectiveness
Practicable, defined, 325, 354
Prescribed forms, 776–777
Private-sector. *See also* Nonpublic entities
　accounting hierarchy, 312, 314–317
　financial statements by predecessor accountant that has ceased operations, 369–371
　unaudited financial statements, 343, 344–345
Pro forma financial information
　assumptions used, 599
　comfort letters concerning, 485
　evidence, 599
　examination engagement, 597–600
　examination report, 600–603
　financial statements, 571–573. *See also* Financial forecasts and projections
　guidelines, 596
　management representations, 600
　negative assurance, 596
　objectives of examination engagements, 597
　objectives of review engagements, 597
　procedures checklist, 598
　read pro forma financial information, 600
　reporting, 600–604, 631–632
　review engagement, 597
　review report, 600–602, 603–604
　SSAE-10 (Attestation Standards: Revision and Recodification), 595–597
　understanding underlying transactions, 598
Professional skepticism, 20–21, 22–24, 86, 175
Proficiency of the independent auditor, 14–15, 467, 544
Projections. *See* Financial forecasts and projections
Promulgated quality control component checklist, 8–10

Public-sector companies
　accounting hierarchy, 312, 315–316
　comparative financial statements, 770–771, 775
　MD&A reporting, 640–641, 658, 662
　reporting to the SEC, 523–524
　unaudited financial statements, 340–341, 344
　warehouses, 538–539

Q

Qualitative Characteristics of Accounting Information (FAS-2), 48, 299
Qualitative Characteristics of Misstatement, 53–54, 61
Qualitative materiality, 52–53, 61–62
Quality control checklist, 8–10
Quantitative
　audit risk, 50–51, 52
　materiality, 52–53

R

Ratios, in analytical procedures for review engagement, 164–166
Real estate financial statements, 442, 445
Reasonable assurance, 21
Reaudit engagements, 76–77
Registration statement, 500, 662
Regulation S-B in MD&A engagements, 641
Regulation S-K
　filings under federal securities statutes, 502
　letters for underwriters, 471, 473–474, 489
　MD&A engagements, 641
Regulation S-X, letters for underwriters, 482, 485
Regulators
　access to working papers, 232, 234–235, 541
　filing requirements of governmental authorities, 406–407

Index

Reissued reports
  comparative financial statements, 762, 766–769
  dating of, 382–383
  difference from reprinting, 369
  going concern paragraph, 238, 246
  by predecessor auditor, 367–368
Related parties. *See also* SAS-45
  client disclosure, 213–215
  determination of, 210–211
  disclosures. *See* FAS-57
  evaluation of transactions, 209–210
  examples, 210–211
  identification of, 211–213
  substantiation of representation, 213
Relationship
  plausibility of data, 159
  between specialists and clients, 218–219
Relationship of Generally Accepted Auditing Standards to Quality Control Standards (SAS-25), 7–10
Report. *See also* Financial Statement(s)
  auditor's. *See* Auditor's report
  by-product, 387
  general-use, 384
  reissued. *See* Reissued reports
  restricted use, 384
Report on controls placed in operation and tests of operating effectiveness (PPPO/TOE report), 130–136
  defined, 130
  example, 137–139
  preparation procedures, 132–133
  qualified, 134–135
Report on policies and procedures placed in operation (PPPO report), 130–136
  defined, 130
  example, 136–137
  preparation procedures, 132–133
  qualified, 134–135
Reportable conditions
  defined, 140, 616
  examples, 145–147
  identification of, 141–142
  report, 147

Reporting
  compliance attestation engagement, 622–623
Reporting Comprehensive Income (FAS-130), 349
Reporting on Comparative Financial Statements. *See* SSARS-2
Reporting on Condensed Financial Statements and Selected Financial Data (SAS-42), 18, 415–418
Reporting on an Entity's Internal Control Structure Over Financial Reporting. *See* Internal Control Review Engagement
Reporting on Financial Statements Prepared for Use in Other Countries. *See* SAS-51
Reporting on Information Accompanying the Basic Financial Statements in Auditor-Submitted Documents. *See* SAS-29
Reporting standards, 5
  in accordance with GAAP, 309
  applicability of accounting principles, 469
  in association with financial statements, 340–344
  audited financial statements, 353–354
  change in reporting entity, 323–324
  checklist, 319–320, 326–335, 353–354, 385
  compilation and review, 680–681
  format of standard auditor's report, 346
  special reports, 447–448, 449–451, 452–454, 455–457
Reports on Audited Financial Statements. *See* SAS-58
Reports on the Application of Accounting Principles. *See* SAS-50
Reports on the Processing of Transactions by Service Organizations. *See* SAS-70
Representation, oral, 227–228
Representation letters. *See* Letters, representation
Reprinting of audit report, 369

Required Communications of Material Weaknesses in Internal Accounting Control. *See* SAS-20
Responsible party, 571
Restatement
 of auditor's reports, 369–370
 of financial statements, 323–324, 402–403
Restricted-use reports, 384
Restricting the Use of an Auditor's Report. *See* SAS-87
Retroactive restatement, 320–321
Review of financial statements. *See* Financial statement review
Review services, 668
Risk. *See also* Fraud
 assessment. *See* Risk assessment
 attestation, 624–625. *See also* Risk, attestation
 audit. *See* Audit risk
 control. *See* Control risk
 detection. *See* Detection risk
 inherent. *See* Inherent risk
 material misstatement. *See* Material misstatement
 sampling, 258–260, 271, 276–278
Risk, attestation, 547, 549–550
 defined, 624–625
 management's assertions, 676–678
Risk assessment
 changes in, 98–99
 defined, 97
 effect of internal audit function, 121
 internal control, 98–99
 obtaining understanding of, 105
Robert Morris Associates, 777
Rules of Conduct. *See also* Code of Professional Conduct
 for professional services, 16–17

S

SAB-99, 62–63, 65
Sampling. *See also* SAS-39
 attribute, 258, 260–273
 audit. *See* SAS-39
 block, 264
 documentation, 273
 haphazard, 264–265
 nonsampling plans, 256–257
 nonstatistical. *See* Sampling, nonstatistical
 random, 263
 representative, 263
 risk, 258–260, 265, 271
 size, 265, 267–268
 statistical. *See* Sampling, statistical
 substantive tests, 258–259, 273–296
 systematic, 263–264
 tests of controls. *See* Tests of controls in sampling
 tolerable misstatement, 278–279
 variable, 258, 273–281, 296
Sampling, nonstatistical, 257–258
 risk, 271
 size, 267–268
 substantive tests. *See* Tests, substantive for sampling
 tests of controls. *See* Tests of controls in sampling
Sampling, statistical, 257–258
 of inventory, 186
 risk, 265, 271–272
 sample size, 267–269
 substantive tests. *See* Tests, substantive for sampling
 tests of controls. *See* Tests of controls in sampling
SAS-1 (Codification of Auditing Standards and Procedures)
 adherence to GAAP, 309–310
 consistency of application of GAAP, 318–324
 dating of auditor's report, 205, 381–383
 due professional care, 20–24
 filings under Federal Securities Statutes, 383
 generally accepted accounting principles, 311
 generally accepted auditing standards, 4–6
 independence, 16–19
 interim financial reports, 523

Index

inventories, 185–191
lack of conformity with GAAP, 406–407
nature of the general standards, 13
part of audit performed by other auditors, 76, 77, 128, 398–405, 519–520
predecessor and successor auditors, 76–77
procedures checklist, 185, 427
for public warehouses, 538–539
responsibilities of independent auditor, 3–4
subsequent discovery of facts. *See* Subsequent discovery of facts
subsequent events, 426–431
training and proficiency of the independent auditor, 14–15
SAS-8 (Other Information in Documents Containing Audited Financial Statements), 408–410, 594
selected financial data, 417
unaudited voluntary disclosures, 255
SAS-11 (Using the Work of a Specialist), 216. *See also* SAS-73
SAS-12 (Inquiry of a Client's Lawyer Concerning Litigation, Claims, and Assessments), 217, 223–224
audit inquiry letter to lawyer, 225–227, 228–231
guidelines for use of a lawyer, 15
identification of litigation, claims, and assessments, 225
inclusion in auditor's workpapers, 233
non-response from lawyer, 228
oral representations, 227–228
procedures checklist, 224
written representation when client has not consulted lawyer, 206
SAS-19 (Client Representations)
inclusion in auditor's workpapers, 233
interim financial reports, 515–516
SAS-20 (Required Communications of Material Weaknesses in Internal Accounting Control), 140. *See also* SAS-60
SAS-21 (Segment Information), 152–153, 336
SAS-22 (Planning and Supervision), 32, 81
audit programs included in auditor's workpapers, 234
compilations and reviews, 678
using the work of a specialist, 217
SAS-25 (The Relationship of Generally Accepted Auditing Standards to Quality Control Standards), 7–10
SAS-26 (Association with Financial Statements), 339–340
compilation and review, 676
examples, 344–345
reporting checklist, 340
reporting on comparative financial statements, 764–765
unaudited financial statements, 340–344
SAS-29 (Reporting on Information Accompanying the Basic Financial Statements in Auditor-Submitted Documents), 411
additional information, 412
condensed financial information, 415
consolidated information, 412–413
independence requirements, 18
procedures checklist, 411–412
supplementary information, 413–414
SAS-31 (Evidential Matter), 151. *See also* SAS-80
financial statement assertions, 49, 103, 115–116, 153–154
in MD&A examinations, 639
procedures checklist, 152
reliability of evidence, 171
substantive tests, 153–154
sufficient evidential matter, 152–153
SAS-32 (Adequacy of Disclosures in Financial Statements), 325, 357

SAS-37 (Filings under Federal Securities Statutes), 417, 499–500
  procedures checklist, 500
  registration statement, 500, 503–504
  review of documents, 503
  review procedures, 501–502
  unaudited financial information, 502–503
SAS-39 (Audit Sampling), 256. *See also* Sampling
  documentation of sampling procedures, 273
  nonsampling plan, 256–257
  nonstatistical sampling, 257–258, 267, 271
  PPPO/TOE report by service auditors, 131
  risk, 258–260
  statistical, 257–258, 265, 267–268, 271–272
  substantive tests, 296
  tests of controls. *See* Tests of controls in sampling
  tolerable rate of deviation, 266–267, 269
SAS-41 (Working Papers), 232
  access by regulators, 234–235
  documentation, 280–281
  exposure draft replacement, 232
  fieldwork standards have been observed, 233–234
  governmental audits, 533
  interim financial reports, 516
  procedures checklist, 232–233
  sampling procedures, 273
SAS-42 (Reporting on Condensed Financial Statements and Selected Financial Data), 18, 415–418
SAS-43 (Omnibus Statement on Auditing Standards)
  changes in format of cash flow statement, 321–322
  generally accepted auditing standards, 4–6
SAS-45 (Omnibus Statement on Auditing Standards-1983)
  audit procedures for oil and gas information, 421–422
  related parties, 209–215
  substantive tests prior to balance sheet date, 67–71
SAS-46 (Consideration of Omitted Procedures after the Report Date), 303–305
SAS-47 (Audit Risk and Materiality in Conducting an Audit), 32, 48–51, 81, 194. *See also* SAS-82
  determining risk at financial statement level, 50–54
  determining risk at individual account-balance or class-of-transactions level, 54–59
  factors in determining risk, 51
  management representations, 203
  planning and supervision, 32
  substantive tests used to determine audit risk, 59–61
SAS-48 (The Effects of Computer Processing on the Examination of Financial Statements), 32, 151
SAS-49 (Letters for Underwriters), 499–500. *See also* SAS-72
SAS-50 (Reports on the Application of Accounting Principles), 465–466
  accumulation of sufficient information, 467–468
  auditor's preparation for audit, 467
  compilation and review, 676
  example of accountant's report, 470
  predecessor and successor accountants, 781
  procedures checklist, 466–467
  reporting standards, 469
SAS-51 (Reporting on Financial Statements Prepared for Use in Other Countries), 392
  audit report, 393–397
  foreign auditing standards, 393
  general standards, 393
  independence requirements, 18
  procedures checklist, 392

Index

SAS-52 (Omnibus Statement on Auditing Standards-1987 [Requirement Supplementary Information]), 419
   minimum procedures, 420–421
   modification of audit report, 421–425
   oil and gas reserve information, 421–422
   procedures checklist, 419–420
SAS-54 (Illegal Acts by Clients), 91–96
   appropriate audit procedures, 93–94
   AU 317, 66
   communication with audit committee, 95–96
   determine effect on audit report, 96
   effects on financial statements, 92–93
   evaluation of results of performing procedures, 94–95
   examples of information indication of illegal acts, 93
   illegal acts, defined, 91
   material weaknesses, 145
   oral communication included in auditor's workpapers, 234
   procedures checklist, 93
   suspicion of illegal acts, 94
SAS-55 (Consideration of Internal Control in a Financial Statement Audit), 97
   application to small and mid-sized entities, 117
   components, 97–101
   control activities, 97, 99
   control environment, 98
   determination of control risk, 108–109
   documentation of control risk, 113
   documentation of understanding of internal controls, 108
   effect of IT on understanding, 107–108
   expectation, 158
   factors, 97–102
   governmental audits, 533
   information and communication, 98, 99–100
   internal control, described, 97–98
   internal control limitations, 101
   internal control reporting, 618
   monitoring, 98, 100
   PPPO/TOE report by service auditor, 131
   procedures checklist, 102–103
   procedures used to obtain understanding, 106–107
   report included in auditor's workpapers, 234
   risk assessment, 97, 98–99, 194–196
   substantive tests, 114–115, 161–163
   tests of controls, 109–113
   understanding of internal control, 103–108, 115–116, 126–127
SAS-56 (Analytical Procedures), 156
   analytical procedures for a review engagement, 164–170
   interim financial reports, 515
   MD&A engagements, 657
   planning the engagement, 157–158
   plausibility of data, 159
   procedures checklist, 156–157
   reliability of data, 159
   substantive tests, 159–163
SAS-57 (Auditing Accounting Estimates), 248
   accounting estimate, defined, 248
   GAAP requirements, 252
   identification of factors requiring estimates, 249–250
   interim financial reports, 515
   procedures checklist, 249
   testing reasonableness of estimates, 250–251
SAS-58 (Reports on Audited Financial Statements), 346. *See also* Auditor's report
   auditor's opinion, 407
   comparative financial statements, 365–366
   example, 348–349
   foreign financial statements, 396
   inventory counts, 360–361

SAS-58, *cont.*
    limited reporting engagement, 362, 377–378, 445
    matters that can be emphasized, 364
    notes on subsequent events, 428
    omission of cash flow statement, 357, 375–376
    reporting standards checklist, 353–354
    scope limitations, 359
    standard auditor's report format, 346–347
    statements to include, 346–347
    unqualified report, 349
SAS-59 (The Auditor's Consideration of an Entity's Ability to Continue as a Going Concern), 238, 246
    compilation and review, 677
    disclosures in the audit report, 242–246
    evaluation, 246–247
    examples of events raising substantial doubt, 239–240
    financial statement compilations, 694
    management's plans to mitigate adverse conditions, 240–241
    procedures checklist, 238–239
SAS-60 (Communication of Internal Control Related Matters Noted in an Audit), 140
    by-product report, 387
    compliance attestation engagements, 628
    deficiencies in internal control, 616
    fraudulent acts, 89
    governmental audits, 533
    inclusion in auditor's workpapers, 233
    material weakness, 143–145, 147–149
    procedures checklist, 141
    reportable conditions, 140, 141–142, 145–147
    reports to audit committee, 142–143
SAS-61 (Communication with Audit Committees), 297
    by-product report, 387
    details to include, 299, 300–302
    form of communication required, 298
    procedures checklist, 298
    report included in auditor's workpapers, 234
SAS-62 (Special Reports), 442
    basis of accounting other than GAAP, 443–448, 460–461
    by-product report, 387
    compilation and review, 677
    compliance with contracts or regulations, 452–458, 462–464
    contractual agreement, 455
    engagements excluded from SSAE-10, 563, 620
    filing requirements of governmental regulatory authorities, 406–407
    financial statement accounting methods, 203
    financial statement content requirements, 44, 340, 341–342
    financial statement defined, 443–444
    incomplete presentations, 455
    independence requirements, 18
    modifications to reports, 459–460
    prescribed form of report, 459
    presentation not in accordance with GAAP or OCBOA, 457–458, 463–464
    reporting standards, 447–448, 449–451, 452–454, 455–457, 457–458
    special-purpose financial statements, 385–386, 455
    specified elements of financial statements, 448–451, 461–462
    using the work of a specialist, 217
SAS-64 (Omnibus Statement on Auditing Standards-1990), 243, 402
    report, 243
SAS-65 (The Auditor's Consideration of the Internal Audit Function in an Audit of Financial Statements), 118, 194
    assessing objectivity and competence, 119–120

Index

assessment factors, 122
compliance attestation engagements, 628
degree of reliance, 121–122
design of substantive procedures, 121
effect on assessed risk, 121
evaluation of internal audit function, 119–123
internal control of entity, 608
MD&A information, 640
procedures checklist, 118–119
understanding of internal control, 120
understanding of monitoring, 106
work of predecessor auditor in reaudit engagements, 77
SAS-67 (The Confirmation Process), 171
    accounts receivable confirmation, 178–179, 234
    confirmation request forms, 172–174
    confirmation requests, 171–179
    financial statement assertions, 172
    procedures checklist, 171
    unconfirmed balances, 177
SAS-69 (The Meaning of "Present Fairly in Conformity with Generally Accepted Accounting Principles" in the Independent Auditor's Report), 311–313, 348
    acceptable accounting principles, 467–468
    compilation and review, 677
    concepts of adequate disclosure, 445
    financial accounting hierarchy, 312, 316–317
    financial statements deviating from GAAP, 445
    GAAP, defined, 406–407
    private-sector accounting hierarchy, 312, 314–315
    public-sector accounting hierarchy, 312, 315–316
SAS-70 (Reports on the Processing of Transactions by Service Organizations), 124–125

    engagements excluded from SAS-75 requirements, 477
    engagements excluded from SSAE-10, 563
    independence requirements, 18
    investments, 196
    PPPO report, 130–136
    PPPO/TOE report, 130–136, 137–139
    service auditor, 125, 129–136
    user auditor, 125–129
SAS-71 (Interim Financial Information), 505–506
    in accordance with GAAS, 506–508
    accountant's report, 518–524, 526–527
    accountant's responsibilities, 506
    accounting changes, 510–512
    analytical procedures, 515–516
    appropriate accounting principles, 509–512, 520–521
    communication with audit committee, 517–518
    disclosure modification, 521
    engagement letter, 508–509, 525–526
    going concern, 521
    independence requirements, 18
    independent auditor, appointment of, 29
    knowledge of internal controls, 514
    modifications, 519, 521–522
    planning the engagement, 512–514
    pre-engagement planning, 506
    procedures checklist, 508
    reports accompanying audited financial statements, 523–524
    subsequent events, 522
    summarized financial statements, 512
    using the work of others, 519–520, 527
SAS-72 (Letters for Underwriters and Certain Other Requesting Parties), 385, 471–472. *See also* SAS-76; SAS-86
    applicability of, 472–474

SAS-72, *cont.*
  comfort letters. *See* Comfort letters
  engagements excluded from SSAE-10, 563, 620
  forward-looking information, 619
  representation letter, 474, 490
SAS-73 (Using the Work of a Specialist), 216–217
  in attest engagements, 545
  circumstances for use, 217
  compliance attestation engagements, 628
  determination of transfer of assets, 221–222
  effect on audit report, 220–221
  examples of circumstances to use specialist, 216
  extent that the work should be used, 220
  guidelines, 15
  MD&A information, 640
  qualifications of specialists, 218–219
  relationship to client, 218–219
  work of predecessor auditors in reaudit engagements, 77
SAS-74 (Compliance Auditing Considerations in Audits of Governmental Entities and Recipients of Governmental Financial Assistance), 143, 531–533
  engagements excluded from SSAE-10, 563, 620
  independent auditor, appointment of, 29
  procedures for audit, 531–532
  regulatory reporting requirements, 452
SAS-75 (Engagements to Apply Agreed-Upon Procedures to Specified Elements, Accounts, or Items of a Financial Statement), 386–387
  compilation and review, 677
  independent auditor, appointment of, 29
  for a portion of entity's financial statements, 451

SAS-90 (Auditing Standards) replacement, 441
SAS-76 (Amendments to Statement on Auditing Standards No. 72, Letters for Underwriters and Certain Other Requesting Parties), 471, 473–474
SAS-77 (Amendments to Statements on Auditing Standards No. 22, "Planning and Supervision," No. 59, "The Auditor's Consideration of an Entity's Ability to Continue as a Going Concern," and No. 62, "Special Reports"), 32, 243, 245
SAS-79 (Amendments to Statements on Auditing Standards No. 58, "Reports on Audited Financial Statements"), 363
SAS-80 (Amendment to Statement on Auditing Standards No. 31, Evidential Matter), 151, 154
SAS-81 (Auditing Investments). *See also* SAS-92
  superseded by SAS-92, 192
SAS-82 (Consideration of Fraud in a Financial Statement Audit), 80–90. *See also* SAS-47
  AU 316, 48, 66, 91
  audit impact from risk factor assessment, 86–88
  audit procedures due to fraudulent misstatement, 88
  communication of fraudulent acts, 89
  in compliance attestation, 625
  documentation of audit results, 89
  evaluation of audit risk after engagement is complete, 88–89
  fraud factors related to industry conditions, 83
  fraudulent financial reporting, 80–90
  management representations, 204
  management's characteristics and influence over the control environment, factors related to, 82–83

Index

misappropriation of assets, 80–81, 84–86
modification of audit approach, 86, 87–88
operating characteristics and financial stability, 83–84
procedures checklist, 81
risk assessment, 81, 82
SAS-83 (Establishing an Understanding with the Client)
   documentation of understanding, 29
   engagement letter, 30–31
   procedures checklist, 27–31
   understandings of engagement, 27–29
SAS-84 (Communications Between Predecessor and Successor Auditors), 72–79, 76–77
   audit evidence, obtaining of, 75–76
   communications before audit engagement, 73–74
   communications helpful in audit planning, 74
   comparative financial statements, 768–769
   cooperation between predecessor and successor auditors, 74–75, 78–79
   discovery of misstatements in previous financial statements, 77
   evidence to support beginning account balances, 76
   fraud in financial statement audit, 90
   MD&A information, 636–637
   misstatements, audit procedures related to discovery of, 77
   procedures checklist, 72–73
   reaudit engagements, 76–77
SAS-85 (Management Representations), 200–201
   evaluation of inconsistencies, 205–206
   letters, 206–208
   MD&A, 649
   procedures checklist, 201
   written, 201–205

SAS-86 (Amendment to Statement on Auditing Standards No. 72, Letters for Underwriters and Certain Other Requesting Parties), 471, 483
SAS-87 (Restricting the Use of an Auditor's Report), 384–385
   basis of reporting criteria, 385–386, 388–389
   by-product report, 387
   reporting standards checklist, 385
   scope of engagement, 386–387, 389–391
SAS-88 (Service Organizations and Reporting on Consistency), 124, 127
SAS-89 (Audit adjustments), 203, 297
   independent auditor, appointment of, 27
SAS-90 (Audit Committee Communications), 297, 298, 299–300
SAS-91 (Federal GAAP hierarchy), 316–317
SAS-92 (Auditing Derivative Instruments, Hedging Activities, and Investments in Securities), 192–193
   assessment of control risk, 195
   design appropriate substantive procedures, 196
   procedures checklist, 193
   understanding derivative securities, 194
SAS-93 (Omnibus Statement on Auditing Standards-2000), 72, 346, 441
SAS-94 (The Effect of Information Technology on the Auditor's Consideration of Internal Control in a Financial Statement Audit), 97
   benefits of ITT controls, 101–102
   control activities, 99
   planned assessed level of control risk, determining, 109
   tests of controls, 110
Scope deficiencies, 460
Scope limitation
   in attest engagements, 553–554
   in auditor's report, 360–362, 376–377

Scope limitation, *cont.*
 internal control reports, 616
 in prospective financial statements, 582
 review of financial statements, 710–711
 in using work of a specialist, 221
 when client's lawyer does not respond, 228
Scope modification in interim financial information, 519
SEC. *See* Securities and Exchange Commission
Section 11 investigation, 472
 shelf registrations, 477–478, 499, 502
 updating representation letter, 205
Section 11(a), 499–500
Securities, investments, 192
Securities Act of 1933, 502. *See also* SAS-37
 applicability of SAS-8, 417
 experts in documents, 499, 502
 letters for underwriters, 471, 472
 MD&A, 646
 representation letters, 474
Securities and Exchange Commission (SEC)
 communication with audit committees, 298, 299
 filing of financial statements, 667, 678
 filing of unaudited financial statements, 342–344, 344–345
 filings under statutes. *See* SAS-37
 financial statements, 667, 678
 interim financial information by public companies, 523–524
 letters for underwriters, 471
 MD&A, 641, 662–663
 selected financial data, 417
Securities Exchange Act of 1934, 298, 408, 502
 report engagements excluded from SSAE-10, 620
Securities statutes, filings under. *See* SAS-37

Segment disclosures, 151–153, 336
Segment Information (SAS-21), 152–153, 336
Service auditor, 125, 129–136
Service organizations, 124, 136. *See also* SAS-70
 control risk, 127–128
 internal control, 126–127
 services that affect substantive procedures, 196–197
 use of subservice organizations, 125, 136, 196
Service Organizations and Reporting on Consistency (SAS-88), 124, 127
Service Organizations (SAS-70), 385
Shelf registrations, 477–478, 499, 502
Shopping for opinions, 465, 781
Single Audit Act of 1984, 237
Skepticism, 20–21, 22–24, 86, 175
Small business enterprise, material weaknesses, 147–149
Solvency
 in attest engagements, 554
 reports on, 541
SOP 82-1 (Accounting and Financial Reporting for Personal Financial Statements), 783–784
SOP 92-4 (Auditing Insurance Entities' Loss Reserves), 216
Special Reports. *See* SAS-62
Specialist, using the work of. *See* SAS-73
SQCS-2 (System of Quality Control for a CPA Firm's Accounting and Auditing Practice), 7–10
SQCS-3 (Monitoring a CPA Firm's Accounting and Auditing Practice), 7–10, 9
SSAE-1 (Codification of Statements, on Standards for Attestation Engagements). *See also* SSAE-10
 superseded by SSAE-10, 541
SSAE-2 (Reporting on an Entity's Internal Control Structure Over Financial Reporting). *See also* SSAE-10
 superseded by SSAE-10, 541

Index

SSAE-3 (Compliance Attestation). *See also* SSAE-10
  superseded by SSAE-10, 541
SSAE-4 (Agreed-upon Procedures Engagements). *See also* SSAE-10
  superseded by SSAE-10, 541
SSAE-5 (Amendments to Statement on Standards for Attestation Engagements No.1, Attestation Standards). *See also* SSAE-10
  superseded by SSAE-10, 541
SSAE-6 (Reporting on an Entity's Internal Control Over Financial Reporting: An Amendment to Statement on Standards for Attestation Engagements No. 4). *See also* SSAE-10
  superseded by SSAE-10, 541
SSAE-7 (Establishing and Understanding with the Client). *See also* SSAE-10
  superseded by SSAE-10, 541
SSAE-8 (Management's Discussion and Analysis). *See also* SSAE-10
  superseded by SSAE-10, 541
SSAE-9 (Amendments to Statement on Standards for Attestation Engagements Nos. 1, 2, and 3). *See also* SSAE-10
  superseded by SSAE-10, 541
SSAE-10 (Attestation Standards: Revision and Recodification), 541. *See also* Agreed-Upon Procedures (AUP) Engagements; Attestation Engagements; Compliance Attestation Engagement; Financial Forecasts and Projections; Internal Control Review Engagement; Management's Discussion and Analysis (MD&A); Pro Forma Financial Information
  attest engagement, 541–543
  AUP engagements, 563–564
  compliance attestation, 620–621
  financial forecasts and projections, 571–573
  internal control review, 605–606
  MD&A information, 635
  pro forma financial information, 595–597
  procedures checklist, 637
SSAE Interpretations
  (August 1987)—Defense Industry Questionnaire on Business Ethics and Conduct, 541, 543
  (February 1988)—Responding to Requests for Reports on Matters Relating to Solvency, 554
  (February 1992)—Responding to Requests for Reports on Matters Relating to Solvency, 541
  (February 1997)—Reporting on an Entity's Internal Control Over Financial Reporting: Attestation Engagements Interpretations of Section 400, 605, 619
  (July 1990)—Applicability of Attestation Standards to Litigation Services, 541, 543
  (May 1996)—Providing Access to or Photocopies of Working Papers to a Regulator, 541, 551
SSARS. *See* Statements on Standards for Accounting and Review Services
SSARS-1 (Compilation and Review of Financial Statements), 667
  engagement letters, 674–675
  financial statement, defined, 443–444, 668
  financial statement examples, 669–670
  financial statement submission defined, 672–673
  independence, 702
  level of service rendered, 769–770
  personal financial statements, 782–783
  types of compilations, 684
  withdrawing from engagement, 682–683
SSARS-2 (Reporting on Comparative Financial Statements), 762–763
  comparative financial statements, defined, 762

SSARS-2, *cont.*
  level of service rendered, 769–770, 775
  periods are compiled or reviewed, 763–763, 772–773
  procedures checklist, 763
  reissued reports, 762, 767
  reports by predecessor accountants, 766–769, 774–775
  revised reports, 767, 773
  status of client has changed, 770–771, 775
SSARS-3 (Compilation Reports on Financial Statements in Certain Prescribed Forms), 776–778
SSARS-4 (Communication Between Predecessor and Successor Accountants), 767, 768–769, 779
SSARS-6 (Reporting on Personal Financial Statements Included in Written Personal Financial Plans), 782–783
SSARS-7 (Omnibus Statement on Standards for Accounting and Review Services-1992), 667, 780
SSARS-8 (Amendments to Statement on Standards for Accounting and Review Services No. 1, Compilation and Review of Financial Statements-2000), 667
  departure from GAAP, 702
  departure from OCBOA, 702
  engagement letter, 702
  financial statement notes, 704–705
  financial statement submission defined, 672–673
  independence, 702
  third party defined, 696–698
  types of compilations, 684
SSARS Interpretation 1 (SSARS-1, SSARS-7)—Omission of Disclosures in Reviewed Financial Statements (December 1979), 667, 715
SSARS Interpretation 1 (SSARS-2)—Reporting on Financial Statements That Previously Did Not Omit Substantially All Disclosures (November 1980), 762
SSARS Interpretation 1 (SSARS-3)—Omission of Disclosures in Financial Statements Included in Certain Prescribed Forms (May 1982), 776, 777
SSARS Interpretation 1 (SSARS-4)—Reports on the Application of Accounting Principles (August 1987), 779, 781
SSARS Interpretation 1 (SSARS-6)—Submitting a Personal Financial Plan to a Client's Advisers (May 1991), 782, 783
SSARS Interpretation 2 (SSARS-1, SSARS-7)—Financial Statements Included in SEC Filings (December 1979), 667, 678
SSARS Interpretation 3 (SSARS-1, SSARS-7)—Reporting on the Highest Level of Service (December 1979), 667, 681
SSARS Interpretation 4 (SSARS-1, SSARS-7)—Discovery of Information After the Date of Accountant's Report (November 1980), 667, 695, 716
SSARS Interpretation 5 (SSARS-1, SSARS-7)—Planning and Supervision (August 1981), 667, 673
SSARS Interpretation 6 (SSARS-1, SSARS-7)—Withdrawal from Compilation or Review Engagements (August 1981), 667, 691
SSARS Interpretation 7 (SSARS-1, SSARS-7)—Reporting When There Are Significant Departures from Generally Accepted Accounting Principles (August 1981), 667, 716
SSARS Interpretation 8 (SSARS-1, SSARS-7)—Reports on Specified Elements, Accounts, or Items of a Financial Statement (November 1981, amended November 1988), 667, 669
SSARS Interpretation 9 (SSARS-1, SSARS-7)—Reporting When Man-

Index

agement Has Elected to Omit Substantially All Disclosures (May 1982), 667, 692
SSARS Interpretation 10 (SSARS-1, SSARS-7)—Reporting on Tax Returns (November 1982), 667, 671
SSARS Interpretation 11 (SSARS-1, SSARS-7)—Reporting on Uncertainties (December 1982), 667, 694
SSARS Interpretation 12 (SSARS-1, SSARS-7)—Reporting on a Comprehensive Basis of Accounting Other than Generally Accepted Accounting Principles (December 1982), 667, 695
SSARS Interpretation 13 (SSARS-1, SSARS-7)—Additional Procedures (March 1983), 667, 689
SSARS Interpretation 14 (SSARS-1, SSARS-7)—Reporting on Financial Statements when the Scope of the Accountant's Procedures Has Been Restricted (April 1984; withdrawn April 1990), 668
SSARS Interpretation 15 (SSARS-1, SSARS-7)—Differentiating a Financial Statement Presentation from a Trial Balance (September 1990), 668, 670–671
SSARS Interpretation 16 (SSARS-1, SSARS-7)—withdrawn by issuance of SSARS-7, 668
SSARS Interpretation 17 (SSARS-1, SSARS-7)—Submitting Draft Financial Statements (September 1990), 668, 680
SSARS Interpretation 18 (SSARS-1, SSARS-7)—Special-Purpose Financial Presentations to Comply with Contractual Agreements or Regulatory Provisions (September 1990), 668, 675
SSARS Interpretation 19 (SSARS-1, SSARS-7)—Reporting When Financial Statements Contain a Departure from Promulgated Accounting Principles That Prevent the Financial Statements from Being Misleading (February 1991), 668, 714
SSARS Interpretation 20 (SSARS-1, SSARS-7)—Applicability of Statements on Standards for Accounting and Review Services to Litigation Services (May 1991), 668, 672
SSARS Interpretation (November 1980)—Reporting on Financial Statements That Previously Did Not Omit Substantially All Disclosures, 692
SSASE 5-Amendments to Statement on Standards for Attestation Engagements No.1, Attestation Standards, 541
SSCS (Statements on Standards for Consulting Services), 556
Staff Accounting Bulletins, 312
Standards
   consistency. *See* Consistency standards
   fieldwork, 5
   GAAS. *See* Generally Accepted Auditing Standards
   general, 5
   reporting. *See* Reporting standards
Statement of cash flows, 321–322, 375–376. *See also* FAS-95
Statement of position (SOP). *See* specific SOP
Statement on Auditing Standards (SAS), 676. *See also* specific SAS
Statement on Quality Control Standards (SQCS), 676. *See also* specific SQCS
Statement on Standards for Attestation Engagements (SSAE), 409. *See also* specific SSAE
Statements of Financial Accounting Concepts No. 2 (Qualitative Characteristics of Accounting Information), 62
Statements on Standards for Accounting and Review Services (SSARS),

SSARS, *cont.*
339, 668, 677–678. *See also* specific SSARS
  compilation service, 668
  review service, 668
Statements on Standards for Consulting Services (SSCS), 556
Stratification, defined, 276
Submission of financial statements, 672–673
Subsequent discovery of facts, 432–437
  financial statement compilation, 695
  financial statement corrections, 322
  financial statement reviews, 716
  misstatements in previous financial statements, 77
  restatement adjustments, 370
Subsequent events, 426–429
  audit program, 429–431
  in compliance attestation engagement, 629
  in interim financial reports, 522
  internal control reports, 617
  MD&A, 646–647, 657, 663
  period, 500
  shelf registration statements, 477–478, 499, 502
Subservice Organizations, 125, 136
Substantial doubt. *See also* SAS-59
  disclosures in the audit report, 242–246
  examples of conditions and events, 239
Sufficient evidential matter, 152–153
Suitably supported assumptions, 576–578, 585
Supervision. *See* Planning the engagement
Supplementary information, 419–425. *See also* SAS-29; SAS-52
  financial statement compilations, 696
  financial statement reviews, 716–717
  oil and gas, 419
Suspension of Certain Accounting Requirements for Oil and Gas Producing Companies (FAS-25), 421
System of Quality Control for a CPA Firm's Accounting and Auditing Practice (SQCS-2), 7–10

T

Tax
  accruals, 151, 155, 361
  financial statements prepared on income tax basis, 442, 446
  income, accounting for, 217
  income, accounting for in interim periods, 505
  returns, reporting on, 667, 671
Tests, substantive
  analytical procedures, 159–163
  for control risk, 114–115
  defined, 114
  for derivatives and securities, 197–199
  for determining audit risk, 57, 59–61
  effects by Service Organizations, 196–197
  of financial statement assertions, 153–154, 197–199
  management representations, 196
  prior to balance sheet date, 67–71
  procedures checklist, 67–68
  sample workpapers, 71
  sampling. *See* Tests, substantive for sampling
  by service auditor, 128
  types of, 67
Tests, substantive for sampling
  documentation, 280–281
  misstatements, 278–279, 280, 287, 291–293
  objectives, 274
  population, 274–275, 276, 279
  procedures checklist, 273–274, 281
  risk, 258–260, 276–278, 283–287, 288–289
  sample size, 276, 282, 289–291, 293–296
  sampling technique, 275
Tests of controls
  MD&A, 643

Index

sampling risk. *See* Tests of controls in sampling
support for planned assessed level of control risk, 109–113
Tests of controls in sampling
  detective, 262
  deviation conditions, 262, 269
  objectives, 261–262
  period covered by test, 262
  population, 262, 263, 267, 292–293
  preventive, 262
  procedures checklist, 260–261
  risk, 258–260, 265, 271
  sample size, 265, 282
  selection of sample, 263–264
Third party defined, 696–698
Tolerable misstatement in sampling, 278–279
Tolerable rate of deviation in sampling, 266–267, 271
Trial balance, 668, 670–671
Trier of fact, 672

U

U. S. Office of Management and Budget, OMB Circular A-123, 384
Uncertainties. *See also* Going concern
  disclosure, 203
  reporting, 362–364, 667, 694, 715

Unqualified report, 349
Updating, 366–367, 762
Updating representation letter, 205
User
  auditor, 125129
  organization, 125
Using the Work of a Specialist (SAS-11), 216. *See also* SAS-73
Using the work of others for interim financial reports, 519–520, 527

W

Warehouses, auditing of, 538–539
Withdrawing from engagement, 682–683
Working Papers, 232–237. *See also* SAS-41
Workpapers. *See also* Documentation
  in attest engagements, 555
  bridging, 233
  communications between predecessor and successor auditors, 74–75
  reaudit engagements, 76–77
  for regulators, 232, 234–237, 541
  substantive test, 69–70, 71

Y

Yellow Book. *See* Government Auditing Standards

About the CD-ROM

System Requirements

- IBM PC or compatible computer with CD-ROM drive
- Windows 95 or higher
- Microsoft Word 7.0 for Windows or compatible word processor
- 2.5 MB available on hard drive

The CD-ROM provided with the 2002 *Miller GAAS Guide* contains electronic versions of the more than 100 exhibits presented in the book.

Subject to the conditions in the license agreement and the limited warranty, which are reproduced at the end of the book, you may duplicate the files on this disk, modify them as necessary, and create your own customized versions. Installing the disk contents and/or using the disk in any way indicates that you accept the terms of the license agreement. The data disk is intended for use with your word processing software.

The list of the CD-ROM Contents is also available on your disk in a file called "_contents.rtf." The listing includes each individual example disclosure and identifies its location in a particular file.

CD-ROM Contents

File	File Name	File Type
Exhibit AU 230-1—Professional Skepticism	AU230-01	RTF
Exhibit AU 310-1—Engagement Letter	AU310-01	RTF
Exhibit AU 311-1—Audit Engagement Planning Checklist	AU311-01	RTF
Exhibit AU 311-2—Prospective Client Evaluation Form	AU311-02	RTF
Exhibit AU 311-3—Audit Questionnaire Checklist—Continuing Engagement	AU311-03	RTF
Exhibit AU 311-4—Audit Engagement Supervision Checklist	AU311-04	RTF
Exhibit AU 313-1—Sample Workpaper Format	AU313-01	RTF
Exhibit AU 315-1—Letter of Understanding between Predecessor and Successor Auditor	AU315-01	RTF
Exhibit AU 315-2—Client Consent and Acknowledgment Letter	AU315-02	RTF
Exhibit AU 319-1—Relationship of Financial Statement Assertions and Relevant Internal Controls	AU319-01	RTF
Exhibit AU 319-2—The Application of Internal Control Concepts to Small and Mid-Sized Entities	AU319-02	RTF
Exhibit AU 324-1—Report on Controls Placed in Operation at a Service Organization	AU324-01	RTF
Exhibit AU 324-2—Report on Controls Placed in Operation at a Service Organization and Tests of Operating Effectiveness	AU324-02	RTF
Exhibit AU 325-1—Examples of Possible Reportable Conditions	AU325-01	RTF
Exhibit AU 325-2—Example of a Report on a Reportable Condition	AU325-02	RTF

File	File Name	File Type
Exhibit AU 325-3—Examples of Possible Material Weaknesses—Small Business Enterprise	AU325-03	RTF
Exhibit AU 325-4—Example of a Separate Report on Material Weaknesses	AU325-04	RTF
Exhibit AU 329-1—Documentation of the Effect of Analytical Procedures on the Planning of Substantive Audit Procedures	AU329-01	RTF
Exhibit AU 329-2—Analytical Procedures for a Review Engagement	AU329-02	RTF
Exhibit AU 330-1—Positive Confirmation	AU330-01	RTF
Exhibit AU 330-2—Negative Confirmation	AU330-02	RTF
Exhibit AU 330-3—Obligation under Long-Term Leases	AU330-03	RTF
Exhibit AU 330-4—Mortgage Obligation	AU330-04	RTF
Exhibit AU 330-5—Audit Program—Confirmation of Accounts Receivable	AU330-05	RTF
Exhibit AU 330-6—Summary of Accounts Receivable Confirmation Statistics	AU330-06	RTF
Exhibit AU 331-1—Audit Program: Inventory Observation Procedures	AU331-01	RTF
Exhibit AU 331-2—Confirmation Request for Inventory Held by Another Part	AU331-02	RTF
Exhibit AU 333-1—Management Representation Letter	AU333-01	RTF
Exhibit AU 337-1—Illustrative Audit Inquiry Letter to Legal Counsel	AU337-01	RTF
Exhibit AU 337-2—Illustrative Audit Inquiry Letter to Legal Counsel Whereby Management Has Requested That the Lawyer Prepare the List of Pending or Threatened Litigation, Claims, and Assessments	AU337-02	RTF
Exhibit AU 339-1—Letter for Regulatory Agency That Requests Access to Audit Workpapers	AU339-01	RTF

CD-ROM Contents

File	File Name	File Type
Exhibit AU 341-3—Evaluating an Entity's Ability to Continue as a Going Concern	AU341-03	RTF
Exhibit AU 350-6—Required Sample Size for Nonstatistical Substantive Tests of Details	AU350-06	RTF
Exhibit AU 350-7—Audit Judgment Factors Used in Nonstatistical and in Statistical Sampling to Determine Sample Size for Tests of Controls	AU350-07	RTF
Exhibit AU 350-8—Audit Judgment Factors Used to Determine Sample Size for Substantive Tests	AU350-08	RTF
Exhibit AU 380-1—Topic and Nature of Communications with the Client's Audit Committee	AU380-01	RTF
Exhibit AU 390-1—Omission of Engagement Procedures Discovered after the Report Date	AU390-01	RTF
Exhibit AU 411-1—Private-Sector Accounting Hierarchy	AU411-01	RTF
Exhibit AU 411-2—Public-Sector Accounting Hierarchy	AU411-02	RTF
Exhibit AU 411-3—Federal GAAP Hierarchy	AU411-03	RTF
Exhibit AU 431-1—Checklist Disclosure Questionnaire	AU431-01	RTF
Exhibit AU 431-2—Engagement Program for SOP 94-6	AU431-02	RTF
Exhibit AU 504-1—Disclaimer of Opinion on Unaudited Financial Statements	AU504-01	RTF
Exhibit AU 504-2—Disclaimer of Opinion on Unaudited Financial Statements That Are Prepared on a Comprehensive Basis of Accounting Other Than Generally Accepted Accounting Principles	AU504-02	RTF
Exhibit AU 504-3—Disclaimer of Opinion on Unaudited Financial Statements Because the Accountant Is Not Independent	AU504-03	RTF

File	File Name	File Type
Exhibit AU 504-4—Description of a Compilation in a Separate Paragraph When Reporting on Audited and Unaudited Financial Statements in Comparative Form	AU504-04	RTF
Exhibit AU 504-5—Description of a Review in a Separate Paragraph When Reporting on Audited and Unaudited Financial Statements in Comparative Form	AU504-05	RTF
Exhibit AU 508-2—Qualified Auditor's Report	AU508-02	RTF
Exhibit AU 508-3—Adverse Auditor's Report	AU508-03	RTF
Exhibit AU 508-4—Qualified Auditor's Report Because Statement of Cash Flow Is Omitted	AU508-04	RTF
Exhibit AU 508-5—Qualified Auditor's Report Because of a Scope Limitation	AU508-05	RTF
Exhibit AU 508-6—Disclaimer Report	AU508-06	RTF
Exhibit AU 508-7—Auditor's Report Only on the Balance Sheet	AU508-07	RTF
Exhibit AU 508-9—Auditor's Report on Comparative Financial Statements	AU508-09	RTF
Exhibit AU 508-10—Auditor's Report on Comparative Financial Statements with Different Opinions	AU508-10	RTF
Exhibit AU 508-11—Auditor's Report When a Predecessor Auditor's Report Is Not Presented	AU508-11	RTF
Exhibit AU 532-1—Restricted Audit Report on Special-Purpose Financial Statement Presentation	AU532-01	RTF
Exhibit AU 532-2—Restricted Audit Report on Financial Statements Prepared Pursuant to a Loan Agreement	AU532-02	RTF
Exhibit AU 532-3—Restricted Audit Report on Specified Accounts of a Financial Statement	AU532-03	RTF

CD-ROM Contents

File	File Name	File Type
Exhibit AU 534-1—U.S.-Style Standard Auditor's Report	AU534-01	RTF
Exhibit AU 543-1—Reference to the Work of Another Auditor in the Audit Report	AU543-01	RTF
Exhibit AU 543-2—Example of Inquiry by the Other Auditor Directed to the Principal Auditor	AU543-02	RTF
Exhibit AU 543-3—Example of Principal Audit's Response to Inquiry Made by Other Auditor	AU543-03	RTF
Exhibit AU 560-1—Subsequent Events Audit Program	AU560-01	RTF
Exhibit AU 561-1—Discovery of Facts after the Date of the Report	AU561-01	RTF
Exhibit AU 623-1—Special Report on Cash-Based Financial Statement	AU623-01	RTF
Exhibit AU 623-2—Special Report on an Account in a Financial Statement	AU623-02	RTF
Exhibit AU 623-3—Special Report on Whether Certain Terms of a Debt Agreement Have Been Observed	AU623-03	RTF
Exhibit AU 623-4—Special Report on a Statement of Assets Sold and Liabilities Transferred	AU623-04	RTF
Exhibit AU 623-5—Special Report on Financial Statements Prepared Pursuant to a Loan Agreement	AU623-05	RTF
Exhibit AU 625-1—Accountant's Report on the Applicability of Accounting Principles	AU625-01	RTF
Exhibit AU 634-1—Representation Letter from Requesting Parties	AU634-01	RTF
Exhibit AU 634-2—Sample Comfort Letter	AU634-02	RTF
Exhibit AU 711-1—Description of Status of Review Report Incorporated through Reference in a Registration Statement	AU711-01	RTF

File	File Name	File Type
Exhibit AU 722-1—Engagement Letter for a Review of Interim Financial Information	AU722-01	RTF
Exhibit AU 722-2—Accountant's Report on Interim Financial Information	AU722-20	RTF
Exhibit AU 722-3—Review Report with Reference to the Work of Another Accountant	AU722-03	RTF
Exhibit AT 101-03—Checklist for an Examination Report on a Subject Matter	AT101-03	RTF
Exhibit AT 101-04—Checklist for an Examination Report on an Assertion	AT101-04	RTF
Exhibit AT 101-05—Checklist for a Review Report on a Subject Matter	AT101-05	RTF
Exhibit AT 101-06—Checklist for a Review Report on an Assertion	AT101-06	RTF
Exhibit AT 101-07—Examination Report—Subject Matter	AT101-07	RTF
Exhibit AT 101-08—Examination Report—Assertion	AT101-08	RTF
Exhibit AT 101-09—Review Report—Subject Matter	AT101-09	RTF
Exhibit AT 101-10—Review Report—Assertion (Restricted Distribution)	AT101-10	RTF
Exhibit AT 201-01—Checklist for an AUP Report	AT201-01	RTF
Exhibit AT 201-02—AUP Engagement Report	AT201-02	RTF
Exhibit AT 301-01—Standard Report on an Examination of a Forecast	AT301-01	RTF
Exhibit AT 301-02—Standard Report on an Examination of a Projection	AT301-02	RTF
Exhibit AT 301-04—Standard Report on a Compilation of Projected Financial Statements	AT301-04	RTF
Exhibit AT 301-05—Report on an AUP Engagement for Prospective Financial Statements	AT301-05	RTF

CD-ROM Contents

File	File Name	File Type
Exhibit AT 401-03—Examination Report on Pro Forma Financial Information	AT401-03	RTF
Exhibit AT 401-04—Review Report on Pro Forma Financial Information	AT401-04	RTF
Exhibit AT 501-02—Examination on the Effectiveness of an Entity's Internal Control over Financial Reporting	AT501-02	RTF
Exhibit AT 501-03—Examination on the Written Assertion on the Effectiveness of an Entity's Internal Control over Financial Reporting	AT501-03	RTF
Exhibit AT 601-01—AUP Report on an Entity's Compliance with Specified Requirements	AT601-01	RTF
Exhibit AT 601-03—Examination on an Entity's Compliance with Specified Requirements	AT601-03	RTF
Exhibit AT 601-04—Examination on Management's Assertion Concerning Compliance with Specified Requirements	AT601-04	RTF
Exhibit AT 701-01—Examination Report on and Entity's MD&A Presentation	AT701-01	RTF
Exhibit AT 702-01—Review Engagement Report on and Entity's MD&A Presentation	AT702-01	RTF
Exhibit AR 100-3—Engagement Letter in a Noncontinuing Compilation Engagement	AR100-03	RTF
Exhibit AR 100-4—Standard Review Engagement Letter	AR100-04	RTF
Exhibit AR 100-5—Engagement Letter in a Noncontinuing Review Engagement	AR100-05	RTF
Exhibit AR 100-6—Client Representation Letter for a Compilation Engagement	AR100-06	RTF
Exhibit AR 100-7—Client Representation Letter for a Review Engagement	AR100-07	RTF

File	File Name	File Type
Exhibit AR 100-8—Client Representation Letter for a Review Engagement (Alternative Illustration)	AR100-08	RTF
Exhibit AR 100-9—Compilation Program—Continuing Engagement	AR100-09	RTF
Exhibit AR 100-10—Compilation Program—Noncontinuing Engagement	AR100-10	RTF
Exhibit AR 100-11—Review Program—Continuing Engagement	AR100-11	RTF
Exhibit AR 100-12—Review Program—Noncontinuing Engagement	AR100-12	RTF
Exhibit AR 100-13—Review Questionnaire Checklist—Continuing Engagement	AR100-13	RTF
Exhibit AR 100-14—Inquiry Checklist for a Review Engagement	AR100-14	RTF
Exhibit AR 100-15—Analytical Procedures for a Review Engagement	AR100-15	RTF
Exhibit AR 200-1—Report on Comparative Financial Statements Where All Periods Have Been Compiled	AR200-01	RTF
Exhibit AR 200-2—Report on Comparative Financial Statements Where All Periods Have Been Reviewed	AR200-02	RTF
Exhibit AR 200-3—Report on Comparative Financial Statements Where the Current Period Is Reviewed and the Prior Period Is Compiled	AR200-03	RTF
Exhibit AR 200-4—Additional Paragraph to a Compilation Report on the Current Period That Refers to the Prior Period That Had Been Reviewed	AR200-04	RTF
Exhibit AR 200-5—Explanatory Paragraph Added to a Current Report That Refers to a Change in a Previous Report Issued by the Accountant	AR200-05	RTF

CD-ROM Contents

File	File Name	File Type
Exhibit AR 200-6—Separate Paragraph Added to the Current Report That Refers to the Predecessor Accountant's Compilation Report	AR200-06	RTF
Exhibit AR 200-7—Separate Paragraph Added to the Current Report That Refers to the Predecessor Accountant's Review Report	AR200-07	RTF
Exhibit AR 200-8—Compilation Report on Comparative Financial Statements That Omit Substantially All Disclosures But Where the Prior Year Had Originally Been Reviewed by the Accountant	AR200-08	RTF
Exhibit AR 200-9—Report on Comparative Financial Statements Where the Current Year Is Compiled and the Prior Year Is Audited	AR200-09	RTF
Exhibit AR 300-1—Compilation Report on Financial Statements Included in a Prescribed Form	AR300-01	RTF
Exhibit AR 600-1—Alternative Accountant's Report on Personal Financial Statements Included in Written Personal Financial Plans	AR600-01	RTF